1

Experience Reading

Suzanne Liff
Nassau Community College

Joyce Stern
Nassau Community College

Mc Graw Hill

Connect
Learn
Succeed™

D1214844

Connect
Learn
Succeed™

Published by McGraw-Hill, an imprint of The McGraw-Hill Companies, Inc., 1221 Avenue of the Americas, New York, NY 10020.

This book is printed on acid-free paper.

1 2 3 4 5 6 7 8 9 0 RJE/RJE 10 9 8 7 6 5 4 3 2 1

ISBN: 978-0-07-329238-0 (Student's Edition)
MHID: 0-07-329238-9 (Student's Edition)
ISBN: 978-0-07-329241-0 (Instructor's Edition)
MHID: 0-07-329241-9 (Instructor's Edition)

Sponsoring Editor: *John Kindler*
Marketing Manager: *Jaclyn Elkins*
Developmental Editors: *Anne Leung and Deborah Kopka*
Production Editor: *Rachel J. Castillo*
Supplements Editor: *Sarah Colwell*
Manuscript Editor: *Barbara Hacha*
Cover Designer and Design Manager: *Jeanne Schreiber*
Text Designer: *Amanda Kavanagh, Ark Design*
Illustrator: *Ayelet Arbel*
Photo Researcher: *Sonia Brown*
Buyer: *Louis Swaim*
Composition: *11/13 Sabon by Laserwords Private Limited*
Printing: *45# New Era Matte Thin, R. R. Donnelley & Sons/Jefferson City, MO*

Vice President Editorial: *Michael Ryan*
Publisher: *David S. Patterson*
Director of Development: *Dawn Groundwater*

Cover: © James Balog/Stone/Getty Images

Library of Congress Cataloging-in-Publication Data

Liff, Suzanne.
    Experience reading. Book 1/Suzanne Liff, Joyce Stern. — 1st ed.
        p. cm.
    Includes bibliographical references and index.
    ISBN-13: 978-0-07-329238-0 (alk. paper)
    ISBN-10: 0-07-329238-9 (alk. paper)
    ISBN-13: 978-0-07-329241-0 (alk. paper)
    ISBN-10: 0-07-329241-9 (alk. paper)
    1. College readers. I. Stern, Joyce D. II. Title.
    PE1417.L523 2011
    808'.0427—dc22

                                                      2010052882

Actively

Activities that are tied to each skill level offer students multiple opportunities to interact with the reading and receive immediate feedback.

Identifying, Marking, and Annotating Supporting Details: Activity

Choose a highlight color:

| None | Supporting Details |

flying. These dreams sometimes became myths, stories, and art. In a Greek myth, a king trapped Daedalus and his son, Icarus, in a maze. Daedalus made wings of wax so that they could fly away, but Icarus flew too close to the sun. His wings melted, and he fell into the sea. A coin of ancient Babylonia showed the king flying on an eagle's back. The Inca claimed that one of their ancestors had wings and could fly.

Perhaps the first people to get off the ground were the Chinese. In about 1000 B.C., they made large kites that carried men to spy on enemy troops. In about 1100, in Turkey, a man made wings of pleated fabric. He jumped from a tower and fell to his death. Centuries later, a man in France built wings that flapped

You have added 2 out of 11 highlights. | Instructions | Submit

Steps in Evaluating an Author's Argument: Activity

Choose a highlight color:

| None | Either-Or | Personal Attack | Appeal to Ignorance |

I have not seen one study to prove that these new social programs will not work.

How can you argue for more funding for Child Protective Services when I have seen you spank your own son?

Anyone who does not support the current homeland security policy supports terrorism.

Buy our anti-aging moisturizer or continue to watch your wrinkles grow.

If you yourself have to wear makeup, then why should I believe that your skin

You have added 2 out of 5 highlights. | Instructions | Submit

"Connect Reading gives [students] more study options and a fresh perspective to listen and learn from."
–Yvette Daniel, Central Georgia Tech.

Critically

LiveInk, a research-based technology, increases the reader's comprehension, which leads to improved synthesis and understanding of information, the foundation of critical thinking.

When Not Asking for Directions Is Dangerous to Your Health

by Deborah Tannen

If conversational-style
    differences
        lead to troublesome outcomes
            in work
        as well as private settings,
there are some work settings
    where
        the outcomes of style
            are a matter
                of life and death.

Health-care professionals
    are often
        in such situations.

So are airline pilots.
Of all the examples
    of women's and men's
        characteristic styles
            that I discussed
                in *You Just Don't Understand*,
    the one that
        (to my surprise)
            attracted the most attention

"When Not Asking for Directions Is Dangerous to Your Health," Deborah Tannen

Click to Read in Live Ink® for a better grade

Learn More about Live Ink

If conversational-style differences lead to troublesome outcomes in work as well as private settings, there are some work settings where the outcomes of style are a matter of life and death. Health-care professionals are often in such situations. So are airline pilots.

Of all the examples of women's and men's characteristic styles that I discussed in *You Just Don't Understand*, the one that (to my surprise) attracted the most attention was the question "Why don't men like to stop and ask for directions?" Again and again, in the responses of audiences, talk-show hosts, letter writers, journalists, and conversationalists, this question seemed to crystallize the frustration many people had experienced in their own lives. And my explanation seems to have rung true: that men are more likely to be aware that asking for directions, or for any kind of help, puts them in a one-down position.

With regard to asking directions, women and men are keenly aware of the advantages of their own style. Women frequently observe how much time they would save if their husbands simply stopped and asked someone instead of driving around trying in vain to find a destination themselves. But I have also been told by men that it makes sense not to ask directions because you learn a lot about a neighborhood, as well as about navigation, by driving around and finding your own way.

To my father, Nathan Brandell. For six years, he never wavered in his query, "How's the book coming?" inspiring perseverance and kindling love. Here it is, Dad.

– Suzanne Liff

To my children, Eric and Robyn, for their love, support, and encouragement.

– Joyce Stern

Brief Table of Contents

Table of Contents

Chapter 3
The Power of Words: *Understanding College Vocabulary* 68

Chapter 4
Get the Big Picture: *Identifying the Main Idea in College Reading* 92

Chapter 8

A Tangled Web: *Assessing Internet Sources*   224

Chapter 9

Put the Pieces Together: *Organizing Information for Reading and Studying*   238

Chapter 10
Make Your Mark: *Becoming an Effective Test Taker 268*

part three Modules: Theme-Based Reading
Selections 284

Module 1
Readings About the Code of Conduct 284

Module 2
Readings About Resilience   316

Module 3
Readings About Diversity and Tolerance 352

Module 4
Readings About School and Learning 386

Module 5
Readings About the World of Work   424

Module 6
Readings About Physical Health and Well-Being 462

Module 7
Readings About Emotional Well-Being   490

Module 8
Readings About Relationships   522

Appendixes

Take the Leap with
Experience Reading!

Experience Reading engages students personally, actively, and critically through an integrated print and digital program designed to prepare them for college—and lifelong—reading. Here's how:

Personally

Experience Reading invites students to make the connection between their lives and reading.

Scaffolded modules help students move from guided to independent reading with selections that are personal and relevant to their lives. By helping students move from practicing to applying, the modules meet a program's goals of making students independent readers.

Self-Monitored Reading
Reading Selection 2

Should the Legal Drinking Age Be Lowered to 18?
Yes! Drinking 'Licenses' Promote Responsible Behavior

By David J. Hanson

This is the first of two essays, presented as paired readings, in a professional publication for college faculty called On Campus. *It presents one point of view on whether or not the legal drinking age should be lowered. What do you think? David J. Hanson is professor emeritus of sociology at the State University of New York at Potsdam.*

connect

Powered by Connect, Video Scenarios demonstrate how course concepts apply to the student's everyday life. In this video about inferences and drawing conclusions, students are asked to identify each concept in action. The students will have the opportunity to see what they caught and missed.

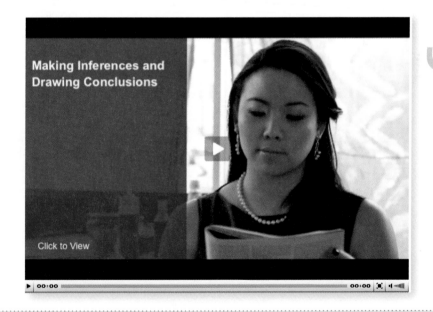

Experience Reading!

Actively

Experience Reading makes students active participants in their learning. Students are provided with hands-on experience in testing their knowledge and applying it to their lives.

try it and apply it activities get students to think about what they've learned. Being aware of how one learns (metacognition) enables students to actively and critically understand "What did I learn, how did I learn it, and how can I use it in the future."

Utilizing symbols such as this pause button, students are given a visual cue as to what they should be doing. In this case they are to pause and think about what they have learned. ▼

try it and apply it! 7-9 **Detecting Negative Connotations**

Directions: Underline the words that you think have a negative connotation in each of the following sets of items. Discuss your answers with your classmates. You may discover that some perceptions of words differ from culture to culture.

1. economical, penny-pinching, cheap
2. heavyset, overweight, obese
3. ignorant, unschooled, naive
4. immature, childish, childlike
5. impulsive, spontaneous, hasty
6. inquiring, nosy, snoopy
7. snicker, laugh, cackle
8. mature, over-the-hill, geezer
9. talk, babble, gossip
10. sly, skillful, calculating

connect

Powered by Connect, activities allow students multiple opportunities to interact with the reading skills and receive immediate feedback.

In this activity students are asked to read some text and then highlight those sentences that offer inferences and those that do not.

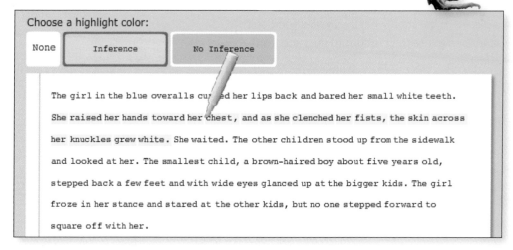

Choose a highlight color:

| None | Inference | No Inference |

The girl in the blue overalls curled her lips back and bared her small white teeth. She raised her hands toward her chest, and as she clenched her fists, the skin across her knuckles grew white. She waited. The other children stood up from the sidewalk and looked at her. The smallest child, a brown-haired boy about five years old, stepped back a few feet and with wide eyes glanced up at the bigger kids. The girl froze in her stance and stared at the other kids, but no one stepped forward to square off with her.

Collaborative learning experiences are stimulating learning experiences. Opportunities to discuss and respond to reading material with peers and in small groups fosters personal confidence and social skill growth, while developing a sense of community and belonging. Collaborative learning opportunities are found throughout the text, identified by the following icon: . Many exercises are structured so that they can be completed individually, in pairs, or in small groups.

Experience Reading!

Critically

Experience Reading encourages students to think critically, to question what they know and don't know, and then to use their insight to read and learn more effectively.

Each **scaffolded module** is arranged from least to most challenging, taking students from Guided Reading to Self-Monitored Reading, to Independent Reading. Students build on skills previously learned and apply them to future concepts.

Guided Reading
Reading Selection 1

Courtship and Mate Selection
By Richard T. Schaefer

This article is adapted from an introductory sociology textbook. Within a chapter titled "The Family and Intimate Relationships," it describes different cultural views about selecting a life partner for marriage.

Self-Monitored Reading
Reading Selection 2

Friendship: Awkward Encounters of the Friendly Kind
by Carlin Flora

This excerpt is taken from an article published in a popular magazine called Psychology Today. As you read it, consider the nature of some of your own friendships. Are any of the situations familiar?

Independent Reading
Selection 3

The Last Word: Growing up Bin Laden
by Naiwa bin Laden, Omar bin Laden, and Jean Sasson

This book excerpt discusses a son's recollections of childhood experiences with his dad. As you read, consider what you know about the father, Osama bin Laden. What do Omar's stories reveal about their relationship?

connect™

Comprehension is improved with Connect. *Experience Reading* uses the research-based LiveInk technology to increase the student's reading comprehension, which leads to improved synthesis of information, the foundation of critical thinking.

Check out the Live Ink Video at http://www.liveink.com/learnmore.php

Check out a Connect Reading demonstration at http://marcomm.mhhe.com/Connect/features/connectreading.php

"A Letter to My Teacher,"
Kate Boyes

Dear Professor,
   I didn't belong in college.

I should have told you that.

My father
   dropped out of school
     after third grade.

My mother
   went through twelfth grade,
but her family thought
   she was a little uppity
     for doing so.

Like my mother,
   I finished high school,
and immediately got married
    and started having babies.

DIAGNOSTIC SCORE	COMPLETE YOUR TEST	CORRECT	PERCENTAGE
1. The Main Idea		--	--
2. Supporting Details		--	--
3. The Author's Purpose		--	--
4. The Author's Tone		--	--
5. Figurative Language		--	--
6. Patterns of Organization		--	--
7. Making Inferences and Drawing Conclusions		--	--
8. Bias		--	--
9. Fact and Opinion		--	--
10. Evaluating Author's Reasoning and Evidence		--	--
11. Scanning, Skimming, and Speed-Reading		--	--
12. Reading Textbooks		--	--
13. Vocabulary		--	--
14. Study Skills		--	--
AVERAGE		--	--

connect™

Powered by Connect, Individual Learning Plans are targeted to each student's specific needs, and offer a systematic examination of all aspects of reading, from the author's purpose and tone to making inferences and drawing conclusions.

Previewing is taught as skill to successful reading. Using the acronym THIEVES (Title, Headings, Introduction, Every first sentence in every paragraph, Vocabulary and visuals, End of chapter questions, Summary) students are aided in learning and synthesizing the skills they need to be successful, critical readers.

T Title—The title identifies the topic, theme, or author's thesis, or argument. Think about the title. What do you already know about it? Turn the title into a question that you can look for an answer to as you read.

H Headings—Headings are the gateways into each section of the chapter or selection. Like the title, they can be turned into questions that give you a reason for reading that section of the text. When you make a question out of a heading, try to connect it to the title. Notice the subheadings as well. They can often provide the answers to questions you make from the headings.

I Introduction—The introduction to a chapter can fill you in on a subject by providing important background information. Make sure you read it. If you are reading a selection, read the first paragraph to find out what is going to be discussed.

E Every first sentence in every paragraph—The first sentences in textbook paragraphs are often the topic sentences or main ideas of the paragraphs. Thus, you will gain a lot of information about the subject by reading them. You will also encounter selections without any headings, so the first sentences of the paragraphs will be your entry into the content. They will help you predict what the author will discuss.

V Vocabulary and Visuals—The language of the discipline in which you are reading will probably be new and unfamiliar, so get ready to increase your vocabulary every time you read. If you take a moment to look at new words ahead of time, it will help you to move through the selection more smoothly when you are reading. Notice the words, often given with their definitions, at the beginning of a chapter, boldface within the text, written in the margin, or reviewed at the end. Highlight these words. Say them aloud. Read their definitions.

Visuals—Textbooks provide pictures, or visuals, that explain and illustrate what is being taught, so be sure to look at them before you read the text. Read the captions, titles, descriptions, and keys. Many people remember and understand best when they can "see" a visual presentation of an idea. Common visuals include: photographs, drawings, graphs, figures, charts and tables, cartoons, and maps.

E End-of-Chapter Questions—Reading these questions will give you a good idea of what the author believes it is important to know. You also establish a purpose for reading: to find the answers to these questions or to gain enough knowledge from the chapter to apply the information and develop a thoughtful response to them. Reading and answering end-of-chapter questions can also help you prepare for exams.

S Summary—Reading the summary first means you will have a lot of background knowledge and information already in your head when you read the chapter, which makes it easier to understand. Be sure to check out the chapter to see if a summary exists.

Jump in and Teach with
Experience Reading!

Resources available for use with this text support both new and veteran instructors, whether they favor traditional text-based instruction or a blend of traditional and electronic media. The First Edition text and support materials provide complementary experiences for instructors and students. All of these components are built around the core concepts articulated in the text to promote a deeper understanding of reading. This type of integration gives instructors the flexibility to use any of the text-specific electronic or print materials knowing they are completely compatible with one another. Please see your McGraw-Hill sales representative for information on policy, price, and availability of the following supplements.

Online Learning Center for Instructors. The password-protected instructor side of the Online Learning Center (www.mhhe.com/experience_reading) contains the Instructor's Manual, Test Bank files, PowerPoint Presentations, and other valuable material to help you design and enhance your course. See more information about specific assets below. Ask your local McGraw-Hill sales representative for password information.

Instructor's Manual, by Jim Bernarducci of Middlesex Community College. This comprehensive guide provides all the tools and resources instructors need to present and enhance their developmental reading course. The Instructor's Manual contains suggested activities and best practices for teaching the course, learning objectives, interesting lecture and media presentation ideas, student assignments and handouts. The many tips and activities in this manual can be used with any class, regardless of size or teaching approach.

Test Bank, by Nicole Williams of Community College of Baltimore County. The test bank contains more than 400 multiple-choice items and 60 short-answer questions, classified by cognitive type and level of difficulty, and keyed to the appropriate key concept and page in the textbook. All questions are compatible with EZ Test, McGraw-Hill's Computerized Test Bank program.

PowerPoint Presentations, by Pamela Huntington and Lenice Wilson of Merced College. These presentations cover the key points of each chapter. They can be used as is, or you may modify them to meet your specific needs.

Ways to
Experience Reading!

Create

Craft your teaching resources to match the way you teach! With McGraw-Hill Create, you can easily rearrange chapters, combine material from other content sources, and quickly upload content you have written, such as your course syllabus or teaching notes. Find the content you need in Create by searching through thousands of leading McGraw-Hill textbooks. Arrange your book to fit your teaching style. Create even allows you to personalize your book's appearance by selecting the cover and adding your name, school, and course information. Order a Create book and you'll receive a complimentary print review copy in 3–5 business days or a complimentary electronic review copy (eComp) via email in about one hour. Go to www.mcgrawhillcreate.com today and register. Experience how McGraw-Hill Create empowers you to teach your students your way.

CourseSmart This text is available as an eTextbook at www.CourseSmart.com. At CourseSmart your students can take advantage of significant savings off the cost of a print textbook, reduce their impact on the environment, and gain access to powerful web tools for learning. CourseSmart eTextbooks can be viewed online or downloaded to a computer. The eTextbooks allow students to do full text searches, add highlighting and notes, and share notes with classmates. CourseSmart has the largest selection of eTextbooks available anywhere. Visit www.CourseSmart.com to learn more and to try a sample chapter.

Tegrity

Tegrity Campus is a service that makes class time available all the time by automatically capturing every lecture in a searchable format for students to review when they study and complete assignments. With a simple one-click start and stop process, users capture all computer screens and corresponding audio. Students replay any part of any class with easy-to-use browser-based viewing on a PC or Mac. Educators know that the more students can see, hear, and experience class resources, the better they learn. With Tegrity Campus, students quickly recall key moments by using Tegrity Campus's unique search feature. This search helps students efficiently find what they need, when they need it, across an entire semester of class recordings. Help turn all your students' study time into learning moments immediately supported by your lecture.

Professional Acknowledgments

We are tremendously grateful to the following instructors whose insightful contributions during the development and production of *Experience Reading* have improved it immeasurably.

Manuscript Reviewers

Albany Technical College
Tomekia Cooper

Anne Arundel Community College
Kerry Taylor

Baltimore City Community College
Carol Anne Ritter

Bowling Green Community College
Brenda Miller
Jeanette Prerost

Brevard Community College–Melbourne
Kathleen Carlson

Bronx Community College
Joseph Todaro

Broward College–South
Gary Kay

Camden County College
Donna Armstrong
Christine Webster

Catawba Valley Community College
Kay Gregory

Community College of Baltimore County–Catonsville
Rachele Lawton
Nicole Willams

Community College of Baltimore County–Essex
Sharon Hayes

Cedar Valley College
Janet Brotherton

Central Georgia Technical College
Yvette Daniel

Central Piedmont Community College
Patricia Hill-Miller

Citrus College
Beverly Van Citters

Community College of Denver
Marta Brown
Yvonne Frye

Delaware Technical Community College–Dover
Martha Hofstetter

El Camino College
Inna Newbury

Florence-Darlington Technical College
Hattie Pinckney

Fullerton College
Amy Garcia

Gloucester County College
Birdena Brookins

Gray's Harbor College
Kathy Barker

Greenville Technical College
Toi Graham
Mahalia Johnson

Harold Washington College
Amelia Lopez

Henry Ford Community College
Pamela Kaminski

Hillsboro Community College
Aimee Alexander-Shea

Houston Community College–Southeast
Patricia Dennis-Jones

Illinois Central College
Nikki Aitken

Imperial Valley College
Deirdre Rowley

JS Reynolds Community College
Eric Hibbison
Nancy Morrison

Jackson State Community College
Letitia Hudlow

Lansing Community College
Leslie Lacy

Lone Star College–North Harris
Wei Li

Merced College
Pamela Huntington
Lenice Wilson

Miami Dade College–Kendall
Billy Jones

Miami Dade College–Wolfson
Jessica Carroll

Middlesex County College
James Bernarducci
Gertrude Coleman

Minneapolis Community and Technical College
Kim Zernechel

Navarro College
Shari Waldrop

Niagara County Community College–Sanborn
Joan Mooney

Normandale Community College
Denise Chambers

North Lake College
Tamera Ardrey

Northwest Vista College
Sharla Jones

Owens Community College
Margaret Bartelt

Palm Beach Community
College–Lake Worth
Catherine Seyler

"This is going to be my next textbook–it is exciting, energetic, presents basic skills in an excellent format and in a logical sequence!!"

– **Bonnie Arnett,** Washtenaw Community College

Passaic County
Community College
Linda Bakian

Prince George's
Community College
Marcia Dawson
Gwendalina McClain-Digby
Mirian Torain

Pulaski Technical College
Lynetta Doye
Betty Raper

Richard J Daley College
Shirley Carpenter

St John's River Community
College–Palatka
Linda Black
Julie Kelly
Theresa Kleinpoppen

St. Petersburg College
Patricia Windon

Saint Philips College
Raymond Elliot

South Texas College
Florinda Rodriguez

Tacoma Community College
Lydia Lynn Lewellen
John Sandin

Tallahassee Community
College
Laura Girtman

Tarrant County College–
Northeast
Karen Harrel

Tidewater Community
College–Norfolk
Wanda Stewart

University of Texas at
Brownsville
Herman Pena

University of Texas at El Paso
Cheryl Baker Heller
Andrea Berta

Valencia Community College–
West
Karen Cowden
Tracy Harrison
Dawn Sedik

Wake Technical Community
College
Cheryl Burk

Washtenaw Community
College
Bonnie Arnett

Design Reviewers

Albany Technical College
Tomekia Cooper

Baltimore City
Community College
Carol Ann Ritter

Brevard Community
College–Melbourne
Kathleen Carlson

Catawba Valley
Community College
Kay Gregory

Central Georgia Technical
College
Yvette Daniel

Community College of
Baltimore County–Catonsville
Rachele Lawton
Nicole Williams

Community College of
Baltimore County–Essex
Sharon Hayes

Community College of Denver
Marta Brown

Greenville Technical College
Toi Graham

Harold Washington College
Amelia Lopez

Illinois Central College
Nikki Aitken

Imperial Valley College
Deirdre Rowley

Jackson State Community
College
Letitia Hudlow

Merced College
Pamela Huntington

Miami Dade College–Kendall
Billy Jones

Middlesex County College
James Bernarducci

Normandale Community
College
Denise Chambers

Prince George's Community
College
Gwendalina McClain-Digby
Mirian Torain

Pulaski Technical College
Lynetta Doye

St John's River Community
College–Palatka
Linda Black
Julie Kelly

St. Petersburg College
Patricia Windon

Saint Philips College
Raymond Elliott

South Texas College
Florinda Rodriguez

Tallahassee Community
College
Laura Girtman

Tarrant County College–
Northeast
Karen Harrel

University of Texas at
Brownsville
Herman Pena

University of Texas at El Paso
Cheryl Baker Heller
Andrea Berta

Wake Technical Community
College
Cheryl Burk

Washtenaw Community
College
Bonnie Arnett

Cover Reviewers

Anne Arundel Community
College
Kerry Taylor

Central Georgia Technical
College
Yvette Daniel

Central Piedmont Community
College
Patricia Hill-Miller

Citrus College
Beverly Van Citters

Commonwealth School of
Western Kentucky University
Jeanette Prerost

Community College of
Baltimore County
Sharon Hayes
Nicole Williams

Delaware Technical and
Community College
Martha Hofstetter

El Camino College
Inna Newbury

Grays Harbor College
Kathy Barker

Harold Washington College
Jennifer Meresman

Illinois Central College
Shari Dinkins

Imperial Valley College
Michael Heumann

J. Sargeant Reynolds
Community College
Eric Hibbison
Nancy Morrison

Jackson State Community
College
Letitia Hudlow

Merced College
Pamela Huntington

Miami Dade College
Jessica Carroll

Minneapolis Community &
Technical College
Kim Zernechel

Niagara County Community
College
Joan Mooney

Normandale Community
College
Denise Chambers

North Lake College
Tamara Ardrey

Northwest Vista College
Sharla Jones

Owens Community College
Marge Bartelt

Prince George's Community
College
Marcia Dawson
Gwendalina McClain-Digby
Mirian Torain

Pulaski Technical College
Betty Rape

Richard J. Daley College
Shirley Carpenter

St. Johns River Community
College
Terrie Kleinpoppen

"An interesting way of teaching students the strategies required to understand reading. Finally something I don't have to work at creating."

– Florinda Rodriguez, South Texas College

St. Petersburg College
Patricia Windon

Tacoma Community College
Lydia Lynn Lewellen
John Sandin

Tallahassee Community
College
Laurie Girtman

Tarrant County College
Karen Harrel

University of Texas at
Brownsville
Herman Pena

University of Texas at El Paso
Cheryl Baker Heller

Valencia Community College
Dawn Sedick

Developmental Reading Symposia Attendees

Every year, McGraw-Hill conducts several Developmental Reading Symposia that are attended by instructors from across the country. These events are an opportunity for editors from McGraw-Hill to gather information about the needs and challenges of instructors teaching the course. They also offer a forum for the attendees to exchange ideas and experiences with colleagues whom they might not otherwise have met. The feedback we have received has been invaluable and has contributed—directly or indirectly—to the development of *Experience Reading*.

Borough of Manhattan Community College
Mark Hoffman

Broward Community College
James Rogge

Cedar Valley College
Janet Brotherton

Central Texas College
Phyllis Sisson

Chattanooga State Community College
Sarah Kuhn

Cincinnati State Technical & Community College
Sandi Buschmann

College of the Desert
Gary Bergstrom

Daytona State College
Sandra Offiah-Hawkins

Delaware Technical Community College–Dover
Ted Legates

El Camino College
Cynthia Silverman

Fullerton College
Amy Garcia

Greenville Technical College
Mahalia Johnson

Guilford Technical Community College
Bart Trescott

Harper College
Judy Kulchawik

Jackson State Community College
Letitia Hudlow

Lonestar College North Harris
Wei Li

Miami Dade College–Kendall
Sylvia Orozco

Miami Dade College–North
Leighton Spence

Miami Dade College–Wolfson
Majorie Sussman

Moraine Valley Community College
Joe Chaloka

Mountain View College
Julie Sepulveda

Navarro College
Shari Waldrop

Normandale Community College
Denise Chambers

Northeast Lakeview College
Wendy Crader

Prince George's Community College
Gwendalina McClain-Digby

Pulaski Technical College
Betty Raper

Saint Phillips College
Janet Flores

St. Petersburg College
Diane Reese

San Jacinto College South
Joanie DeForest

Santa Fe College
Laurel Severino

South Texas College
Romaldo Dominguez

Suffolk Community College
Nancy Gerli

Tallahassee Community College
Christine Barrileaux

Valencia Community College–West
Tracy Harrison

Westchester Community College
Lori Murphy

Personal Acknowledgments

We would like to extend our deepest appreciation to the many energetic individuals who help make *Experience Reading* possible. At McGraw-Hill, we'd like to thank John Kindler, Dawn Groundwater, Rachel Castillo, Sonia Brown, Jeanne Schreiber, and Marty Moga for all their efforts. Thanks also to Gillian Cook, Deborak Kopka, Barbara Hacha, and Anne Leung for their fine manuscript work. Finally, we would like to thank our students at Nassau Community College for providing us with inspiration.

About the Authors

Suzanne Liff is an Associate Professor in the Department of Reading and Basic Education at Nassau Community College. A former district-wide chairperson of secondary Special Education, Suzanne holds advanced degrees in Special Education and in Educational Administration and Supervision. She has taught preschoolers through adult learners, focusing on the learning, affective, behavioral, and metacognitive needs of students. She has presented to parents and colleagues, locally and nationally, on topics including cognitive and learning style differences, college reading and study strategies, effective classroom management, successful transition from high school to college, developmental learning communities, and social and emotional intelligence and the developmental learner. Her original works have been published for college-wide distribution as well as in professional juried journals. Professor Liff's work always links affective components with learning theory to yield academic success and scholarly joy. She teaches several developmental college reading classes, holds leadership positions on developmental reading and faculty development committees in higher education, and maintains a private practice for psycho-educational evaluation and intervention. She coordinates a unique initiative called IDEAS, which integrates basic academic skill development within all disciplines of college study. Professor Liff is an honorary life member of SEPTA. She is the recipient of the 2003 Faculty Distinguished Achievement Award for outstanding scholarly and professional accomplishment and the SUNY Chancellor's Award for Excellence in Teaching, 2007.

Joyce Stern is an Associate Professor in the Department of Reading and Basic Education at Nassau Community College. An educator for over thirty-five years, Professor Stern holds an advanced degree in TESOL from Hunter College. She is currently serving as the coordinator of her college's Learning Community Program and is involved in the design, implementation, and assessment of learning communities for liberal arts, career and technical education, ESL, and developmental students. She also wrote the curriculum for the English Language Institute, a language immersion program for entry-level second language learners. For her work at the college, she has been recognized by the college's Center for Students with Disabilities for her dedication to student learning and was the recipient of the 2008 NISOD Award in recognition for her achievement of excellence in teaching and leadership. She has also been awarded several Perkins Grants to develop learning communities for career and technical education students and recently participated in the STAR Grant to support nursing students in their professional studies.

chapter

Start Strong
Taking Charge of Your Success in College

In this chapter

you will learn to

- Build your strengths
- Be a successful college student
- Discover your learning style
- Engage with your school

A New Journey

An old saying goes, "Today is the first day of the rest of your life." If you are reading these lines, then you are, indeed, at the beginning of a new journey—a new opportunity to learn and develop the skills you will need to succeed in college.

Reading is probably the most important of the academic skills. Your professors expect you to learn material by reading about it, all on your own. You will read to study. You will read to better understand your class work. You will read in order to do research and write your papers. You will read, hopefully, because you are so interested in the subject that you just can't get enough of it!

The stronger you are as a reader, the stronger you will be as a student. Like driving a car, after you learn, it is up to you to do it well. You are in charge. You decide when to start and when to stop. You determine your destination, your route, how quickly you will move, and how often you set out. You decide what to do to make your "drive" safe and enjoyable. You are behind the wheel.

3

Building Your Strengths

Being a strong, independent reader is one of several abilities you will want to strengthen as you set out for success in college. Mastering the reading skills and strategies in this book will empower you. What are the other skills? Educators in the field of higher education have identified important skills that will help you start strong in college and stay strong and capable throughout your experience. Before reading about these skills in the following section, write a list of the skills you think are needed to succeed in college. Share your thoughts with a classmate or the rest of your class.

_____

_____

_____

_____

Next, read about the topic of student success in this article from *Campus Life*. What "secrets for college success" does writer Josh Johnson reveal through his conversations with three college professors? Take a look at the questions that follow the selection before you read. Answer the questions after you read. We will discuss these and other "secrets" later in this chapter.

Study Secrets for College Success

By Josh Johnson

Tomorrow's the test, and your professor warned it would be the biggest thing since the Tickle-Me-Elmo craze.

You were sitting in the front row yesterday when he described this monster in all its gory details. Forty multiple-choice questions, just to "warm up the pencils," the professor had said. He smiled. You didn't.

"Oh, and there will also be a few short-answer questions, about a paragraph each—as a warm-up for the essay question."

"Essay? How long should that be?" you asked.

"As long as it takes to completely answer the question," was his reply.

This isn't high school anymore, you thought to yourself as you walked away (back to your dorm room).

And now you're at your desk. It's 11 p.m. The monster's tomorrow. Scattered about the desk are a textbook, study guide, notes from class, and notes written to the guy next to you during class. You don't know where to start. It doesn't occur to you at the time, but far more goes into acing a test than what was studied the night before.

That's what the professors say, at least. They'll tell you there are (essentially) three areas that contribute to success on a given test, and even more importantly, to the knowledge you draw from each class as a whole:

1. Know your professor.
2. Manage your time.
3. Study effectively.

Know Your Professor

"When you take a class, you need to master the professor as much as the material," says Dr. Rick Mann, vice president for academic affairs at Crown College in St. Bonifacius, Minnesota.

"Master a professor? How does that work?" you might ask. Mann says successful students first identify the things a professor gives priority to, and then they figure out how to communicate this information back to the prof in the method he or she requires.

But how do you know what a prof is looking for?

"Just ask," Mann says. "They won't bite."

He says students often think wrongly that faculty members don't want to talk to them. But that's not true. He says he values visits from his students—even when they don't have class-related questions.

"Go see a prof if for no other reason than so you'll know how to approach them when there *is* a reason," Mann says. "Stop by their offices often. Then when you really need help, it won't be so uncomfortable. Professors really value student initiative."

"Professors are real people," says a college dean in Texas. "And most of the time, they're real nice people."

Virginia Lettinga, associate professor and director of academic enrichment and support at Bethel College in St. Paul, Minnesota, says that connections with friends and professors are key ingredients to a successful student.

"Those connections make you feel like you are in the swing of college—if you feel like you belong here, you'll do well," Lettinga says. "Research shows that if you study like an animal but don't make friends or meet your profs, you'll likely drop out after your first year."

Manage Your Time

So, back to that monster test you're studying for. As long as you review the right material the night before the test, you'll succeed, right?

Not necessarily. Since that's probably not the only class you're taking, you may have reading to do for another class, as well as a paper to write for still another. Or worse.

Jarstfer warns: "Expect that you may have three tests on the same day, and you're not going to be able to study for all three the night before. You really need to start studying for them the week before. . . .

Incoming students tend to think they can do things at the last minute, and in high school they probably could. But it's better to plan ahead rather than throw something together at the last minute." Efficient **time management** is critical to college success and survival.

Unfortunately, though, planning ahead in college can be tough, considering the heavier class load and increased responsibility, not to mention more social options. Jarstfer says that every year students overcommit their time. Surrounded by so many good options, it's hard for them to say no.

"But it's OK to say no," Jarstfer says. "You don't have to be involved in everything. You need only to do the things that are in keeping with your goals and talents."

You'll want to find time for a social life, of course, and for your job, but not at the expense of your studies. Do your best to work social activities, as well as your work, around your academic schedule.

"Block out time to study for just about every course, just about every day," Lettinga says. "The reason they give you a syllabus is so you can see the whole semester and can divide (80) pages of reading into reasonable portions. Eighty pages in a single blow would mean you read the entire evening, and that's not the way the mind remembers and retains well."

Many professors agree it's helpful to immediately transfer all the due dates from your syllabus into your daily planner. If daily planners don't work for you, find something else—whatever it takes for you to

keep track of your tests and assignments as you budget time for studying and homework.

Study Effectively

OK, let's rewind a little bit. It's not the night before the test. Instead, you have planned ahead and are taking your whole Saturday afternoon to prepare for next Thursday's exam.

But there's a problem. You're a recovering procrastinator with study skills that revolve around your short-term memory and an uncanny ability to cram. *How in the world,* you wonder, *does anybody go about studying in such a way that information can be retained over the long haul?*

One of the first steps is to determine how you best learn. Do you get more information from reading the textbook, or from studying figures in the textbook, or from vocabulary flashcards?

"Some students come to me and say, 'I've read this three times, and it just doesn't stick,' and I say, 'Quit reading it then!'" Jarstfer says. "If you don't get it by reading it, don't read it over and over again. If you would get it better by studying the pictures and diagrams and lists, study those."

In seeking to retain knowledge, Lettinga suggests that a pencil is actually a far greater complement to reading than a highlighter. And since students own their own books in college, scribbling notes in the margins of textbooks isn't only allowed, it's encouraged. After each reading assignment, she says students should write a short summary of the information. This will help them to encapsulate the main idea of the reading in a way a highlighter could only dream of.

"I've had students who have highlighted almost every single word in every single book," Lettinga said. "Highlighting can be really counterproductive if you do that. But if you summarize and reframe an idea in your own words, that makes you understand. Highlighting just gives you a batch of bright words."

Other things to keep in mind while studying:

1. **Environment**—Find several good places to study; just don't make them too comfortable. That means you probably shouldn't study in bed, where you're likely to fall asleep. It also means being realistic about the stuff you surround yourself with. "If you cover your studying area with pictures of people from home, the Rocky Mountains where you wish you could be, your dog, your girlfriend, I promise, it will distract you," she says. "There's all that stuff reminding you of what you'd rather be doing."

2. **Been there, done that**—Mann gives a good reminder: "All of these classes have been taken before." Because of this, he says, upperclassmen can be a perfect resource in learning how to master not only the material, but the professor's expectations. Be sure to ask those older students.

3. **Teaching method**—Jarstfer notes that many professors say they've learned the most since they've been teaching students. In order to explain the material to someone else, students have to understand the ideas themselves. Whether it's a classmate or a stuffed animal—as Jarstfer said one successful student used—teaching the material to someone else can pay big dividends in learning and retention.

4. **Attendance**—"One of the best and easiest things you can do is go to every class. It is a rare student who cannot go to class and do well," Mann says.

Test Time

Tomorrow's the test, but you're ready. You've managed your time well, and you've studied appropriately. You know your professor and his expectations, and though he wouldn't provide a word count for the essay, he's pointed you in a direction for success.

That monster he promised? It's no longer the Godzilla it might have been. In fact, it's looking more like Elmo all the time.

(Johnson 2002)

Please refer to the reading as you respond in complete sentences to the following questions:

1. What three areas that contribute to learning success were identified by the professors in this article?
   The three areas that contribute to learning success are knowing your professors, managing your time, and studying effectively.

2. Identify one recommendation in the area of knowing your professor that you believe you would do.
   Answers will vary.

3. What is one idea in the section on managing your time that you believe is important?
   Answers will vary.

4. Name two suggestions in the area of studying effectively that you will use this semester.
   Answers will vary.

Being a Successful College Student

As you may have concluded, being successful in college includes adopting certain behaviors that will strengthen your ability to manage and master your course work. It is certainly beneficial to begin college academically prepared, being able to read, write, think critically, and do research are definite advantages. These academic skills will grow as you learn and apply other skills that support your college experience.

To be a strong, successful student, you will need to

- Set—and reset—goals.
- Manage your time effectively.
- Control your concentration.
- Monitor your progress.
- Study and read.
- Connect with your professors as well as your fellow students.

Set Your Goals

Goals are your intentions—what you plan to accomplish. The simple act of stating a goal is the first step to achieving it. So go right ahead and say your goals out loud!

You can develop goals for the long term, intermediate term (as steps toward a longer-term goal), or short term. For example, one long-term goal you have most likely set for this class is to pass it satisfactorily. A short-term goal might be to complete the assignment that is due for next class. An intermediate goal might be to transfer all the assignments and their due dates from your syllabus into your planner by the weekend.

Short-term, intermediate, and long-term goals also can be applied to longer time periods. For instance, a short-term goal could be to pass all your classes this semester with a C+ or better. Your intermediate goal could be to earn your Associate of Arts degree in three years, emphasizing the social sciences in your electives. You may establish the long-term goal of transferring to a four-year college and majoring in psychology. We continue to set goals as we move through our experiences. Perhaps after you graduate with a degree in psychology, your new long-term goal will include working as a counselor in a public school as you go on to earn a graduate degree in psychology.

The more specifically you state your goals, the more meaningful they become. For example, rather than saying you will pass all your tests, you can establish a clearer objective by saying, "I will get at least an 85 percent on my math exam." Instead of saying, "I'll study this week," you can develop a goal that will really help you succeed: "I will rewrite my class notes after each class this week, and ask and answer two possible test questions for each set of notes."

try it and apply it! 1-1   Set Your Goals

Directions: Identify at least one short-term, one intermediate, and one long-term goal for yourself for this academic year.

Time Frame	Goal(s) for This Year
Short-Term	
Intermediate	
Long-Term	

try it and apply it! 1-2   Set Your Goals for a Class

Directions: Now be more specific. Identify goals, as described previously, for this or another class you are taking this semester.

Class: _____

Time Frame	Semester Goals
Short-Term	
Intermediate	
Long-Term	

Remember to review your goals periodically. You want to be sure you are on track. You might also decide to revise your goals along the way. For example, although unsure at the start, you may sense that you are understanding the material and performing much better in your health class than you had at first anticipated. You initially planned to "Pass with a C." Now you believe you can do better, so you set a higher goal. In this situation, it would be fine to adjust your grade objective to a B or better.

Sometimes you will make changes in some goals in order to accommodate other changes in your life. For example, you might need to adjust the number of classes you will take next semester to make room for more hours at work. Adjust your intentions in one area to make time for goals in another. Make your goals realistic enough to attain, but flexible enough to allow you to achieve success. Commitment to your goals will affect other decisions you make in life. You might need to put some things on hold as you pursue certain objectives. For example, if your goal is to get an A in English, you need to study, read, and prepare your essays, rather than go out the night before assignments are due.

Keep this in mind

Set Your Goals

- Goals put you in charge of your own life and build character.
- Set short-term, intermediate, and long-term goals.
- Write down your goals, and refer to them periodically.
- Set goals that are realistic and doable.
- Make your goals as specific as possible so you can monitor your progress.
- Adjust your goals when necessary, but stay focused.
- Be sure to allow enough time to do what is necessary to reach each goal.

Manage Your Time

What is always moving, but once it passes it can never come back?
What do many people waste, but always wish they had more of?
What will appear if "Emit" looks in a mirror?

The answer to all these questions is . . . Time!

Here's another question: What is the number one life skill students need in order to succeed in college? The answer is the ability to manage their time. Interestingly, although college students spend about half as many hours in class as high school students do, they are expected to study and complete assignments a great deal more *outside* of class. In general, for every three-credit class you take, you should spend twice that, or six hours, completing assignments and studying for the class on your own each week. Many students express great joy at not having to "go to school" so many hours of the day when they are in college, but it is very important that, when building your schedule, you block out the periods of time needed for studying and completing work for each class.

How well do you manage your time? Complete this short survey. For each statement, write the number in the space provided that best describes you. Then add up your total score.

Time Management Survey

Scale	Never 1	Seldom 2	Sometimes 3	Often 4	Always 5

1. _____ I submit my assignments and projects on time.
2. _____ I remember important test and assignment due dates.
3. _____ I record my assignments and test dates in a planner.
4. _____ I complete my assignments before I go out and have fun.
5. _____ I allot sufficient time to complete each assignment.
6. _____ I review class material each day.
7. _____ I keep my schedule flexible so that I can have more time to study before midterms and finals.
8. _____ I arrive before the class session begins.

_____ **Total Score**

If you scored 40, you have **excellent** time management skills.
If you scored 30–39, you have **above average** time management skills.
If you scored 20–29, you have **average** time management skills.
If you scored 10–19, you have **below average** time management skills.
If you scored 1–9, you have **poor** time management skills.

Do the results match the impressions you have of yourself? Don't feel badly if you did not score as well as you hoped. Managing time is a skill most students need to improve upon in college. When they do, they juggle academic life much better. So how can you do this?

Think of the acronym PLANS, presented next, to remind you of important strategies you can use to help manage your time.

PLANS

P **P**urchase a **p**lanner.

L **L**ook at all your course syllabi. **L**ocate important dates. **L**og these into your planner at the beginning of each semester.

A **A**llocate enough time in your week to not only **a**ttend class, but to complete **a**ssignments, and **a**rrive on time!

N **N**ote due dates and work backward in planning your time. Think: "When do I need to begin this, and how much do I need to do each night so it will be prepared on time?"

S **S**chedule yourself.

P **Purchase of a college planner is one of the best ways to improve the quality of your time management skills.** Along with your textbooks, it is one of the most important investments you can make at the beginning of each semester. Have it with you always. Because college students have so many assignments to complete, papers to write, presentations to make, quizzes and tests to take, family obligations to meet, and work schedules to juggle, it's impossible to remember everything. Your college planner serves as a central organizer. Numerous planners are available at the campus bookstore, so you can select the one that best suits your needs. You can find these organizers online as well.

L **Look at all your course syllabi at the beginning of a semester, highlight the important dates: due dates for important assignments, tests and quizzes, midterm and final exams, and even vacations!** Next, allocate time to transfer these into your planner on the appropriate dates. This will give you a realistic sense of what your semester will be like. Then, as you check your planner regularly—at least once a week—you will know what is due, when it is due, and you'll be able to plan your life accordingly.

A **Allocate enough time in your planner or schedule to complete reading assignments, study for exams, or write papers.** Some students find it a good idea to stay on campus an extra hour or two daily to finish up tasks before going home or to work. Sometimes a period between classes is actually helpful, because you can use it to study or complete assignments. Over-schedule, rather than under-schedule, time for study.

It's important to include your work and personal responsibilities in your schedule as well. These often take up much of your time. And don't forget to allocate some downtime! You need opportunities to relax, enjoy time with family and friends, and do the things you love. Building a schedule that takes all this into account will provide you with a realistic and workable weekly plan.

Arrive to classes on time. Being punctual says a lot about you to your professors and classmates: you are responsible and organized. Make any adjustments in your schedule or start times for classes if this presents a problem.

N **Note due dates for assignments and work backward to find out when you should start preparing for a test or researching for an essay.**

S **Make schedules to help you organize your time.** Assign yourself tasks as though you were your own professor. Use daily, weekly, or monthly schedules to "see" your activities and the amount of time you have to complete them.

try it and apply it! 1-3   Time Management Scenarios

Directions: Break up into groups. You have 15 minutes to discuss your assigned scenario. As a group, you need to identify the poor time-management skills presented in your scenario and develop a better plan for the characters involved. Assign a director to lead the discussion, a note-taker to complete the form that follows, and a timekeeper/taskmaster to make sure the group adheres to the time limits and stays on task. The note-taker is responsible for reporting back to the class.

Scenario 1

Carolina is meeting with her academic advisor to schedule her classes for next semester. This is the last day she can register for classes. She explains to her advisor that she works every day, but could begin evening classes at 5:30 p.m. The advisor schedules three classes for her, but these are not the classes she had wanted to take. Going against the advisor's advice, Carolina adds one more class to her schedule in order to be considered a full-time student. Now she will attend classes four nights a week. What do you think of Carolina's decisions? What could she have done differently?

Scenario 2

On the first day of class, Michael's English professor distributes the course syllabus. The first assignment, involving reading an essay and writing a response, is due on Friday. Mike hasn't bought the textbook yet and is not sure when his financial aid will come through. He also has to buy textbooks for three other classes. How could he complete the first assignment?

Scenario 3

It is Wednesday afternoon, and Daniel has an oral presentation to prepare for his Psychology 101 class tomorrow at 9:00 a.m. Dan also wants to head for Chandler's tonight, where his closest friend, Jason, is playing lead sax in a band. All his friends are planning to go to the first show at 8:00 p.m. Dan hasn't even started working on his presentation or thought about what he is going to say. What should he do?

Scenario 4

Myra has never missed an episode of *Lost,* and the season finale is on tonight. However, she has two more chapters to read in history for class tomorrow. She has about 20 minutes before the show begins. What should she do?

Scenario 5

It's now Thursday evening. Jana has a midterm in chemistry next Monday, and her best friend is having a party tomorrow night. On Saturday, she will be working all day, and on Sunday she is taking her younger sister shopping for a Halloween costume. What is the best way to manage her time so that she can do well on this test?

Scenario 6

It's only three weeks into the semester, and Brian has already been late three times for his Friday morning English class. On Thursday evenings, he usually gets together with his high-school friends and plays pool, getting to bed at about 2:00 a.m. On Friday mornings, he staggers into class 15 minutes after the session has begun. Most of the

(continued)

(*continued*)

time, he has forgotten his textbook. What should he do differently if he wants to pass this course?

Scenario 7

The college campus is really huge and finding a parking spot is a terrible problem. Ben's first class is at 11:00 a.m., and by that time, most of the good spaces are taken. He typically drives around for 20 minutes looking for a spot and eventually ends up parking in a lot far from his first class. He races across campus on foot, usually arriving to class late. His professor has issued him a final warning. If he is late to class one more time, he will be dropped from class. Is there anything Ben can do?

Scenario # _____

Brainstorm a list of possible ways to avoid the situation.

1. _____
2. _____
3. _____
4. _____
5. _____

Now use your list to generate a solution.

_____
_____
_____
_____
_____

Keep this in mind

What Does a Good Time Manager Do?

- Sets specific and realistic personal and academic goals.
- Purchases and uses a planner for personal, academic, and work obligations.
- Reviews all course syllabi and enters important dates in the planner.
- Develops a weekly and monthly schedule.
- Arrives to classes on time.
- Does not underestimate the time needed to complete tasks.
- Modifies schedules when necessary.
- Makes time to relax and exhale.

Control Your Concentration

College freshman often say that staying focused is a major problem in class and when studying. Their minds wander and before they know it, 10 minutes in class have passed but they haven't heard a thing! Or they find themselves in the middle of a chapter but can't recall one thing they have just read.

How can you control your **concentration** and make yourself a stronger student? To improve your listening, reading, and studying skills, an important step is to recognize what distracts you and interferes with your concentration.

The art of concentration, no matter if you are studying psychology or playing sports, is to reduce or eliminate distractions and focus on the task at hand. The exercise below will help you identify your distractions. Then continue reading for helpful hints for enhancing concentration.

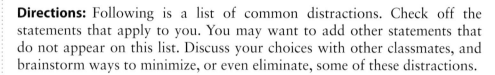 **1-4**   **Identify What Distracts You**

Directions: Following is a list of common distractions. Check off the statements that apply to you. You may want to add other statements that do not appear on this list. Discuss your choices with other classmates, and brainstorm ways to minimize, or even eliminate, some of these distractions.

Common Distractions Checklist

____ 1. I am worried about paying for college.

____ 2. I am concerned about paying off my loans.

____ 3. I am worried about meeting my expenses.

____ 4. I am working full time.

____ 5. I am helping in my family's business.

____ 6. I think about finding a place to live.

____ 7. I am worried about taking care of my siblings, children, or parents.

____ 8. I am worried about flunking out.

____ 9. I don't want to lose my financial aid.

____ 10. I am worried about making new friends in college.

____ 11. I miss my high school friends.

____ 12. I think about my boyfriend/girlfriend.

____ 13. I want to go back to my country. I miss my family and friends.

____ 14. I am suffering from migraines.

____ 15. I always get hungry when I do my work.

____ 16. My little brother/sister always comes into my room and bothers me.

____ 17. My cell phone keeps ringing.

____ 18. My neighbors play loud music.

____ 19. The TV is always blasting in the den.

____ 20. I listen to my iPod while I am studying.

____ 21. I fall asleep while I am studying.

(continued)

(continued)

___ 22. I daydream a lot.

___ 23. I like to sit in the back of the classroom.

___ 24. I go out to drink a beverage, to eat a snack, or to smoke a cigarette during the lecture.

___ 25. I finish my assignments while I am in another class.

___ 26. I am often texting on my cell phone.

___ 27. _____

___ 28. _____

___ 29. _____

___ 30. _____

Hints for Enhancing Concentration
When You Are Outside of Class

- **Study in a quiet and comfortable environment.** Select a place that is designated for reading and studying. The college library provides large tables or individual desks. On a nice day, a quiet place on campus might be just the right spot for you. Even your dorm room, when your roommate is out, might be an ideal location to study.

- **Create your own study area.** At home, find a comfortable working space where others will not bother you. Gather all your study materials together, make sure there is adequate lighting, turn off your cell phone, TV, and music player (unless background music helps you concentrate). Minimize visual distractions, such as pictures, your computer, or an open window.

- **Establish a regular weekly schedule.** Find the best time to read and study. Most people are more alert and able to concentrate during the day and early evening. However, if you have other responsibilities, such as work or family, you might have to plan to study early in the morning or later at night.

- **Set reading and study goals, and be positive and realistic.** Some college reading may not be challenging or interesting; however, to pass your class and meet graduation requirements, you will need to do the work. In addition, if you know you have difficulty concentrating, begin with short study periods and increase them gradually over time.

■ **Take breaks.** Divide assignments into manageable chunks. Reward yourself with a small break. Step away from your studies and do something different for a short period of time.

When You Are in Class

■ **Before lectures, look over notes from the previous session.** This will remind you about what you have learned and help you to predict what will be discussed in the current lecture.

■ **Read ahead.** It is always a good idea to read the chapters in your textbook that relate to what is going to be covered in the next lecture. By doing so, you will become an active listener who can participate in discussions and ask questions.

■ **Show interest during lectures.** Sitting in the back of the room, putting your head on the desk, or looking out of the window will make it more difficult to concentrate. Behave as though you are concentrating! Select a seat toward the front of the class. Try to answer questions and take part in the discussion. Your involvement will help you concentrate. It will also show the instructor that you are actively listening and participating in class.

■ **Be active and take notes.** Focus on the instructor's lesson by asking questions and taking notes. If you are part of a group, get involved. Don't sit back and let others do the work.

■ **Resist distractions.** Turn off your cell phone, and put it away so you will not be tempted to view your messages. Position yourself away from disruptive classmates.

■ **Minimize taking breaks in the middle of lectures.** Students miss valuable material when they leave class to answer calls or to get a drink. Instructors generally schedule breaks when classes meet for long blocks of time, so wait for that designated break.

Sometimes you may find that you cannot eliminate certain distractions that interfere with your performance in college and your general well-being. Test anxiety, concerns about money, and personal and health problems can be very serious. You may benefit from outside or professional support. You may want to ask your professor for an appropriate place on campus to get advice. Find out about the location and hours of the following support services on your campus:

■ students with disabilities office   ■ financial aid office

■ career counseling   ■ health services

■ educational counseling   ■ international student services

- job placement counseling
- psychological counseling center
- transfer counseling
- child care services
- academic advisement center

Monitor Your Progress

One of the most *wonderful* things about college is that you are more independent than ever. One of the most *challenging* things about college is that you are more independent than ever! Yes, it's the good news, and, sometimes, the problem. But you can handle it.

Before college, it is likely that several people in your life were keeping track of how you were doing in school. Parents, guardians, teachers, guidance counselors, and school administrators might have gotten involved in your progress and well-being. They would watch out for you and step in to set limits and give you advice and support, whether you asked for them or not. Many people had access to your records, and if you were entitled to support, it simply came your way.

It is different in college. Many people will call about you and lend support, but it is up to you to seek them out. Your records, grades, and any documentation of disability or special needs are not shared unless you give your permission. Your professors and administrators will not speak to anyone in your personal life about you unless you allow it. And you will not get help unless you ask for it. If services exist at the college that could support you, such as a reading or writing center, you must make an appointment on your own to access that support.

This means that you are responsible for monitoring, or watching over, your own progress in college. You need to judge how things are going and make changes when they are needed. This is especially important for each of your classes. You need to keep track of your grades within each class throughout every semester. Even within individual assignments, you will need to check that you are really learning the material. Your need to be your own support system! If you ever answer the question "How are you doing?" with "I don't know" or "I have no idea," it's time to learn some self-monitoring skills. The checklist on page 19 will help you.

try it and apply it! 1-5   Monitor Your Progress

Directions: Here is a checklist of questions to help you monitor your behavior and progress in school. Read each question carefully and check *Always, Sometimes,* or *Never* as it applies to you. Then read the comments that follow.

Checklist: How Am I Doing?

Task	Always	Sometimes	Never
1. Do I plan my schedule to include time during the week to complete all of my course work?			
2. Do I review all of my course outlines at the start of each semester so that I know where I am headed in each class?			
3. Do I enter important due dates from the syllabus into my own planner at the beginning of the semester?			
4. Do I break long assignments into manageable parts and assign these to myself on a weekly basis?			
5. Do I check off assignments after I have completed them?			
6. Do I make sure I never miss a class?			
7. Do I arrive at all of my classes on time?			
8. Do I ask questions in or after class when I need to clarify something that has been said in class?			
9. Do I prepare well for exams and stop studying only when I am sure I know the material?			
10. Do I record all my grades on exams and assignments as I receive them so I have a running record?			
11. Do I make appointments to meet with my professors when I am unclear about an assignment or confused by a topic?			
12. Do I find out in a timely manner what I may have missed in class because of an unavoidable absence?			
13. Do I schedule personal and social events around the completion of my assignments?			
Total Number of Checks in Each Column			

- **If you identified between 10 and 13 items in the *Always* column,** you are already doing a fine job of self-monitoring. Notice any items where you selected *Sometimes* or *Never* and try including them this semester.

- **If you scored between six and nine items in the *Always* column,** you are doing fairly well in self-monitoring but should set goals in three or four areas to get even better.

- **If you scored five or fewer items in the *Always* column,** you need to take much better charge of your self-monitoring. Consider ways to incorporate the behaviors into your regular college routine. Focus on the items you checked as *Never* and try to include them in your college routine. Set personal goals in these areas for the semester. Meet with an advisor or counselor to get support.

try it and apply it! 1-6   **Monitor Your Progress**

Directions: Using the questions in the preceding survey, write a list of 13 behaviors you could practice to help you monitor your progress in college. The first one is done for you. *Answers may vary. Sample answers provided.*

1. Plan a schedule that includes time to get my course work done.

2. *Review all my course outlines at the beginning of each semester.*

3. *Enter important due dates from the syllabus into my own planner at the start of each semester.*

4. *Break long assignments into manageable parts and assign these to myself on a weekly basis.*

5. *Check off assignments after I have completed them.*

6. *Never miss a class.*

7. *Arrive on time for all my classes.*

8. *Ask questions in or after class when I don't understand something or want to learn more.*

9. *Prepare well for exams and don't stop studying until I can say I know the material.*

10. *Record all my grades on tests and assignments so I have a record of all of them.*

11. *Make appointments to meet with my professors when I am unclear about an assignment or confused about a topic.*

12. *Find out what I have missed in class when I was unavoidably absent.*

13. *Schedule personal and social plans around the completion of my assignments.*

The behaviors on the checklist are those of a student who is "doing the right thing." Let that student be you. If you realize that you never or only sometimes do a particular task as a successful student would, modify your behavior to be more in control and in charge of your learning. Be your own monitor. Take care of yourself. This will definitely improve your chances for academic success and help you feel better at the same time.

try it and apply it! 1-7   Monitor Your Progress

Directions: Go back to your responses to the "How Am I Doing?" checklist. Look at the items that you do only *Sometimes* or *Never*. Select one of these tasks and write it below. Then indicate how you will approach this task in order to be more successful this semester.

A self-monitoring task I need to improve this semester is _____

_____

To address this task I will

_____

_____

_____

Keep this in mind

Advantages of Monitoring Your Progress

- You will feel in control of your academic life.
- You will make adjustments when needed.
- You will know when to ask for help.
- You will be better prepared for exams and classes.
- You will improve your overall performance in school.

Discover Your Learning Style

What comes to mind when you hear the word "style"? Maybe you think of the type of clothing a person wears, his or her mannerisms, or even personality. Do you have a friend who is talkative, loves to dance, and is often working on a project? Perhaps you have another who is quiet, enjoys reading and painting, and always helps you come up with solutions to your problems. You and your friends have different approaches to managing your lives.

As individuals, we also have different approaches in the way we learn. Educators have researched and studied the different **learning styles** we use to complete tasks or acquire knowledge. In fact, these styles in learning are reflected in the way we deal with our lives, because they are rooted in our brain and life experiences.

One helpful model of learning styles for students is the **VAT/K Model.** Each letter stands for a general learning style or preference a person is likely to have and use.

V stands for Visual. Visual learners prefer to learn from things they can see and study visually. They tend to think in pictures and create and use mental images to remember information. Thus, in reading, a visual learner will appreciate the use of pictures, charts, diagrams, and illustrations. In class, a visual learner benefits from the use of PowerPoint presentations, videos, transparencies, and models.

A stands for Auditory. Auditory learners prefer to learn by listening. Generally, auditory learners can interpret the meaning of the language they hear and sense the impact of tone of voice and expression. Often, an auditory learner will transform written material into aural material, as in reading or studying aloud. Hearing the information, or even attaching it to melody, often helps the auditory learner recall it later. An auditory learner may enjoy lectures, class discussion, verbal arguments, and debate.

T/K stands for Tactile/Kinesthetic. Tactile/kinesthetic learners learn best by touching, feeling, moving, and doing. They prefer a "hands-on" approach, getting physically involved in the learning process. Thus, in class, they are likely to enjoy laboratory experiences, role-playing, puzzles, and working with or creating models. Often, the active process helps focus attention and increases recall of the information involved in the experience.

What is your learning style? Knowing your learning style preference will help you select the **learning strategies** that work best for you. To help you find out, complete the following exercise.

try it and apply it! 1-8   Identify Your Learning Style

Directions: Read the word in the first column titled "When you . . ." Then, going across each row, circle the questions to which you answer "Yes." These are grouped under the headings Visual, Auditory, and Kinesthetic/Tactile. You may answer "Yes" in all three categories for some items. However, you will probably find that you write "Yes" in one column more than you do in the others. This column represents your preferred learning style. After you complete the exercise, answer the questions that follow.

Learning Styles

When you...	Visual	Auditory	Kinesthetic & Tactile
Spell	Do you try to see the word?	Do you sound out the word or use a phonetic approach?	Do you write the word down to find if it feels right?
Talk	Do you talk sparingly but dislike listening for too long? Do you favor words such as *see*, *picture*, and *imagine*?	Do you enjoy listening but hesitate to talk? Do you use words such as *hear*, *tune*, and *think*?	Do you gesture and use expressive movements? Do you use words such as *feel*, *touch*, and *hold*?
Concentrate	Do you become distracted by untidiness or movement?	Do you become distracted by sounds or noises?	Do you become distracted by activity around you?
Meet someone again	Do you forget names but remember faces or remember where you met?	Do you forget faces but remember names or remember what you talked about?	Do you remember best what you did together?
Contact people on business	Do you prefer direct, face-to-face, personal meetings?	Do you prefer the telephone?	Do you talk with people while walking or participating in an activity?
Read	Do you like descriptive scenes or pause to imagine the actions being described?	Do you enjoy dialogue and conversation or hear the characters talk?	Do you prefer action stories, or are you not a keen reader?
Do something new at work	Do you like to see demonstrations, diagrams, slides, or posters?	Do you prefer verbal instructions or talking about a task with someone else?	Do you prefer to jump right in and try it?
Put something together	Do you look at the directions and the picture?	Do you read aloud?	Do you ignore the directions and figure it out as you go along?
Need help with a computer application	Do you seek out pictures or diagrams?	Do you call the help desk, ask a neighbor, or growl at the computer?	Do you keep trying to do it, or do you try it on another computer?

Adapted from Colin Rose (1987).

What is your dominant learning style? Does this correspond with what you already know about yourself? Explain.

Answers will vary.

try it and apply it! 1-9

Select Learning Strategies to Match Your Style

Directions: Now that you have identified your learning style preference, you can select strategies for learning and study that match your style. Following are several strategies grouped according to the style they complement. First, find your identified style and read through the recommended strategies. Check off those you think you could do to support your learning. Then look through the strategies that are listed in the other two categories. Even though they may not represent your predominant learning style, you may find some that work for you as well.

Visual Learning Strategies

_____ Pay attention to diagrams, sketches, semantic maps, photographs, charts, and other visual representations of your course material. Look at these during your studying and use them to help you recall the information.

_____ Transfer your lecture notes or information from reading selections into visual representations of your own. Create your own word maps, flow charts, and diagrams from which to learn your material.

_____ Watch video recordings about the subjects you are studying.

_____ Color code your notes or portions of your textbook, using different color highlighters to designate different kinds of information. For example, highlight main ideas in blue and examples in yellow.

_____ Create symbols to represent key information you are learning.

_____ Sit in class where you can easily see the board, screen, or other visual representations of the instruction.

Auditory Learning Strategies

_____ Use your class notes to recite the day's lecture aloud.

_____ Read important points from your textbook aloud while studying.

_____ Listen to audio recordings of the subjects you are studying.

_____ Discuss your subjects with friends after class.

_____ Be part of a study group that meets regularly.

Tactile/Kinesthetic Learning Strategies

_____ Participate in classes where you can move about and/or be actively involved, such as laboratory classes, hands-on art classes, or physical education classes.

_____ Take a lot of notes; keep busy in class.

_____ Move around as you study. It's OK to recite the information you are learning as you walk.

_____ Study while you exercise or power walk.

_____ Make your own study tapes.

_____ Create flash cards or study cards that you can manipulate or maneuver while reviewing.

Other preferences in the way you study also reflect your personal learning style. One area to think about is the surroundings in which you prefer to learn—the environment. Consider the following environmental factors, and check off the situation that reflects your preferences. Then when you make arrangements to study, you can incorporate these factors.

Sound

_____ I prefer to study in a quiet area.

_____ I prefer to study with some background noise or music.

Light

_____ I prefer soft, dim light.

_____ I prefer bright light while concentrating.

Temperature

_____ I like to study in a cool room.

_____ I like to study in a warm place.

Time

_____ I do my best studying in the morning.

_____ I study best later in the day.

Design

_____ I study best sitting at a desk.

_____ I like an informal, relaxed study arrangement, such as a soft chair, or pillows and carpet on the floor.

Keep this in mind

Evaluating the Effectiveness of Your Learning Style

It's possible that sometimes the learning style you prefer is not always the most effective for you. For example, you may enjoy listening to music while you study, but if you find yourself singing along to a song rather than focusing on your task, you should turn off the sound. Or if you think it best to study at night, but you fall asleep before finishing the assigned material, you should study earlier, because your preference is not serving your goals. Be honest with yourself, and do what you need to do to succeed.

Engage with Your School

In addition to all the skills and strategies you want to develop to support your learning, one of the best things you can do for yourself in college is to connect with your school and those in it. The more you engage with your studies, peers, and professors, the more you are likely to meet your collegiate goals.

Connect with Your Campus

Find out about the clubs and activities on campus. You will be amazed at the range of extracurricular activities available. Ongoing programs are likely to cross every area of academic study, interest, and sport. If you get involved in some, you will meet other students who share interests similar to yours.

Check out the special events, lectures, seminars, and guest speakers. Also, become familiar with the services available to you on campus, ranging from tutorial support to job placement, computer training to health services, advisement to psychological counseling. As you make a campus "your" campus, you will feel more at home and connected, and this feeling will help you to stick to your goals, even when things seem difficult.

Connect with Your Professors

Throughout your college years, you will come in contact with many professors. You may like some more than others. Some professors will teach in a style that works particularly well for you. For example, if you are a visual

learner, you may enjoy a professor who uses a lot of PowerPoint slides in class. Some professors may share anecdotes and call for a lot of discussion, whereas others may focus only on the content of the subject. Some professors will involve the class in a lot of activity, and others will offer only lectures. You are likely to perceive certain professors as being more open to engaging personally with students. It is up to you to understand the requirements and expectations of each professor, both academically and in terms of classroom behavior. Do your very best to meet those expectations.

In any case, it is a good idea to make yourself known to your professors. If you can, introduce yourself before or after a class. Ask questions or share comments. Take advantage of a professor's office hours, the time the professor is available to meet with students. Use this time to clarify your assignments and be sure you are on the right track. Visit a professor before an exam to be sure you are studying the right material. If you have the opportunity, make appointments to make up exams or hand in work when you have been absent. If you are experiencing difficulty in class, don't hesitate to share this with your professor. He or she will appreciate your openness and can offer support.

Finally, you may find a professor with whom you feel especially comfortable. You might want to seek out this professor with a problem or concern about any aspect of your college experience. He or she may be able to help you directly or advise you as to where you can go for additional support.

Connect with Your Peers

Having friends and acquaintances is an important part of your overall well-being, especially when entering a new environment like college. Connecting with other students will not only make you feel more at home and secure on campus, it will also create an important support base and resource for your studies.

Although your campus may appear very diverse, everyone there has at least one thing in common: They are all attending the same school! College is a wonderful opportunity to reach out and connect with others, even if, or perhaps, especially if, they "appear" different from you. Aside from forging potential friendships, engaging with your fellow students can ultimately support your learning. Even if you prefer to study alone, leave some time to review material with a fellow student. Join a study group. Participate in class discussions. If your professor forms groups or teams in your classes, try to take an active role, even if it means leaving your "comfort zone" for a little while. If you feel comfortable, try to find at least one person in each of your classes with whom you can connect if you are absent or have a question about something in class.

If you are on a commuter campus, making personal connections may be especially challenging. It is easy to become isolated since most students go to class and then leave immediately for home or work. Try to allow for some social time. Joining a club or attending a special event may be just the vehicle you need to find a friend. The funny thing is that most people who have attended college forget a lot of what they have learned, but the friendships they formed can last a lifetime.

try it and apply it! 1-10   **Engage with Your School**

Directions: Think about how the information you just read can apply to you personally. For each area previously discussed, identify at least one way in which you will make an attempt to take part. Be as specific as possible. Establish them as goals for the semester. Share your responses with a classmate.

1. This semester I will take part in a college-wide activity by _____

    _____

2. This semester, I will engage with a professor by _____

    _____

3. This semester, I will connect with a fellow student by _____

    _____

On Your Way

The chance to start *anything* that you have chosen to do is always a wonderful opportunity. Starting college, as you probably have been told over and over, ranks at the top of the opportunity list. Starting strong—that is, with knowledge, skills, insights, and commitment, will make your journey more pleasant. Of course, you will grow and learn along the way, but it is always helpful to gain insight from those who have already taken that road.

The following brief article, from a textbook by Robert Feldman called *Power Learning*, recounts the educational experiences of a student named Shante Moore. He eventually received a bachelor's degree from Kansas State University and his master's degree from Georgetown University. Read the selection. Keep track of the factors that led to Moore's success. As you read, notice any similarities you may have with him. Complete the activity that follows.

Have a great semester!

Speaking of Success

By Robert Feldman

It was in the ninth grade that Shante Moore came to the realization that he needed to make some major changes in his life if he wanted to succeed academically.

"I tried to do everything—play sports, work a job, hang out with my friends, as well as balancing my academics," Moore recalled. "But in the ninth grade I didn't do well and my grades suffered. It was a shock to me. I then made a decision to prioritize things and to make my grades the first priority."

He sure did: Moore eventually went on to win a series of academic prizes, including Fulbright and Truman awards. Moore is currently economic commercial officer for the U.S. diplomatic liaison office in Pristina, Kosovo, part of the U.S. Department of State.

Moore's academic and occupational success was brought about not only by hard work, but also by guidance from some good mentors (people who took care to counsel and advise him).

"The grades were important in college, but for me, learning how to make contacts and to network were big challenges," Moore explained. "I'm a very private person so learning how to develop interpersonal skills was a challenge. I thought all I needed to do is get good grades, but it's more than that."

"I was fortunate at Kansas State where we were required to take a public speaking course, and it really helped," he added. "One of my counselors told me to get out and do more, get involved in clubs, activities, and community service. For me, community service was very important because it dovetailed nicely with my interests and values.

"In addition, particular mentors have been very important to me. I always had the support of my family but I needed the support of mentors who really guided me," Moore said. "I wouldn't have won the Fulbright or Truman awards without them."

Moore attributes his academic success to three main factors.

"Prioritization is very important," he noted. "You have to choose two or three things and focus on them. Second, time management is crucial, because it's always a challenge to find the time to study. And, finally, there's preparation."

"The challenge," he said, "is finding the time to study, work hard, and get good grades."

(Feldman 2009)

try it and apply it! 1-11

Starting Strong with Behaviors Leading to College Success

Directions: Answer the following questions based on the preceding reading selection and ideas you have gotten from reading this chapter.

1. What was the major cause of the academic problems Moore experienced in ninth grade?

   He felt that he was trying to do too many things at once, playing sports, hanging out with friends, working, and studying.

2. What did Moore decide to do?

   He decided to prioritize his time and make his studies the most important thing.

3. How do you know his decision paid off?

   He went on to win two academic prizes called the Fulbright and Truman awards.
   He also earned two degrees, a bachelor's and a master's, and holds an important job in the government.

(continued)

(continued)

4. In addition to working hard to get better grades, to what does Moore attribute his success?

   He thinks that his development of interpersonal skills, which he used in clubs, activities,

   and community service, was important. He also thinks that his connections with people

   who served as mentors, or advisors to him, was most helpful.

5. At the conclusion of the article, what are the three main factors to which Shante Moore attributes his academic success?

   First, prioritize the things on which you want to focus; second, develop time-management

   skills to find the time to study; and third, work hard to complete tasks and be prepared for

   school and all its challenges.

6. What strategies do you intend to put into place this semester based on ideas from this selection, or throughout the chapter?

   Answers will vary.

Start Strong: Taking Charge of Your Success in College

- Begin learning and applying skills and strategies that support your success from Day 1!
- Set personal and realistic short- and long-term goals. Be as specific as you can, and make adjustments to your goals when needed.
- Do whatever it takes to manage your time. Prioritize your studies. Buy a planner!
- Eliminate distractions that interfere with studying productively.
- Monitor your progress. Keep track of how you are doing in all your classes.
- Identify your personal learning style. Use your self-knowledge to select strategies that work best for you in your studies.
- Get involved! Engage in campus activities, with your professors, and with fellow students.

Key Terms

auditory
concentration
goals
kinesthetic

learning strategies
learning style
monitor your progress

tactile
time management
visual

chapter

2

Get Ready to Read
Active Reading Strategies for Managing College Texts

In this chapter

you will learn to

- Become an active reader
- Understand metacognition
- Survey your college reading
- Access your prior knowledge
- Preview readings of different genres
- Read for a purpose by asking and answering questions

- Manage your reading
  Highlight
  Annotate
  Take marginal notes

Find out more about the learning process in Module 4.

Develop Skills While Reading About the
Learning Process

How did I learn to speak? Why can my 10-year-old brother do so many more things than my 5-year-old cousin, but he can't understand any of the subjects I am learning in college? Why am I so strong in math, but have a tough time with writing? Why am I motivated to learn some things, but not others? Ron isn't as smart as Karina—why does *he* get the A's? How did I come to believe in the things that I do?

We all have questions about how we learn: mentally, socially, and emotionally. A wide range of ideas exists about what happens when learning takes place. Some of these ideas are called learning theories. A **learning theory** looks at the influences and experiences that account for the development of knowledge, skills, values, and worldview. Much has been researched and written about the learning process by educators, psychologists, and scientists. Enjoy finding out about aspects of how we learn and develop while you learn and improve your capabilities as an active reader.

Become an Active Reader

What comes to mind when you think of reading? If it has been a challenge for you over the years, you might respond, "Ugh!" or "Please, no!" If you enjoy curling up with a good book to relax, or, with the help of your imagination, to "visit" another world or time, then of course you will think of reading as a positive experience: pleasurable, soothing, interesting, or even exciting.

Generally, those who feel good about reading understand the dynamic nature of the reading process. There's nothing passive about it. Reading is full of activity. It requires far more than turning to page one, sitting back, and moving your eyes. There is much to do before, during, and after reading. If you learn to become an active reader, you will surely answer the opening question in a positive way. Let's find out how.

What Do Active Readers Do?

Before reading, active readers check out the entire book to discover the features it offers. They think about what they already know about a subject and what they would like to learn. Active readers look over individual chapters in a systematic way to preview the main points and predict what will be discussed.

As they read, active readers are always thinking about what they are reading, often visualizing the material. They ask questions about the content—establishing a purpose for reading it—to discover the answers to their questions. They monitor their progress along the way. They recognize when something is unclear or confusing to them, and they stop to reread or question the material in order to understand it, allowing them to move on to the next section.

Active readers read with a pen, pencil, and/or a highlighter in hand. They mark up their textbooks—highlighting or underlining key points, writing notes in the margin, and identifying key vocabulary terms.

While reading, active readers are never alone. Who are they with? The author! They "talk" with the author, not literally, but in their minds. They question, challenge, or even disagree with the author. They show this by writing comments in the places where they question an author's argument, disagree with a point, find an answer to a question they developed during previewing, or want to note information from their own experience that relates to the text.

Active readers adjust how quickly they read, based on the purpose or difficulty of the assignment.

After reading, active readers don't just close a book and walk away. They think about what they have read. They might reflect a few moments about the message of a novel or about a character that meant the most to them. Perhaps they jot down key points or write a short summary to note the most important points in a textbook chapter, or write questions about the material to ask their professor. Often, when the reading is finished, the reflection begins.

Metacognition

Being aware of what you do and do not understand as you read is part of a process known as metacognition. **Metacognition** is the capacity to think about your own thinking. It comes from the terms *meta,* meaning going beyond, transcending, or being more comprehensive, and *cognition,* refer-ring to thought and mental processes. Active readers use metacognition con-stantly. They think about how well they are learning and what they can do to best meet their learning goals.

It is very important to have metacognitive skills—to be conscious of your own level of understanding while you are reading. You need to be mindful of how your new learning fits into your broader understanding of a topic. Metacognition helps you remember what you are reading. Your analysis of your thinking makes what you read meaningful, personal, and relevant to you. It helps you take different steps and try different strategies as you study, until you are satisfied that you understand the material. When you understand the material, your ability to use and remember the new information is greatly improved.

Throughout this textbook, activities have been created to help you use metacognition. At places where it is most important, you will see the symbol at the beginning of this section. It is a reminder to you to think about your thinking—to be especially aware of your own learning process and to take responsibility for your learning.

In the pages that follow, you will learn and practice important strategies to help you become an active and purposeful reader.

Survey Your Textbooks

Although we live in a technological age, and so much of what we need to learn can be accessed through the push of a button, the good old textbook continues as a primary means of obtain-ing knowledge in college. Most classes have assigned textbooks and students are required to read them. Just check out those lines at the bookstore! More often than not, you will be expected to read textbooks inde-pendently. You are held responsible for the content that is assigned, whether or not your professor covers the material in class. So it is extremely important that you develop the skills to *independently* manage your text-book reading.

Just as you would "check out" all the fea-tures of any electronic equipment you pur-chase before you start to use it, you need to check out the features of each of your col-lege textbooks. This is called **surveying the textbook.** Each book is different. You need

to know what each offers, how it is organized, what features it includes, and where each feature is located. After you know this information, you can use your textbook efficiently and effectively as a study tool and a resource. Take off that plastic wrap, write your name on the inside cover, and spend some time getting acquainted with each text.

try it and apply it! 2-1   Identifying Textbook Features

Directions: The following features are common to most textbooks, although each is not necessarily found in every book. Look through the list. Then, based on your experience, try completing the definitions by writing in the correct feature on the line provided. Check your answers on page 38 when you are finished.

Title Page	Glossary
Table of Contents	Appendix
Preface	Bibliography
Subject Index	Webliography
Name Index	Acknowledgments

1. The _____glossary_____ is an alphabetical listing of terms and their definitions used within the textbook. It is generally found in the back of the book.

2. The _____title page_____ appears at the front of the text and lists the title of the book and the names of the author and publisher.

3. In the _acknowledgments_ section, the author expresses appreciation or gratitude to those who have supported the writing of the text.

4. The _table of contents_ is a sequential or chronological listing of the sections, units, chapter names, and chapter parts, as well as their page numbers, found at the beginning of the book. Looking this feature over will give you a good overview of the topics you will be studying.

5. The _____subject index_____ is at the back of a book. It is an alphabetical listing of the topics, subjects, ideas, terms, and names mentioned in the text, and the page(s) on which each is located.

6. The _____preface_____ is a brief essay at the beginning of the book. The author uses this to present a personal message to the reader, including the author's reasons for writing, a relevant anecdote, aims, hopes, or expectations. Sometimes the organization of the chapters is reviewed.

7. Usually placed at the end of the main text, the _____appendix_____ is a compilation of various charts, graphs, tables, lists, maps, or documents to which reference is made throughout the text. Sometimes answer keys are found here as well.

8. The _____bibliography_____ is an alphabetical listing, by author, of printed sources used in the creation of, or cited in, the text. Textbook writers may obtain information from other texts or articles, and give credit to those sources, just as you would in writing a paper.

9. A _____webliography_____ is an alphabetical listing of electronic sources used in the creation of, or cited in, the text.

10. The _____name index_____ is a listing of the significant people, researchers, or contributors mentioned in the content of the textbook.

try it and apply it! 2-2   Survey This Textbook

Directions: Now check out *this* textbook. What features does it include? List five of them in the following chart, along with the page numbers on which they are found. What information about the text does each one help you to understand?

Feature	Page No.	What I Learned About This Textbook
1. *Answers will vary.*		
2.		
3.		
4.		
5.		

Access Your Prior Knowledge

As you open up your textbook to the first chapter, sit down to read a magazine article, or tackle the essay that has been assigned in your history class, you need to take one specific step before you begin.

People understand and learn best when they attach new material to information that they already know. Think about it. If you know a lot about sports, then reading a magazine article on the latest NFL draft picks will make a lot of sense to you. You will connect any new information to your prior knowledge about football. If you are familiar with the law and the correctional system, then an introductory text on criminal justice will be generally comprehensible to you.

Before you read anything, it is important to think about what you already know about the subject. Surprisingly, you probably do know *something* about most topics or issues that will come your way in college reading. Before you read, ask yourself, "What do I already know about this?" and recite the answers.

For the reading assignments in all your classes, take a moment to consider what knowledge or information you already have about the topic. In this textbook, you will be asked to actively think about what you already know about the topics of reading selections and to list that information or to write a short paragraph about it before you read. You will be amazed how this simple step will help you in learning the new material to come.

Answers to Try It and Apply It 2-1: 1-glossary, 2-title page, 3-acknowledgments, 4-table of contents, 5-subject index, 6-preface, 7-appendix, 8-bibliography, 9-webliography, 10-name index

try it and apply it! 2-3   Access Prior Knowledge

Directions: The following are concepts related to intellectual development and learning theory. They appear as titles or headings in reading selections later in this chapter. Next to each, write *anything* you may know related to the concept. You will come upon them in excerpts throughout this chapter. The last title is that of a complete chapter in the appendix of this book, which you will be applying these skills to later in this chapter. Compare your responses with those of your classmates.

Long-term memory *Answers will vary.* _____

_____

Multiple intelligences _____

_____

Tip-of-the-tongue phenomenon _____

_____

Motivation for learning _____

_____

Memory and eyewitness testimony _____

_____

Bilingual education _____

_____

Learning styles _____

_____

Avoidance learning _____

_____

The benefits of higher education _____

_____

Keep this in mind

Accessing Prior Knowledge

- **Get acquainted with every textbook you use each semester.** The more you know about each one, the better you can use it to support your success in class.
- **Always think about what you already know about a topic before you begin reading about it.** You will learn new information more efficiently if you can connect it to knowledge you already have about a subject.

Preview Your Reading

Another important strategy you can use to prepare yourself for reading is to preview the material you have been assigned. *Previewing* means to look over a reading assignment before you actually read it. Just as the previews, or coming attractions, for movies give you an overview of what they are all about, and what you might expect when you actually watch them, previewing a selection or chapter will do the same for your reading experience.

Previewing will do the following:

- **Familiarize you with the subject matter you are about to read.** This helps to get you ready for your reading, serving as a "warm-up." It will help you ease your way into the material.
- **Supply you with additional prior knowledge about a topic.** As mentioned earlier, this prior knowledge is so important, especially when you are reading about a new or challenging topic. Even if you don't know much about a topic ahead of time, previewing will provide you with some useful information.

Title—*The title identifies the topic, theme, or author's thesis, or argument.* Think about the title. What do you already know about it? Turn the title into a question that you can look for an answer to as you read.

Headings—*Headings are the gateways into each section of the chapter or selection.* Like the title, they can be turned into questions that give you a reason for reading that section of the text. When you make a question out of a heading, try to connect it to the title. Notice the subheadings as well. They can often provide the answers to questions you make from the headings.

Introduction—*The introduction to a chapter can fill you in on a subject by providing important background information.* Make sure you read it. If you are reading a selection, read the first paragraph to find out what is going to be discussed.

Every first sentence in every paragraph—*The first sentences in textbook paragraphs are often the topic sentences or main ideas of the paragraphs.* Thus, you will gain a lot of information about the subject by reading them. You will also encounter selections without any headings, so the first sentences of the paragraphs will be your entry into the content. They will help you predict what the author will discuss.

Vocabulary and Visuals—*The language of the discipline in which you are reading will probably be new and unfamiliar, so get ready to increase your vocabulary every time you read.* If you take a moment to look at new words ahead of time, it will help you to move through the selection more smoothly when you are reading. Notice the words, often given with their definitions, at the beginning of a chapter, boldface within the text, written in the margin, or reviewed at the end. Highlight these words. Say them aloud. Read their definitions.

Visuals—*Textbooks provide pictures, or visuals, that explain and illustrate what is being taught, so be sure to look at them before you read the text.* Read the captions, titles, descriptions, and keys. Many people remember and understand best when they can "see" a visual presentation of an idea. Common visuals include: photographs, drawings, graphs, figures, charts and tables, cartoons, and maps.

End-of-Chapter Questions—*Reading these questions will give you a good idea of what the author believes it is important to know.* You also establish a purpose for reading: to find the answers to these questions or to gain enough knowledge from the chapter to apply the information and develop a thoughtful response to them. Reading and answering end-of-chapter questions can also help you prepare for exams.

Summary—*Reading the summary first means you will have a lot of background knowledge and information already in your head when you read the chapter, which makes it easier to understand.* Be sure to check out the chapter to see if a summary exists.

■ **Help you establish a purpose for your reading.** You may think that your reason for reading is to complete an assignment—to answer questions posed by your instructor or questions in the text. That is true, in part. But even if you don't have a specific written assignment, by previewing a selection you can anticipate important questions that will be addressed in it. Developing these questions *yourself,* before you read, will help focus and guide you. Your purpose for reading, then, is so that you can answer questions *you* have created based on the text, and answer others that occur to you as you read. You'll come to understand this process in greater depth as we move along.

The way you preview will vary, depending upon the kind, or genre, of reading you are dealing with.

Previewing College Textbook Chapters: Apply THIEVES

What should you look at ahead of time to give you all this information? An acronym (a word made from the first letters of several words) that can help you remember the parts of a selection you should preview is THIEVES. Think about "stealing" information from a text before you read it. Be greedy! Follow the diagram on page 40 as you preview a chapter or reading.

try it and apply it! 2-4 Guided Preview of a Textbook Chapter Section

Directions: Take out your highlighter and turn to the complete textbook chapter in the appendix of this text, titled "Expand Your Emotional Intelligence" (page A-21). Preview the first part of the chapter through the section "Emotional Intelligence and Maturity" (pages A-21–A-24), by applying the THIEVES method with the help of the following directions and questions. Carefully and thoughtfully move through the chapter:

■ Read the title and introduction.

■ Highlight the headings of the sections you preview.

■ Highlight the subheadings.

■ Underline the first sentence in each paragraph within each section.

■ Circle the boldface vocabulary, and read the sentence in which it is presented to get an idea of the meaning.

■ Stop and review visuals, charts, graphs, and so on. Highlight titles and captions.

■ Read any end-of-chapter questions.

(continued)

(*continued*)

1. What is the **title** of the chapter? *Expand Your Emotional Intelligence*
   Turn the title into a question: *What is emotional intelligence? How can I expand it?*

2. Write three learning objectives the author hopes you will achieve by reading the chapter. *Answers will vary.*

3. Is there an **introduction?** *Yes* How many paragraphs is it? *Three* Read the introduction. Then write one important piece of information you learned from it. *Answers will vary.*

4. Highlight the first **major heading,** which indicates the first topic to be discussed. Turn it into a question and write your question here.
   What is emotional intelligence, and what does it have to do with maturity?

5. Read the **first sentence in each paragraph** under the first major heading. Then answer the following questions.

   a. What is emotional intelligence?
       It is the ability to understand and manage yourself and relate effectively to others.

   b. What ability is necessary for school and job success?
       The ability to regulate emotions.

6. Highlight the next **heading** in this section and then answer the following questions.

   a. What three components are listed in it that help you understand the meaning of "Character"? *Integrity, Civility, and Ethics*

   b. What question(s) do you think will be answered by reading this section? *What are integrity, civility, and ethics? What do they have to do with character?*

7. Read and highlight the first sentence in each paragraph in this section. Then answer the following questions.

   a. What is the Golden Rule? *Treating others as we want to be treated.*

   b. What is civility? *It is a set of tools for interacting with others with respect, kindness, and good manners, or etiquette.*

   c. What are ethics? *The principles of conduct that govern a group or society.*

   d. Whose "tough decisions" will you be reading about?
       Peggy, Rey, and Tora

8. What is the next heading? *Responsibility*

9. Read and highlight the first sentence in each paragraph in this section. Look at Figure 2.1 as well. Highlight the caption. Then answer the following two statements:

   a. Name three areas of responsibility in which you are successful.
   Answers will vary.

   b. Name three areas of responsibility in which you would like to improve.
   Answers will vary.

10. Preview the section "Self-Control" beginning on page A-28. (Read each subheading and highlight the first sentence in each.) How many tips are given to help maintain self-control?

    Seven

    For each tip, write a question you think will be answered in the reading. Connect each to the topic indicated in the heading "Self-Control," when possible. The first one is completed for you.

    a. <u>How can I calm down to maintain self control?</u>

    b. *What should I clarify and define for self-control?*

    c. *How do I listen with empathy and respect?*

    d. *What does it mean to use "I" statements?*

    e. *How does focusing on one problem help with self-control?*

    f. *What is a win-win solution?*

    g. *How can I reward positive behavior to maintain self-control?*

11. What is the last major heading in the section on emotional intelligence and maturity? *Self-esteem and Confidence*

12. Read and highlight the first sentence in each paragraph and the first sentence in each bullet. Then answer the following questions:

    a. What is self-esteem? *It is how you feel about yourself.*

    b. What is the benefit of having positive self-esteem? *It gives the self-confidence that allows people to be more open to new experiences and accepting of different people.*

    c. Name three ways in which confidence develops. *Answers will vary.*

try it and apply it! 2-5 Monitored Preview of a Textbook Chapter Section

Directions: Continue applying THIEVES to preview the next section of the chapter: "A Positive Attitude and Personal Motivation" (pages A-30 to A-42). Read and highlight each major heading and subheading. This time, write your questions from headings directly in the text, next to or above the heading. Continue reading and highlighting the first sentence in each paragraph, noting vocabulary and visuals. When you are finished, answer the following questions using only the information from your preview. You may look back to check your answers.

1. In what three areas is your success impacted by having a positive attitude?

    school, career, and life

2. What is the definition of motivation?

    Motivation is the inner drive that moves you to action.

3. What are four results of a positive attitude?

    enthusiasm, vitality, optimism, and a zest for living

4. What are the outcomes of a negative attitude?

    It drains you of enthusiasm and energy, and it leads to absenteeism, tardiness, and impaired mental and physical health.

5. What are the basic physiological needs at the base of Maslow's pyramid?

    breathing, food, water, and sleep

6. What is at the top of Maslow's Hierarchy of Needs?

    self-actualization

7. List 10 strategies to increase your motivation.

    (1) act as if you are motivated, (2) use affirmations, (3) use visualizations, (4) use goals as motivational tools, (5) understand expectations, (6) study in teams, (7) stay physically and mentally healthy, (8) learn to reframe, (9) reward yourself, (10) make learning relevant

8. What is visualization?

    Visualization is seeing things in your mind's eye by organizing and processing information through pictures and symbols.

9. What does reframing mean?

    Reframing is choosing to see a situation in a new way.

10. What are three major benefits of higher education?

    It encourages critical thinking, it is a smart financial investment, and it prepares you for a job.

11. What will you learn by "reading" the bar graph in Figure 2.4?

I will learn how a person's annual income changes based on how much education he or

she has.

12. By quickly glancing at the graph, what general conclusion can you make?

The more education a person has, the greater his or her income will be.

try it and apply it! 2-6 Independent Preview of a Textbook Chapter Section

Directions: Now complete the chapter preview by applying THIEVES to the last major section, called "Overcome Obstacles," and the chapter summary (pages A-43 to A-46). Based on your preview, write three of your own preview questions you believe will be answered in the reading. Then write three points of information you learn from previewing this portion.

Three Preview Questions

1. *Answers will vary.*
2. _____
3. _____

Three Points of Information

1. _____
2. _____
3. _____

Previewing Magazine Articles and Essays

You will apply similar strategies to preview magazine articles and essays that are assigned in your classes. Magazine articles are generally written about current topics in our world and society. They are often informative and can be serious or lighthearted. Essays generally provide an author's perspective or point of view on a topic or issue. Sometimes they are a creative reflection about a topic or the author's life. Other essays attempt to persuade a reader to change his or her beliefs and/or take action. In these, an author strongly expresses an opinion throughout the selection, which is stated in the **thesis.**

Although articles and essays are not formatted in the same way as college textbooks, and do not have many of the features that appear in textbook chapters, you can look at certain elements in preparation for reading. These include the title, introduction, headings, introductory sentences, a concluding paragraph, and, perhaps, visuals.

try it and apply it! 2-7   **Preview an Essay**

Directions: The highlighted portions in the following essay indicate what you should read and think about during your preview. Read over those portions. Place a check after each to monitor yourself. Then answer the questions that follow. You will see just how much background knowledge previewing can provide.

"Learning Disorder"? Just Say No!

By Jan Hunt

1   My heart goes out to those children who have been labeled "ADHD" ("attention-deficit and hyperactivity disorder"), the latest "learning disability" label. Many educators and researchers now believe that these children and their families have been profoundly deceived by the use of these labels. Dr. Thomas Armstrong, a former learning disabilities specialist, changed professions when he "began to see how this notion of learning disabilities was handicapping all of our children by placing the blame for a child's learning failure on mysterious neurological deficiencies in the brain instead of on much needed reforms in our system of education."

2   "ADD" and "ADHD" are fictions. They are nothing less than self-fulfilling pseudo-diagnoses, used as an excuse to give children powerful drugs so they can be fitted into the unnatural environment of a classroom. Overburdened teachers and parents made anxious by the school institution have unrealistic and unfair expectations about what a "normal" child should be able to do. The high energy of many young children—especially boys— is normal for a healthy child. A child's natural energy is something to celebrate, not a problem that we need to fix with mind-altering drugs. It is only a problem when we force children into a boring environment where they have little voice or power.

3   The abnormality is in the school, not in the child. It is normal and natural for a healthy child to be active and energetic, much more so than our society wants us to believe (see "The Child Who Never Sits Still" by Robert Mendelsohn).

4   Subjective and unreliable behavioral observations by those who hold to society's skewed expectations of what "normal" behavior should look like in a classroom (meaning, behavior that meets the needs of the teacher and ignores the needs of the child) is a far cry from a "diagnosis." As neurologist Fred Baughman wrote: "Twenty-five years of research, not deserving of the term 'research', has failed to validate ADD/ADHD as a disease." And the "cure" is so dangerous. Ritalin is a form of speed, with many potential dangers and side effects—even death. As reported by *The*

Australian, "Children as young as five have suffered strokes, heart attacks, hallucinations and convulsions after taking drugs to treat attention deficit hyperactivity disorder."[1]

5   If ADD and ADHD were true diseases, surely they would be found in the same proportion in all populations of children. Yet neither of these so-called "diseases" are seen in homeschooling families unless the child has recently been in school. Homeschooling parents would have no reason to force unnatural behavior like sitting still for long periods or studying something that is of little interest to them that day. Compassionate parents understand and celebrate a child's natural energy and enthusiasm. In such an environment, there are no "learning disorders." The National Institutes of Health admitted in 1998, ". . . . We do not have an independent, valid test for ADHD, and there are no data to indicate that ADHD is due to a brain malfunction."

6   It is one of our society's greatest ironies that the same educators who admonish children to "just say no" to drugs are at the same time handing out powerful drugs to millions of children for a fictional disorder in an attempt to counter the very normal reactions of healthy children to an abnormal environment.

7   The fault is not within our children, but in our society's attitudes toward them. A healthy child is naturally active, curious, and even rambunctious. When will we let a 6-year-old act like a 6-year-old and not expect him to act like he's 36? When will we let children be children?

(Jan Hunt, "'Learning Disorder'? Just Say No!,"
http://www.naturalchild.org/jan_hunt/learning_disorder.html)

[1]Clara Pirani, "Child Drugs Linked to Heart Attack," *The Australian,* March 27, 2006.

1. What is the article discussing?
    Labeling children ADD and ADHD and considering their natural behavior as a kind of
    learning disability

2. What can you tell about Jan Hunt's opinion about ADD from the title?
    She doesn't think we should call it a learning disorder.

3. In the introductory paragraph, who does the author believe has been deceived and what does the author seem to be calling for?
    The author believes the children who have been labeled ADHD and their families have been
    deceived. The writer calls for changes in our educational system.

4. Again, in paragraphs 2 and 3, who or what does the writer find at fault?
    The writer believes that the schools are abnormal, not the children.

5. What is the author criticizing in paragraph 4?
    The writer is criticizing observations of children in the classroom that say that their behaviors
    are abnormal because they are not acting the way the teachers would like them to.

6. Can you explain the "irony" (twist or unexpected outcome) the author states in paragraph 6?
    That educators who want kids to say "no" to drugs are willing to load them up with drugs
    to change their behaviors, which are totally healthy because the children do not fit into the
    "abnormal" environment of school.

(continued)

(*continued*)

7. How does the last sentence in the concluding paragraph re-state the author's overall view?

It says that we should let kids be kids. They are naturally active and curious, and schools and society should change, and not change them.

Previewing Newspaper Articles

Information about the most current developments in your local community and in the larger world are written in news articles that are published in newspapers. Most newspapers are fact-based, reliable, and up-to-date sources of information. They are published regularly, usually daily. The purpose of news articles is to inform readers of current events in a straightforward manner.

Newspaper articles are written in a *journalistic style,* which moves from the main points to specific details. They are generally "front loaded." Within the first paragraph or two, you will usually find out the *who, what, when, where, why,* and *how* of the story. The remainder of the article provides details to help the reader understand an event in more depth. Below is a graphic representation of the news article format.

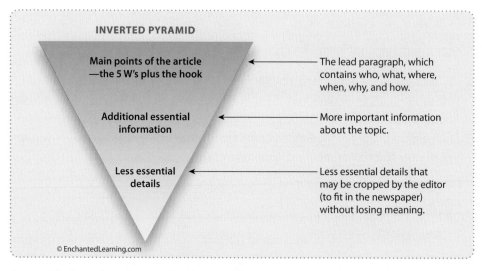

Copyright EnchantedLearning.com. Used by permission.

When you preview a newspaper article, where should you focus? *In the beginning, of course!* Read the title, sometimes called the headline, and then the first few paragraphs. These elements should give you the most important points. If you are reading to do research, you can tell from the headline and first few paragraphs if the article is likely to be a good source for you. If you are reading for pleasure, you will have enough information to know if you are interested and would like to continue.

try it and apply it! 2-8 Preview a Newspaper Article ⏸

Directions: Preview the following brief newspaper article from the *New York Times* on some research about learning in young children. Read only the first two paragraphs. Then answer the questions that follow.

Children: Self-Control Presages Math Gains in Young

By Nicholas Bakalar

A simple five-minute behavioral test for children entering kindergarten can predict significant gains in mathematics skills over the course of the year, researchers have found.

Claire Cameron Ponitz, a research associate at the University of Virginia, led a group that tested 343 children with the Head-Toes-Knees-Shoulders task, in which children perform the opposite of an oral command (for example, the correct response for "touch your toes" would be to touch your head). Higher scores, the researchers write in the May issue of *Developmental Psychology,* indicate a greater ability to control and direct one's own behavior, an ability essential for success in the structured environment of a kindergarten class.

Those with higher scores on the fall test generally reached higher scores in all areas in the spring, but showed significant gains compared with other children only in mathematics, not in literacy or vocabulary.

What's a parent to do? "We know that consistency and giving children opportunities to control their own behavior helps them develop self-regulation skills," Dr. Ponitz said. "Playing games like red light, green light, or following through with consequences for violations of family rules—these are things that have been shown to be related to self-regulation in early childhood."

1. **Who** is this article about? *researchers at the University of Virginia*

2. **What** is this about? *a five-minute behavioral test for children entering kindergarten*

3. **What** can the test do? *It can predict significant gains in math skills.*

4. **When?** *over the course of the school year*

5. **How** did they do the research? *343 children had to perform the opposite of an oral command in the Head-Toes-Knees-Shoulders task.*

6. **What** did the results indicate? *Higher scores indicate a greater ability to control and direct one's own behavior, which is necessary for success in the structured environment of kindergarten.*

7. **How** did they prove the connection? *Children with higher scores on the test in the fall reached higher scores in all areas in the spring, but significantly higher gains in math.*

Previewing Novels and Nonfiction Books

The inside and/or outside covers of a book jacket provide information about the characters, action, or type of novel you have chosen (mystery, historical fiction, classic literature, romance, adventure, and so on). You are likely to also find out a little about the author, perhaps with a photo. Publishers often include comments from reviewers, all positive, of course, to entice you into reading (and perhaps purchasing) the book. Nonfiction books, such as memoirs, biographies, autobiographies, and those on topics of interest, are also marketed with book jackets, so you can gather information on these selections as well. Softcover versions of books will include this information on the covers or first few pages of the book.

Inside the book you may find acknowledgments or a dedication page, in which authors honor someone important to them. A writer who wants to introduce the work in a certain way may include a prologue. Some books contain a table of contents, including chapter titles that may help you get an idea of the action or topics. Preview this to get an idea of what is to come.

Reading the first chapter is an active and helpful way to preview a book you are about to read. You may get an idea of the characters and the setting. You will gain a sense of the writer's style, and a taste of what is to come. Reading the first chapter is often the way those who read for pleasure will determine whether they want to go ahead or select something else. Ready yourself for reading even more by thinking about what you may already know about the topic you anticipate will be discussed, or relating personally to the ideas that are revealed.

try it and apply it! 2-9   Preview a Book (Memoir)

Directions: Next, you will find information from the book jacket of the popular memoir by Mitch Albom, called *Tuesdays with Morrie*. This book jacket is followed by the first chapter. Read these, and then respond to the questions that follow.

Tuesdays with Morrie: An Old Man, a Young Man, and Life's Greatest Lesson

By Mitch Albom

Maybe it was a grandparent, or a teacher, or a colleague. Someone older, patient and wise, who understood you when you were young and searching, helped you see the world as a more profound place, gave you sound advice to help you make your way through it.

For Mitch Albom, that person was Morrie Schwartz, his college professor from nearly twenty years ago. . . .

> "This is a sweet book of a man's love for his mentor. It has a stubborn honesty that nourishes the living."
>
> (Robert Bly, author of *Iron John*)

"I love this book. I've been telling all my friends 'You have to read this.' Mitch Albom was given a wonderful gift from his teacher Morrie Schwartz and now we have the great pleasure of auditing the same class. This is a true story that shines and leaves you forever warmed by its afterglow."

(Amy Tan, Author of *The Joy Luck Club*)

Contents

(continued)

(*continued*)

Chapter One
The Curriculum

The last class of my old professor's life took place once a week in his house, by a window in the study where he could watch a small hibiscus plant shed its pink leaves. The class met on Tuesdays. It began after breakfast. The subject was The Meaning of Life. It was taught from experience.

No grades were given, but there were oral exams each week. You were expected to respond to questions, and you were expected to pose questions of your own. You were also required to perform physical tasks now and then, such as lifting the professor's head to a comfortable spot on the pillow or placing his glasses on the bridge of his nose.

Kissing him good-bye earned you extra credit.

No books were required, yet many topics were covered, including love, work, community, family, aging, forgiveness, and, finally, death. The last lecture was brief, only a few words.

A funeral was held in lieu of graduation.

Although no final exam was given, you were expected to produce one long paper on what was learned. That paper is presented here.

The last class of my old professor's life had only one student.

I was the student.

(Albom 1997)

1. Who are the key characters in this book?
    the professor, Morrie Schwartz, and the author, Mitch Albom

2. What topics can you anticipate you will read about?
    the meaning of life, love, work, community, family, aging, forgiveness, death

3. Interestingly, what is the author's "final project" for being "in class" with his old professor? *the book,* Tuesdays with Morrie

4. Right from the start, what do you know about what happens to Morrie? *He dies.*

5. What terms does the author use to suggest that his conversations with Morrie are similar to being in a class in school?
    subject, grades, questions, extra credit, graduation, paper, professor, student

6. If you can, identify a person from whom you learned lessons about life. What did you learn? *Answers will vary.*

7. Do you think you would want to read this book? Why or why not?
    Answers will vary.

You will adapt your previewing to meet the needs of each assignment. When the reading is new and unfamiliar, an extensive preview will help you gain background knowledge, provide you with the motivation to read, and prepare you for reading the assignment in depth.

Keep this in mind

Previewing a Reading

- **Remember—Previewing doesn't take that long, and can make a huge difference in your capacity to understand a reading.** Try not to skip it as a first step, especially when you are going to read about a topic that is new or unfamiliar to you.
- **Adjust your preview to suit the kind of selection you are reading.**

Reading with a Purpose: Ask and Answer Your *Own* Questions

Think back to your high school days, or even to elementary school. Whenever you were asked to read, you were usually asked to answer questions. Hopefully, you looked at those questions ahead of time, to have them in your mind while you read. You might have even stopped to write down the answers when you came upon them.

In college, you will be assigned quite a lot of reading and be expected to know and use the content. Sometimes your professors will assign questions for you to answer, and sometimes they won't. Whether or not you are given questions doesn't matter: Assign yourself the questions!

Creating your own questions, before and while you read, is a great way to keep you active and connected to your reading. If you formulate questions, you will have them in your mind, and they will give you a purpose for reading: to find out the answers. As you read you will also be *thinking*.

You can create four kinds of questions to help you become an active, thoughtful reader:

- preview questions
- guide questions
- monitoring questions
- study questions

Preview Questions

Preview questions are the general questions you create when you read the title, headings, and subheadings of your text. You turn these into questions by attaching words such as *What, How, Where, Why, Who,* and *When* to the heading.

For example, in "Expand Your Emotional Intelligence," the textbook chapter you previewed earlier, you read a heading called, "Emotional Intelligence and Maturity." Before you read the material that follows, you could ask yourself, "What is emotional intelligence? What does emotional intelligence have to do with maturity?" Later on, in a section on "Positive Attitude," a heading reads, "Motivational Strategies." You might think, "What does this mean? What are some motivational strategies? What do they have to do with a positive attitude?" Seeing the next heading, "The Benefits of Higher Education," the logical question to have in your mind while reading would be, "What are the benefits of a higher education?" By creating these questions from the title, headings, and subheadings before you read, you can look for the answers as you read. Later on in this chapter, we discuss ways you can write these questions directly in the reading selection itself.

Guide Questions

Guide questions involve a similar process. Here you focus on important sentences, often the first ones in paragraphs, and turn them into questions to guide your reading. Your goal will then be to find the answers to these questions as you read. For example, one paragraph in the social and emotional intelligence chapter begins with the sentence, "You will be more motivated to succeed if you understand what is expected of you in each class." You might wonder, "How can I find out what is expected of me? What should I do?" and read to discover the answer. In another portion of the text, early in a paragraph it says, "Abraham Maslow, a well-known psychologist, developed the theory of a hierarchy of needs." Here you might ask, "What does *hierarchy* mean? What did Maslow's theory state?" You would then read with the purpose of finding the answer to these questions.

Creating such guide questions is a *thinking* process. Although we will practice these in writing, most often you will keep guide questions in your mind. Later in this chapter we will discuss how you will highlight and mark the answers in your text.

Monitoring Questions

Have you ever read a chapter, and when you got to the end realized that you just didn't get any of it at all? What a waste of your precious time. To avoid this kind of outcome, use **monitoring questions.**

Monitoring questions are questions you ask yourself to find out how you are doing *as you read.* You use them to check your understanding of what you are reading along the way. They help ensure that you are reading with real understanding rather than just moving your eyes along the page.

When you monitor your comprehension, you stop, reflect, and recite. Do this at the conclusion of each paragraph. Do you know the answer to your guide question? Can you think it, recite it, or even write it (see the next section on annotation)? Can you state the most important point about what you just read?

A more general way to monitor yourself is to stop a moment at the end of a paragraph or section and ask yourself, "Do I understand what I just read?" If your answer is something like, "No, not really," then you will need to go back and reread, probably more slowly. A good way to challenge yourself here is to see if you can paraphrase the passage, or put it into your own words.

Keep this in mind

Many students like to place a check at the conclusion of each text passage to indicate that they have stopped and asked and answered monitoring questions to their satisfaction. The check means they have given themselves "permission" to move on.

Study Questions

You create **study questions** after you complete an assigned reading. You may want to review the material or start preparing for an exam. Making study questions is your chance to play the professor. To ask intelligent, meaningful questions, you must have a fairly good understanding of the subject the question is about. Good study questions show that you understand the subject and recognize the important topics and their relationship to one another. Think of the questions your professor might ask on an exam. It's a great feeling when these study questions actually turn up on the test!

Sometimes your preview or guide questions tap the important test items. Pay close attention to the subheadings in a text. For example, in the chapter you previewed, when you came upon the subheading "The Benefits of Higher Education," you likely asked the preview question, "What are the benefits of higher education?" That very same question would be an excellent study question to use for review and preparation for a test on the chapter. By reading this portion and looking at the subheadings, you learn that three major benefits are discussed; a more specific study question you could challenge yourself with would be, "Identify *three* important benefits of higher education."

In addition to questions based on your reading, two other types of study questions are very important for you to create: *discipline-specific vocabulary questions* and *essay questions*.

Discipline-Specific Vocabulary Questions Expanding your knowledge of words, concepts, and processes—the terminology specifically related to the subjects you are studying—is an important part of college learning. In your textbooks, important words may be referred to as **vocabulary words** or **key terms.** When you study, you should always create questions that ask you to identify the meaning of these important terms.

In addition, your courses will include important **concepts** and **processes.** These are ideas and procedures or systems related to a particular discipline. They involve a more extensive explanation.

Key terms, vocabulary words, concepts and processes are often **boldface,** *italicized,* or highlighted in your texts. You should consider these important terms when creating study questions. For example, when creating study questions for the chapter "Expand Your Emotional Intelligence," you would want to ask yourself to define and explain the following:

■ Key terms such as *civility, maturity,* and *empathy*

   Example: What is a civility?
   Example: Define maturity.
   Example: What does empathy mean?

■ Concepts such as *emotional intelligence* and *using affirmation*

   Example: Explain the components of emotional intelligence.
   Example: How can using affirmations improve motivation?

■ Processes such as *reframing* and *team studying*

   Example: How does reframing work?
   Example: How can we develop team studying?

try it and apply it! 2-10   Creating Discipline-Specific Vocabulary Questions

Directions: Return to the chapter "Expand Your Emotional Intelligence." Write discipline-specific vocabulary questions for two terms, two concepts, and two processes you discovered in your preview on the lines below. Then answer your own questions!

Key Terms

Question 1: *Answers will vary.* _____

Definition: _____

Question 2: _____

Definition: _____

Concepts

Question 1: _____

Answer: _____

Question 2: _____

Answer: _____

Processes

Question 1: _____

Answer: _____

Question 2: _____

Answer: _____

Keep this in mind

> To improve your general understanding of a reading, circle or highlight *any* words in the text that you do not understand, even if they aren't directly related to your topic of study. You can look these up in a dictionary, or use context clues to help your comprehension and strengthen your vocabulary in general.

Essay Questions   Essay-type questions require you to go further in demonstrating your understanding of what you have read. They ask you to think about, **analyze,** and even apply your broader knowledge of the material in your writing. These often appear as stated objectives in the beginning of textbook chapters. With practice, you can become very good at predicting the essay questions appearing on exams. You might even anticipate essay questions based on information you learn from your preview. Using the headings and subheadings to guide you, try to create significant essay-type questions for yourself. For example, a subheading in the social and emotional intelligence section is "Character First: Integrity, Civility, and Ethics." A good essay question tapping this content might be:

> Discuss the meaning of integrity, civility, and ethics. Explain how they relate to good character and their impact on academic success.

Reread the portions of the text that will help you answer your own questions. In doing so, you will challenge yourself in a very meaningful way, and you may even come up with the exact test questions you will see on your next exam. Important essay questions based on a student's reading of "Expand Your Emotional Intelligence" might include the following:

- Identify and describe the five levels of Maslow's Hierarchy of Needs.
- Explain how people can develop greater self-confidence.
- Compare and contrast using visualizations with using affirmations.
- List and explain five strategies to foster self-control.

Essay questions often begin with, or may include, one of the terms listed in the following box. It is important to know the differences among these terms to respond accurately to a question. The exercise that follows will help you learn what each specific term is asking you to do. See Chapter 10 for more about essay questions.

Analyze	**Evaluate**	**Prove**
Compare	**Explain**	**Summarize**
Contrast	**Identify**	**Trace**
Discuss	**Justify**	

try it and apply it! 2-11   Study Terms and Definitions

Directions: Fill in the blanks below with a word from the text box above. The first letter or letters of the term is provided. When you finish, you will have the definitions of all the terms. Be sure to learn them.

1. To argue in support of a decision, concept, or action, by giving reasons or evidence in favor of it is to j*ustify*___ it.

2. To break something into its component parts to understand it and its workings and patterns is to a*nalyze*___ it.

3. To show similarities and differences between things or ideas is to com*pare*___ them.

4. To provide information briefly, covering all important major points but omitting details and examples is to s*ummarize*___ it.

5. To name or list features, elements, or characteristics is to i*dentify*___ them.

6. To provide logical and convincing arguments or support for an idea, action, or situation is to pr*ove*___ it.

7. To show how things or ideas are different is to con*trast*___ them.

8. To examine something in a broad, thorough way, providing key questions, issues, evidence, and information is to ex*plain*___ it.

9. To discuss the strengths and weaknesses of something, its value, and its benefits, is to ev*aluate*___ it.

10. To make something clear or meaningful, to clarify something by reviewing how it works or why it does is to d*iscuss*___ it.

11. To list and describe the steps or stages in the development of an idea or process is to t*race*___ them.

try it and apply it! 2-12   Ask Questions for Active Reading

Directions: Use the following guidelines to preview and read the next selection, "The Theory of Multiple Intelligences." Read it actively by asking and answering your own questions. There are several places for you to enter your questions and responses in the margins and in the space below the text. Place a check in the box after each paragraph when you think that you have understood it and are ready to move on.

1. Create Preview Questions

Before you read it, preview the selection. Write three preview questions based on the title and the headings on the lines provided beneath the title and headings. Keep these questions in mind when you read.

2. Make Guide Questions

Now start to read the selection. STOP after you read the first sentence of each paragraph. Underline it. Think of a specific question that the sentence makes you think will be answered in the paragraph. Write this in the space provided in the margin next to the opening sentence. Then, read the paragraph. As you read, CIRCLE any terms that are unfamiliar to you or that you think are important words connected to the topic of multiple intelligence. When you get to the end of the paragraph, STOP and write an answer to the question you wrote in the margin.

3. Ask Yourself Monitoring Questions

As you finish each paragraph, ask yourself, "Did I understand what I just read?" and "Should I continue?" If the answer is Yes, go on. Place a check in the box at the end of the paragraph to indicate you are comfortable with your understanding of the material. If your answer is No, go back and reread the paragraph more slowly.

4. Design Study Questions

At the conclusion of your reading, list at least three terms you believe are important to know to understand this selection. Next, write three essay-type questions that cover the most important points made by the author. Then, challenge yourself to write answers to them.

5. Peer Discussion

Compare your responses with those of another student and discuss any differences between them.

The Theory of Multiple Intelligences

Answers may vary. Sample answers provided.

Preview Question(s): *What are multiple intelligences? What is the theory about them?*

Howard Gardner is a psychologist and Professor at Harvard University's Graduate School of Education, as well as Co-Director of Harvard Project Zero. Dr. Gardner claims that all human beings have multiple intelligences. These multiple intelligences can be nurtured and strengthened, or ignored and weakened. He believes each individual has nine intelligences.

Q: *Why do I need to know about Howard Gardner? What did he do?*

The Nine Intelligences

Preview Question: *What are the nine intelligences?*

Verbal-Linguistic Intelligence includes well-developed verbal skills. These are language-based skills. Verbal-linguistic intelligence also embraces sensitivity to the sounds, meanings, and rhythms of words. Clearly then, those who write and/or speak well are strong in this area.

Q: *What is verbal-linguistic intelligence?*

(continued)

(continued)

Q: *What is mathematical-logical intelligence?*

  Mathematical-Logical Intelligence is the ability to think conceptually and abstractly. It includes the capacity to discern logical or numerical patterns. Scientific researchers and mathematicians are likely to be strong in this intelligence.

Q: *What is musical intelligence?*

  Musical Intelligence is another ability. It is the capacity to produce and appreciate rhythm, pitch, and timbre. Composers, musicians, and singers have strong musical intelligence.

Q: *What is visual-spatial intelligence?*

  Visual-Spatial Intelligence refers to the capacity to think in images and pictures, to visualize accurately and abstractly. We often think of artists, architects, planners, engineers, and those involved in graphic design as having strong visual-spatial abilities.

Q: *Who has bodily-kinesthetic intelligence?*

  Bodily-Kinesthetic Intelligence is the ability to control one's body movements and to handle objects skillfully. Athletes are particularly strong in this intelligence. Dancers, artists, and craftsmen need this capacity as well.

Q: *What are the two personal intelligences?*

  There are two "personal" intelligences. *Interpersonal Intelligence* is the capacity to detect and respond appropriately to the moods, motivations, and desires of others. This capacity is an important component in developing social skills. Those who work with others, of course, would benefit from interpersonal intelligence. *Intrapersonal Intelligence* refers to the capacity to be self-aware and in tune with one's inner feelings, values, beliefs, and thinking processes. Knowing one's self and managing one's emotions strengthens the well-being of most people.

Q: *What are the two other intelligences identified by Gardner?*

  Years after identifying the first seven intelligences, Gardner named two others. *Naturalist Intelligence* is the ability to recognize and categorize plants, animals, and other objects in nature. *Existential Intelligence* involves sensitivity and the capacity to tackle deep questions about human existence, such as the meaning of life, why do we die, and how did we get here.

Developing the Theory

Preview Question: *How did Gardner develop his theory? What made him create it?*

Q: *Who were the people Gardner studied to develop his theory?*

  Based on his study of many people from many different walks of life in everyday circumstances and professions, Gardner developed the theory of multiple intelligences. He performed interviews with and brain research on hundreds of people, including stroke victims, prodigies, autistic individuals, and so-called "idiot savants." These are people who are seemingly undeveloped in most of the intellectual areas except one or two, in which they behave in an extraordinary manner. For example, a child who doesn't speak or relate to others, but can play the piano like Mozart. Howard Gardner defined the first seven intelligences in FRAMES OF MIND (1983). He added the last two in INTELLIGENCE REFRAMED (1999).

Educational Impact

Preview Question: *What is the impact of Gardner's theory of multiple intelligences on education?*

According to Gardner, all human beings possess all nine intelligences in varying amounts. These intelligences are located in different areas of the brain. They can work independently or together. Each person has a different intellectual composition. Those who teach must recognize this. People can be exceptionally strong in one or more areas and not others. Educators can improve education by addressing the multiple intelligences of students. This has important implications for the way they teach and the kinds of assignments they offer their students. The best instruction will vary the way information is presented and give opportunities to learners to experience and demonstrate their learning from their intellectual strengths. According to Gardner, these intelligences may define the human species.

Q: How can people have all nine intelligences?

Now that you have completed the reading, write three questions on the lines below that you predict a professor would ask students about the selection.

Answers will vary. Sample answers provided. 1. What are the nine intelligences? Briefly explain each. 2. What did Gardner do to develop his theory? 3. Why do teachers need to understand the theory?

How did it feel to read actively and with purpose? Hopefully, it felt pretty good. Yes, you spend more time thinking about your reading, but you are also putting that additional time to very good use if you come away with a complete understanding of what you have read.

Keep this in mind

Reading with a Purpose

- **Remember—Don't continue reading for very long without checking your understanding of the material.** You don't want to come to the conclusion of a chapter and wonder what you just read. Monitor yourself by stopping periodically, paragraph by paragraph, to check your understanding.
- **Reread sections that are difficult or confusing.**
- **Give yourself permission to continue when you are satisfied that you have understood the content.**
- **When you have focused for long periods, especially on difficult material, you might want to take a break before continuing.**

Manage Your College Reading: Highlight, Annotate, and Make Marginal Notes

Never read empty handed! Have a pen, pencil, or highlighter with you. Reading in college is about thinking and learning. You always want to be ready to "jump in" and note important points to learn, remember, or consider in the text. Though students sometimes hesitate to write in their books, hoping to get a higher price when selling them back to the bookstore, it truly is in your best academic interest to respond directly to the reading by marking your texts. Here's why.

College reading, especially textbooks, contains a lot of information. As you read, you want to think about and identify the important content and have it stand out from the rest. That way, when you go back to review the material, to write about it or study it, you will need to focus only upon the information you identified as being most important. It's a real time-saver.

Highlighting, annotating, and writing marginal notes are three active reading strategies that ask you to think and make decisions as you read. Using these techniques together, you can turn your textbook into a user-friendly review book.

Highlighting

Highlighting involves using markers to make important information stand out. The problem with highlighting, however, is that many students over-

highlight, ending up with a pink or yellow page! They highlight so much that it is impossible to tell what information is significant. The remedy for this is: *Do not highlight as you read*. Wait. When you have completed reading a paragraph, decide what is the most important information. This will probably include the topic sentence and major supporting details; then go back and highlight that information.

Read and highlight all the boldface information as well, including chapter titles, headings, subheadings, and key vocabulary words. You might ask, "Why should I highlight these if they are already boldface?" They are boldface because they are important information. Highlighting them when you reread enables you to capture them in your net of important information.

You have already begun the highlighting process in the preceding section on previewing.

Annotating and Marginal Notes

Annotating is a more in-depth method of identifying main ideas, important details, and key vocabulary terms. You use it in combination with highlighting. When you annotate, you still underline important points, but you also write notes and use symbols to explain why you have done so and to identify important types of information.

You have already begun the process of annotating by writing preview and monitoring questions, and marking within the text. You can annotate *within the text*, and/or *in the margins* of the pages (marginal notes). For example, within the text you might circle important vocabulary words and underline their definitions. When you come upon a list of related points in the text, number the items directly in the text. Place stars next to important points and put question marks next to statements you doubt or find confusing.

Use the margin to label the topics and subtopics discussed in each paragraph. Words like *definition, causes, effects, advantages, benefits, goals, problems, reasons,* or *examples* can indicate that a list follows, and it would be useful to number that list. For example, the word *benefits* in an article on higher education might be followed by a list of reasons why it is important to go to college.

Annotating is also your opportunity to respond personally to the material. In the margin you can write comments like *I disagree, No way, Amazing, Yes!* or *Check this later.*

Develop your own list of annotation symbols, and get in the habit of using them regularly as you read. After a while, you will never be able to read textbook material without that pen or pencil in your hand.

Here is an example of one student's system of annotation. You might choose to use some of these ideas, or develop your own.

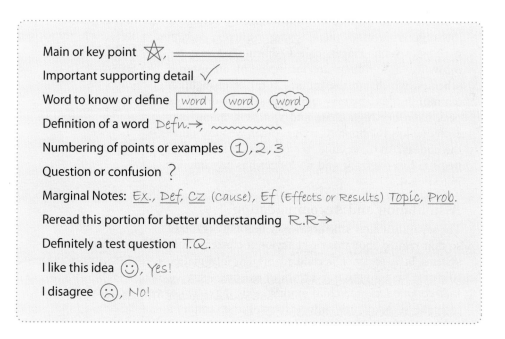

Look at the following paragraphs adapted from a psychology textbook. They begin a discussion of the work of Jean Piaget, a famous psychologist who studied the development of intelligence in children. You will learn more about Piaget's stages of development if you take an introductory psychology class. Notice how the highlighting, annotation, and marginal notes draw your attention to the most important topics and key points.

What is

A Stage Approach: Piaget's Theory ?

Piaget's Research

For nearly sixty years, Swiss psychologist Jean Piaget (1896–1980) devoted himself to understanding the development of children's intelligence. His careful observation of infants and children has provided a comprehensive account of mental development. His ideas have served as the basis for much of our knowledge about how a child's mind grows. Piaget produced a strict stage theory of development, in which a child actively constructs his or her knowledge of the world. As a child develops, the mind undergoes a series of reorganizations. With each reorganization, the child moves into a higher level of mental functioning. Three psychological processes are vital to intellectual growth: ① the use of schemes, ② assimilation, and ③ accommodation.

Stage Theory of Development

3 Processes Needed (T.Q)

Schemes ✓

Schemes- Defn.

Newborns know nothing about the objects and people that make up their world or how their own actions affect those objects. But they begin almost immediately to acquire this knowledge by acting on the objects around them, using recurrent action patterns which Piaget called schemes. Grasping, throwing, and rolling are examples of an infant's schemes, which are the infant's form of thought. A ten-month-old baby may explore gravity by dropping peas from her high chair and watching intently as each one hits the floor. As we get older, we internalize these ideas. An older child, then, knows that dropped items fall to the floor and no longer has any interest in testing it.

Examples
• Infants

• 10 mos

• older child

Assimilation ✓ and Accommodation ✓

The separate action schemes slowly become organized so that related thoughts or behavior is clustered into systems. In *assimilation,* a child adapts new information so that it fits into the framework of existing schemes. In *accommodation,* a child modifies existing schemes to make sense of new information. For example, a baby already sucks from a nipple on a bottle, so at first he will suck from a cup to drink (assimilation). Doing this makes the milk run down his chin, so he adjusts his mouth to eventually drink from a cup successfully (accommodation).

Assimilation Defn.

Accommodation Defn.

Ex. assimilation

accommodation

try it and apply it! 2-13 Highlighting and Annotating

Directions: Now turn to "Expand Your Emotional Intelligence," in the appendix. Actively read below the subheading "Character First: Integrity, Civility, and Ethics" (on page A-23). Stop at the end of each paragraph to highlight and annotate. Then compare your work to the excerpt. Make modifications or additions in your own annotation based on your review of the model that follows.

Character First: Integrity, Civility, and Ethics

Good character is an essential personal quality for true success in school, work, and life. A person of good character has a core set of principles that most of us accept as constant and relatively noncontroversial. These principles include fairness, honesty, respect, responsibility, caring, trustworthiness, and citizenship. Recent surveys of business leaders indicate that dishonesty, lying, and lack of respect are top reasons for on-the-job difficulties. If an employer believes that an employee lacks integrity, all of that person's positive qualities—from skill and experience to productivity and intelligence—are meaningless. Employers usually list honesty or good character as an essential personal quality, followed by the ability to relate and get along with others. A number of books have been written by successful top executives who claim that good character, honesty, and a strong value system are what make you an effective leader. All the corporate scandals seen in the news lately are testimonials that business leaders with poor values will eventually meet their demise.

Character

Important in the Business World

Essential

Following The Golden Rule (treating others as we want to be treated) is a simple way to weave integrity and civility into our everyday lives. The word *integrity* comes from the Latin word *integre,* meaning "wholeness." Integrity is the integration of your principles and actions. In a sense, people who have integrity "walk the talk." They consistently live up to their highest principles. Integrity is not adherence to a rigid code but, rather, an ongoing commitment to being consistent, caring, and true to doing what is right. Not only is integrity understanding what is right, but it is also the courage to do it even when it is difficult.

defn. Integrity

Civility is a set of tools for interacting with others with respect, kindness, and good manners, or etiquette. However, civility is more than good manners and politeness. It includes the many sacrifices we make each day in order to live together peacefully. Empathy—understanding and compassion for others—is essential for integrity and civility. You can practice civility in your classes by being on time, turning off your cell phone, staying for the entire class, and listening to the instructor and other students when they speak.

Civility in the classroom

Keep this in mind

Highlighting and Annotating

- **Be prepared! Read with your highlighter and pen and pencil in hand.** Be ready to mark important information in your text.
- **Don't overhighlight!** Be selective. Read the entire paragraph before deciding what matters most and is important to note.
- **Develop a personal system of annotating** that you apply to all your reading. Be creative, and enjoy the process.

Get Ready to Read: Active Reading Strategies for Managing College Texts

wrap it Up

Remember that reading is a *process* that includes all the activities before, during, and after you read.

- **Before you begin using your textbooks, survey them all** to learn their organization and features.
- **Always think about what you already know about a topic** before you start to read about it.
- **Preview your selections.** Vary your strategy based on what you are reading: textbooks, articles, essays, newspapers, or literature.
- **Establish your purpose for reading** portions of your textbook by creating your own guide questions based on titles, headings, and introductory sentences in paragraphs.
- **Periodically stop and reflect upon your understanding.** Reread portions when you are unsure.
- **Always read with a pen, pencil, or highlighter in hand.** Interact with the content of your textbooks. Note important information, terms, or ideas by annotating, highlighting, and writing marginal notes.
- **Check your understanding of the material** by asking and answering your own questions based on the most important points in a chapter.

Key Terms

acknowledgments	contrast	glossary
analyze	discuss	guide questions
annotating	evaluate	heading
appendix	explain	index
compare	first sentence in	introduction
concepts	each paragraph	justify

key terms   processes   title
learning theory   prove   title page
major heading   study questions   trace
metacognition   summarize   vocabulary words
monitoring questions   surveying the textbook   webliography
preface   table of contents
preview questions   thesis

3

The Power of Words
Understanding College Vocabulary

In this chapter

you will learn to

- Use the following context clues to learn the meaning of new words:

    Definition clues

    Synonym clues

    Contrast and antonym clues

    Example clues

    Inference clues

- Understand the meaning of discipline-specific vocabulary and academic vocabulary

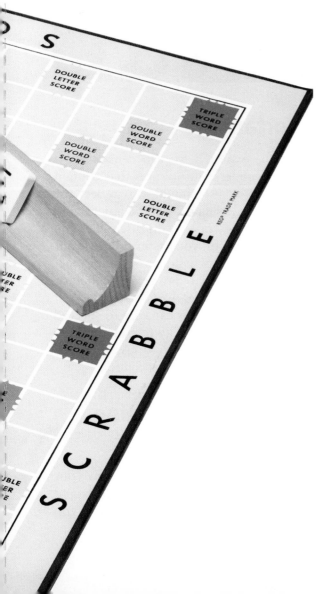

Develop Skills While Reading About
Diversity

The concept of **diversity** includes acceptance and respect for each individual's unique differences, whether they are related to race, ethnicity, gender, sexual orientation, socioeconomic status, age, physical abilities, religious beliefs, political beliefs, or other ideologies. It is about our understanding of one another and embracing each other so that we can benefit and grow from the richness of our shared experiences.

Few societies have a more diverse population than the United States; our nation is truly a multiracial, multiethnic, and multicultural society. In addition, today there is no one type of student on U.S. college campuses. The diverse student body includes people from a broad range of age, color, culture, language, and ability. The overall numbers of nontraditional-age students, military veterans, students returning to college, single parents, older adults, and evening students are increasing, too. Find out more about diversity and tolerance in Module 3.

Why Vocabulary Is Important

In your college course work, you will be expected to read densely written textbooks, write scholarly essays, and understand lectures that contain academic language. In fact, the language *you* use should also reflect the vocabulary of the disciplines you are studying. Using the right language, and having a broad vocabulary that includes the key words of the disciplines you are studying, will significantly affect how successful you are in college. Your ability to understand what you hear in lectures or discussions and your capacity to understand college-level material is directly related to your vocabulary.

A strong vocabulary also leads to benefits in other areas of your life. It will improve your future career opportunities and your capacity to succeed and advance in your work. More importantly, your ability to communicate effectively will go a long way in making good first impressions when you meet new people, whether they are friends, employers, or colleagues.

Using Context Clues to Learn the Meaning of Words

As you read college textbooks, essays, and articles that pertain to your course work, you will come across many new and unfamiliar words and terms. If you depend only upon your prior experience with a word, you may or may not understand its specific meaning in the material you are reading. In addition, if you stop to look up every new word you encounter, you can waste a lot of time and maybe even come up with the wrong definition. However, if you use the **context clues** in a reading, you will probably be able to guess what a word means or understand enough to be able to continue to read efficiently and effectively. Following is a good strategy to help you understand and learn new and unfamiliar words:

1. Circle new words or those used in an unfamiliar way as you encounter them.
2. Use context clues to get a general understanding of their meaning.
3. Complete the reading.
4. Look the new words up in a dictionary.

There are five commonly used types of context clues:

- definition clues
- synonym clues
- contrast and antonym clues
- example clues
- inference clues

Definition Clues

A **definition clue** is a hint provided in the text, which leads the reader to the meaning of a word. It may be the most obvious way an author helps you to understand new words, especially discipline-specific terminology or the meaning of words commonly found in college textbooks. Often the term being defined is in bold or italic font, and the definition follows immediately after it. Signal words and punctuation are also used to indicate that a definition is being given.

Signal words—words and phrases such as *is, are, means, can be defined as, refers to, involves, that is,* and *in other words*—-indicate that a definition of a term is about to be provided. The examples that follow show how signal words and punctuation can help you understand new words or terminology.

Example 1

> **Stereotypes** are broad generalizations about members of a group that do not recognize individual differences within the group. (Adapted from Schaefer 2007)

The signal word *are* tells the reader that a definition of the term in bold print will follow. Therefore, the word **stereotypes** means *broad generalizations about all members of a group that do not recognize individual differences within the group.*

Example 2

> **Prejudice** involves a negative attitude toward a cultural group based on little or no experience. (Adapted from Hybels and Weaver II 2009)

The signal word *involves* tells the reader that a definition of the word in bold print will follow. Therefore, **prejudice** means *a negative attitude toward a cultural group based on little or no experience.*

The definition of a word or term may also be set off by **punctuation cues,** such as parentheses, commas, and dashes, or it may follow a comma or dash. Note the way punctuation is used in the sentences that follow:

Example 3

> Sometimes, prejudice results from **ethnocentrism**—the tendency to assume that one's own culture and way of life represent the norm or are superior to all others. (Adapted from Schaefer 2007)

The dash after the word in bold print indicates that a definition will follow, so **ethnocentrism** means *the tendency to assume that one's own culture and way of life represent the norm or are superior to all others.*

Example 4

> One important and widespread form of prejudice is **racism,** the belief that one race is superior and all others are inferior. (Adapted from Schaefer 2007)

In this example, the information after the comma provides the reader with information about the boldface word; that is, the word **racism** means *the belief that one race is superior and all others are inferior.*

In some textbooks, **special font clues** are used to signal that a definition of a term is being presented; for example, words are presented in *italic*, **bold**, or colored font.

Example 5

> Prejudice often leads to **discrimination,** the denial of opportunities and equal rights to individuals and groups because of prejudice or other reasons. (Adapted from Schaefer 2007)

In this example, the word being defined, discrimination, is in bold, and the words in italic that follow tell the reader the meaning of the term. So **discrimination** can be defined as *the denial of opportunities and equal rights to individuals and groups because of prejudice or other reasons.*

try it and apply it! 3-1   Using Definition Clues

Directions: Underline the definition clues used in these sentences. Then write the clues and the meanings of the boldface words on the lines provided.

1. The term **race** is generally used to refer to obvious physical differences that set one group apart from another. (Adapted from Feldman 2009)

    Clue(s): *is*

    Meaning: *obvious physical differences that set one group apart from another*

2. **Culture** (the learned behaviors, beliefs, and attitudes that are characteristic of an individual society or population, and the products people create) influences our view of others, and how we treat them in turn. (Adapted from Feldman 2009)

    Clue(s): *parentheses*

    Meaning: *the learned behaviors, beliefs, and attitudes that are characteristic of an individual society or population, and the products people create*

3. We learn about other cultures through **cultural competence**—the knowledge and understanding of others' customs, perspectives, and history. (Adapted from Feldman 2009)

    Clue(s): *dash*

    Meaning: *knowledge and understanding of others' customs, perspectives, and history*

4. As a college student, you can learn about other cultures through courses in **anthropology**, the science of human beings . . . and their ancestors through time and space and in relation to physical character, environmental and social relations, and culture. (By permission. From Merriam-Webster's Collegiate® Dictionary, 11th Edition © 2010 by Merriam-Webster, Incorporated (www.Merriam-Webster.com))

    Clue(s): *comma*

    Meaning: *the science of human beings and their ancestors through time and space and in relation to physical character, environmental and social relations, and culture*

5. You can also **expand your horizons** by spending a semester abroad: in other words, living in another country will broaden your outlook and understanding about life in another culture. (Adapted from Feldman 2009)

    Clue(s): *in other words*

    Meaning: *broaden your outlook and understanding about life*

6. Sometimes, you can participate in **in-service learning**—a process whereby students learn and develop through active participation in organized service experiences that actually meet community needs—by becoming involved in the tutoring of middle-school students whose native language is not English. (Adapted from Feldman 2009)

(continued)

(continued)

Clue(s): *dashes*

Meaning: *a process whereby students learn and develop through active participation in organized service experiences that actually meet community needs*

7. It is important not to make **conjectures** about who people are, which may <u>involve</u> making guesses about a person's ethnicity, religion, or background. (Adapted from Feldman 2009)

    Clue(s): *comma, involve*

    Meaning: *guesses*

8. Even if people appear very different on the surface, they may exhibit many **commonalities;** <u>that is to say</u>, they may have <u>the same</u> fears and anxieties as you, and they may <u>share similar</u> goals and dreams. (Adapted from Feldman 2009)

    Clue(s): *that is to say, the same, share similar*

    Meaning: *similarities, sameness*

9. The most important thing about differences is that we must **embrace** them—accept them and not reject them. (Adapted from Feldman 2009)

    Clue(s): *dash*

    Meaning: *accept*

10. Celebrate **diversity**, the differences in gender, race, ethnicity, sexual orientation, physical disabilities, learning styles, and all learning disabilities, and you will be richer and wiser for it. (Adapted from Ferrett 2010)

    Clue(s): *commas*

    Meaning: *the differences in gender, race, ethnicity, sexual orientation, physical disabilities, learning styles, and all learning disabilities*

Synonym Clues

Another way an author can tell you what a word means is by providing a synonym for it. A **synonym** is a word that has the same or a similar meaning as the targeted term.

> Signal words such as *and* and *or* are used to indicate that a synonym is being provided. Punctuation cues such as commas, dashes, or parentheses may also be used to signal that a synonym of an unfamiliar term is being provided.

Example 1

> Native Americans are often the subject of **stereotyping,** or labeling.

The word in bold print is followed by *or*, so that another word for **stereotyping** is labeling.

Example 2

> American Indians are often the target of stereotypes in the United States as they struggle to meet their most basic needs and maintain their cultural background in a **hostile** modern world, or a society that shows feelings of ill will. (Adapted from Hahn 2007)

The term in bold print is followed by *or*. The word *or* signals that a synonym of the target word will follow, so a phrase that means **hostile** is *showing ill will*.

Example 3

> Some people believe that American Indians are **stoic**—unemotional.

The term in bold print is followed by *a dash*, so a synonym for **stoic** is unemotional.

Example 4

> We should be careful not to judge American Indians because, like other communities, they **yearn** for and strongly desire the traditional values of an earlier day. (Adapted from Hahn 2007)

The term in bold print is followed by *and*, a signal word that tells the reader a synonym might follow. A similar meaning for **yearn** is *strongly desire*.

try it and apply it! 3-2   Using Synonym Clues   ⑪

Directions: Underline the clue word or punctuation used to signal the synonym for the boldface word. Write the clue and the meaning of the word on the lines provided.

1. In a **pluralistic** society, <u>or</u> one based on mutual respect for one another, even a minority group is allowed to express its own culture and still participate without prejudice in the larger society. (Adapted from Schaefer 2007)

    Clue: *or* _____

    Meaning: *based on mutual respect for one another* _____

2. Government programs, such as affirmative action, have been developed to **recruit,** <u>or</u> attempt to acquire the services, of minority group

    (continued)

(*continued*)

members or women for jobs, promotions, and educational opportunities. (Adapted from Schaefer 2007)

Clue: *or*

Meaning: *attempt to acquire the services of people*

3. Many people **resent** and feel insulted or injured by this program because they feel it merely shifts the discrimination to another group. (Adapted from Schaefer 2007)

Clue: *and*

Meaning: *feel insulted or injured by*

4. Discriminatory practices and prejudice continue to **pervade** (spread through) nearly all areas of life in the United States. (Adapted from Schaefer 2007)

Clue: *parentheses*

Meaning: *spread through*

5. The labeling of Latino children as underachievers or learning disabled can act as a self-fulfilling **prophecy,** affecting their future opportunities. (Adapted from Schaefer 2007)

Clue: *comma*

Meaning: *future and what will be*

6. Bilingual education and ESL course work are educational approaches aimed at easing the **transition,** or movement, of Latino children and others whose first language is not English to a new cultural experience. (Adapted from Schaefer 2007)

Clue: *or*

Meaning: *movement from one state to another*

7. Asian Americans are often seen as the **model** or ideal minority because they have succeeded economically, socially, and educationally. (Adapted from Schaefer 2007)

Clue: *or*

Meaning: *ideal*

8. Some Asian Americans find this stereotype unfair and blame the media for its **proliferation,** especially by spreading the great number of myths through television programming. (Adapted from Warner and Hilliard 2010)

Clue: *comma*

Meaning: *spreading a great number*

9. Despite the stereotype that most Arab Americans are of the Islamic **denomination,** or religious group, most are not. (Adapted from Schaefer 2007)

Clue: *or*

Meaning: *religious group*

10. In spite of their great diversity, Arab Americans have been subject to **profiling** <u>and</u> are being singled out for criminal activities, especially since the attacks of September 2001. (Adapted from Schaefer 2007)

    Clue: *and*

    Meaning: *to be singled out for possible criminal acts or behavior*

Contrast or Antonym Clues

You can also determine the meaning of an unfamiliar word by noting a word or phrase in the sentence that means just the opposite of it (an antonym).

Signal Words That Show Contrast

different from, differ, but, yet, however, although (though), even though, nevertheless, while, whereas

In the following sentences, contrast clues will give you hints about the words in bold print:

Example 1

Whereas an **adolescent** may be denied a job because he or she is inexperienced, an elderly person might be refused a position because he or she is too old. (Adapted from Schaefer 2007)

The word *whereas* shows a contrast, so **adolescent** means the opposite of elderly or *someone who is young*.

Example 2

Research indicates that older people who have a favorable or positive image of aging live longer; nevertheless, the media continue to portray the **adverse** effects of growing old. (Adapted from Schaefer 2007)

The word *nevertheless* also indicates a contrast. In other words, **adverse** means the opposite of positive. It means *unfavorable or negative*.

try it and apply it! 3-3   Using Contrast Clues

Directions: Underline the signal words for contrast or antonym clues for the words in bold print. Then write the clues and the meaning of the words in the spaces provided.

1. In the workplace, older workers have begun to feel that they are bearing a **disproportionate** share of the layoffs, <u>as opposed</u> to the lesser amount received by younger workers. (Adapted from Schaefer 2007)

(continued)

(continued)

Clue: *as opposed*

Meaning: *unequal amount*

2. In a controlled experiment conducted by AARP, younger applicants received many **affirmative** responses to their resumes, while the older applicants who sent out comparable resumes got a great deal of unfavorable responses. (Adapted from Schaefer 2007)

Clue: *while*

Meaning: *favorable*

3. Today, many elderly people have strong financial assets to provide for them in their retirement; however, there are still many who are **impoverished.** (Adapted from Schaefer 2007)

Clue: *however*

Meaning: *not having strong financial assets, poor*

4. Traditional gender roles portray men as dominant and tough, while labeling women as **submissive** and soft. (Adapted from Schaefer 2007)

Clue: *while*

Meaning: *not dominant, giving in*

5. Some have claimed that the use of the word homophobia, a fear and prejudice against homosexuality, is **pejorative;** nevertheless, sociologists have still not succeeded in replacing it with a less offensive or insulting word. (Adapted from Schaefer 2007)

Clue: *nevertheless*

Meaning: *offensive, insulting*

6. When considering homophobia, it is important to consider the difference between prejudice and **discrimination.** Although many college students have prejudices about gays, they do not necessarily act on these prejudices in a manner that would interfere with their rights. (Adapted from Schaefer 2007)

Clue: *difference, although*

Meaning: *act on prejudices in a way that would interfere with a person's rights*

7. Students enrolled in "Psychology of Prejudice" showed **substantial** evidence of reduction in prejudice toward gays, in contrast to "Introductory Psychology," in which there was a minimal decrease. (Adapted from Pettijohn and Walzer 2008)

Clue: *in contrast to*

Meaning: *significant*

8. Sexism, the belief that one sex is superior to the other, is still increasing; however, there have been attempts to **curtail** this ideology through the establishment of Title VII of the Civil Rights Act of 1964 and sexual harassment policies. (Adapted from Schaefer 2007)

Clue: *however*

Meaning: *to make less*

9. In the military, women are often **banned** from combat duty, whereas men are permitted to engage in all maneuvers on the battlefield.

   Clue: *whereas*

   Meaning: *are not permitted*

10. One of the most obvious concerns about combat is that women are perceived as weak, while men are considered **brawny**. (Adapted from Schaefer 2007)

    Clue: *while*

    Meaning: *have physical strength, not weak, strong*

Example Clues

Sometimes, authors provide examples to illustrate the meaning of unfamiliar words.

Signal Words That Indicate Examples Are Being Used

for example, for instance, such as, like, consist, including

Read the sentences below to see how the examples provide information that clarifies the meanings of the words in bold print.

Example 1

The disruption of a combat unit's **esprit de corps** is cited as a reason for banning women from front lines; for example, during the Revolutionary War, George Washington was convinced that females were distracting and greatly impacted the spirit of comradeship among officers. (Adapted from Brinkley 2007)

In this sentence, the writer provides an example to help the reader understand the unfamiliar expression and uses the word *spirit* as a synonym for **esprit de corps**.

The meaning of **esprit de corps** is spirit.

Example 2

Many historians point out that there are vast **archives** of information about women achieving much on the battlefield in combat roles, such as Deborah Sampson in the Revolutionary War; Sarah Rosetta Walkman during the Civil War; Lt. Col. Eileen Collins during the invasion of Panama; and Col. Kelly Hamilton during the 1991 Gulf War. (Source information from "Women in the Military in the Americas," Wikipedia)

Here the author uses examples to make the point that **archives** are filled with information from the past. The meaning of **archive** is a place where public records or other historical documents are kept.

try it and apply it! 3-4   Using Example Clues

Directions: Underline the example clues in the following sentences. Then write the meaning of the boldface words on the lines provided.

1. Throughout history, the disabled were frequently seen as a **menace** to society. For example, in Japan more than 16,000 women with disabilities were involuntarily sterilized with government approval from 1945 to 1995. Sweden apologized for the same action taken against 62,000 citizens in the 1970s. (Adapted from Schaefer 2007)

   Meaning: *threat, danger*

2. In the early 1960s at the University of California at Berkeley, the very first **advocacy** group for the rights of the disabled on college campuses succeeded in winning two important initiatives, which consisted of securing college admissions for students with disabilities at the college and establishing independent living centers, which later became a model for hundreds of others. (Adapted from Schaefer 2007)

   Meaning: *arguing in favor of, supporting*

3. The Americans with Disabilities Act (ADA) of 1990 has done a great deal to **level the playing field** for the disabled, including making available to them many opportunities to attend college programs, live in dorms, attend lecture halls, and engage in recreational activities with their nondisabled classmates. (Adapted from Hahn 2007)

   Meaning: *to give everyone the same advantages or opportunities*

4. This law prohibits discrimination against people with disabilities in all **sectors** of the economy, such as employment, transportation, public accommodations, and telecommunications. (Adapted from Schaefer 2007)

   Meaning: *a distinct part, especially of society*

5. The responsibility for **enforcing** the ADA has been given to several federal agencies, including the Equal Employment Opportunity Commission, which oversees the employment of people with disabilities, and the Department of Transportation, which is responsible for administering the transportation requirements. (Adapted from Schaefer 2007)

   Meaning: *putting or keeping in force; compelling obedience to*

6. New on the agenda for the disabled is the concept of visitability, which focuses on designing housing so that it is **accessible** to visitors with disabilities through the inclusion of no-step entrances, wide doorways, and grab bars in the bathrooms. (Adapted from Schaefer 2007)

   Meaning: *easy to approach or enter*

7. In many colleges, a major role of disability services personnel is to **collaborate** with faculty, <u>including</u> instructors, academic counselors, department chairs, and <u>administrators</u>, to help students become independent learners.

   Meaning: *work together* _____

8. An effective **pedagogy** for learning disabled students attending college is Universal Design for Instruction (UDI), which <u>includes</u> straightforward and simple <u>instruction</u>, materials in <u>digital</u> format, and an instructional approach that requires communication among students and between faculty and students. (Adapted from Scott, McGuire, & Shaw 2001)

   Meaning: *instructional methods* _____

9. An <u>example</u> of simple and **intuitive** instruction is providing a grading <u>formula</u> for papers or projects to clearly state performance expectations. (Adapted from Scott, McGuire & Shaw 2001)

   Meaning: *immediate understanding* _____

10. It is also important for faculty to design an instructional **climate** that is welcoming and inclusive; <u>for instance,</u> instructors should include statements on their syllabuses that affirm the needs of students with disabilities, which respect diversity, which emphasize the expectation of tolerance, and encourage all students to discuss learning needs with their teachers. (Adapted from Shaw et al. 2001)

    Meaning: *environment, atmosphere* _____

Inference Clues

Sometimes, there are no definitions, synonyms, antonyms, or examples to give you a clue to the meaning of an unfamiliar word. But don't give up. Continue to read the passage to see if you can get a general sense of the meaning of the word by drawing **inferences** or conclusions from the information the author provides.

Example 1

Gender, race, and class stereotypes of Asian Americans in the **media,** especially those depicted in popular movies, give the impression of what Asian Americans are really like to other Americans as well as to Asian Americans themselves. In prime time television, the roles of Asian Americans are often shown as those of professionals in medicine and scientific research. (Source information from "Asian Americans and the Media: Perpetuating the Model Minority")

From these sentences, we can conclude that the **media** has something to do with movies and television.

Example 2

Since the September 11 tragedy, there has been an increasing mood of **xenophobia** in Europe and beyond. Many hate crimes against Muslims, Arabs, and others mistaken for Arabs have occurred. (Adapted from Schaefer 2007)

From these two sentences, we learn that **xenophobia** results from fear of immigrants or people from other countries. The 9/11 attack was perpetrated by Muslim extremists; consequently, there was an increase in the fear of all foreigners, especially those of Arab descent.

try it and apply it! 3-5   Using Inference Clues

Directions: See if you can figure out the meanings of the boldface words by using inference clues from the surrounding text. Then write the meanings of the words on the lines provided.

1. According to a recent study by Children Now, television-viewing during the "family hour" is the least ethnically diverse, with only one in eight programs having a mixed cast. This sends highly **skewed** messages about diversity in America to viewers, especially children. (Adapted from www.childrennow.org)

    biased or distorted

2. Journalism groups have recently started new training initiatives, backed by media firms and organizations to **boost** the numbers of minority managers and executives. Only a very small percentage of all newspaper managers are from minority groups, according to the American Society of News Editors. (Adapted from www.asne.org)

    increase

3. The **burgeoning** need to improve cross-cultural communication has resulted from changes in the workplace. These include U.S. businesses expanding into world markets; people now being connected by the Internet, email, and electronic bulletin boards to other people they have never seen face-to-face; and changing immigration patterns. (Adapted from Hybels and Weaver II 2009)

    growing

4. Some people do not know about other cultures, and some do not want to know. There is no doubt that lack of knowledge can **inhibit** intercultural communication. (Adapted from Hybels and Weaver II 2009)

    prevent

5. Overweight children are **stigmatized** by their peers as early as age 3, and even face discrimination from their parents and teachers, giving them a quality of life comparable to people with cancer. (Adapted from Associated Press, "Overweight Kids Face Widespread Stigma," July 12, 2007)

    labeled socially undesirable

6. Youngsters who report teasing, rejection, **bullying,** and other types of abuse because of their weight are two to three times more likely to report suicidal thoughts, as well as to suffer from other health issues such as high blood pressure and eating disorders, researchers said. (Adapted from Associated Press, "Overweight Kids Face Widespread Stigma," July 12, 2007)

    verbal or emotional abuse

7. An **alarming** finding of this research was that obese children had [quality of life] scores comparable with those of children with cancer, the researchers reported. (Adapted from Associated Press, "Overweight Kids Face Widespread Stigma," July 12, 2007)

    disturbing

8. Dr. Xavier Pi-Sunye reports that the "discovery of a fat gene" is "a welcome step forward from thinking of obesity as a psychological or personality disorder to thinking of it as a biologically determined genetic illness over which an individual has less direct control. This should remove some of the social stigma from being fat, and may **diminish** some of the discrimination fat people endure." (Burns 1995)

    lessen

9. Little People of America, at its annual conference in Brooklyn this week, has called for the Federal Communications Commission to **ban** the use of the word "midget" on broadcast TV. "Growing up as a little person because you're different, you experience the ups and downs of some cruelties and prejudices. How many times have people I don't know come up to me and wanted to pick me up?" said Clinton Brown, 27. (Adapted from Maloney 2009)

    prohibit by law

10. Michael Petruzzelli, president of the group's Long Island chapter, said physical accommodations for little people have come a long way, but "we haven't made those social changes to take those **offensive** words out of our vocabulary." (Adapted from Maloney 2009)

    hurtful or harmful

Using Context Clues

Clues	Look For	Example
Definition	is, are, means, can be defined as, refers to, involves, that is, in other words	**Stereotypes** are unreal generalizations about all members of a group that do not recognize individual differences within the group.
	dashes, commas, parentheses	One important and widespread form of prejudice is **racism,** the belief that one race is supreme and all others are inferior.

(continued)

(continued)

Clues	Look For	Example
	italic, boldface, different colors	Prejudice often leads to **discrimination,** the denial of opportunities and equal rights to individuals and groups because of prejudice or other reasons.
Synonym	and, or	We should be careful not to judge Native American Indians because, like other communities, they **yearn** for and strongly desire the traditional values of an earlier day.
Contrast/ Antonyms	different from, differ, however, although, though, nevertheless, while, whereas	Traditional gender roles portray men as dominant and tough yet women as **submissive** and soft.
Example	for example, for instance, such as, like, to illustrate	The ADA prohibits discrimination against people with disabilities in all **sectors,** such as in employment, transportation, public accommodations, and telecommunications.
Inference	Another sentence before or after the unfamiliar word that may provide additional information	Some people do not know about other cultures, and some do not want to know. There is no doubt that lack of knowledge can **inhibit** intercultural communication.

Discipline-Specific Vocabulary

As you will discover in college, each area of study, or discipline, has its own **discipline-specific vocabulary**—terminology, or technical words specific to the subject.

For example, students who study sociology will encounter words or terms such as *norms, ethnocentrism, power elite,* and *groupthink.* These words will often appear in boldface or italic type in the body of the text. They are typically followed by definitions, explanations, and examples, because authors realize you are learning a new subject and want to support you in this process. They may also appear in the margins, in text boxes, or in the introduction or summary section of the chapter. Discipline-specific terms are usually defined in the glossary of a textbook as well. It is your responsibility to master these new terms. Your active involvement in class discussions and activities will give you an opportunity to use and learn these new words.

You should also pay close attention to the possibility of terms having more than one meaning. For example, you know that the definition of the word **mean** as an adjective is *rude and bad-tempered,* and as a noun it is a way or method (means of transportation) or explanation or significance (the meaning of a word). However, in sociology or mathematics, the term **mean** is defined as *a number calculated by adding a series of numbers and then dividing by the number of values or the average.* To recognize differences in meaning such as this, it is necessary to think about the content of the selection you are reading.

Read the following excerpt from the sociology textbook titled *Sociology* by Richard T. Schaefer. Notice how many of the vocabulary terms are related to the field of sociology. Circle these in the text.

> Sociologists frequently distinguish between racial and ethnic groups. The term racial group describes a group that is set apart from others because of physical differences that have taken on social significance. Whites, African Americans, and Asian Americans are all considered racial groups in the United States. Unlike racial groups, an ethnic group is set apart from others primarily because of its national origin or distinctive cultural patterns. In the United States, Puerto Ricans, Jews and Polish Americans are all categorized as ethnic groups.
>
> (Adapted from Schaefer 2007)

Academic Vocabulary

In addition to discipline-specific vocabulary, all college textbooks use words known as **academic vocabulary.** *The Academic Word List* (AWL) (Coxhead 2000) identified and compiled 570 word families commonly appearing throughout academic writing. In the reading modules in Part Three of this textbook, the academic words found in all of the selections are identified and used in practice exercises. As you read, you will see how important it is to know the meanings of these words in order to understand assigned readings.

> Anti-Semitism—that is, anti-Jewish prejudice—has often been vicious in the United States, although rarely so **widespread** and never so formalized as in Europe. In many cases, Jews have been used as scapegoats for other people's failures. Not surprisingly, Jews have not reached equality in the United States. **Despite** high levels of education and **professional** training, they are still conspicuously absent from top management of large **corporations.** Until the late 1960s many prestigious universities **maintained restricted** quotas that limited Jewish enrollment. In addition, private and social clubs and fraternal groups frequently limited their membership.
>
> (Adapted from Schaefer 2007)

You were probably familiar with many of the words in bold in the excerpt. However, you may still need to learn some words, such as maintained (keep up, continue) and restricted (limited). Sometimes, you will be able to determine their meaning using the surrounding words. Other times, you will need to consult a dictionary. You will find it helpful to keep a running list of the new academic vocabulary words you encounter in the reading selections in this text. List them with their definitions and different word forms. Study them. You will find them used across the disciplines in textbooks and lectures. They will also be useful for college writing assignments.

AWL Words and Related Word Forms

Corporation
Professional, professionally
Despite
Restrict, **restricted,** restrictive
Maintain, **maintained,** maintenance
Widespread

---

try it and apply it! 3-6   Integrating Vocabulary Strategies

Directions: The vocabulary words in this exercise come from a section in a sociology textbook that discusses the status of women worldwide. Using context clues, select the *best* definition for each of the words in bold print.

__c__ 1. A detailed overview of the **status** or position in society of women worldwide, issued by the United Nations in 2000, noted that women and men live in different worlds.
   a. category
   b. type
   c. position
   d. condition

__d__ 2. These worlds differ in terms of **access** to education and work opportunities, as well as in health, personal security, and human rights.
   a. the operation of reading or writing stored information
   b. a way of entering or leaving
   c. the act of approaching or entering
   d. the right to obtain or make use of or take advantage of something

__a__ 3. The Hindu culture, for example, makes life especially **harsh** for widows. If the husband dies, the widow becomes the property of the husband's family, and in many cases, may end up working as an unpaid servant.

  a. cruel and severe
  b. simple and comfortable
  c. inconsiderate and unkind
  d. unpleasantly cold

_d_ 4. In other families, the widow is simply **abandoned** and left penniless.
  a. vacant
  b. discontinued
  c. supported
  d. deserted

_a_ 5. Regardless of the culture, women everywhere suffer from **second-class** status.
  a. inferior
  b. superior
  c. decreased
  d. private

_c_ 6. It is estimated that women grow half of the world's food, but they **rarely** own land.
  a. sometimes
  b. always
  c. almost never
  d. occasionally

_b_ 7. Women **constitute,** or make up, one-third of the world's paid labor force, but are generally found in the lowest-paying jobs.
  a. make off with
  b. represent
  c. manufacture
  d. set up

_d_ 8. Single-parent households headed by women, which appear to be **surging** in many nations, are typically found in the poorest sections of the population.
  a. declining
  b. decreasing
  c. opposite
  d. increasing

_a_ 9. The **feminization** of poverty has become a global issue.
  a. a bias against women
  b. giving a feminine appearance to
  c. becoming a woman
  d. causing a male to take on feminine characters

_b_ 10. As in the United States, women around the world are **underrepresented** politically.
  a. proportionate representation
  b. inadequate representation
  c. sufficient representation
  d. misrepresented

try it and apply it! 3-7   Using Context Clues and Word Parts

Directions: The following selection continues to explore the status of women, especially in the United States (adapted from Schaefer 2007). Read each paragraph. Then underline the clues that help you understand the words in bold print. Finally, select the best definition for each word in bold print in the exercises that follow each portion of the textbook.

Despite these challenges, women are not responding **passively.** They are mobilizing, individually and **collectively,** as a group. The feminist movement of the United States was born in upstate New York, in a town called Seneca Falls. On July 19, the first women's rights convention began, attended by Elizabeth Cady Stanton, Lucretia Mott, and other **pioneers** in the struggle for women's rights. The first wave of feminists, as they are currently known, faced disrespect and **scorn** as they fought for legal and political equality for women. They were not afraid to risk **controversy** on behalf of their cause; in 1872, Susan B. Anthony was arrested for attempting to vote in the presidential election.

The first wave of feminists fought for legal and political equality for women, such as the right to vote.

_c_ 1. **passively**
    a. peacefully
    b. actively
    c. not participating readily
    d. not influenced

_b_ 2. **collectively**
    a. individually
    b. as a group
    c. formed by collection
    d. singly

_a_ 3. **pioneers**
    a. one who takes part in the beginnings of a plan or project
    b. a person who is among those who first settle a region
    c. one who ventures into unknown or unclaimed territory
    d. an organism that successfully establishes itself in an infertile area

_b_ 4. **scorn**
    a. praise
    b. disrespect
    c. difficulty
    d. battles

_d_ 5. **controversy**
    a. jail
    b. physical fights
    c. discrimination
    d. discussion of issues

    Ultimately, the early feminists won many victories, among them the **ratification** and approval of the Nineteenth Amendment to the Constitution, which gave women the right to vote in national elections beginning in 1920. But **suffrage** did not lead to other changes in women's social and economic position, and in the early and middle twentieth century, the women's **movement** became a much less powerful force for social change.

_b_ 6. **ratification**
    a. disapproval
    b. approval
    c. strengthening
    d. denial

_d_ 7. **suffrage**
    a. the right to freedom
    b. a great deal of suffering
    c. a change for independence
    d. the right to vote

(continued)

(*continued*)

_c_ 8. **movement**
   a. rapid progress of events
   b. abundance of events or incidents
   c. a series of actions intended toward a particular end
   d. a particular manner of moving

The second wave of feminism in the United States emerged in the 1960s and came into full force in the 1970s. As more and more women became aware of sexist attitudes, they began to challenge male **dominance.**

_a_ 9. **dominance**
   a. the disposition of an individual to claim control in dealing with others
   b. high status in a social group, usually acquired as the result of violent behavior
   c. the normal tendency for one side of the brain to be more important than the other in controlling certain functions
   d. disadvantages and drawbacks caused because of men

Over the past several decades, the women's movement has undertaken public protests on a wide range of **issues,** including the passage of the equal rights amendment; government **subsidies** for child care that would help lower expenses for working mothers; affirmative action for women and minorities; federal **legislation** outlawing sex discrimination in education; greater representation of women in government, and rights to legal abortion.

Secretary Clinton
United States

_c_ 10. **issues**
    a. something that is printed or published and distributed
    b. a quantity of something that is officially offered for sale
    c. a point whose decision is of special or public importance
    d. the passage of the equal rights amendment

_a_ 11. **subsidies**
    a. financial assistance
    b. money for child care
    c. charity for working mothers
    d. a tax write-off

_b_ 12. **legislation**
    a. the act of legalization
    b. the making or giving of laws
    c. punishment for illegal actions
    d. official forbiddance

The Power of Words: Understanding College Vocabulary

- Don't just rely on *familiar* meanings when reading college material.
- Don't look up every new word in the dictionary as you read. It slows down your reading process and makes you lose concentration. Use context clues to guess the meaning of unfamiliar words while reading.
- Don't hesitate to ask your professor to explain new and unfamiliar words and terminology.

Key Terms

academic vocabulary
context clues
contrast and antonym
  clues
definition clue

example clues
inference clues
punctuation cues
signal words

special font clues
synonym
synonym clue

chapter

4

Get the Big Picture
Identifying the Main Idea in College Reading

In this chapter

you will learn to

- Identify topics in reading
- Determine the stated main idea in paragraphs or longer selections
- Formulate the unstated or implied main ideas in paragraphs and longer selections
- Identify the overall main idea or thesis of a selection

Develop Skills While Reading About

Physical Health and Well-Being

Your physical health is an important component of your overall health. Physical health relates to the design and operation of your body and your body's characteristics. These include weight, strength, coordination, and resistance to disease. Your physical well-being is influenced by the choices you make in your lifestyle: how you socialize, the quality of your diet, your intake of alcohol, your use of substances like tobacco or drugs, and how much exercise you do. Your physical well-being is also impacted by other dimensions of health, including your emotions. (You will have an opportunity to read about emotional health in Chapter 5.)

Enjoy learning about your physical health and well-being as you develop your ability to identify the main idea in all you read. Find out more about your physical health and well-being in Module 6.

The Main Idea

Imagine you have just returned from a week's vacation in the Bahamas. Your plane is taxiing to the gate. This was your first "real" vacation in years, and you had the best time of your life. You were busy every minute of every day, until all hours of the evening, swimming, surfing, parasailing, snorkeling, hiking, shopping, eating out, dancing—you just didn't stop. Moments before you disembark the plane, your cell phone rings. It's Ron, your best friend, who has never been out of the country. He has eagerly awaited your return.

"How was it? Tell me all about it!" he implores.

You have about 30 seconds to explain. How can you possibly share a week's worth of fun in the sun in just a sentence or two? There certainly is no time to go into detail. What you need to do here is relay the central message about your vacation: the main idea. You might say something like, "It was amazing. I went swimming, surfing, and shopping during the day, and went out every night. I'll tell you all about it as soon as I get back home."

College reading requires you to identify and understand the key concept or major point an author is making, without getting bogged down in the details. This is called the **main idea.** Whether you are reading a paragraph, an essay, an article or a textbook chapter, your ability to understand and express the main idea presented by the author is critical.

Each paragraph in a reading contains a key point or main idea, usually expressed in a sentence called the **topic sentence.** Topic sentences often appear at the beginning of a paragraph, but can also be found in the middle or at the end of a paragraph. The main ideas of paragraphs work to support the overall point, or main idea, of an entire selection. In class discussion, you may hear the main idea of a paragraph referred to as

- the gist
- the key point
- the central idea
- the main point

In longer reading selections, the main idea of the entire piece is called the **thesis,** or **thesis statement,** and it usually appears near the end of the introductory paragraph. This is the main point the author will discuss throughout the course of the essay, article, or textbook chapter.

Being able to identify the main idea of a paragraph or longer reading is an important and helpful skill because it

- gives you the big picture—a frame of reference so that all the details within a paragraph or reading will come together and have meaning
- tells you the most important point the author wants you to understand
- establishes a *purpose* for your reading—understanding the main idea is always an important goal for any reader
- enables you to take good notes while you read
- prepares you to write a summary or create an outline after you read
- prepares you to convey the gist of the reading to a professor or classmate

Two Steps to Identify the Main Idea

You need to complete two important steps to identify the main idea of a reading. The first is to identify the topic of the selection you are reading. The second is to determine the most important, overall point the author is making about that topic, combine the main point with the topic, and state it *in a complete sentence*. This is the main idea. Sometimes a sentence stated by the author does this. Sometimes you will create it on your own.

Step 1: Identify the topic

Step 2: Determine the most important overall point about the topic, combine it with the topic, and state in the result in a complete sentence.

Step 1: Identify the Topic

Whether you are reading a paragraph or a chapter, the first step to identify the main idea is to recognize or name the **topic** of the selection. The topic is the subject. It can be a broad term or idea. The rest of the paragraph or chapter tells all about it. Even individual sentences have topics; these are the subjects of the sentence.

When looking for the topic, ask yourself, "Who or what is this about?" Some students find it helpful to think of the topic as the title of their reading selection.

The topic

- can be a single word, a few words, or a phrase
- is *not* a sentence
- is often repeated several times within a paragraph or selection
- can be the same term or phrase or different words that mean the same thing
- is often seen in the title or heading
- may appear in boldface or italic type
- sometimes is not actually stated, but may be identified through reasoning

The Topic of a List Even a list has a topic. The same thinking you use to identify the topic of a list can be used to identify the topic of a sentence, a paragraph, or a reading. Look at the following list of terms related to health:

    sore throat
    runny nose
    cold symptoms
    watery eyes
    general fatigue

Do you notice that one item in the list seems to cover or describe all the others? That item is the subject, or topic, of the list. Which item is the topic?
cold symptoms

Here is a list of items, *without a topic*. To identify the topic on your own, think about a heading that would work as a title for the list. You will use the same thinking in your reading when an author does not directly state the topic.

running

power walking

weight training

bicycling

kick boxing

What is the topic? What heading could you put at the top of the list?

ways to exercise
_____

try it and apply it! 4-1   Identify the Topic of a List

Directions: Read the following lists of terms related to our physical health and well-being. One of the words in each list is the topic, the word that includes all the other items. Underline the topic of each list.

1. opium, <u>narcotics</u>, heroin, morphine, codeine
2. whole grains, berries, nuts, fish, <u>healthy foods</u>
3. influenza, <u>infectious diseases</u>, tuberculosis, mononucleosis, pneumonia
4. traffic, test anxiety, <u>causes of stress</u>, relationship problems, lack of sleep
5. losing weight, exercising, <u>ways to lower blood pressure</u>, restricting the use of salt, limiting the drinking of alcohol
6. insomnia, <u>sleep disorders</u>, narcolepsy, sleep apnea, sleep walking
7. herpes, AIDS, <u>sexually transmitted diseases</u>, gonorrhea, syphilis
8. <u>facilities for health care</u>, hospitals, nursing homes, clinics, doctor's offices

try it and apply it! 4-2   Identify the Topic of a List

Directions: On the line following each list of terms, write a broad or general term that identifies the topic of the list.

1. potatoes, cucumbers, broccoli, turnips *vegetables* _____
2. physicians, nurses, physician assistants, dentists *health-care providers* _____
3. dieting, exercising, eating healthy foods, getting enough sleep *ways to stay healthy* _____
4. bulimia, anorexia, purging, binging *eating disorders* _____
5. McDonald's, Wendy's, Taco Bell, Burger King *fast food restaurants* _____

The Topic of a Sentence To identify the topic of a sentence, apply the same kind of thinking you did to identify the topic of a list. Look for the general subject that takes in, or refers to, the rest of the sentence. Determine who or what the sentence is about.

try it and apply it! 4-3   Identify the Topic of a Sentence

Directions: Now read the following sentences. Underline the subject, or topic, of each one. Ask yourself, "Who or what is the sentence about?"

1. Regular exercise, doing yoga, eating properly, and getting enough sleep, in addition to talking about your problems, are all <u>effective strategies for reducing stress</u>.

2. It is common knowledge that a runny nose, watery eyes, aches and pains, and a listless feeling are all <u>symptoms of a cold</u>.

3. An inflammatory process, <u>hepatitis</u>, occurs in the liver and can be caused by viruses and alcohol abuse, among other factors.

4. There are <u>many reasons people choose to be celibate</u> rather than engage in a sexually intimate relationship.

5. Even if you can't afford a gym membership, you can work out at home, ride a bike, or take physical education classes at school as a <u>way to stay fit and active</u>.

6. Concern is growing regarding the role of <u>childhood immunizations</u> in the development of serious childhood health problems.

7. <u>Contact with pathogens</u>, such as viruses, bacterium, and fungi, is responsible for the transfer of diseases.

8. <u>Medical treatments on college campuses</u> may be on an inpatient or outpatient basis.

9. Although not popularly identified as beneficial, <u>fats</u> are an important nutrient in our diets because they provide a concentrated form of energy.

10. Rope climbing, weight lifting for strength, and sprinting are <u>short-duration activities</u> that quickly cause muscle fatigue.

The Topic of a Paragraph Each paragraph in a reading selection has its own topic. In fact, writers create new paragraphs as they shift from topic to topic within a selection. Think of a paragraph as a small "package" containing information about a topic or subject. To identify the topic of a paragraph, ask yourself, "Who or what is the paragraph about?" The following hints will also help:

- Often, the term or form of the term that is **repeated** throughout the paragraph is the topic.
- **Synonyms** for the term that identifies the topic may be used.
- **Pronouns** may be used to refer to the topic that has been identified.
- The topic is likely to be the word or phrase that could serve as a **good title** for the paragraph.

You can also make a broad topic more precise or exact by connecting it with the specific aspect that is being discussed. For example, an author could be writing about illegal drugs, but if the focus is their use by teens, then the topic could be stated as *illegal drug use among teenagers*.

try it and apply it! 4-4   Identify the Topic of a Paragraph

Directions: Read the following paragraphs adapted from a textbook on college success, called *Peak Performance*. Select the best topic for each from the choices provided.

Paragraph 1

Experts say that exercise is one of the best ways to reduce stress, relax muscles, and promote a sense of well-being. Most people find that they have more energy when they exercise regularly. Make exercise a daily habit and top priority in your life.

(Ferrett 2010)

  b 1. The topic of the paragraph is
- a. reducing stress
- b. exercise
- c. prioritizing your life
- d. energy

Paragraph 2

It is hard to believe that anyone would smoke cigarettes after hearing and viewing the public awareness campaigns that present the risks of cigarette smoking. Smoking cigarettes causes major health problems for those who smoke, as well as for those exposed to it through second-hand smoke. Smoking cigarettes is directly responsible for 87 percent of all lung cancer cases and causes emphysema and chronic bronchitis.

Nonsmokers married to smokers have a 30 percent greater risk for lung cancer than those married to nonsmokers. Cigarette smoking-related diseases cause about 430,700 deaths each year in the United States.

(Adapted from Ferrett 2010)

_d_ 2. The topic of the paragraph is
   a. lung cancer
   b. health problems in the United States
   c. cigarette smoking
   d. the health risks of cigarette smoking

Paragraph 3

Nothing reduces stress like a hearty laugh or spontaneous fun. Discovering the child within helps us release our natural creativity. Laughing produces endorphins, natural chemicals that strengthen the immune system and produce a sense of well-being. Laughter also increases oxygen flow to the brain and causes other physical changes. It just feels good to chuckle!

(Adapted from Ferrett 2010)

_c_ 3. The topic of the paragraph is
   a. having fun
   b. reducing stress
   c. the benefits of laughter
   d. strengthening the immune system

Paragraph 4

Addictive behavior comes in many forms and is not relegated to substance abuse solely. Just as an alcoholic feels happy when drinking, a food addict feels comforted when eating, a sex addict gets a rush from new partners, a shoplifter feels a thrill with getting away with stealing, an addictive shopper feels excited during a shopping spree, a gambler feels in control when winning, and a workaholic feels a sense of importance while working late each night. Addiction is an abnormal relationship with an object or event and is characterized by using a substance or performing a behavior repeatedly. Behavior that is addictive usually starts as a pleasurable act or means of escape, and progresses into a significant problem.

(Adapted from Ferrett 2010)

_a_ 4. The topic of the paragraph is
   a. addictions
   b. alcoholism
   c. causes of addictive behavior
   d. substance abuse

try it and apply it! 4-5   Identify the Topic of a Paragraph

Directions: Now, identify the topic of each paragraph on your own. Look for the term or the form of the term that is repeated throughout the paragraph. Synonyms, words with similar meanings, or pronouns may be used. Phrases that restate the topic may also appear. Underline them. Then write the topic of each paragraph on the line provided.

Paragraph 1

Though it may be difficult and require some changes, eating right is one of the best things you can do to stay well. You should avoid processed foods, and instead, eat a variety of "whole" foods, including fruits, vegetables, and grain products. Healthy eating also demands that you avoid foods that contain a lot of sugar and salt. To eat healthy, seek a diet low in fat and cholesterol. Remember that less is often more when it comes to developing a healthy diet. You don't need to walk away stuffed from every meal! Read labels and pay attention to the hidden contents in various foods. For example, many low-fat foods contain a great deal of sugar and salt. Being a healthy eater also means trying to schedule three regular meals daily.

(Adapted from Feldman 2009)

1. What is the topic of the paragraph? _healthy eating or eating right_

Paragraph 2

Do you feel as if you don't get enough sleep? You probably don't. Most college students are sleep deprived, a condition that causes them to feel fatigued, short tempered, and tense. Sleep deprivation makes staying alert in class nearly impossible. Ultimately, insufficient sleep leads to declines in academic and physical performance. You can't do your best at anything if you're exhausted—or even tired.

(Adapted from Feldman 2009)

2. What is the topic of the paragraph? _sleep deprivation_

Paragraph 3

Often, the solution to the problem of sleep deprivation is to simply allow yourself more time to sleep! Most people need about eight hours of sleep each night. Besides sleeping more, there are some simple changes you can make that will help you to sleep better. Exercising regularly will help. Also, going to bed around the same time every night will give your body a regular rhythm and make sleep a habit. Try to use your bed only for sleeping, and not as an all-purpose area for study, watching TV, and eating. Let your bed be a trigger for sleep. Other remedies for not enough sleep include avoiding caffeine after lunch and drinking a glass of milk at bedtime. Milk contains a natural chemical that makes you drowsy.

(Adapted from Feldman 2009)

3. What is the topic of the paragraph? *remedies for sleep deprivation, how to get more sleep*

Paragraph 4

Close to 20 million people in the United States are alcoholics, and college students make up their fair share of the total. Alcoholics, individuals with serious alcohol-abuse problems, become dependent on alcohol, experiencing a physical craving for it. The alcohol-addicted person continues to drink despite serious consequences. Furthermore, he or she develops a tolerance for alcohol and must drink increasing amounts to experience the initially positive effects that alcohol brings about.

(Adapted from Feldman 2009)

4. What is the topic of the paragraph? *alcoholics*

The Topic of a Longer Passage   Writers create new paragraphs as they shift from topic to topic within a selection. When the topic changes, it's time to write a new paragraph. Although the topics of individual paragraphs will vary, entire selections have one overriding topic. In longer selections, paragraphs usually contain a subtopic of the broader topic, or subject, of the entire selection. For example, if you are reading about the benefits of exercise for your physical well-being, each paragraph might discuss a different benefit.

Apply strategies similar to those you used earlier to identity the topic of a lengthier reading selection. Ask yourself, "Who or what is this entire selection about?" "What overall topic is common to all of the paragraphs?" Look for words and terms that are repeated or that refer to the same subject throughout the text. Think of a good title for the entire selection. That is likely to be the topic.

It is helpful to note the topic of each individual paragraph, and see how, when viewed together, they help you identify the topic of the whole passage or selection.

try it and apply it! 4-6   Identify the Topic of a Longer Passage

Directions: Read the following textbook passages about health and well-being. While you are reading each selection, stop to identify the topic of each paragraph. Note and underline terms that are repeated or presented more than once or in different ways. Then ask yourself, "What is the overall topic of all the paragraphs included in the selection?" and write the answer on the line provided.

Selection 1

To maintain good health and energy, it is important to get enough sleep. Although amounts vary from one person to the next, most people need between six and nine hours of sound sleep each night.

The key to getting enough rest is not to be concerned about the number of hours of sleep that you require but, rather, whether or not you feel rested, alert, and energized. Some people wake up rested after five hours of sleep; others need at least nine hours to feel energized and refreshed.

If you wake up tired, try going to bed earlier for a night or two and then establish a consistent bedtime. Avoid foods with caffeine later in the day. Notice if you are using sleep to escape conflict, depression, or boredom. It is also important to find time to relax each day. Being rested and getting enough sleep is an important factor of your overall physical and emotional health.

(Adapted from Ferrett 2010)

1. The overall topic of the selection is *getting enough rest or sleep*

Selection 2

In the United States today, between 5 and 10 million females, and about 1 million males, are struggling with eating disorders. **Eating disorders** refers to medically identifiable and dangerous conditions, including anorexia, bulimia, and binge eating, brought about by difficulties with body image, body weight, and food selection. College students are included in the at-risk population for these illnesses. Athletes, models, actors, in fact, any group in which success is influenced by weight and attractiveness, are also at risk for the development of an eating disorder.

Jill is a young woman who began exercising vigorously, and cutting down on her food intake tremendously, after a difficult semester at school. She had broken up with her boyfriend and had been involved in a car accident that totaled her car, though she wasn't seriously hurt. She continued to lose weight until her family insisted that she get counseling and weigh in at the health center every day. Jill didn't think she had an eating disorder because she wasn't obsessed with being thin. However, she was diagnosed with anorexia nervosa.

Though not everyone with the eating disorder of anorexia is the same, there is a profile of those who tend to become anorexic. Most anorexics are white, young, middle-class women who have a distorted body image and want to be thin. Some anorexics are perfectionists, grew up in families with high expectations, and feel overwhelmed that they cannot meet these expectations. They turn to something that they can control—their food intake and their weight.

Bulimia is another eating disorder. It involves binge eating and purging through forced vomiting or the use of laxatives. It can cause long-term dental issues and serious health problems. It can even lead to death. Often, people with eating disorders also suffer from depression, anxiety, or substance abuse.

The National Association of Anorexia Nervosa and Associated Disorders says about 8 to 10 million people in the United States have an eating disorder. Though 95 percent of people with an eating disorder are women, such disorders are on the rise in men. Research suggests that about 8 of every 100 college-age women have, or will develop, an eating disorder.

If you are dealing with an eating disorder, or you suspect a friend or family member is struggling with a disorder with diet, seek help immediately. Several treatment options are available, including individual, group, and family counseling. Treatment can range from inpatient hospitalization to outpatient support groups. Medications are also available.

(Adapted from Ferrett 2010)

2. **What is the topic of the entire selection?** *eating disorders*

(continued)

(continued)

Selection 3

Let's look at health in a holistic way. Health has several aspects, so we must recognize it as multidimensional. We will examine six components of health that interact with each other and allow us to engage in the wide range of life experiences.

We rely on the physical and structural characteristics of our bodies to accomplish the daily activities of our life. Among these physical characteristics are our body weight, visual ability, strength, coordination, endurance, susceptibility to disease, and powers to recover from illness. These physical dimensions of health are very important to our well-being.

We also have certain emotional characteristics that can help us through the demands of daily living. The emotional dimension of health includes our ability to see the world in a realistic manner, cope with stress, remain flexible, and compromise to resolve conflict.

A third dimension of health includes social skills. Our earliest experiences in social skills occur in our family relationships, school experiences, and peer group interactions. These begin the development of our "social" health. Social connections into adulthood generate further development and refinement of skills. The relationships in college enhance the social dimensions of health for all students.

The abilities to think about and act on information, clarify values and beliefs, and make decisions rank among the most important aspects of total health. For many college-educated persons, these intellectual components of health may prove to be most satisfying of all the dimensions.

There are other dimensions of health to consider. The spiritual dimension encompasses religion and belief systems, including our relationship with other living things in the universe, the nature of human behavior, and the need and willingness to serve others. The occupational dimension reflects the importance of the workplace to people's well-being. Lastly, some would add an environmental dimension. This is impacted by the quality of the land, air, and water around us.

(Adapted from Hahn et al. 2007)

3. **What is the topic of the entire selection?** *the many dimensions or components*
    of health

Step 2: Determine the Main Idea

After you have determined the topic of a paragraph or reading selection, ask yourself, "What is the most important point the author is making about the topic in the selection?" This is the main idea. The main idea is a statement that includes the topic and the author's most important or general idea about it.

The main idea

- must be a complete sentence.
- must include the topic of the paragraph or selection.
- may be stated directly in the text.
- may not be stated directly but implied.

In the second paragraph you read in Try It and Apply It 4–5 (page 100), the topic is *sleep deprivation* and the main idea is: *Sleep deprivation is a significant problem for college students.* In the third paragraph, the topic is *remedies or solutions for sleep deprivation* and the main idea is: *There are several remedies to deal with the problem of sleep deprivation.* How do you go about finding the main idea of a paragraph after you have identified the topic?

Finding the Stated Main Idea in Paragraphs: Topic Sentences   The *main idea* is the most important point a writer wants to make about the topic. When the main idea is stated directly in a paragraph, it is called the topic sentence. Yes, topic sentences do appear as the *first* sentences of paragraphs. This is often the case in college textbook writing or other forms of informative writing. However, don't be fooled. Be aware that the topic sentence may appear *anywhere* in a paragraph: at the beginning, in the middle, or at the end. Sometimes, when an author wants to restate or emphasize the main point, he or she will open and close with the main idea. Remember, the main idea is not always stated in the first sentence.

The following paragraphs are all about alcohol abuse. Each paragraph has a point to make about one aspect of that topic. The point, or main idea, of each paragraph is expressed in the topic sentence. The rest of the paragraph adds information or details about that main idea. Notice the location of each topic sentence.

Example 1: Topic Sentence as the First Sentence

- *TOPIC SENTENCE*
- _____
- _____

> **Recently, a high amount of alcoholism has been found among adult children of alcoholics.** It is estimated that these children are about four times more likely to develop alcoholism than children whose parents are not alcoholics. Even those who do not become alcoholics may have a difficult time adjusting to everyday living.

(Adapted from Hahn et al. 2007)

Here the author states the most important point at the beginning, and then goes on to add more specific information. In many paragraphs, this information often includes examples that illustrate and explain the main point.

Example 2: Topic Sentence in the Middle

■ _____
■ _____
■ *TOPIC SENTENCE*
■ _____
■ _____

To respond to this problem, support groups have been formed. These attempt to help the grown-up children of alcoholics avoid developing the same drinking problems as their parents. **Support groups for the adult children of alcoholics play a very strong role in preventing the continuation of abuse.** These groups include Al-Anon and Adult Children of Alcoholics. Experts agree that adult children of alcoholics who believe they have come to terms with their feelings can sometimes face lingering problems.

(Adapted from Hahn et al. 2007)

If an author is continuing a discussion from a previous paragraph, or wants to provide some background information to lead into the next point, the topic sentence of the new paragraph may not appear until the middle, as in this example, and more supportive information or examples will follow.

Example 3: Topic Sentence at the End

■ _____
■ _____
■ _____
■ _____
■ _____
■ *TOPIC SENTENCE*

For decades, women have used less alcohol and had fewer alcohol-related problems than men. However, evidence is now showing a change. A greater percentage of women are choosing to drink. Some groups of women, especially younger women, are drinking more heavily. The increased number of females entering treatment centers is reflecting this change. **Studies indicate that drinking among women is on the rise and currently there are almost as many female alcoholics as men.**

(Adapted from Hahn et al. 2007)

When an author wants to build up to his or her main point, he or she may provide related and background information first and lead up to the topic sentence that is stated at the very end of the paragraph.

Example 4: Topic Sentence at the Beginning and the End

■ *TOPIC SENTENCE*

■ _____

■ _____

■ _____

■ _____

■ *TOPIC SENTENCE RESTATED*

> **College drinking has become a major social and health problem in the United States.** Students consume more than 430 million gallons of alcohol every year. One hundred fifty-nine thousand of today's first-year college students will drop out of school for alcohol- or other drug–related problems. The average student spends $900 on alcohol each year, compared with $450 on textbooks, and almost one-third of college students admit to having missed at least one class because of their alcohol use. What they may not know is that one night of heavy drinking can impair the ability to think abstractly for up to 30 days. **The abuse of alcohol among college students is becoming a problem of increasing concern in the nation today.**

(Adapted from Ferrett 2010)

When an author wants to emphasize his or her main point, you may find a topic sentence both at the beginning and the conclusion of a paragraph. The main idea that was stated in the first sentence is restated using different words.

Keep this in mind

Recognizing Topic Sentences

To be sure you have correctly identified the topic sentence in a paragraph, remember these important points:

■ The sentence must include the topic of the paragraph.
■ The sentence must include the main idea about the topic.
■ The sentence must be broad or general enough to encompass the key points or details in the rest of the paragraph.
■ The sentence is *not* a detail that supports the main idea.
■ The sentence is *not* an example.

try it and apply it! 4-7 Identifying Topic Sentences in Paragraphs

Directions: The following paragraphs discuss a component of our physical health and well-being—body weight. Read each paragraph. Determine the topic of each and consider the most important overall point the author is making about it. Then go back and highlight or underline the topic sentence in each paragraph. Beneath each paragraph, identify the topic and then write the topic sentence on the line provided.

Paragraph 1

<u>Weight management is a significant health problem in America</u>. Obesity in the United States has risen at an epidemic rate during the past 20 years. One of the current national health objectives is to reduce the amount of obesity among adults to less than 15 percent. Research indicates that the situation is worsening rather than improving. An estimated 65 percent of adult Americans are either overweight or obese.

(Adapted from Hahn et al. 2007)

1. The topic of the paragraph is *weight management*
2. The stated main idea is *Weight management is a significant health problem in America.*

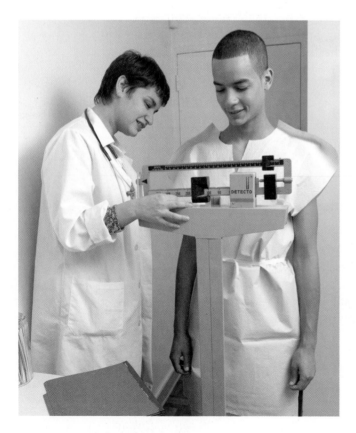

Paragraph 2

There are greater problems associated with obesity than there are with not being attractive or being able to easily participate in sports. <u>Experts cite significant dangers to health and wellness that stem from obesity.</u> Among the health problems caused by or made worse by obesity are increased risks during surgery, high blood pressure, heart disease, stroke, type 2 diabetes, several forms of cancer, and joint problems. Obesity also contributes to complications during pregnancy, gallbladder disease, and a general increased risk for dying. Because it is so closely associated with ongoing medical conditions, experts now recommend that obesity itself be defined and treated as a chronic disease.

(Adapted from Hahn et al. 2007)

1. The topic of the paragraph is *obesity* _____
2. The stated main idea is *Experts cite significant dangers to health and wellness that* _____ *stem from obesity.* _____

Paragraph 3

What is the difference between being overweight and being obese? Doctors usually define overweight as a condition in which a person's weight is 1–19 percent higher than normal, while in obesity a person's weight is 20 percent or more above the normal weight. This is based on the use of a standard height-weight chart. (Morbid obesity refers to being 50–100 percent above normal weight, or more than 100 pounds above normal.) Some clinicians continue to use standard height-weight scales to determine when weight is excessive; however, more precise techniques to determine body composition are now available.

(Adapted from Hahn et al. 2007)

1. The topic of the paragraph is *the difference between overweight and obesity* _____
2. The stated main idea is *Overweight is a condition in which a person's weight is 1–19* _____ *percent higher than normal, while in obesity a person's weight is 20 percent or more above* _____ *the normal weight.* _____

Paragraph 4

A national survey showed that 41 percent of men were dissatisfied with their weight, with many of these men wanting to gain weight and increase muscle mass. Nearly half of American women are unhappy with their weight. Many feel this way even though they are actually within a healthy weight range. While the average American woman wants to lose 11 pounds, the average American man wants to lose 1 pound, or is happy with his weight. Overall, men report feeling more comfortable with their weight and experience less pressure to be thin than women.

(Adapted from Hahn et al. 2007)

1. The topic of the paragraph is *the differences between men and women in their* _____ *satisfaction with their weight* _____
2. The stated main idea is *Overall, men report feeling more comfortable with their* _____ *weight and experience less pressure to be thin than women.* _____

(continued)

(continued)

Paragraph 5

Though men are not as unhappy with their weight as women are, they seem to have another concern. <u>Men do tend to have the desire to be more muscular.</u> They want to be more "cut," bigger, and stronger. Men with this preoccupation obsessively lift weights for hours a day, sometimes sacrificing important social relationships, jobs, or physical health.

(Adapted from Hahn et al. 2007)

1. The topic of the paragraph is *men's desire for muscles*
2. The stated main idea is *Men do tend to have the desire to be more muscular.*

Paragraph 6

<u>Despite the range of health problems that are caused, more and more men in the United States are using steroids and other supplements to increase muscle mass.</u> Research suggests that 2 to 3 million American males have used steroids and/or other dietary additives. The use often begins in the teenage years, or even earlier. Steroid use can result in serious side effects. These include psychiatric problems and aggressive behaviors while using steroids, and depressive symptoms from withdrawal. It is shocking how parents, teachers, and even trained clinicians often remain unaware of steroid use, despite these obvious physical and personality changes. <u>The increased use of steroids and related dietary supplements to enhance muscle mass in men is a serious health concern for this country's medical community.</u>

(Adapted from Hahn et al. 2007)

1. The topic of the paragraph is *steroid use among men*
2. The stated main idea is *Despite the range of health problems that are caused, more and more men in the United States are using steroids and other supplements to increase muscle mass. The increased use of steroids and related dietary supplements to enhance muscle mass in men is a serious concern of this country's medical community.*

Finding the Stated Main Idea in Longer Reading Selections: Thesis Statements A *thesis statement* is the main idea of a longer selection. You can think of it very much like the topic sentence of a paragraph. It is the most general point the author is making or discussing throughout the entire selection. In some way, all the paragraphs within the selection support or tell about that main point or thesis.

Often the thesis of a selection or article is stated in the first, or introductory, paragraph. As an active college reader, you will want to keep the thesis in mind as you identify the more specific points of each paragraph that explain or provide details about it. Like a main idea, the thesis must be a complete sentence. It includes the topic of the selection and the most important point the author is making about the topic.

Take another look at a passage you read when learning to identify the topic of a selection on page 102 (reprinted next). Reread it. This time, write the topic of each paragraph in the margin. Underline the topic sentence in each paragraph. Then think about which sentence in the selection includes the topic and the most important overall point the author is making.

Eating Disorders

In the United States today, between 5 and 10 million females, and about 1 million males are struggling with eating disorders. **Eating disorders** refers to medically identifiable and dangerous conditions, including anorexia, bulimia, and binge eating, brought about by difficulties with body image, body weight, and food selection. College students are included in the at-risk population for these illnesses. Athletes, models, actors, in fact, any group in which success is influenced by weight and attractiveness, are also at risk for the development of an eating disorder.

Eating Disorders

Jill is a young woman who began exercising vigorously, and cutting down on her food intake tremendously, after a difficult semester at school. She had broken up with her boyfriend and had been involved in a car accident that totaled her car, though she wasn't seriously hurt. She continued to lose weight until her family insisted that she get counseling and weigh in at the health center every day. Jill didn't think she had an eating disorder because she wasn't obsessed with being thin. However, she was diagnosed with anorexia nervosa.

Jill, as an example of a person with anorexia nervosa

Though not everyone with the eating disorder of anorexia is the same, there is a profile of those who tend to become anorexic. Most anorexics are white, young, middle-class women who have a distorted body image and want to be thin. Some anorexics are perfectionists, grew up in families with high expectations, and feel overwhelmed that they cannot meet these expectations. They turn to something that they can control—their food intake and their weight.

"Typical" anorexic

Bulimia is another eating disorder. It involves binge eating and purging through forced vomiting or the use of laxatives. It can cause long-term dental and serious health problems. It can even lead to death. Often, people with eating disorders also suffer from depression, anxiety, or substance abuse.

Bulimia

The National Association of Anorexia Nervosa and Associated Disorders says about 8 to 10 million people in the United States have an eating disorder. Though 95 percent of people with an eating disorder are women, such disorders are on the rise in men. Research suggests that about 8 of every 100 college-age women have, or will develop, an eating disorder.

Numbers of people with eating disorders

If you are dealing with an eating disorder, or you suspect a friend or family member is struggling with a disorder with diet, seek help immediately. Several treatment options are available, including individual, group, and family counseling. Treatment can range from inpatient hospitalization to outpatient support groups. Medications are also available.

Treatments for eating disorders

(Adapted from Ferrett 2010)

As you may recall, the topic of this selection was *eating disorders*. The thesis statement is in the first paragraph. It is: **Eating disorders refers to medically identifiable and dangerous conditions, including anorexia, bulimia, and binge eating, brought about by difficulties with body image, body weight, and food selection.** Notice how the thesis statement includes the topic and makes a broad, general statement about it. In this case, it includes the definition. All the following paragraphs discuss a specific aspect of the thesis. Some focus on specific disorders. Others tell about the numbers of people with eating disorders. The last paragraph speaks about treatments for eating disorders.

If you were using this selection as source information for a paper, you might choose to paraphrase, or put in your own words, the thesis statement. You might also choose to expand the thesis statement by referring to information that you identified as the topics, or main ideas, of the paragraphs. Thus, you could restate the thesis in your own words as: *Eating disorders, including anorexia nervosa, bulimia, and binge eating, impact millions of Americans, especially women, and should be treated as serious medical conditions.*

try it and apply it! 4-8   Identifying Main Ideas and the Thesis Statement

Directions: Actively read the following longer selections. As you read each selection, write the topic of each paragraph in the margin. Underline or highlight the stated main idea of each paragraph. Then review this information to select the best thesis statement for each selection from the list of options that follow it. Be careful. Many of the answer choices are true, but only one in each set is the thesis statement of the entire selection.

A. Sexually Transmitted Infections

Sexually transmitted infections

Sexually transmitted infections, or STIs, are spread through sexual contact with an infected partner. A person may be infected yet appear healthy and symptom free. STIs include AIDS, chlamydia, genital herpes and warts, gonorrhea, and syphilis.

The effect of STIs

Despite public health efforts and classes in health and sexuality, STIs continue to infect significant numbers of young adults. Even if treated early, STIs are a major health risk and can have a devastating effect on your life. They result in damage to the reproductive organs, infertility, or cancer.

Preventing STIs

There are several guidelines one can follow to avoid contracting any STI. Be sure to know your partner. Find out about a prospective partner's health. No matter what the other person's health status is, explain that you always use safety precautions and do so. Remember that abstinence, or not engaging in sexual activity, is the only totally effective method of preventing the spread of STIs and pregnancy. It is vital to know the facts, the latest treatments, and the ways you can protect your body.

(Adapted from Ferrett 2010)

__c__ 1. **The thesis statement of the selection is**
   a. STIs.
   b. There are many different kinds of STIs.
   c. Though STIs continue to be a significant health problem, there are several steps one can take to avoid them.
   d. Abstinence is the only effective method in preventing the spread of STIs.

B. How Does Diet Influence Health?

Diet has an important effect on health. For instance, there is a strong connection between heart disease and the amount of salt and animal fat in one's diet.

Diet and Health

Certain foods support good health. Fruits, vegetables, whole grains, complex carbohydrates, and dietary fiber often have beneficial health effects. Vitamins A, C, and E, which we get from plants, seem to have anticancer effects.

Foods that support good health

Eating too much food is a significant dietary health factor in developed countries and among the well-to-do everywhere. Sixty percent of all U.S. adults are now considered overweight, and the worldwide total of obese or overweight people is estimated to be more than 1 billion. Every year in the United States, 300,000 deaths are linked to obesity.

Overeating and obesity

One in three U.S. children will become diabetic unless many more people start eating less and exercising more. The odds are worse for Black and Hispanic children. Nearly half of them are likely to develop the disease. And among the Pima tribe of Arizona, nearly 80 percent of all adults are diabetic. A poor diet has a significant impact on the development of many diseases, including diabetes.

Diabetes and a poor diet

(Adapted from Cunningham and Cunningham 2008)

<u>b</u> 2. **The thesis statement for this selection is**
   a. Many Americans and those in well-to-do countries are overweight and in poor health.
   b. Diet plays a major role in the health and well-being of humans.
   c. Many people suffer from diabetes because of a poor diet.
   d. Certain foods are far more beneficial to our health and well-being than others.

Keep this in mind

Identifying the Thesis

How can you be sure you have identified the thesis of a selection? Here are some important tips:

- The thesis must include the overall topic of the selection and the most important, general point the author is making about it.
- It must be a complete sentence.
- It is likely to be located in an introductory paragraph in a textbook selection, newspaper or magazine article, or essay.
- It must be broad or general enough to encompass the key points discussed in the entire selection.
- It is *not* an example.
- Remember that just because a statement is true, that does not make it the thesis!

Implied Main Ideas

Every paragraph contains a main idea. The content of the paragraph supports an overall point or key thought. Surprising as it many seem, however, **the main idea is not always stated directly in a topic sentence.** In this case, the key point or thought is called the **implied** or **unstated main idea.** When you are speaking with someone who does not state his or her point directly in the conversation, you can infer it by thinking about all of the information he or she does share. Similarly, you can find the implied main ideas in your reading material.

As an active reader, you can work out the main idea of a paragraph. First, you need to identify the topic. Then note the information, or details, the author provides to tell about it. You use this information to determine the most important overall point the author wants you to know. After you understand the implied or unstated main idea of a paragraph, you can express it using your own words. You will learn more about working with the details of a paragraph in Chapter 5.

To determine an implied main idea, follow these steps:

Step 1: As you read the paragraph, circle repeated words or phrases that indicate the topic.

Step 2: Underline the important points of information that tell more about that topic.

Step 3: Think about how these points or details may be related. Ask yourself, "What overall point does the information help me understand about the topic?"

Step 4: Create the main idea statement by making a sentence in which you state the topic and then tell the most important point the writer is making about it.

Step 5: Add your own words or terms to explain the idea when necessary.

Here is a paragraph that contains an unstated main idea. Apply the preceding steps to formulate the main idea.

(Illegal Drug Use)

Did you know that almost 80 percent of people in their mid-twenties have (tried illegal drugs?) Sadly, (taking illegal drugs) tempts many young people. It is important to have the facts about the many downsides of (illegal drug use) For example, certain patterns of behavior among marijuana users, especially adolescents, show loss of memory and intellectual reasoning. Marijuana releases five times more carbon dioxide and three times more tar into the lungs than tobacco does. (Crack addiction) can occur in less than two months of occasional use. The cost of (drug abuse) to American society is almost $50 billion a year.

(Adapted from Ferrett 2010)

So, who or what is the paragraph about? Perhaps, you circled these words: *illegal drugs, taking illegal drugs, illegal drug use, crack addiction,* or *drug abuse.* The topic then is *illegal drug use.* Now, review the paragraph and the sentences you underlined.

What is the most important point about illegal drug use that the author is making in this paragraph? The details focus on *the negative impact to our health and to society.* To state the main idea, combine the answers to the two questions, "Who or what is the paragraph about (the topic)?" and "What is the most important point about the topic the author is making in this paragraph?" The implied main idea of the paragraph is:

> **Illegal drug use *(the topic)* causes serious social and health problems.** *(the overriding point)*

Note: The author of the paragraph did not actually use the word "health." As the reader, based on the details, you can incorporate that word to help you explain the main idea.

Sometimes the implied, or unstated, main idea is formulated by combining two sentences in a paragraph. Both are important, but each on their own does not tell the whole point. Together they do.

Read the following paragraph on cold remedies. Notice the two sentences in italic type within the paragraph. These could be connected to cover the major points expressed. Restate them as a single sentence to identify the implied main idea. Write it on the line provided.

> *At this time there is no effective way to prevent colds.* In 1999 a medication, Pleconaril, appeared to be effective in reducing how severe and long-lasting colds became once the initial symptoms had developed. However, in 2002 the Food and Drug Administration did not allow approval of Pleconaril. This was due, in part, to the negative reactions shown by some women who used the drug while they were taking oral contraceptives (birth control pills). *There are, however, some over-the-counter cold remedies that can help you manage a cold.* These come in liquid, tablet, and gel cap form. They will not cure your cold, but may lessen the discomfort associated with it.
>
> (Adapted from Hahn et al. 2007)

Implied main idea: *At this time there is no effective way to prevent colds, but some over-the-counter cold remedies can help you manage a cold.*

The most important point of the paragraph is that we do not currently have an effective way to prevent colds, but that remedies sold in stores can help us to manage cold symptoms. You should have written . . . *At this time there is no effective way to prevent colds, but some over-the-counter cold remedies can help you manage a cold.*

Keep this in mind

Determining the Main Idea

How can you be sure you have formulated a main idea statement that works for your selection?

- It must be a complete sentence.
- It must include the general topic or topics of the paragraph or selection.
- It must state the most important overall point the author is making about the topic.
- It may *not* be a specific detail or example.
- It would work well as the first sentence of the paragraph if you were to add it.

try it and apply it! 4-9   Identifying Implied Main Ideas in Paragraphs

Directions: Apply the preceding strategy to the following paragraphs. For each paragraph, circle the repeated words and phrases that indicate the topic. Underline the portions that indicate the main point the author is making. Write the topic on the line provided. Then formulate the implied main idea and write it on the line below the paragraph. **Remember to mention the topic and the most important point the writer is making.**

Paragraph 1

We all get (colds). Most of us (treat the symptoms of a cold) with over-the-counter remedies. These won't cure the cold, but may lessen the discomfort. Sometimes colds persist. You may experience prolonged, (more serious cold symptoms). For example, you may have a fever above 103 degrees Fahrenheit, experience chest heaviness or aches, shortness of breath, cough up mucus, or have a persistent sore throat or hoarseness. In these cases with more (long lasting and severe symptoms), it is advisable to contact a physician.

(Adapted from Hahn et al. 2007)

Topic: *treating cold symptoms*

Unstated main idea: *Some cold symptoms are mild and can be treated with over-the-counter medications, while more severe and long-lasting symptoms should be treated by a doctor.*

Paragraph 2

Influenza, or the flu, is a severe, contagious disease caused by viruses. Most young adults can cope with the milder strains of influenza that appear each winter or spring. However, pregnant women and older people—especially older people with additional health complications, such as heart disease, kidney disease, emphysema, and chronic bronchitis—are not as capable of handling this viral attack. People who regularly come into contact with the general public, such as teachers, should also consider annual flu shots.

(Adapted from Hahn et al. 2007)

Topic: *how different people deal with influenza*

Unstated main idea: *People cope with the flu in different ways and should take precautions based on their particular health situation.*

Paragraph 3

We now know that colds are transmitted most readily by hand contact. Hands transmit infectious agents when they touch the eyes, nose, or mouth. You should wash your hands frequently. How often you wash your hands is important. Wash your hands not only when they are dirty, but before, during, and after you prepare food, and before and after you use the bathroom. You should also wash your hands after touching animals or animal waste, or right after a period of frequent hand shaking. Of course, you should wash more often when someone in your home is sick.

(Adapted from Hahn et al. 2007)

Topic: *hand washing*

Unstated main idea: *Washing your hands often will help prevent the transmission of infectious diseases.*

Paragraph 4

Mononucleosis, called "mono" by most (and the "kissing" disease, though it is actually not highly contagious), is a viral infection in which the body produces an excessive amount of

(continued)

(continued)

white blood cells. The acute symptoms of mono can appear long after it has been contracted, and include weakness, headache, low-grade fever, swollen glands, and sore throat. Fatigue and depression are sometimes reported as side effects. College students who contract mono can be forced into a long period of bed rest during a semester when they can least afford it. Other common diseases can be managed with little interference into life activities, but the overall weakness and fatigue that come with mono sometimes require a month or two of rest and recuperation.

(Adapted from Hahn et al. 2007)

Topic: *mononucleosis*

Unstated main idea: *Mono, unlike other diseases, often leads to weakness and fatigue that require a long period of rest for recuperation.*

Paragraph 5

We have spent considerable amounts of effort and money to control the major outdoor air pollutants, but we have only recently become aware of the dangers of indoor air pollutants. The Environmental Protection Agency has found that indoor concentrations of toxic (poisonous) air pollutants are often higher than outdoors. Furthermore, people generally spend more time inside than out, and therefore are exposed to higher doses of these pollutants. Cigarette smoke, as well as other chemical compounds that are illegal, are found in indoor spaces.

(Adapted from Cunningham and Cunningham 2008)

Topic: *indoor air pollutants*

Main Idea: *In addition to outside air pollutants, there are many dangerous indoor air toxins, including cigarette smoke and illegal chemicals.*

Paragraph 6

The effect of environmental tobacco smoke, smoke that stays in the air from smoking, on the health of children seems well established. The children of parents who smoke are twice as likely as children of nonsmoking parents to experience bronchitis or pneumonia during the first year of life. In addition, throughout childhood, these children will experience <u>more wheezing and coughing</u> than will children whose parents do not smoke. <u>Middle ear infection is also significantly more common</u>.

(Adapted from Hahn et al. 2007)

Topic: *effect of environmental smoke on children*

Main Idea: *Children of parents who smoke are around environmental smoke and suffer increased health problems throughout their childhood.*

Paragraph 7

Ritalin is a prescription <u>stimulant drug</u> that is typically prescribed to children, adolescents, and young adults <u>to help them focus attention</u> if they cannot concentrate. There is concern about its <u>abuse on college campuses.</u> Studies have shown that <u>one in every five college students has used Ritalin illegally.</u> Students who take it <u>without a prescription</u> are using the drug <u>to help increase their concentration during late-night studying sessions, to obtain a "high," or to suppress their appetites.</u>

Topic: *Ritalin*

Main Idea: *There is a growing concern about the illegal use of Ritalin by college students to help with studying, to get high, or to suppress eating.*

Paragraph 8

Like any drug, Ritalin has side effects. Some are very serious when the drug is taken illegally. Students may not realize they can occur. They include <u>nervousness, insomnia</u> (the inability to sleep), <u>loss of appetite, headaches, increased heart rate, dry mouth, perspiration, and feelings of superiority,</u> being better than others. Higher doses can result in more damaging reactions including <u>tremors, convulsions, paranoia, and/or a sensation of bugs crawling under the skin.</u> These health risks are considerably <u>higher if Ritalin is snorted. Death can occur from abusing Ritalin. Students are often unaware</u> of the severity, or even the existence, of these side effects.

Topic: *the side effects of Ritalin*

Main Idea: *Most college students who take Ritalin illegally are unaware of the many serious side effects that can occur.*

try it and apply it! 4-10   Identifying Stated and Implied Main Ideas in Longer Selections

Directions: Read the following excerpts. Identify the main idea of each paragraph by locating the topic sentence *or* by identifying the topic, noting important content, and formulating the implied main idea. Underline the topic sentence and important details, and circle repeated words that indicate the topic. Then write the main idea for each paragraph on the line that follows it. Finally, select the most general or *overall main point* of the entire selection. This will be the thesis of the selection. It is not stated completely, but is implied by combining the topic and main ideas.

A. Making Exercise a Part of Your Life

Exercise produces a variety of benefits. Your body will run more efficiently. You'll have more energy. Your heart and circulatory system will run more smoothly, and you'll be able to bounce back from stress and illness more quickly.

1. **Main Idea:** *There are many benefits to exercise.*

Exercising will be a chore if you don't enjoy what you are doing. You will end up avoiding it, and losing its benefits. So it is important to choose a type of exercise that you like.

2. **Main Idea:** *It is important to choose a type of exercise that you like.*

Your daily life offers many opportunities to exercise. Use these to do so. Take the stairs instead of the elevator. Leave your car at home and walk to campus or work if that is possible. When you're on campus, take the longer way to reach your destination. The gym is not the only place where you can get moving. The more activity you integrate into your life, the better.

3. **Main Idea (Implied):** *Use the many opportunities that present themselves in your daily life to exercise.*

Exercising with others brings you social support and turns exercise into a social activity. Make exercise a paired or group activity. You'll be more likely to stick to a program if you have a regular "exercise date" with a friend.

4. **Main Idea:** *Make exercise a paired or group activity.*

Doing the same thing over and over again can become boring. The same is true for doing the same kind of exercise day after day. Choose different sorts of activities that will involve different parts of your body and keep you motivated.

For example, for cardiovascular fitness that supports your heart and circulatory system, you might alternate between running, swimming, biking, or using a cardio training machine. Varying your exercise routine will keep it interesting.

5. **Main Idea:** *Varying your exercise routine will keep it interesting.*

One note of caution before you begin your exercise program. It is a good idea to have a physical checkup, even if you feel you're in the peak of health. This is especially true if you're starting an exercise regimen after years of inactivity. You might consult a personal trainer at a gym to set up a program that gradually builds you up to more vigorous exercise.

(Adapted from Feldman 2009)

6. **Main Idea (Implied):** *Before beginning any exercise program, it is a good idea to have a physical checkup, especially if you have been inactive for a long time.*

_b_ 7. **The overall main idea or thesis of the selection is that**
   a. Exercise is good for you.
   b. Because of its many benefits, exercise should be built into the routines of our daily lives.
   c. Before beginning any exercise program, one should consult with a physician.
   d. If you don't vary your exercise routine and make it a group activity, you are not likely to follow it.

B. Nicotine

Despite the clear evidence of its dangers, smoking remains a significant health problem. Smoking causes lung damage and increases the risks of developing cancer, emphysema, and a host of other diseases. Many doctors say that the single best change people can make to improve their health is, if they smoke, to stop smoking.

1. **Main Idea:** *Smoking continues to be a significant health problem.*

Why do people smoke when the evidence is so clear about its risks? There are a variety of reasons. Smoking is sometimes viewed as a kind of initiation into adulthood, a sign of growing up. In other cases, teenagers see smoking as "cool," a view promoted by movies and television shows from the past. Some see it as an act of rebellion, purposely doing what is known to be harmful.

2. **Main Idea (Implied):** *Despite evidence about the risks, people begin to smoke for a variety of reasons.*

(continued)

(*continued*)

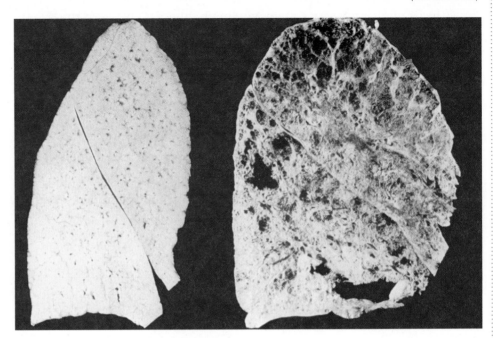

The addictive nature of nicotine makes smoking a difficult habit to kick. The effects of smoking are deadly: at left, a healthy lung; at right, a diseased lung.

The problem is that, no matter what reason persuades a person to try out a few cigarettes, smoking can quickly become a habit. A major ingredient of tobacco—nicotine—is an addictive drug. An addictive drug produces a biological or psychological dependence. The absence of the drug leads to a craving for it that may be nearly irresistible.

3. **Main Idea (Implied):** *Smoking becomes a habit due to the addictive nature of nicotine, a major ingredient of tobacco.*

Smoking is one of the hardest addictions to break. Health professionals offer several suggestions for breaking the smoking habit. These include remaining smoke free for one day at a time, rather than thinking about the long term. The all-purpose remedy, exercise, will make you feel better physically and take your mind off smoking. Avoid others who smoke. Reward yourself in some way for every day, or week, that you don't have a cigarette. Enroll in a quit-smoking program to receive the support of others who are in the same boat as you are. Lastly, use nicotine patches or chew nicotine gum.

4. **Main Idea:** *Health professionals offer several suggestions for breaking the smoking habit.*

Another suggestion is to use your power of imagination. Picture blackened, rotting lungs filled with smoke. Then think about the fresh, pink lungs that you'll have after you've stopped smoking. Visualizing both the consequences of a bad habit, and the results of the change in behavior, can help.

(Adapted from Feldman 2009)

5. **Main Idea (Implied):** *Visualizing the consequences of smoking and then of breaking the habit can help you quit smoking.*

<u>c</u> 6. **The overall main idea, or thesis, of the selection is that**
   a. Smoking is very addictive and despite warnings, people continue to smoke.
   b. Visualizing the consequences of smoking can help you stop.
   c. Smoking is a significant health problem because of the addictive quality of nicotine, but there are many suggestions on how to quit.
   d. People begin to smoke for various reasons, including a desire to appear grown up and to seem cool.

Get the Big Picture: Identifying the Main Idea in College Reading

wrap it Up

Getting the main idea will help you discover the most important points of textbook paragraphs and chapters, reading selections, articles, or essays. Remember the following points:

- **Just because a statement is factual or accurate doesn't necessarily mean it is the main point.**

- **Don't be distracted by familiar or amusing statements.** These may be interesting but may not reflect the author's most important point.

- **Stay focused on the text and not on your own opinions on the topic.** Remember the main idea is what the author *says or implies about* the subject. It's not your viewpoint.

- **Don't assume the first sentence will be the topic sentence.** Remember it can be located anywhere within a paragraph.

- **Identifying and writing the main ideas of your assigned reading is a simple and effective way to take notes and prepare for exams.** You will learn more about this is in Chapter 10.

- **Identifying and writing the main ideas will help you write summaries of your reading.** You will learn more about this is in Chapter 9.

Key Terms

implied

main idea

thesis

thesis statement

topic

topic sentence

unstated main idea

chapter

5

Lend Some Support
Locating and Using
Important Details

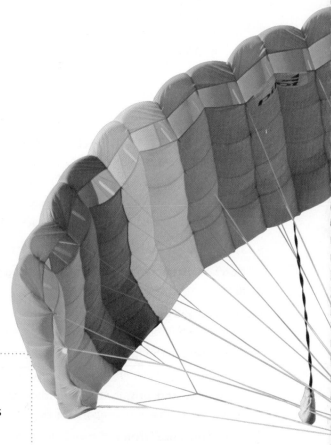

In this chapter

you will learn to

- Identify major and minor supporting details
- Recognize different types of transitions
- Use transitions to locate supporting details
- Use details to aid your studying

Develop Skills While Reading About
Emotional Wellness

Emotional wellness relates to how people show their feelings, deal with stress, manage problems, and accept changes. Emotionally well people maintain a generally positive attitude about life and its challenges. They are self-aware and self-accepting while remaining flexible and continually open to personal development. They can function independently but are aware of personal limitations and seek the help and support of others. They form interpersonal relationships based on mutual trust and respect and maintain satisfying relationships with others. Find out more about emotional health and well-being in Module 7.

125

The Importance of Supporting Details

In the last chapter, you read about physical well-being. So let's suppose that you didn't feel well and went to see your doctor.

The doctor asks, "What brings you here today?"

"Doctor, I'm just not feeling right," you reply.

"Well, you will have to share more details if you want me to help you."

You elaborate: "This morning I woke up with a major headache, so I felt my head and sure enough, I had a fever. Then, I began to have the chills, and my arms and legs started to feel achy. Oh, yeah, my throat started to feel scratchy last night."

"Well, now that I have all the details, I just have one more question. Did you get a flu shot in the fall?"

You say, "No. I don't think so."

"Well then, let me check you out and take a throat culture. The symptoms you are complaining about are all typical of the flu, and we're seeing a lot of cases right now. It's the most likely reason for why you're not feeling well."

At the beginning of this conversation, you presented your general complaint. However, for the doctor to make a clear diagnosis, she needed more information about your complaint. In fact, the doctor needed *more* than the big picture; she needed the *details*. Providing all your symptoms helped the doctor make a proper diagnosis.

Details that tell you the *how, what, when, where, why,* and *how much* information about the main idea are called **supporting details.** They provide you with examples, facts and statistics, explanations, or reasons that back up the author's point.

Identifying Supporting Details

Not all details are equally important. **Major supporting details** directly explain and support a writer's main point, whereas **minor supporting details** provide additional information about the major details. Becoming a good reader requires you to learn how to find supporting details and separate the more important ones from the less important ones.

Sometimes, a single sentence provides enough details to help you understand the main point. These details often appear as a list or series of examples.

Personal stressors are events or conditions that may have a negative impact on an individual's life, such as suffering from a serious illness, being unable to find a job, or experiencing the divorce or separation of parents.

In this sentence, the topic is personal stressors. The main idea is: "Personal stressors are events or conditions that may have a negative impact on an individual's life." The details, which help you understand what the writer means by a personal stressor, are

- suffering from a serious illness
- being unable to find a job
- experiencing the divorce or separation of parents

try it and apply it! 5-1 — Identifying Supporting Details in Sentences

Directions: Read the following sentences. Then underline the supporting details.

1. Catastrophic events, including <u>tornadoes</u>, <u>hurricanes</u>, and <u>plane crashes</u>, have a clear end point, which sometimes makes coping more manageable.
    (Adapted from Feldman 2009)

2. Some stressors, however, are so traumatic that they have long-lasting effects, as found in <u>Holocaust survivors</u>, <u>Vietnam veterans</u>, and <u>rape victims</u>.
    (Passer 2007)

3. Daily hassles, such as <u>waking up at 5 a.m.</u>, <u>missing the bus</u>, or <u>getting to class on time</u> generally produce the least amount of stress.

4. Stress causes many physical responses, which include <u>a faster heart beat</u>, <u>rapid or shallow breathing</u>, and an <u>increase in sweating</u>.
    (Adapted from Feldman 2009)

5. When we experience stress, our body becomes more susceptible to disease, ranging from the <u>common cold</u> and <u>headaches</u> to <u>cancer</u>, <u>strokes</u>, <u>heart disease</u>, and <u>diabetes</u>.
    (Adapted from Feldman 2009 and Passer 2007)

As you read a paragraph, keep in mind the author's main point. In this way, you will be reading to discover how the author explains, or elaborates upon his or her major thought. In the following exercise, you will distinguish between relevant and irrelevant supporting details.

try it and apply it! 5-2 — Identifying Supporting Details in Paragraphs

Directions: Each of the following topic sentences states the writer's main thought. It is followed by details that may or may not support his/her point. Read each sentence and indicate the detail that does ***not*** support, explain, or develop the author's main idea.

(continued)

(continued)

_a_ 1. Psychological health is connected to having a positive self-esteem or a good sense of your own value or worth.

(Adapted from Hahn 2007)

a. You are critical of yourself.
b. You have self-confidence.
c. You feel good about yourself.
d. You have pride in yourself.
e. You treat yourself with self-respect.

_b_ 2. People with low self-esteem see themselves in a negative way.

(Adapted from Hahn 2007)

a. They might develop eating disorders.
b. They often have a fever accompanied by chills.
c. They may suffer from depression.
d. They could have substance abuse problems.
e. They may criticize themselves or others.

_e_ 3. Laughter is an important part of emotional wellness.

(Adapted from Hahn 2007)

a. It gets rid of stress.
b. It reduces pain.
c. It makes you want to be creative.
d. It decreases fear.
e. It makes you feel more depressed.

_d_ 4. Nurture, the effect of where you were brought up and live, can have a negative impact on your emotional health.

a. It can prevent you from making friends.
b. It can cause problems with your job.
c. It may result in trouble at school.
d. It can promote self-esteem and confidence.
e. It can contribute to a broken marriage.

_e_ 5. Nature or inherited qualities also contribute to psychological health. You may have heard one of following statements at one time or another:

a. She is serious like her mother.
b. He is funny like his father.
c. Lenny is a born comic.
d. Her grandmother suffered from depression.
e. Robert has never held a job for more than six months.

Major Supporting Details in Paragraphs

As you learned in Chapter 4, all paragraphs contain a topic and a main idea. To identify the topic, ask yourself: What is the whole paragraph about? To recognize the main idea, ask yourself: What does the author say about the topic? To identify the major supporting details, ask yourself: How does the author explain, develop, or prove his or her main point?

To see the relationship between all the parts in a paragraph, look at the following basic outline:

> **Topic**
> > **Main Idea**
> > > Supporting Detail 1
> > > Supporting Detail 2
> > > Supporting Detail 3

Now read the following paragraph:

> (1) Psychologically healthy people are not perfect, but they know how to deal with their stress and failures. (2) They can take of themselves and function independently, as well as work with others. (3) They accept their mistakes and life's disappointments. (4) They express concern for and trust in others. (5) They lead a healthy lifestyle that includes regular exercise, good nutrition, and a sufficient amount of sleep.
>
> (Adapted from Hahn 2007)

Applying the strategies you learned in Chapter 4, you can determine that the topic of the paragraph is *psychologically healthy people*. The main idea is located in the first sentence (the topic sentence). The remainder of the paragraph, sentences 2–5, provides supporting details about the author's main point—that psychologically healthy people know how to deal with their stress and failures.

Following is an outline of the paragraph. It includes the topic, main idea, and supporting details.

> **Topic:** psychologically healthy people
> > **Main Idea:** Psychologically healthy people are not perfect, but they know how to deal with their stress and failures.
> > > **Supporting Detail 1:** They can take of themselves and function independently, as well as work with others.
> > > **Supporting Detail 2:** They accept their mistakes and life's disappointments.
> > > **Supporting Detail 3:** They express concern for and trust in others.
> > > **Supporting Detail 4:** They lead a healthy lifestyle that includes regular exercise, good nutrition. and a sufficient amount of sleep.

Notice how all the supporting details in this paragraph relate back to the main idea. There are no unrelated or random sentences. A paragraph is like an *umbrella*. The topic is the tip of the umbrella, the main idea is the canopy of the umbrella and covers the entire surface, and the supporting details are the ribs, all of which fall under the umbrella and support the canopy.

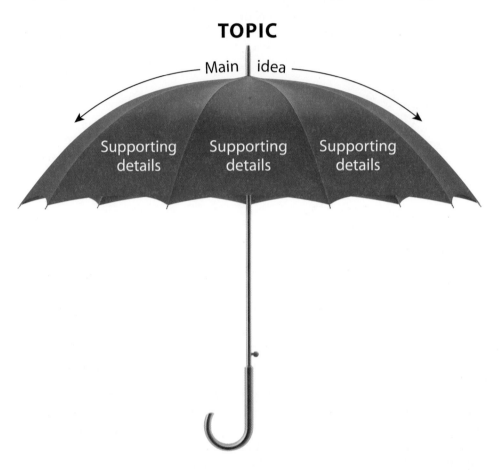

You can also visualize or see the relationship of main ideas to supporting details in the following diagram:

The supporting details listed in the outline are called major supporting details because they explain the main idea.

try it and apply it! 5-3 — Locating Major Supporting Details

Directions: Read each paragraph, and then complete the outline that follows using the major supporting details.

1. Many holocaust survivors are still troubled by high levels of fear and anxiety. Those who were children during the war and lost their families continue to experience fears about what will happen to their spouses or children when they are out of sight. Depression and crying spells are common. They also feel insecure about forming relationships.

(Adapted from Passer 2007)

Main Idea: Many holocaust survivors are still troubled by high levels of fear and anxiety.

Major Supporting Details

1. Those who were children during the war and lost their families continue to experience fears about what will happen to their spouses or children when they are out of sight.
2. Depression and crying spells are common.
3. They also feel insecure about forming relationships.

2. Unemployment can also lead to long-term stress. Some who lose their jobs may never regain their self-confidence even after they find new employment. Others may constantly fear being let go at their next job. Still others may find a major decrease in satisfaction at home and with their families.

(Adapted from Passer 2007)

Main Idea: Unemployment can also lead to long-term stress.

Major Supporting Details

1. Some who lose their jobs may never regain their self-confidence even after they find new employment.
2. Others may constantly fear being let go at their next job.
3. Still others may find a major decrease in satisfaction at home and with their families.

3. The emotional stress of losing a spouse can contribute to a decrease in physical well-being. Bereaved widows begin to show an increase in mortality rates compared to most married people who have not lost a spouse. Bereaved husbands, who tend to respond with greater feelings of distress, show an even greater increase in mortality rates. Within one year of a spouse's death, about two-thirds of bereaved people decline in health.

(Adapted from Passer 2007)

Main Idea: The emotional stress of losing a spouse can contribute to a decrease in physical well-being.

(*continued*)

(continued)

Major Supporting Details

1. *Bereaved widows begin to show an increase in mortality rates compared to most married people who have not lost a spouse.*

2. *Bereaved husbands, who tend to respond with greater feelings of distress, show an even greater increase in mortality rates.*

3. *Within one year of a spouse's death, about two-thirds of bereaved people decline in health.*

4. Sometimes, people experiencing stress seem to age before our eyes, especially women who have children with a chronic illness (infantile paralysis, autism). These women show evidence of weakened muscles. In addition, their skin becomes wrinkled. Their eyesight starts to fade. Most significantly, their ability to think, reason, and solve problems decreases.

(Adapted from Passer 2007)

Main Idea: Sometimes, people experiencing stress seem to age before our eyes, especially women who have children with a chronic illness.

Major Supporting Details

1. *show evidence of weakened muscles*

2. *skin becomes wrinkled*

3. *eyesight fades*

4. *their ability to think, reason and solve problems decreases*

5. Stress can also contribute to health breakdowns by causing people to engage in risky behavior. When experiencing stress, for example, a person with diabetes may fail to take his or her medication or refrain from exercising, both of which are crucial in controlling the disease. Stress can also lead people to smoke, use drugs, or drink alcohol. College freshmen may adopt poor sleep habits resulting in an increase in illness, failing grades, and the possibility of being academically dismissed from school.

Main Idea: Stress can also contribute to health breakdowns by causing people to engage in risky behavior.

Major Supporting Details

1. *A person with diabetes may fail to take his/her medication or refrain from exercising.*

2. *Stress can also lead people to smoke, use drugs, or drink alcohol.*

3. *College freshmen may adopt poor sleep habits resulting in an increase in illness, failing grades, and the possibility of being academically dismissed from school.*

Minor Supporting Details in Paragraphs

Details that further explain the major supporting details are called minor supporting details. These details provide additional information about a major supporting detail. The following outline will help you see the differences between major and minor supporting details.

> Topic
> **Main Idea**
> **Major Supporting Detail 1**
>   Minor Supporting Detail 1
>   Minor Supporting Detail 2
> **Major Supporting Detail 2**
>   Minor Supporting Detail 1
> **Major Supporting Detail 3**

Read the following paragraph to see how major and minor supporting details work together to support the main idea:

(1) Psychologically healthy people are not perfect, but they know how to deal with their stress and failures. (2) They can take care of themselves and function independently, as well as work with others. (3) They accept their mistakes and life's disappointments. (4) For example, students who do not get the grade they expect on an English paper plan to do a better job next time. (5) Psychologically healthy people express concern for and trust in others. (6) They lead a healthy lifestyle that includes regular exercise, good nutrition, and a sufficient amount of sleep. (7) For instance, they join a gym or take a weekly yoga class.

(Adapted from Hahn et al. 2007)

Here is an outline of the paragraph:

Main Idea: Psychologically healthy people are not perfect, but they know how deal with their stress and failures.

> **Major Supporting Detail 1:** They can take of themselves and function independently, as well as work with others.

> **Major Supporting Detail 2:** They accept their mistakes and life's disappointments.

>> **Minor Supporting Detail 1:** For example, if a student does not get the grade he/she expects on an English paper, the student plans to do a better job next time.

> **Major Supporting Detail 3:** Psychologically healthy people express concern and trust for others.

> **Major Supporting Detail 4:** They lead a healthy lifestyle that includes regular exercise, good nutrition, and a sufficient amount of sleep.

>> **Minor Supporting Detail 1:** They join a gym or take a weekly yoga class.

You can also visualize, or see, the relationship of major and minor supporting details in a map (see page 134). Notice how major details 2 and 4 are further developed through minor supporting details. All these details are connected to the main idea.

try it and apply it! 5-4   Distinguishing Between Major and Minor Supporting Details

Directions: Determine the main idea of each paragraph, and identify the major and minor supporting details. Insert the details in the map that follows the paragraph.

1. A positive attitude results in enthusiasm, vitality, and optimism in school, at work, and in your career. First, in school, a positive attitude will provide you with a sense of purpose and direction. Upon entering college, you make an appointment with an advisor and select a possible major. In addition, at work, a positive attitude will result in higher productivity. You will even have time to take your lunch breaks instead of working through them just to get your job done. Finally, in your career, that same attitude will lead you to greater creativity in solving problems and finding solutions. You will be recognized for your accomplishments and rewarded for your efforts.

(Adapted from Ferrett 2010)

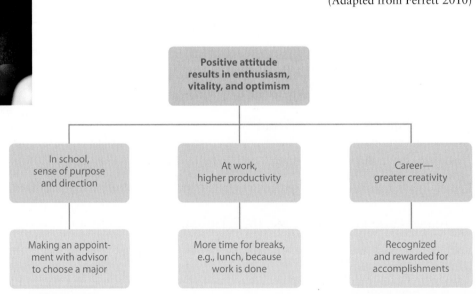

2. A negative attitude can drain your enthusiasm and energy. People who feel angry and blame others are helpless to make any changes. For example, some students blame instructors for poor grades and feel that nothing will help them pass their class. Some may see a difficult situation as potentially lasting forever. If their store is not showing a profit this month, they are ready to close it down. Others may focus on the negative in people and situations. They focus on other people's flaws and often see the same in themselves. They might think about the negative aspects of going away to college, a bad decision they made to pursue a career in medicine, or even that it is a bad idea to go on a diet.

    (Adapted from Ferrett 2010)

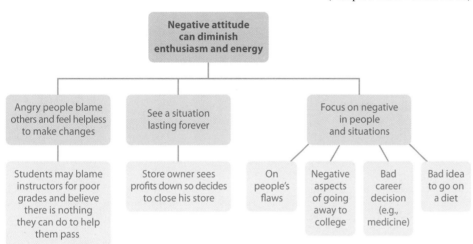

3. Motivation is the inner drive that moves you to action. Even if you are not really motivated, act as if you are already motivated. Consider your posture. You should try standing straight with your shoulders back. Notice the facial expressions you are using. Try smiling. Look at the kinds of friends you keep. Surrounding yourself by people who have a good attitude helps motivate you.

    (Adapted from Ferrett 2010)

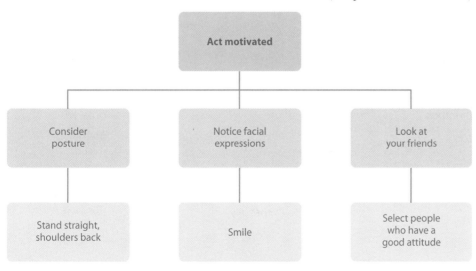

Using Transitions to Locate Supporting Details

Often, a writer will introduce supporting details by using transitional words. **Transitions** are words or phrases that help the reader to anticipate what is coming next and tell what kind of information will be presented. Look for words that signal the relationship between the supporting details and the main idea or that serve as signposts to each detail.

Read the following paragraph about student stress. You will see how the phrases *for instance, another example*, and *final example* signal that author is going to provide examples as details to support his main point.

> Going to college has been compared to crossing over to a new culture where one needs to learn new customs. When students enter college for the first time, they meet up with new challenges, especially stressors. *For instance,* students often face homesickness. *Another example* is that some students have to deal with long-distance relationships. A *final example,* and probably the greatest source of stress, is balancing work, home, and school.
>
> (Adapted from Hahn et al. 2007)

The following chart lists common transitions you will encounter in your college reading.

Common Types of Transitions

Addition	Example	Reasons	Sequence	Comparison	Contrast
and	for example	as a result	after, afterward	just as, just like	however
also	for instance	because	before	like, likewise	in contrast
another	including	consequently	by the time	similarly	on the other hand
besides	specifically	for this reason	during	in the same way	unlike
finally	such as	since	first, second, etc.		but
furthermore	to illustrate	therefore	finally		conversely
in addition	namely	thus	later		otherwise
first, first of all, last			next		on the contrary
moreover, next			then		nonetheless
other			meanwhile		instead
too			eventually		whereas

Types of Transitions

Different types of transitional words and phrases are used to indicate that an author is going to provide certain types of supporting details, such as additional items, examples, explanations or reasons, sequences of events, or comparison and contrast.

Additional Items

Some of the most commonly used transitions in college reading are words that signal additional items. These words indicate that an author is continuing with the same idea and is going to provide more supporting details.

Common Addition Transitions

and	furthermore	last
also	besides	finally
another	another	
in addition	other	

try it and apply it! 5-5   Addition Transitions

Directions: Underline the transitions in the following paragraph that signal additional items, and complete the outline that follows.

Balancing work, home, and school is a major stressor for college students today. More than two-thirds of college students work full time or part time while going to school. <u>In addition</u>, between 5 and 10 percent of college students also have children. <u>Furthermore</u>, the number of women over 25 years of age has grown by over 500 percent over recent years.

(Adapted from Hahn et al. 2007)

Main Idea: Balancing work, home, and school is a major stressor for college students today.

Supporting Details

1. *More than two-thirds of college students work full time or part time.*

2. *Between 5 and 10 percent of college students have children.*

3. *The number of women over 25 years of age has grown by over 500 percent.*

Examples

In college textbooks, examples are used to help students understand concepts (health promotion, social and emotional intelligence, and body image), problems (mood disorders, body dysmorphic disorder, and obesity), or processes (achieving psychological health, maintaining a healthy weight, or preventing infectious diseases).

Common Example Transitions

for example	such as	including
for instance	to illustrate	specifically

try it and apply it! 5-6   Example Transitions

Directions: Underline the transitions in the following paragraph that signal examples, and complete the outline that follows.

College students with young children at home have to juggle family responsibilities and the coordination of their school schedules. One way to alleviate this stress is to look for good child care. For example, many college campuses offer excellent child care programs, which can be used while students are taking classes. These programs are generally located on campus so that you can easily be reached should a problem arise. In addition, some programs may allow you to visit your children during specially designated times. Such a program would certainly serve to alleviate stress and worries and help you concentrate on your schoolwork.

Main Idea: To alleviate stress, college students with young children should explore good child care options.

Major Supporting Details: *child care programs on campus*

Minor Supporting Details:

Programs are located on campus so that you can easily be reached should a problem arise

Some programs may allow you to visit your children during specially designated times.

Explanations and Reasons

Writers of textbooks often provide explanations or reasons to support their main points. You will often find supporting details that offer explanations in persuasive or argumentative writing. Authors support their opinions by providing reasons for their ideas, beliefs, or actions.

Common Explanation and Reason Transitions

because, since, therefore, thus, consequently, as a result, so, if

try it and apply it! 5-7 **Explanation and Reason Transitions**

Directions: In the following paragraph, notice how explanations are provided to help you understand the impact of test anxiety on college success. Underline the transitions in the paragraph that signal reasoning or explanation, and complete the outline that follows.

> Test anxiety is a major source of stress for college students and contributes to poor academic achievement. <u>Since</u> students are so nervous and distressed, they tend to make more mistakes. They often make more errors in spelling and add information incorrectly. <u>Because</u> students are sometimes fidgety, they may not read directions carefully and end up doing poorly on exams. <u>If</u> students become nauseous or headachy before a test, they may not show up for exams at all.

(Adapted from Hahn et al. 2007)

(continued)

(*continued*)

Main Idea: Taking tests is one of the greatest sources of stress for college students.

   Major Supporting Detail 1: *Since students are so nervous and distressed, they tend to make more mistakes.*

      Minor Supporting Detail: *They often make more errors in spelling and add information incorrectly.*

   Major Supporting Detail 2: *Because students are sometimes fidgety, they may not read directions carefully and end up doing poorly on exams.*

   Major Supporting Detail 3: *If students become nauseous or headachy before a test, they may not show up for exams at all.*

Sequence

When writers want to explain the order in which events occurred or the steps in a process, concept, or theory, they use sequential transitions.

Common Sequence Transitions

first, later, next, finally, after, when, during, once

---

try it and apply it! 5-8   Sequence Transitions

Directions: Read the following paragraph that explains the steps involved in making changes in one's behavior. Underline the words that signal sequence, and then complete the outline that follows.

Another common stressor for college students is math anxiety. There are a number of steps you can take to help you overcome this problem. First, if necessary, take any required remedial course work during your first semester because it will help you develop a solid arithmetic foundation, and minimize future stress and anxiety. Then, on your first day of classes, locate your college's math center, just in case you need to go there during the semester. It might also be a good idea to set up an appointment at the beginning of the semester so that you can become familiar with the services. Once the semester begins, make sure you review all your notes on a daily basis.

Research says that you will recall 50 percent of your lectures if you look over your material immediately after class but only 20 percent if you review it 24 hours later.

(Adapted from Hahn et al. 2007)

Main Idea: There are a number of steps you can follow to overcome math anxiety.

Major Supporting Detail 1: *First, if necessary, take any required remedial course work during your first semester because it will help you develop a solid arithmetic foundation, and minimize future stress and anxiety.*

Major Supporting Detail 2: *Then, on your first day of classes, locate your college's math center, just in case you need to go there during the semester.*

    Minor Supporting Detail: *It might also be a good idea to set up an appointment at the beginning of the semester so that you can become familiar with the services.*

Major Supporting Detail 4: *Once the semester begins, make sure you review all your notes on a daily basis.*

    Minor Supporting Detail: *Research says that you will remember 50 percent of what you heard if you look it over immediately after class but only 20 percent if you review it 24 hours later.*

Comparison and Contrast

If writers want to show how a previous idea is similar to one that follows, they use transitions such as *like* or *similarly*. If they want to talk about the differences between items or ideas, they use transitions such as *unlike* or *in contrast*.

Common Comparison and Contrast Transitions

Comparison	
like	in the same manner
likewise	also
similarly	too

Contrast	
unlike	while
but	whereas
yet	although
however	even though
nevertheless	on the other hand
still	in contrast

try it and apply it! 5-9   **Comparison and Contrast Transitions**

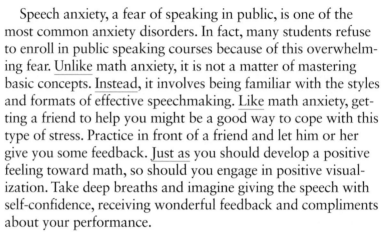

Directions: Read the following paragraph about speech anxiety. Underline the transition words that signal the comparison and/or contrast of major supporting details. Then complete the chart using details from the selection.

Speech anxiety, a fear of speaking in public, is one of the most common anxiety disorders. In fact, many students refuse to enroll in public speaking courses because of this overwhelming fear. <u>Unlike</u> math anxiety, it is not a matter of mastering basic concepts. <u>Instead</u>, it involves being familiar with the styles and formats of effective speechmaking. <u>Like</u> math anxiety, getting a friend to help you might be a good way to cope with this type of stress. Practice in front of a friend and let him or her give you some feedback. <u>Just as</u> you should develop a positive feeling toward math, so should you engage in positive visualization. Take deep breaths and imagine giving the speech with self-confidence, receiving wonderful feedback and compliments about your performance.

(Adapted from Hahn et al. 2007)

Speech Anxiety	Math Anxiety
1. Learn *styles* and *formats* of effective speechmaking.	1. Learn *basic math concepts*.
2. Get a *friend* to help you practice. Allow him/her to give you feedback.	2. Enlist the assistance of a *friend*.
3. Take *deep breaths*; imagine giving the speech, receiving wonderful *feedback*.	3. Use *positive* visualization.

Studying Supporting Details

You borrow a friend's college textbook and discover that everything is highlighted in yellow. You are impressed that your friend has read the chapter for homework; however, you realize that because everything is highlighted, it is difficult for you to decide which information is important.

Because college textbooks contain so much information, it is virtually impossible to remember everything. After studying Chapter 4, you know it's important to understand the main ideas of a selection. In this chapter, you have learned that major and minor supporting details also provide significant information to help in comprehension. So, what's important?

As you read, you should use the major supporting details to understand the main ideas, and use the minor supporting details to get more information about the corresponding major details. When you mark your textbook, it's usually best to focus only on the major supporting details; otherwise, nothing will stand out as important. These major supporting details are the details you should study for tests.

try it and apply it! 5-10   Studying Supporting Details

Directions: Read the paragraphs that follow and underline the transition words that help you locate the supporting details. Then answer the questions about the main ideas and major and minor supporting details.

A. Psychological Disorders

A great many people suffer from psychological or mental disorders. In fact, an estimated 22 percent of Americans, about one in five, suffer from a diagnosable mental disorder. Moreover, large-scale population studies indicate that anxiety disorders are the most prevalent, affecting 17.6 percent of Americans during their lifetime. In addition, four of the leading causes of disability in the United States are mental disorders, such as depression, bipolar disorder, obsessive compulsive disorder, and schizophrenia.

(Adapted from Hahn 2007 and Passer 2007)

_d_ 1. What percentage of Americans suffer from mental disorders?
   a. 17.6%
   b. 5%
   c. over 25%
   d. under 25%

_c_ 2. Which mental disorder is the most prevalent?
   a. depression
   b. bipolar disorder
   c. anxiety
   d. schizophrenia

_b_ 3. How many people suffer from anxiety disorder during their lifetime?
   a. 22%
   b. 17.6%
   c. 4%
   d. one out of 5

_a_ 4. All of the following are leading causes of disability *except*
   a. anxiety disorder
   b. obsessive compulsive disorder
   c. depression
   d. bipolar disorder

(continued)

(*continued*)

B. Depression

Depression, an emotional state of sadness ranging from mild discouragement to utter hopelessness, can be tied to certain stages of life. <u>Because</u> you are an adolescent, you may be faced with trying to face new responsibilities of freedom and adulthood. Many college students suffer from depression at this time. <u>If</u> you are facing middle age, you may be experiencing feelings about lost youth or an unrealized career. <u>As</u> an elderly person, the loss of physical strength, illness, and the death of friends and loved ones may cause depression.

(Adapted from Ferret 2010)

___c___ 1. Depression can be defined as
   a. mild discouragement
   b. utter hopelessness
   c. a psychological state of sadness
   d. a stage of life

___d___ 2. Depression can be connected to the following stages of life:
   a. adulthood
   b. old age
   c. adolescence
   d. all of the above

___c___ 3. According to this paragraph, college students experience depression because
   a. They are facing unrealized careers.
   b. They are losing body strength.
   c. They are encountering new responsibilities.
   d. They are losing friends.

___b___ 4. As a senior citizen, you may feel depressed because of
   a. new responsibilities
   b. personal illness
   c. old age
   d. unfulfilled dreams

C. Depression and Suicide

Major depression, a psychological disorder that lasts more than a couple of weeks, can lead to suicide. The best predictor of suicide attempts in both men and women is a verbal or behavioral threat to commit suicide. <u>Other times</u>, the threat is more subtle, as when a person expresses hopelessness about the future, withdraws from others or from favorite activities, gives away treasured possessions, or takes unusual risks. <u>Other</u> important risks are a history of previous suicide attempts and a detailed plan that involves a lethal method. Substance use and abuse <u>also</u> increase suicide risk.

(Adapted from Passer 2007)

_d_ 1. A major depression can be defined as
    a. a psychological disorder of short duration
    b. a behavioral threat that leads to suicide
    c. hopelessness and risk taking
    d. a disturbance in mental health of more than 14 days

_a_ 2. What is the main idea of this paragraph?
    a. Major depression can lead to suicide.
    b. The best predictor of suicide attempts in both men and women is a verbal or behavioral threat to commit suicide.
    c. A history of previous suicide attempts and a detailed plan that involves a lethal method is the most important predictor of suicide.
    d. Substance use and abuse increase suicide risk.

_c_ 3. The preliminary indicator of suicide include all of the following *except*
    a. telling someone about your plans to kill yourself
    b. using drugs or alcohol in excess
    c. taking risks like applying for a new job
    d. having prior suicide attempts

_a_ 4. According to the writer, expressing hopelessness about the future is considered an example of _____.
    a. a subtle threat of suicide
    b. the best predictor of suicide
    c. one of several important risks
    d. major depression

try it and apply it! 5-11
Identifying Major and Minor Supporting Details in Longer Passages

Directions: Actively read the following selections on emotional wellness. Underline any transition words that point out the major or minor supporting details. Then answer the questions at the end of each passage.

A. Panic Disorder

In contrast to generalized anxiety disorder, which involves chronic tension and anxiety, panic disorders occur suddenly and unpredictably. The onset of panic disorder generally appears in late adolescence or early adulthood, unlike generalized anxiety disorder, which tends to occur in childhood and adolescence.

Both of these disorders can markedly interfere with daily functioning. Many people who suffer recurrent panic attacks develop agoraphobia, a fear of public places, because they are

(continued)

(continued)

afraid they will suffer an attack in public. In extreme cases, they remain homebound for years at a time.

Even more common are occasional panic attacks. A survey of Canadian students indicated that 34 percent reported having at least one unexpected panic attack, especially during times of stress, especially around final exam periods. These students would not be diagnosed with panic disorder unless they became fearful of having future attacks or developed maladaptive behavior, such as agoraphobia.

(Adapted from Passer 2007)

_a_ 1. What is the major difference between panic disorder and generalized anxiety disorder?
    a. the general onset of symptoms
    b. the effects on people's daily functioning
    c. the gender that is mostly affected
    d. the symptoms

_b_ 2. All these details about panic disorders are true *except*
    a. They occur without warning.
    b. They generally begin to appear in adolescence.
    c. They may develop into other phobias.
    d. They generally appear during times of stress.

_c_ 3. Panic disorder is diagnosed
    a. after a person experiences a single attack
    b. after a person remains home for years at a time
    c. when a person becomes afraid of having subsequent attacks
    d. when a person experiences a great deal of stress

_c_ 4. Why might people who experience panic attacks develop agoraphobia?
    a. because they are afraid of public places
    b. because they are apprehensive about taking tests
    c. because they are worried about having future attacks
    d. because they are concerned about their future

B. Posttraumatic Stress Disorder

Posttraumatic Stress Disorder (PTSD) is a severe anxiety disorder that results from being exposed to traumatic or catastrophic events, such as wars, battles, or natural disasters. For example, Vietnam veterans who spent a significant amount of time in combat and were wounded may have recurrent flashbacks of these events. In addition, civilians who have experienced war may be vulnerable. The survivors may feel extreme guilt for having survived while others did not.

Traumas caused by human actions, such as war, rape, and torture, tend to cause more serious reactions as compared to natural disasters, such as hurricanes and earthquakes. Women exhibit twice the rate of PSTD following exposure to traumatic events as compared to men. Women were more likely to develop depressive disorders and alcohol-related problems in the future.

Terrorist acts can take a heavy toll in PSTD symptoms for survivors. Interviews with 1,008 adult residents of Manhattan revealed that 7.5 percent experienced symptoms associated with PTSD in the 5 to 8 weeks following the September 11, 2001 attacks. In those living closest to the World Trade Center, the PTSD rate was 20 percent.

(Adapted from Passer 2007)

_d_ 1. PTSD may be experienced by
a. witnesses to catastrophic events
b. victims of natural disasters
c. survivors of traumatic occurrences
d. all of the above

_b_ 2. According to this passage, people who suffer from posttraumatic stress disorder may experience all of the following *except*
a. flashbacks
b. drug problems
c. depression
d. guilt

_c_ 3. It has been shown that people experience more severe PTSD symptoms as a result of which of the following factors?
a. PTSD is caused by a natural disaster.
b. The person experiencing PTSD is male.
c. PTSD is the result of wars, rape, or torture.
d. A depressive disorder is already present.

_c_ 4. Statistics indicate that the September 11 terrorist attacks
a. caused a decrease in PTSD
b. showed that proximity to the attack site had no effect on the PTSD rate
c. revealed that the rate of PTSD more than doubled for those who lived near the World Trade Center
d. indicated that all Manhattan residents experienced PTSD after the September 11 attacks

C. Attention Deficit/Hyperactivity Disorder

In attention deficit/hyperactivity disorder (ADHD), problems may take the form of inattention, hyperactivity/ impulsivity, or a combination of the two. This disorder occurs <u>more</u> frequently among boys than among girls. Boys are <u>more</u> likely to exhibit aggressive behavior and impulsive behavior, <u>whereas</u> girls will primarily show inattentiveness. Studies have

(continued)

(continued)

shown that for 50 to 80 percent, the problem persists into adolescence. In addition, for 30 to 50 percent, it continues into adulthood. In adults, it usually manifests itself in occupational, family, and interpersonal problems.

In spite of a great deal of research, the causes of this disorder still remain unknown. Genetic factors are probably involved. For example, there seems to be a greater occurrence of ADHD among identical twins than in fraternal twins. In addition, when we examine adoptive children, we see that the biological parents are more likely to have ADHD than their adoptive ones. Environmental factors, such as inconsistent parenting, may also account for ADHD.

(Adapted from Passer 2007)

The most effective treatment for ADHD involves a multimodal approach. This includes counseling and coaching the individual to provide strategies and structure in life. Additionally, it may include the administration of drugs, such as Concerta, Ritalin, or Adderall.

(Adapted from Hahn 2007)

_d_ 1. The manifestation of ADHD may appear as
   a. problems at work, and with relationships
   b. inattentiveness in class
   c. aggressive behavior at school
   d. all of the above

_a_ 2. How do boys and girls who have ADHD differ?
   a. They each exhibit different types of behavior.
   b. Their first symptoms occur at different stages of development.
   c. For boys, the problems persist into adulthood.
   d. Girls will have more problems in school.

_b_ 3. Which of the following statements are *not true* according to this passage?
   a. Eighty percent of those who suffer from ADHD continue to have problems throughout their lives.
   b. At least one-third of those who have ADHD continue to experience symptoms as adults.
   c. Research is working on a cure for ADHD.
   d. Research has confirmed inconsistent parenting as the number one cause of ADHD.

_d_ 4. The best way to treat ADHD is
   a. with the administration of Ritalin, Concerta, or Adderall
   b. by learning coping techniques
   c. through the use of daily planners and organizers
   d. combining counseling, education, and drug therapy

Lend Some Support: Locating and Using Important Details

Understanding the supporting details in a paragraph will help you make more sense of the main idea, so when you read you should follow these tips:

- **Distinguish between main ideas and supporting details.** The main idea states the overall message of the paragraph, whereas the supporting details help explain, develop, or support what an author is saying in his or her main point.

- **Distinguish between major and minor supporting details.** The major supporting details provide evidence about the main idea, and the minor supporting details give more information about the major supporting details. Minor supporting details follow the major detail they describe.

- **Look for transition words or expressions that signal different types of details that will follow.**

- **If there are no transition words, see how the information relates to the main idea.** Does it add information, provide examples, describe a time or order of events, describe a process, or explain why the author is making his or her main point?

- **Study major supporting ideas.** Don't just focus on the main ideas. In college reading, the major supporting details are important because they provide specific information about the main idea. Read them carefully. Not only will these details help you understand better, but they will also be important to learn for tests.

Key Terms

major supporting details   supporting details
minor supporting details   transitions

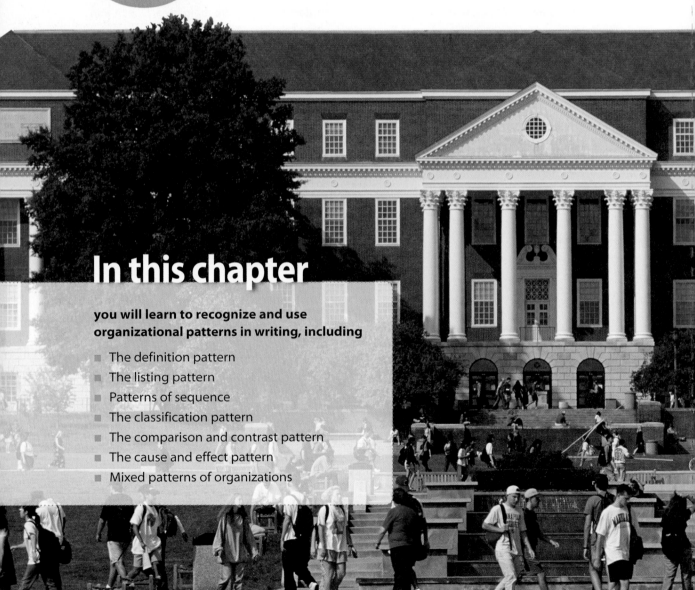

chapter

6

Chart the Course
Identifying and Integrating Writing Patterns

In this chapter

you will learn to recognize and use organizational patterns in writing, including

- The definition pattern
- The listing pattern
- Patterns of sequence
- The classification pattern
- The comparison and contrast pattern
- The cause and effect pattern
- Mixed patterns of organizations

Develop Skills While Reading About the
Code of Conduct

Like many organizations, businesses, and institutions, colleges establish rules and expectations regarding the behavior and activities of those on campus. They set standards based not only on the law, but also on the moral and ethical values that they embrace and want their students to embrace as well.

If you look through your college catalogue, you are likely to find sections that discuss the ways students are expected to conduct themselves. These will include statements about acceptable behavior within classes; respect for authority, property, and fellow students; attendance policies; regulations about the use of alcohol, drugs, and tobacco on campus; definitions of cheating and plagiarism; and statements about harassment, sexism, racism, and bigotry. In college and on the job, it is important to be aware of the expectations and consequences of these and related issues. This knowledge is not just to avoid problems, but also to gain a better understanding of what it means to be a responsible member of a community.

Enjoy learning about codes of conduct on college campuses, as well as in the business world, as you develop your ability to identify and use written organizational patterns to improve your comprehension in reading. Find out more about codes of conduct in Module 1.

151

Organizational Patterns in Writing

In this chapter you will learn how to recognize and identify the organizational writing patterns used by authors. An **organizational pattern** refers to the way in which an author arranges the information and details he or she presents. Noticing and identifying different patterns will help you become a stronger reader. You will be better able to recognize main ideas, predict where the author is going, organize the information you are learning, and recall it later on. These are important tools for a college-level reader!

To understand organizational patterns in writing, it helps to think about the strategies people use every day to manage their lives or to communicate information. For example, you might ask your professor to explain the meaning of, or *define,* a term he has used in a lecture. Before starting a busy day, you might write a *list* of all the things you want to accomplish. Perhaps you put that list in a particular *sequence* or order to be sure you get to the most important items. Many of us tend to pay our bills by separating, or *classifying,* them into categories: Take care of this immediately, next pay these, save those for next month! Before you buy your next car, you are likely to visit several dealerships or websites and *compare* the features and prices of all the vehicles. When you are caught in an unexpected hailstorm on your way to school, you may wonder about the *cause* of the hailstorm and try to calm yourself as you experience its *effects* on your nerves: the hailstorm caused you to be late, and the hailstones have put several cracks in the windshield of your new car!

Writers use strategies like these to organize the information they present in their texts, especially in textbooks. However, whether fiction or nonfiction, informative or humorous, writers *define* terms, *list* items, *sequence* events, *categorize* or *classify* information, make *comparisons and contrasts,* and show *causes and effects.* Following is a list of the most common writing patterns, and a brief description of each.

Common Patterns of Organization

Definition	The author explains the meaning of new terms or concepts.
Listing or Enumeration	The author presents a list of items or concepts for which the order is *not* important.
Sequence	The author presents a series of events, items, or ideas in a particular order or time frame.
Classification	The writer breaks larger groups or topics into subgroups or categories.
Comparison and Contrast	The author shows how items or ideas are similar to one another and/or different from one another.
Cause and Effect	The author presents reasons for an event or condition and/or outcomes and results of an event.

You use these same patterns in your everyday life when you think and communicate, so they should be fairly easy to understand and remember.

try it and apply it! 6-1   Identifying Organizational Patterns

Directions: Fill in the organizational pattern in the spaces provided. Look at the preceding list of Common Patterns of Organization to help you complete the scenario.

Shana is entering her freshman year. She is very ethical and wants to be sure she has a thorough understanding of the meaning of the term *plagiarism*. Thus, she is after the complete _definition_ of it. She begins by writing down her plan in order, or _sequence_. She reads a chapter on plagiarism in a Freshman Experience textbook. She better understands what constitutes plagiarism after reading the various examples the author has _listed_, one after another, in the explanation. The author then describes the various kinds of plagiarism, by _classifying_ the examples into different categories. These include copying directly from a text, not using quotation marks or including citations, using the work of another student, and taking another person's ideas without giving them credit. Reading on, Shana learns what drives some students to plagiarize: what _causes_ someone to stoop to that level. She also finds out about the serious consequences, or _effects_, of plagiarizing. Finally, Shana reads through two sample papers, one containing correctly quoted and cited sources, and the other including plagiarized material and no documentation. By _comparing_ and _contrasting_ the two versions, Shana is better able to understand the meaning of plagiarism. She now is ready to research and write with the confidence that she will not be violating the college's code of conduct on plagiarism.

Organizational Patterns in Textbook Writing

Now that you have the general idea of how organizational patterns work, you can apply this knowledge to your reading. Identifying the organizational pattern an author is using helps you formulate the main idea of paragraphs and chapters and enhances your overall comprehension. As you learn about each pattern, you will also come to recognize clue words, called **signal words,** that suggest a particular writing pattern is being used.

The excerpts that follow are taken from texts written for college freshmen about college life and experiences.

Definition Pattern

Authors of textbooks know their readers are likely to be unfamiliar with the language they use and the concepts they discuss, so they will often **define,** or provide an explanation of, the meaning of new terms and ideas, both in the context of the writing as well as in sidebars and lists. Entire paragraphs may be devoted to defining a term or identifying a concept or idea. Thus, the main idea of an entire paragraph might, in fact, be a definition.

Signal Words and Phrases for Definitions

is
means
refers to
can be defined as
is called
also known as
which states that
or (followed by a synonym for the less familiar term)

Notice the signal words in the following sentences.

- The term **discrimination** *refers to* treating someone differently based on specific characteristics such as age, sex, or skin color.

- **Sexism** *is defined as* the belief that one gender or sex is **inferior,** *or* less valuable than the other.

- **Prejudice** *is* a negative feeling directed at a person or group based on pre- conceived opinions or judgments.

Punctuation is often used to signal that a definition is being provided. Notice how different punctuation marks are used to set off the definitions of the term *conduct* in the following examples.

- **Commas:** Colleges are concerned about student **conduct,** *the manner in which students behave in class and on campus.*

- **Dashes:** Jackson was brought before the dean of students because his **conduct**—the *behavior he exhibited in classes*—was deemed unaccept- able by all his professors.

- **Parentheses:** A recent national study on student **conduct** (*their modes of behavior on campuses*) was carried out to identify the most significant concerns among faculty.

- **Colon:** To get acquainted with college policies, it is important to read the Code of Conduct: *the standard for behavior on campus, which includes expectations, regulations, and consequences for violation of these rules.*

try it and apply it! 6-2   Practice with Definition

Directions: Read the following paragraphs. Underline any signal words or punctuation cues for definition. Then answer the questions.

A.   Sexual harassment in the workplace is a form of sex discrimination that violates the Civil Rights Act of 1964. It applies to employers with 15 or more employees, as well as employment agencies, labor organizations, and the federal government. Unwelcome sexual advances, requests for sexual favors, and other verbal or physical conduct of a sexual nature constitute sexual harassment when the conduct affects a person's employment, interferes with their work performance, or creates an intimidating, hostile, or offensive work environment.

(Adapted from The U.S. Equal Employment Opportunity Commission, Sexual Harassment, www.eeoc.gov/types/ sexual_harassment.html, 8/09)

1. What is the organizational pattern of the paragraph? *definition*

2. What term is being defined?
    sexual harassment in the workplace

3. What is the meaning of the term? *a form of sex discrimination that violates the Civil Rights Act, including unwanted sexual advances, requests for sexual favors, and verbal or physical conduct of a sexual nature when the conduct affects a person's employment, interferes with their work performance, or creates an intimidating, hostile, or offensive work environment*

HINT: To identify the main idea of the paragraph, combine the key term with its definition. Thus, the main idea is that *Sexual harassment in the workplace* (term being defined) *is a form of sex discrimination that violates the Civil Rights Act, including unwanted sexual advances, requests for sexual favors, and verbal or physical conduct of a sexual nature when the conduct affects a person's employment, interferes with their work performance, or creates an intimidating, hostile, or offensive work environment.* (definition).

(continued)

(continued)

B.　Profanity violates a moral code on campus. Profanity <u>refers to</u> cursing, swearing, or abusive speech. It is expected that students verbally, as well as behaviorally, conduct themselves with integrity.

1. What is the organizational pattern of the paragraph? *definition*
2. What term is being defined? *profanity*
3. What is the meaning of the term? *cursing, swearing, or abusive speech*
4. What is the main idea of the paragraph? *The main idea is that profanity, including cursing, swearing, or abusive speech, is a violation of a moral code on campus.*

C.　If you feel you are a victim of any kind of discrimination at work, including sexual harassment, there are several different paths you can take to file a complaint with the United States Equal Employment Opportunity Commission. Though the EEOC does not accept charges online or over the phone, you can begin the process this way. Online, you can access and fill out a questionnaire, which you can then print and use for the next step. Over the phone, you will be asked several questions and then sent follow-up paperwork to complete. You can also contact the agency directly by mail. Be sure to include information that identifies you and your employer, a description of the discriminatory event that tells where, when, and possibly why it occurred, your signature, and your contact information. If you prefer, you can also go directly to a local EEOC office and file a complaint in person. Each field office has its own procedures for appointments, so be sure to check before you go. Bring as much documentation with you as possible. You can also bring a friend.

(Source: www.eeoc.gov)

1. What is the organizational pattern of the paragraph? *listing*
2. What is the topic of the paragraph? *paths to file a complaint about discrimination at work*
3. What is the main idea of the paragraph? *There are several options you have for filing a complaint of discrimination.*
4. What are the four methods for initiating a complaint of discrimination offered by the EEOC? *online, by phone, through the mail, in person*

(**Note:** Just like in a math text, examples are provided to help you better understand the term being defined. Do not confuse the example with the definition and or/the main idea itself.)

Listing or Enumeration Pattern

Writers use the **listing or enumeration pattern** when their purpose is to identify a list of items, ideas, or concepts. The order in which they are presented is not significant. You can remember the items in any order; the important part is to note all the items included in the listing.

Sometimes an author will number items, label them *a, b, c,* and so on, or even use the words *first, second,* or *third* in a simple list. It is up to you, as the reader, to understand that those words or numbers are being used to organize the list but do not necessarily convey a particular order to the listing.

Signal Words and Phrases for Listing or Enumeration

and	last
also	in conclusion
another	there are
furthermore	a number of
additionally	three, five, etc.
in addition	many
first	several
second	various
third	ways
finally	

Numbers, bullets, and letters are often used to indicate the items in a list.

try it and apply it! 6-3   Practice with Listing or Enumeration

Directions: Read the following paragraphs. Be alert for a sentence, often the topic sentence, that identifies the list that is going to be presented. Highlight that sentence or write the title of the list in the margin. Underline any signal words for listing or enumeration. Annotate the items in the list by numbering them within the paragraph. Use your understanding of the list being presented to formulate the main idea.

Example

At Gering Community College, there is zero tolerance for any infraction of academic integrity. Cheating of any kind is unacceptable and students are responsible for knowing the behaviors that constitute cheating and/or plagiarism.

(continued)

(continued)

Plagiarism is portraying the work or words of another as one's own. This includes presenting the words of an author without proper citation or quotation, or downloading any or all portions of content material from online sources and presenting it as one's own. Cheating includes copying another student's paper or exam responses, or fabricating sources for papers. Cheating also includes using notes or texts of any kind during an exam when prohibited, or surreptitiously gleaning information from electronic sources such as a cell phone or digital device during an exam.

The topic of this paragraph is cheating or plagiarism. The second sentence in the paragraph is the topic sentence, identifying both the main idea of the paragraph, and the list that is being generated. The paragraph lists the behaviors that constitute cheating or plagiarism, so the predominant pattern is listing, or enumeration. If you haven't already done so, number the items in the list directly in the paragraph. That is the best way to annotate when you encounter a selection with a list. Now, from your annotation, complete the list that follows.

Behaviors That Constitute Cheating or Plagiarism

a. *cheating on a test*

b. *copying a student's paper or theme*

c. *copying an author's work without citing the source*

d. *making up false sources*

e. *downloading papers from the Internet and presenting them as one's own work*

f. *using cell phones or digital cameras during exams to get information*

A.   Sexual harassment in the workplace can occur in a variety of circumstances. The victim as well as the harasser can be a man or a woman. The victim doesn't have to be of the opposite sex. Interestingly, the victim does not have to be the person harassed, but could be anyone affected by the offensive conduct. Furthermore, unlawful sexual harassment may occur without economic injury to the victim, nor the firing of the victim. Lastly, the harasser's conduct must be unwelcome.

(Adapted from The U.S. Equal Employment
Opportunity Commission, www.eeoc.gov)

1. What is the organizational pattern of the paragraph? *listing or enumeration*

2. What is the topic of the paragraph? *circumstances for sexual harassment at work*

3. What is the main idea of the paragraph? *Sexual harassment can occur in a variety of circumstances in the workplace.*

4. Complete the following notes to identify the list embedded in the paragraph.

Circumstances of Sexual Harassment at Work

a. *victim or harasser can be a man or woman*

b. *victim can be of the same sex*

c. *victim can be anyone who is affected by the offensive conduct, not just the person who is harassed*

d. *harassment can occur without economic injury or getting fired*

e. *The harasser's conduct must be unwelcome.*

  B. A person committing sexual harassment on the job can be one of several individuals. The harasser might very well be the victim's supervisor, but not necessarily. The harasser could be an agent of the employer or even a supervisor in another area. A co-worker, on the victim's same level of employment, could be the harasser. Even a non-employee who enters the workplace could commit harassment.

(Adapted from U.S. Equal Employment Opportunity Commission, www.eeoc.gov)

1. What is the organizational pattern of the paragraph? *listing or enumeration*
2. What is the topic of the paragraph? *sexual harassers at work*
3. What is the main idea of the paragraph? *Many people can be considered as a harasser in the workplace.*
4. Complete the following notes to identify the list embedded in the paragraph.

Potential Harassers in the Workplace

a. *a supervisor or boss*

b. *an agent of the employer*

c. *a supervisor in another area*

d. *a co-worker*

e. *a non-employee*

  C. If you feel you are a victim of sexual harassment at work, there are several routes you can take to file a complaint. Don't keep it to yourself. One avenue is a hotline that is set up for such a purpose. Call it. Another option is to contact the human resources department within your company or institution. You may also want to speak to your boss or supervisor. As an employee, you should have the option of talking with a male or female company representative. It's always a good idea to document the harassment by writing down the incident or incidents.

(Adapted from *Sexual Harassment and Discrimination in the Workplace*, www.employer-employee.com/sexhar1.htm, 8/09)

1. What is the organizational pattern of the paragraph? *listing or enumeration*
2. What is the topic of the paragraph? *routes to take to file a complaint about sexual harassment*

(continued)

(continued)

3. What is the main idea of the paragraph? _You have several options for filing a_
   complaint of sexual harassment in the workplace.

4. Complete the following notes below to identify the list embedded in the paragraph.

Filing a Sexual Harassment Complaint at Work

a. *Call a hotline.*

b. *Contact the human resources department.*

c. *Speak with your boss or supervisor.*

d. *Talk with a male or female company representative.*

Sequence Pattern

As you read, you will come upon lists in paragraphs or selections in which the order of the items does matter very much. In that case, you would identify the writing pattern as one of **sequence**.

The order of items, or their sequence, can be arranged in several ways: chronological order, process order, spatial order, or order of importance.

Chronological Order   When events are listed according to the time they occurred, the writer is using a **chronological,** or time, **order.** Here the author wants you to understand the background or development of an event or concept. For example, how your college has grown and expanded over the years or the history of the advancements in health care would likely be presented in chronological order.

Signal Words and Phrases for Chronological Order

date (February 24, 1997)
times (6:00 p.m., 15 minutes, 2 years, a decade)
lasting for
beginning in
since
until
during
soon after
formerly
currently
presently

try it and apply it! 6-4   **Practice with Chronological Order**

Directions: Read the following paragraphs. Underline any signal words for chronological order. Then answer the questions.

A.   For <u>almost 40 years</u>, most states voluntarily set their minimum drinking age law at 21. Colleges put these laws into their codes of conduct. But at the height of the Vietnam War <u>in the early 1970s</u>, 29 states began lowering their drinking age to match the new military enlistment and voting age. Drinking ages varied from 18 to 20; they sometimes even varied based on the alcohol being consumed (e.g., 18 for beer, 20 for liquor). The results of this "experiment" were fairly immediate and hard to miss. The lowered drinking age caused an increase in alcohol traffic fatalities and injuries. As a result, <u>by 1983</u>, 16 states voluntarily raised their drinking age back to 21—a move that immediately decreased drinking and driving traffic fatalities incidents. Then, <u>on July 17, 1984</u>, President Reagan signed into law the Uniform Drinking Age Act that directed all states to make 21 the legal drinking age within five years. <u>By 1988</u>, the minimum drinking age was 21 in all states, which is where it should remain.

(Adapted from Brief History of the Drinking Age, www.why21.org/history)

Did you recognize that the predominant organizational pattern is sequence, and in particular, chronological sequence? Write five phrases that signaled the chronological order to you.

(continued)

(continued)

1. *for almost 40 years* _____
2. *in the early 1970s* _____
3. *by 1983* _____
4. *on July 17, 1984* _____
5. *by 1988* _____

Notice how you can use time order to help you find and state the main idea.

1. What is the organizational pattern of the paragraph? *sequence/chronological order*

2. What is the topic of the paragraph? *the drinking age*

3. What is the main idea of the paragraph? *Lowering the drinking age in the 1970s led to increased auto-related fatalities and injuries, throughout the 1980s all states eventually changed the minimum drinking age to 21.*

B.   Youth drinking rates have also declined since the Uniform Drinking Age law went into effect. The 2006 *Monitoring the Future* study shows American youth's alcohol consumption declining, although alcohol use continues to be widespread. The research on the minimum drinking age from 1960 to 2000 shows that establishing the age 21 minimum drinking age laws actually decreased underage consumption of alcohol. Even over the past 15 years, since the age 21 minimum drinking age laws were passed, the percentage of 8th, 10th, and 12th graders who report drinking alcohol in the past year decreased 38 percent, 23 percent, and 14 percent, respectively. These percentages show significant drops in teens' alcohol use in those grade levels.

(Adapted from Brief History of the Drinking Age, www.why21.org/history)

1. What is the organizational pattern of the paragraph? *sequence/chronological order*

2. What is the topic of the paragraph? *youth drinking rates*

3. What is the main idea of the paragraph? *Over the past 50 years, as the minimum drinking age has been lowered, the percentage of underage drinkers has declined.*

Process Order Pattern   Process order identifies the steps followed for an event or process. You see this organizational pattern often in the life sciences, where there are stages of development, or in government or at school, where there are procedures to follow. For example, during the registration period on campus, you may need to go through various procedures and steps, including meeting with an advisor, checking course availability, selecting courses, and paying the tuition bill.

Signal Words and Phrases for Process Order

first	after that	stages
second	subsequently	progressions
third	following	sequence
then	lastly	series
next	finally	continuum
finally	steps	

try it and apply it! 6-5   Practice with Process Order

Directions: Read the following paragraph. Circle any signal words for process order. Annotate the steps in the process by numbering them within the paragraph. Answer the questions that follow.

It is important that every business have a sexual harassment policy. If there is none to be found at your workplace, then you might get involved in helping to create one. The first step is to write a policy, clearly defining sexual harassment and identifying behaviors that constitute it. Be sure to include the

(continued)

(continued)

consequences for such actions, which should include termination of employment and possible legal or criminal charges. (At this point),[2] getting the advice of an attorney is often warranted. (Next), be sure to[3] make the policy known to all employees. It's even a good idea to[4] have everyone sign the policy. The policy can become part of an employee handbook, posted on bulletin boards, and mailed to all via email or sent through interoffice memo. (Additionally), be sure to[5] inform employees of the steps for dealing with harassment, including filing a sexual harassment complaint. (Finally), be sure [6] to review the policy, at least annually, with all employees.

(Some source information from www.ehow.com/print/ how_2140066_create-sexual-harassment-policy.html)

Recognizing that the predominant pattern here is sequential, with a focus on process, will help you formulate the main idea. The topic of the paragraph is the steps needed to create a sexual harassment policy at work. Thus, the main idea of the excerpt is several steps should be followed, in a specific order, to create a sexual harassment policy at work.

Briefly, paraphrase the steps in the following section. Use your annotations to help you.

Creating a Sexual Harassment Policy at Work

Step 1. *Write a sexual harassment policy.* _____

Step 2. *Have it reviewed by an attorney.* _____

Step 3. *Make the policy known to all employees.* _____

Step 4. *Have everyone sign it.* _____

Step 5. *Inform employees about dealing with harassment and filing complaints.* _____

Step 6. *Review the policy annually.* _____

Spatial Order Pattern   Writers use **spatial order** to describe the location of objects or items in relation to one another. It is often used in descriptive writing so that the reader can visualize a setting. For example, "Gazing at the shore from his rowboat in the center of the lake, Jake viewed the soft sands, black-topped by the cluster of trees, and the rolling hills in the far distance. . . ." You encounter spatial order in textbooks as well. For example, to identify the parts of the heart or locations of the different lobes of the brain, a spatial description might be included. When you study a map of your college campus to find the location of the physical education complex, you are thinking spatially.

Signal Words and Phrases for Spatial Order

above	lined up
below	linear
beneath	circular
to the left	separated by
to the right	leading to
behind	leading away from
adjacent to	next to
aligned	in a row

try it and apply it! 6-6   Practice with Spatial Order

Directions: Read the following paragraph. Try to visualize the locations, and their relationship to one another, as you read. Underline any signal words for spatial order. Then answer the questions.

Students should be aware of the "mixed company" visitation restrictions on campus in student living areas. The north side of each quadrangle on campus is reserved for male residence halls and the south side dorms are for women. Guests may not enter residence halls, lobbies, rest rooms, or living areas of the opposite sex on campus without written, authorized permission. Passes may be obtained from entry monitors at the reception desk. When visiting a residence hall of the opposite sex, guests are not permitted to go beyond the first floor lobby. This is the area just to the left and right of entry, and does not include areas beyond the doors within each space. The men's and the women's residence halls have visiting hours posted on the bulletin boards to the left of the reception desk, before reaching the elevators.

1. What is the topic of the paragraph? *the mixed company restrictions in residential areas on campus*

2. What is the main idea of the paragraph? *Students must be knowledgeable about the restrictions for visiting members of the opposite sex on campus and the locations that are permissible.*

(continued)

(continued)

3. Describe the only area in which visitation is permitted. <u>*It is in the lobby, just to the left and right of the entry and not beyond any other doors.*</u>

4. Where can one find the hours for visitation? <u>*On the bulletin boards just to the left of the reception desk, before the elevators.*</u>

Order of Importance Pattern   Sometimes items, reasons, or causes listed in a reading selection vary in their degree of significance, and writers use **order of importance** to indicate which is the most important item, the next most important, and so on. This organizational pattern appears often in essays or persuasive writing, as well as in textbooks. For example, there may be three primary reasons why students begin to drink alcohol at college, but one is the most important. Of four causes for students dropping out of college, one may occur the most often, another may be infrequent, and two may be somewhere in the middle. Authors generally present items in order of importance in the following two ways:

Descending order refers to moving from most important to least important.
Ascending order refers to moving from least important to most important.

Signal Words and Phrases for Order of Importance

most important	minor
least important	also
secondary	

try it and apply it! 6-7   **Practice with Order of Importance**   ⏸

Directions: The following paragraph discusses ways to avoid plagiarism. Based on the author's use of order of importance, can you rank these *from most important to least important?* Read the paragraph. Underline any signal words for order of importance, and number the recommendations. Then complete the chart that follows. There may be some variation in order after you get past the two points the writer considers most important.

    The best way to avoid plagiarism is to be very, very careful. Several guidelines can help you. <u>First of all</u>, be sure to keep accurate records as you are taking notes. Keep a record of

your sources. <u>Further</u>, learn effective methods of paraphrasing, or putting information into your own words. You need to do more than just rearrange the words and choose synonyms for them. Even when you do paraphrase, it is <u>also</u> necessary to cite the source of the facts or ideas that you are using. <u>Another</u> recommendation is not to rely on a single source. It's too easy to make use of the same wording and terminology without being aware of it. <u>Remember</u> to use quotation marks, even in your notes. Don't <u>forget</u> that you must cite the material you find on the Internet. <u>Toward the top of the list here</u> is that you never even think about buying a paper that someone is offering to sell. No, no, no! <u>Most importantly</u>, *always* cite the sources and distinguish between your ideas, quotations, and your paraphrases of other's ideas in your final presentation. Don't use anything you've written down in your notes until you identify the source.

(Adapted from Feldman 2009)

Guidelines for Avoiding Plagiarism

1. *Always cite the sources and distinguish between ideas, quotations, and paraphrasing in the final paper.*
2. *Never buy a paper online!*
3. *Cite material from the Internet.*
4. *Use quotations marks, even in notes.*
5. *Don't rely on only one source for a paper.*
6. *Learn how to paraphrase.*
7. *Cite even when you are paraphrasing.*
8. *Keep track of sources while taking notes.*

Classification Pattern

In many of your classes, you will find yourself learning the material by breaking larger topics into categories: this is called **classification.** The process is similar to the way you select courses for registration. There may be requirements that direct you to take classes within a certain category, such as the Arts and Humanities (which include English, Communication, and Drama), Mathematics (Calculus, Trigonometry, and Statistics), and the Physical Sciences (Astronomy and Physics). When you look through the course catalogue, you see that courses are not listed in random order; rather, they are subdivided into these major areas of study. Even within each major area, further subdivisions exist. For example, in English you will find literature classes. These can include French Literature, Literature about Women, or Novels of the Twentieth Century.

When an author identifies the categories of a larger entity, he or she is using the writing pattern of classification. Recognizing that the larger group is viewed or organized into subcategories will help you understand and identify the main point. Although an author may list the categories, it is important for you to understand that the key pattern is classification, and the list has been used to present categories and subcategories of the topic.

Signal Words and Phrases for Classification

groups
levels
kinds
categories
type
subsets
divided into
broken into
This can be divided into three categories . . .
There are four types of . . .
We can break this down into two major groups . . .

Charts are often used to explain classification and categories.

try it and apply it! 6-8   Practice with Classification

Directions: Read the following paragraphs. Note any signal words for classification. Circle major categories. Then, underline the subcategories within each major category. Answer the questions that follow.

A.   Jefferson College expects students to set high standards. Thus, proper behavior is expected in several major areas, including morality, personal habits and lifestyle choices, and social life. Under morality, it is important that students understand and obey the college's expectations regarding academic integrity, honesty, stealing, harassment, the use of profanity, and respect for privacy. In the area of personal habits, the school has strict rules regarding the use of alcohol and drugs, gambling, and tobacco products. It is expected that students adhere to our dress code that expects them to dress modestly, maintain a neat, well-groomed appearance, and wear proper attire during classes and labs. Because students are expected to demonstrate wholesome conduct at all times, the code of conduct regarding dating and social conduct must be reviewed and understood. This includes where and how students engage with one another, both on and off campus. It also speaks to visitation regulations within dormitories.

This paragraph opens by listing some general areas in which college policies have been set. It then moves on to identify more specific aspects of each area.

1. What is the organizational pattern of the paragraph? *classification*

2. What is the topic of the paragraph? *standards of behavior at Jefferson College*

3. What is the main idea of the paragraph? *There are several areas at Jefferson College in which standards of behavior have been set.*

4. List the major categories under which behavioral standards have been set. Next to each, write two examples of subcategories.

   a. *morality—stealing, honesty*

   b. *personal habits and lifestyle—alcohol/drugs and gambling*

   c. *social life—where and how students engage, visitation rules*

   B.   Should you feel that you have any of the symptoms that warn of an addiction to drugs or alcohol, you should seek professional help. Addictions to these substances are extremely difficult to deal with on your own. There are several paths of support you can consider. One is through the college. Most colleges provide services to help you overcome addiction. They include college health services, counseling centers, and mental health centers. Another area of support can be found within the community. Sometimes located in hospitals and sometimes independently run, drug treatment centers or clinics can provide help. You can also check for local listings for Alcoholics Anonymous or Narcotics Anonymous. A third venue of support is through government hotlines. The federal government provides extensive information about drug and alcohol use. You can visit the National Council on Alcoholism and Drug Dependence website at www.ncadd.org for help with alcohol and drug problems.

1. What is the organizational pattern of the paragraph? *classification*

2. What is the topic of the paragraph? *kinds of support for problems with drugs and alcohol*

3. What is the main idea of the paragraph? *There are three primary areas to turn to for problems with alcohol and drugs: college health services, local drug treatment centers and clinics, and government hotlines.*

Graphics, such as tables, charts, and semantic maps, are often used to depict the classification of a body of information. An image can clearly and simply present the key categories, subcategories, and important components or details of a larger idea or concept.

try it and apply it! 6-9   **Practice with Classification and Graphics**

Directions: Use the following chart to learn about the various types of illegal drugs, their street names, effects, and health hazards.

Illegal Drugs

Drug	Street Name	Effects	Withdrawal Symptoms/ Health Hazards
STIMULANTS **Cocaine** **Amphetamines** Benzedrine Dexedrine Methamphetamine	Coke, blow, snow lady, crack Speed Speed Meth	Increased confidence, mood elevation, sense of energy and alertness, decreased appetite, anxiety, irritability, insomnia, transient drowsiness, delayed orgasm	Apathy, general fatigue, prolonged sleep, depression, disorientation, suicidal thoughts, agitated motor activity, irritability, bizarre dreams
DEPRESSANTS **Alcohol** **Barbiturates** Nembutal Seconal Phenobarbital **Rohypnol**	Booze Yellowjackets, yellows Reds Roofies, rope, "date-rape drug"	Anxiety reduction, impulsiveness, dramatic mood swings, bizarre thoughts, suicidal behavior, slurred speech, disorientation, slowed mental and physical functioning, limited attention span Muscle relaxation, amnesia, sleep	Weakness, restlessness, nausea and vomiting, headaches, night-mares, irritability, depression, acute anxiety, hallucinations, seizures, possible death Seizures
NARCOTICS **Heroin** **Morphine**	H, hombre, junk, smack, dope, crap, horse Drugstore dope, cube, first line, mud	Anxiety and pain reduction, apathy, difficulty in concentration, slowed speech, decreased physical activity, drooling, itching, euphoria, nausea	Anxiety, vomiting, sneezing, diarrhea, lower back pain, watery eyes, runny nose, yawning, irritability, tremors, panic, chills and sweating, cramps

HALLUCINOGENS
Cannabis
  Marijuana
  Hashish
  Hash oil
 	
MDMA
 	
LSD
	Bhang, kit, ganja, dope, grass, pot, smoke, hemp, joint, weed, bone, Mary Jane, herb, tea
	
	Ecstasy
	
	Acid, quasey, microdot, white lightning
		Euphoria, relaxed inhibitions, increased appetite, disoriented behavior
		
		Heightened sense of oneself and insight, feelings of peace, empathy, energy
		
		Heightened aesthetic responses, vision and depth distortion, heightened sensitivity to faces and gestures, magnified feelings, paranoia, panic, euphoria
			Hyperactivity, insomnia, decreased appetite, anxiety
			
			Depression, anxiety, panic attacks
			
			Anxiety, depression, flashbacks

(Feldman 2009, 407)

1. What are the four major types of illegal drugs shown in the chart?
    stimulants, depressants, narcotics, and hallucinogens

2. What are three kinds of depressants? *alcohol, barbiturates, and rohypnol*

3. Name three types of barbiturates. *nembutal, seconal, and phenobarbital*

4. What type of drug tends to create euphoria and relaxed inhibitions?
    cannabis

5. What type of drugs may cause seizures ? *rohypnols or roofies*

6. What are the health hazards of ecstasy? *depression, anxiety, and panic attacks*

7. On the following lines, write three questions of your own that could be answered by "reading" the chart. Share these with your classmates.

Responses will vary.

Comparison and Contrast Pattern

Authors often want you to understand the relationships among topics and ideas. One way they do this is by highlighting comparisons and contrasts.

Comparisons are similarities or likenesses. **Contrasts** show differences. Thus, the **comparison and contrast pattern** in writing emphasizes likeness and differences between two or more concepts, events, or ideas. If only similarities are noted, you might say the pattern is entirely comparison. If only differences are discussed, the pattern is contrast.

For example, a college experience textbook discussing diversity might point out how students from different cultures on campus are still, surprisingly, very much alike. A section on different types of degree programs might point out the similarities and differences between two- and four-year schools.

Signal Words and Phrases for Comparison

similarly	both	less than
likewise	same	more important
along the same vein	more than	less important

Comparisons are also indicated by adding endings to descriptive words, such as happ*ier*, bigg*er* than, small*er* than, the wis*est,* and so on.

Signal Words and Phrases for Contrast

on the contrary	unlike
in contrast	opposite
in opposition	opposed
however	different
nevertheless	pro and con
whereas	support and refute
although	advantages and disadvantages
on the other hand	strengths and weaknesses
while	benefits and problems

try it and apply it! 6-10   Practice with Comparison and Contrast

Directions: Read the following paragraphs. Underline any signal words for comparison and contrast. Try to identify the main idea by noting the comparison and contrast pattern in the writing.

A.   In keeping with the belief that the body is an important and sacred entity, both alcohol and drugs have no place in the life of college students. Consequences for their use will be dealt with similarly. We are a drug-free and alcohol-free work and educational environment. The possession and/or use of intoxicating beverages and illegal drugs is strictly prohibited. Students may not engage in drinking, handling, possessing, or giving away intoxicants including beer, wine, ale, etc. Likewise, the possession and/or use of drugs not prescribed by a physician or the possession of drug paraphernalia is strictly prohibited. Violation of these restrictions will result in the same penalty: automatic suspension from the college. Students will not be reinstated for at least the remainder of the semester.

1. This is a paragraph of comparison. What is being compared in this paragraph? *the penalties for possession or use of both illegal drugs and alcohol on the campus*

2. What is the main idea of the paragraph? *The penalties for using or possessing both illegal drugs or any kind of alcoholic beverages are the same at the college, an automatic suspension for a least one semester.*

The next paragraphs present different interpretations of the same situation. Read them to identify the topic of the selection and the overall point. Underline the writing pattern signal words and notice the predominant organizational pattern. This will help you formulate the main idea and answer the questions that follow.

The Case of the Opposing Perspectives

B.   It started out innocently, as a date to study for an exam. However, it turned wrong. Here is what Bob had to say:
"Patty and I were in the same statistics class. She usually sat near me and was always very friendly. I liked her and thought maybe she liked me too. Last Thursday I suggested that she come to my place to study for midterms together. She agreed immediately.
That night everything seemed to go perfectly. We studied for a while and then took a break. I could tell that she liked me, and I was attracted to her. I started kissing her. She seemed to really like it. We started touching each other and it felt really good. Suddenly she pulled away and said, "Stop." I figured she didn't want me to think that she was easy or loose. I just ignored her

protests and eventually she stopped struggling. I think she liked it, <u>but</u> afterwards she acted bummed out and cold."

Patty, <u>on the other hand</u>, had a <u>very different</u> view of their encounter. Here is what she said:

"I knew Bob from my statistics class. He's cute and we are both good at statistics, so when a tough midterm was scheduled, I was glad that he suggested we study together. It never occurred to me that it was anything except a study date. Everything went well at first. We got a lot of studying done in a short time. When he suggested we take a break I thought we deserved it.

Well, all of a sudden he started acting romantic and began kissing me. I liked the kissing, <u>but</u> then he started touching me below the waist. I pulled away and tried to stop him <u>but</u> he didn't listen. After a while I stopped struggling. He was hurting me and I was scared. He was so much bigger and stronger than I. I couldn't believe it was happening to me. I didn't know what to do. He actually forced me to have sex with him. Looking back, I should have screamed or done something besides trying to reason with him, but it was so unexpected. I couldn't believe it was happening."

(Adapted from Feldman, *Power Learning*, p. 419)

1. What is the organizational pattern of the excerpt? <u>*comparison and contrast*</u>

2. What is the topic of the excerpt? <u>*how Bob and Patty viewed the same situation*</u>
   differently, perhaps the topic of date rape

3. What is the main idea of the excerpt? *A woman and a man had very different*
   interpretations of their sexual encounter when they had gotten together to study for an exam.

4. What is one set of contrasting points of view presented in this selection?
   Answers will vary.

Graphics, such as charts, tables, and graphs are often used to visually illustrate how factors compare and contrast.

try it and apply it! 6-11   Practice with Comparison and Contrast and Graphics ⏸

A. Directions: Look at the bar graph titled "Percentage of Adults Ages 25–64 Who Have Completed Higher Education, 2007." Refer to it to answer the questions that follow.

1. In what way are the percentages being compared? *They are being compared*
   according to the countries the adults are from.

2. Which country has the largest percentage of adults who have completed a college education? *the United States*

(*continued*)

(continued)

Percentage of Adults Ages 25-64 Who Have Completed Higher Education, 2007

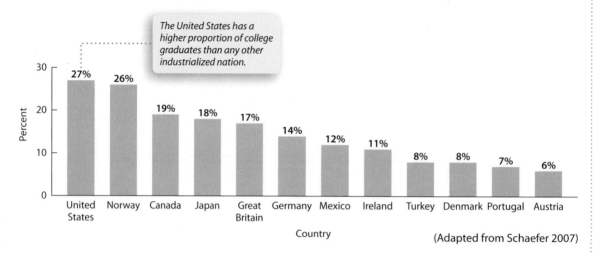

The United States has a higher proportion of college graduates than any other industrialized nation.

(Adapted from Schaefer 2007)

3. In which country is the percentage the lowest? *Austria*

4. What interesting bit of information do you learn about the United States in the note provided? *The United States has a higher proportion of college graduates than any other industrialized nation.*

5. What overall conclusion can you draw from these comparisons? *The United States is the most highly educated industrialized nation.*

B. Directions: The following bar graph compares and contrasts the percentages of students who were binge drinkers in 2001. Look at it carefully and then answer the questions that follow.

Percentage of students who were binge drinkers in 2001

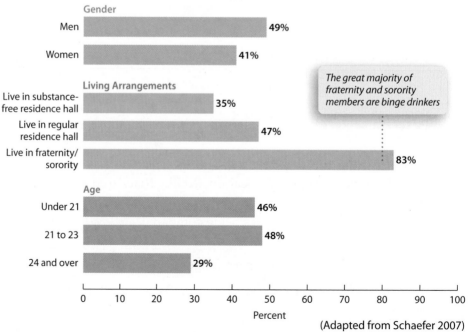

The great majority of fraternity and sorority members are binge drinkers

(Adapted from Schaefer 2007)

1. In what three general areas are the comparisons being made?
   according to gender, living arrangements, and age

2. In what living arrangement was there the greatest amount of binge drinking? *sorority and fraternity houses*

3. Which gender had the greater amount of binge drinking? *men*

4. What age group had the highest amount of binge drinking? *21–23*

5. What occurred as the students got older? *The amount of binge drinking declined.*

Cause and Effect Pattern

When a writer wants to help you understand the reasons something happened or the results of an event, he or she will use a **cause and effect writing pattern.** You might read about the events (*causes*) leading up to a student withdrawing from college, global warming, or poverty in the inner city, or you might read about the results (*effects*) of binge drinking, being sexually harassed, or violating the code of conduct.

Signal Words and Phrases for Cause

reason	is due to
cause	results from
creates	leads to
because	

Signal Words and Phrases Used for Effect

effect	consequence	thus
result	leads to	therefore
outcome	resulted in or from	consequently
response	created	as a result

try it and apply it! 6-12   Practice with Cause and Effect

Directions: Read the following paragraphs. Underline any signal words for cause and effect. Then answer the questions.

A.   Why is it important to be concerned about alcohol and other drug use on campuses? Far too often, alcohol and other drug use leads to tragedy. Deaths resulting from alcohol poisoning and from alcohol-related incidents have occurred on all types of

(continued)

(*continued*)

campuses in recent years. Use and abuse of these substances is a factor in many accidents, injuries, vandalism, and crime on campuses. It is frequently a causal factor when students encounter problems with their course work.

(Adapted from Alcohol and Drug Use on College Campuses, www.yesican.gov/drugfree/alcabuse.html, 8/11/09)

1. What is the organizational pattern of the paragraph? *cause and effect*
2. What is the topic of the paragraph? *results of alcohol and drug abuse on campus*
3. What is the main idea of the paragraph? *Alcohol and drug use on college campuses causes negative, sometimes tragic results.*

4. Some of the results of substance abuse on campus mentioned by the author include
    a. *alcohol poisoning*
    b. *death*
    c. *accidents*
    d. *injuries*
    e. *vandalism and crime*
    f. *problems with course work*

    B.   Furthermore, penalties for plagiarism are severe. In many colleges, plagiarism results in a comment on your transcript or can result in expulsion. You could even face legal charges because almost all published material is copyrighted, which means that it is someone's *intellectual property:* It is legally owned by the writer, and/or the publisher, of the published material. If an author learns that you have used his or her writing as your own, the author has the right to take you to court and sue for damages.

(Feldman 2009)

1. What is the organizational pattern of the paragraph? *cause and effect*
2. What is the topic of the paragraph? *the consequences of plagiarism*
3. What is the main idea of the paragraph? *There are several severe consequences or penalties for plagiarizing.*

Mixed Patterns

Your goal in recognizing writing patterns is not just to "label" paragraphs but to help you understand the content and most important points. Indeed, many paragraphs use more than one writing pattern to make a point. Yes, one may be dominant, but keep your eyes open for others as well. As you recognize them, you will be able to identify additional important points of information.

   For example, although the dominant pattern in the preceding paragraph was cause and effect, the author inserted an element of definition by introducing the term *intellectual property* in his explanation.

try it and apply it! 6-13   **Practice with Mixed Patterns**

Directions: The following paragraph is about academic dishonesty. It is a good example of a paragraph that opens with one pattern but concludes with another. Read it to see if you can identify the major patterns that are used. Answer the questions that follow.

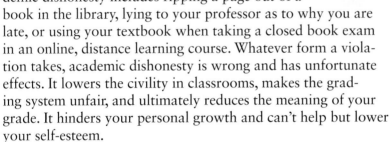

Academic honesty is one of the foundations of civility in the classroom as well as in society. Unless the work you turn in under your own name is your work, you are guilty of academic dishonesty. Violations of academic honesty take many forms. They may involve plagiarism, copying another's work and passing it off as your own. They may also include using a calculator when it's not allowed, discussing the answers to a question, copying a computer file when it's unauthorized, taking an exam for another person, or stealing an exam. Academic dishonesty includes ripping a page out of a book in the library, lying to your professor as to why you are late, or using your textbook when taking a closed book exam in an online, distance learning course. Whatever form a violation takes, academic dishonesty is wrong and has unfortunate effects. It lowers the civility in classrooms, makes the grading system unfair, and ultimately reduces the meaning of your grade. It hinders your personal growth and can't help but lower your self-esteem.

(Adapted from Feldman 2009)

1. In the beginning of the paragraph, the author identifies several examples of academic dishonesty. The primary organizational pattern here is: <u>listing</u>

2. Midway through the paragraph, the author says, "Whatever form a violation takes, academic dishonesty is wrong and has unfortunate effects." This signals to you that the writer is shifting to the pattern of: <u>cause and effect</u>

3. Combine these two patterns to complete the following sentence to identify the main idea of the paragraph.

   Violations of academic honesty come in <u>many different forms</u>, but whatever the form, it is <u>wrong</u> and has many unfortunate <u>consequences, effects, outcomes, or results</u>

4. List at least three examples of academic dishonesty. <u>Answers will vary.</u>
   <u>plagiarism, cheating on an exam, copying a computer file, stealing an exam</u>

5. Identify at least two results of academic dishonesty stated by the author.
   <u>Answers will vary. Reduces the civility of a classroom, reduces the meaning of grades, lowers self-esteem, hinders personal growth</u>

keep this in mind

Organizational Patterns in Writing

Pattern	Purpose	Signal Words	Helpful Hints
Definition	Explore the meaning of new terms or concepts	*is, means, refers to, is defined as, is called, is known as, or, which states, that*	Terms in textbooks are often boldface, italicized, or set apart by punctuation.
Listing or Enumeration	Present a list of items or ideas for which the order is not important	*and, also, another, further, furthermore, additionally, firstly, next, last in conclusion*	Items may be numbered, though numbers do not signify a specific order. Writers also often use bullets or letters to enumerate.
Sequence	Presents a series of events, items, or ideas in a particular order		Some signal words are interchangeable and may indicate more than one type of sequence.
■ **Chronological**	Organized according to time	dates, times—*lasting for, since, beginning in, until, during, soon after, formerly, currently, presently*	Knowing the actual sequence of details is critical to understanding the main idea of a piece.
■ **Process**	Organized according to the steps or stages followed	*first, second, third, then, now, after that, subsequently, following, lastly, steps, stages, progressions, sequence, series, continuum*	Numbering items within your annotation of text is very helpful.
■ **Spatial**	Organized according to position "in space" to show location or objects in relation to one another	*above, below, beneath, next to, adjacent to, to the left/right, aligned, behind, circular, separated by, leading away, in a row*	
■ **Order of Importance**	Organized according to value from most important to least important or vice versa	*most/least important, most/least significant, minimal/maximum value*	
Classification	Break larger categories into subcategories	*several groups, many types, kinds, subsets, categories, families*	For studying, it helps to transfer narrative text of classification to a graph or other visual organizer.
Comparison	Show how items or ideas are similar to one another	*similarly, likewise, along the same lines, both, this, too*	

Contrast	Show how items are different from one another	*on the contrary, however, in contrast, in opposition, unlike, although, however, whereas, on the other hand, unlike*	"Opposite" listings signal contrast (that is, *pro and con, advantages and disadvantages, support and refute, positives and negatives, in favor of and opposed to*).
Cause and Effect	Identify reasons or motives for an event or condition and/or the outcomes and results of an action or event	*reasons, causes, because, is due to, leads to, creates, motivates, because of, is due to results from, the effect, the results, the responses, the outcomes, the findings, the consequences*	Causes and effects may be "listed"; be aware of the more important pattern that focuses on causes and/or effects.

Chart the Course: Identifying and Integrating Writing Patterns

- ■ **Recognizing organizational patterns will help you discover an author's purpose for writing:** to provide the definition or meaning of terms, list items, sequence items or events in a particular order, classify information, compare and contrast ideas or items, explain causes and/or results.

- ■ **Knowing the patterns will support your comprehension and help you formulate the main ideas of a reading.**

- ■ **Realizing that writers often provide examples to help explain can help you identify the main idea.** Sometimes, the examples are key details for you to learn. More often, the examples are there to help you understand key points or new terms.

- ■ **Do not assume a paragraph or selection is primarily organized in a listing pattern just because it includes lists or because points of information are presented one after the other.** Try to dig deeper to recognize the purpose of the writing and what the author wants you to know.

Key Terms

ascending order
cause and effect writing pattern
chronological order
classification
comparison and contrast pattern
comparisons
contrasts
define

descending order
listing or enumeration pattern
organizational pattern
order of importance
process order
sequence
signal words
spatial order

7

You Be the Judge
Becoming a Critical Reader

In this chapter

you will learn to

- Make inferences
- Determine the author's purpose for writing
- Consider the audience
- Distinguish fact from opinion
- Detect the writer's tone
- Recognize bias in writing
- Evaluate the author's argument
- Identify and interpret figurative language

Develop Skills While Reading About
Relationships

College is a place to develop your intellectual skills, broaden your understanding of the world, immerse yourself in major areas of study, and prepare for a career. However, when most college graduates look back on their college years, it is the relationships they formed there that often matter most and that they remember the best.

For many, college opens up a new world of personal connections. You constantly meet new people. You interact with fellow students, professors, advisors, counselors, and campus personnel. Likely, your college is more diverse than your high school. The interactions you have with your professors are on a different level than those you had with your high school teachers; they are adult-to-adult.

Some of the relationships you form while in college may become very significant in your life. Perhaps, you will find a best friend, boyfriend or girlfriend, spouse, or life partner.

Your college years offer you an opportunity to develop social skills that will help you in your future relationships. You will experience different styles of interacting, whether in the cafeteria, in your classroom, on the field, or at the workplace. Hopefully, you will leave college as a stronger communicator, a better team player, and a more effective conflict and stress manager.

This chapter presents reading excerpts and selections that reflect a variety of relationship experiences, from friendship to marriage and from conflict to divorce. Learn a little more about relationships as you develop your skills in critical reading. Find out more about relationships in Module 8.

Being a Critical Reader

Every day, we are bombarded with advertisements, news stories, scientific research, and websites, to name a few sources of information. How can we tell what is true? Should we take all this information at face value, or should we question the source, the motives of those presenting it, and the implications of the arguments it contains? Active and engaged thinkers evaluate everything they learn from these sources and arrive at their own conclusions based on the evidence.

This is also true of critical readers. Critical readers do not take everything they read as statements of fact. They are active and thinking readers who go beyond understanding the literal meaning of a selection to arrive at thoughtful conclusions based on the evidence. While reading, they make inferences, determine the author's purpose for writing, distinguish between facts and opinions, detect the tone of the writing, recognize the author's point of view or bias, evaluate arguments, and make sense out of figurative language.

Based on the information that is gathered or gleaned from a reading, critical readers discover the answers by themselves and draw their own conclusions about what is stated.

Making Inferences

An **inference** involves using what you already know in order to choose the most likely explanation from the facts or information at hand. You make inferences all the time in your daily life. If you observe a wet floor in your kitchen, for example, you might conclude that a leak exists or that something has spilled.

Here's another situation where inference skills are called into play: With the widespread use of cell phones today, it's not unusual to hear just one side of a conversation. Very often, a person standing nearby can make inferences about to whom the speaker is talking, what the speaker is talking about, what the other person is saying, and how both the caller and receiver of the call are feeling.

Imagine you are standing outside the cafeteria, and you overhear the following conversation. The speaker is a casually dressed male student. He is constantly running his fingers through his hair as he speaks.

"I don't know why I did it."

"She doesn't mean a thing to me. It was a stupid mistake. I offered her a ride home from school, and things went from there."

"Of course, I care about your feelings."

"You didn't give me a chance to explain."

"I'll make it up to you. Please give me another chance."

Think about the answers to the following questions. They will help you make inferences about the one side of the conversation you heard.

1. To whom is the speaker talking?
2. How does the young man feel?
3. How does the other person feel?
4. What has he done?
5. Why is he sorry?
6. What does he want the other person to say?
7. What does the other person say?

Did you figure out that the guy is talking to his girlfriend? The young man is nervous—he is running his fingers through his hair—about being confronted by his girlfriend because she found out he cheated on her (sentences 1, 2, and 3). He apologizes and wants to explain why he was unfaithful, and he begs her forgiveness. But she won't listen to him (sentence 4). Does his girlfriend seem to be understanding? Do you think she forgives him?

Now see if you can fill in the missing lines from the preceding dialogue, and write them below.

He: I don't know why I did it.

She: *Answers will vary.*

He: She doesn't mean a thing to me. It was a stupid mistake. I offered her a ride home from school, and things went from there.

She: _____

_____

He: Of course, I care about your feelings.

She: _____

_____

He: You didn't give me a chance to explain.

She: _____

_____

He: I'll make it up to you. Please give me another chance.

She: _____

_____

Making inferences based on what you read utilizes a similar reasoning process. You use your prior knowledge to conclude what an author is saying, *but not directly stating,* based on the information that is presented. In a sense, you are *reading between the lines* when you make inferences. You have already used inferential thinking in Chapter 3, when you used context clues to make inferences about the meanings of new and unfamiliar words, and again in Chapter 4, when you formulated the implied main idea based on the details provided. When you read, apply the following thinking strategies to help you make accurate inferences:

- Be sure to understand the literal meaning of the text.
- Notice the author's choice of details and examples.
- Think about what the details and examples "add up to."
- Consider what may have been omitted, or left out.
- Draw a conclusion based on the information or data that is presented. Don't "jump to conclusions" without that evidence!
- Check the accuracy of your inference by reviewing the material. Think about the logic of your conclusion based on the information that is presented.

Read the following sentences, which introduce the topic of establishing relationships and communicating with advisors and faculty. Think about the inferences that you can draw about the author's views based on the information included in each sentence.

Example 1

Develop relationships with your instructors and advisors, just as you would with your supervisors at work.

Think about your role with supervisors at work and compare it to developing a relationship with your instructors or advisors. Based on this sentence, you might have inferred that you should:

- develop a professional relationship
- be respectful

- exhibit a positive attitude
- be responsible and accountable for your actions

Example 2

> In general, the job of a college advisor is to give you guidance about the registration process, course selection, and graduation requirements.

From this sentence, you may have inferred that college advisors will be able to provide you with guidance about

- what classes to take
- how to select a major
- which courses will fulfill requirements of selected majors
- how to create a schedule
- how to complete your degree for graduation

When making inferences, be careful not to go beyond what is stated. If you do, you will be making an **assumption,** or accepting a statement as true without evidence to support it. For example, based on Example 2, it would be inaccurate to infer that a college advisor would provide information about

- where you can find out information about extracurricular activities and clubs
- where to get a job on campus
- how to apply for financial aid

Keep this in mind

Remember to draw conclusions and make inferences *based on what is stated*, not based on your own opinions or attitudes. Check back in the text to verify or locate information that supports your conclusions, and don't make assumptions based on your opinions. Ask yourself if your inference is logical and reasonable. When you do this, your inferences are more likely to be accurate and valid.

try it and apply it! 7-1 Practice with Inferences in Sentences

Directions: Read the following sentences. Think about the inferences you can draw about the author's view based on the information included. Several possible inferences are listed after each sentence. Underline *all* the inferences that are valid based on the information that is stated in the sentence. You might want to work with a classmate to verify which are the valid inferences.

(continued)

(continued)

1. Advisors are particularly busy during the beginning of each term, as well as when the course schedule comes out. (Adapted from Feldman 2009)

   a. The beginning of the semester is a good time to show up without an appointment.

   b. Advisors are not available to see students after the semester begins.

   c. It's always a good idea to make an appointment with your advisor, especially during advisement periods and the start of each semester.

   d. Advisors are never too busy to see students.

2. Never go unprepared to an appointment with your college advisor. (Adapted from Feldman 2009)

   a. Bring all your textbooks with you when you meet with your advisor.

   b. Compile a list of some of the courses you plan to take.

   c. Always bring your parents or a good friend along with you.

   d. Read through the college catalogue before you meet with your advisor to find out about different majors.

3. No matter how helpful your advisor is (or unsupportive, for that matter), remember that *you* are ultimately responsible for your academic career. (Feldman 2009)

   a. If you are not happy with a course you are taking, you shouldn't blame your advisor.

   b. If you don't like your advisor, you can select another one.

   c. Take responsibility for your own learning.

   d. The job of a counselor is to ensure and facilitate your academic success.

4. Some colleges discourage personal relationships between students and faculty.

   a. You can meet your professor off campus for lunch.

   b. You should meet with your professor in his or her office.

   c. You should develop a professional relationship with your instructor.

   d. You can call faculty at home.

5. Most instructors will provide you with extra help if you take the initiative. (Ferrett 2010)

   a. They might give you feedback on your assignments if you ask.

   b. They will ask you if you need help.

   c. They will always be available to help you review for exams during their office hours.

   d. They will expect you to approach them for assistance.

6. Instructors are more supportive of students who come to class regularly, show responsibility, and stand out in class.

    a. <u>If you always arrive late to class, teachers will be less willing to provide you with extra help.</u>

    b. <u>If you hand in assignments on time, you can usually depend on your teachers for additional assistance.</u>

    c. Only instructors can provide extra help in course work.

    d. Students who show obvious interest in class can always count on their professors to provide them with individual tutoring sessions.

7. A coach or an instructor might be willing to serve as your mentor, one who is a role model, supports your goals, and takes an interest in your personal and professional development.

    a. <u>He or she might become your advisor.</u>

    b. <u>He or she might help you find an internship off campus.</u>

    c. <u>He or she may inquire about any personal situations that impact your college success.</u>

    d. <u>He or she might be able to guide you in making career choices.</u>

8. When emailing your advisor, professor, or mentor for assistance, don't forget to use the proper etiquette—rules of behavior—common in face-to-face communication. (Adapted from Ferret 2010)

    a. <u>Be polite.</u>

    b. <u>Use proper greetings.</u>

    c. It is not necessary to say "Thank you."

    d. The use of slang is permissible.

9. Although you may be used to text messaging in lowercase letters, proper email etiquette calls for writing email to college faculty the same way you would write a business memo. (Adapted from Ferrett 2010)

    a. Write your entire message in capital letters.

    b. Include emoticons to express your emotions and feelings.

    c. <u>Use a spell checker before sending.</u>

    d. <u>Reread the email at least once.</u>

10. Learning how to form bonds with your advisors, instructors, and classmates will make you successful in college, at work, and in personal relationships.

    a. <u>Building rapport with others in college will help you forge better relationships with friends and family.</u>

    b. It will help you get a raise at your job.

    c. <u>You will have better relationships with co-workers and supervisors.</u>

    d. You will get better grades.

try it and apply it! 7-2 **Practice with Inferences in Paragraphs** ⏸

Directions: Read the following paragraphs. Think about the inferences you can draw about the author's view based on the information included. Several possible inferences are listed after each paragraph. Underline *all* the inferences that are valid based on the information that is stated.

1. Few of us lead our lives in isolation. There's a reason for this: Relationships with others are a significant component of our sense of well-being. The help of friends and relatives helps us feel good about ourselves. In fact, studies have found that our physical and psychological health may suffer without relationships. For example, people who have friends recuperate faster from illnesses than those who do not.

(Adapted from Feldman 2009)

   a. Having relationships contributes to the establishment of self-esteem.
   b. Relationships are important to both our physical and emotional health.
   c. With the assistance of friends and family, illnesses can be cured without medical intervention.
   d. If we do get sick, we get better faster if we have a supportive network of friends and family.

2. Our relationships with others also help us understand who we are. To understand our own abilities and achievements, we compare them with those of others who are like ourselves. Our attitudes, beliefs, and values are influenced—and shaped—by others.

   a. We are who we are largely because of the people with whom we come in contact.

   b. Our parents shape our lives.

   c. Our classmates help shape our lives, too.

   d. When we compare our achievements with others like ourselves, we may also understand our own shortcomings.

3. Making friends requires you to accept others as they are, not as you would like them to be. Do not impose conditions on accepting others. Keep in mind that no one is perfect and that everyone has good and bad qualities. (Adapted from Feldman 2009)

   a. You don't have to accept a friend's flaws.

   b. Select your friends based on their good qualities.

   c. Don't be afraid to tell your friends about the qualities that you do not like.

   d. You should not expect your friends to change for you.

4. Not everyone makes a good friend. People who put you down consistently or behave in ways that violate your personal standards are not friends. Choose your friends based on the good feelings you have when you are with them and the concern and care that they show you. Friendship is a two-way street.

   a. Try to be friends with all those you encounter.

   b. You should abandon friendships that make you feel bad about yourself.

   c. If you want your friends to be nice to you, you should also act kindly to them.

   d. Be accepting of a friend's criticism because he or she is concerned about you.

5. A college roommate is not always a friend. Nevertheless, it is important to create an open environment for communicating needs, problems, and solutions. Don't mope or whine about a grievance or leave nasty notes. Communicate honestly and kindly. It's important that you understand each other's views and expectations and try to work out conflicts. (Adapted from Ferrett 2010)

   a. It is not advisable to make friends with your college roommate.

   b. Maintain a friendly and cordial relationship with your college roommate.

   c. If your roommate likes to have the dishes done after each meal, try to comply with his or her wishes.

   d. Look for a new roommate if you can't resolve your conflicts.

Determining an Author's Purpose for Writing

To completely understand and evaluate what you read, it is important to determine the author's **purpose**, or reason, for writing. This information will provide greater insight into what you are reading and will alert you as to whether you should question the material. The four primary purposes for writing are to

- inform
- instruct
- entertain
- persuade

Depending on their purpose, authors use different kinds of language to express their thoughts. They may choose to include or omit information, and the tone or mood of their writing will also vary. A good question to ask yourself to determine an author's purpose for writing is, "Why did the author write this? To inform me about something? To teach me how to do something? To amuse or entertain me? To persuade or convince me about an action or an issue?"

Writing to Inform

Most textbooks are written with the purpose of informing college students about a particular discipline. Newspaper and magazine articles and entries in reference books are written to inform as well. Some nonfiction writing is also intended to familiarize readers about subjects as varied as the lives of famous people, significant historical events, and developments in technology. Generally, this type of nonfiction writing presents information in an unbiased and objective manner, without the inclusion of the writer's opinion. Here is an example:

> Sociologists and other social scientists have begun to consider the impact of technology on socialization, especially as it applies to family life. The Silicon Valley Cultures Project studied families in California's Silicon Valley (a region with a large technology industry) for 10 years beginning in 1991. The researchers are finding that families are socialized into multitasking (doing more than one task at a time) as the social norm; devoting one's full attention to one task—even eating or driving—is less and less common on a typical day.
>
> (Adapted from Schaefer 2007)

Writing to Instruct

In college, you are also likely to encounter material written with the purpose of instructing you in how to do something. For example, a biology laboratory manual guides you through a process of study or experimentation; a math textbook teaches you how to do equations; and a freshman composition book instructs you on the writing process. Similar writing is found in cookbooks and in "how-to" magazine articles. In writing to instruct, the sequence of steps involved in a process is often important, so it is advisable to read through all the steps or procedures in a process before beginning a specific task. Here is an example:

The Six Steps to Strategic Flexibility

Strategic flexibility means that you use your repertoire of communication behaviors to best address a particular situation. Suppose you are in an unfamiliar situation. You will not find yourself in an uncomfortable position if you draw upon the best skills you have already learned. This is a characteristic of effective leaders and participants. The first step is to anticipate or think about potential situations and requirements that might arise from them. Second, assess the factors, elements, and conditions of the situations in which you find yourself. Third, evaluate the value of these factors and determine how they might have an impact on your skills and abilities. Fourth, carefully select the most appropriate skills and behaviors that will be used. Fifth, apply relevant skills. Finally, reassess your actions based on your own observations and feedback from others.

(Adapted from Hybels and Weaver II 2009)

Writing to Entertain

Authors write novels, short stories, and essays to entertain and encourage their readers to think about things in new ways. They may amuse you and make you laugh, or shock you and make you cry. This type of writing can stimulate your imagination, impart a meaningful message, and teach you life lessons. Here is an example from the novel, *The Kite Runner* by Khaled Hosseini:

One
December 2001

I became what I am today at the age of twelve, on a frigid overcast day in the winter of 1975. I remember the precise moment, crouching behind a crumbling mud wall, peeking into the alley near the frozen creek. That was a long time ago, but it's wrong what they say about the past, I've learned, about how you can bury it. Because the past claws its way out. Looking back now, I realize I have been peeking into that deserted alley for the last twenty-six years.

(Hosseini 2003)

Writing to Persuade

Authors often use writing to express their points of view on issues. Here their purpose is to **persuade,** or convince, the reader to agree with them. Effective persuasive writers usually support their viewpoint with data and statistics, so their writing appears to be primarily informative. But be careful, and be critical. Though persuasive writing may include accurate information, it may also be one-sided and opinionated. It is important to recognize this distinction. A critical reader should always be able to see the difference between informative and persuasive writing.

Editorials, political speeches, and argumentative essays are examples of persuasive writing. As a critical reader, it is important to recognize the purpose to persuade, especially when the content is presented as informative and objective. Think about infomercials you have seen on television. They appear to alert you to the latest breakthroughs in losing weight, getting rid of headaches, or becoming a homeowner. However, their real goal is to convince you to buy a product or invest your money. In the same way, print advertisements may seem to be informative reports about a product or opportunity, but there is always a hidden agenda: to convince you to buy, join, or commit your time or money in some way to the product or organization being advertised. Following is an example of persuasive writing:

Mediation Is Best Method for "Good" Divorce

Parents who choose the course of the "good" divorce must select a process for ending the relationship. The adversarial process, or going to divorce court, is guaranteed not to promote the cooperation, communication, and accommodating behaviors that are necessary for parents to co-parent after they are no longer married. The adversarial process increases stress for children because it often increases the level of conflict between parents and raises uncertainties about future contact with each parent. A non-adversarial method of dispute resolution, such as mediation, is less likely to add to the emotional trauma and is better suited to future co-parenting. In divorce mediation, the spouses sit down in the same room with each other and with a neutral mediator. With the mediator's help, they work through all the issues needed to be resolved, so the two of them can get through their divorce and on with their separate lives.

(Wilson 2009)

Considering the Audience

It is also important to consider the **audience** for whom an author is writing: the people whom the author wants to reach with his or her message. Textbooks are intended for an audience of college students, and their purpose is to inform or instruct. Popular magazines and newspaper articles are written for the general public, and their purpose is to entertain. Academic journals, such as the *New England Journal of Medicine* or the *Law Review*, are written for professionals in the fields of medicine and law, respectively, and are likely to be informative or persuasive.

You will notice differences in the language used in writings about the same topic, depending on the intended audience. The word choice used in a popular magazine article or on an Internet site that discusses relationships, for instance, will be simpler than that in your college communications or sociology textbooks.

try it and apply it! 7-3   **Determining the Author's Purpose for Writing and the Intended Audience**

Directions: Read the following article on divorce. Then answer the questions that follow.

Splitsville:

Coping When Parents Divorce

By Linda Bernstein

Erin was 11 at the time of her parents' divorce, and, she says, "It ruined my life." Looking at Erin, who is now 18, you probably wouldn't think her life is ruined. She captained the cross-country team at her high school outside of Denver, was coeditor of her high school yearbook, and scored a scholarship to the University of Colorado at Boulder. When she talks about her life, she names dozens of friends, and she is excited about her new start at college. Erin, however, is focusing on what she believes she lost: the nice house where her family lived, all her aunts, uncles, and grandparents on her father's side of the family—and her father, too.

"When my dad left, he really left. He moved several states away, where he married another woman and had a new family," Erin explains. Her father's family was so angry at Erin's mother that they cut off contact, even with Erin and her siblings. The family had to move to a smaller house, and Erin's mother had to find a full-time job because money was tight. At first, Erin would see her dad on vacations, but she says his new wife "doesn't like us, especially now that she has her own kids." Erin hasn't seen her father in three years and refused to pick up the phone when he called on her birthday.

Just as you aren't responsible for your parents' split, you can't do anything to make them get back together—or even like each other. However, experts have several recommendations that can help you deal with the divorce, whether it happened when you were little, only recently, or is going to happen soon.

Don't keep your feelings bottled up. "You're part of the divorce too. It's affecting you as much as your parents," Hueckel emphasizes. Ask your parents to set a time when you can speak to them, preferably together. Be prepared with a list of your questions and concerns. And don't be reluctant to tell them how you're feeling. If there is constant bickering and you feel as if you are "stuck" in between your parents, let them know how that is affecting you. They're the grown-ups, after all.

(Adapted from Bernstein 2008)

1. What is the purpose of the paragraph?
   to inform

2. Who is the intended audience? Support your answers with details from the article.
   Children and adolescents. The article discusses the experiences of a person whose parents divorced, and the author's reference to "you" suggests it is directed to other young people who may be in the same position.

3. What is the main idea?
   Divorce has a negative impact on children, but there are ways of coping with it.

try it and apply it! 7-4

Determining the Author's Purpose for Writing and the Intended Audience

Directions: Read the essay, "I Want a Wife," by Judy Syfers Brady on the roles of men and women in marriage. Then answer the questions that follow.

I belong to that classification of people known as wives. I am A Wife. And, not altogether incidentally, I am a mother.

Not too long ago a male friend appeared on the scene from the Midwest fresh from a recent divorce. He had one child, who is, of course, with his ex-wife. He is obviously looking for another wife. As I thought about him while I was ironing one evening, it suddenly occurred to me that I, too, would like to have a wife. Why do I want a wife?

I would like to go back to school so that I can become economically independent, support myself, and, if need be, support those dependent upon me. I want a wife who will work and send me to school. And while I am going to school I want a wife to take care of my children. I want a wife to keep track of the children's doctor and dentist appointments. And to keep track of mine, too. I want a wife to make sure my children eat properly and are kept clean. I want a wife who will wash the children's clothes and keep them mended. I want a wife who is a good nurturant attendant to my children, arranges for their schooling, makes sure that they have an adequate social life with their peers, takes them to the park, the zoo, etc. I want a wife who takes care of the children when they are sick, a wife who arranges to be around when the children need special care, because, of course, I cannot miss classes at school. My wife must arrange to lose time at work and not lose the job. It may mean a small cut in my wife's income from time to time, but I guess I can tolerate that. Needless to say, my wife will arrange and pay for the care of the children while my wife is working.

I want a wife who will take care of *my* physical needs. I want a wife who will keep my house clean. A wife who will pick up after my children, a wife who will pick up after me. I want a wife who will keep my clothes clean, ironed, mended, replaced when need be, and who will see to it that my personal things are kept in their proper place so that I can find what I need the minute I need it. I want a wife who cooks the meals, a wife who is a *good* cook. I want a wife who will plan the menus, do the necessary grocery shopping, prepare the meals, serve them pleasantly, and then do the cleaning up while I do my studying. I want a wife who will care for me when I am sick and sympathize with my pain and loss of time from school. I want a wife to go along when our family takes a vacation so that someone can continue to care for me and my children when I need a rest and a change of scene.

I want a wife who will not bother me with rambling complaints about a wife's duties. But I want a wife who will listen to me when I feel the need to explain a rather difficult point I have come across in my course of studies. And I want a wife who will type my papers for me when I have written them.

I want a wife who will take care of the details of my social life. When my wife and I are invited out by my friends, I want a wife who will take care of the babysitting arrangements. When I meet people at school that I like and want to entertain, I want a wife who will have the house clean, will prepare a special meal, serve it to me and my friends, and not interrupt when I talk about the things that interest me and my friends. I want a wife who will have arranged that the children are fed and ready for bed before my guests arrive so that the children do not bother us. I want a wife who takes care of the needs of my guests so that they feel comfortable, who makes sure that they have an ashtray, that they are passed the hors d'oeuvres, that they are offered a second helping of the food, that their wine glasses are replenished when necessary, that their coffee is served to them as they like it. And I want a wife who knows that sometimes I need a night out by myself.

I want a wife who is sensitive to my sexual needs, a wife who makes love passionately and eagerly when I feel like it, a wife who makes sure that I am satisfied. And, of course, I want a wife who will not demand sexual attention when I am not in the mood for it. I want a wife who assumes the complete responsibility for birth control, because I do not want more children. I want a wife who will remain sexually faithful to me so that I do not have to clutter up my intellectual life with jealousies. And I want a wife who understands that *my* sexual needs may entail more than strict adherence to monogamy. I must, after all, be able to relate to people as fully as possible.

If, by chance, I find another person more suitable as a wife than the wife I already have, I want the liberty to replace my present wife with another one. Naturally, I will expect a fresh, new life; my wife will take the children and be solely responsible for them so that I am left free.

When I am through with school and have acquired a job, I want my wife to quit working and remain at home so that my wife can more fully and completely take care of a wife's duties.

My God, who *wouldn't* want a wife?

1. What is the purpose of the paragraph?

   to persuade

2. Who is the intended audience? Support your answers with details from the article.

   the general public

3. What is the main idea?

   She believes that the role of women in marriage is distinctly different and unfair.

Distinguishing Between Facts and Opinions

When evaluating reading material, a critical reader should be able to tell the difference between facts and opinions. This skill is especially important when you are evaluating arguments in persuasive writing.

Facts

Facts are statements that can be proven to be true. They are based on direct evidence, actual experience, or observation. Facts may include dates, statistics, percentages, and numbers. Often, writers will cite the source of facts that they include in their work. They may do this by providing the source in parentheses after the statement of fact or including a statistic that supports it.

> Writers also use words and phrases to introduce factual or cited information:
>
> according to
> as reported in the . . .
> cited in . . .
> as documented in . . .
> as published in . . .

Look at the following statements of facts about the benefits of a college education. Notice that they are supported by additional data or by common knowledge that can be verified.

- According to the U.S. Census Bureau, over the course of a person's work life, those with a high school degree earn an average of $1.2 million; those with an associate's degree earn about $1.6 million; those with a bachelor's degree earn about $2.1 million.

- A 1998 Institute for Higher Education Policy report examines the benefits college graduates enjoy. These include more money in savings accounts, improved personal and professional growth, better quality of life for their children, better ability to make decisions as a consumer, and more interests outside of work.

- Research also consistently shows a clear relationship between completing higher education and good health. This is true both for the individual and for his or her children. (Adapted from Porter 2002)

try it and apply it! 7-5   Identifying Facts

Directions: Read the following list of statements of fact about marriage, adapted from a sociology textbook (Schaefer 2007, 301–303). Underline the words or phrases that indicate that the details are factual.

1. Currently, <u>over 95 percent</u> of all men and women in the United States marry at least once during their lifetimes.
2. <u>Until the 1960s</u>, some states outlawed interracial marriages.
3. Nevertheless, the number of marriages between African Americans and Whites in the United States has increased <u>more than seven times</u> in recent decades, jumping from <u>51,000 in 1960</u> to <u>416,000 in 2003</u>.
4. Moreover, <u>25 percent</u> of married Asian American women and <u>12 percent</u> of Asian American men are married to a person who is not of Asian descent.
5. Marriage across ethnic lines is even greater among Hispanics; <u>27 percent</u> of all married Hispanics have a non-Hispanic spouse. (Bureau of the Census 1998, 2004).

Opinions

An **opinion** is the belief, point of view, or feeling of a writer about a particular topic or issue. Opinions can be valid and worth consideration, especially if they are the viewpoints of an expert in a relevant field of study and are backed up with facts. In this case, they are called **informed opinions.** For instance, if a psychologist gave an opinion about an aspect of divorce or marriage, you might consider his or her observations and statements to be informed opinions.

Beware of expressions or phrases containing the word *fact*. Unless the author provides direct evidence that can be verified to support these statements, they may actually be opinions. Here are two examples of opinions.

> *The fact* is people who live together before getting married are more likely to get divorced.

> Friends are valuable in college. *In fact*, you cannot truly enjoy college life without them.

Many authors want to make it clear that they are expressing an opinion. When this is the case, they use qualifying signal words and phrases. The following box shows a list of some commonly used words and phrases.

Signal Words and Phrases for Opinions

In my opinion, I think, feel, believe, suspect, conclude, assume, hope, wish . . .

We must, should, need to, have to . . .

It is important, imperative, necessary . . .

The only way, the best way, the most important way . . .

Maybe, hopefully, probably, apparently, seemingly, likely, perhaps usually, often, sometimes, on occasion

Additionally, the use of **adjectives,** words that interpret, label, or modify nouns (*pretty* woman, *ugly* argument, *unsafe* encounter, *dangerous* relationship) or **adverbs** that modify a verb (speak *softly,* tread *carefully,* speaks *harshly*) indicates that a personal judgment is being made about a topic.

> I am always *happiest* when I am in a relationship.
>
> Being in a committed relationship can be *stressful.*
>
> Children of divorce speak *harshly* about their childhood.

The use of adjectives and adverbs in these examples shows how different people can have varying opinions about the same topic.

The use of the future tense (*will, would*) may also be an indication that an opinion is being presented, because no one can accurately predict the future.

> The number of interracial marriages *will* double by the year 2025.

Clearly, mate selection is unpredictable, and although some patterns of social behavior seem to be changing, we cannot consider this a statement of fact. This sentence explains why the previous sentence cannot be considered a fact.

try it and apply it! 7-6   Determining Opinions

Directions: Read the following list of sentences. Each reflects a personal opinion on the topic of love. Underline the words or phrases that indicate opinion. Then, add some statements of opinion of your own about love and relationships to complete the list, and underline the words you used to reveal your viewpoint.

1. Love <u>may</u> be one of the most <u>elusive</u> yet widely <u>recognized</u> concepts that <u>describe</u> some level of attachment between two people. (Adapted from Hahn 2007)

2. Relationships <u>must</u> be built on trust. We <u>need</u> to be able to count on others and feel that they will be open with us.

3. <u>The only way</u> for a relationship to survive is if the partners are <u>honest</u> with one another.

4. Your life does not <u>have to</u> be an open book—it's the <u>rare</u> individual who has no secrets whatsoever—but <u>it is important</u> to be honest about your fundamental beliefs, values, and attitudes.

5. I also truly <u>believe</u> that mutual support, loyalty and acceptance are <u>essential</u> components of a <u>good</u> relationship.

6. If a relationship is to survive, it <u>will</u> need to grow, develop and change.

7. We <u>need</u> to accept change as a fundamental part of relationships and build upon that change. In fact, we <u>need</u> to welcome change. Although change brings challenges with it, it also <u>helps</u> us to understand ourselves and our own place in the world more accurately. (Adapted from Feldman 2009)

8. *Answers may vary.* _____

9. _____

10. _____

Facts and Opinions

In your college reading, you will be expected to distinguish between fact and opinion so that you can question and evaluate the validity and reliability of the information presented. The excerpt that follows is taken from a sociology textbook. Pay attention to how the author includes both opinions and facts to discuss marriage.

> Currently, certain trends regarding marriage are evident. (opinion) The most obvious of these is the age at first marriage. (fact) Today, men are waiting longer to marry. (fact) The median age at first marriage for men is 27 years. (fact) In addition, these men are better educated than in the past and are more likely to be established in their careers. (fact) Women are also waiting longer to get married and tend to be more educated and career oriented than in the past. Recent statistics indicate that the median age at first marriage for women is 25 years. (facts)
>
> (Adapted from Hahn 2007)

try it and apply it! 7-7   Distinguishing Facts from Opinions

Directions: Read each of the following sentences about the current trends in divorce. Decide if the statements are facts or opinions. Write F (fact) or O (opinion) in the spaces provided.

O 1. Divorce statistics are difficult to interpret.

F 2. In the United States and many other countries, divorce began to increase in the late 1960s, but then leveled off and has since decreased since the late 1980s.

O 3. This trend may be due in part to the aging of the baby boomer generation and the corresponding decline in people of marriageable age.

O 4. But it also indicates an increase in marital stability in recent years.

(continued)

(continued)

<u>O</u> 5. Getting divorced obviously does not sour people on marriage.

<u>F</u> 6. About 60 percent of all divorcees in the United States have remarried.

<u>O</u> 7. Women are less likely than men to remarry because they often retain custody of the children after a divorce, which complicates remarriage.

<u>O</u> 8. Some people regard the nation's high rate of remarriage as an endorsement of the institution of marriage. (Adapted from Schaefer 2007)

try it and apply it! 7-8   Distinguishing Facts from Opinions

Directions: Read the following paragraph about divorce and its long-lasting effects on children. Decide if the sentences are facts, opinions, or informed opinions. Then, write fact, opinion, or informed opinion in the spaces provided.

According to a recent study, only 67 percent of children in the United States grow up with both biological parents in the home. (*fact*_____) The fact that many children of divorce report great suffering and yet are within the normal range psychologically has somehow been taken as evidence that the suffering from divorce does no damage. (*opinion*_____) Early research conducted by sociologists suggests the negative effects of divorce on children are confined to the first few years following a break-up. (*informed opinion*_____) A group of parents who were surveyed believe that the effects of divorce may linger much longer into adulthood. (*opinion*_____) As a matter of fact, one respondent was quoted as saying that children who come from a divorced home are more likely to get divorced themselves. Others believe that children will eventually adjust to the change in family structure after divorce and go on to live normal lives. (*opinion*_____) Researcher and sociologist Paul R. Amato (2001) agrees that divorce can affect children into adulthood, but he thinks that the potential for harm has been exaggerated. (*informed opinion*_____)

(Adapted from Schaefer 2007)

Detecting the Tone

Another important aspect of critical reading is detecting tone. In spoken English, we can hear expression in a speaker's voice or observe facial expressions and body language. The speaker may also use words or expressions that reflect his or her attitude. For example, here is a dialogue between a boss and his employee. "Listen" to it, and note the tone of their conversation.

Boss: You're an hour late. If you're going to work here, you have to be on time.

Employee: I'm sorry, my car wouldn't start.

Boss: That's not a reason for being late. You should have called.

Employee: I tried, but . . .

Boss: When work starts at 9 a.m., you must be here at 9. If you can't make it on time, you should look for another job. Next time you are late, don't bother coming in.

In this dialogue, the listener can detect the superior (boss) and subordinate (employee) roles at work. The boss is angry because his employee has reported to work late. The boss is clearly in control throughout the conversation, and he is making judgments about the employee's failure to arrive on time. There is also an air of certainty in his language, which leaves little room for the employee to say anything that would convince the boss that his excuse is acceptable or plausible. The employee is apologetic and attempts to make an excuse for his lateness, but he is cut off by his boss. This dialogue probably left the employee feeling defensive, angry, and frustrated at being unable to explain himself.

Here is another version of the dialogue between the same boss and his employee. See if you can detect a different tone in this conversation. Describe it following the dialogue.

Boss: You're an hour late! What happened?

Employee: My car wouldn't start.

Boss: Weren't you near a phone?

Employee: Every time I tried to call, I was put on hold. I decided that it would be faster if I walked to work rather than try to get through to you.

Boss: When people come in late, I am always worried that we will fall behind in production. Wasn't there any other way you could have contacted me?

Employee: I guess I could have emailed you, but I was so panicked that I didn't think about that. If this ever happens again, I'll surely know what to do.

Boss: Good. Now let's get to work. We have a lot to do!

(Adapted from Hybels and Weaver 2009)

There is a more equal status in this dialogue between the boss and the employee. The boss is willing to listen to his employee. He is not passing judgment on his employee. He is attempting to help the employee solve his problem of arriving late should such a circumstance arise in the future.

In written English, you can also detect the mood or attitude of the writer; however, because you cannot *hear* the author's voice or *observe* his or her body language, you have to rely on the language and the author's choice of words. The mood or attitude expressed in a piece of writing is called the **tone**. A writer may use neutral words or emotional words to express feelings about a subject of issue.

Detecting tone can also be helpful in determining an author's purpose. The table on the facing page provides examples of purposes and possible tones to address each.

Take a look at the following two textbook excerpts from *Communicating Effectively* by Hybels and Weaver II, which illustrate how detecting tone helps you to understand an author's purpose.

> Defensive communication occurs when one partner tries to defend himself or herself against remarks or behaviors of the other. A researcher, in a classic article, came up with six categories of defensive communication and supportive strategies to counter each of them.
>
> (Hybels and Weaver II 2009)

In the preceding example, the writer's tone is straightforward, neutral, factual, and informative. The writer provides details based on research and citations that can be accessed for verification and further reading. The purpose is to inform. A direct, straightforward, neutral tone is fairly typical of college textbooks.

In the next example, taken from the same communications textbook, the writer's tone is also direct but somewhat informal. It is part of a textbook feature called "Working Together," which provides activities that encourage group learning and discussions of key concepts. You will notice there are instructions to follow and an example of how the activity might proceed. The purpose here is to instruct.

> Imagine that you have caught your partner in a bold-faced lie, and it is clear that he or she cannot deny it, explain it away, or otherwise retreat from this situation. Go around your group, and have each member supply first a defensive statement and then a supportive statement of the same level—or a supportive statement designed to offset, dispel or otherwise ameliorate the defensive one. For example . . .
>
> (Adapted from Hybels and Weaver II 2009)

Sometimes, you have to be careful to distinguish between the inclusion of negative words, or words that suggest a negative response, and the overall tone of a piece of writing. In the passage that follows, you will read about evaluating online relationships. Underline the negative words. Are the writers being objective or critical?

> When you are using the Internet, and when your goal is to evaluate an online relationship, the key is to move slowly. The potential for lies, deceit, half-truths, hidden agendas, and misunderstandings is real, and they are more likely to reveal themselves over time. What are the red flags to look for?
>
> (Adapted from Hybels and Weaver 2009)

The words *lies, deceit, half-truths, hidden agenda, misunderstanding* and *red flags* indicate negative actions; however, the tone is objective and the purpose is to inform.

Tone and Purpose

Purpose: Inform and Instruct

Tones

factual: based on fact

formal: written using academic conventions, not casual

neutral: not supporting a particular side or position, unbiased

objective: not influenced by personal feelings; based on fact

straightforward: direct, honest

Purpose: Entertain

Tones

amusing: pleasing in a light-hearted way

carefree: playful

comical: causing laughter

dramatic: filled with emotion

humorous: funny, witty

ironic: mocking; conveying a humorous or angry meaning

joyful: happy

laughable: comical, amusingly ridiculous

light-hearted: free from care

ridiculous: extremely silly

romantic: preoccupied with love, expressing love

sentimental: influenced more by emotion than by reason

witty: using words in a clever and funny way

uplifting: offering or providing hope

Purpose: Persuasive

Tones

accusing: charging with wrongdoing

angry: extremely upset

blaming: accusing

compassionate: having or showing concern for feelings of another

condemning: blaming

critical: inclined to find fault

cynical: bitter, distrustful

disapproving: passing unfavorable judgment

distressed: upset

frustrated: displaying feelings of discouragement

impassioned: strongly emotional

judgmental: authoritative and often having critical opinions

negative: disagreeable, marked by features of opposition, hostility, or pessimism

opinionated: stubborn, biased, prejudiced

outraged: angry, extremely offended

pessimistic: no hope, seeing the worst side of things

sarcastic: bitter, making fun of things

subjective: placing emphasis on one's own attitudes and opinions

supportive: promoting the interests of a particular idea

upbeat: cheerful and happy

worried: concerned

Denotation and Connotation

Tone can also be understood by thinking about the meaning of words. Most words have two levels of meaning. The **denotation** is the literal meaning, the one you find in a dictionary. The **connotation** of a word refers to the emotions, attitudes, or perceptions related to the word. For example, the words *thrifty* and *cheap* have the same denotation, yet how we perceive the meanings of these words, or their connotations, is quite different. *Thrifty* has a positive meaning. A *thrifty* person is one who is careful with money and doesn't want to waste it, whereas a *cheap* person is one who doesn't want to spend money at all.

Notice the difference in meaning when *slim* or *skinny* is used in the following pair of sentences.

> Lisa, the *slim* young woman sitting in the rear of the classroom, was the first to hand in her exam.

Lisa's body can be admired for its beauty.

> Carolyn, the *skinny* brunette who sits next to the window, finished the math final during the first hour.

Carolyn is noticed for being thin, maybe too thin.

A good reader carefully considers both the positive and negative connotations of words in order to determine the tone of a reading selection.

try it and apply it! 7-9 **Detecting Negative Connotations**

Directions: Underline the words that you think have a negative connotation in each of the following sets of items. Discuss your answers with your classmates. You may discover that some perceptions of words differ from culture to culture.

1. economical, <u>penny-pinching</u>, <u>cheap</u>
2. heavyset, <u>overweight</u>, <u>obese</u>
3. <u>ignorant</u>, <u>unschooled</u>, naive
4. <u>immature</u>, <u>childish</u>, childlike
5. <u>impulsive</u>, spontaneous, <u>hasty</u>
6. inquiring, <u>nosy</u>, <u>snoopy</u>
7. <u>snicker</u>, laugh, <u>cackle</u>
8. mature, <u>over-the-hill</u>, <u>geezer</u>
9. talk, <u>babble</u>, <u>gossip</u>
10. <u>sly</u>, skillful, calculating

try it and apply it! 7-10   Detecting Tone

Directions: Read the following statements about relationships. Pay particular attention to the author's choice of words and their connotations. Select the answer that best describes the tone of each statement.

_d_ 1. Marcello was having a great experience at college, but he missed his family and friends back home.

    a. frustrated
    b. romantic
    c. upbeat
    d. nostalgic

_a_ 2. The level of grief at the funeral for the three brothers killed in the drunk-driving accident was profound. No one uttered a word at the gravesite as the burial service began.

    a. solemn
    b. supportive
    c. compassionate
    d. distressed

_d_ 3. I've been waiting here for you for three hours. Where are you?

    a. formal
    b. judgmental
    c. negative
    d. annoyed

_c_ 4. Let's head out to the beach for a day of fun-filled action.

    a. amused
    b. witty
    c. carefree
    d. humorous

_b_ 5. "It's our anniversary and Blanche is expecting a magical evening, so I decided to put her in a box and saw her in half." (Adapted from *Newsday*, Aug. 29, 2009)

    a. sarcastic
    b. comical
    c. amusing
    d. subjective

_c_ 6. "I knew my marriage was over when my car was dirty." (Adapted from *Newsweek*, Oct. 20, 2007)

    a. distressed
    b. worried
    c. amusing
    d. blaming

(continued)

(continued)

___c___ 7. "Living together is not only immoral but a sure path to divorce."
   a. pessimistic
   b. supportive
   c. critical
   d. straightforward

___a___ 8. Employers have rejected prospective employees based on Facebook profiles, so be careful what you post.
   a. concerned
   b. condemnatory
   c. disapproving
   d. ridiculous

The author's tone and the connotation of words he or she uses can influence your reaction to a piece of writing. An angry tone can be distracting and lead you to dismiss a person's opinion on an issue or topic, whereas a straightforward and well-reasoned tone can convince you of an author's argument. However, as a critical reader, you will sometimes have to separate the "feelings" a writer evokes in you from the arguments the writer makes, so that you can evaluate the ideas and viewpoints more objectively.

Keep this in mind

- Pay attention to the author's language and choice of words.
- Determine how the author feels about his subject.
- Evaluate how shades of meaning affect you as the reader.

Recognizing Bias

Tone and the connotation of words can also reveal an author's **bias,** or tendency to believe in a particular viewpoint. College students do not expect their textbooks to be biased. Instead, they sometimes believe that the facts and figures in them should not be questioned, because they were written by experts in a variety of academic disciplines. Nevertheless, textbooks have been written that show clear bias on the part of the author. For example, some history textbooks have omitted coverage of racism or events related to black history and have ignored major contributions by women to society. Even foreign-language textbooks, which usually focus on the positive aspects of other cultures, sometimes contain bias and propaganda. Consequently, good readers check to see what authors include, leave out, or emphasize in their writing.

By their very nature, essays, editorials, and magazines articles are more likely to include bias. Very often, in these types of writing, the author presents a particular viewpoint or opinion.

It is especially important to look for bias when a writer addresses a controversial issue. As the word *controversy* suggests, these issues generate different points of view. If the writer presents only one perspective, he or she is revealing bias. A biased piece can draw a reader into an author's perspective. The reader may begin to "feel" instead of "think" about the subject.

Bias is not always bad. A writer may have a strong leaning in favor of a particular point of view. If he or she provides a well-grounded argument, which is supported by facts and addresses alternative views, this may present a valuable point of view.

College students are often asked to research or read about issues of controversy in today's society. To recognize bias you should do the following look:

- Determine the author's purpose. Consider whether it is to persuade you of one specific point of view.
- Notice whether the author presents only one side of the argument.
- Look for counterarguments. If these are not presented and discussed, this is a strong indication of bias.
- Distinguish between facts and opinions. If only opinions are provided, there is bias.
- Examine the tone and the connotation of the words used; strong feelings in one direction may indicate bias.

As a critical reader, be sure you consider texts carefully. You will want to form your own opinions and judgments about the issues you explore.

try it and apply it! 7-11   **Recognizing Bias in Writing**

Directions: The following editorial discusses the changing structure of the American family. Read the whole piece first, and then go back and answer the questions after each paragraph.

Family-Unfriendly Policies

Mortimer B. Zuckerman

1. You will hear a lot about the American family in the election campaign. For most of us, that calls up an image of a man and wife and two or three children. Forget it. Unfortunately, the social pattern of the American family has lost its place. Households of unmarried couples and households without children outnumber "American family" households. What a shame. And only about 20 percent of families fit into the traditional structure with father as the only breadwinner.

    a. What is the main idea of the paragraph?
    The American family has changed for the worse.
    _____

    b. Is the author biased? Explain.
    Yes, the author is biased in favor of a traditional two-parent household, one male and one
    female. He believes the partners should take on traditional roles.

    c. What words and phrases indicate that the author is biased?
    The author makes statements such as "Forget it," "Unfortunately," and "What a shame."
    _____

2. Here is what has been happening: In the 1950s, 80 percent of adults were married; today, roughly 50 percent are. Why? Partly because people are delaying marriage, with the median age for a first marriage rising by four years for men and about five years for women. Second, divorce rates have more than doubled since the 1960s as marriage evolved from a sacrament to a contract. Third, millions more cohabit before marriage. Fourth, births to unmarried mothers, white and black, have risen from 5 percent in 1960 to about 35 percent today. So the new American family is a household with fewer children, with both parents working, and with mothers giving birth to their children at an ever older age, having fewer children, and spacing them further apart.

    a. What is the main idea of this paragraph?
    There are several reasons for the changes in the makeup of the American family.
    _____

    b. What is the author's tone?
    His tone is critical.
    _____

    c. Is the author biased? Explain.
    Yes. By saying that marriage has changed from "a sacrament to a contract" and listing other
    demographic changes, he reveals his negative judgments about the American family today.

3. This is not good news. It is the children who are most affected. The stable family of two biological parents—surprise, surprise!—turns out to be the ideal vessel for molding character, for nurturing, for establishing values, and for planning for a child's future. By comparison, the children of single parents or broken families do worse at school and in their careers. Marriage, or the lack of it, is the best single predictor of poverty, greater even than race or unemployment.

   a. What is the main idea of this paragraph?

   That children from two parent families do better than those from single parent or divorced
   families.

   b. Is the author biased? Explain.

   Yes, this is one-sided; no opposing viewpoints are presented. In addition, the author does not
   provide facts to support his opinions.

4. The startling increase in the number of those who grow up with only one parent has markedly added to poverty among children, shifting poverty from the old to the young. Children in mother-only families are more likely than those with two parents to be suspended from school, to have emotional problems, to become delinquent, to suffer from abuse, to take drugs, and to perform poorly on virtually every measure.

   a. What is the main idea of this paragraph?

   Children in mother-only families suffer more from poverty and display a range of problematic
   behaviors.

   b. Is the author biased? Explain.

   Yes, he doesn't address opposing viewpoints and only focuses on the negative effects of single
   parenthood.

5. Working moms are also a problem. In the past, about 40 percent of those surveyed thought that a wife should help her husband's career rather than have one of her own. Now, 81 percent think she should have her own career, and 70 percent think that both husband and wife should earn money. Parental time with children has dropped from about 30 hours a week to around 17—yet 70 percent believe that children are not affected negatively by having a working mother unless they are under school age. Moreover, it is shocking that the vast majority of working mothers now say that even if the family did not need the income, they would continue working.

   a. What is the main idea of this paragraph?

   The increase in the number of working mothers has had a negative impact on child
   rearing.

   b. Is the author biased? Explain.

   Yes. The bias is the belief that mothers should not work outside the home because it decreases
   time spent with children and is detrimental to them.

(continued)

(*continued*)

6. The dramatic shift in family structure and values is unlikely to change. But the bulk of the nation's greatest social problems would benefit from nurturing a more traditional American family. We can't afford to contribute to an a la carte menu of sex, love, and childbearing. We must emphasize the benefits for all from the package deal of marriage.

   a. What is the main idea of this paragraph?
      Many social problems would be solved if we promote a more traditional model of the American family.

   b. Is the author biased? Explain.
      Yes. The author assumes that most of our social problems stem from the changes in family structure. He does not consider any other possible causes.

Now answer the following questions about the entire article.

7. What issue is discussed in this editorial?
   changes in the structure of American families

8. What is the author's point of view on the issue?
   The author believes the change from a traditional to modern family structure has had a destructive impact, especially on children.

9. What is the overall tone? List some of the words that reveal the tone.
   critical and alarmed: forget it, What a shame! (para. 1); Surprise, surprise! (para. 3); startling (para. 4); It is shocking. (para. 5); We can't afford…(para. 7).

10. Is the author biased? Explain.
    Yes. He mostly presents his own opinion. He does not consider opposing viewpoints. His tone is critical and alarmed, and he is not objective.

11. How did this article make you think or feel?
    Answers will vary.

12. Would you use this article for a college paper, or would you search for other articles? Explain your answer.
    Answers will vary.

Source Citation: Zuckerman, Mortimer B. "Family-Unfriendly Policies (present American family structure) (Editorial)." *U.S. News & World Report* 143.13 (Oct 15, 2007): 72.

try it and apply it! 7-12 Recognizing Bias in Writing ⏸

Directions: Go back and read "I Want a Wife" by Judy Syfers Brady on pp. 194–195. Read it carefully to discern the bias, and then write the answers to the following questions.

1. What is the overall tone? List some of the words that reveal the tone.

    The overall tone is sarcastic. Emphasis on the role of the wife as subservient to her husband—
    "take care of 'my' physical needs"; the listing of all the tasks a wife performs "pleasantly" for
    her husband— "I want a wife who will plan the menus, do the necessary grocery shopping,
    prepare the meals, serve them pleasantly, and then do the cleaning up while I do my studying."

2. Is the author biased? Explain.

    Yes. She presents only her viewpoint of the inequitable role of the wife. She does not consider
    what a husband might do for a wife.

3. How did this article make you think or feel?

    Answers will vary.

4. Would you use this article for a college paper, or would you search for other articles that present a less biased viewpoint?

    Answers will vary.

Evaluating the Author's Argument

An **argument** is the author's thesis or position on an issue as well as the reason or evidence the author uses to support his or her main point. When reading a selection that presents an author's point of view on an issue, you not only want to identify the argument but also evaluate the author's development of it. Assessing the quality of the author's argument is an important tool for a critical reader. Here are some factors to consider:

- **Adequacy of Coverage:** Is there is enough information to support the argument? Does the writer provide logical reasons, backed up with valid evidence, to support his or her position on the issue? Does the author present counterarguments and answer them? Some words or phrases that indicate the author is explaining counterarguments include *however, on the other hand, in contrast, an opposing viewpoint is, on the contrary, another view, opponents say.*

- **Relevancy:** Does all the information directly relate to the issue being discussed?

- **Objectivity:** Does the author present the material in an unbiased, objective manner? If the author writes in a subjective, personal way, it can distract the reader from the looking for evidence to support the author's points. Look out for the use of the first-person, "I."

■ **Currency:** Does the author present information that is up-to-date? The writer must take into account the latest findings, research, and information available about an issue.

■ **Authority:** Does the author have professional qualifications and expertise in the field that he or she is discussing? This adds a degree of authority to the author's argument.

■ **Strength of the Evidence:** Does the author offer sufficient support for the argument? Valid types of support include the following:

   ■ personal experiences
   ■ expert or informed opinions
   ■ citations
   ■ historical documentation
   ■ statistical data
   ■ research
   ■ facts

Keep this in mind

- Determine if the author has any political beliefs that may affect his or her objectivity.
- Notice details that are included or overemphasized, and think about details that have been omitted.
- Observe the author's language for evidence of bias.
- Look for statements of opposing viewpoints that are expressed in a fair manner.
- Assess the quality of a writer's argument if you personally agree with his/her viewpoint.

try it and apply it! 7-13   Practice with Critical Reading

Directions: Read this essay from *Newsweek*. Then answer the critical reading questions that follow.

So Where's the Epidemic?

Kathleen Deveny

1   The number of families in our position is actually much smaller than you might think.

2   It's become a rite of each school year, a masochistic little ritual that I can't resist. As soon as my daughter's school sends out the parent directory, I open it immediately.

I may glance at the teacher photos, but I'm really looking for divorced families. We're easy to spot: those painfully obvious entries with two addresses listed next to the student's name. This year, we are the only one in my daughter's class. It's not that I'd wish this on any family. But if divorce is an epidemic in America and half of all marriages fail, how come I so rarely meet other divorced parents? Have I landed in an episode of "Mad Men"?

3   The mystery apparently extends beyond my Brooklyn neighborhood. "The 50 percent thing doesn't seem to be my reality," says Debbie Zeitman, 47, a divorced mom who lives with her 15-year-old son in Venice, Calif. "I'm surprised by how relatively uncommon it seems to be." Dorothy Lloyd, the divorced mother of an 11-year-old girl in Highland Park, Ill., says most families where she lives are "more of the traditional kind, both parents at home."

4   We're not imagining things. The number of families in our position—thankfully—is much smaller than you might think. Only 10 percent of the nation's children were living with a divorced parent in 2004, according to my calculation using the most current available U.S. Census data. That doesn't include kids living with parents who have remarried, or parents who have never married. But it doesn't feel like a national crisis, either.

5   That's partly because the divorce rate is dropping—and has been for some 25 years. The oft-repeated statistic that one in two marriages ends up in divorce isn't exactly right. It's based on the annual marriage rate per 1,000 people, compared with the annual divorce rate. In 2005, the marriage rate was 7.5 per 1,000 people, while the divorce rate was 3.6 per 1,000, according to the National Center for Health Statistics. But since the people who get married in any given year usually are not the same people who get divorced (OK, maybe a few), the statistic isn't very meaningful. Even if you look at divorces among married couples, the rate has declined from a peak of 22.8 divorces per 1,000 in 1979 to 16.7 divorces in 2005.

6   Thanks to later marriages, smaller families, longer life expectancy and the fact that unhappy couples tend to divorce faster than they used to, the number of children affected by each divorce is also shrinking. In 1968, the average divorce affected 1.34 kids, according to Betsey Stevenson and Justin Wolfers, both assistant professors at the University of Pennsylvania's Wharton School. By 1995, that number was 0.91, about the same level as 1950. And in general, divorce rates are lowest among those with a college degree, according to Stevenson. She thinks that may be because educated women tend to marry later, and the older you are when you get married, the more durable your marriage seems to be.

(continued)

(*continued*)

1. What issue is discussed?
   the divorce rate in America

2. What is the author's point of view on the issue?
   Based on her research, she believes the divorce rate is not increasing and certainly not at an
   alarming rate.

3. How does the author support her opinion? Is the material mostly fact or opinion?
   She uses a combination of facts and opinions. She provides her own observations and those
   of divorced women in different parts of the country and facts from the 2004 U.S. Census about
   the small number (10 percent) of children living with divorced parents, and notes the decline
   in divorce rate from the National Center for Health Statistics. She cites the work of Stevenson
   and Wolfers, assistant professors at Wharton, for information about the numbers of children
   affected by divorce and other conclusions they have made about why rates may be declining.

4. What authorities does the author cite in supporting her opinion? Is her selection of
   authorities biased?
   2004 U.S. Census; National Center for Health Statistics; Stevenson and Wolfers, assistant
   professors at Wharton. Her selection is mostly one-sided, with very little concrete evidence to
   explain why most people think divorce rates are climbing and have reached epidemic proportions.

5. What is the author's purpose?
   to persuade

6. Who is the intended audience?
   the general public

7. What is the tone? Underline some words or phrases in the text that support your
   answer. How do you think her tone and use of language impact her argument?
   Answers will vary. Tone could include: positive, upbeat, and optimistic: I don't wish this on
   anyone. Thankfully, thanks to

8. What are the author's credentials or qualifications to write this article? Do you think
   they are substantial?
   Answers will vary. She is a writer. She is also divorced and a mother of a young daughter.

9. How did this article make you feel? Do you agree with the author? Do you find her
   points convincing? Explain.
   Answers will vary.

Understanding Figurative Language: Inferring the Meaning Behind Words

In addition to making inferences about the information you read, you will
also have to draw conclusions about the words a writer uses. Writers often
use **figurative language,** language that is not literally true but conveys ideas

in a creative and imaginative way. In writing about the Internet, for example, someone might say, "James *is cruising the electronic highway*." Here the writer is comparing the use of the Internet to driving on a highway, using figurative language to suggest an image of someone quickly moving through the complex man-made network of the computer. An author's use of figures of speech and choice of words shapes how his or her writing portrays the world and conveys ideas, so you should be sensitive to these choices and what they mean.

Introductory textbooks are typically written in a straightforward manner. Because their purpose is to inform and instruct, authors tend to use literal language in order to be as clear and concise as possible. However, even within textbooks and academic writing, figurative language may be used.

Those people were at the **bottom of the social heap.**

Those people came from the lowest social class.

The xylem also serves as **a piping system, bringing** water and nutrients up from the roots into the plant.

The xylem is responsible for the transport of water and nutrients from the roots and throughout the plant.

Figurative language is also used in many other genres of college reading, including literature and poetry.

The five most commonly used figures of speech are metaphor, simile, hyperbole, personification, and idiom.

Metaphor

A **metaphor** compares two things that are dissimilar to create a mental image that conveys a point or provides a vivid description. Authors use a form of the verb *to be*, saying something *is* or *was* something else, to show the comparison.

Example

Your homework is a **nightmare.** (Your assignment is terrible, maybe poorly written.)

You are **my sunshine.** (You make me happy.)

Following is a literary example from William Shakespeare's play *As You Like It*.

"All the world's a stage,
And all the men and women merely players;
They have their exits and their entrances . . ."

In this famous speech, the character in the play compares the *world* to a *stage*. Notice how the metaphor is extended because the author also uses additional language related to plays, such as *players* or actors, and *exits* and *entrances*.

Simile

A **simile** is another figure of speech in which two essentially unlike things are compared; however, unlike a metaphor, it is often in a phrase introduced by *like* or *as*. Some similes are used so often that they have become part of our everyday conversation or writing. For example, phrases such *as quiet as a mouse, as pretty as a picture, as hard as a rock. eat like a bird*, and *swim like a fish* are common similes.

Examples

Bob doesn't seem very smart, but he is **as sharp as a tack**. (He is, in fact, very smart or intelligent.)

Those two girls are **like two peas in a pod**. (The girls are very similar.)

As the instructor entered the classroom, she muttered under her breath, "This class looks **like a three-ring circus**." (There is a lot of noise and chaos in the class.)

When he got the tools out, he was **as precise and thorough as a surgeon**. (He is very skillful.)

Here is an example of a simile from literature:

"The blast echoes through the street of my father's house. Hassan slumps to the asphalt, his life of unrequited loyalty drifting from him **like the windblown kites** he used to chase." (Hosseini 2003)

"It wasn't so much the whistling itself, Laila thought later, but the seconds between the start of it and the impact. The brief and interminable time of feeling suspended. The not knowing. The waiting. **Like a defendant about to hear the verdict**." (Hosseini 2007)

Notice how metaphors and similes enrich the writing and make it more interesting. In fact, by using metaphors and similes, authors can create special effects and vivid images for their readers.

Personification

When authors use **personification,** they attribute human qualities to non-human beings or inanimate objects. The phrases *the roar of the ocean* and *the whisper of the wind* are examples of personification. Oceans don't have the capacity to roar, and the wind certainly cannot whisper; neither one has vocal chords. However, describing actions in this manner is creative and imaginative. It is often more powerful than simply saying that the ocean was loud or the wind was blowing softly.

Here are some other examples of personification:

The camera **hates** me. (I don't look good in photographs.)

Opportunity **knocked** at my door. (This was a great opportunity.)

Time **never waits** for anyone. (Time continues to pass and you can't control it.)

The sun **was playing hide and seek** among the clouds. (It was a partly-sunny day with clouds.)

Hyperbole

Hyperbole is the use of exaggerated language to make a strong point or to provide emphasis. It is commonly used in spoken language—for example, "I told you a million times!" Using an expression that exaggerates the facts, the speaker is emphasizing a degree of concern or frustration and makes a strong statement. It is the same in written language. A writer may exaggerate, especially when he or she is expressing a strong opinion. Here are some examples of hyperbole:

I will **die** if my professor calls on me. (I will be embarrassed.)

His brain is the **size of a pea.** (He is not very smart.)

I'm doing a **million** things right now. (I am very busy.)

She's **light years** from finishing her project. (She is a long way from finishing the project.)

try it and apply it! 7-14   Understanding Figurative Language

Directions: In the following sentences, look for figurative language. Then write the choice that best explains the meaning. Remember that figurative language usually brings a picture to the reader's mind. Use that picture to help you understand the meaning of the figurative language.

_b_ 1. Her **icy gaze** penetrated me.
   a. cold
   b. not friendly
   c. shiny and slick
   d. not warm

_d_ 2. He wasn't able to **digest** anything the nurse had just told him.
   a. consume
   b. summarize
   c. study
   d. understand

_b_ 3. He is an upstanding **pillar** of his community.
   a. looks like a stone
   b. a supporting or upstanding member
   c. is a rock
   d. appears tall and strong

_a_ 4. I am **on top of the world**; I just received a scholarship.
   a. extremely happy
   b. very tired
   c. so dizzy
   d. really afraid

_d_ 5. Last night, I was awakened by the **growling thunder.**
   a. peaceful silence
   b. barking noises
   c. crashing sound
   d. rumbling boom

_c_ 6. His father has a mind **like a computer.**
   a. He has a good memory.
   b. He can multitask.

(continued)

(*continued*)

    c. He thinks in a powerful manner.

    d. He is very resourceful.

_c_ 7. Taking drugs is **like playing with fire**.

    a. It can burn your fingers.

    b. It is hot.

    c. It is dangerous.

    d. It can wipe you out.

_b_ 8. Stop crying. You are acting **like a baby**.

    a. You appear youthful.

    b. You are immature.

    c. You always need your mommy.

    d. You are always hungry.

_b_ 9. Stop complaining. You always have **a million excuses** for not doing your work.

    a. You always have another reason.

    b. You don't have any good explanations.

    c. You should come up with a better excuse.

    d. You should apologize this time.

_b_ 10. When he stood up, **his head touched the clouds**.

    a. The young man is light-headed and dizzy.

    b. The young man is extremely tall.

    c. The young man was wearing a big hat.

    d. The young man was standing on a mountain top.

try it and apply it! 7-15   Understanding Figurative Language in Literature

Directions: Novels are filled with figurative language, words and phrases that depart from their literal meanings. These devices help writers make comparisons between concrete or familiar objects and unfamiliar ideas or objects in order to explain them. They also enable writers to create vivid, even poetic descriptions.

In the novel *The Kite Runner*, by Khaled Hosseini, the author uses many examples of figurative language. They enhance his writing and provide the reader with vivid descriptions of the characters' emotions, feelings, and needs. In the following quotations, underline the figures of speech, and then write about the idea or picture the author is trying to convey.

1. That was a long time ago, but it's wrong what they say about the past, I've learned, about how you can bury it. Because <u>the past claws its way out</u>.

   Experiences or events that happened in the past are not easily forgotten. They continue to affect you long after they happened.

2. "I know, I know. But he's always buried in those books or shuffling around the house <u>like he's lost in some dream</u>."

He is often preoccupied and lost in his own thoughts.

3. "<u>Children aren't like coloring books</u>. You don't get to fill them in with your favorite colors."

You don't get to choose the qualities or personalities of your children, or you can't make your children be what "you" want them to be.

4. There was a <u>monster in the lake</u>. It had <u>grabbed Hassan by the ankles</u>, <u>dragged him to the murky</u> bottom. I was that monster.

There is something horrifying or terrifying in the lake. It is attacking and tormenting Hassan and trying to kill him. It turns out that he himself is the tormenter. He is causing his own suffering and responsible for his own pain.

5. Baba believed Carter had unwittingly done more for communism than Leonid Brezhnev. "He's not fit to run this country. It's <u>like putting a boy who can't ride a bike behind the wheel of a brand new Cadillac</u>."

He is inexperienced. It was a risky venture.

Idioms

Many students enter college with the hope of meeting new people and making friends. Here's what you might hear some students on campus saying:

Yesterday, I had lunch with one of my classmates, but today he **gave me the cold shoulder** in class.

My roommate **has such a sunny disposition**. No matter what time I trudge into the dorm, she never complains.

Just because you **got up on the wrong side of the bed**, don't yell at me.

Charlene always **welcomes her friends with open arms**.

These expressions, or **idioms**, often add interest and sometimes a dash of humor to spoken English. Most native speakers are familiar with many of them and use them often in conversations. Nonnative speakers, however, may struggle with idioms because they are not easily translated and may not be found in standard dictionaries. Because idioms are informal, they are not commonly used in college textbooks, but they may be used in anecdotes, fiction, and nonacademic articles. To understand this kind of figurative language, both native and nonnative speakers of English should use the context of the sentence or passage where it appears.

try it and apply it! 7-16   Using Idioms

Directions: Idiomatic expressions can be used to describe emotions and behaviors. Read the following sentences and then select the best definition from the text box to explain the meaning of the idiom in each.

> create a disturbance
> help out
> everyone agrees
> angry today about something that
>   occurred in the past
>
> wants revenge for a grievance, resents
> confrontational
> make peace
> out of control

1. After fighting for weeks, James and Bob decided **to bury the hatchet.**
   make peace

2. George does not get along well with others at work; he always trying **to make waves.**
   create a disturbance

3. Karla was having difficulty finding someone to care for her toddler while she was in school, so I offered **to lend her a hand** on Tuesday mornings.
   help out

4. My neighbor always has **an axe to grind** with me; if she's not complaining about the noise level, then she is arguing with me about the property lines.
   want revenge for a grievance, resent

5. Robert has **a chip on his shoulder;** he can't forget about the time I didn't invite him to a barbeque a few years back.
   angry today about something that occurred in the past

6. Tyron is constantly **in your face.**
   confrontational

7. I think it's time to report him to my supervisor before things **get out of hand.**
   out of control

8. We are all **on the same page** about the importance of tolerance and respect in the classroom.
   everyone agrees

Using Figurative Language

Figure of Speech	Definition	Example
Metaphor	A direct comparison between two dissimilar objects or ideas	*My kitchen is the size of a postage stamp.* *No man is an island.*
Simile	A comparison between two unlike objects or ideas, using "like" or "as"	*. . . float like a butterfly* *. . . sting like a bee*
Personification	Attributing human qualities to nonhuman beings or inanimate objects	*The rain kissed her face.* *The tropical storm slept for two days before it hit the coast.*
Hyperbole	Exaggerated language to make a point or provide emphasis	*His books are piled to the ceiling.* *My cell phone rang a million times before I answered it.*
Idioms	A figurative expression whose meaning has evolved within a particular language or people. The origin may be obscure.	*It's a good thing James held his tongue. (didn't say anything)* *saw the handwriting on the wall. (realized something would happen)*

You Be the Judge: Becoming a Critical Reader

Throughout this chapter, you have learned about concepts that will help you be a more critical reader. The following chart lists questions you should ask yourself to go beyond the literal meaning of the text and read critically.

Questions to Ask Yourself	Critical Reading Concept
■ Based on what the author states, what can I conclude? ■ What does the writer imply by omitting certain points? ■ What does he or she mean or suggest here?	This is inference.
■ Can the information be verified or checked out in a reliable source? ■ Are there statements that are introduced by phrases like *according to, as reported in the . . . , cited in . . . , as documented in . . . , and as published in . . . ?*	These are facts.

(continued)

(*continued*)

wrap it **Up**

■ Is the writer presenting his or her own viewpoint on an issue? Are there statements that start with words or phrases, like *I think, feel, believe, suspect, conclude, assume, hope, wish . . . We must, should, need to, have to . . . It is important, imperative, necessary . . . The only way, the best way, the most important way . . . apparently, presumably, this suggests, possible, can, may, and might?*	These are opinions.
■ Why is the author writing this selection? ■ Does the author want to *inform* me about the topic, *teach* me how to do something, *entertain* me, or *persuade* me to go along with his or her opinion?	This is the author's purpose.
■ For whom is the article or text intended? ■ Does the author write in a way that will appeal to a certain group or readership, or is it for the general population?	This is the writer's intended audience.
■ What mood or feeling is conveyed by the author's writing? ■ How does the writer's choice of words and the connotation of those words reflect his or her point of view about a topic?	This is the tone of the writing.
■ What is the effect of the tone? ■ Does the author use a lot of positive words to describe his or her own viewpoint? ■ Does the author present opposing viewpoints? ■ Does the author use a lot of negative words to describe opposing viewpoints? ■ What impression does this language make? ■ Does the author include, omit or emphasize details?	These questions will help you discover bias.

Questions to Ask Yourself	Critical Reading Concept
■ Is there adequate information?	This will help you evaluate the author's arguments.
■ Is all the information relevant?	
■ Is the author objective?	
■ Does the author present updated information and current research?	
■ Does the author have credentials in the field in which he/she is writing?	
■ Does the author provide strong evidence to back up his or her point of view?	
■ Does the author address counterarguments in a fair, evenhanded way and answer them?	

Key Terms

adjectives	denotation	metaphor
adverbs	facts	opinion
argument	figurative language	personification
assumption	hyperbole	persuade
audience	idioms	purpose
bias	inference	simile
connotation	informed opinions	tone

chapter

8

A Tangled Web
Assessing Internet Sources

In this chapter

you will learn to

- Find information on the Internet
- Evaluate web resources
- Document your sources
- Understand the value of the Internet

Develop Skills While Reading About
Emotional and Physical Health

Achieving and maintaining a healthy psychological and physical well-being will help you deal with the rigorous demands of college course work. If you are suffering from headaches, you may find it difficult to concentrate during lectures. If you are exceptionally tired when it's time to complete assignments or study for tests, you may find yourself missing deadlines or performing poorly on exams. If you are overworked and stressed out, your immune system may be compromised, and you may become more susceptible to the flu or other infections, which may result in missing many class sessions and falling behind in course work.

The first step to managing your health is awareness. Being aware of your moods, habits, and changes in your body is very important in determining whether you can handle a situation by yourself or whether you need to seek professional or medical advice. (Adapted from Ferrett 2010)

Today, medical advice is also widely available on the Web. From information offered by doctors, hospitals, and federal health agencies to personal experiences about illnesses, diseases, and drug interactions, you can find out about practically everything you want to know without leaving your home or incurring high medical expenses. Under what circumstances would you choose to use the Web to get medical advice? Find out more about emotional and physical health in Modules 6 and 7.

Finding Information on the Internet

The Internet provides a wealth of information on just about every topic imaginable. If you want to find out what's up with your friends from high school or a former co-worker, log on to Facebook. If you want to learn how to plant tulip bulbs in your backyard, locate the best price for an HDTV, or read a review on a new movie release, just type in your subject on Google or your favorite search engine, and everything you want to know will be at your fingertips.

Attempting to locate old friends, fun projects, best prices, or good movies is pretty simple to do. However, suppose you want to find information about a new allergy medication your doctor has just prescribed. You want to know, for example, if the symptoms you are experiencing are typical or perhaps more serious. Would you just type in your search term on Google? If you do, you may find yourself taking advice from an unreliable source and not from a health professional. That is because material on the Internet can be posted by anyone. Accessing medical information from an unknown source can potentially be very harmful to your health.

Smart consumers verify a site's credibility and find out who is responsible for the content posted on it. They look for health information on sites sponsored by hospitals, medical schools, or physicians. In addition, they check that the information is current. Reliable medical websites are regularly reviewed and updated, and the date of the most recent update or review is clearly posted. Three good sources for medical advice are the following:

- www.healthfinder.gov—This is a government website, where you can find information and tools to help you stay healthy. It provides the most up-to-date information and provides reliable sources on a wide range of health topics selected from more than 1,600 government and nonprofit organizations.

- www.nih.gov—The National Institutes of Health is part of the U.S. Department of Health and Human Services. It is the primary federal agency for conducting and supporting medical research.

- www.mayoclinic.com—The Mayo Clinic is a not-for-profit medical practice dedicated to the diagnosis and treatment of virtually every type of complex illness.

Evaluating Web Resources

In the previous chapter, you learned how to read between the lines and evaluate college reading material found in textbooks, anthologies, and periodicals. Today, however, a great deal of academic resource material can be found on the Internet, and if you are like most college students, you rely heavily on the Internet for your research. So like any smart consumer, you must be a good critical reader and verify sources to determine whether they contain material appropriate for inclusion in college papers and projects.

Information on the Web is mostly free and accessible, but it is also unregulated and unmonitored. Because the Internet is open to anyone, you always have to check for *purpose* and *authority, currency,* and *accuracy* of the source you are considering. Other techniques for evaluating the usefulness of websites are the same as those used for assessing printed material (see Chapter 7). These skills include being able to distinguish between fact and opinion, understand the author's purpose, determine the intended audience, understand tone, and recognize bias.

As you learn about how to evaluate Internet sources, we will consider the topic of health, because the information you glean about it will not only be useful for college research but also to your well-being. You may also find you are asked to read about health issues in health education, psychology, sociology, and even English composition courses.

Purpose and Authority

The **purpose** and **authority** of a website can be determined by checking the following:

- the domain name
- the purpose of the website
- the author or sponsor of the site
- the credentials of the author or sponsor

The Domain Name   Examine the **URL** (uniform resource locator), the location of the file and the site's official address. The URL includes the **domain,** the category to which the site belongs. For example, in the two URLs that provide good sources for medical advice, www.healthfinder .gov and www.nih.gov, the domains are .gov. Before you go further, glean as much information as you can from the URL and the domain. Choose a domain that is most useful and reliable for your research project. URLs ending in .gov, and .edu are often reliable sources of information. Many of those ending in .com are set up for commercial reasons, so review them carefully, keeping in mind they are trying to sell a product. If the URL contains a name, it may be someone's personal page, and the information may not be suitable for your research. You can limit your search to a specific domain by using an advanced search option. See the Common Domains table on page 228.

The Purpose of the Website   To find out more information about a site you have selected, click Home or About Us to learn about the **purpose** of the website—the mission of the organization or business—and the contributors.

A website can have one or more purposes. It can be designed as

- a personal web page
- a company or organization website
- an educational or public service information site

Common Domains

.gov (government): This domain is restricted to use by government, government agencies, or government officials. It is administered by the General Services Administration (GSA). It is a reliable source of information. It may contain studies, statistical data and analysis, and reports.

.edu (education): These educational sites provide information from colleges and universities. You will need to determine whether the information is written by an expert or by a college student. A reliable site may offer research studies and the opinions of academic scholars.

.org (organization): Anyone can register for a .org domain; there are no requirements for registration. In fact, in many instances .org is used for commercial sites.

Organizations can also be nonprofit agencies or unaffiliated groups. Therefore, if you have heard of a group before—for example, Greenpeace or Amnesty International—the site may provide reliable information. However, many nonprofit groups are concerned with social issues and promote a particular point of view. Be cautious. These sites have their own agendas, so their information might be biased.

.com (commercial): Commercial sites can be business or personal sites. You need to investigate these sites further to see if the information on them is reliable. Many commercial sites are looking to promote their goods and services, so they give information only about the products they sell or the services they offer to consumers.

- a site for scholarly research
- an entertainment site
- an advertising site
- a site for electronic commerce
- a forum for ideas, opinions, and points of view

If you find a lot of advertisements or requests to sell you products, you should consider viewing another site.

The Author or Sponsor of the Site Because anyone can post information on the Internet, a reliable source must have a named author(s) whose credentials are stated or a **sponsor**—an organization, business, or advertiser who is funding the site.

The Credentials of the Author or Sponsor **Credentials** indicate whether a person is an expert in the field he or she is writing about. Credentials can consist of an advanced degree in the discipline, a record of research in the field, or job-related experience. If this information is not available on the

page you open, go to the home page or check About Us. If you do not believe a writer is an authority or expert in the field he or she is writing about, or if no author is listed, you should check out another site. Many useful web pages appear on .org sites, which indicate their affiliation with the group sponsoring them. You need to read about these organizations to determine the reliability and usefulness of the material on the site.

Some popular sites provide disclaimers—statements denying responsibility—about their material so readers know ahead of time how valid or accurate they can expect the information to be. Wikipedia, for instance, is a popular website used by many college students. A careful reader should click About Wikipedia to learn about this source. Do you think Wikipedia is a good source of information? Would you include details from this website in your college research or use it to get information about your health? Read the following disclaimer from the Wikipedia site:

> Wikipedia is an online open-content collaborative encyclopedia, that is, a voluntary association of individuals and groups working to develop a common resource of human knowledge. The structure of the project allows anyone with an Internet connection to alter its content. Please be advised that nothing found here has necessarily been reviewed by people with the expertise required to provide you with complete, accurate or reliable information. That is not to say that you will not find valuable and accurate information in Wikipedia; much of the time you will. However, **Wikipedia cannot guarantee the validity of the information found here.** The content of any given article may recently have been changed, vandalized or altered by someone whose opinion does not correspond with the state of knowledge in the relevant fields.

As you have just read, contributions to Wikipedia are not carefully monitored in terms of validity and accuracy. Therefore, it is *not* a good source for college research. It is also not a reliable source for medical advice because there is no way to ascertain whether the information is provided by a medical professional or is up-to-date.

Not all sites provide such disclaimers, so your job as a critical reader is not only to find information online but also to evaluate websites and draw your own conclusions about them based on the information provided.

try it and apply it! 8-1   **Checking the Purpose and Authority of a Website**   ⏸

Directions: Visit the following websites that deal with the topic of health. Write down details that provide information about the purpose and authority of each site.

Answers will vary. Sample answers provided.

1. **www.drugs.com**

   Drugs.com is a resource for drug and related health information that provides objective, comprehensive, and up-to-date information for both consumers and healthcare professionals. It is not an online pharmacy. The Drugs.com drug-information database is powered by four independent leading medical-information suppliers: Wolters Kluwer Health, Physicians' Desk Reference, Cerner Multum, and Thomson Micromedex.

2. **www.webmd.com**

   Staff includes experts in medicine, journalism, and health communication. Independent Medical Review Board includes medical experts.

3. **www.nida.nih.gov**

   The National Institute on Drug Abuse (NIDA) is part of the National Institutes of Health (NIH), a component of the U.S. Department of Health and Human Services.

4. **www.eDrugSearch.com**

   Provides tools and resources to help consumers make decisions when purchasing online medication. Directs consumers to licensed international pharmacies and can currently access more than 100,000 online medication listings. Based in San Antonio, eDrugSearch.com is led by Cary Byrd, entrepreneur and advocate but not a medical professional.

5. **www.drugboat.com**

   Internet division of a fully licensed overseas pharmacy. Run by a "dedicated" team which has responsibility for all aspects of technology, supply-chain management, and customer service. They do not provide advice about taking medication.

Currency

Evaluate the currency of a website by checking

- the date on the website
- the date the page was revised
- the status of the links

Currency refers to the date on which information was posted or the last time a web page was updated. You should also check to see if links on the page work; this will let you know if the author or sponsor is still maintaining the page. If a link leads to an error message, be cautious about the quality of the information on the original page. Depending on your subject, it may be important to have current information. You certainly do not want to include outdated details on a current issue in a research report.

try it and apply it! 8-2   Checking the Currency of a Website

Directions: Visit the following websites that contain information about influenza. Because the strain of the flu varies from year to year, it is important that the information provided about it is up-to-date. Locate the details that will provide information about the currency of each website, and write them below.

1. www.cdd.gov *The Center for Disease Control, last updated July 13, 2009*
2. www.fda.gov *The Food and Drug Administration, news release is current*
3. www.who.int *The World Health Organization, copyright 2009*
4. www.medicinenet.com *updated daily*
5. www.influenza.com *last updated June 29, 2007*

Accuracy

Unlike print resources, web resources are less likely to have editors or fact-checkers, so it is a good idea to apply what you have already studied in your textbooks, learned from your lectures, or read about in periodicals or newspapers to the information on the Web. If information on the site does not match information obtained from other sources, it may be inaccurate. You should evaluate the material in the same way you learned to evaluate print material in Chapter 7: distinguish between fact and opinion, identify the tone, be alert to connotations of the language used, and look for signs of bias. You should also check for grammatical or spelling errors, which can indicate that a site is a less-reliable source. If the information meets all the preceding criteria, you can feel comfortable about including it in your research. Otherwise, explore other Internet sites and evaluate them in the same way.

Use these guide questions to help you evaluate the **accuracy,** or validity of a website.

1. How does the information compare to what you already know?
2. Are opinions or facts offered?
3. What is the tone of the text? Do you detect bias?
4. Does the author include a list of works cited?
5. Are there any spelling or grammatical errors?

Here is a checklist you can use to evaluate websites you are considering using for research on a topic.

Checklist for Evaluating Websites

1. Does the URL contain any information that gives you a clue to its source?
Check the ones that apply.
_____ An individual's name
_____ The name of a familiar company, organization or institution
_____ No/Cannot find information on site

2. What is the domain?
_____ .gov
_____ .edu
_____ .com
_____ .org
_____ Other _____

3. Do you think another domain would provide you with better information?
_____ Yes   Which one(s)? _____
_____ No   Why? _____

4. What is the purpose of the website? Check all those that apply.
_____ Personal page
_____ Forum for an organization or nonprofit agency
_____ Forum for ideas or opinions
_____ Informational site, e.g., governmental, nonpartisan site (offering no opinion), or online encyclopedia
_____ To sell a product or provide a service
_____ Entertainment
Other _____

5. Is the author of the page mentioned?

_____ Yes

_____ No

6. Are the qualifications of the author or group listed?

_____ Yes

_____ No

7. Do they indicate the author is an expert?

_____ Yes   What are his/her qualifications? _____

_____ No   _____

8. Is there a date on the page, or has the page been updated?

_____ Yes _____

_____ No

9. Are the links broken?

_____ Yes

_____ No

10. Is the article related to your topic?

_____ Yes

_____ No

11. Does the information appear to be similar to what you have read on other sites?

_____ Yes

_____ No

12. Does the information match what you already know?

_____ Yes

_____ No

13. Are opinions or facts offered?

_____ Yes

_____ No

14. Can you discern tone or connotations that indicate bias?

_____ Yes

_____ No

15. Are there any spelling or grammatical mistakes?

_____ Yes

_____ No

16. Does the author include a list of works cited?

_____ Yes

_____ No

(continued)

(continued)

17. Based on your responses to this survey, is this a good source for your college research?

_____ Yes

_____ No

Why?

_____

_____

_____

try it and apply it! 8-3   Evaluating Websites

Answers will vary. Sample answers provided.

Directions: Evaluate each of the following websites on the topic of mental health using the Checklist for Evaluating Websites. State whether you would use this site for research, and explain why or why not.

1. www.mentalhealth.com

   The site is updated (1995–2009). Dr. Phillip W. Long, a psychiatrist, is the sole creator and developer. He has not received any recent recognition in the field of psychiatry (last in 1996). In his mission statement, he expresses an angry tone about how pharmaceutical companies manipulate doctors and the public. He offers computerized diagnostic therapy on this site and maintains another site, mytherapy.com, which contains ads for home heating oil. I would not use this site for research.

2. www.nimh.nih.gov

   The National Institute of Mental Health, a component of the U.S. Department of Health and Human Services. It is updated regularly. I would use this site for research.

3. www.nami.org

   The National Alliance for Mental Illness, celebrating its 30th anniversary, with 1,200 affiliates in all 50 states, including D.C. and Puerto Rico. It provides annual reports and has as its mission the focus on awareness, education, and advocacy. Its board and staff members are health professionals with a great deal of experience. I would use this site for research.

4. www.english.illinois.edu/maps/depression/about.htm

   This site does not contain any information on emotional health. Instead, it focuses on The Great Depression, a period in American history that spanned 1929–1939. I would not use it for mental health research.

5. www.queendom.com

   Queendom.com is a subsidiary of PsychTests AIM Inc., a company that develops products and

   services centered around an extensive battery of psychological assessments to be used by

   therapists, students, researchers, professors, marketers, and Human Resources professionals.

   It also has an Internet dating site, MatchScale. The site also contains many ads, and it touts

   that many of its assessment tools can be "fun" for its users. I would not use this site for

   research.

   Now, based on your evaluations, which site(s) is appropriate for a college research project? Why?   *Answers may vary.*

   Numbers 2 and 3

   _____

   _____

   _____

   _____

   _____

Document Your Sources

After you have selected an online resource that meets the previously discussed criteria, you need to accurately record the source of information so that you can include it in your research paper or project. It is particularly important to record the title of the article, the author(s) name, the name of the website, the name of the sponsor of the site, the URL (so that you can locate the source again at a later point in your research), and the date you accessed the site. Keep this information in a notebook, write it down on an index card, clip it into a file, or type it into a word-processing program.

Although information on the Internet is available to everyone, and as a student you can freely use the periodical databases of your college's library, you still must give credit to *all* the sources you use. This information is considered intellectual property, so whether you quote or paraphrase it, you still need to **document** it. If you use material by an author and do not give him or her credit, you are guilty of **plagiarism** (passing other people's ideas off as your own). In fact, a student who plagiarizes can be placed on academic probation or even expelled from an institution.

To avoid plagiarism and its consequences, online resources, like print resources, need to be cited. The way in which you cite information depends on the discipline you are studying. English, foreign languages and some humanities departments use the Modern Language Association (MLA) documentation format. Psychology and some social sciences departments use the American Psychological Association (APA) guidelines.

The Value of the Internet

Internet material can be valuable for academic research. The number of resources on the Web continues to grow. Academic and scholarly journals, news organizations offering up-to-date developments, and online encyclopedias are added daily. However, effective evaluation of online resources must be part of your college research; otherwise, you may include unreliable or inaccurate information. You also should not limit your research to digitized sources. Print sources are still lining the shelves of your college library. In fact, some of them may be more relevant to your research. For example, you can locate primary sources there, and nothing quite compares with turning the dusty pages of an old volume that has been kneaded by hundreds of hands. More importantly, a trip to your library can help you enlist research specialists and college librarians, who can help guide you to all kinds of valid resources, including the Web.

A Tangled Web: Assessing Internet Sources   wrap it Up

- Remember not all resources on the Internet are created equal.
- Great variations exist in the quality of the resources you access.
- Evaluate the strengths and weaknesses of the resources.
- Check their purpose and authority, currency, and accuracy.
- When in doubt, leave it out.
- Use appropriate or required styles for citing all resources.
- Avoid plagiarism.

Key Terms

accuracy

authority

credentials

currency

domain

document

plagiarism

purpose

sponsor

URL

9

Put the Pieces Together

Organizing Information for Reading and Studying

In this chapter

you will learn to organize the information from your reading by

- Paraphrasing
- Outlining
- Summarizing
- Using visuals to organize information

Develop Skills While Reading About the
World of Work

Most students enter college today with the hope of developing skills that will prepare them for a career. Others enroll in college to retool their skills in order to get a higher salary or to find a new career. Even if you are one of the many students who start out with an "undecided" major, you should spend your time in college taking courses and exploring majors that may eventually lead you down the path to a potential career. However, do not fret if you don't find the ideal major right away. In fact, on average, students change their majors at least three times during their college years. For now, it is just important to see how the courses you are taking provide you with the skills that will prepare you for the world of work. Find out more about the world of work in Module 5.

Organizing Information

Almost everything you do in life requires good organizational skills. Whether it's filing unpaid bills to ensure timely payment, or keeping a calendar of upcoming events, plans, exams, or business meetings so that you won't miss course deadlines or disappoint family, friends, or colleagues, being organized will make you more efficient and productive.

In college reading, being organized means that you have organized the information from your reading so that you will later be able to retrieve it to prepare for exams, papers, or projects. Organizing information will save you time and energy and help you to avoid the frustration of doing the same thing over again—rereading your textbook!

Three important ways to organize or review information from college reading are *outlining, mapping,* and *summarizing.* The method you select often depends upon the nature of the reading material, the purpose for reviewing textbook information, or your preference for a particular strategy. All three strategies require you to paraphrase.

Paraphrasing is restating an author's material using your own words. An accurate paraphrase shows you have read and understood the material and helps you to recall important information for exams. In fact, according to research, putting material into your own words actually helps you remember it better.

Following are some tips for writing a paraphrase.

Writing a Paraphrase

1. Read through the entire section or paragraph you want to paraphrase so that you understand the context.
2. Read the sentence you will be paraphrasing to get a general understanding of it.
3. Identify the main idea of the sentence.
4. Note key details that support the main idea of the sentence.
5. Use synonyms or phrases that have the same meaning as the word you are paraphrasing.
6. Note the grammatical structure of the original sentence and consider rearranging it while maintaining the author's meaning.
7. Look away from the text and try paraphrasing what you have just read.
8. Check the accuracy of your paraphrase by substituting it for the sentence in the text. It should make sense and fit in with the rest of the ideas.
9. Do not add your own opinion.
10. Acknowledge the source of your paraphrase.

Read the following passage from a business textbook, and then read the example paraphrase that follows.

Because communication is so important, business wants people with good communication skills. Evidence of the importance of communication in business is found in numerous surveys of executives, recruiters, and academicians. Without exception, these surveys have found that communication (especially written communication) ranks at or near the top of the business skills needed for success.

(From Lesikar 2008)

Paraphrase Example

According to surveys and business professionals, communication is very important in today's workplace; therefore, businesses require that people possess good communication skills, especially in written communication.

You can see how the main ideas were included, some repetitious examples were cut, and the language was simplified and restructured.

try it and apply it! 9-1 Paraphrasing

Directions: Read each of the following paragraphs that continue the discussion of the importance of communication skills in the workplace. Then reread each numbered sentence, and write a paraphrase of it in the space provided.

Answers will vary. Sample answers provided.

A. Typical of these surveys is one by Robert Half International of the 1000 largest employers in the United States. According to 96 percent of the executives surveyed, today's employees must have good communication skills to advance professionally. Most recently, NFI Research, a private organization that regularly surveys over 2,000 executives and senior managers, found that 94 percent rank this skill as the most important for them to succeed today and tomorrow. The *Wall Street Journal* also stated, "To stand out from the competition, you must demonstrate the unwritten requirements that are now most in demand: leadership and communication . . ."

(Lesikar 2008)

1. Typical of these surveys is one by Robert Half International of the 1000 largest employers in the United States. According to 96 percent of the executives surveyed, today's employees must have good communication skills to advance professionally.

   In a survey of executives conducted by Robert Half International, almost all participants indicated the need for workers to have good communication skills in order to earn promotions.

(continued)

(continued)

2. Most recently, NFI Research, a private organization that regularly surveys over 2,000 executives and senior managers, found that 94 percent rank this skill as the most important for them to succeed today and tomorrow.

   A more recent survey showed that almost 95% of business professionals felt that the possession

   of good communication skills is essential for peak job performance.

3. The *Wall Street Journal* also stated, "To stand out from the competition, you must demonstrate the unwritten requirements that are now most in demand: leadership and communication . . ."

   According to the Wall Street Journal, people must demonstrate leadership qualities and

   good communication skills if they want to be competitive.

B. Unfortunately, business' need for employees with good communication skills is all too often not fulfilled. Most employees, even the college trained, do not communicate well. In fact, surveys show, that in the opinion of their employers, even managers and their executives who think they communicate well often fall short. Effective communicators, therefore, are in high demand.

(Lesikar 2008)

1. Unfortunately, business' need for employees with good communication skills is all too often not fulfilled.

   Businesses don't always have employees with good communication skills.

2. Most employees, even the college trained, do not communicate well.

   College graduates do not always possess good communication skills.

3. In fact, surveys show that, in the opinion of their employers, even managers and their executives who think they communicate well often fall short.

   Surveys of employers have even reported that management staff are lacking in

   communication skills.

4. Effective communicators, therefore, are in high demand.

   Consequently, there is a great need for those who have good communication skills.

C. The communication shortcomings of employees and the importance of communication in business explain why you should work to improve your communication skills. Whatever position you have in business, your performance will be judged by your ability to communicate. If you perform (and communicate) well, you are likely to be rewarded with advancement. And the higher you advance, the more you will need your communication ability. The evidence is clear: Improving your communication skills improves your chances of success in business.

(Lesikar 2008)

1. The communication shortcomings of employees and the importance of communication in business explain why you should work to improve your communication skills.

    Since communication is essential for a job and because not all employees have good

    communication skills, you should be able to see why it is critical to learn to communicate well.

2. Whatever position you have in business, your performance will be judged by your ability to communicate.

    In every sector of business, you will be evaluated based on the ways you communicate with others.

3. If you perform (and communicate) well, you are likely to be rewarded with advancement.

    Your ability to communicate well will help you move up the ladder to success.

4. And the higher you advance, the more you will need your communication ability.

    Your need for excellent communication skills will be even greater as you advance professionally.

5. The evidence is clear: Improving your communication skills improves your chances of success in business.

    It is clear that honing one's communication skills will lead to greater achievement and

    advancement in the world of work.

Keep this in mind

Writing a Paraphrase

- Always refer back to the selection so that you can use the context to help you paraphrase accurately.
- Objectively state what the author says without adding any personal feelings about the topic.
- Focus on explaining what the author says or means using your own words rather than merely rearranging the existing words of the author.
- Use paraphrasing when you take notes, outline, map, and summarize.

Outlining

Outlining is a writing technique that visually illustrates the hierarchy of main ideas and supporting details in a piece of writing. In other words, it shows the relative importance of ideas and details and how they are related to one another. This strategy helps you organize textbook information and assists you in studying and recalling what is most important to know. It is also a good way to synthesize information from several reading sources or from your lecture notes and textbook. This method works well for students who learn material in an orderly and sequential manner. Outlines are a particularly effective way to organize information from disciplines that focus on process, time order, or classification (such as chemistry, history, and biology).

The outline should be simple. The best way to do this is to focus on the main ideas and corresponding details. Include only what you think you will be required to remember. Don't forget to paraphrase, or use your own words. To create an effective outline, follow these guidelines.

Writing an Outline

1. Read the text carefully, and then annotate it.
2. Create an outline title that reflects the overall topic of the selection.
3. List the main ideas you highlighted or annotated.
4. List the major supporting details for each main idea.
5. Include minor supporting details (facts, dates, or examples) the author uses to provide support for major supporting details. Remember your outline should show the importance and relationship between ideas.
6. Indicate the connection between main ideas and the details that support them using Roman numerals (I, II, III), capital letters (A, B, C), Arabic numbers (1, 2, 3), and lowercase letters (a, b, c).

Here is an example of the outline format:

Title

I. First Major Topic
    A. First Main Idea
        1. First Major Supporting Detail
            a. First Minor Supporting Detail
            b. Second Minor Supporting Detail
        2. Second Major Supporting Detail
    B. Second Major Idea

II. Second Major Topic

Here is a paragraph from *Peak Performance: Success in College and Beyond* about résumés. It is followed by a sample outline.

The purpose of a résumé is to show connections among your strengths, accomplishments, and skills and the needs of a company or employer. The résumé is a critical tool because it is a first impression, and first impressions count. Your résumé is almost always the first contact an employer will have with you, since many companies now initially screen potential candidates through online application submission. You want it to stand out, to highlight your skills and competencies, and to look professional. Computer programs and online services can help you format your résumé, and résumé classes may be offered in the career center of your college.

(Ferrett 2010)

Sample Outline

I. The purpose of a résumé

    A. Shows connections with the needs of the employer

        1. Strengths

        2. Accomplishments

        3. Skills

   B. Provides first impression to employer

   1. Make it stand out.

   2. Highlight skills and competencies.

   3. Make it look professional.

II. Seek help for formatting of résumé.

   A. Computer programs

   B. Online services

   C. College career center

try it and apply it! 9-2   Outlining

Directions: Read the following excerpt about the general components of a résumé, and annotate the reading as suggested by the acronym THIEVES, in Chapter 2. Then complete the outline that follows.

Although you may not be actively looking for a job right now, it's good practice to have at least a draft résumé in your portfolio to build upon. This preparation will make creating a polished version an easier task. Although the final format of your résumé may depend upon the preferences of your prospective employers or career field, you will more than likely include the following components:

1. Write your full name, telephone number, cell number, and email address. If you have a temporary or school address, also include a permanent address and phone number. Don't include marital status, height, weight, health, interests, a picture or hobbies unless you think they are relevant to your job.

2. It is not essential to include a job objective on your résumé unless you will accept only a specific job. As a new college graduate, you may not want to limit your job prospects to one job objective. If you do not list a job objective, you may use your cover letter to relate your job to the specific job for which you are applying.

3. List the title of your last job first and a brief description of your duties. Don't clutter your résumé with irrelevant jobs. You can elaborate on specific duties you performed at each job in your cover letter or at the interview.

4. List your highest degree first, including schools attended, dates, and major fields of study. Include educational experience that may be relevant to the job, such as certification, licensing, advanced training, intensive seminars, and summer study programs or institutes. Don't list individual courses on your résumé. If you have taken

some specific courses that relate directly to the job for which you are applying, list them in your cover letter.

5. List awards and honors that are related to the job or that indicate excellence. Arrange them by displaying your best award or honor first.

6. List activities in which you participated on and off campus. These activities should highlight your capacity to help others, your willingness to give of your own time, and a demonstration of your leadership skills.

7. List professional memberships to organizations you have joined, speeches you have presented, or research projects you conducted, especially in your field of interest.

8. You should also include three to five references that will provide prospective employers with information about your scholarship, job experience, and character. Academic references can be obtained from instructors or advisors. Club advisors, coaches, or fellow members of a professional organization can provide good character references.

(Adapted from Ferrett 2010)

Components of a Résumé

I. Personal Information

   A. Name

   B. Telephone and cell number.

   C. *Email* _____

   D. *Temporary or school and permanent addresses* _____

II. *Job Objective* _____

III. Work Experience

   A. Begin with most recent job

   B. *Include a brief description of duties* _____

IV. *Educational Background* _____

   A. Begin with highest degree

   B. Include all schools attended, dates, and major areas of study

   C. Include education relevant to job

      1. certification

      2. licensing

      3. *advanced training* _____

      4. *intensive seminars* _____

      5. *summer study or institutes* _____

(continued)

(*continued*)

    V. *Awards and Honors* _____

       A. Related to job application
       B. Best award or honor first

    VI. Campus and Community Activities

       A. Highlight capacity to help others
       B. Show your willingness to give of your own time
       C. *Demonstrate your leadership skill.* _____

    VII. Professional Membership and Activities

       A. Organizations
       B. Speeches
       C. *Research Projects* _____

    VIII. References

       A. *Include three to five* _____
          1. *Scholarship* _____
          2. *Job Experience* _____
          3. *Academic* _____
             a. *Instructors* _____
             b. *Advisors* _____
          4. *Character* _____
             a. *club advisors* _____
             b. *coaches* _____
             c. *fellow members of a professional organization* _____

Keep this in mind

Writing an Outline

- Write an outline after you have read and annotated the material.
- Read over the highlighted sections and marginal notes, and then select the main ideas of each section.
- Create a hierarchy of information through indenting and using Roman numerals, letters, and numbers.
- Use phrases or sentences, whichever you prefer, for each line in your outline.
- Use your *own* words.

Summarizing

Summaries are shorter or condensed versions of important points in a longer passage and contain limited details. Writing a summary is an important way to organize information after you have finished an assigned textbook reading. It demonstrates your overall comprehension of what you have read. Following are some tips for writing an effective summary.

Writing a Summary

1. A summary should be brief, no more than a quarter of the length of the original material. The goal is to paraphrase the author's main ideas, using your own words, and to present them in the same order they appear in the original.
2. Include the title of the selection and the name of the author.
3. Carefully read the entire selection you plan to summarize. Next, reread it, and highlight and annotate the main points.
4. Write a sentence that restates the overall main idea, or thesis.
5. Briefly state each major supporting detail.
6. Use transition words that show you understand the relationships between the details you are including.
7. If necessary, add minor supporting details that help explain the major supporting details. For instance, include significant examples, facts, and definitions of important terms.
8. If the author presents an opinion about one of the main points, include this in your summary; however, do not include your own opinions.
9. End your summary with a concluding sentence that restates the overall main idea.
10. Present the ideas and details in the order they appear in the original text.

The following is a sample summary of the excerpt about résumés in Try It and Apply It! 9-2:

Create a rough draft of your résumé now so that you can tweak it when you are ready to apply for a job. Include the following basic components in your résumé: identification and contact information, position, work history, education, achievements and distinctions, volunteer work, affiliations, and names of references.

In college, you may be asked to research news articles and write summaries of them. The details of a general news article answer *wh-* questions (*who, what, when, where,* and *why*). These answers form the content of news stories that follow what is known as *journalistic style*.

Writing a Summary of a News Article

To write a summary of a news article, answer the following *wh-* questions:

Who is the article about?

What happened?

When did the event happen?

Where did it occur?

Why did it happen?

How did it happen?

Your summary of the article will be a synthesis of the answers to these questions.

try it and apply it! 9-3   Creating a Summary of a News Article

Directions: Read the following news article about finding a career. Answer the *wh-* questions and then write a summary of the article.

New Class at CSUSM Helps Students Find Career Path:

Tests Help People Sort Among Thousands of Occupations

By Jeff Rowe

At the Cal State San Marcos career center, counselors say perhaps the most frequent question students ask at graduation is "Now what?"

Getting a degree can turn out to be a far different challenge from finding a vocation and launching a career; and so, mindful that thousands of college grads still have not identified their calling in life, CSUSM this semester began offering what it calls its "Value Improvement Program" (VIP) for third-year business students. "The class gives students places to explore rather than producing an 'aha' moment," said Regina Eisenbach, associate dean of the College of Business Administration at CSUSM.

She said the school heard of a similar career program at a university in Ohio and thought: "This is a great idea." Many CSUSM students are the first in their families to attend college, she said, and often lack an orientation toward professional careers or knowledge of networking, résumé construction, interviewing and business etiquette. The class meets every other week. Pamela Wells leads many of the class sessions; she is associate director of the university's career center. Business school students tend to be better oriented than those in other colleges, she says, because they already have at least decided on a broad career field. In arts and sciences, though, as many as 40 percent of the students have not honed in on a career field, she says. Wells and other career counselors say the "aha" career-discovery moments come slowly. . . .

VIP class is non-credit, but nonetheless incorporates plenty of tests. In these, students learn to identify their strengths, interests and aspirations. In a recent class, students learned about six major career areas. The categories, synopses and examples of the occupations in each category were: Realistic: Practical over abstract—Military, ranger, police; Artistic: Imagination and creativity—Museum curators, writers; Social: Community service—Teachers, social workers, nurse; Enterprising: Business, risk-takers—Entrepreneurs, athletes; Conventional: Structured, practical procedures—dental hygienist; Investigative: Solving complex problems, preference for data and ideas over people—Computer programmers, scientists. Yet as many students seemed to realize in discussion during the class, their interests, hopes and aspirations often straddle two or more of those broad categories. And then they're faced with sorting out which of the thousands of occupations in each category might fit them. . . .

Source: "New Class at CSUSM Helps Students Find Career Path: Tests Help People Sort Among Thousands of Occupations." *North County Times* (Escondido, CA) (Oct 9, 2009): NA.

Who? _Cal State San Marcos Career Center_

Answers may vary.

What? _Began offering a noncredit course titled "Value Improvement Program" for third-year business students to identify their strengths, interests, and aspirations._

Where? _California_

When? _Fall 2009_

How? _Students meet every other week and learn about and discuss different careers in business, networking strategies, résumé writing, the interview process, and business etiquette._

Why? _Business students are more goal-oriented, but many have not narrowed down their choices to a particular career._

Summary: _In Fall 2009, the Cal State San Marcos Career Center in California began offering a noncredit course titled "Value Improvement Program" to identify the strengths, interests, and aspirations for third-year business students. These students are generally more goal-oriented than arts and sciences majors, although many have not narrowed down their particular career paths in the business field. Every other week, these students meet together to learn about and discuss different careers in business, networking strategies, résumé writing, the interview process, and business etiquette._

Keep this in mind

Writing a Summary

- Keep your summary simple, concise, and complete.
- Include the author and the title.
- Use the highlighted and annotated sections of your reading to identify key ideas and supporting details.
- Add the minor supporting details that are the most important.
- Avoid adding your personal opinions or details not in the text.
- Use transition words to make your summary easy to understand.
- Summarize a news article using the answers to the *wh-* questions.

Using Visuals to Organize Information

A **graphic organizer** is a visual or graphic display of the organization of information of your reading. It can be used to assess your understanding of reading material or as a tool to illustrate concepts or show the relationship between concepts in a text for reading and study. Some graphic organizers that we will discuss in this chapter include concept maps, tables, timelines, process diagrams, flowcharts, and Venn diagrams.

Concept Maps

Creating a **concept map** is another way to show the relationship between ideas and concepts and to organize information from your textbooks. Maps are especially useful for visual learners and students with a creative flair. You can use different colored markers and draw pictures or symbols to help you remember what is important to learn. Unlike an outline, it takes less space to map a chapter; in fact, an entire textbook chapter can be mapped on *one* page. You can even add details from other sources, including supplementary reading materials, information you gleaned from a film or field trip, and your class notes. Other maps, also known as graphic organizers, can be used to show specific organizational patterns.

Here are four simple steps for creating a concept map:

1. Write the topic in the center of your page.
2. Select the major points and arrange them so they radiate from the topic at the center (see Figure 9-1) or appear below it (see Figure 9-2). Use circles or rectangles for these main points.
3. For each main point, add the major and minor details that support it.
4. There is no standard method for mapping, so you can use lines or arrows to connect the supporting details to the main ideas. Just make sure that minor details connect to major details and major details connect to main ideas.

Here is a commonly used format for concept maps followed by a concept map for components of a résumé.

Figure 9-1   Sample Concept Map

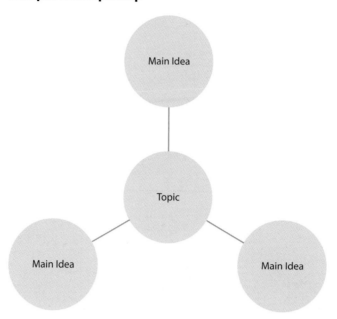

Figure 9-2   Example Concept Map for Résumé Components

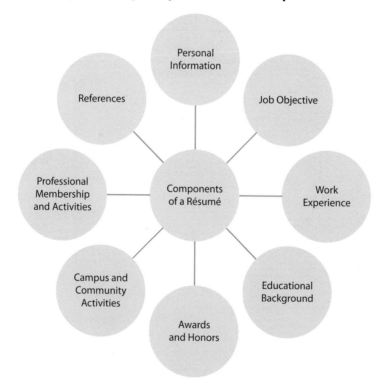

Following is another commonly used format for concept maps followed by a concept map that shows what information about your education should be included in a résumé.

Figure 9-3 Sample Concept Map

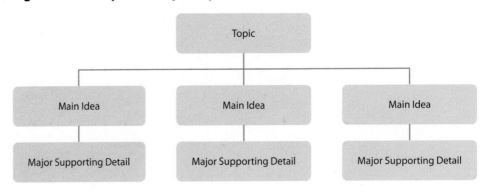

Figure 9-4 Example Concept Map for Educational Background

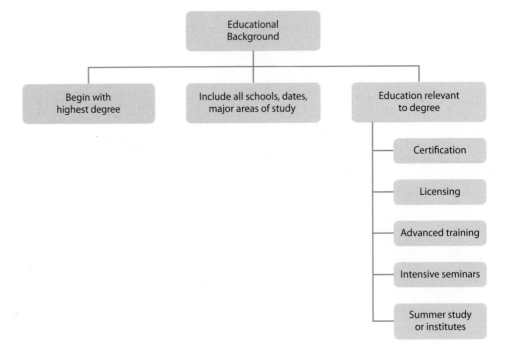

try it and apply it! 9-4   Creating a Concept Map

Directions: Read and annotate each passage. Then complete the concept maps that follow using details from the readings.

A. Interviewing and Nonverbal Communication

Just as the résumé is important for opening the door, the job interview is critical for putting your best foot forward and clearly articulating why you are the best person for the job. Here are some interview strategies that will help you make full use of nonverbal skills:

1. A good first impression is important and can be lasting. If you arrive late, you have already said a great deal about yourself. Make certain you know the time and location of the interview. Allow time for traffic delays and to find a parking space.

2. Being too familiar can be a barrier to a professional interview. Don't sit too close to the interviewer. Don't talk or sit until the interviewer does.

3. Because much of our communication is nonverbal, dressing properly for the interview is important. In most situations, it will be safe if you wear clean, pressed, conservative business attire in a neutral color. Pay special attention to grooming.

(continued)

(continued)

Make sure your nails and hair are clean, neat, and trimmed. Women should keep makeup light and not wear an excessive amount of jewelry that might be distracting.

4. Avoid nervous habits, such as tapping your pen, chewing on your pencil, playing with your hair, or covering your mouth with your hand. Don't chew gum, pick your cuticles, or bite your nails.

5. Look people in the eye and speak with confidence. Your eyes reveal much about you; use them to show interest, poise, and sincerity.

(Adapted from Ferrett 2010)

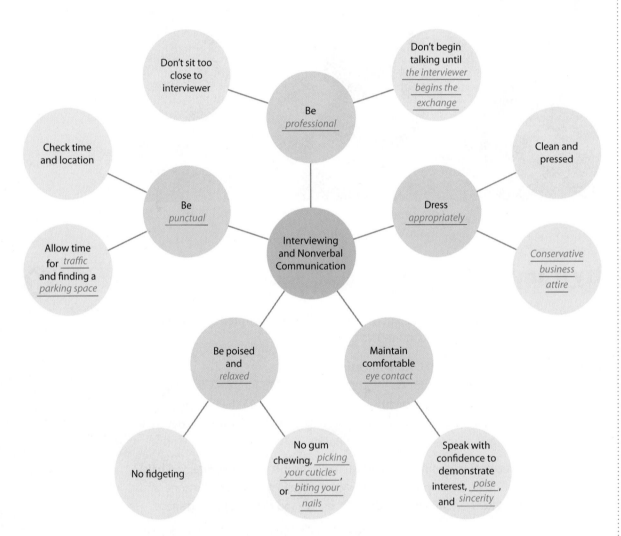

B. Here are some other tips that will be an asset during the interview process.

■ Request a job description from the personnel office to find out exactly what qualifications and skills are required. Learn about the company for which you are interviewing. Check out the company's website to find out about the company's mission statement, the product it makes, or the services it offers.

- Show how you can make a contribution to the company. Do not focus on asking about benefit packages, salary requirements, and vacation time.

- Expect open-ended questions, such as "What are your career goals?" and "Tell me about your best work experience." Decide in advance what information and skills are pertinent to the position and reveal your strengths.

- Although it's always important to stress your strengths, remember to be honest. Dishonesty or exaggeration can later haunt you when someone checks your references or your educational background.

- A follow-up thank you letter is especially important. It shows your gratitude, and it also serves to remind the interviewer of your sincere interest in the position. Send the thank you note no later than one day after your interview.

(Adapted from Ferrett 2010)

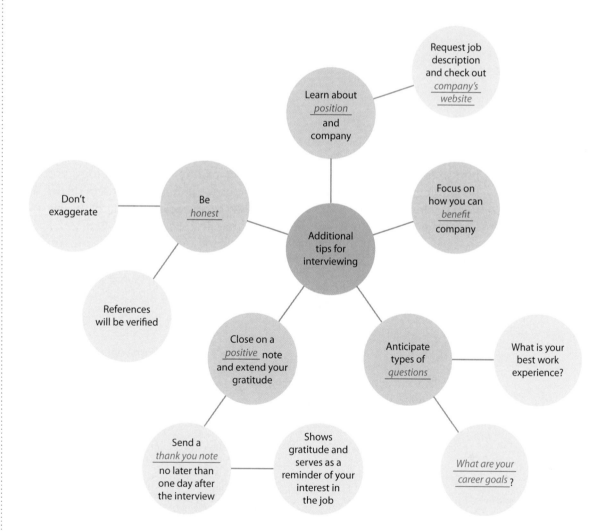

Tables

Tables are used to organize large amounts of information into an easy-to-read format; they are ideal for summarizing. They are often used at the end of textbook chapters to gather all the information that has been discussed in an easy-to-read format. They can also be used to compare and contrast information. In the workplace, especially in sales, tables are used to compare the amount of money generated by salespersons in a particular company. In the table that follows, the sales manager compares and contrasts the total revenue of sales for three of his salespeople. Notice the headings, columns, and rows, which are characteristic of tables.

Representative	July Sales	August Sales	Increase
Charles B. Brown	$32,819	$33,517	$698
Thelma Capp	$37,225	$39,703	$2,478
Bill E. Knauth	$36,838	$38,198	$1,360

(Adapted from Lesikar 2008)

Timelines

Textbook authors use **timelines** to highlight dates or to show a sequence of events that have been discussed in the text. You can use timelines to organize information you learned in a chapter. For example, in psychology, you may be reading about the significant people and the impact of their theories on the development of modern psychology. In history, you might be learning about the events that led up to and ultimately caused World War I.

The following timeline shows the chronology, or sequence in time, of some important events in the history of business from 1700 to 1800.

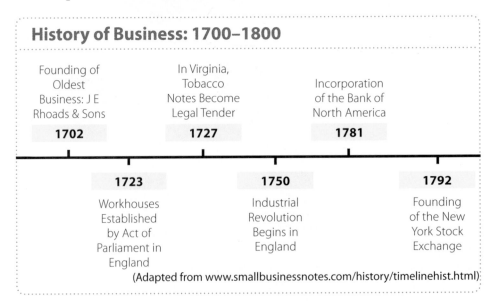

History of Business: 1700–1800

Founding of Oldest Business: J E Rhoads & Sons	In Virginia, Tobacco Notes Become Legal Tender	Incorporation of the Bank of North America
1702	**1727**	**1781**

1723	**1750**	**1792**
Workhouses Established by Act of Parliament in England	Industrial Revolution Begins in England	Founding of the New York Stock Exchange

(Adapted from www.smallbusinessnotes.com/history/timelinehist.html)

Process Diagram or Flow Chart

A **process diagram** or **flow chart** helps you to visualize the steps in a process. Understanding processes is part of every college discipline. For example, in political science, you may learn how a bill becomes a law; in biology, you might study how the body digests food; and in criminal justice, you could find out what happens when a person is charged with a crime.

Here is a flow chart that illustrates the process of searching with Google (Lesikar 2008).

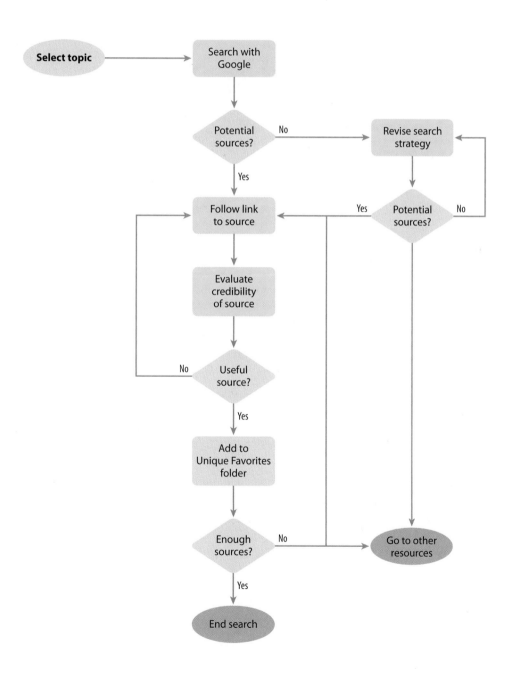

Venn Diagrams

A **Venn diagram** is an effective way to show comparison and contrast. Information is arranged within two large intersecting circles, each labeled with the name of one of the concepts you are comparing. In the intersecting, or overlapping, part, you write the similar attributes or characteristics of each concept and in the non-intersecting parts of the circles, the differences between them. Below is a Venn diagram that compares two job offers. Which job would you select?

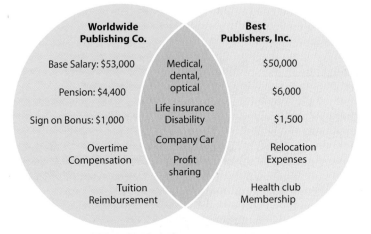

Worldwide Publishing Co.	Medical, dental, optical	Best Publishers, Inc.
Base Salary: $53,000		$50,000
Pension: $4,400		$6,000
Sign on Bonus: $1,000	Life insurance Disability	$1,500
Overtime Compensation	Company Car Profit sharing	Relocation Expenses
Tuition Reimbursement		Health club Membership

Keep this in mind

- Create your graphic organizers after reading and annotating a selection.
- Select the type of organizer that best suits your purpose.
- Allow enough space for details.
- Use any shapes you want. Be creative and have some fun.
- Use colored ink, special print, or illustrations to enhance retention of the material.

try it and apply it! 9-5   Using Graphic Organizers

Directions: Read each of the following passages about the workplace and annotate them. Then complete the graphic organizer that follows each reading selection.

1. **Finding an Employer**

You can use a number of sources to assist you in finding a place of business where you will begin or continue your career. Your choice of sources will probably depend on the stage of your career. For example, if you are just beginning your career, you might consider visiting your college's career center. Many career centers provide the services of excellent job search counselors, maintain extensive directories of major companies, and offer interviewing opportunities. Campus career centers often hold annual career fairs, at which students can meet up with companies that are looking for new graduates or locate opportunities for summer internships. Another great source is online databases. Monster.com offers job opportunities throughout the country, with new opportunities listed daily. In addition to using online sources, you can request that job notices be sent to you directly by websites. These sites use tools called personal search agents. Using a filter based on a confidential file you have completed for the site, these tools find jobs that match your profile and send you an email about these jobs. Some job seekers approach prospective employers directly, either by a personal visit or email. Personal visits are appropriate if the company has an employment office. Email contacts typically include a résumé and cover letter.

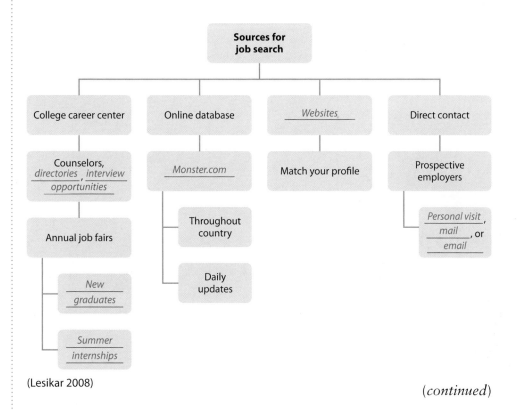

(Lesikar 2008)

(continued)

(*continued*)

2. **Making Formal Speeches**

The most difficult kind of oral communication at work is making a formal speech. Most of us do not feel comfortable speaking in front of others; however, you can learn speech techniques and put them into practice.

First, you must determine the topic of your presentation. In some cases, you will be assigned a topic, usually in your area of expertise. If you are not assigned a topic, you should be guided by three basic factors: your background and knowledge, the interests of your audience, and the occasion of your speech. After you have decided on your topic, the next step is to research your topic in a library, online, in the company files, or from people in your own company or other companies. When you have that information, you are ready to begin organizing your speech. The introduction of your speech should prepare the listeners to receive the message and arouse some interest in your topic. To arouse interest, you might begin by telling a human interest story, present a credible quotation or ask questions. The body of your speech should organize your information based on factors or issues. You also need to use clear transitions so that the listener can follow the different points and not be confused. Your speech should end by drawing a conclusion, which is where you bring together all that you have presented to achieve

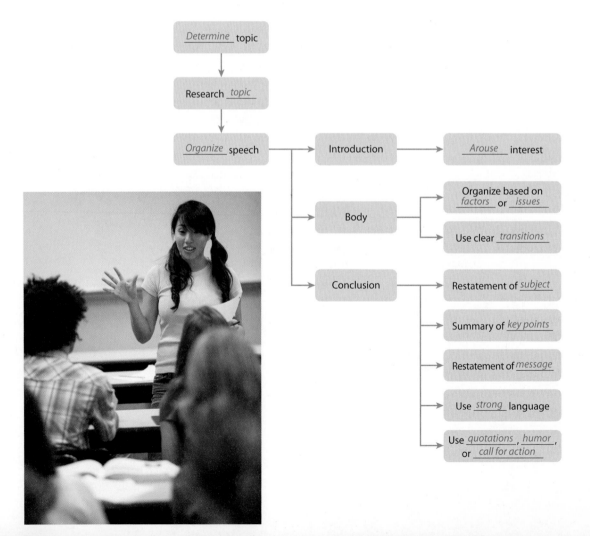

whatever goal the speech has. You should consider including the three elements in your closing: a restatement of the subject, the summary of the key points, and a restatement of the main message. Present the conclusion in strong language—in words that will get attention and be remembered. In addition, you can conclude with a quote, a bit of humor, or a call for action.

(Adapted from Lesikar 2008)

3. **Determining the Method of Presentation**

With the speech organized, you are ready to prepare your presentation. At this time, you need to decide whether to present the speech extemporaneously, memorize it, or read it.

Extemporaneous presentation—delivered without notes or papers—is the best and most effective way of presenting a speech. Using the notes you prepared, you review all the information, making no attempt to memorize it all. This type of presentation sounds the most natural to the listener and requires a great deal of planning and practice.

The most difficult method is memorizing. Although it, too, requires a great deal of preparation, it may not always bring about the best results. When you memorize a speech, you are usually memorizing words rather than ideas. As a result, if you make a speech and forget a couple of words, you may become confused and flustered.

The third presentation method is reading. Unfortunately, most of us tend to read aloud in a monotone voice. We can also miss punctuation marks, fumble over words, or lose our place. One effective way to practice this method is to read into a recorder and listen to yourself. Then practice your delivery until it sounds most natural.

(Adapted from Lesikar 2008)

Method of Presentation	Planning and Practice	Effectiveness
Extemporaneous	Use _notes_. Rehearse information. _Don't memorize_. _Requires a lot of practice_.	Sounds most _natural_
Memorizing	Focus on _ideas_, not just words.	May _not_ bring about the best results
Reading	Practice reading into _tape recorder_. Practice until your voice sounds most _natural_.	May sound _monotonous_

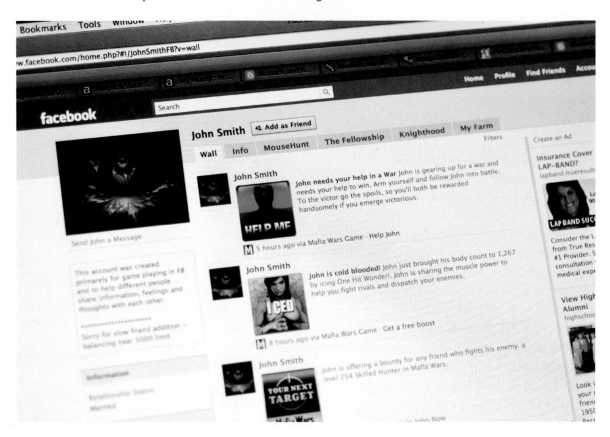

try it and apply it! 9-6 Organizing the Information   ⏸

Answers will vary. **Directions:** After you read each excerpt, decide on the best way to organize the information in it. Create an outline, write a summary, or draw a graphic organizer for each on separate sheets of paper.

Excerpt 1

Virtual Competence Is Vital in the Workplace: Online Communication Tools, Such as Facebook, Develop Important Work Skills.

By Nicole Haggerty, Richard Ivey School of Business

LONDON, Ontario, July 2 (AScribe Newswire)—When the Ontario government banned thousands of its employees from using the social networking site Facebook during work a couple of years ago, opponents of the move argued the workers were deprived of a powerful tool.

Recent research from Nicole Haggerty, an assistant professor of information systems at the Richard Ivey School of Business, now shows that online activities, such as communicating on Facebook, result in skills that are valuable in the workplace. "Managers should recognize that the capabilities people develop using daily life technologies are often transferable to the workplace. The interesting, collaborative, socially-oriented things that people do in their personal lives may actually create a foundational skill set that's valuable at work," said Haggerty. "When an organization bans something for short-term productivity reasons, it may be stifling the development of capabilities that are valuable in the long run."

Haggerty and Yinglei Wang, an Ivey graduate, have developed the concept "virtual competence," which refers to the degree of self-confidence in one's ability to use the technologies and collaborative tools now found in the workplace. While technology skills are important in the workplace, their research shows virtual competence also has a positive correlation with job satisfaction and job performance.

According to Haggerty, as companies invest money in technologies and collaborative tools, they need to think about the kinds of employees and skill sets that are best suited for today's workplace.

> **Source:** "Virtual Competence Is Vital in the Workplace: Online Communication Tools, Such as Facebook, Develop Important Work Skills." *Ascribe Higher Education News Service* (July 2, 2009): NA.

Excerpt 2

Notable Events in Business in American History

In February 1928, stock prices began to rise and continued, except for a few temporary lapses, for the next year and a half. In the autumn of 1929, the great bull market began to fall apart. Towards the end of October, stock prices began to decline at an alarming rate. Finally, on October 29, "Black Tuesday," all efforts to save the market failed, which helped trigger the Great Depression. It took over a decade for the market to fully recover, and many changes in the ways of conducting business and new federal policies resulted from this period in history.

As the economy sank because of the Great Depression, consumers became price-sensitive at a level never experienced before. In the 1930s, the first U.S. supermarket, King Kullen, was opened. King Kullen was seen as more than a convenience. It meant affordable food for families hurt by the depression. By 1936 there were 17 King Kullen supermarkets bringing in about $6,000,000 in annual sales. A leader in employee relations, King Kullen surprised the food industry by giving its employees insurance, vacation and pay raises in the late 30s. By 1940 it was New York's premier supermarket.

(*continued*)

(continued)

The Stock Market Crash and the Great Depression also brought about some new federal policies, which were initially created as relief for those people who were out of work. In 1934, FDR, as part of The New Deal, signed the bill for the Federal Housing Administration (FHA). The FHA provided some relief in the form of insuring mortgages for new construction and home repairs. Then, in 1939 the Social Security Act, which had created a system of unemployment and temporary assistance from the government, issued its first check.

(Adapted from Brinkley and www.kingkullen.com)

Put the Pieces Together: Organizing Information for Reading and Studying

In this chapter, you learned the importance of organizing information after you have read it. Whether you choose to write outlines or summaries or to create graphic organizers of sections or complete chapters from textbooks, you should always utilize effective paraphrasing.

Paraphrase	A restatement of an author's ideas, used in summarizing, outlining, and mapping
Outline	A hierarchical arrangement of an author's ideas going from general to specific
Summary	A condensed version of an author's main points
Concept Map	A general graphic or visual representation of the organization of an author's main ideas and details
Table	A graphic organizer used to organize large amounts of information
Timeline	A graphic representation used for sequence or order of events over time
Process Diagram	A graphic organizer used to show steps in a process
Venn Diagram	Intersecting circles used to analyze similarities and differences

Key Terms

concept map   process diagram   table
graphic organizer   or flow chart   timeline
outlining   summary   Venn diagram
paraphrase

Make Your Mark
Becoming an Effective Test Taker

In this chapter

you will learn to

- Prepare for exams
- Understand the different kinds of exam formats
- Reduce test anxiety

Prepare for Exams

Let's begin with an "exam." Circle your response to the following questions.

1. When should you begin studying for an exam in one of your classes?
   a. the night before
   b. the week before
   c. each day once classes have begun
   d. the morning of the test

2. Which of the following will impact your ability to succeed on exams?
   a. attending class regularly and asking questions
   b. taking good notes and reviewing them after each class
   c. completing assigned and recommended reading throughout the term
   d. all of the above

3. Because everyone takes the same exam, all students should study in the same manner.
   True or False

Each of the preceding questions represents important points about preparing for exams. The answer to question 1 is *c*. In actuality, you begin preparing for exams on the first day of class! Focus on the course goals and stay on top of the material from day one. The more connected and involved you are with the course material right from the start, the better prepared you will be for exams.

Certainly, the correct response to question 2 is *d*. Attending class regularly keeps you on track and in control because you know what's going on. Steady completion of assignments throughout the semester, effective note taking, participation in discussions, and asking questions keeps you involved with the material and also makes class time enjoyable. Being active in class builds a strong foundation that you can rely on when you begin to review material for an exam.

Review is the important word here. Studying for a test should not be the first time you encounter the material on your own. Studying is a time for *relearning* material you have already understood and applied. Keep this in mind as you plan your weekly schedule of tasks throughout the term. Make time to actively read your assigned material and review your notes regularly each week, if not each evening, to prepare yourself for the inevitable test.

The statement in question three is definitely *false*. It is important for you to **understand your preferred learning modality and learning style.** Review page 21 on "Discover Your Learning Style" in Chapter 1 to make sure you are aware of how *you* learn best. Let the process of studying be personal and work for you. Read the chart that follows to refresh your understanding.

Learning Modality/Style	Suggestions for Exam Preparation
Auditory	Recite information out loud.
Verbal	Write out information.
Visual	Draw charts, semantic maps, and simple outlines. Create "pictures" in your mind on which you can attach information.
Tactile-Kinesthetic	Walk around while you study. Highlight and annotate text.
Social	Form a study group with friends and meet regularly.

Ways to Prepare for an Exam

Here are some additional suggestions to consider when preparing for your exams.

- **Speak with your professor.** Your professor can set you on the right path when it comes to selecting the correct material that will be covered on an exam. Your professor may give you a better understanding of the kinds and number of questions that will be asked and the format of the test.

- **Rehearse for the specific type of exam you will be taking.** Structure your study in a similar format as the exam. For example, for essay exams, *plan, outline,* and *write* out essays based on the questions you anticipate will be asked. If you know the exam will have a "fill in the blank" portion with a list of choices, study with a list of choices. If on a math exam you need to "show your work," you should include every step as you solve practice problems to prepare for the test. If "spelling counts," particularly on foreign language exams, be sure to write and correctly spell all your terms as you study.

■ **Gather your study material.** Be sure you have all the sources of information on which the exam will be based. These include your textbooks, handouts, lecture notes, and feedback on previous exams and assignments.

■ **Organize the test material.** Whenever possible, break large amounts of information into categories, so that you are not just remembering one unrelated fact after another. For example, if you were studying the nervous system in biology or psychology, you would divide this large topic into the central nervous system, the peripheral nervous system, and the autonomic nervous system. You might relate each system to a different portion of the brain and then review disorders in each system. The point is to cluster your information into related areas of study; then organize it into major and minor points.

■ **Study over a longer period of time than you think you need.** As we said at the beginning of this chapter, start studying further in advance of the exam than you might think necessary. This way you can study for shorter periods of time, covering less material during each session. Most of us learn best by breaking large units of information into smaller, more manageable parts. After you have organized the information, use your planner to assign yourself specific areas to study at specific times before the exam. Make sure you review previous units briefly each time before you move on to the next unit.

■ **Understand the material you are learning, rather than simply memorize it.** Focusing on the meaning of the information will improve your ability to learn and remember it.

■ **Intend to remember!** Although this may seem obvious, it is important to be conscious of your goal to learn or commit something to memory. It will make a difference in accomplishing your objective.

■ **Read simpler versions of the material presented in your textbook.** Consider initially reading material written at a lower reading level than your text or a "review" book on the material you are learning. This review can help you gain background knowledge that will help you later in learning the material at a higher level.

■ **Create mnemonic (memory) devices.** Devise *your own* acronyms, acrostics, and simple graphic aids to help your recall. It is usually allowed, assuming you are permitted to write notes on your test paper, to jot down your mnemonics at the beginning of a test. This way you have them available during the exam.

   ■ An **acronym** is a word formed from the initial letters of each component of a list, organization, or process. For example, THIEVES is an acronym for recalling the steps for previewing a reading selection. Can you recite them? (Look back to page 40.) Can you name the colors of the light spectrum (Red, orange, yellow, green, blue, indigo, and violet) by remembering the name of ROY G. BIV? Psychology students can remember R.J. Sternberg's elements of love: passion, intimacy, and commitment, by remembering to PIC their boyfriend or girlfriend. HOMES is an acronym used to recall the Great Lakes (Huron, Ontario, Michigan, Erie, and Superior).

Many acronyms have become commonly used words themselves. Did you know that NASCAR is actually an acronym for the National Association for Stock Car Auto Racing and SCUBA is an acronym for Self-contained Underwater Breathing Apparatus?

■ An **acrostic** is a memorable phrase or sentence in which the first letter of each word triggers a memory of a part of a list or series. Sometimes these are nonsensical, making them easier to remember. *Keep ponds clean or frogs get sick* has helped many biology students remember the classification system of Kingdom, Phylum, Class, Order, Family, Genus, Species. Try to name the planets of the solar system, in their order from the sun, by relying on the first letter of each word in the following sentence as a clue: *My very earnest mother just served us nine pickles* (Mercury, Venus, Earth, Mars, Jupiter, Saturn, Uranus, Neptune, Pluto). Here's an acrostic for those Great Lakes: *Some men hate each other.*

■ If you recall information visually, using **graphic aids** can be very helpful. Make simple charts or graphs to show the key elements of a model, system, or process. These can help you recall them and trigger your memory for the related details. (See Chapter 9 for more on graphic organizers.)

■ **Seek support if you are having difficulty understanding the material.** Your professors are usually available to help you, especially during their office hours. Your school also may provide tutoring services. Don't hesitate to take the help available!

Understand Exam Formats

Generally, in-class exams include two types of questions: objective questions and essay questions. Find out the format of the test in advance from your professor, so you can better prepare for it.

Objective Questions

Objective questions generally tap your *knowledge* of specific information, though they may also ask you to apply your *understanding* of information. Usually, an objective question has only one correct response. The most commonly used kinds of objective questions are multiple choice, fill in the blank (also known as *cloze* when included within paragraphs or reading selections), true/false, matching, and short answer.

Multiple-Choice Questions   Professors often choose a **multiple-choice format** for exams. In this case, you are asked to select the best answer from four to five possible responses. You might be asked to enter your responses on a grid sheet or fill in the corresponding circle so that grading can be done mechanically.

Tips for Responding to Multiple-Choice Questions

- **Read each question carefully.** Pay close attention to words that may change the answer you choose, particularly if the question asks you to identify the response that is *not* true. For example:

Which of the following is *not* a portion of the three-stage memory model?

    a. sensory memory

    b. invented memory

    c. short-term memory

    d. long-term memory

The correct response is invented memory. As you work through this question, you may think to yourself, "Which *are* the components of the three-stage memory model?" As you recall that sensory, long-term, and short-term memory are the major components, you will conclude that the answer to the question is the choice *b*.

    This is another way the question could be phrased:

All of the following are part of the three-stage memory model *except:*

Again, the answer is choice *b*. This is another way of asking you to identify the item that is *not* something.

- **When multiple-choice questions ask you to fill in a blank, be sure to read past the blank until the end of the sentence or paragraph.** The context will help you identify the correct answer choice.

- **Anticipate the answer first, *without* looking at the choices.** Then, see if your response, or a version of it, is presented as a possible option. If it is, you are likely to be correct.

- **Read all the possible choices to be sure you choose the *best* possible answer.** The first choice may seem right, but you might discover a more accurate response as you read on.

- **Use the process of elimination to narrow your choices.** Cross out choices you know are incorrect. The odds are more in your favor if you are selecting one out of two or three choices, rather than one out of four.

- **When unsure, eliminate choices that present an all-or-nothing response.** Life tends not to exist in absolutes. Thus, consider passing on choices that include *always, all, never, only,* or *no one*. However, bear in mind that this *could be* the case. This strategy doesn't *always* work!

- **Mark questions you are unsure of and return to these later.** Sometimes, by working your way through the rest of the exam, you will pick up, or even recall, information that is helpful to you.

- **If you are *sure* that two choices are correct, even if you are not sure of the others, selecting "all of the above," if it is given as a choice, is likely to be the correct response.**

Cloze Questions   Many standardized tests used for college placement or to measure competence use a **cloze format** (also known as fill in the blank). Blanks, representing sections of missing information, are included in

sentences, paragraphs, or longer selections, and possible answers for completing them are presented in a multiple-choice format.

Tips for Responding to Cloze Questions

■ **Whether or not choices are provided, always try to complete the response on your own first.** Say the word "blank" aloud as you read through to the end of the sentence so that you can "hear" how it sounds. If choices are provided, find the one that most closely matches your prediction. For example, consider the following sentence on a psychology exam:

Having only a brief duration, _____ is the stage in which the recognized information enters into our consciousness from sensory memory.

You might think "quick stage" or "early stage" could fit in the blank. Suppose you are provided with the following word bank from which to choose your response:

short-term memory	intermittent-stage memory	long-term memory

You would look for the choice that most closely corresponds to your idea. In this case, *short-term memory* is the correct response.

■ **If you have no idea what the answer is, reread the sentence, substituting different choices in the blank.** Decide which seems to work best. You can use the process of elimination here as well. The more choices you elimi-nate, the better your chances are for selecting the correct response.

■ **If you are provided with choices, mark these off as you use them.** Check to see if you are provided with more options than will be actually used. This way you won't be concerned if you have some left over.

■ **Watch for grammatical clues.** The sentence that you complete must be grammatically accurate, as well as factually correct. Pay attention to the part of speech that is needed (adjective, noun, verb, etc.). Notice if the missing word must begin with a vowel, as it would if it is preceded by *an*, or if it needs to be singular or plural.

True/False Questions   In true or false questions, you are asked to decide whether a statement is accurate or inaccurate. Because the only two options are true or false, you have a 50 percent chance of responding correctly. Fol-lowing are some suggestions to strengthen even those odds.

Tips for Responding to True/False Questions

■ **If any part of the statement is false, then the statement is false.** If you are unsure, and a statement contains terms such as *all, always, everyone* or *never, nothing,* or *no one,* you may do best to mark it false. Likewise, statements that are more qualified—that is, they contain words such as *perhaps, may, some,* or *might*—are more likely to be true. For example, *All students consume caffeine to stay alert* is false. *Some students con-sume caffeine to stay alert* is true.

■ **Read statements with two or more parts closely.** Even though one part of the statement may be true, if the second part is not, the statement must be considered false. For example, consider this sentence: *Kinesthetic learners like to move around during study, while social learners prefer to study quietly and alone.* Though the first portion of the sentence is correct, the second portion is not, so the statement is false.

Matching Questions   This format generally presents two lists, such as terms and definitions, causes and effects, or synonyms or antonyms. You must pair or match the items.

Tips for Responding to Matching Questions

■ **Read all the items in both lists before responding.** Although an initial choice may seem correct, as you move along you may find a better response. You also want to have an overall sense of your choices before you begin making your matches.

■ **Complete the matches you are sure of first.** This narrows your choices for the remaining items.

■ **Keep track of your responses.** Check off or circle items you use so the num-ber of remaining choices narrows as you move along. Do not completely cross out items you have used so that you can no longer read them! You might need to rethink items and return to previously selected matches.

Short-Answer Questions   These are questions that tap your understand-ing or recall of material in a quick, direct way. Choices are not provided. You either know the material or you don't! For example, "What memory trick, or mnemonic device, is a word formed from the first letters of a series of other words, such a PEMDAS or SCUBA?" Here, the answer is "acronym."

Tips for Responding to Short-Answer Questions

- **The amount of space provided may be a clue for the length of the answer.**
- **If these questions are part of a larger exam, and you are not sure of a response, work through the rest of the exam.** The information that it covers may help you recall your response. The answer may even be within another portion of the test itself.
- **Don't leave any blanks. Give it your best shot.**

Essay Questions

Essay questions ask you to respond to a question or series of questions in a written format. Expect to write answers that range from one paragraph to several paragraphs in length, depending on the nature of the questions.

This type of question usually goes beyond your understanding and recall of facts. It typically asks you to explain, integrate, and apply that knowledge.

Essay questions are posed in a variety of ways. It is important to understand what each question asks you to do. Read the table on page 278 to distinguish the different tasks an essay question is asking you to do.

Tips for Responding to Essay Questions

- **Read all the essay questions as part of your exam preview.** Jot down any ideas related to the questions that you may think of as you complete other portions of the test.
- **Annotate the essay questions.** Number the various tasks or criteria that may be part of a question. Underline key words in the directions or content of the question. Notice how the essay question that follows has been annotated to help the test taker be sure he or she is addressing all the required components.

  1. Compare and contrast long-term and short-term memory. Discuss the 2. neurological basis for each and 3. how each plays a role in the learning process. 4. Include examples in our daily lives that relate to each.

- **Create a brief graphic organizer of your ideas before you begin writing.** (See Chapter 9.) A simple outline, chart, or concept map may help you recall your ideas and organize your essay ahead of time. This will serve as a guide that you can refer to after you begin composing your essay.
- **Pay attention to your time.** Be sure you allocate enough time to complete your written responses. Also, consider dividing the time up so you can complete the following tasks:
  - *Plan and organize your information before you actually begin to write* (10–25% of your time). Create a brief outline or map in which you identify your key points and important supporting details. Realize that this planning time is not wasted time but an important part of your composing process.
  - *Write your response* (60–80% of your time). Write as legibly as you can, so you won't need to use your revision time to repair messy handwriting!

Terms Used in Essay Questions

Term	What the Term Is Asking You to Do
Describe	Provide details about a given place, time, or situation. **Describe** the social climate in the United States during the years prior to the Civil Rights Movement.
Identify	Name or list something. In an essay question, it is often combined with another task. **Identify** the stages of sleep and **explain** the importance of each.
Summarize	Identify the key points or elements of an issue, event, process, etc. and tell about each briefly. **Summarize** the biological reasons as to why we forget information.
Explain	Provide the reasons, rationale, or process behind a behavior. **Explain** how sleep deprivation impacts the emotional and physical well-being of humans.
Compare	Show how things are similar. **Compare** the impact of mass media on children today with the impact of mass media on children in the 1950s.

Contrast	Show how things are different.
	    Contrast the codes of conduct in schools today with those of the nineteenth century.
	Often, comparison and contrast are included in the same question.
	    Compare and **contrast** the similarities and differences between large universities and small private colleges.

Justify	Provide the reasons or causes for an action or behavior. **Justify** the creation of an all-year school calendar in public schools across the country.
Discuss	Explain and describe the issue or topic. Include different perspectives and viewpoints. **Discuss** the concerns of those who are opposed to lowering the drinking age for alcoholic products.
Evaluate/ Assess	State your opinion or make a judgment about a situation or actions related to it. Back up your view with information or facts. **Assess** the impact of the Internet on the quality of student performance in high school English classes.
Trace	Provide a sequential or chronological overview that identifies key elements in the development of a concept, object, or living creature. **Trace** the development of psychological therapies over the last century.

- *Proofread, edit, and revise* (10–20% of your time). Here is your time to check word use, capitalization, punctuation, spelling, and perform a quick content review. Try not to make major adjustments here. Your preplanning should help you avoid major organizational pitfalls. Polish and add any additional relevant thoughts that make your essay stronger or clearer.

For example, if you have an hour to complete one essay, you might allow 6 to 15 minutes to plan it, 36 to 48 minutes to actually write it, and 6 to 12 minutes to proofread, edit, and revise it.

- **It is often best to begin with a thesis statement that states the main idea or point of your response.** Generating a thesis statement helps bring clarity to your response and helps you stay focused on your key point and purpose.
- **Follow the same strategies you have learned for writing a good composition.** Include an introduction in which you provide brief background information and state your thesis. Then include your body paragraphs that explain and support your thesis, and include a clear topic sentence in each. Conclude your essay with a restatement of your thesis.

try it and apply it! 10-1   Understanding Test Formats

Directions: Take the brief "test" that follows. Each question uses a different question format. Answer the question, and then write the question format in the parentheses.

1. When answering true/false questions, even if only a small portion of the statement is untrue, the response should be marked *false* _____
   (*cloze/fill in the blank*) _____

2. Circle the choice below that is not an example of an "objective" test question. (*multiple choice*) _____
   a. multiple choice
   b. (essay)
   c. fill in the blank
   d. matching

3. What percentage of the time you have to write an essay should you allocate for proofreading, editing, and revising your work? *10–20%* _____
   (*short answer*) _____

4. Write a paragraph in which you identify three different tasks often asked in an essay question. Discuss what each expects you to do and give an example of each question. (*essay*)
   Answers will vary _____
   _____
   _____

Reduce Test Anxiety

For some students, the stress and worry of an exam is worse than the exam itself. Remember, feeling somewhat nervous before a test is absolutely normal. It represents your concern and care about succeeding, which probably has motivated you to work hard and study. That's a good thing! Although it would be unrealistic to expect to walk into an exam entirely relaxed, let's consider some strategies to lessen the anxiety.

Tips for Reducing Test Anxiety

- **First and foremost, be prepared for the exam.** Even though you may still have the jitters on test day, you will be far less stressed if you know you have done your best to prepare. Be sure to pack the supplies that you need for the exam, such as pencils, pens, calculators, and batteries for the calculator.

- **Study for the exam over several days, rather than the night before.** Review your class material daily and complete your homework assignments on time. *Studying for an exam should not be the first time you attempt to learn material.* In other words, avoid cramming! Just the nature of cramming for a test at the last minute lends itself to stress. You are likely to feel overwhelmed by the sheer quantity of material you attempt to learn or review in too short a period of time. If the process keeps you up late the night before test day, it has done even greater damage because you need your rest.

- **Get a good night's sleep before an exam.** Avoid the rationalization that you can relax by going out late and partying. Save that reward for the night after the exam. You should enter an exam rested, not exhausted.

- **Eat a light meal before your test.** Don't go into a test hungry. This deprivation can impact your energy level and ability to focus, and can even cause headaches.

- **Try to arrive at class a little early the day of an exam.** You don't want to rush or worry over being late. Leave yourself enough time so you can exhale and relax a bit before an exam is distributed. You have a better chance of selecting a seat that you prefer and "calming down" before you must get to work.

- **Sit apart from others if possible.** This position will give you some "space" and lessen the potential for distraction by your classmates. **Plan to be the last person to leave the exam room.** Take all the time that is afforded to you. Don't be upset if someone, or everyone, leaves earlier than you.

- **Take a few minutes to preview your exam.** Look over the entire test first. This preview will help you know what's in store and to pace yourself. Perhaps you will take care of portions you find easiest first, building your confidence. Previewing the test can also help you recall ideas or terms you will use throughout the test.

- **Read all directions slowly and carefully.** In a question with multiple tasks, you might number them to be sure you answer them all. Check off each portion as you complete it.

- **Write down mnemonics, key words, simple lists, or formulas that you expect will be needed in the margin or on paper provided.** That way you won't be concerned about forgetting them.

- **If you need to, take a "breather" midway.** Literally take a deep breath or two, and stretch your hands if you have been writing intensely.
- **Ask questions you may have during the exam, if permitted.** Don't assume this is not permitted; you may have an opportunity to clarify something about the test format that is confusing to you.
- **Have a watch with you so you can keep track of the time.** Some professors may not permit cell phone use, even to check the time.
- **Some students find it relaxing to chew gum, suck on a piece of candy, or sip a drink during an exam.** If food and drink is permitted, and if it works for you, go ahead.
- **Try to remove the notion that any one test or assignment will "make or break" your grade.** Your grades are usually determined using several measures of your achievement. Keep this in mind if you find yourself getting very nervous about a particular exam.
- **Believe in yourself!** If you have prepared and studied for your exam, wish yourself well, trust in your capabilities, and feel empowered.

The passage below lists and describes some common student practices that, unfortunately, add stress during exam time rather than minimize it. It is adapted from a website article titled *Studying Mistakes: How to Make Finals More Stressful*, by Elizabeth Scott (About.com. 11/09). Do any apply to you?

try it and apply it! 10-2   Reducing Test Anxiety

Directions: Read the following selection. Then respond to the questions that follow.

Making Exams *More* Stressful

Pulling "All-Nighters"

Many students, especially those who work best with deadlines, find themselves staying up all night studying. Going through the next day exhausted, many may wonder if it's worth it. Do the benefits of an all-night study session outweigh the sleepiness and fuzzy thinking that generally characterize the next day? Research says 'no'. A recent study found that students who regularly pulled all-nighters tended to have lower GPAs than those who didn't. The study also found that most students didn't stay up studying because they *had* to, but because it was 'kind of fun,' or a rite of passage. This is good news because it means that most students, armed with the understanding that all-nighters aren't associated with higher grades, can stop.

(*continued*)

Powering Down the Caffeine

Decades ago, truck drivers and students in the throes of finals season considered taking caffeine pills or powering down the Mountain Dew to stay awake when they wanted to be up all night. More recently, many 'energy drinks' have sprung up on the market, and are gaining popularity with students who want to have extra energy for extra studying. While energy drinks may be tempting, and some evidence shows that they can enhance performance in the short term (especially for those who aren't habitual consumers), there are drawbacks as well. Caffeine can give your energy level a temporary jolt, but that can be accompanied by a later crash that leaves you feeling completely drained. Studies show that students who consumed energy drinks may also experience headaches or even heart palpitations. Also, caffeine stays in your system for many hours longer than you may expect, which can interfere with sleep, making it difficult to sleep when you need to. This can leave you exhausted rather than refreshed in the morning, and potentially causing a self-perpetuating cycle. Finding natural ways to get extra energy, such as a healthy diet and exercise, as well as quality sleep on a regular basis, is the best way to maintain enough energy to tackle finals.

Having Study Parties with Your Fun Friends

While it seems like a great idea to get together and study with your friends, if you're not careful you may find yourself wasting valuable study time accomplishing nothing but some muted fun. With the wrong mix of people, group studying can turn into a gossip session.

Even meeting in the wrong place, such as a busy restaurant, can offer enough distraction to sabotage your efforts. It's best to stick with the library or another quiet place that presents the right atmosphere and is conducive to studying. Study groups can be wonderfully successful, but be sure to think long and hard before organizing one. Choose people who are responsible and committed, and be sure that you maintain the same level of commitment to studying. You can all celebrate your good grades when finals are over.

Waiting Until the Last Minute

This is an obvious risk if you really think about it. First, you always run the risk of not finishing in time, and being unprepared. Second, you greatly increase your chances of needing to try some of the other items on this list, such as powering down the caffeine or pulling all-nighters. Finally, hasty 'cramming' tends to encode information into your short-term memory, but the knowledge doesn't always remain memorized; you cheat yourself out of a true education. A wiser choice for those who work best with deadlines is to give yourself a deadline that's really a week or so before your 'real' deadline—this gives you a burst of motivation, but also some wiggle room.

Constantly Reminding Yourself What's at Stake

Remembering the importance of a test's outcome can be a good motivator for studying. However, too much focus on the outcome can backfire. If you're the type of person who is already pretty conscientious, and the idea of doing poorly on the test is starting to cause significant test anxiety, it may be time to shift your focus. This is because being overly anxious about a test's outcome can actually cause you to do poorly, or to score lower than you normally would. To avoid obsessing, try some positive affirmations, visualizations, or tips on overcoming test anxiety.

Sources: Haskell CF, Kennedy DO, Wesnes KA, Scholey AB. Cognitive and Mood Improvements of Caffeine in Habitual Consumers and Habitual Non-Consumers of Caffeine. *Psychopharmacology,* June 2005.

Malinauskas BM, Aeby VG, Overton RF, Carpenter-Aeby T, Barber-Heidal K. A Survey of Energy Drink Consumption Patterns among College Students. *Nutrition Journal,* October 2007.

Musch J, Bröder A. Test Anxiety Versus Academic Skills: A Comparison of Two Alternative Models for Predicting Performance in a Statistics Exam. *British Journal of Educational Psychology.* March 1999.

1. **List five behaviors of college students that increase test anxiety.**
    1. Pulling all-nighters, 2. Ingesting too much caffeine, 3. Wasting time while "studying" with friends, 4. Leaving studying and preparation to the "last minute," 5. Obsessing on the outcome or importance of an exam.

2. **Identify one behavior that you have or have had a tendency to do. How will you change it?**
    Responses will vary.

Make Your Mark: Becoming an Effective Test Taker

There are many behaviors and strategies you can apply to become a strong, confident test taker. Review this chapter to identify techniques that you will adopt for yourself.

■ **Consider the suggestions to better prepare for exams and try them out.** Make some changes and evaluate their impact on your success throughout the semester. Use different strategies in different classes.

■ **Practice creating mnemonic devices and strategies throughout the term, when you are not under the pressure of midterms and finals.** You can find out which mnemonic devices work best for you.

■ **Anticipate and create your own essay questions using the various terms presented.** Being able to create potential test questions shows that you know what is important. If you have "no idea" what the potential questions are, you should go back to the material and work with it until you do. Then, practicing the written response before the exam will take your preparation even further.

■ **Consider the suggestions to reduce test anxiety.** Remember that exercise, rest, and healthy diet will go a long way to reduce stress about exams and everything else in your life!

Key Terms

acronym
acrostic
cloze format
essay questions

graphic aids
multiple-choice
    format

short-answer
    questions

Readings About the Code of Conduct

Get Acquainted with the Issue

Perhaps you have seen war movies in which American soldiers say to their captors, "I am only required to give you my name, rank, service number, and date of birth." This order comes from *The Six Articles of the Code of Conduct* of the U.S. military. This code of conduct is the legal guide for the behavior of military members who are captured by hostile forces.

Although other organizations, institutions, businesses, and professions in American society may not be engaged in such life-threatening situations, many still establish a set of rules outlining the responsibilities and appropriate behaviors for their staff. These strict rules of behavior serve as a guide for their decision making and setting of procedures, and at the same time protect the rights of individuals who work for them. In the article "Bounced from Preschool," you will read about a young student who does not follow the rules of conduct outlined by his school. In "Lying as America's Pastime," you find out about the inappropriate behavior of some college students. Finally, in "Navigating the Minefield of Harassment at Work," you will discover the rules of proper etiquette in the workplace.

Guided Reading

Bounced from Preschool:
Nursery School Delinquents?

Some Tots Are Getting the Heave-Ho for Unruly Behavior

By Thomas Fields-Meyer

This selection from People *magazine talks about certain changes in preschool policies and programs.*

◀◀ before you read

Think about what you already know about a topic before you begin reading. Then when you begin to read, you will be able to attach your new learning to this background knowledge and more easily understand the new information. (See Chapter 2, page 38.)

Discuss or write your responses to the following questions about your *own* experiences with preschool.

1. Did you attend preschool? If so, what experiences do you recall?
2. What are some of the reasons parents send their children to preschool today?
3. In your opinion, what is the role of preschool?

Prepare to Read

Preview the selection "Bounced from Preschool," using the THIEVES strategy on page 40.

Exercise 1   Previewing

Directions: Complete the following items.

1. Take a look at the selection and check off all the items that are available to you for preview.

   _X_ Title

   ___ Headings

   _X_ Introduction

   _X_ Every first sentence in each paragraph

   ___ Visuals/vocabulary

   ___ End of chapter questions

   _X_ Summary/concluding paragraph

2. Actively preview the selection by reading and highlighting the items you have checked.

3. Based on your preview, place an "X" next to all those items you predict will be discussed in the selection.

   ___ a. Preschoolers are becoming juvenile delinquents.

   ___ b. A solid education begins with a preschool experience.

   _X_ c. Preschoolers are getting kicked out for inappropriate conduct.

   _X_ d. Some nursery programs are helping preschoolers adapt to school.

   ___ e. Therapists are assisting young children in changing their behavior.

   _X_ f. There are changes in the nature of preschool education.

Check Out the Vocabulary

You will find the following vocabulary words in bold type in the reading selection. Do you know what some of these words mean? Knowing the meaning of all these words will increase your understanding of the material.

addressed	aggressive	drive	expelled	magnet school
affiliated	agitation	empathizing	launch	shirking

| **Exercise 2** | **Checking Out the Vocabulary** |

Directions: Look at each word taken from the reading selection. Read the sentences that follow. The first is from the selection, with a hint to its meaning, and the second one uses the word in an additional context. Choose the best definition for the word, and write the letter of the definition you select on the line provided.

_c_ **1. agitation**

- Renee Tucker spoke to a therapist who suggested a possible reason for William's **agitation** . . . (para. 2) (HINT: Reread sentence 1 in paragraph 1.)
- I usually feel jittery before exams; my advisor believes this **agitation** is due to my fear of failing out of college.

  a. anger
  b. childish behavior
  c. physical restlessness
  d. movement

_c_ **2. launch**

- Having to leave preschool seems a bad way to **launch** one's academic career . . . (para. 3) (HINT: For some children, preschool is the beginning of one's formal education.)
- According to research, enrolling in a freshman seminar is one of the most effective ways to **launch** one's college career.

  a. throw forward
  b. send off
  c. begin, give a start
  d. enjoy a midday meal

_c_ **3. expelled**

- A 2005 Yale University study estimated that more than 5,000 U.S. preschoolers are **expelled** each year—a rate three times higher than in elementary or high schools. (para. 3) (HINT: The prefix *ex-* means *out of*, as from a specified place or source, as in the word *ex*it, a place you go out from.)
- Robert was **expelled** from school because he had been caught selling papers over the Internet.

  a. welcomed
  b. blown out
  c. forced to leave
  d. graduated

_a_ **4. shirking**

- The trend troubles some experts, however, who say too many schools are **shirking** their responsibility by tossing out, rather than dealing with, tots who act up in class or fall behind in their schoolwork. (para. 4) (HINT: *Rather than* means *the opposite*.)

- Many professors contend that any students who **shirk** their responsibility to complete an assignment should not be allowed to attend class.

  a. avoiding one's duty
  b. accepting one's responsibility
  c. facing one's obligation
  d. tricking someone

_a_ 5. **drive**

- Behind the **drive** to expel is the changing nature of preschool itself. (para. 5) (HINT: Think about the cause of expulsions from preschool.)
- Hank's desire to complete college in four years **drove** him to attend both winter and summer sessions.

  a. pressure
  b. action
  c. rush
  d. trip

_d_ 6. **empathizing**

- . . . schools . . . are forcing an overly academic curriculum on little ones at the expense of teaching such basic skills as dealing with frustration or **empathizing** with classmates . . . (para. 5) (HINT: The prefix *em-* means *in* or *within*. The root *path* or *pathos* means feeling.)
- Although I passed the English and math portions of the college's entrance exam, I **empathized** with my friend who had to take several noncredit courses before she could enroll in credit-bearing course work.

  a. misunderstanding
  b. feeling frustrated
  c. calling upon
  d. understanding

_a_ 7. **affiliated**

- **Affiliated** with Tufts University, the center benefits from its financial support. (para. 8) (HINT: Why does the center receive money from Tufts University?)
- Students in the business and marketing program enroll in internships provided by **affiliated** local businesses.

  a. created a close connection
  b. became friends
  c. joined a club
  d. originated or came from

_c_ 8. **addressed**

- Happily, William Hewett's behavior has been effectively **addressed**. (para. 9) (HINT: Look beyond the familiar meaning of the word *address*, which means to write the directions for a place or destination. Use context clues.)

- Professor Marks recommended that I visit the student center, where the counseling staff **addressed** my issues with time management.

  a. made a speech
  b. made preparations for
  c. dealt with or discussed
  d. overlooked

_d_ **9. magnet school**

- Kangaroo Korner . . . has become a **magnet school** for mainstream tots kicked out of other programs. (para. 9) (HINT: Some words in English take on a meaning that is related to their commonly used definitions. What do you think a "magnet school" is?)

- As a high school student, I attended a special **magnet school** in Philadelphia for the arts and humanities.

  a. a school for students who are interested in the sciences
  b. an attractive school built on a large piece of property
  c. a school that attracts the attention of parents
  d. a school with a specialized program that attracts students throughout a region

_d_ **10. aggressive**

- Since starting there in August, William, now 3, has had no incidents of hitting or other **aggressive** behavior . . . (para. 9) (HINT: Use context clues. Is hitting an example of good behavior?)

- According to the college's code of conduct, **aggressive** behavior that interferes with the safety and security of the students and instructor is not tolerated.

  a. disrespectful conduct
  b. masculine traits
  c. forceful activities
  d. destructive or hostile behavior

▶ as **you read**

Establish Your Purpose

Now you are ready to read and annotate the selection "Bounced from Preschool." Focus on major points of information. Read to discover the reasons for expelling young children from preschool.

Actively Process While You Read: Guided Reading

Stop and think about the information as you read.

Exercise 3   **Processing While You Read**

Directions: Answer the questions that appear in bold type at the conclusion of each paragraph. This will help you monitor your reading process and understand the material.

Answers may vary. Sample answers provided.

from the pages of

Bounced from Preschool: Nursery School Delinquents?

Some Tots Are Getting the Heave-Ho for Unruly Behavior

By Thomas Fields-Meyer

1   Just two weeks into the school year, Renee Tucker got a call: Anthony Jr., 4, refused to stay in his seat or listen to instructions. The preschool director, Tonya Elliott of the New Creative Child Care Center in Suitland, Md., suggested the boy had ADHD (Attention Deficit Hyperactivity Disorder) and recommended Tucker take him for an evaluation. She made a doctor's appointment right away, but before the date arrived, Elliott spoke to her again. "She said she couldn't handle him anymore," Tucker recalls. "She said he needed more one-on-one attention. I was blown away."

Why was Anthony Tucker asked to leave his preschool?

He refused to stay in his seat or listen to instructions, and the preschool director could not handle him anymore.

2   Renee Tucker spoke to a therapist who suggested a possible reason for Anthony's **agitation**: The boy was still dealing with the death of his father, Anthony Sr., who was killed in an auto accident a year earlier. Tonya Elliott says, "We had asked [Tucker] to work with us," but she felt "there was something else needed with Anthony that we could not do for him."

According to the therapist, why was Anthony acting out?

Anthony was still dealing with the trauma of his father's death.

3   Having to leave preschool seems a bad way to **launch** one's academic career, but Anthony is hardly alone. A 2005 Yale University study estimated that more than 5,000 U.S. preschoolers are **expelled** each year—a rate three times higher than in elementary or high schools. While the study was the first of its kind and no other statistics are available, experts say there's little doubt preschool expulsions are on the rise.

What does the Yale University study tell us about school expulsions?

More than 5,000 U.S. preschoolers are expelled each year—a rate three times higher than in elementary or high schools. The numbers of school expulsions among preschoolers is increasing.

4   Schools say they are forced to take such action when a student's behavior—such as hitting, biting or throwing things—interferes with the smooth running of the class. The trend troubles some experts, however, who say too many schools are **shirking** their responsibility by tossing out, rather than dealing with, tots who act up or fall behind. "We are creating a group of children who are very likely to come to kindergarten with serious problems," says Dr. Jack Shonkoff, dean of Brandeis University's School for Social Policy and Management.

Why are some young children being kicked out of nursery school programs?

Children are expelled for poor behavior, such as hitting, biting, or throwing things, which interferes with the smooth running of the class.

How do experts respond to this action?

Experts feel that schools are not responding adequately and appropriately to these children's behaviors. They should be doing more because these children may later develop more serious problems.

5   Behind the **drive** to expel is the changing nature of preschool itself. While a generation ago most kids didn't start nursery school until age 4, today many begin half- or even full-day programs as young as 2 or 3—a developmental stage not known for good behavior. And with the ever-increasing pressure to achieve, some schools—often at the insistence of parents—are forcing an overly academic curriculum on little ones, instead of teaching such basic skills as dealing with frustration or **empathizing** with classmates, experts say. "Some of these centers pride themselves on the fact that your kid will count or know the alphabet by Christmas," says Dr. Barbara Howard, a developmental pediatrician at the Johns Hopkins School of Medicine. "Maybe that's not what you want."

What are the changing goals of preschool programs that have contributed to the increase of school expulsions?

Today, preschools are focusing more on developing academic skills and not concentrating on teaching basic skills like dealing with frustration or empathizing with classmates.

What skills are children missing when they are enrolled in preschool at ages 2 or 3?

They have not yet learned the skills that teach them about good behavior.

6   Catherine Hewitt remembers her surprise earlier this year when her 2 1/2-year-old son, William, began coming home from preschool with notes from his teacher telling her of his poor conduct. "It seemed like every other day, they were telling me he hit this kid or pushed this one or was fighting for a toy," says Hewitt, 43, an Oakville, Connecticut, nurse's aide. "I thought he was just being a typical little boy."

How did Catherine Hewitt learn about her son's behavioral problem in school?

Her son began coming home from preschool with notes from his teacher telling her of his poor conduct.

7   Administrators at Rainbowland Nursery School Center, in nearby Watertown, saw things differently. Patty Forbes, executive director of Rainbowland, says William "couldn't figure out how to play with others. We had a hard time keeping him focused." Within six months of the first bad report, they told William's parents that the boy—who has a slight speech delay but no diagnosed learning or behavioral problem—would have to attend school elsewhere. "Going there was like a second home for him," Hewitt says. "I felt very badly."

Why was William asked to leave Rainbowland?

Because he couldn't figure out how to play with others, and the school had a hard time keeping him focused.

8   Some schools are taking a different approach. When kids at Tufts Educational Day Care Center in Somerville, Mass., regularly show unacceptable behavior, the school draws up a contract listing the behaviors and consequences—but never expels. **Affiliated** with Tufts University, the center benefits from solid financial support. But elsewhere, says Dr. Harvey Karp, an assistant professor of pediatrics at UCLA School of Medicine, preschool teachers often do not have the training to deal with many common toddler problems—yet are pressured by administrators and tuition-paying parents to do whatever it takes to keep the class running smoothly. "I'm all in favor of responding to inappropriate behavior," Karp says. "But you have to do it in the most effective way."

In what ways are other preschool programs dealing with undesirable behaviors?

When children show unacceptable behavior, the school draws up a contract listing the behaviors and consequences—but never expels.

According to this article, who is to blame for not handling disruptive student conduct?

Teachers and administrators of preschools.

9   Happily, William Hewitt's behavior has been effectively **addressed**. After getting a list of other preschool programs from his old school, his parents enrolled him in Kangaroo Korner, a school founded for Down Syndrome kids but which, in recent years, has become a sort of **magnet school** for mainstream tots kicked out of other programs. Since starting there in August, William, now 3, has had no incidents of hitting or other **aggressive** behavior and is on track to enroll in kindergarten when he turns 5, says director Catherine Risigo-Wickline. And Catherine Hewitt couldn't be happier. "When I ask [the teachers] how he's doing, they say, 'Wonderful—he's a little angel.'"

How did William's behavior improve and why?

His parents enrolled him in Kangaroo Korner, a preschool that enrolls many students who have been kicked out of other preschools. Since starting there in August, William has had no incidents of hitting or other aggressive behavior and is on track to enroll in kindergarten. The teachers are involved in monitoring his progress and his behavior, and they think he is doing well and is a well-behaved child.

■ ■ ■

 **after you read**

Review Important Points

Going over major points immediately after you read, while the information is fresh in your mind, will help you recall the content and record key ideas.

| Exercise 4 | **Reviewing Important Points** |

Directions: Answer the following questions based on the information provided in the selection. You may need to go back to the text and reread certain portions to be sure your responses are correct and can be supported by information in the text. Write the letter of your choice in the space provided.

_b_ 1. **What is the author's overall message in this selection?**

   a. Children are kicked out of preschool because their teachers cannot deal with them.
   b. Children are expelled from preschool because their disruptive behavior interferes with student learning.
   c. Some children are bounced from preschool because schools are fearful that these children may become juvenile delinquents.
   d. Preschool children are expelled because of parent complaints.

_c_ 2. **Schools say they are expelling preschoolers for all the following reasons *except* that they:**

   a. are displaying unacceptable behavior.
   b. are ruining the class.
   c. are running the class.
   d. are not keeping up with the rest of the class.

_b_ 3. **In paragraph 3, a Yale University study indicated:**

   a. More high school students are being expelled from school.
   b. The number of nursery school expulsions is increasing.
   c. The number of preschool expulsions will rise to 5000 in 2005.
   d. There are fewer students kicked out of preschool than elementary or secondary schools.

_d_ 4. **According to this article, another reason that may account for an increasing numbers of expulsions in preschool is:**

   a. Children are starting preschool at age 4 or older.
   b. Children are pressured to attend preschool before age 4.
   c. Children cannot count from one to ten or recite the alphabet.
   d. Children are not emotionally prepared to acquire academic skills.

_c_ 5. **Educational experts say that some of the blame for school expulsions lies with:**

   a. parents.
   b. other classmates.
   c. teachers.
   d. therapists.

_d_ 6. **Some other schools, however, are using a different approach to discipline young children. They are:**

   a. accepting some undesirable behavior.
   b. training their teachers to handle poor behavior.
   c. expelling only those students who display persistent bad conduct.
   d. creating a contracts that list behaviors and their consequences.

_c_ **7.** After William Hewett was kicked out of preschool:

    a. He attended a special school for students with Down Syndrome.

    b. His parents took him to UCLA Medical Center for an evaluation.

    c. He was enrolled in Kangaroo Korner and is now doing well.

    d. He returned to Rainbowland six months later.

_b_ **8.** The stories of the two preschoolers illustrate:

    a. how parents interfere with their children's education.

    b. why preschool children are being expelled from school.

    c. where preschoolers can go if they are kicked out of school.

    d. who to speak with when preschoolers are having trouble in school.

_b_ **9.** The overall organizational pattern of this article is:

    a. time order.

    b. cause and effect.

    c. listing.

    d. definition.

_c_ **10.** From this article, we can infer that:

    a. Parents should not send their children to preschool.

    b. Nursery schools should not be permitted to expel preschoolers.

    c. Parents should be aware of a school's code of conduct.

    d. Students who have behavioral problems in preschool are likely to become juvenile delinquents.

Organize the Information

Organizing the information you have learned from a reading selection shows you have understood it and have the ability to restate the material in a different way. You can use this reorganized material to help you study for exams and prepare for written assignments. (See Chapter 9.)

| **Exercise 5** | **Organizing the Information** |

Directions: Using the reading selection, make a list of *five* behaviors that may result in the expulsion of preschoolers from preschool.

Answers may vary.

1. refusing to stay in their seats 2. not listening to the teacher 3. hitting 4. biting

5. throwing things 6. fighting 7. interrupting instruction

Integrate the Vocabulary

Make the new vocabulary presented in the reading *your* vocabulary. In addition to learning the meaning of new words, you should also learn related word forms.

Exercise 6A	**Using Context Clues**

Directions: For each sentence, select the word from the text box on p. 286 that is a synonym for the word or words in parentheses and best completes the sentence. Then write the word or a form of the word in the space provided.

1. The Study Skills Center helped me (deal with) _address_____ my fear of taking tests.

2. The college freshman was (kicked out) _expelled_____ from the university because he copied his English paper from the Internet.

3. College security guards are notified immediately when (hostile) _aggressive_____ behavior, such as name-calling or shoving and pushing is displayed anywhere on the campus.

4. After my friend's father passed away, I (understood and became aware of) _empathized_____ with her feelings of grief and sadness, and so I called her regularly just to check in.

5. Melanie's (inescapable pressure) _drive_____ to pass the state reading exams on the first try was related to her desire to complete her associate's degree in two years and transfer to a four-year college.

6. When Bob felt (restless) _agitated_____ from studying, he would crumple up his notes and fling them into the garbage can.

7. The syllabus for my American history course states the following: Students must hand in work as assigned. Students who (avoid a task) _shirk_____ this responsibility will lose 10 points for each session past the due date.

8. Weill Medical College and the Graduate School of Cornell University maintain close (associations, connections) _affiliations_____ with New York Presbyterian Hospital, Memorial Sloan-Kettering Cancer Center, and the Hospital for Special Surgery.

9. If you want to (begin, get off to a good start) _launch_____ a successful career in business, you should get an MBA.

10. There are a variety of (schools with a special program that attract students from all over) _magnet_____ _schools_____ in Miami, many of which offer programs in the areas of art, music, theater, science, business, and technology.

Exercise 6B	**Learning Synonyms or Similar Expressions**

Directions: Writers often use synonyms or other expressions to restate important terms in selections. Scan the article and list the synonyms for *expel.* Then check the dictionary or a thesaurus for additional synonyms.

Located in the Text: Words that mean *expel:* _bounce from, kick out, toss out_____

Found in the Dictionary or Thesaurus: Synonyms for *expel:* _discharge, dismiss, drop_____

Make Personal Connections Through Writing and Discussion

When you make your new learning relevant to yourself in some way, it becomes more meaningful and easier to remember. Whenever you read, try to connect to the content on a personal level. How does it relate to you? How can you apply what you have read to other situations? What else would you like to know?

| **Exercise 7** | **Making Personal Connections Through Writing and Discussion** |

Responses will vary.

Think about yourself in relation to the article you have just read. Apply the information you learned from the reading and respond to the following questions in your journal.

1. Create your own list of *five* good ways that parents can monitor their children's behavior in preschool.

TIPS FOR PARENTS

1. _____
2. _____
3. _____
4. _____
5. _____

2. Locate the *Code of Conduct* for your college. Make a list of five inappropriate behaviors and their consequences. Arrange them in the table that follows.

Code of Conduct for _____
(Name of your college)

Inappropriate Behavior	Consequence
1.	
2.	
3.	
4.	
5.	

Self-Monitored Reading
Reading Selection 2

> ## Lying as America's Pastime
> By Joe Saltzman

This selection, from USA Today, *discusses the reasons why people tell lies.*

◀◀ before you read

Answer the following questions before you read the selection. *Answers will vary.*

1. What do you consider to be a lie?

   _____

   _____

2. Is there ever a time in which it is appropriate to tell a lie? If so, explain.

   _____

   _____

3. Have you ever told a white lie? If so, provide some examples.

   _____

   _____

Prepare to Read

Preview the reading selection by applying the THIEVES strategy (Chapter 2, p. 40).

| Exercise 1 | **Previewing** |

Based on your preview, respond to the following questions:

1. What kind of a lie is used to protect someone's feelings?
   a white lie
   _____

2. What percentage of Americans occasionally do not tell the truth?
    90%

3. Why are most people not truthful?
    They are afraid or embarrassed of telling the truth.

4. What does the word plagiarism mean?
    passing off another's work as your own

Check Out the Vocabulary

You will encounter the following vocabulary words in bold type in this reading.

adulterers	corrupt	entail	plagiarism
attribution*	deceptions	fabrication	reprimanded
condemnation	enhanced*	integral*	urge

*Denotes a word from the Academic Word List

Exercise 2   **Checking Out the Vocabulary**

Directions: Look at each boldface word taken from the reading selection. Use the context of the sentence and the hint provided to select the best definition from the choices listed. Write the letter of your choice on the line provided.

d **1. urge**

They (parents) also **urge** their offspring to leave their teeth under the pillow so the Tooth Fairy will reward them. (para. 1) (HINT: The information after *so that* gives the purpose of the action in the first part of the sentence.)

a. ask
b. convince
c. discourage
d. persuade

a **2. entail**

White lies **entail** false compliments ("I love that dress on you"), lazy excuses ("I'll call you back tomorrow"), and broken promises ("I won't ever do that again"). (para. 2) (HINT: What makes people tell white lies?)

a. involve
b. result in
c. exclude
d. end up

_c_ **3. corrupt**

We cheat on our income tax returns because the tax laws are **corrupt**. (para. 2) (HINT: The prefix *co-* means *together*. The root word *rupt* means *broken.*)

a. acceptable
b. unlawful
c. damaging
d. legal

_d_ **4. condemnation**

. . . many of this country's citizens are extremely religious, believing in God, Satan, and a Bible that is very specific in its **condemnation** of lying. (para. 4) (HINT: How do most religions feel about the act of lying?)

a. clear definition
b. commonplace
c. lack of support
d. strong disapproval

_d_ **5. adulterers**

Adulterers—some surveys indicate that a significant percentage of married men and women have affairs—must lie constantly, and they lie to the people they say they love the most: spouses, children, best friends, and co-workers." (para. 3) (HINT: Look at the information in between the dashes, which provides additional information about *adulterers.*)

a. adult men and women
b. men who have affairs
c. women who engage in extramarital activities
d. married men or women who cheat on their spouses

_c_ **6. reprimanded**

If we are caught doing something wrong, we will be **reprimanded**, fired, or even sent to jail. (para. 4) (HINT: What happens when you get caught doing something wrong?)

a. much praised
b. totally forgiven
c. severely criticized
d. amply rewarded

_a_ **7. plagiarism**

Plagiarism—passing off another's work as your own—and fabrication have become commonplace . . . (para. 5) (HINT: The use of dashes in writing indicates providing a definition of an unfamiliar word or giving additional information.)

a. passing off another's work as your own
b. committing a literary crime
c. commonplace, not out of the ordinary
d. passing off work to someone else

_d_ **8. fabrication**

Plagiarism—passing off another's work as your own—and **fabrication** have become commonplace . . . (para. 5) (HINT: What does *fabrication* refer to in this sentence?)

a. writing something
b. constructing something
c. handed in something
d. making something up

_d_ **9. enhanced**

Staff writers on such well-known publications as the *New York Times* and *New Republic* have made up or improperly **enhanced** stories. (para. 5) (HINT: Why do authors want to enhance their writing? What purpose will this serve?)

a. lengthened
b. harmed
c. reinforced
d. intensified

_d_ **10. attribution**

In broadcast news, pieces are lifted out of print publications without **attribution** or apology. (para. 5) (HINT: If you copy or use someone else's writing, what are you supposed to do?)

a. paying tribute to the author
b. not paying for material
c. acting without shame
d. giving credit to the author

_d_ **11. integral**

Lying has become such an **integral** part of society that no one seems outraged by it anymore, even when that lie has extraordinary and painful consequences. (para. 6) (HINT: When using *such . . . that,* the details after the word *that* give the result of the condition in the first part of the sentence.)

a. unimportant
b. understated
c. individual
d. essential

_b_ **12. deceptions**

The end justifies any means, any lies, any **deceptions,** any dishonest behavior. (para. 6) (HINT: Look at the other words listed with *deceptions.*)

a. foolishness
b. dishonesty
c. truthfulness
d. indecencies

 **as you read**

Establish Your Purpose

Now, read and annotate the selection below, and focus on the major points of information.

Actively Process While You Read: Self-Monitored Reading

Monitor your comprehension as you read. Be sure to stop to reflect at the conclusion of each paragraph, and ask yourself the following questions:

- Did I understand what I have just read?
- What is the main idea of the paragraph?
- Am I ready to continue?

Exercise 3   **Processing While You Read**

Directions: Highlight the most important points in each paragraph. Then write the key topics and main ideas in the spaces provided in the margins. Finally, underline or number the supporting details in the text.

Lying as America's Pastime
By Joe Saltzman

---

1   EVERYBODY LIES. From the president of the U.S. to Congress to the smallest citizen in the country, we are a nation of liars. Parents still try to teach their children not to do so. They retell the story of George Washington and the cherry tree or recite Proverbs 6:16–19 to make their point. Yet, with the same breath, they tell their kids that, if they are not good, Santa Claus will not bring them any presents. They also **urge** their offspring to leave their teeth under the pillow so the Tooth Fairy will reward them. Youngsters discover at an early age that avoiding the truth will keep them out of trouble: "I didn't do it; she did." "It wasn't my fault." "I don't know why the toilet overflowed. It just did."

Notes
Topic _____
_____
_____
Main Idea _____
_____
_____
_____

2   White lies are rationalized by young and old alike as a way of being kind to people. They **entail** false compliments ("I love that dress on you"), lazy excuses ("I'll call you back tomorrow"), and broken promises ("I won't ever do that again"). As we grow older, the rationalizations for lying become more complex. We cheat on our income tax returns because the tax laws are **corrupt**. "The check is in the mail" buys some extra time in paying a late bill; besides, what is the harm? Putting on a resume that you graduated from college when you did not seems fair because you were just a few units shy of getting a diploma before you had to quit school because you ran out of money.

Topic _____
_____
_____
Main Idea _____
_____
_____

Notes

Topic _____

_____

_____

Main Idea _____

_____

_____

_____

3   One survey determined that 90% of Americans lie under certain circumstances. Others show that many of this country's citizens are extremely religious, believing in God, Satan, and a Bible that is very specific in its **condemnation** of lying. Yet, members of the clergy have been caught in mistruths concerning financial dealings, corrupt practices, and pedophilia (the Catholic Church hierarchy long denied such behavior even took place). **Adulterers**—some surveys indicate that a significant percentage of married men and women have affairs—must lie constantly, and they lie to the people they say they love the most: spouses, children, best friends, and co-workers. Our lying to each other has become a way of life.

Topic _____

_____

_____

Main Idea _____

_____

_____

_____

4   Most of us lie out of fear or embarrassment. If our resumes are not impressive, we are afraid we will not get that job. If we are caught doing something wrong, we will be **reprimanded,** fired, or even sent to jail. Some rationalizations just keep growing, making the liar almost appear noble and kind of heart: "I don't want my wife to find out I'm having an affair because it would hurt her and the children." "I cheat on my tax return because the government is using my tax dollars to wage an unjust war that is killing innocent people." "I'm a good person and the lie really didn't hurt anybody. In fact, it saved a lot of bruised feelings."

Topic _____

_____

_____

Main Idea _____

_____

_____

_____

5   **Plagiarism**—passing off another's work as your own—and **fabrication** have become commonplace, especially in student papers at all levels of American education. Moreover, it has seeped into the media. Writers of nonfiction books and memoirs have been caught lying about past events. Staff writers on such well-known publications as the *New York Times* and *New Republic* have made up or improperly **enhanced** stories. In broadcast news, pieces are lifted out of print publications without **attribution** or apology. Few electronic or Internet news media bother checking quotes or facts that they steal from other publications. Most of the students or journalists caught red-handed seem more frustrated that they were caught than apologetic for what they have done. Some do not seem to understand that using other people's work without attribution or simply fabricating quotes and facts is dishonest.

Topic _____

_____

_____

Main Idea _____

_____

_____

_____

6   Lying has become such an **integral** part of society that no one seems outraged by it anymore, even when that lie has extraordinary and painful consequences. So, when the president or a congressman is caught in a lie, the public seems to accept it as just business as usual. It turns out that it does not really matter what the real reasons were for going to war in Iraq. The end justifies any means, any lies, any **deceptions,** any dishonest behavior.

Joe Saltzman, "Lying as America's Pastime," *USA Today (Magazine)* 135.2734 (July 2006): p. 25(1).

■ ■ ■

⏭ after **you read**

Review Important Points

Going over the major points immediately after you have read, while the information is fresh in your mind, will help you recall the content and record key ideas.

| Exercise 4 | **Reviewing Important Points** |

Directions: Choose the best answer for each of the following questions using information provided in the selection. Write your answers in the spaces provided.

_b_ 1. The topic of the reading selection is:

    a. cheating.

    b. lying.

    c. white lies.

    d. plagiarism.

_c_ 2. The main idea of this article is:

    a. All Americans lie.

    b. 90% of Americans lie under certain circumstances.

    c. Lying has become an integral part of American society.

    d. Plagiarism has become commonplace, especially on college campuses.

_b_ 3. The author supports his main point by providing:

    a. definitions of lying, cheating and plagiarism.

    b. examples of dishonest behavior.

    c. consequences of immoral actions.

    d. facts and statistics.

_b_ 4. In paragraph 1, when parents tell their children about Santa Claus and the Tooth Fairy, they are:

    a. trying to teach their kids not to lie.

    b. telling lies.

    c. preserving the truth.

    d. teaching their children about the importance of honesty.

_d_ 5. The main idea of paragraph 2 is that telling white lies is a way of:

    a. protecting one's friends from getting hurt.

    b. enhancing one's resume to get the job you want.

    c. cheating on tax returns and resumes.

    d. providing a reasonable but untrue reason for one's behavior.

_d_ 6. According to the surveys cited in this article, all of the following statements are true *except:*

    a. Most Americans lie occasionally.

    b. Many Americans lie because of religious convictions.

    c. Adulterers must lie constantly.

    d. Members of a church have never been caught in a lie.

_c_ 7. According to the selection, which of the following rationalizations about why we lie are *not* true?

    a. fear of losing a job

    b. fear of hurting someone else's feelings

    c. embarrassment about going to jail

    d. dread of feeling ashamed

b 8. **Which of the following states the main idea of paragraph 5?**

    a. Plagiarism is a form of cheating.
    b. Plagiarism is widespread.
    c. College students plagiarize their papers from the Internet.
    d. College students do not believe that plagiarism is wrong.

c 9. **Based on the reading, when students are caught plagiarizing someone else's work, they:**

    a. apologize for what they have done.
    b. simply fabricate a new paper and resubmit it.
    c. may not always realize that it's wrong to copy from another's writing.
    d. are often not aware of the consequences.

a 10. **The last sentence in paragraph 6, "The end justifies any means, any lies, any deceptions, any dishonest behavior" means:**

    a. Some people believe that achieving their goals is so important that lying or other dishonest behavior is acceptable, even necessary.
    b. People act dishonestly in order to get what they want.
    c. In the end, people always tell lies, instead of the truth.
    d. The Bush administration was dishonest about its reasons for going to war in Iraq.

Organize the Information

Organizing the information from a reading selection shows you have understood it and can restate the material in your own way.

Exercise 5   **Organizing the Information**

Directions: Using your notes, complete the following summary. Write your answers in the spaces provided.

One survey determined that 90% of Americans (1) *lie* _____ under certain circumstances. Parents are lying to their children when they tell them about Santa Claus or the Tooth Fairy. Politicians lie to the voters when they make promises they know they can't keep, and even clergymen have been caught in (2) *mistruths* _____ about financial dealings. (3) *White lies* _____, especially, are rationalized by young and old alike as a way of being kind to people. In fact, most people lie out of (4) *embarrassment* _____ or fear. (5) *Plagiarism* _____ is another type of deception. It is defined as the passing off another's work as your own. This (6) *deceptive* _____ behavior has become commonplace at all levels of (7) *education* _____. Students are often not aware that plagiarism is (8) *wrong* _____. Lying has become such an (9) *integral* _____ part of American society that most people truly believe that the end justifies any (10) *means* _____.

Integrate the Vocabulary

Make the new vocabulary *your* vocabulary.

Exercise 6A	**Using Context Clues**

Directions: Locate a word from the text box in Exercise 2 (p. 298) that best completes the following sentences. Then write the word, or a form of the word, in the spaces provided.

1. Anne _urged_ Prof. Waverly to give her an extension on the history paper because she had not completed the citations.

2. Being an effective reader _entails_ using good previewing strategies.

3. According to the college's code of conduct, plagiarism is considered _corrupt_ and can result in expulsion.

4. Engaging in any unlawful activities on college campuses, such as selling drugs or carrying a weapon, is _condemned_ .

5. Upon John's return to class, Prof. James _reprimanded_ him for his excessive absences.

6. Instead of telling her professor the truth about why she had missed her final exam, Karen _fabricated_ an elaborate story.

7. The use of descriptive details and college level vocabulary _enhances_ academic student writing.

8. The English professor reminded his students to _attribute_ credit to all their sources, including Internet sites; otherwise, they will receive a failing grade.

9. An _integral_ part of successful academic study is effective time management.

10. Any attempt to provide _deceptive_ or false information on a college application form can result in denial of admission.

11. According to a recent survey, three-quarters of all high school and college students admit to _plagiarism_ , the stealing of ideas or words of another and passing them off as one's own.

12. In the American Legal System (LAW 102), we learned that in most states _adultery_ is not grounds for divorce.

Exercise 6B	**Learning Synonyms and Other Word Forms**

Directions: Writers often use synonyms or other expressions to restate important terms in selections. Scan the article and list the synonyms for *lies*. Then check the dictionary or a thesaurus for additional synonyms.

Located in the Text: Words that mean *lies:* _skirting the truth, false, cheat, fabrication, fabricating, deception_

Found in the Dictionary or Thesaurus: Synonyms for *lies:* _deceit, dishonesty, falsehood, misrepresentation, myth, tale, perjury, slander_

You may also see the same word, especially for the topic, used in different forms. Now scan the article for the different forms of the following word, and write them in the space provided.

Lie: _lies, liars, lying_

Make Personal Connections Through Writing and Discussion

Connect to the content on a personal level. How does it relate to you? How can you apply what you have read to other situations?

Responses will vary.

| **Exercise 7** | **Making Personal Connections Through Writing and Discussion** |

Think about yourself in relation to the article you have just read. Apply the information you learned from the reading and respond to the following questions in your journal.

1. Read your college's policy on plagiarism and summarize it.

_____

_____

_____

_____

_____

2. In small groups, discuss your answers to the following questions with other students, and then share your responses with the whole class.

   - Have you ever noticed someone cheating on an exam? If so, provide some details.
   - How common is it for students to copy papers off of the Internet? How can colleges prevent plagiarism?
   - Why is there so much academic pressure to succeed or get to the top of the class?
   - How can we create a culture of trust and honesty on college campuses?

Independent Reading
Reading Selection 3

Navigating the Minefield of Harassment at Work
By Hanah Cho

When Betty Buck attended her first state convention as the company's leader, she was surrounded by men who used bad language, disrespected her, and failed to treat her as their peer. So Buck told them she wouldn't stand for their behavior.

⏪ before you read

⏸

Answer the following questions before you read the selection.

1. At school or in the workplace, has anyone ever spoken to you in a way that made you feel uncomfortable?

    _____
    _____

2. Did you tell anyone about this experience? If so, to whom did you confide in?

    _____
    _____

3. Were any actions taken against this individual? If so, what happened? Were you satisfied with how this situation was handled?

    _____
    _____

Prepare to Read

Now, preview the essay "Navigating the Minefield of Harassment at Work," on page 310, using the THIEVES strategy.

| **Exercise 1** | **Developing Preview Questions** |

Directions: Based on your previewing, write *three* questions you anticipate will be answered in the selection.

Answers may vary.

1. _____

2. _____

3. _____

| **Exercise 2** | **Check Out the Vocabulary** |

Directions: You will encounter the following words in boldface in the reading selection.

| advocates* | discrimination* | harassment | peer | stereotypes |
| define* | disparaging | offensive | pervasive | taunts |

*Denotes a word from the Academic Word List

Read each of the following sentences in which a vocabulary word from the selection appears in bold. Select the best definition of the word from the choices provided. Write the letter of your choice on the line provided.

_c_ **1. disparaging**

At a training meeting, a man told her that she belonged "at home and in the kitchen." Her strategy was to ignore the **disparaging** remark. (para. 2)

a. kind and respectful
b. caring and concerned
c. degrading and belittling
d. complimentary and praising

_d_ **2. peer**

But when Buck attended her first state convention as the company's leader, she was surrounded by men who used rude language, disrespected her and failed to treat her as their **peer.** (para. 3)

a. inferior status
b. superior rank
c. family member
d. of equal rank or standing

_b_ **3. stereotypes**

As far as women have come in the workplace, they still face gender **stereotypes,** sexist attitudes, and inappropriate behavior on the job. (para. 4)

a. types of recording equipment used by engineers
b. an oversampled, conventional idea of someone or something

c. inappropriate behavior at work by women

d. personality types of engineers

a 4. **taunt**

Many women find themselves using various strategies for dealing with bad behavior: deciding which **taunts** or teasing comments are better left ignored, which call for a quick response and which need to be taken to a higher level. (para. 4)

a. teasing

b. haunting

c. pleasing

d. laughter

d 5. **offensive**

Or should they speak up at the first occurrence of an **offensive** comment or inappropriate behavior? (para. 5)

a. leading to harm

b. making satisfied

c. resulting in opposition

d. causing displeasure

c 6. **advocates**

Women's rights **advocates** say female employees—or for that matter, male workers—don't have to accept any behavior they find offensive, regardless of whether it meets the legal definition of sexual harassment. (para. 6)

a. opponents

b. lawyers

c. supporters

d. adversaries

a 7. **harassment**

Women's rights advocates say female employees—or for that matter, male workers—don't have to accept any behavior they find offensive, regardless of whether it meets the legal definition of sexual **harassment.** (para. 6)

a. persistent and annoying conduct

b. favorable and complimentary requests

c. constant and persistent behavior

d. defensive and angry actions

b 8. **discrimination**

Under federal law, sexual harassment is a type of **discrimination** defined by the U.S. Equal Employment Opportunity Commission as "unwelcome sexual advances, requests for sexual favors, and other verbal or physical conduct of a sexual nature." (para. 8)

a. displaying indifference

b. making a difference in treatment or favor

c. accepting behavior

d. unwelcome sexual advances

_a_ **9. pervasive**

In order to meet the legal definition, workplace experts and lawyers say, employees typically must prove that the conduct was **pervasive,** not limited to one situation, and produced an unfriendly or threatening work environment. (para. 9)

a. present everywhere
b. limited in action
c. persuasive
d. unimportant

_d_ **10. define**

Buck's two 20-something daughters plan to join their mother in the family business. And Buck's advice is simple: "Believe in yourself and don't let others **define** you." (para. 17)

a. outline the boundaries of
b. take advantage of
c. explain the meaning or translate
d. explain the essential qualities

 **as you read**

Establish Your Purpose

Read and annotate the selection below using the guidelines for active reading, and focus on the major points of information.

Actively Process as You Read: Independent Reading

 Monitor your comprehension as you read. (See Chapter 2, page 54.) Be sure to stop to reflect at the conclusion of each paragraph. Highlight the most important points. Write your notes, responses, or questions in the margins.

> ## Navigating the Minefield of Harassment at Work
> ### By Hanah Cho

1   When Betty Buck took over her family's beer-wholesaling business in 1985, she quickly found herself putting up with men who [caused her trouble] because she was a woman.

2   At a training meeting, a man told her that she belonged "at home and in the kitchen." Her strategy was to ignore [these] **disparaging** remarks.

3   But when Buck attended her first state convention as the company's leader, she was surrounded by men who used rude language, disrespected her and failed to treat her as their **peer.** So Buck told them she wouldn't [put up with] their behavior. . . .

The Usual Victims: Women

4   As far as women have come in the workplace, they still face gender **stereotypes,** sexist attitudes and inappropriate behavior on the job. Many women find themselves using various strategies for dealing with bad behavior: deciding which **taunts** [or teasing] are better left ignored, which [call for] a quick response and which need to be taken to a higher level.

5   Such gray areas present a problem for female employees: How much should they put up with before taking action? Or should they speak up at the first [occurrence] of an **offensive** comment or [inappropriate] behavior? . . .

6   Women's rights **advocates** say female employees—or for that matter, male workers—don't have to [accept] any behavior they find offensive, regardless of whether it meets the legal definition of sexual **harassment.**

7   But [situations that occur from] office politics, peer pressure and fear of being [considered] a troublemaker play a [part] in the choices women make, experts say. . . .

What the Law Says

8   Under federal law, sexual harassment is a type of **discrimination** defined by the U.S..Equal Employment Opportunity Commission as "unwelcome sexual advances, requests for sexual favors, and other verbal or physical conduct of a sexual nature."

9   In order to meet the legal [definition], workplace experts and lawyers say, employees typically must prove that the behavior was **pervasive**, [not just occasional], and produced [an unfriendly or threatening] work environment.

10   The victim as well as the harasser can be a man or a woman, and sexual harassment does not have to involve the opposite sex. Experts say harassment cases typically involve a male offender and a female victim. Of the 12,679 sexual harassment charges filed with the EEOC in the 2005 fiscal year, less than 15 percent were filed by men.

11   But even with federal and state sexual harassment laws and company policies in place, women still face tough decisions. . . .

Harassment's Gray Areas

12   What [makes up] improper or disrespectful behavior sometimes is in the eye of the person. Therefore, workplace experts say, there's no one-size-fits-all rule on when good-natured teasing or flirting, for example, crosses the line.

13   Even though an off-color joke or a suggestive comment may [not fit] the legal definition of sexual harassment, such behavior [goes against] professional workplace rules of behavior, said Amy Oppenheimer, a California-based lawyer and business consultant who specializes in sexual harassment training.

14   A company can [create] a good policy on sexual harassment prevention and workplace conduct that spells out what type of behavior is and is not expected on the job, she said. . . .

15   In the 20 years since Buck took over her father's company, the industry has become more welcoming to women, she said.

16   Men want the workplace atmosphere to change because "they want their daughters in the business," and women are taking on leadership roles in the industry, Buck

said. She is set to become the first chairwoman of the National Beer Wholesalers Association in September.

17   Buck's two 20-something daughters plan to join their mother in the family business. And Buck's advice is simple: "Believe in yourself and don't let others **define** you."

■ ■ ■

▶▶ after you read

Exercise 3   **Answering Your Preview Questions**

Directions: Look back at the questions you posed before you read the selection. If you have discovered the answers, write them on the lines provided.

Answers will vary.

1. _____

_____

2. _____

_____

3. _____

_____

Exercise 4   **Reviewing Important Points**

Directions: Choose the best answer for each of the following questions using information provided in the selection. You may need to go back to reread certain sections to be sure your responses are accurate.

_c_ 1. The title of this selection indicates that:

a. sexual harassment occurs only in the workplace.

b. it's easy to detect sexual harassment.

c. it's often difficult to determine inappropriate behavior in the workplace.

d. employers get angry when employees report sexual harassment.

_a_ 2. The overall topic of the selection is:

a. sexual harassment in the workplace.

b. sexual harassment among women.

c. Betty Buck's experience with sexual harassment.

d. sexual harassment.

_d_   3. **In paragraph 2, the author provides an example of:**
   a. complimentary remarks.
   b. amusing remarks.
   c. appropriate behavior.
   d. gender stereotypes.

_c_   4. **Although women have come a long way in the workforce, they:**
   a. often receive lower pay than men.
   b. are always ignored for higher positions.
   c. are still forced to deal with offensive language or bad attitudes from men.
   d. generally encounter difficulty finding jobs.

_a_   5. **In paragraph 5, "grey areas" refers to:**
   a. situations that are not clearly acts of sexual harassment.
   b. problems that only women encounter.
   c. requests of unwanted sexual favors.
   d. actions in the workplace that employers must respond to immediately.

_d_   6. **Sexual harassment in the workplace may be experienced by:**
   a. female employees.
   b. male workers.
   c. employers.
   d. all of the above.

_d_   7. **Sexual harassment is regulated by all of the following _except:_**
   a. the EEOC.
   b. company policies.
   c. state laws.
   d. women's rights advocates.

_b_   8. **One way to prevent sexual harassment in the workplace is for employers to:**
   a. listen in on the conversations of all employees.
   b. set up clear guidelines for appropriate behavior.
   c. fire all those who do not follow company guidelines.
   d. hire only male employees.

_d_   9. **Betty Buck's message to women in the workplace is to:**
   a. ignore teasing and flirting.
   b. learn the definition of sexual harassment.
   c. take on leadership roles in the workplace.
   d. speak up about sexual harassment incidences.

_a_   10. **From paragraphs 15–17, we can conclude that incidences of sexual harassment may:**
   a. deter women from entering certain areas of business.
   b. encourage women to enter Buck's industry.
   c. create more leadership opportunities for men.
   d. strengthen father-daughter relationships.

| **Exercise 5** | **Organizing the Information** |

Directions: Using your notes and annotations in the text, complete the outline of paragraphs 8–10.

Navigating the Minefield of Harassment at Work

I. Federal Law—U.S. Equal Opportunity Commission

   A. Definition of Sexual Harassment

      1. Unwelcome *advances*

      2. Requests for *sexual favors*

      3. Verbal or physical conduct of *a sexual nature*

   B. Proof of Sexual *Harassment*

      1. *Pervasive* behavior

      2. Produces an *unfriendly* or threatening
       environment

   C. *Victims* of Sexual Harassment

      1. Male or female

   2. May not involve the opposite sex, but typically *male offender and*
      female victim

   3. 2005: 12,679 cases reported, *85%* of victims
      were female

| **Exercise 6** | **Using Context Clues** |

Directions: Using context clues, select the word from the text box on p. 308 that best completes each of the following sentences.

    One *pervasive* belief throughout the United States is the *stereotype* that men are better drivers than women. Even so, insurance companies in New York State are now requiring young men under the age of 25 to pay higher premiums.

    Last week, I was driving Marvin across the busy streets of Manhattan. As I turned the first corner, he covered his eyes, pulled down his hat, and muttered some *offensive* comment like, "You must have grown up in New Jersey." Not that there is anything wrong with New Jersey, but I am a native New Yorker and passed my driving test on the first try.

    Advocates for women's rights say that females still have a long way to go before *discrimination* against women and such *disparaging* remarks about women's inferior qualities are totally eliminated. In the meantime, next time you find yourself sitting next to a gentleman who just can't refrain from *taunting* you about your driving skills, pull over to the curb, bat your eye lashes ever so gently, and hand him over the keys to your car. Then, sit back and watch him squirm as he tries to navigate the road, maneuver across the busy intersections, and read the street signs all at the same time.

Exercise 7	**Making Personal Connections Through Writing and Discussion**

Directions: Think about yourself in relation to the article you just read.
Responses will vary.

1. Under Title IX of the Education Amendment of 1972, colleges are mandated to create a clear policy on sexual harassment. Read your college's policy and answer the following questions:
   a. What is considered sexual harassment?
   b. What are some gray areas?
   c. What are the procedures to report incidences of sexual harassment?

2. Discuss what you believe to be the cause of sexual harassment on college campuses. Consider the gender and rank among faculty and the administration, and the interaction between faculty and students.

3. In addition to written policies about sexual harassment, what else could colleges do to prevent sexual harassment on campuses?

⸢°reflect AND respond⸥

Having read the selections about *codes of conduct*, you now have a broader and better understanding of the topic.

Directions: Complete a journal response for this module. Read the following questions. Select two to which you would like to respond. Then write your responses on a separate piece of paper. Write at least one page.

1. What did you learn about codes of conduct?

2. How does this information apply to you? Make connections with your own experience(s). What do these readings make you think about?

3. How can you relate what you have read to other situations? Make connections to other readings, course work, or current events.

4. What else would you like to know about this topic?

Readings About Resilience

Get Acquainted with the Issue

Most students come to college with the hopes and dreams of being successful in their studies. However, they cannot always anticipate adversities that could prevent them from achieving their goals. Consider the loss of a much-needed job or the ineligibility for financial aid, which can seriously impact one's finances, or a personal illness or a death in the family, which can also seriously affect one's concentration and attendance. Are these examples of failures, or are they just bumps in the road? Are they reason enough to drop out of school? Defining resilience, or the ability to cope with difficulties, will go a long way in dealing with these and other unexpected obstacles.

In this module, we present three selections on the topics of adversity and resilience. The first, "Reversal of Fortune: Attitude Can Reroute Adversity," discusses how experiences with a failure can serve as a positive opportunity for change. The next selection, titled "Decoding Dyslexia: Dyslexia Sabotages the Reading Skills of Millions of People," describes the experience of a young woman who has worked hard to overcome her disability. In the final selection, "Confessions of a Quit Addict," the author takes us through her difficult journey to self-discovery and happiness.

Guided Reading
Reading Selection 1

Reversal of Fortune:
Attitude Can Reroute Adversity
By Alice Steinbach

This selection first appeared in Pulitzer Prize winner Alice Steinbach's book, The Miss Dennis School of Writing and Other Lessons from a Woman's Life. *In this essay, Steinbach shares a lesson about the value of challenges and adversity.*

before you read

Think about what you already know about a topic before you begin reading. Then you will be able to attach your new learning to this background knowledge and more easily understand the new information. See Chapter 2, page 38.

Discuss or write responses to the following questions about your *own* experience with adversity and resilience.

1. Describe a situation in which you failed to reach a goal. How did this experience make you feel?
2. Describe an experience in which you were successful.
3. Which of these experiences made you feel better about yourself? Explain.

Prepare to Read

Preview the essay "Reversal of Fortune" using the THIEVES strategy in Chapter 2, page 40.

Exercise 1   Previewing

Directions: Complete the following items.

1. Take a look at the selection and check off all the items that are available to you for preview.

    _X_ Title

    ___ Headings

    _X_ Introduction

    _X_ Every first sentence in each paragraph

    ___ Visuals/vocabulary

    ___ End of chapter questions

    _X_ Summary/concluding paragraph

2. Actively preview the selection by reading and highlighting the items you have checked.
3. Based on your preview, place an "X" next to all those items you predict will be discussed in the selection.

    ___ a. daily radio show programs

    ___ b. mountain climbing strategies

    _X_ c. mistakes

    _X_ d. successes and failures

    ___ e. addictive behavior from drug and alcohol use

    _X_ f. adversity

    ___ g. Harvard Business School admission

Check Out the Vocabulary

You will find the following vocabulary words in bold type in the reading selection. Some are repeated more than once in the text. Do you know what these words mean? Knowing the meaning of all these words will increase your understanding of the material.

accolades	distinction*	quantum leap	unattributed
adversity	emerged*	shelf life	
confront	erudite	summit	

*Denotes a word from the Academic Word List

Exercise 2   Checking Out the Vocabulary

Directions: Look at each word taken from the reading selection. Read the sentences that follow. The first is from the selection, with a hint to its meaning, and the second one uses the word in an additional context. Choose the best definition for the word, and write the letter of the definition you select on the line provided.

_a_ **1. erudite**

• "You know this job never gets easier," said this **erudite** and learned man who for years has presided over an extremely popular call-in show. (para. 2) (HINT: Use a synonym clue; another word for *erudite* is *learned*. Also, *for years* indicates experience and acquired knowledge.)

• My anthropology professor is such an **erudite** scholar that he has translated several ancient Sanskrit poems into English.

   a. scholarly and knowledgeable
   b. fearful and concerned
   c. curious and inquisitive
   d. elderly and experienced

_c_ **2. adversity**

• Written by a young man I know quite well, the letter concerned itself with the idea that **adversity** might offer, in the long run, more rewards than getting what you thought you wanted. (para. 4) (HINT: What is the opposite of getting rewards?)

• In today's economic downturn, it is all too common to hear about **adversities**, such as job loss, mortgage foreclosures, or bankruptcies.

   a. differences or similarities
   b. successes or failures
   c. hardship and suffering
   d. disagreements or disparities

_a_ **3. unattributed**

• Then last week, in what seemed a curious completion of the philosophy beneath both these remarks, I came across this **unattributed** quotation on mountain climbing: "Today is a new day; you'll get out of it just what you put into it. If you have made mistakes, even serious mistakes, you can make a new start whenever you choose. For the thing we call failure is not the falling down but the staying down." (Para. 6 and 7) (HINT: There is no mention of who made the statement.)

- Using improper citations and including **unattributed** material to essays or papers is considered plagiarism.
    - a. unknown source
    - b. not considered a cause
    - c. uncharacteristic of
    - d. qualified

_d_ **4. distinction**

- Few of us can claim the **distinction** of not knowing the sting of falling down, of "failure" . . . (para. 8) (HINT: Look at *few of us*.)
- Jaime had the **distinction** of being the only graduate this year to receive high honors in math, biology, and English.
    - a. dreadful mistake
    - b. high quality
    - c. visible signs
    - d. special or unique characteristic

_d_ **5. quantum leap**

- "But most people I know—including myself—can point to a disappointment or a failure that resulted in what I would call a **quantum leap** of self-knowledge and self-confidence . . ." (para. 9) (HINT: This is a contrast clue. Disappointment usually leads to lack of self-confidence, but instead, it results in developing self-confidence and acquiring self-knowledge.)
- The discovery of a vaccine would mark a **quantum leap** in the fight against cancer.
    - a. minor improvement
    - b. abrupt change
    - c. tremendous decline
    - d. sudden advancement

_b_ **6. accolades**

- Honors and **accolades** are wonderful. (para. 15) (HINT: Read the following sentence. A *promotion* is an example of what you might get as a reward for a successful achievement on the job.)
- Prof. Smart received **accolades** for his scholarly presentation at the National Association for Developmental Education conference in March 2010.
    - a. lessons or values
    - b. a sign of praise and recognition for achievements
    - c. prizes and certificates
    - d. monetary awards

_d_ **7. shelf life**

- "It's taken me a long time to understand that prizes and honors, while wonderful to receive, have a short **shelf life**," says one successful journalist. (para. 12) (HINT: Here it is used in the figurative sense.)

- The buzz about my high score on an aptitude test had a short **shelf life,** for the next day, I was still an underpaid substitute teacher.

  a. is perishable and will spoil easily
  b. length of time remaining on the shelf
  c. duration of time a product will be suitable for selling
  d. period of time in which something will have an impact

b   **8. confront**

- It is quite a painful experience to **confront** the loss of some trapping or another that seems bound up with success. (para. 13) (HINT: The writer expresses her feelings about not achieving success as a *loss*; that is, she does not receive the benefits that go along with the success.)

- When Stewart failed to hand in his history paper on time, he had to **confront** the possibility that his professor might drop him from the course.

  a. to express dissatisfaction
  b. to be forced to deal with a difficult situation
  c. to challenge someone face to face
  d. to present an opposing idea

c   **9. emerged**

- But eventually what **emerged** from the digging was a sense of something similar to freedom. (para. 14) (HINT: Read the previous paragraph about the result of digging deeper about the meaning of success and failure.)

- After a period of investigation, it **emerged** that a student from the college had hacked into the computer system.

  a. rose to the surface
  b. plunged into
  c. became evident
  d. came into existence

d   **10. summit**

- It is written somewhere that you can stand on the **summit** for only a few moments, then the wind blows your footprints away. (para. 17)

- After an exhausting hike up to the **summit** of the mountain, the students and their physical science professor rested for a well-deserved lunch.

  a. top level meeting
  b. lowest point
  c. sandy beach
  d. the highest point or apex

▶ as **you read**

Establish Your Purpose

Now you are ready to read and annotate the selection "Reversal of Fortune." Focus on major points of information. Read to learn about the effects of success as compared to failure.

Actively Process While You Read: Guided Reading

Stop to think about the information as you read.

Exercise 3   **Processing While You Read**

Answers may vary. Sample answers provided.

Directions: Answer the questions that appear in bold type at the conclusion of each paragraph. This will help you monitor your reading process and understand the material.

> ## Reversal of Fortune:
> ## Attitude Can Reroute Adversity
> ### By Alice Steinbach

1   It was a few minutes before air time and the talk-show host was about to begin his daily radio program. He poured himself a cup of coffee and then, turning to me, said something surprising:

2   "You know this job never gets any easier," said this **erudite** man who for years has presided over an extremely popular call-in show. "Every time I go on the air, I have to overcome a fear that I'll fail; that the show won't be any good."

How does the talk show host feel before he goes on the air?

He is afraid that the show won't be a success, and he will be considered a failure.

3   He paused. "But I've found something interesting about failing. And that is, you can build on success but you really learn only from failure."

What does the host discover?

He discovers that you can learn from adversities.

4   A few days later, a letter arrived that seemed, in a way, to continue this line of thought. Written by a young man I know quite well, the letter concerned itself with the idea that **adversity** might offer, in the long run, more rewards than getting what you thought you wanted. My correspondent wrote:

5   "What I guess I'm learning from my difficult situation is a deeper sense of who I am. And what I'm capable of when it comes to handling disappointment. I think—at least I hope—I'll come out of this a stronger person."

What does the correspondent learn from his experience with adversity?

He discovers that you can learn more from failure than from success. From failure, you can acquire self-knowledge and develop ways to cope with difficult situations.

6   Then last week, in what seemed a curious completion of the philosophy underlying both of these remarks, I came across the **unattributed** quotation in a book on mountain climbing:

7   "Today is a new day; you'll get out of it just what you put into it. If you have made mistakes, even serious mistakes, you can make a new start whenever you choose. For the thing we call failure is not the falling down but the staying down."

What does the author learn from the quotation in the mountain climbing book?

She learns the definition of failure. Failure is not being unsuccessful; it is accepting failure and not doing anything about it.

8   Few of us can claim the distinction of not knowing the sting of falling down, of "failure." The promotion not gotten; the honor not won; the job lost; the praise denied—we've all known the loss of self-esteem that comes with such moments. And because the wound of failure is a deep one, we seldom risk sharing our feelings about such moments.

Why are people unwilling to discuss their failures with others?

Failure is a painful experience that people feel uncomfortable sharing.

9   "Success does not necessarily build character—sometimes it doesn't even build self-confidence," says a friend one judged by the world to be successful. "But most people I know—including myself—can point to a disappointment or a failure that resulted in what I would call a **quantum leap** of self-knowledge and self-confidence. The confidence comes from knowing that you can get through 'failure' and come out stronger on the other side."

Where does confidence come from?

Confidence comes from the knowledge of getting through failure.

10   Still, she admits that it is a "painful process to go through."

11   Some successful people find that they become "addicted" to honors and **accolades.** And when they don't get them—when they're just doing well at their job—not sensationally well—they feel depressed.

How do some people feel about success?

They become obsessed with seeking success. It becomes such a driving force that when they don't get the recognition they want, they feel depressed.

12   "It's taken me a long time to understand that prizes and honors, while wonderful to receive, have a short **shelf life,**" says one successful journalist. "I have found that the sense of achievement you can get from 'winning' needs to be constantly renewed. It's easy to feel good about yourself when you're winning. It's not winning that's hard. But that's when you learn to dig deeper and do your best work. Not for the rewards of success but for the rewards of self-respect."

What does the author learn about success?

The feelings associated with achieving success do not last long, and new achievements must be accomplished to receive further recognition.

13   A few years back, I found myself needing to dig deeper (and not for the first time in my life) to find a firmer foundation upon which to build my understanding of what success is and what failure is. And my friend was right: It is quite a painful experience to **confront** the loss of some trapping or another that seems bound up with success.

Why is it painful to experience failure?

Because there are many rewards that accompany success, and one who fails does not get these rewards, such as a promotion, a bonus, or an award.

14   But eventually what emerged from the digging was a sense of something similar to freedom. A realization that there's a feeling of accomplishment and success that comes from mastering the pain of failure. And then getting on with the job.

How can failure become a good experience?

When you master failure, you learn that you can handle failure, you are resilient, and you can move on and not be stuck.

15   Honors and **accolades** are wonderful. Promotions are wonderful. Success—however you define it—is wonderful. But none of them, in my experience, really teaches you anything of lasting value about yourself.

16   **Adversity,** on the other hand, can be an inspirational teacher.

What is the most significant value of adversity?

Adversity teaches you about yourself.

17   It is written somewhere that you can stand on the summit for only a few moments, and then the wind blows your footprints away.

Did the author say this before? What does it mean?

Success has a short shelf life.

18   Life is like that, too.

19   Harvard Business School probably doesn't teach that to its MBAs. But you know what? Maybe it should.

What should Harvard Business School teach its MBAs?

The school should teach its students the value of success and failure, especially the importance of adversity in terms of inspiring learning, building confidence, and establishing a sense of accomplishment.

Source: Adapted from "Success and Failure," *The Miss Dennis School of Writing and Other Lessons from a Woman's Life* by Alice Steinbach, pp. 69–71. 1966 The Bancroft Press.

■ ■ ■

 after you read

Review Important Points

Going over the major points immediately after you have read, while the information is fresh in your mind, will help you recall the content and record key ideas.

| Exercise 4 | **Reviewing Important Points** |

Directions: Answer the following questions based on the information provided in the selection. You may need to go back to the text and reread certain portions to be sure your responses are correct and can be supported by information in the text. Write the letter of your choice in the space provided.

_d_   1. **What is the overall message of this selection?**
  a. You can turn your good fortune into money.
  b. You can overcome your fear of heights by climbing mountains.
  c. Harvard Business School should offer courses in overcoming adversity.
  d. You can build on success, but you can learn only from failure.

_a_   2. **To explain the author's main point, Steinbach provides quotations from all of the following** *except:*
  a. Harvard Business School.
  b. a radio talk show host.
  c. a successful journalist.
  d. a mountain climbing book.

_d_   3. **The writer uses the _____ organizational pattern to discuss the topic of success and failure.**
  a. definition
  b. sequence/chronology
  c. classification
  d. cause and effect

_b_   4. **The talk show host:**
  a. is confident that his show will remain on the air.
  b. has learned that you can benefit from failure.
  c. is not afraid of failure.
  d. has learned a lot from success.

_a_   5. **How did the journalist feel?**
  a. Adversity can help you learn how you can deal with a difficult situation.
  b. He wishes he were a stronger person.
  c. He cannot cope with adversity.
  d. In the long run, adversity leads to success.

_c_ 6. In paragraph 7, a good paraphrase for the quotation from the book on mountain climbing about "falling down and staying down" might be:

   a. If you injure yourself, don't get up.
   b. Do not feel depressed because you fell down.
   c. We are defeated only if we don't have the resiliency to begin anew.
   d. If you are not a good mountain climber, you should take up another activity.

_d_ 7. According to paragraphs 8–10, failure is:

   a. a way of showing one's feelings.
   b. not a painful experience.
   c. part of the passage of life.
   d. a way that many people make personal gains.

_c_ 8. In paragraphs 12 and 17, the author says that receiving honors and accolades:

   a. can be addictive.
   b. can lead to depression.
   c. are short lived and fleeting moments.
   d. can contribute to self-esteem.

_b_ 9. From paragraph 14, we can infer that success and a sense of accomplishment can be derived from:

   a. doing a good job at work.
   b. overcoming failures.
   c. getting a new position.
   d. tolerating pain well.

_c_ 10. According to this essay, what teaches us about self-worth?

   a. mountain climbing
   b. accolades and honors
   c. failures and adversities
   d. failure and success

_d_ 11. Which of the following statements can we infer from the reading?

   a. Adversity can teach us a great deal about ourselves.
   b. We can develop self-confidence from the knowledge of overcoming failure.
   c. Adversity promotes success.
   d. All of the above.

_d_ **12. The tone of this essay is:**

    a. angry.
    b. sarcastic.
    c. humorous.
    d. sincere.

Organize the Information

Organizing the information you have learned from a reading selection shows you have understood it and have the ability to restate the material in a different way. You can use this reorganized material to help you study for exams and prepare for written assignments. (See Chapter 9.)

Exercise 5   **Organizing the Information**

Directions: Fill in the following table with details from the reading on success and failure.

Success	Failure
1. Success does not necessarily build _character._	1. Failure offers more rewards. It is a tremendous _learning_ experience.
2. It does not build self-_confidence._	2. It helps you develop a deeper sense _of who you are._
3. It has a short _shelf life_ and must be constantly renewed.	3. You can experience a _quantum_ leap of self-knowledge and self-confidence from getting through failure.
4. Some people are _addicted_ to honors and accolades.	4. It can be a painful _experience._
5. Some become _depressed_ when they are not doing sensationally well.	5. You get a feeling of _accomplishment_ from mastering the pain of failure and making a new start or getting on with the job.

Integrate the Vocabulary

Make the new vocabulary presented in the reading _your_ vocabulary. In addition to learning the meaning of new words, you should also learn related word forms.

Exercise 6A   **Using Context Clues**

Directions: For each sentence, select the word from the text box on p. 319 that is a synonym for the word or words in parentheses and best completes the sentence. Then write the word or a form of the word in the space provided.

1. After Jane completed all her remedial course work, she made a (tremendous stride) _quantum leap_____ in her studies and graduated with a 4.0 GPA.

2. Yesterday, I came across an (unidentified) _unattributed_____ quotation on adversity.

3. (A scholarly) An _erudite_____ professor of economics from Harvard Business School spoke at our graduation ceremony. He spoke about the effects of the economic downturn and new career opportunities.

4. Dealing with the (problems) _adversity_____ of losing my financial aid could have been devastating to my college studies if I had not already applied for a bridge loan.

5. Jenna White received an honor (of special recognition) _distinction_____ for her essay, "Diversity in the College Classroom," published in the *Journal of Community Colleges*.

6. (Having to deal with the possibility) _Confronted with_____ losing his academic scholarship, Justin quit his part-time job to devote more of his time to his studies.

7. The members of the Student Council received (praise) _accolades_____ from the president of their college for their successful "Going Green" initiative on campus.

8. The (highest point) _summit_____ of Robert's legal career came at the early age of 32 when he received a tenured position at Yale Law School.

9. After Robert received his position, he continued to get letters of recognition and praise from scholars all over the world in law for two years. He had never expected his success to have such a long (last for a period of time) _shelf life_____, but it did.

10. What (became evident) _emerged_____ from his experience was that obtaining a position at a prestigious college was going to open doors to many other opportunities in the field of law.

Exercise 6B   **Learning the Meaning of Hyphenated Words**

Directions: In this essay, the author used four hyphenated words beginning with "self." Use your knowledge of word parts to define these words from the essay (marked with an asterisk) and other words that begin with "self." Match the words in the first column with their definitions in the second one. Then write the letter in the spaces provided.

_j_ 1. self-centered   a. causing harm to oneself

_g_ 2. self-concept   b. designed to permit learning at the student's own level of performance

_h_ 3. self-confidence*   c. a proper regard for oneself as a human being

_i_ 4. self-conscious   d. able to provide for yourself without the help of others

_f_ 5. self-esteem*   e. understanding of one's own capabilities, character, feelings, or motivations

_a_ 6. self-inflicted   f. satisfaction in oneself

_e_ 7. self-knowledge*   g. having the image or perception of yourself

_b_ 8. self-paced   h. confidence in oneself and in one's powers and abilities

_c_ 9. self-respect*   i. excessive or uncontrollable concern about your appearance

_d_ 10. self-sustaining   j. concerned solely with one's own desires, needs, or interests

Make Personal Connections Through Writing and Discussion

When you make your new learning relevant to yourself in some way, it becomes more meaningful and easier to remember. Whenever you read, try to connect to the content on a personal level. How does it relate to you? How can you apply what you have read to other situations? What else would you like to know?

| **Exercise 7** | **Making Personal Connections Through Writing and Discussion** |

In small groups, or as a personal reflection, consider this question: In what ways can a person become more resilient or recover more quickly during difficult times? List at least five ideas or strategies. Then share your thoughts with the rest of the class.

1. _____   *Answers will vary.*

2. _____

3. _____

4. _____

5. _____

Self-Monitored Reading
Reading Selection 2

Decoding Dyslexia: Dyslexia Sabotages the
Reading Skills of Millions of People

By Sean McCollum

In this article, from Scholastic Choices, *the author discusses the impact of dyslexia and how one woman refuses to let her disability stop her from pursuing her education and reaching her goals. How do you think this story relates to you?*

⏪ before you read

Answers will vary.

Answer the following questions before you read the selection.

1. Dyslexia can be defined as a learning disability that involves difficulties in acquiring and processing language. Do you or someone you know have dyslexia? What problems have you or someone you know encountered in school, college, or at work?

    _____

    _____

2. What recommendations do you have for someone who is dyslexic?

    _____

    _____

3. Does your college provide accommodations for students with disabilities?

    _____

    _____

Prepare to Read

Preview the reading selection by applying the THIEVES strategy (p. 40).

Exercise 1   **Previewing**

Based on your preview, respond to the following questions:

1. How would you describe the brain of a dyslexic?
    They are perfectly healthy, but the "software" is less compatible with the way reading is taught.

2. What can a dyslexic do to make up for his/her disability?
    Retrain the brain and use other learning strategies to make up for the disability.

3. Describe Kristin's struggle with school.
    Her learning disability impacted her academic success. Nevertheless, she wanted to go to college and found a school, Beacon College, which was devoted to teaching learning-disabled students. There she received personalized help in overcoming her dyslexia. Later, she continued her studies at Webster University.

Check Out the Vocabulary

You will encounter the following vocabulary words in bold type in this reading.

anxiety	compensate*	devoted*	harbored
assemble*	cope	excel	retrieving
compatible	detection*	excluded*	ridicule

*Denotes a word from the Academic Word List

Exercise 2   **Checking Out the Vocabulary**

Directions: Look at each boldface word taken from the reading selection. Use the context of the sentence and the hint in parentheses to select the best definition from the choices listed. Write the letter of your choice on the line provided.

_b_ **1. excluded**

"I felt very **excluded** and alone, like I was being punished," Kristen tells *Scholastic Choices*. (para. 1) (HINT: What does the prefix *ex-* mean as in the word *exit*?)

a. expelled
b. left out
c. accepted
d. suspended

_b_ **2. ridicule**

"Kids would **ridicule** me and say things like, 'Why do you have to sit in the back of the class?' Or 'What are you, stupid?'" (para. 1) (HINT: Look at what the kids say.)

a. question or inquire
b. tease or taunt
c. show anger or act irate
d. act silly or foolish

_a_ **3. cope**

The condition cannot be cured, but dyslexics can develop the ability to **cope** with it and improve their reading. (para. 3) (HINT: Dyslexia can't be cured, but what can be done to improve reading comprehension?)

a. deal with difficulties
b. imitate perfectly
c. cover up imperfections
d. take action

_b_ **4. excel**

Dyslexic brains are perfectly healthy. Many dyslexics **excel** in math, art, mechanics, and sports—areas that don't require strong language skills. (para. 5) (HINT: What does the word *excellent* mean?)

a. do poorly
b. perform extremely well
c. select carefully
d. fail or not pass

_d_ 5. **compatible**

In dyslexic brains, the "software" is less **compatible** with the way reading is usually taught. (para. 7) (HINT: Look at the comparison between PCs and the Macintosh computer.)

a. consistent and steady
b. friendly and agreeable
c. existing together in harmony
d. designed to work together

_b_ 6. **retrieving**

Dyslexics have more difficulty **retrieving** the meaning for the words they see written down. (para. 7) (HINT: Read the next sentence.)

a. setting something right
b. recalling something from memory
c. locating data
d. restoring to its original condition

_b_ 7. **anxiety**

The struggle to read often leads to feelings of embarrassment, **anxiety,** and failure. (para 8) (HINT: What is an emotional effect of dyslexia? See the examples.)

a. fatigue and weariness
b. uneasiness and worries
c. shyness and reticence
d. doubt and uncertainty

_d_ 8. **assemble**

This approach carefully teaches them how to break apart and **assemble** syllables. (para. 9) (HINT: Use contrast clues.)

a. call to order
b. look like
c. sit in one place
d. fit together

_b_ 9. **detection**

Early **detection** makes the rewiring process much easier. (para. 10) (HINT: Look for a synonym in the next sentence.)

a. mystery
b. screening
c. investigation
d. intervention

_c_ **10. compensate**

Besides retraining their brains, dyslexic students can use other learning strategies to **compensate** for their disability, including listening to books on tape, writing papers by dictating words to a computer equipped with special software, having tests read to them, and being given extra time to complete tests. (para. 11) (HINT: Use example clues.)

  a. repay
  b. take over
  c. make up
  d. atone

_c_ **11. harbored**

Even so, Kristen earned B's and C's and **harbored** a dream of going to college. (para. 13) (HINT: Look at the surprising contrast between Kristin's struggles and her dreams.)

  a. sheltered her emotions
  b. retreated from an idea
  c. held as a thought or feeling
  d. obsessed with a thought or feeling

_d_ **12. devoted**

Beacon is the only accredited four-year U.S. college **devoted** to teaching learning-disabled undergraduates. (para. 14) (HINT: Why was Kristin able to improve her reading level at Beacon?)

  a. displayed feelings of strong affection
  b. showed feelings of dedication
  c. made a formal commitment
  d. set apart for a specific purpose

▶ as you read

Establish Your Purpose

Now, read and annotate the selection on page 333 using the following questions for active reading, and focus on the major points of information.

Actively Process While You Read: Self-Monitored Reading

Monitor your comprehension as you read. (See Chapter 2, page 54.) Be sure to stop to reflect at the conclusion of each paragraph, and ask yourself the following questions:

- Did I understand what I have just read?
- What is the main idea of the paragraph?
- Am I ready to continue?

| Exercise 3 | **Processing While You Read** |

Directions: Highlight the most important points in each paragraph. Then write the key topics and main ideas in the spaces provided in the margins. Finally, underline or number the supporting details in the text.

Decoding Dyslexia: Dyslexia Sabotages the Reading Skills of Millions of People
By Sean McCollum

Notes

Topic _____
Main Idea _____
_____

1   The color of Kristen Seaman's fourth-grade reading book was red. Her classmates had higher-level orange ones. The teacher also made Kristen sit in the back of the classroom. "I felt very **excluded** and alone, like I was being punished," Kristen tells *Choices*. "Kids would **ridicule** me and say things like 'Why do you have to sit in the back of the class?' Or 'What are you, stupid?' After a while I started wondering, 'Maybe they're right.'"

Topic _____
Main Idea _____
_____

2   They were wrong. A learning disability called dyslexia was the source of Kristen's problems in school. Dyslexia is a disorder of the brain that makes it difficult for a person to read and write properly. The word "dyslexia" is of Greek origin and means "difficulty with words." People are born with dyslexia, which often runs in families.

Topic _____
Main Idea _____
_____

3   The National Institutes of Health estimates that 15 percent of people in the United States have some degree of dyslexia. The condition cannot be cured, but dyslexics can develop the ability to **cope** with it and improve their reading.

Word Work

Topic _____
Main Idea _____
_____

4   "Reading is one of the most important and complex tasks that people learn to do," says Nancy Hennessy, past president of the International Dyslexia Association. "Writing is a code that involves sounds and letters that represent meaning. Most kids can figure out that code, but for dyslexics that code is impossible to crack."

Topic _____
Main Idea _____
_____

5   Dyslexic brains are perfectly healthy. Many dyslexics **excel** in math, art, mechanics, and sports—areas that don't require strong language skills. Their brains, though, have trouble connecting the sounds of letters and syllables to words written on a page.

Topic _____
Main Idea _____
_____

6   These brain differences are "like the difference between PCs (personal computers) and Macintosh computers," says Michael Ryan, a psychologist in Grand Rapids, Michigan, who has dyslexia. "Both are very good computers, but each uses different software to process written language."

Topic _____
Main Idea _____
_____

7   In dyslexic brains, the "software" is less **compatible** with the way reading is usually taught. Dyslexics have more difficulty **retrieving** the meaning for the words they see written down. "It's like they have a library full of words, but no card catalogue to find them," Ryan says.

Outcasts

Topic _____
Main Idea _____
_____

8   Dyslexia can have emotional consequences, too. The struggle to read often leads to feelings of embarrassment, **anxiety,** and failure. Dyslexics dread being called on to

read in class. They fall behind friends and classmates in their studies. Sometimes they lash out in frustration or just give up. "I had this terrible insecurity that I didn't measure up," Kristen says. "I had a very poor self-image."

9   Fortunately, once dyslexia is diagnosed, the person suffering from it can get help. One approach is multisensory reading instruction. A trained teacher uses sight, sound, and even touch to help students connect letters and syllables to the sounds they represent. Dyslexic students learn the specific rules—and the many exceptions—about sounding out words. This approach carefully teaches them how to break apart and **assemble** syllables. Over time, it can actually "rewire" the dyslexic brain so it can decode words better.

Notes
Topic _____
Main Idea _____
_____

10   Early **detection** makes the rewiring process much easier. Experts like Hennessy and Ryan would like to see every school screen for dyslexia in the earliest grades. "If we catch it early, we could save these kids a lot of heartache, as well as millions of dollars in special education and other costs," Ryan says.

Topic _____
Main Idea _____
_____

11   Besides retraining their brains, dyslexic students can use other learning strategies to **compensate** for their disability, including listening to books on tape, writing papers by dictating words to a computer equipped with special software, having tests read to them, and being given extra time to complete tests. Increasingly, schools are making these resources available.

Topic _____
Main Idea _____
_____

School Struggle

12   Kristen continued to struggle even after she was diagnosed with dyslexia. By the end of middle school she was cutting classes. "I was miserable," Kristen says. Her school's special-education program wasn't able to teach dyslexic students, she says.

Topic _____
Main Idea _____
_____

13   Even so, Kristen earned B's and C's and **harbored** a dream of going to college. Wanting help finding colleges that had special support for learning-disabled students, Kristen went to see her guidance counselor. The counselor told her that she wasn't "college material." "That just made me more determined," Kristen recalls.

Topic _____
Main Idea _____
_____

14   Through her own research, Kristen found Beacon College. Beacon is the only accredited four-year U.S. college **devoted** to teaching learning-disabled undergraduates. "It was also in Florida, and I like warm weather," Kristen adds. "I graduated high school by the skin of my teeth with a fourth-grade reading level. I cried when Beacon accepted me, believe me."

Topic _____
Main Idea _____
_____

15   At Beacon College, Kristen received personalized help in overcoming her dyslexia. She raised her reading ability to a 12th-grade level by the time she graduated last year. She takes pride in having read all of the Harry Potter books.

Topic _____
Main Idea _____
_____

16   Now 22, Kristen is studying at Webster University in St. Louis, Missouri. She is working toward a master's degree in mental-health counseling. She takes one class per term to manage the heavy reading load. "I want to help teenagers who are dealing with emotional problems or learning disabilities," she says. "I want to help them get the resources they need."

Topic _____
Main Idea _____
_____

Source: Sean McCollum, "Decoding Dyslexia: Dyslexia Sabotages the Reading Skills of Millions of People," from *Scholastic Choices* magazine, October 2006 issue. Copyright © 2006 by Scholastic Inc. Reprinted by permission of Scholastic Inc.

■ ■ ■

 **after you read**

Review Important Points

Going over the major points immediately after you have read, while the information is fresh in your mind, will help you recall the content and record key ideas.

Exercise 4   Reviewing Important Points

Directions: Choose the best answer for each of the following questions using information provided in the selection. Write your answers in the spaces provided.

_d_ 1. **The overall topic of this article is:**
   a. dyslexic brains.
   b. learning disabilities.
   c. dyslexia screening.
   d. dyslexia and resilience.

_a_ 2. **What is the overall message of this article?**
   a. Dyslexics can overcome adversity through determination, hard work and resilience.
   b. At the present time, dyslexia cannot be cured.
   c. Early detection of dyslexia is critical.
   d. Dyslexia results in emotional problems.

_b_ 3. **The primary purpose of the author is to:**
   a. persuade the reader to become aware of his/her disability.
   b. inform the reader about dyslexia, its adversities, and the importance of resiliency.
   c. instruct the reader how to compensate for learning disabilities.
   d. entertain the reader through Kristin's story.

_d_ 4. **From paragraph 1, we can infer that in fourth grade:**
   a. Kristin's classmates knew she had dyslexia.
   b. Kristin's teacher used specially designed reading techniques for dyslexics.
   c. Kristin liked sitting in the back of the room.
   d. Kristin had not yet been screened for dyslexia.

_d_ 5. **According to paragraph 2, which of the following statements are true about dyslexia?**
   a. It is inherited.
   b. Other family members may be dyslexic.
   c. People with dyslexia will experience difficulty in school.
   d. All of the above.

_c_ 6. **The main idea of paragraph 3 is:**
   a. Dyslexia is widespread.
   b. Dyslexia can be cured.
   c. Dyslexics can learn to deal with their disability.
   d. The NIH conducted a survey on dyslexia.

_c_ 7. **From paragraphs 4 and 5, we can infer that dyslexics may have difficulty with:**
   a. computer science and mathematics.
   b. physical education requirements.
   c. English composition course work.
   d. music or art electives.

_c_ 8. **In comparing the dyslexic's brain to a PC and a Mac, we can learn that a dyslexic's brain:**
   a. is not healthy.
   b. cannot decode words.
   c. requires a different method of retrieving words.
   d. works like a computer.

_a_ 9. **According to this article, in addition to difficulty with reading and writing, dyslexics can experience:**
   a. fear and embarrassment of being called upon to read in class.
   b. anxiety of performing in front of classmates.
   c. insecurities about their appearance.
   d. failures in holding jobs or maintaining relationships.

_d_ 10. **Experts in dyslexia claim that early screening is important because it:**
   a. saves money spent on purchasing special material.
   b. provides additional funds to train professionals.
   c. helps parents understand their children's needs.
   d. spares children from having academic and psychological problems.

_d_ 11. **When did Kristin make the most strides in overcoming her difficulties with reading comprehension?**
   a. in fourth grade
   b. in middle school
   c. in high school
   d. in college

_c_ 12. **Why does Kristin want to become a mental health counselor?**
   a. She wants to improve her reading skills.
   b. She would like to be trained as a multisensory reading specialist.
   c. She wants to help students like herself learn to cope.
   d. She would like to conduct research on dyslexia.

_a_ 13. **Kristin's story illustrates how:**

   a. Dyslexics struggle with their learning disabilities.
   b. Dyslexics do not succeed.
   c. Early diagnosis and intervention can benefit young children.
   d. Approaches such as multisensory instruction help students.

_b_ 14. **The author uses the _____ pattern of organization to relate Kristin's experiences with dyslexia.**

   a. definition
   b. chronological (time)
   c. listing
   d. spatial

_b_ 15. **The overall tone of this article is:**

   a. critical.
   b. optimistic.
   c. persuasive.
   d. pessimistic.

Organize the Information

Organizing the information from a reading selection shows you have understood it and can restate the material in your own way.

Exercise 5	**Organizing the Information**

Directions: Fill in the blanks in the right column with details from the selection on dyslexia.

Dyslexia

Definition	■ Greek: difficulty with _words_
Causes	■ Disorder of the _brain_ , which makes it difficult to _read_ and _write_
Effects	■ Inherited, common in _families_
	■ Difficulty with schoolwork
	■ Feelings of _embarrassment_ , _anxiety_ and _fear_
	■ _Poor_ self-image
Treatment	■ _Multisensory_ reading instruction to retrain brain
	■ Listen to books _on tape_
	■ Write papers using special software, which is _voice-activated_
	■ Have tests _read_
	■ Get extra _time for tests_

Integrate the Vocabulary

Make the new vocabulary *your* vocabulary.

Exercise 6	**Using Context Clues**

Directions: Locate a word from the text box in Exercise 2 (p. 331) that best completes the following sentences. Then write the word, or a form of the word, in the spaces provided.

1. Because I do not come from the same town as my suitemates, I often feel *excluded* _____ from their conversations about friends back home.

2. I tried to print my paper on the computer in the library, but it seems that my computer at home is not *compatible* _____.

3. The nurse informed me that if the flu is *detected* _____ within the first 24 hours, a dose of the medicine TAMIFLU can be taken to possibly shorten the duration of the virus.

4. Although I am not a great writer, I try to *compensate* _____ for my lack of creativity by writing coherently and proofreading carefully before I hand in my papers.

5. The Math Lab is solely *devoted* _____ to students who are taking remedial course work, whereas the Math Center is for all math students.

6. Mara was often the subject of *ridicule* _____ by her friends because of her outrageous style of dress.

7. When I can't *cope* _____ with all my reading assignments, I take a short break from my studies and go to the gym for a workout.

8. Although I am not a great math student, I *excel* _____ in the social sciences.

9. While I am studying anatomy and physiology, I use mnemonic or memory devices and techniques to help me *retrieve* _____ the information for tests.

10. I often feel *anxious* _____ when I read aloud, so I asked my professor not to call on me to read. Now I am more at ease.

11. I asked my brother to lend me money for books this semester, but he still *harbored* _____ anger against me for taking six months to pay him back the last time I borrowed some cash.

12. The apparel design students were ready to *assemble* _____ the costumes they had designed for the upcoming fashion show.

Make Personal Connections Through Writing and Discussion

Connect to the content on a personal level. How does it relate to you? How can you apply what you have read to other situations?

| **Exercise 7** | **Making Personal Connections Through Writing and Discussion** |

Responses will vary.

1. Kristin's guidance counselor did not display any empathy toward her and her disability and, in fact, discouraged her from attending college. Pretend you are Kristin, and you have now completed your master's degree in mental health counseling. Write a letter to your high school counselor and tell him how he or she should treat future students with dyslexia differently.

2. Find out what accommodations your college provides for students with disabilities.

3. Working in pairs, prepare a list of 10 questions you can use to conduct an interview with a counselor or professional who works with disabled students. Make an appointment to visit this individual. You and your partner will gather the information and organize it into a summary. Share your summary with your classmates. The class can work together synthesizing all the information and submit the revised essay to the student newspaper or a local paper.

4. Does your college offer a degree in disability studies? If so, describe the course of study. What are some career options for a degree in such a major?

Independent Reading
Selection 3

> ## Confessions of a Quit Addict
> ### By Barbara Graham

In this essay, a woman talks about the lessons she learned from quitting. After living a carefree life of traveling and adventure for years, she realizes that quitting was not the ultimate freedom but another trap where one had no family, friends, career, or home.

  before you read

Answer the following questions before you read the selection.

1. What do you think about quitting? Does it bring to mind any negative thoughts? Have your family or friends influenced the way you feel?

_____
_____
_____

2. Have you or someone you know ever quit a team, resigned from a job, left school, or abandoned a project? What happened to you or the other individual? Was it a good decision? Did it bring about any changes?

_____

_____

_____

Prepare to Read

Preview the essay "Confessions of a Quit Addict" by Barbara Graham, using the THIEVES strategy.

| **E x e r c i s e 1** | **Developing Preview Questions** |

Directions: Based on your previewing, write *three* questions you anticipate will be answered in the selection.   *Answers may vary.*

1. _____

2. _____

3. _____

| **E x e r c i s e 2** | **Checking Out the Vocabulary** |

Directions: You will encounter the following vocabulary words in boldface in this reading.

alienated	confirmation*	inevitably*	tenacious
apprentice	conventions*	lucrative	upheavals
collaborator	dwelling	mantra	

*Denotes word from Academic Word List

Read each sentence from the selection in which a vocabulary word from the selection appears in bold. Then select the best definition of the word from the choices provided. Write the letter of your choice on the line provided.

_c_ 1. **confirmation**

The year was 1967, and Leary's battle cry was for me more a **confirmation** of what I already believed than a call to action. (para. 1)

   a. a religious ceremony

   b. a right administered to a baptized person

   c. a statement of evidence

   d. a denial or opposition

_c_ 2. **tenacious**

I was stubborn, **tenacious** in my devotion to the people and things I loved, disrespectful of everything else. (para. 2)

a. tough
b. accepting
c. stubborn
d. devoted

_b_ **3. mantra**

"When one jumps over the edge, one is bound to land somewhere," wrote D.H. Lawrence, and for a long time this was my **mantra.** (para. 3)

a. sacred prayer
b. guiding principle
c. common saying
d. favorite song or tune

_a_ **4. collaborator**

It didn't take long for me to find a **collaborator,** a master of disappearing acts who made me look like a rookie. (para. 4)

a. someone who will cooperate or work together
b. a person who is willing to conspire
c. a highly experienced participant
d. a magician or sorcerer

_d_ **5. apprentice**

I became his loyal **apprentice,** and during the summer of 1968, shortly after Bobby Kennedy and Martin Luther King Jr. were gunned down, we sold everything we owned and quit our jobs, our friends, our apartment, the urban jungle, America and the blight of Vietnam, and fled to Europe. (para. 4)

a. favorite girlfriend
b. sincere friend
c. one who is beginning to learn a trade
d. one who is beginning to learn

_a_ **6. dwelling**

We crisscrossed the United States, went north to British Columbia, and lived in every conceivable sort of **dwelling** from tenements and tents to farmhouses and plywood shacks. (para. 4)

a. a place to reside or inhabit
b. an outdoor living space
c. an apartment or high-rise building
d. a poverty-stricken region

_d_ **7. lucrative**

But something always went wrong: It rained too much (British Columbia), the cost of living was too high (Colorado), the air wasn't pure enough (Southern California) or we couldn't find work that was meaningful, not to mention **lucrative** enough to make a living (everywhere). (para. 4)

a. useful and advantageous
b. sufficient and adequate

c. insufficient and poorly paid
d. profitable and well paid

_c_   8. **inevitably**

In that moment I knew that I no longer had it in me to continue feeding on fantasies of a future that **inevitably** turned to dust. (para. 5)

a. consequently
b. automatically
c. surely
d. out of necessity

_b_   9. **conventions**

It had taken thousands of miles and one child for me to understand that the quitting I took for freedom was as much of a trap as the social **conventions** we were trying to escape. (para. 6)

a. formal meetings, such as between states or countries
b. practices and procedures widely accepted in a group
c. meetings for members of a group
d. relationships between societies

_b_   10. **alienated**

After seven years, I felt sad, spent, and more **alienated** than ever—from Brian, from the rest of the world, and, most frighteningly, from myself. (para. 6)

a. unfriendly
b. isolated
c. afraid
d. negative

_a_   11. **upheavals**

Upheavals, startling turns, and unpredictable shifts have all come unbidden—especially when I've been at my most settled. (para. 8)

a. disturbances
b. high places
c. ascension
d. changes

▶ as **you read**

Establish Your Purpose

Read and annotate the selection using the guidelines for active reading. When reading a narrative essay, picture the setting and the plot events in your mind. Become familiar with the characters and the story line. Make note of the sequence of events and the culminating idea.

Actively Process as You Read: Independent Reading

Monitor your comprehension as you read. (See Chapter 2, page 54.) Stop and reflect at the conclusion of each paragraph. Highlight the most important points. Write notes, responses, or questions that come to mind in the margin.

Confessions of a Quit Addict
By Barbara Graham

The year is 1967, and America is fighting a war far away from its shores in Vietnam. A counterculture develops that questions the current state of society. It opposes war and promotes freedom of lifestyles, including sex and drugs, which mainstream society considered escapism or simply quitting.

1   By the time I heard Timothy Leary chant "Turn on, tune in, drop out" from the stage of New York's Fillmore East, I had already quit college. The year was 1967, and Leary's battle cry was for me more a **confirmation** of what I already believed than a call to action.

2   I had never been much good at doing things that didn't arouse my passion. Even when I was a young girl, it was obvious that I had been born without the stick-to-it, nose-to-the-grindstone gene. I was stubborn, **tenacious** in my devotion to the people and things I loved, disrespectful of everything else. There was no in-between. In high school I got straight A's in English and flunked math. When it came time for college, I enrolled at NYU because it was the only way I could think of to live in Greenwich Village and get my parents to pick up the tab. But I rarely made it to classes and dropped out one month into my sophomore year.

3   That was the first time I felt the rush of quitting, the instant high of cutting loose, the biochemical buzz of burning my bridges. The charge had to do not with leaving college for something else, but with leaving, period—the pure act of making the break. Suddenly, it seemed possible to reinvent myself, to discard my old life like last year's outfit and step into a new one—free from the responsibilities and relationships that had dragged me down. I got an unlisted telephone number and warned my parents to stay away. 'When one jumps over the edge, one is bound to land somewhere,' wrote D.H. Lawrence, and for a long time this was my **mantra.**

4   It didn't take long for me to find a **collaborator,** a master of disappearing acts who made me look like a rookie. Brian was ready to morph one life into the next on the turn of a dime. I became his loyal **apprentice** and during the summer of 1968, shortly after Bobby Kennedy and Martin Luther King Jr., were gunned down, we sold everything we owned and quit our jobs, our friends, our apartment, the urban jungle, America and the blight of Vietnam, and fled to Europe. But our new life didn't quite match our dreams: As winter neared, we found

ourselves living in a rusty old van on the outskirts of Rome, hungry and cold and hard up for cash. From there, we boarded a freighter for Puerto Rico—which turned out not to be what we'd imagined, either—especially after the little episode with customs officials over a speck of hashish. Still, a pattern had been set: living in one place, dreaming of another, working at odd jobs (mine included secretary, salesgirl, cocktail waitress, draft counselor, nude model, warehouse clerk, candle maker), earning just enough money to get us to the next destination. We crisscrossed the United States, went north to British Columbia, and lived in every conceivable sort of **dwelling** from tenements and tents to farmhouses and plywood shacks. Sometimes, I'd grow attached to a place and plant a garden, thinking that this time things would work out and we'd stay forever—or at least long enough to see the flowers bloom. But something always went wrong: It rained too much (British Columbia), the cost of living was too high (Colorado), the air wasn't pure enough (Southern California) or we couldn't find work that was meaningful, not to mention **lucrative** enough to sustain us (everywhere).

5   For a long time it didn't matter that we weren't happy anywhere, because the rush of heading off into the unknown and starting over was more potent and trippy than anything we smoked and we just kept going—even after our son, Clay, was born. But one day, in the mountains of Northern California, when our latest scheme for finding True Happiness—living close to nature, in a house we built, near another family—fell apart, I just snapped. In that moment I knew that I no longer had it in me to continue feeding on fantasies of a future that **inevitably** turned to dust. That night I made this entry in my journal: 'I'm so sick of listening to ourselves talk about what's going to be—plans, plans, plans. I want to live in the present for once, not in the future. I mean live, settle down, make a home for my son.' I had understood finally that the problem wasn't in the places we went or the people we found there but in ourselves. We could shed our surroundings but not our own skin. No matter who or what we left behind, our private demons followed, and our differences with one another erupted like a sleeping volcano the minute we stopped running. In the end, there was nowhere left to go, no place left to leave behind, no one left to say good-bye to except each other.

6   It had taken thousands of miles and one child for me to understand that the quitting I took for freedom was as much of a trap as the social **conventions** we were trying to escape. Together, Brian and I had been so busy saying no to everything that might limit our options that, except for Clay, we'd neglected to say yes to anything. We had no careers, few friends, and no place to call home. Moreover, what had begun as a journey to find our 'true' selves, independent of other people's expectations, had turned into an addictive cycle of fantasy and failure, followed by another stab at seeking something better. After seven years, I felt sad, spent, and more **alienated** than ever—from Brian, from the rest of the world, and, most frighteningly, from myself. More than anything, I longed to land somewhere.

7   Still, I don't consider myself a "recovering" quitter. That would put too negative a spin on an act that is sometimes the best, most honest, and most creative response

to a life situation, as well as a tremendous source of energy and power. What's more, in the years since Brian and I went our separate ways, I've walked away from a marriage and a number of significant relationships, bailed out of college a second time (just a few credits shy of getting my degree), and moved back and forth across the country twice. As for my relationship to the workforce, it officially ended 15 years ago when I left a long-term (for me—it lasted all of eight months) position as the publicist for an outpatient leper clinic. I simply could not deal with a life in which I was expected to show up at the same place at the same time five days a week and not take frequent naps. So I did what any self-respecting jobaphobic would do: I became a writer.

8   Over the years, I've also come to understand that even if I don't go chasing after change, it will do a perfectly good job of finding me. **Upheavals,** startling turns, and unpredictable shifts have all come without warning—especially when I've been at my most settled. Besides, I've watched enough people I love die to know that no matter how hard we try to be the authors of our own stories, life itself will eventually have its way and quit us.

9   And though sometimes I miss the rush of cutting loose—and, God knows, the impulse still arises—I've learned that, for the most part, it's impossible to travel deep and wide at the same time. Now it's simply more interesting, more richly satisfying, to mine my life just as it is, with all of its wild imperfections and—for the most part at least—lack of drama. My family, my home, close friendships, the natural world, and the worlds I create in my work constantly surprise me with their nourishment—a thick and complex root system I might never have known if I hadn't stopped cutting the ties that bind.

Source: Adapted from "Confessions of a Quit Addict" by Barbara Graham. This essay originally appeared in the Sept.–Oct. 1996 issue of *Utne Reader.*

■ ■ ■

 ## after you read

| **Exercise 3** | **Answering Your Preview Questions** |

Answers may vary.   **Directions:** Look back at the questions you posed before your read the selection. If you have discovered the answers, write them on the lines provided.

1. _____

_____

2. _____

_____

3. _____

_____

| Exercise 4 | **Reviewing Important Points** |

Directions: Choose the best answer for each of the following questions using the content provided in the reading. You may need to go back to reread certain sections to be sure your responses are accurate.

_b_ 1. The overall message of the reading is:

a. If you quit college, you should travel around the world.
b. You can learn a great deal about yourself from quitting and failure.
c. Quitting is an addictive behavior.
d. Leaving your parents and friends is a painful experience.

_a_ 2. The author reveals her attitude about *quitting* through:

a. her actions and behavior.
b. the dialogue in the essay.
c. her physical appearance.
d. her friend's reactions.

_c_ 3. Why did the author have little trouble following the advice of Timothy Leary, who encouraged people in society to "Turn on, tune in, drop out"?

a. She had run away from home when she was a child.
b. She had already graduated from NYU in 1967.
c. She was always a bit of a nonconformist, mostly following her own passions.
d. She had a big fight with her parents when she quit college.

_d_ 4. Who becomes the author's collaborator in her journey to escape?

a. her parents
b. her son
c. her best friend
d. her boyfriend

_b_ 5. While traveling, Brian and Barbara's day-to-day routine can best be described as:

a. establishing roots and making friends wherever they go.
b. living in one place and dreaming of another.
c. trying to earn enough money to build their dream home.
d. working at odd jobs until a better opportunity comes along.

_a_ 6. In paragraph 5, after moving to many different places, the author finally realizes that the problem was not in the places but:

a. within herself.
b. with her boyfriend.
c. with her parents.
d. in the jobs they took.

_c_ 7. According to paragraph 6, what does the author learn from her nomadic life and traveling?

a. She wants to continue traveling.
b. She wants to become a writer.

    c. She needs to belong somewhere.
    d. Traveling is not good for raising children.

d **8. What has Barbara accomplished since she left Brian?**

    a. She has become more interested and satisfied with her life.
    b. She has gotten closer to her family.
    c. She has established new relationships.
    d. All of the above.

a **9. Why does she say she is not a "recovering" quit addict?**

    a. She still has the impulse to quit and feels it is the driving force behind her uniqueness and unconventional qualities.
    b. She has never gone or has the intention of going for rehabilitation.
    c. She will never recover from her failure to meet the expectations of herself and her parents.
    d. She is still addicted to quitting.

b **10. In the end, how does the author feel about quitting?**

    a. It is not for everyone.
    b. It can be a learning experience.
    c. It is never a good solution to a problem.
    d. It always hurts the people you love.

d **11. The overall tone of this essay is:**

    a. persuasive.
    b. critical.
    c. humorous.
    d. ironic.

Exercise 5   **Organizing the Information**

Directions: Read the essay again. Then complete the summary about Barbara's first journey, narrated in paragraphs 1–6, with words or phrases from the selection.

In this essay, Barbara Graham describes her journey to find true *happiness*, independent of the expectations of others. By the time she had heard Timothy Leary's chant in 1967, she had already *quit college*. This was the first time she had experienced the *power* of quitting and the instant high of cutting loose. Together with Brian, her *collaborator*, she set out to find a new life in places like Europe, *Puerto Rico*, *the United States*, and *Canada*. Their pattern had been set: living in one place and *dreaming of another*, working at odd jobs, earning just

enough money to survive and get to the next location. However, after their latest _fantasy_ to build their dream
house close to _nature_ failed, Barbara realized that
she wanted to live in the present, _not in the future_. She had
finally understood that the problem lay not in the places they traveled to but _in themselves_. In the end, she and Brian split up.
Her long journey yielded no careers, _few friends_, and
no place to call home. She felt sad and _alienated_
—from Brian, from the rest of the world, and most frighteningly
from herself.

Exercise 6	**Integrating the Vocabulary**

Directions: Because this essay discusses the topic of quitting, the author uses
many words, expressions, and idiomatic language that relate to this action.
The repetition of expressions about quitting also creates coherence in the
writing. Write an original sentence with each of the following on a separate
sheet of paper. Then submit your work to your instructor or another student
for review, revision, and feedback:

burn one's bridges

cut loose

cut ties

drop out

make the break

Are you familiar with any other words or expressions that mean _quit?_
You may check a dictionary or thesaurus for synonyms or related expressions, and then list at least five of them:

1. _bail out_
2. _fall by the wayside_
3. _forfeit_
4. _step down_
5. _throw in the towel_

In this essay, a couple of expressions mean the opposite of _quit._ For
example, in paragraph 2, the author describes herself as being born without the _stick-to-it_ or _nose–to-the-grindstone_ gene? Do you know any other
antonyms for _quit?_ Check a dictionary or thesaurus and list five:

1. _be determined_
2. _endure_
3. _hang tough_
4. _persist_
5. _stay the course_

Exercise 7   **Making Personal Connections Through Writing and Discussion**

Responses will vary.   **Directions:** Think about yourself in relation to the essay you just read.

1. Form two groups and debate the pros and cons of quitting. A small group of "unbiased" listeners led by the instructor can judge the winner of the debate.

2. Discuss the impact of a nomadic and freewheeling lifestyle on raising children.

3. Write a 500-word essay in which you describe the power of quitting, cutting ties, and moving around.

reflect AND respond

Now that you have read three selections related to *adversity and resilience*, you have a broader and better understanding of the topic.

Directions: Complete a journal response for this module. Read the following questions. Select two to which you would like to respond. Write your responses on a separate piece of paper. Write at least one page.

1. What did you learn about success and failure, adversity and quitting?

2. How does this information apply to you? Make connections to your own experience. What do these readings make you think about?

3. What else would you like to know about some of the topics discussed in this module?

Readings About Diversity and Tolerance

Get Acquainted with the Issue

Our nation is a rich tapestry of many heritages, but we struggle with how to embrace all of this cultural diversity. We still make distinctions about various cultural groups by referring to them as Latino-Americans, Asian Americans, or Native Americans instead of just saying "Americans." We still hold stereotypes, have prejudices, and engage in discriminatory behaviors when we encounter people who are "unlike" ourselves. Perhaps it's time for all of us to listen to the words of John Hume, a 1998 Nobel Peace Prize Recipient, when he said:

> "Difference is of the essence of humanity. Difference is an accident of birth and it should therefore never be the source of hatred or conflict. The answer to difference is to respect it. Therein lies a most fundamental principle of peace: respect for diversity."
>
> (John Hume, Nobel Lecture, Oslo, December 10, 1998)

In the first article, "Diversity and Tolerance: First Steps Toward a Brighter Future," the author makes an appeal for a more peaceful and tolerant society. In the second article, "Home Alone," the writer reports on the surprising findings of the effects of cultural diversity in the United States. In the final reading, "The Myth of the Model Minority," Philip Chiu discusses different viewpoints about Chinese Americans.

Guided Reading
Reading Selection 1

> ## Diversity and Tolerance: First Steps Toward a Brighter Future
> By Anupreet Kaur

This selection from Skipping Stones *talks about what can happen when we fear diversity. Anupreet Kaur, a 17-year-old girl from India, writes, "While doing research and writing my essay, even I learned a lot about my own deep-rooted prejudices and my intolerance toward people who differ from me. I'm now trying to incorporate the values of tolerance and love in myself and apply them in my own life. I hope that I'm able to inspire readers to be more tolerant towards those whom they cannot like."*

 **before you read**

Think about what you already know about a topic before you begin reading. Then when you begin to read, you will be able to attach your new learning to this background knowledge and more easily understand the new information. (See Chapter 2, page 38.)

Discuss or write your responses to the following questions about your *own* experiences on the topic of diversity and tolerance.

1. Respond to the following statements. Do you agree or disagree with any of them? Explain.

   - People who wear glasses are smart.
   - Women are better cooks than men.
   - All politicians are crooks.
   - All doctors are rich.
   - All tall people are good basketball players.
   - Native Americans live on reservations.

2. Have you ever experienced discrimination because of your age, gender, education level, native language, etc.?

3. What are the benefits of a tolerant society?

Prepare to Read

Preview the selection "Diversity and Tolerance" using the THIEVES strategy on page 40.

on page 40.

Exercise 1   **Previewing**

Directions: Complete the following items.

1. Take a look at the selection, and check off all the items that are available to you for preview.

    _X_ Title

    ___ Headings

    _X_ Introduction

    _X_ Every first sentence in each paragraph

    ___ Visuals/vocabulary

    ___ End of chapter questions

    _X_ Summary/concluding paragraph

2. Actively preview the selection by reading and highlighting the items you have checked.

3. Based on your preview, place an "X" next to all those items you predict will be discussed in the selection.

    _X_ a. Acceptance of differences can lead to tolerance and understanding of one another.

    _X_ b. Resistance to diversity is caused by fear and discomfort with change.

    ___ c. Understanding differences can lead to intolerance.

    ___ d. Making judgments about people promotes diversity.

    ___ e. The world is split into various groups because of the acceptance of diversity and tolerance.

    _X_ f. The differences among us can lead to intolerance.

Check Out the Vocabulary

You will find the following vocabulary words in bold type in the reading selection. Do you know what some of these words mean? Knowing the meaning of all these words will increase your understanding of the material.

autopilot	diversity*	ignorance*	splintered
belittle	ecosystem	labeling*	stereotypes
bigotry	excluded*	prejudice	wary

*Denotes a word from the Academic Word List

Exercise 2	**Checking Out the Vocabulary**

Directions: Look at each word taken from the reading selection. Read the sentences that follow. The first is from the selection, with a hint to its meaning, and the second one uses the word in an additional context. Choose the best definition for the word, and write the letter of the definition you select on the line provided.

_b_ **1. diversity**

- No, because we all long for variety or **diversity.** (para. 1) (HINT: Look for a synonym clue word.)
- Two-year colleges today offer a **diversity** of majors, ranging from liberal arts to allied health sciences to career and technical education studies.
  - a. multicolored flowers
  - b. variety
  - c. excitement
  - d. attraction

_d_ **2. wary**

- But why then, are we so **wary** of the diversity among the people with whom we share this world? (para. 1) (HINT: Look at the contrast clue word.)
- Be **wary** of emails that attempt to get your username and password from email accounts.
  - a. to be concerned
  - b. to be worried
  - c. to be excited
  - d. to be cautious

_a_ **3. ecosystem**

- Just as the biological diversity of an **ecosystem** increases its stability, the diversity among people brings together the resources, talents, and experiences of many people for the mutual benefit of all. (para. 2) (HINT: The word contains the root *eco,* which means *environment* or *habitat.*)
- An oil spill can cause extreme damage to **ecosystems** in the region and beyond.
  - a. a collection of living things and the environment in which they live
  - b. products that are friendly to the environment
  - c. the study of the environment
  - d. a community of people in the environment

_b_ **4. bigotry**

- Sadly, the differences amongst us have always formed the basis of fear, **bigotry** and discrimination, harassment, conflict and even violence. (para. 2) (HINT: Look for a synonym clue word.)
- **Bigotry** can take many forms, and one can be biased against others because of ethnicity, religion, culture and gender.

        a. attack and harassment
        b. discrimination and bias
        c. conflict and disagreement
        d. prejudice and intolerance

_a_ 5. **ignorance**

- Factors like **ignorance**, misunderstanding, misinformation, lack of education and awareness, too, make us resist diversity. (para. 3) (HINT: All of the series of nouns refer to lack of education.)
- **Ignorance** about multiculturalism can contribute to bigotry in the classroom.
  - a. lack of knowledge
  - b. intelligence
  - c. wisdom
  - d. stupidity

_a_ 6. **belittle**

- When we don't understand another's values, lifestyles, beliefs, it becomes easier to **belittle** them. (para. 4) (HINT: The prefix *be-* means *to make or cause*.)
- I believe my classmate **belittled** the A I received on the midterm in psychology because he was envious of my grade.
  - a. scorn or dismiss
  - b. praise
  - c. exaggerate
  - d. disgrace

_c_ 7. **labeling**

- As a result, on the basis of differences, we start putting people into categories and **labeling** them unfairly. (para. 4) (HINT: What happens when we put people in categories? In addition, look at the sentences before and after for more context clues.)
- Some experts in education think that **labeling** students, especially students with disabilities, can be negative in that it depicts the student's deficit and contributes to poor self-esteem.
  - a. branding or putting on a trademark
  - b. attaching a piece of material to something
  - c. putting into a group or category
  - d. calling someone names

_d_ 8. **stereotypes**

- These **stereotypes** are generalized assumptions concerning the characteristics of all members of a particular group. (para. 4) (HINT: Look for a clue word that indicates a definition.)
- A common **stereotype** is that females are not as good as males in math.
  - a. a conclusion based on differences
  - b. a fixed and unvarying form
  - c. a process for making metal printing plates
  - d. a generalization used to describe or distinguish a group

_b_ 9. **prejudice**
- Stereotypes give birth to **prejudice**, i.e., a premature judgment about a group or its members without knowledge or thought. (para. 5) (HINT: Look for a definition clue word.)
- One way to end **prejudice** and discrimination in schools is to promote open discussions on diversity, tolerance, and social justice.
  a. an injury through legal action
  b. an unfair bias
  c. an attitude considered collectively
  d. a state of justice and tolerance

_b_ 10. **splintered**
- As a result, the world now is **splintered** at each and every level. (para. 6) (HINT: This is the main idea. Read the details of the paragraph.)
- Unfortunately, students in the multicultural club **splintered** off into separate clubs, such as the Filipino Cultural Club, the Caribbean Students Organization, the Haitian Students Association and the Muslim Students Association.
  a. to split or break into sharp, slender pieces
  b. to fragment or break off into different groups
  c. to snap off into something
  d. to categorize students into different groups

_c_ 11. **excluded**
- Schools categorize students according to appearance, athletic achievement, style, race and academic achievement, so they are included in one group and **excluded** from another. (para. 6) (HINT: The prefix *ex-* means *out of*.)
- Students labeled as special education often feel **excluded** from mainstream students.
  a. included
  b. kept in
  c. kept out
  d. kept up

_a_ 12. **autopilot**
- This means we reprogram ourselves to treat each other with automatic love and respect and stop all prejudices and biases that have been on **autopilot** for so long. (Para. 8) (HINT: *Auto* is used in forming compound words, such as automobile and autobiography, and means *self*. It is also an idiomatic expression, so think beyond the literal meaning.)
- While I was in law school, I was on **autopilot** with my studies; I spent every waking hour reading in the library.
  a. acting without thinking or reflecting
  b. a special device used for steering buses
  c. a robot that flies a plane
  d. a pilot that has been well trained

as you read

Establish Your Purpose

Now you are ready to read and annotate the selection "Diversity and Tolerance." Focus on major points of information. Read to discover the effects of intolerance.

Actively Process While You Read: Guided Reading

Stop to think about the information as you read.

| Exercise 3 | **Processing While You Read** |

Answers may vary. Sample answers provided.

Directions: Answer the questions that appear in bold print at the conclusion of each paragraph. This will help you monitor your reading process and understand the material.

> ## Diversity and Tolerance: First Steps Toward a Brighter Future
> By Anupreet Kaur

1   "Can you eat the same bread and butter everyday for breakfast, lunch and dinner?" or "Can you wear a single color throughout your life?" No, because we all long for variety or **diversity.** The diversity of multicolored flowers in a nursery, of clothes at a store, of food at a restaurant, of animals at a zoo—all of it attracts and excites us. But why then, are we so **wary** of the diversity among the people with whom we share this world?

Why do we crave diversity in life?

We are attracted to variety because it prevents boredom and monotony and adds excitement to our lives.

2   We humans have different races, religions, cultures, sexual identities, age groups, physical attributes, abilities, beliefs, views, ideas and opinions. We can clearly see this diversity in our homes, our neighborhoods and classrooms, on TV . . . practically everywhere. It enriches and lends beauty to humanity. Just as the biological diversity of an **ecosystem** increases its stability and productivity, the diversity among people brings together the resources, talents, and experiences of many people for the mutual benefit of all. Sadly, the differences amongst us have always formed the basis of fear, **bigotry** and discrimination, conflict and even violence.

Where is diversity found?

It is found in all aspects of life, including race, culture, religion, gender, physical attributes, abilities, beliefs, views, ideas, and opinions, and other ways in which we are unlike.

What are the benefits of diversity?

It brings together the resources, talents, and experiences of many people for the mutual benefit of all.

3   We fear diversity simply because we are used to the way things are, and change makes us feel uncomfortable. Some of us think of it as a threat to our own power. Factors like **ignorance,** misunderstanding, misinformation, lack of education and awareness, too, make us fearful of diversity.

Why are we afraid of diversity?

We are used to the way things are, and change makes us feel uncomfortable. We fear diversity because we view it as a threat to our own power and because of ignorance, misunderstanding, misinformation, lack of education and awareness.

4   When we don't understand another's values, lifestyle or beliefs, it becomes easier to **belittle** them. As a result, on the basis of differences, we start categorizing people, **labeling** them unfairly. These **stereotypes** are generalized assumptions concerning the characteristics of all the members of a particular group. They are reflected in the media and our surroundings in statements like: "All Indians are . . ." or "Old people always . . ." and so on.

What happens when we fear diversity?

We tend to belittle people, categorize them, label them unfairly, and create stereotypes.

5   Stereotypes often give birth to **prejudice**, i.e., a premature judgment about a group or its members, made without proper knowledge or thought. It demonstrates an unfair bias, violating the standards of reason, justice and tolerance. It is this prejudice that has caused us to feel suspicious and hateful and may result in personal bias, discriminatory practices and violence.

What results from stereotypes and how does that make us feel?

Stereotypes lead to prejudice. Prejudice makes us feel suspicious and hateful of others, which may lead to personal biases, discriminatory practices, and violence.

6   As a result, the world is now **splintered** at each and every level. Families are fragmented on the grounds of economic status or personal differences. Schools categorize students according to appearance, athletic achievement, style, race and academic achievement, so they are included in one group and are **excluded** from others. The atmosphere at our workplaces is very formal, and now for the slightest reason, we break up relationships with our neighbors and friends. Gays are harassed or verbally assaulted to an extent that they lead their lives in fear or attempt suicide to escape exclusion. Women, children, senior citizens, the disabled and the economically weak also continue to be the victims of discrimination. Many racial, ethnic and religious groups are victims of hate crimes. Wars, terrorism, bombings, looting, physical assaults, and threatening mail and calls have become all too common.

Provide three examples of how prejudice impacts society:

1. Families are fragmented because of economic status or personal differences. 2. Schools label children according to abilities and skills, which leads to exclusion. 3. Workplace environment is formal. 4. Friendships and relationships are fragile. 5. Many groups are victim to discrimination. 6. There are incidences of hate crimes.

7   Something must be done to change the future, if we are to have a future. This is where tolerance comes into play.

8   Tolerance is a personal decision that stems from the belief that we are the children of one God and share one world. Each one of us is special and deserves to be respected and accepted for who we are. This means, we reprogram ourselves to treat each other with automatic love and respect and stop all prejudices that have been on **autopilot** for so long. Reach out to different people, say, the elderly gentleman sitting beside you on the bus or the neighbor's child who walks with crutches.

What can we do to become a more tolerant society?

Be respectful and accepting of others. Put an end to prejudices. Make overt efforts to change your behavior and attitudes toward diversity.

9   Mahatma Gandhi said, "You must become the change you want to see in the world." So we must be a role model for others and take a firm stand against hatred, bigotry, injustice and inequality. Let us build a peaceful and productive society based on human rights, diversity and inclusion in a spirit of respect, tolerance and mutual understanding. It is a tough job, but it can become a reality.

According to the writer, what does Gandhi's quotation say about how we can promote a more peaceful and productive society?

To create a more tolerant society, individuals need to start by making personal changes in their attitudes and behaviors toward prejudice and injustice. Only then will a change be possible.

Source: Kaur, Anupreet. "Diversity and Tolerance: First Steps Toward a Brighter Future." *Skipping Stones* 18.4 (Sept-Oct 2006): 12(1). Nassau Community College Library - SUNY. 24 July 2009 <http://find.galegroup.com/itx/start.do?prodId=ITOF>.

■ ■ ■

 **after you read**

Review Important Points

Going over major points immediately after you read, while the information is fresh in your mind, will help you recall the content and record key ideas.

Exercise 4   **Reviewing Important Points**

Directions: Answer the following questions based on the information provided in the selection. You may need to go back to the text and reread certain portions to be sure your responses are correct and can be supported by information in the text. Write the letter of your choice in the space provided.

_a_ 1. **What is the thesis of Kaur's essay?**

    a. We need to embrace diversity because intolerance is destructive.

    b. We should stop fearing prejudice because it can lead to discrimination.

    c. We should be a role model for all changes in society.

    d. We should put an end to violence, criminal behavior, and especially terrorism.

_c_ 2. **What is the main idea of paragraph 1?**

    a. None of us can eat the same thing for all meals.

    b. We are all excited by multicolored flowers.

    c. While we all crave diversity, we are fearful of it, too.

    d. There is a great diversity in life.

_d_ 3. **Examples of diversity among people include all of the following** *except:*

    a. abilities, beliefs, ideas, and opinions.

    b. races, religions, cultures.

    c. sexual identities, age groups, physical characteristics.

    d. differences in our houses, neighborhoods, classrooms.

_c_ 4. **According to this essay, what are the advantages of cultural diversity?**

    a. loss of productivity

    b. instability

    c. increased productivity

    d. human resources

_b_ 5. **Why are some people resistant to diversity?**

    a. They are fearful of education.

    b. It threatens their authority.

    c. They are unaware of change.

    d. They lack information about diversity.

_d_ 6. **Misunderstanding leads to:**

    a. making generalized assumptions about people.

    b. categorizing people into separate groups.

    c. belittling people unjustly.

    d. all of the above.

_c_ 7. **What results from stereotyping?**

    a. being just and tolerant

    b. making accurate judgments

    c. becoming prejudiced and perpetrating violent acts

    d. establishing personal practices

_a_ 8. **What is the main idea of paragraph 6?**

    a. Prejudice has impacted all sectors of society.

    b. Families are categorized based on financial status.

    c. Criminal activities have become routine.

    d. Wood is splintered.

_b_ 9. What is the overall pattern of organization?

    a. comparison-contrast

    b. cause-effect

    c. classification

    d. definition and example

_b_ 10. A paraphrasing of Gandhi's statement, "You must become the change you want to see in the world," is:

    a. You must stand for injustice and inequality.

    b. To see any change in society, you must start by taking on responsibility and doing something about it yourself.

    c. You should change what you don't like about society.

    d. You ought to change other people's minds about hatred and bigotry.

Organize the Information

Organizing the information you have learned from a reading selection shows you have understood it and have the ability to restate the material in a different way. You can use this reorganized material to help you study for exams and prepare for written assignments. (See Chapter 9.)

Exercise 5   **Organizing the Information**

Directions: Using the reading selection, complete a cause-effect map with details from the essay that reveal how fear of diversity leads to prejudice and discrimination.

> **Fear of Diversity:**
>
> We are _used to_ _____ the way things are.
> Change makes us feel _uncomfortable_ _____.

↓

> **Resistance to Diversity:**
>
> ■ Ignorance
> ■ _Misunderstanding_ _____
> ■ _Misinformation_ _____
> ■ _Lack of education_ and awareness

↓

> _Stereotypes:_ _____ generalized assumptions concerning the characteristics of all its members of a particular group
>
> ■ Categorize _people_ _____
> ■ Label people _unfairly_ _____
> ■ Reflected in the _media_ _____
> ■ Reflected in statements, like "All women are . . ."

↓

Prejudice: *premature judgment* about a group or its members made *without* proper knowledge or thought.

- Conjures up feelings of *suspicion* and *hatred*.

- Manifested in personal *bias*, *discriminatory* practices and *violence*.

Integrate the Vocabulary

Make the new vocabulary presented in the reading *your* vocabulary. In addition to learning the meaning of new words, you should also learn related word forms.

Exercise 6A   Using Context Clues

Directions: For each sentence, select the word from the text box on p. 354 that is a synonym for the word or words in parentheses and best completes the sentence. Then write the word or a form of the word in the space provided.

1. Roberto was (left out) *excluded* from the list of candidates for the scholarship because he did not have a 3.0 GPA for this past semester.

2. I am often (careful) *wary* of believing a classmate who says he always gets A's but never studies for exams.

3. In my biology class, we read about the importance of preserving the (environment) *ecosystem* in the Amazon.

4. When Alyssa begins to study for her final exams, she is on (task) *autopilot*; she always gets out all her notes, and then stays in her room until she has mastered all the material.

5. Don't (put down) *belittle* someone else's method of studying; we all have different learning styles.

6. (Variety) *Diversity* across campuses—ranging from students of different countries, ethnic groups, and cultures to returning students and veterans—is increasing nationwide.

7. In spite of the richness of diversity, (prejudice) *bigotry* is still rampant, especially among different racial, ethnic, and religious groups.

8. In spite of new evidence that women are scoring higher on aptitude exams that assess analytical skills, society still perpetuates gender (biases) *stereotypes* in education, such as men are better in math and the sciences while women are better in the humanities.

9. Some believe the old adage that (lack of knowledge) *ignorance* is bliss, which implies that peace of mind flows from unawareness.

10. One of the most common terms used by young people to describe others is "loser." That's not a description; it's a (tag) *label*, which can be very hurtful and harmful.

11. Over the last two decades, inclusion has become a critical part of education; nevertheless, children are still (divided) *splintered*

into groups on many levels, such as in remedial classes, special education, and gifted programs.

12. "We are each burdened with (bigotry) _prejudice_____: against the poor or the rich, the smart or the slow, the gaunt or the obese. It is natural to develop (biases) _prejudices_____. It is noble to rise above them."
—Author Unknown

Exercise 6B **Learning Key Words**

Directions: The thesis of an essay presents a writer's opinion on a topic. It is not uncommon for an author to begin and end an essay with the main point. Scan the first and last paragraphs of the reading for language that indicates the significant and important impacts of embracing diversity. Then list the words and phrases below.

Diversity

1. _peaceful and productive society_
2. _human rights_
3. _inclusion_
4. _spirit of respect_
5. _tolerance_
6. _mutual understanding_

A writer also develops his or her main point by providing supporting and relevant details. In this essay, to support her reasons for creating and embracing diversity, Kaur wants the reader to clearly see the negative and destructive aspects of intolerance. She uses many words to discuss intolerance and to show its negative impact on society. Scan the essay for this language and write it in the spaces provided.

Located in the text: Words that refer to **intolerance:** _harassment, stereotypes, bias, bigotry, prejudice, discrimination, belittle, categorize, labeling, hatred, suspicion, injustice, inequality_

Located in the text: Words or phrases that relate to **violence** and criminal behavior: _assaulted, aggression, vandalism, bombings, physical assaults, threatening mail_

Located in the text: Words or phrases that relate to **ignorance:** _misunderstanding, misinformation, lack of education, lack of awareness, without proper knowledge or thought_

Make Personal Connections Through Writing and Discussion

When you make your new learning relevant to yourself in some way, it becomes more meaningful and easier to remember. Whenever you read, try to connect to the content on a personal level. How does it relate to you? How can you apply what you have read to other situations? What else would you like to know?

| Exercise 7 | **Making Personal Connections Through Writing and Discussion** |

Directions: Think about yourself in relation to the article you have just read.   *Responses will vary.*
Apply the information you learned from the reading and respond to the following questions in your journal.

1. In small groups, discuss your answers to the following questions and then report back to the class.

   a. What do you think an individual can do to help reduce bias and stereotyping?

   b. What could local, state, and federal governments do to lessen discrimination?

   c. Can you think of any events in history that were influenced by stereotyping and bias? If so, explain.

   d. How can the media (newspapers, television, movies) help to reduce stereotyping?

2. Write a personal essay beginning with Mahatma Gandhi's famous quotation, "You must become the change you want to see in the world." You may want to discuss a personal change, such as a change in job or career, or a sociological issue, such as women's rights, poverty, homelessness, or health care.

Self-Monitored Reading
Reading Selection 2

Home Alone
By Erica Goode

This selection, from the New York Times Magazine, *discusses a surprising finding about diversity based on a recent study.*

◀◀ before **you read**

Answer the following questions before you read the selection.   *Answers will vary.*

1. In school or at work, with whom do you usually associate? Do you make an effort to meet new people? Do you make plans together after school or work?

   _____

   _____

2. How do you react when you are around strangers? Do you withdraw, or do you engage people in conversations?

_____

_____

3. Are you more likely to trust people of the same race, ethnicity, or religion as yourself?

_____

_____

Prepare to Read

Preview the reading selection by applying the THIEVES strategy (p. 40).

Exercise 1   **Previewing**

Directions: Based on your preview, respond to the following questions:

1. According to Putnam's survey, how does diversity affect the way we live?
   It makes people more distrustful of other races and even their own.

2. How does Putnam evaluate his findings?
   He still believes that diversity has its benefits, and he is hopeful that some of the differences
   will fade in the future.

3. What is some evidence that religious and racial relationships are changing because of diversity?
   There is an increase in interracial and multi-ethnic marriages, especially among youth.

Check Out the Vocabulary

You will encounter the following vocabulary words in bold type in this reading.

anomie	enhanced*	optimistic	pervasive
colleagues*	homogenous	overarching	solidarity
encountering*	irrelevant*		

*Denotes a word from the Academic Word List

Exercise 2   **Checking Out the Vocabulary**

Directions: Look at each boldface word taken from the reading selection. Use the context of the sentence and the hint provided to select the best definition from the choices listed. Write the letter of your choice on the line provided.

_a_ 1. encountering

For decades, students of American society have offered [conflicting] theories about how **encountering** racial and ethnic diversity affects the way we live. (para. 1) (HINT: Read the next sentence.)

a. to come upon or meet with by chance
b. to meet a situation with difficulty
c. to meet a person in conflict or battle
d. run away from a social situation

_b_ **2. solidarity**

Others argue that just throwing people together is rarely enough to [cause] **solidarity:** when diversity increases, they [claim], people tend to stick to their own groups and distrust those who are different from them. (para. 1) (HINT: Continue to read this lengthy sentence and you will find a synonym.)

a. distrust
b. unity
c. stick-to-itiveness
d. companionship

_d_ **3. pervasive**

But what if diversity had an even more complex and **pervasive** effect? (para. 2) (HINT: Read the rest of the paragraph to find out about the pervasive effect on diversity.)

a. distrustful
b. solitary
c. powerless
d. widespread

_c_ **4. colleagues**

This is the unsettling picture that has come out of a huge nationwide telephone survey by the famed Harvard political scientist Robert Putnam and his **colleagues.** (para. 3) (HINT: Other people who work with Robert Putnam.)

a. students
b. colleges
c. associates
d. groups

_b_ **5. anomie**

"Diversity seems to trigger not in-group/out-group division, but **anomie** [social instability resulting from a breakdown of standards and values; personal unrest, alienation, and uncertainty that comes from a lack of purpose or ideals] or social isolation," Putnam writes in the June issue of the *Journal of Scandinavian Political Studies.* (para. 3) (HINT: Look at information in parentheses.)

a. in-group/out-group division
b. social instability or social isolation
c. a breakdown of standards
d. an unsettling picture

_b_ **6. homogenous**

In highly diverse cities and towns like Los Angeles, Houston and Yakima, Wash., the survey found, the residents were about half as likely to trust people of other races as in **homogenous** places like Fremont, Mich., or rural South Dakota. . . . (para. 4) (HINT: *Diverse* is compared to *homogenous*. The root *homo-* means like.)

a. made up of the same genes
b. not of a similar nature
c. diverse quality
d. unified consistency

_a_   7. **enhanced**

[However], diversity has clear benefits, he says, among them economic growth and **enhanced** creativity—more top-flight scientists, more entrepreneurs, more artists. (para. 6) (HINT: Look at what results from "enhanced" creativity, especially after the dashes.)

a. improved
b. beneficial
c. higher value
d. populated

_c_   8. **overarching**

[G]roup divisions can give way to a larger, **overarching** identity. (para. 7) (HINT: *Overarching* is a compound word that contains *over* and *arch*. It is used in a figurative way.)

a. forming an arch above
b. larger and greater
c. encompassing and overshadowing everything
d. unfamiliar and disturbing

_d_   9. **irrelevance**

Half a century later, for most Americans, the importance of religion as a mating test has [lessened] to near **irrelevance,** "hardly more important than left- or right-handedness to romance." (para. 7) (HINT: The prefix *ir-* means *not*. Look at the information after the comma, which gives an example of irrelevance.)

a. nearing extinction
b. increasing significance
c. of great importance
d. lacking importance

_a_ 10. **optimistic**

"If you're asking me if, in the long run, I'm **optimistic**," Putnam says, "the answer is yes." (para. 8) (HINT: When you are optimistic about something, you say *yes* rather than *no*.)

a. hopeful
b. helpless
c. helpful
d. cheerful

 **as you read**

Establish Your Purpose

Now, read and annotate the selection, using the guidelines for active reading, and focus on the major points of information.

Actively Process While You Read: Self-Monitored Reading

Monitor your comprehension as you read. (See Chapter 2, page 54.) Be sure to stop to reflect at the conclusion of each paragraph, and ask yourself the following questions:

- Did I understand what I have just read?
- What is the main idea of the paragraph?
- Am I ready to continue?

Exercise 3 **Processing While You Read**

Directions: Highlight the most important points in each paragraph. Then write the key topics and main ideas in the spaces provided in the margins. Finally, underline or number the supporting details in the text.

Home Alone
By Erica Goode

Notes

1   For decades, students of American society have offered [conflicting] theories about how **encountering** racial and ethnic diversity affects the way we live. One says that simple contact—being tossed into a stew of different cultures, values, languages and styles of dress—is likely to nourish tolerance and trust. . . . Others argue that just throwing people together is rarely enough to [cause] **solidarity:** when diversity increases, they [claim], people tend to stick to their own groups and distrust those who are different from them.

Topic _____

_____

Main Idea _____

_____

2   But what if diversity had an even more complex and **pervasive** effect? What if, at least in the short term, living in a highly diverse city or town led residents to distrust pretty much everybody, even people who looked like them? What if it made people withdraw into themselves, form fewer close friendships, feel unhappy and powerless and stay home watching television in the evening instead of attending a neighborhood barbecue or joining a community project?

Topic _____

_____

Main Idea _____

_____

3   This is the unsettling picture that has come out of a huge nationwide telephone survey by the famed Harvard political scientist Robert Putnam and his **colleagues.** "Diversity seems to trigger not in-group/out-group division, but **anomie** [social instability resulting from a breakdown of standards and values; personal unrest,

Topic _____

_____

Main Idea _____

_____

alienation, and uncertainty that comes from a lack of purpose or ideals,] or social isolation," Putnam writes in the June issue of the *Journal of Scandinavian Political Studies*. "In [other words,] people living in ethnically diverse settings appear to 'hunker down'—that is, to pull in like a turtle."

Notes

Topic _____ **4**

_____

Main Idea _____

_____

In highly diverse cities and towns like Los Angeles, Houston and Yakima, Wash., the survey found, the residents were about half as likely to trust people of other races as in **homogenous** places like Fremont, Mich., or rural South Dakota, where, Putnam noted, "diversity means inviting a few Norwegians to the annual Swedish picnic."

Topic _____ **5**

_____

Main Idea _____

_____

More significant, they were also half as likely to trust people of their own race. They claimed fewer close friends. They were more apt to agree that "television is my most important form of entertainment." They had less confidence in local government and less confidence in their own ability to [influence political decisions]. They were more likely to join protest marches but less likely to register to vote. They rated their happiness as generally lower. And this diversity effect continued to show up even when a community's . . . average income, crime levels, rates of home ownership and a host of other factors were taken into account. . . .

Topic _____ **6**

_____

Main Idea _____

_____

[However,] diversity has clear benefits, he says, among them economic growth and **enhanced** creativity—more top-flight scientists, more entrepreneurs, more artists. But difference is also disconcerting, he maintains, "and people like me, who are in favor of diversity, don't do ourselves any favors by denying that it takes time to become comfortable," Putnam says. . . .

7   [I]n Putnam's view, the findings are neither cause for despair nor a brief against diversity. If this country's history is any guide, what people perceive as unfamiliar and disturbing—what they see as "other"—can and does change over time. . . . [G]roup divisions can give way to a larger, **overarching** identity. When he was in high school in the 1950s, Putnam notes, he knew the religion of almost every one of the 150 students in his class. At the time, religious intermarriage was uncommon, and knowing whether a potential mate was a Methodist, a Catholic or a Jew was crucial information. Half a century later, for most Americans, the importance of religion as a mating test has [lessened] to near **irrelevance,** "hardly more important than left- or right-handedness to romance."

8   The rising marriage rates across racial and ethnic lines in a younger generation, raised in a more diverse world, suggest the current markers of difference can also fade in [importance]. In some places, they already have: soldiers have more interracial friendships than civilians, Putnam's research finds, and evangelical churches in the South show high rates of racial integration. "If you're asking me if, in the long run, I'm **optimistic,**" Putnam says, "the answer is yes."

Notes
Topic _____

Main Idea _____
_____

Topic _____
_____
Main Idea _____
_____

■ ■ ■

▶▶ after you read

Review Important Points

Going over the major points immediately after you have read, while the information is fresh in your mind, will help you recall the content and record key ideas.

| Exercise 4 | **Reviewing Important Points** |

Directions: Choose the best answer for each of the following questions using information provided in the selection. Write your answers in the spaces provided.

_d_ **1. What is the meaning of the title, "Home Alone"?**
    a. Children are often left alone by working parents.
    b. Geographical distance has created loneliness.
    c. Diversity results in strong family bonds.
    d. Diversity drives people to stay within their own networks.

_a_ **2. The main idea of paragraph 1 is located in:**
    a. sentence 1.
    b. sentence 2.
    c. sentence 3.
    d. sentence 4.

_b_ 3. The metaphor "a stew of different cultures" means:

  a. being mixed up with the wrong people.
  b. a society accepting of cultural differences.
  c. being accepted by people from different backgrounds.
  d. being thrown together with the wrong crowd.

_d_ 4. According to Putnam's survey, how does diversity affect the way we live?

  a. We do not trust anybody.
  b. We make fewer friends.
  c. We remain at home.
  d. All of the above.

_a_ 5. In paragraph 3, the simile "people living in ethnically diverse settings appear to 'hunker down'—that is, to pull in like a turtle" means:

  a. withdraw socially from everyone.
  b. hide from others because of fear.
  c. find comfort with family at home.
  d. find warmth in familiar surroundings.

_c_ 6. What is the main idea of paragraph 4?

  a. Racial and ethnic diversity makes people more trustworthy.
  b. The more diverse the people you live around, the more you trust them.
  c. There is a positive relationship between trust and homogeneity.
  d. All of the above.

_c_ 7. All of the following details illustrate that the people surveyed were half as likely to trust people of their own race *except:*

  a. They withdraw from close friends.
  b. They expect the worst from their community and its leadership.
  c. They were more likely to participate in elections.
  d. They spent more time in front of the television.

_d_ 8. Putnam cites _____ as proof that the acceptance of diversity will change over time.

  a. his attendance in high school
  b. his strong religious beliefs
  c. his romantic notions
  d. events in history

_c_ 9. An increase in interracial marriage illustrates:

  a. Religious beliefs among the younger generation are disappearing.
  b. Religion as an important social barrier has increased.
  c. Religion as a significant social division has diminished.
  d. Some religions, especially among evangelical churches, are permitting interracial marriages.

_c_ 10. What is the *overall* pattern of organization of the selection?

  a. comparison and contrast
  b. definition and example
  c. cause and effect
  d. process

Organize the Information

Organizing the information from a reading selection shows you have understood it and can restate the material in your own way.

> **Exercise 5**   **Organizing the Information**

Directions: Using your notes, complete the following summary. Write your answers in the spaces provided.

For decades, students of American society have offered _conflicting_ theories about how racial and ethnic _diversity_ affects the way we live. Some feel experiencing diversity is enough to promote _tolerance_ and trust, whereas others argue that just throwing people together is rarely enough to cause _solidarity_. When diversity increases, they feel people tend to stick to their own groups and _distrust_ those who are different from them.

According to Putnam's survey, diversity seems to trigger alienation and _isolation_. Nevertheless, his findings are neither cause for _despair_ nor a brief _against_ diversity. In some places soldiers have more interracial _friendships_ than civilians, and there is an increase in interracial _marriages_, all of which indicates the barriers due to differences are slowly coming down.

Integrate the Vocabulary

Make the new vocabulary *your* vocabulary.

> **Exercise 6A**   **Using Context Clues**

Directions: Using context clues, locate the word from the text box in Exercise 2 (page 366) that best completes each of the following sentences. Then write the word, or a form of the word, in the spaces provided.

1. The students joined the _solidarity_ march to demonstrate their opposition to sending troops overseas.

2. Prof. Silverman met with her _colleagues_ in the sociology and history departments to discuss a new major in diversity studies.

3. Many ESL students prefer to study English in heterogeneous groups, as opposed to _homogenous_ ones filled with native speakers from their own countries.

4. Our English professor suggested we _enhance_ our essays by using figurative language, such as metaphors, similes, and personifications.

5. Now that I have been admitted to the nursing program, it almost seems _irrelevant_ for me to retake psychology for a better grade.

6.   When I first _encountered_ my classmates, I thought they were cold and unfriendly; nevertheless, after a couple of weeks, we were all meeting for coffee after class.

7.   Problems with plagiarism, especially copying from the Internet, are _pervasive_ across many college campuses.

8.   When new and incoming freshmen arrive at college, it's not uncommon for them to feel a sense of _anomie_, a feeling caused by the absence of family and close friends.

9.   Sonia is currently enrolled in an ESL learning community that has the _overarching_ theme of "tolerance and diversity."

10. Paul is _optimistic_ that he will be completing his associate's degree in May and will be able to continue his education at a four-year college in September.

Exercise 6 B   **Learning Synonyms and Other Word Forms**

Directions: Writers often use synonyms or other expressions to restate important terms in selections. Scan the article and list the synonyms for _diversity_. Then check the dictionary or a thesaurus for additional synonyms.

Located in the Text: Words that mean _**diversity**_: _diverse, racial and ethnic diversity, ethnically diverse, a stew of different cultures, not homogenous, group divisions, racial integration_

Found in the Dictionary or Thesaurus: Synonyms for _**diversity**_: _cultural diversity, dissimilarity, heterogeneity, multicultural, cross-culturalism, ethnic inclusiveness, ethnic mosaic, multiracialism, pluralism_

Make Personal Connections Through Writing and Discussion

Connect to the content on a personal level. How does it relate to you? How can you apply what you have read to other situations?

Exercise 7   **Making Personal Connections Through Writing and Discussion**

Responses will vary.

Directions: Think about yourself in relation to the article you have just read. Apply the information you learned from the reading and respond to the following questions in your journal.

1.   Find out if your college offers courses in tolerance and diversity. Read through the course descriptions, select three courses you might be interested in taking, and write them on the lines provided.

a. _____

b. _____

c. _____

2. According to the author, it's not enough to embrace diversity. We also need to construct new social identities. Write a paragraph in which you suggest one way to accomplish this. Then share your writing with your classmates.

Independent Reading
Reading Selection 3

The Myth of the Model Minority

By Philip Chiu

In the following essay, Chiu discusses the stereotyping of Chinese Americans by the media.

◀ before you read

Answer the following questions before you read the selection.

Answers will vary.

1. Can you think of any ethnic or racial group that has been called a "model" minority?

    _____

    _____

2. Are you familiar with any characteristics that have been used to stereotype or label people of Chinese heritage?

    _____

    _____

3. What does the word "myth" mean? What does this word indicate about the model minority?

_____

_____

Prepare to Read

Preview the reading selection by applying the THIEVES strategy (page 40).

Exercise 1   **Developing Preview Questions**

Directions: Based on your previewing, write *three* questions you anticipate will be answered in the selection. *Answers may vary.*

1. _____
2. _____
3. _____

Exercise 2   **Checking Out the New Vocabulary**

Directions: You will encounter the following vocabulary words in boldface in the reading selection:

amicable	complex*	embezzle	ferocious	media*
citing*	diligently	endeavors	industrious	

*Denotes words from the Academic Word List

Read each of the following sentences in which a vocabulary word from the selection appears in bold. Select the best definition of the word and write the letter of your choice on the line provided.

__c__ **1. diligently**

We read in newspapers how **diligently** they have worked and saved. (para.1)

a. indifferently
b. intelligently
c. actively
d. inactively

__b__ **2. citing**

Now, the press is reporting on rising organized crime on the West Coast and **citing** the Pasadena incident as the latest public demonstration. (para. 2)

a. quoting a passage from a book or reference
b. mentioning as proof or referring to as an example
c. visualizing
d. receiving a traffic violation

_c_ **3. media**

What happened to that law-abiding Chinese American we have heard so much about? Have the **media** been wrong all these years? The answer is a complex one. (para. 3)

a. the general public
b. television producers
c. channels of communication
d. the average citizen

_c_ **4. complex**

What happened to that law-abiding Chinese American we have heard so much about? Have the media been wrong all these years? The answer is a **complex** one. (para. 3)

a. easy
b. psychological
c. complicated
d. factual

_c_ **5. amicable**

And we read about clean, **amicable** or friendly, upright and industrious Chinese Americans who, nearly a century before, had contributed to winning the American West by working day and night in the mines, on the farms, and on the railroads. (para. 5)

a. loving
b. clean
c. friendly
d. brief

_a_ **6. industrious**

And we read about clean, amicable or friendly, upright and **industrious** Chinese Americans who, nearly a century before, had contributed to winning the American West by working day and night in the mines, on the farms, and on the railroads. (para.5)

a. hardworking
b. professional
c. winning
d. building

_a_ **7. ferocious**

The Korean War brought a picture of **ferocious** Chinese troops marching to conquer Asia. (para. 6)

a. brutal and violent
b. peaceful and serene
c. insane and wild
d. tamely and quietly

_c_ **8. scholar**

The newly discovered extraordinary accomplishments of Chinese Americans in the face of prejudice sent **scholars** looking everywhere for answers. (para. 7)

a. scholarship or financial aid
b. higher education
c. expert or academic
d. amateur

_b_ **9. endeavors**

Certainly, I am proud of the academic and economic successes of Chinese Americans and proud that many of us have done so well in the sciences, the arts, law, medicine, business, sports and other **endeavors.** (para. 9)

a. academic success
b. a purposeful undertaking that requires effort
c. athletic skills
d. try or attempt

_a_ **10. embezzle**

A few Chinese Americans steal when they are desperate; a few rape when nature overwhelms them; a few sell drugs when they can see an easy way to make a buck; a few **embezzle** when instant fortunes blind them; a few murder when passions overtake them; and a few commit crimes simply because they are wicked. (para. 10)

a. to steal and use money or property belonging to someone else
b. to murder someone for their money or possessions
c. to commit a crime through gambling
d. to rob blindly

 **as you read**

Establish Your Purpose

Read and annotate the selection, using the guidelines for active reading, and focus on the major points of information.

 ### Actively Process as You Read: Independent Reading

Monitor your comprehension as you read. (See Chapter 2, page 54.) Be sure to stop to reflect at the conclusion of each paragraph. Highlight the most important points. Write notes, responses, or questions that come to mind in the margin.

The Myth of the Model Minority

By Philip Chiu

---

1   For years, Chinese Americans have been labeled as the model minority. We read in newspapers how **diligently** they have worked and saved. We see on television how

quietly they obey the laws and how they stay clear of crime. We learn in magazines how they climb up the economic ladder and how much better than the Caucasian kids their children do in school.

2   But recently, we have been reading about a different side of Chinese American life. In January, *U.S. News* reported on Chinese gangs and their criminal activities. Not long afterward, a gun battle in the quiet streets of Pasadena, CA, left two federal drug agents and two Chinese drug dealers dead. Now, the press is reporting on rising organized crime on the West Coast and **citing** the Pasadena incident as the latest public demonstration.

3   What happened to that law-abiding Chinese American we have heard so much about? Have the **media** been wrong all these years? The answer is a **complex** one.

4   About sixty years ago, the silver screen gave us the evil criminal genius of Fu Manchu. We heard about the dim opium dens and the filthy gambling halls. We saw slanted-eyed, ever obedient little men toiling about with their pigtails freshly cut off. And we wondered just what kind of expression was "long time no see."

5   Then came WW II, and the Chinese became our allies. The picture of a smiling, beautiful Chiang Kai-Shek appeared in every newspaper. And we read about clean, **amicable** or friendly, upright and **industrious** Chinese Americans who, nearly a century before, had contributed to winning the American West by working day and night in the mines, on the farms, and on the railroads.

6   The Korean War brought a picture of **ferocious** Chinese troops marching to conquer Asia. And we learned that the Chinese spoke with forked tongues. They felt no pain when you stuck a needle in their tummies. They ate from their rice bowls with disgusting noises and giggled with delight when they stabbed you in the back.

7   The 1972 Nixon visit to China brought forth a time of high praise for anything Chinese. The newly discovered extraordinary accomplishments of Chinese Americans in the face of prejudice sent **scholars** looking everywhere for answers. And it was in the late 1970s and early 80s that the experts in sociology told the world that the Chinese Americans were the model minority.

8   Is the wind changing its direction again in 1988? I don't know for sure, but I do know as a Chinese American I am glad to see reporting on the underside of Chinese American life. In part, I am tired of hearing how miraculously the well-behaved Chinese Americans have been doing, and I'm sick of reading about those teenage bookworms who have contributed to exceptionally low juvenile-delinquency rates among Chinese American kids. But mostly I am fed up with being stereotyped as either a subhuman or superhuman creature.

9   Certainly, I am proud of the academic and economic successes of Chinese Americans and proud that many of us have done so well in the sciences, the arts, law, medicine, business, sports and other **endeavors**. But it's important for people to realize that there is another side.

10   A few Chinese Americans steal when they are desperate; a few rape when nature overwhelms them; a few sell drugs when they can see an easy way to make a buck; a few **embezzle** when instant fortunes blind them; a few murder when passions overtake them; and a few commit crimes simply because they are wicked.

11   It is about time for the media to report on Chinese Americans the way they are. Some are superachievers, most are average citizens, and a few are criminals. They are only human—no more and no less.

Source: Adapted from Philip Chiu, "The Myth of the Model Minority," *U.S. News & World Report,* May 16, 1988.

■ ■ ■

 **after you read**

| Exercise 3 | **Answering Your Preview Questions** |

Directions: Look back at the questions you posed after previewing the selection. If you have discovered the answers, write them on the lines provided.

Answers will vary.

1. _____

2. _____
   _____

3. _____
   _____

| Exercise 4 | **Reviewing Important Points** |

Directions: Choose the best answer for each of the following questions using information provided in the selection. You may need to go back to reread certain sections to be sure your responses are accurate.

_c_ 1. **What is the thesis of Chiu's essay?**

a. Chinese Americans have been labeled as a model minority for too long.

b. Only some Chinese Americans are superachievers, whereas others are criminals.

c. The media should stop stereotyping Chinese Americans and report on them as ordinary human beings.

d. Americans should stop labeling people from other cultures because this behavior is destructive.

_d_ 2. **In paragraph 1, how are Chinese Americans depicted?**

a. superhuman creatures

b. subhuman beings

c. the model minority

d. a and c

_b_ 3. **The main idea of paragraph 2 is located in:**

a. sentence 1.

b. sentence 2.

c. sentence 3.

d. sentence 4.

_d_ 4. What have been some of the stereotypes used to refer to Chinese Americans over the past 60 years?

    a. ferocious, unfeeling, and disgusting
    b. smiling and friendly
    c. industrious and intelligent
    d. all of the above

_a_ 5. The details in paragraph 4 show that Chinese Americans are:

    a. dishonest and deceitful.
    b. obedient and respectful.
    c. mysterious and enigmatic.
    d. all of the above.

_d_ 6. Which of the following details illustrate the diligent and industrious nature of Chinese Americans?

    a. working day and night in the gambling halls
    b. becoming U.S. allies
    c. tilling the farms in China
    d. building U.S. railways

_a_ 7. In paragraph 6, Chinese Americans are depicted as:

    a. unfeeling and insensitive.
    b. amiable and kind.
    c. brave and strong.
    d. cold-blooded and lacking kindness.

_c_ 8. When were Chinese Americans first referred to as the model minority?

    a. during WWII
    b. after the Korean War
    c. in the late 1970s and early 80s
    d. in 1972 after Nixon's visit to China

_a_ 9. In paragraph 8, what does Chiu mean when he says, "Is the wind changing its direction again?"

    a. Chinese Americans may once again be depicted in a negative way.
    b. Chinese Americans will continue to be portrayed as superachievers.
    c. Global warming might influence the description of Chinese Americans.
    d. A new model minority will be selected in the future.

_b_ 10. Why does Chiu believe it is important to see Chinese people from both sides?

    a. They are superachievers.
    b. They are just human.
    c. They are underachievers.
    d. Chinese Americans are the model minority.

_c_ 11. What does this essay reveal about the nature of stereotyping?

    a. It leads to making generalizations about people from other countries.
    b. It only focuses on bad qualities of others who are different.
    c. It simplifies human complexity.
    d. It is always hurtful and destructive.

_d_ **12.** Chiu begins and ends his essay by blaming _____ for spreading the myth of the model minority.

    a. Chinese Americans
    b. newspapers
    c. scholars
    d. the media

_b_ **13.** What is the *overall* pattern of organization?

    a. cause and effect
    b. comparison and contrast
    c. chronological
    d. definition

Exercise 5   **Organizing the Information**

Directions: Using your notes and annotations in the text, complete the following table with details from the essay.

Chronicle of the Stereotyping of Chinese Americans

Event	Superhuman	Subhuman
60 years ago		_Fu Manchu_ introduced to the movies. Heard about dim _opium dens_ and _filthy_ gambling halls.
WW II	American _allies_. Contributions to the building of the _American West_.	
Korean War		_Ferocious_ Chinese troops marching to conquer _Asia_.
1972 Nixon Visit to China	Discovered _extraordinary_ accomplishments. Became the _"Model Minority"_.	
1988		_Gangs_, gun battles, drug dealing and _organized crime_.

Exercise 6A	**Using Context Clues**

Directions: Using context clues, select the word from the text box on p. 376 that best completes each of the following sentences.

Bullying

1. Almost 30 percent of children in the U.S are involved in bullying as a bully, a target of bullying, or both. Bullying is the act of intimidating a weaker person to make him or her do something. Bullies tend to be confident and have high self-esteem. They can be quite _ferocious_ in their attacks of others, which may include verbal and physical abuse.

2. Children who are bullied are generally anxious and usually have low self-esteem. One study found that the most frequent reason _cited_ by youth for why certain children are bullied is that they "didn't fit in." As a result of bullying, these children cannot work _diligently_ in school and often are not very willing to participate in out-of-school _endeavors_, such as sports or other extracurricular activities. _Scholars_ have found that years later, long after the bullying has stopped, adults who were bullied as children have more depression and poorer self-esteem than other adults.

3. After the 1999 Columbine High School massacre revealed that bullying played a key role in that incident and other school shootings, experts realized the need to pursue bullying research and look at the role of the _media_ in school crime, especially the Internet. New school programs were also developed to reduce and eliminate bullying behaviors. These initiatives focused on tolerating differences and embracing the _complexity_ of all human beings, and promoting positive attitudes toward diversity, including the benefits of developing _amicable_ and friendly relationships, and negative attitudes toward hate-based victimization of people who may be different from the mainstream.

(Adapted from www.safeyouth.org/scripts/faq/bullying.asp)

Exercise 6B	**Using Figurative Language, Idioms, and Expressions**

Directions: The use of figurative language, idioms, and expressions makes descriptions imaginative, colorful, and vivid. Complete each sentence using one of the following idioms or expressions.

To stab someone in the back: to do something harmful to someone who trusted you

To climb the economic ladder: to move to a higher economic status, to achieve financial success

To speak with a forked tongue: to speak in a way which is not honest

To see an easy way to make a buck: to earn money quickly and often in a way that is not honest

"Long time no see": something that you say to greet someone who you have not seen for a long time

1. He *had been stabbed in the back* by people he thought were his friends.
2. The mayoral candidate *is speaking with a forked tongue*, promising major tax cuts he may never be able to deliver.
3. *Long time no see*. It must be at least 10 years since I saw you in high school, and now we are taking chemistry together!
4. Times are hard. You have *to make a fast buck* whenever and however you can.
5. Prof. Jones was so glad to hear that her former business student, Taylor, *had climbed the economic ladder* in the music industry and was already earning a six-figure salary.

Exercise 6C   **Using Compounds**

Directions: Compound words are made up of two or more words that are put together to form a new one. They interrelate in such a way as to create a new meaning, which is very often different from the meanings of the words used separately. For each of the following words, write an original sentence that uses it correctly.

Sentences will vary.

1. **upright** (honest or righteous)
2. **slanted-eye or slant-eye** (offensive term used to refer to a Chinese or Japanese person)
3. **law-abiding** (obeying the law)
4. **underside** (side that is less desirable or reputable)
5. **well-behaved** (having good behavior, polite)
6. **bookworms** (a person devoted to reading or studying)
7. **juvenile-delinquency** (criminal action by a juvenile that is subject to legal action

---

Exercise 7   **Making Personal Connections Through Writing and Discussion**

Responses will vary.

Directions: Think about yourself in relation to the article you just read.

1. Conduct research about one of the following references made in this essay, and share your findings with your classmates.

   ■ Chinese contribution to the building of the Transcontinental Railroad
   ■ Fu Manchu
   ■ Chiang Kai-Shek

- role of the Chinese during World War II
- Korean War
- Nixon's trip to China

2. Access your college's periodical database, and open Lexis-Nexus. Then do a Power Search and look for:

   Lewin, Tamar, "Report Takes Aim at 'Model Minority' Stereotype of Asian American Students," *The New York Times*, June 10, 2008 (L) Final, Tuesday, Section A; Column 0; National Desk; Pg. 18.

   Then, write your answers to the *wh-* questions: *Who? What? Where? When? Why?*

⌐reflect AND respond⌐

Having read the selections about *diversity and tolerance,* you now have a broader and better understanding of the topic.

Directions: Complete a journal response for this module. Read the following questions. Select two to which you would like to respond. Then write your responses on a separate piece of paper. Write at least one page.

1. What did you learn about diversity and tolerance?

2. How does this information apply to you? Make connections with your own experience(s). What do these readings make you think about?

3. How can you relate what you have read to other situations? Make connections to other readings, course work, or current events.

4. What else would you like to know about this topic?

Readings About School and Learning

Get Acquainted with the Issue

Are you aware that many people study not only *in* school but *about* school? Scientists, educators, psychologists, and parents are interested in understanding how we learn, the best ways to teach, the impact of school on our social and emotional well-being, and trends in society and technology that affect education. You are in the educational system right now, and you may continue to be part of it for several years to come. Perhaps you will become an educator. If you are a parent, or intend to be, you will be involved in your child's education.

This module presents three selections on topics related to the field of education. The first is a magazine article called "Mourning the Death of Handwriting." As the title implies, it discusses the gradual decline in the instruction, and demand for, good penmanship in schools and society. The next selection, titled "Sparking Creativity in Your Child," tells about several strategies parents can adapt to nurture the development of creative thinking in their children. The final selection is a short story called "Charles." It creatively depicts the unusual experiences of a little boy and his parents during the first days in kindergarten.

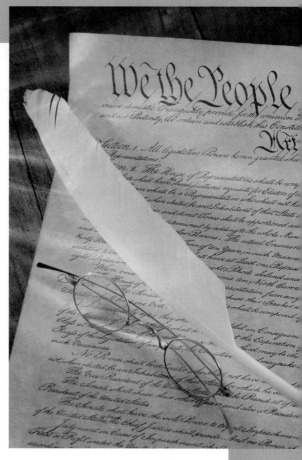

Guided Reading
Reading Selection 1

Mourning the Death
of Handwriting
By Claire Suddath

This article was first published in Time Magazine. *The author includes her own personal experiences as she explores the gradual shift in emphasis on the teaching of handwriting, also known as penmanship, in public schools today.*

 **before you read**

Think about what you already know about a topic before you begin reading. Then, when you begin to read, you will be able to attach your new learning to this background knowledge and more easily understand the new information. (See Chapter 2, page 38.)

Discuss or write responses to the following questions about your *own* experience with handwriting.

1. Do you remember learning penmanship in elementary school? What was it like for you? Were you excited to learn how to write in cursive?

2. Do you enjoy composing in handwritten form, or do you prefer to type on a computer? Are there any types of writing that you think benefit from being handwritten?

3. Since we use word processing so often now, do you think schools should continue to teach children handwriting?

Prepare to Read

Preview the selection, "Mourning the Death of Handwriting," using the THIEVES strategy on page 40.

Exercise 1   **Previewing**

Directions: Complete the following items.

1. Take a look at the selection, and check off all the items that are available to you for preview.

    _X_ Title
    ___ Headings
    _X_ Introduction
    _X_ Every first sentence in each paragraph
    _X_ Visuals/vocabulary
    ___ End of chapter questions
    _X_ Summary/concluding paragraph

2. Actively preview the selection by reading and highlighting the items you have checked.

3. Based on your preview, place an "X" next to the items you predict will be discussed in the selection.

    _X_ a. Why is penmanship dying?
    _X_ b. When did the move away from penmanship begin?
    _X_ c. Why is the art of penmanship continuing to decline?
    _X_ d. Who or what is Zaner-Bloser?
    ___ e. What plans are in development to bring handwriting instruction back to schools?
    _X_ f. Why is the author not bothered by the demise of penmanship?

Check Out the Vocabulary

You will find the following vocabulary words in bold font in the reading selection. Some are repeated more than once in the text. Do you know what these words mean? Knowing the meaning of all of these words will increase your understanding of the material.

clout	distinctive*	insufferable	radical*
demise	documents*	intensified	shunned
dismal	illegible	modifies*	static

*Denotes a word from the Academic Word List

Exercise 2   **Checking Out the Vocabulary**

Directions: Look at each word taken from the reading selection. Read the sentences that follow. The first is from the selection, with a hint to its meaning, and the second uses the word in an additional context. Choose the best definition for the word, and write the letter of the definition you select on the line provided.

_a_ 1. insufferable
  • In grade school, I was one of those **insufferable** girls who used pink pencils and dotted their *i*'s with little circles. (para. 1) (HINT: What does the author's tone imply about this behavior?)

- Because he is known as an **insufferable** bore, not many students register for Professor Conklin's chemistry class.

  a. not to be endured, intolerable
  b. nasty, unkind
  c. pleasant, kindly
  d. interesting, stimulating, motivating

c **2. shunned**

- I am a member of Gen Y, the generation that **shunned** cursive. (para. 1) (HINT: Read the preceding sentence. What did this generation do, rather than write in cursive?)

- Because Carolyn couldn't tolerate any form of cruelty, she **shunned** several members of the sorority who were known to be less than kind to certain people on campus.

  a. embraced, welcomed into one's group
  b. copied, took on as one's own
  c. deliberately avoided
  d. made fun of, put down or mocked

b **3. distinctive**

- People born after 1980 tend to have a **distinctive** style of handwriting. . . . (para. 2) (HINT: The sentence that follows describes the "distinction.")

- No one could miss Aaron, because his appearance was **distinctive:** six feet five inches tall, with a long black beard and always wearing a Mets cap!

  a. formal
  b. of a particular style, unlike others
  c. like the rest, similar to everyone else
  d. unhealthy, harmful

a **4. illegible**

- The knee-jerk explanation is that computers are responsible for our increasingly **illegible** scrawl, but Steve Graham, a special-education and literacy professor at Vanderbilt University, says that's not the case. (para. 2) (HINT: What does scrawl imply? Look at the following sentence. What does it say that kids have not learned to do? What does this suggest?)

- Because Dr. Framer's handwriting was **illegible**, the pharmacist phoned her to verify the amount of medication that she was actually prescribing for the patient.

  a. not able to be read, indecipherable
  b. understood by only a few
  c. clear and well defined
  d. unusual or uncommon, unique

a **5. clout**

- Cursive started to lose its **clout** back in the 1920s. Educators theorized that because children learned to read by looking at books printed in manuscript rather than cursive, they should learn to write the same way. (para. 3) (HINT: Is *clout* something positive or negative? Would cursive be gaining strength or losing it?)

- Since its creation, the Internet has increased its **clout** in society.
  a. power and importance; influence
  b. financial worth
  c. detrimental effects
  d. annoyance, bothersome nature

d 6. **documents**

- The company . . . is named for two men who ran a penmanship school back when most business **documents** were handwritten. . . . (para. 4) (HINT: What would be written in a business?)
- The appendix in my American History textbook contains copies of several important **documents,** including the Constitution, the Amendments, and Lincoln's Gettysburg Address.
  a. intellectual activity such as thinking, reasoning, or remembering
  b. emotional issues, such as anxiety, depression, or love
  c. physical activities, such as running and jogging
  d. original or official written papers

c 7. **modifies**

- [It admits that it] occasionally **modifies** its alphabet according to cultural tastes and needs. (para. 4) (HINT: the phrase *according to* implies some variation.)
- Jennifer **modifies** her hairstyle depending upon her mood; she wears it up when she is happy and lets it hang long when she is feeling down.
  a. destroys
  b. brightens
  c. changes
  d. removes

d 8. **static**

- Handwriting has never been a **static** art. (para. 5) (HINT: Read what the rest of the paragraph tells you about handwriting. What is the overall point? Static is the opposite.)
- Compared to the changes that have occurred in the twentieth century, including electronics and the Internet, the state of communications throughout the nineteenth century now almost seem **static.**
  a. delirious
  b. accepted by others, appreciated
  c. moving around a lot in a frenzied way
  d. stationary, not moving, fixed in one place

_c_ **9. radical**

- One of the most **radical** overhauls was to Q. . . . (para. 6) (HINT: Because the paragraph talks about changes to letter formations, and Q caused so many problems, what would you expect about the kind of change it needed?)
- In order to move the business from the verge of bankruptcy, the new CEO needed to make **radical** changes within its organization.

  a. minor
  b. annoying, problematic
  c. drastic, thorough or extreme
  d. kind and helpful

_c_ **10. dismal**

- The Federal Government's landmark 1983 report, *A Nation at Risk*, on the **dismal** state of public education, ushered in a new era of standardized assessments [in schools]. . . . (para. 9) (HINT: Based on the word *troubling*, would *dismal* be something positive or negative?)
- The weather was so **dismal,** dark, windy, and rainy, that we decided to change our picnic plans and stay indoors.

  a. thrilling, exciting
  b. uplifting and encouraging
  c. bleak, dreary, gloomy
  d. bothersome and annoying

_a_ **11. intensified**

- [It] has **intensified** since the passage in 2002 of the No Child Left Behind Act. (para. 9) (HINT: Does the rest of the paragraph make you think the testing has increased or lessened?)
- Rather than becoming less demanding, Brett felt that the amount of course work required in medical school **intensified** through the years.

  a. became stronger, sharper, more severe
  b. soothed, calmed down
  c. became easier
  d. reverted back to old ways

_c_ **12. demise**

- Cursive's **demise** is due in part to the kind of circular logic espoused by Alex McCarter, a 15-year-old in New York City. (para. 13) (HINT: What does the title of the selection imply has happened to the teaching and use of cursive handwriting?)
- The **demise** of the gang that had been vandalizing schools and churches throughout the neighborhood brought great relief to all of its citizens.

  a. celebration
  b. growth and development
  c. death, downfall
  d. publicity

▶ **as you read**

Establish Your Purpose

Now you are ready to read and annotate the selection, "Mourning the Death of Handwriting." Focus on major points of information. Read to learn what has occurred to cause the "death" of handwriting.

⏸ Actively Process While You Read: Guided Reading

Stop to think about the information as you read.

Exercise 3   **Processing While You Read**

Directions: Answer the questions that appear in bold print at the conclusion of each paragraph. This will help you monitor your reading process and understand the material.

from the pages of

TIME

Mourning the Death of Handwriting
By Claire Suddath

1   I can't remember how to write a capital *Z* in cursive. The rest of my letters are shaky and stiff, my words slanted in all directions. It's not for lack of trying. In grade school I was one of those **insufferable** girls who used pink pencils and dotted their *i*'s with little circles. I experimented with different scripts, and for a brief period I even took the time to make two-story *a*'s, with the fancy overhang used in most fonts (including this article). But everything I wrote, I wrote in print. I am a member of Gen Y, the generation that **shunned** cursive. And now there is a group coming after me. There are a boom of tech-savvy children who don't remember life before the Internet and who text-message nearly as much as they talk. They have even less need for good penmanship. We are witnessing the death of handwriting.

What is the author's main idea in this paragraph?

The main idea is that over time handwriting is becoming less important.

2   People born after 1980 tend to have a **distinctive** style of handwriting: a little bit sloppy, a little bit childish and almost never in cursive. The knee-jerk explanation is that computers are responsible for our increasingly **illegible** scrawl, but Steve Graham, a special-education and literacy professor at Vanderbilt University, says that's not the case. The simple fact is that kids haven't learned to write neatly because no one has forced them to. "Writing is just not part of the national agenda anymore," he says.

Why aren't children able to write in cursive as well as they used to?

Though some say it is because of the computer age, the author believes that we just don't care about it as much as we used to. It's not part of the "national agenda."

3   Cursive started to lose its **clout** back in the 1920s. Educators theorized that because children learned to read by looking at books printed in manuscript rather than cursive, they should learn to write the same way. By World War II, manuscript, or print writing, was in standard use across the U.S. Today, schoolchildren typically learn print in kindergarten and learn cursive in third grade. But they don't master either one. Over the decades, daily handwriting lessons have decreased from an average of 30 minutes to 15.

How does the author explain the gradual decline in cursive writing?

Because books were printed in manuscript, educators thought students should learn to write the same way.

4   Zaner-Bloser, the nation's largest supplier of handwriting manuals, offers coursework through the eighth grade but admits that these days, schools rarely purchase materials beyond the third grade. The company, which is named for two men who ran a penmanship school back when most business **documents** were handwritten occasionally **modifies** its alphabet according to cultural tastes and needs.

According to Zaner-Bloser, generally what is the highest grade level at which handwriting is taught?

Generally, it is not taught beyond the third grade.

5   Handwriting has never been a **static** art. The Puritans simplified what they considered hedonistically elaborate letters. Nineteenth-century America fell in love with loopy, rhythmic Spencerian script (think *Coca-Cola:* the soft-drink behemoth's logo is nothing more than a company bookkeeper's handiwork), but the early 20th century favored the stripped-down, practical style touted in 1894's *Palmer Guide to Business Writing.*

What is the main idea of the paragraph?

The main idea is that handwriting has constantly changed and has become more simplified over the years.

6   The most recent shift occurred in 1990, when Zaner-Bloser eliminated all superfluous adornments from so called Zanerian Alphabet. "They were nice and pretty and cosmetic," says Kathleen Wright, the company's national product manager, "but that isn't the purpose of handwriting anymore. The purpose is to get a thought across as quickly as possible." One of the most **radical** overhauls was to Q, *after* the U.S. Postal Service complained that people's sloppy handwriting frequently caused its employees to misread the capital letter as the number 2.

What is the purpose of handwriting today, which might explain the shift to make it more simple?

The purpose of handwriting is to communicate a thought as quickly as possible.

7   I entered third grade in 1990, the year of the great alphabet change. My teacher, Linda Garcia at Central Elementary in Wilmette, Ill., says my class was one of the last to learn the loops and squiggles. "For a while I'd show my kids both ways," she says. "But the new alphabet is easier for them, so now I just use that one."

8   Garcia, who has been teaching for 32 years, says her children consider cursive a "rite of passage" and are just as excited to learn it as ever. But once they leave her classroom, it's a different story. She doesn't know any teachers in the upper grades who address the issue of handwriting, and she frequently sees her former students reverting to old habits. "They go back to sloppy letters and squished words," she says. "Handwriting is becoming a lost art."

How does the author's third-grade teacher support her point of view in this article?

She tells the author that once children leave her class, their teachers in the upper grades do not address handwriting and her students go back to sloppy writing.

9   Why? Technology is only part of the reason. A study published in the February issue of the *Journal of Educational Psychology* found that just 9% of American high school students use an in-class computer more than once a week. The cause of the decline in handwriting may lie not so much in computers as in standardized testing. The Federal Government's landmark 1983 report, *A Nation at Risk*, on the **dismal** state of public education, ushered in a new era of standardized assessments that has **intensified** since the passage in 2002 of the No Child Left Behind Act. "In schools today, they're teaching to the tests," says Tamara Thornton, a University of Buffalo professor and the author of a history of American handwriting. "If something isn't on a test, it's viewed as a luxury."

What two possible causes for the decline in handwriting are discussed in this paragraph?

One cause is the introduction of word processing and the use of computers. Another is that students must pass standardized tests in other areas of content knowledge, so there just isn't enough time to focus on a "luxury" like penmanship.

Garcia agrees. "It's getting harder and harder to balance what's on the test with the rest of what children need to know," she says. "Reading is on there, but handwriting isn't, so it's not as important." In other words, schools don't care how a child holds her pencil as long as she can read.

What skill takes precedence over handwriting?

Reading

10   Is that such a bad thing? Except for physicians—whose **illegible** handwriting on charts and prescription pads causes thousands of deaths a year—penmanship has almost no bearing on job performance. And aside from the occasional grocery list or Post-it note, most adults write very little by hand. The Emily Post Institute recommends sending a handwritten thank you but says it doesn't matter whether the note is in cursive or print, as long as it looks tidy. But with the declining emphasis in schools, neatness is becoming a rarity.

What question does the author raise in this paragraph?

Is the lack of focus on handwriting really such a terrible thing? Is it really so important after all?

11   "I worry that cursive will go the way of Latin and that eventually we won't be able to read it," says Garcia. "What if 50 years from now, kids can't read the Declaration of Independence (in its original handwritten form)?"

What concern does Ms. Garcia raise here?

That in the future, students won't be able to read documents that were originally penned in cursive writing.

12   I am not bothered by the fact that I will never have beautiful handwriting. My printing will always be fat and round and look as if it came from a 12-year-old. And let's be honest: the Declaration of Independence is already hard to read. We are living in the age of social networks and frenzied conversation, composing more e-mails, texting more messages and keeping in touch with more people than ever before. Maybe this is the trade-off. We've given up beauty for speed, artistry for efficiency. And yes, maybe we are a little bit lazy.

Why isn't the author troubled?

She's not bothered because times have changed, and we have traded off beauty for speed and efficiency in the technological world in which we live.

13   Cursive's **demise** is due in part to the kind of circular logic espoused by Alex McCarter, a 15-year-old in New York City. He has such bad handwriting that he is allowed to use a computer on standardized tests. The U.S. Department of Education estimates that only 0.3% of high school students receive this particular accommodation. McCarter's mother tried everything to help him improve his penmanship, including therapy, but the teenager likes his special status. "I kind of want to stay bad at it," he says. These days, that shouldn't be a problem.

∎ ∎ ∎

 after you read

Review Important Points

Going over major points immediately after you read, while the information is fresh in your mind, will help you recall the content and record key ideas.

Exercise 4   **Reviewing Important Points**

Directions: Answer the following questions based on the information provided in the selection. You may need to go back to the article and reread certain portions to be sure your responses are correct and can be supported by information in the text. Write the letter of your choice in the space provided.

_b_ 1. **What is the overall message of this selection?**

  a. Schools are not doing enough to maintain handwriting standards.
  b. Penmanship is becoming a lost art in our society.
  c. Computers are ruining the ability of students to write neatly.
  d. The current educational system should reemphasize the instruction of handwriting in public schools.

_d_ 2. **In paragraph 1, the thesis of the selection is found:**

  a. in the first sentence.
  b. in the second sentence.
  c. in the middle, beginning with, "I experimented with different scripts. . . ."
  d. in the last sentence.

_c_ 3. **By tracing the demise of handwriting back to the 1920s in paragraph 3, the author uses the organizational pattern of:**

  a. cause and effect.
  b. definition.
  c. sequence/chronology.
  d. classification.

_a_ 4. **What is the topic of paragraph 6?**

  a. changes in handwriting reflecting changes in its purpose
  b. the U.S. postal service
  c. Zaner-Bloser's elimination of fancy details in handwriting
  d. radical overhauls to the letter Q

_d_ 5. **What is the main idea of paragraph 9?**

  a. Technology partly explains the demise of handwriting.
  b. The federal government is highly critical of the educational system today.
  c. Teaching to the test is all we do in this country.
  d. One reason why handwriting instruction has lessened is because it is not a skill measured on standardized tests.

_b_ 6. **In paragraph 9, the author uses the _____ writing pattern by explaining the impact of standardized testing and the passage of the No Child Left Behind Act on the inclusion of handwriting instruction in schools.**

  a. definition
  b. cause and effect
  c. listing
  d. comparison and contrast

_c_ 7. **What does the author imply in paragraph 10?**

  a. Doctors should improve the legibility of their handwriting.
  b. Neatness is becoming a rarity in our schools and we need to address this.
  c. Our lack of focus on handwriting may not be such a negative after all.
  d. Penmanship, in the end, can improve one's job performance.

_a_ 8. That the federal government published the 1983 report called *A Nation at Risk* is an example of a:

   a. fact.
   b. opinion.
   c. informed opinion.
   d. biased statement.

_b_ 9. Toward the conclusion of the selection, especially in paragraph 12, the author reveals her personal point of view by:

   a. providing statistics.
   b. expressing her opinions.
   c. listing facts.
   d. citing other authorities.

_b_ 10. What is the overall tone of the article?

   a. critical and concerned
   b. informational yet lighthearted
   c. worried and pessimistic
   d. sarcastic yet sincere

Organize the Information

Organizing the information you have learned from a reading selection shows you have understood it and have the ability to restate the material in a different way. You can use this reorganized material to help you study for exams and prepare for written assignments. (See Chapter 9.)

| Exercise 5 | **Organizing the Information** |

Directions: Using the content of the reading selection, complete the timeline that follows, which traces the demise of handwriting in the United States.

The Demise of Penmanship Instruction

- 1700s—*Puritans* simplified overdone and elaborate letters.
- Early 20th Century—*Americans favored* the stripped down practical style of the Palmer Guide to Business Writing.
- 1920s—*Cursive began losing its clout because* educators believed that because children learned to read manuscript, they should write the same way.
- World War II Era—*Print writing became* the standard across America.
- 1983—*The federal government's report* A Nation at Risk *emphasizes content area learning, not handwriting, and* standardized testing.
- 1990s—*Zaner-Bloser eliminates* fancy, decorative details from its handwriting alphabet.
- *The focus of handwriting is* to get a thought across as quickly as possible.
- 2002—*No Child Left Behind Act stresses* reading and other skills; handwriting is seen as less important and a luxury.

Integrate the Vocabulary

Make the new vocabulary presented in the reading *your* vocabulary. In addition to learning the meaning of new words, you should also learn related word forms.

Exercise 6   Using Context Clues

Directions: For each sentence, select the word from the text box on p. 388 that is a synonym for the word or words in parentheses and best completes the sentence. Then write it in the space provided.

1. Because Caryn has such a (unique and unlike others) *distinctive* _____ laugh, I knew she was in the audience enjoying the show at the college's latest production of *Mame*.

2. Unfortunately, I didn't have time to print out my paper, so I turned in the handwritten copy. My professor refused to grade it, saying that it did not meet the presentation requirements because my writing was (unable to be decoded for reading) *illegible* _____.

3. Although he was given a "second chance" to stay in class after he was caught cheating on the exam, Wayne was (deliberately avoided) *shunned* _____ by the other students.

4. Even though the forecast was for clearing and sunny skies, the rain seemed to (get stronger and more acute) *intensify* _____ as the evening progressed.

5. For our latest project in Asian History, we were required to locate copies of original (written records of the time) *documents* _____ from which we would cite direct quotes to back up the thesis.

6. Before Marion purchased her wedding gown, she wanted to be sure the seamstress would (alter, change) *modify* _____ the neckline of the dress to her liking.

7. Stuck in the rut of doing the same tasks every day for seven years, Jim felt his life was (going nowhere) *static* _____, and he longed for a career that would bring variety and stimulation into his life.

8. Because the governor had so much (influence and power) *clout* _____ at the start of his first term in office, it was shocking that his results in the election for a second term were so (poor, bleak, dreary) *dismal* _____, leading to the (downfall, ending, death) *demise* _____ of his career in politics.

9. The movie was so tedious and boring that it was just (not to be endured, intolerable) *insufferable* _____ to sit in my seat and stay until the end.

Make Personal Connections Through Writing and Discussion

When you make your new learning relevant to yourself in some way, it becomes more meaningful and easier to remember. Whenever you read, try to connect to the content on a personal level. How does it relate to you? How can you apply what you have read to other situations? What else would you like to know?

| **Exercise 7** | **Making Personal Connections** |

What do you think about the death of handwriting? Who or what do you think is to blame? Is it a problem for society? Does it contribute to the "dumbing down" of our culture, or is it just reflective of change and growth?

In a small group, or personal reflection, consider these questions. Write five conclusions that you, or your group, arrive at after thinking about the questions. Share your thoughts with the rest of the class.

Answers will vary.

1. _____
2. _____
3. _____
4. _____
5. _____

Self-Monitored Reading
Reading Selection 2

> ## Sparking Creativity in Your Child
> By Thomas Armstrong, Ph.D.

This article was originally published in a popular magazine. Its audience is parents interested in the intellectual development of their children. As you read it, consider the author's suggestions. Did you have some of the experiences he advocates in your own childhood? Would you consider them for your own children now, or someday?

◄ before you read

Answer the following questions before you read the selection.   *Answers will vary.*

1. Do you think that parents can make a difference in the intellectual development of their children? In what ways?

   _____
   _____

2. What do you think creativity is? How does a "creative" child behave?

   _____
   _____

3. Is creativity something that can be learned? Do you think schools are responsible for "teaching" students to be creative? How would they do that?

_____

_____

Prepare to Read

Preview the reading selection by applying the THIEVES strategy (p. 40).

Exercise 1   **Previewing**

Directions: Based on your preview, respond to the following questions:

1. Why does the author believe it is important to maintain a connection with the "creative self" often found in childhood?
    It leads to a world of satisfaction and richness that is immeasurable.

2. What can you predict is the purpose of the article?
    The purpose would be to instruct parents about what they can do to foster creativity in their
    own children.

3. Identify three suggestions the author will discuss further to foster creativity in children.
    Answers will vary, including 1. Nourish your own creativity. 2. Avoid judgments or criticism.
    3. Honor your child's individuality. 4. Don't force your children to do things.
    5. Provide materials and experiences that trigger ideas and feelings.

Check Out the Vocabulary

You will encounter the following words in this reading. They are in bold font in the selection. Are you already familiar with some of them? Knowing the meaning of these vocabulary terms will increase your comprehension of the material.

clichés	dialogue	misconceptions	stagnation
contraptions	evoke	novel	unimpeded
conventional*	inevitably*	percussion	uniqueness*

*Denotes a word from the Academic Word List

Exercise 2   **Checking Out the Vocabulary**

Directions: Look at each boldface word taken from the reading selection. Use the context of the sentence and the hint provided to select the best definition from the choices listed. Write the letter of your choice on the line provided.

_c_ 1. novel

Encourage new ways of seeing the world and **novel** ways of doing conventional things. (para. 3) (HINT: Since the topic is creativity, what kinds of ways would likely to be encouraged?)

a. ordinary, everyday

b. fictional, untrue

c. remarkably new and different

d. intrusive, problematic

_b_   **2. conventional**

Encourage new ways of seeing the world and novel ways of doing **conventional** things. (para. 3) (HINT: What kind of thing might the author suggest making novel?)

a. criminal or unlawful

b. ordinary or usual; conforming to accepted standards

c. having to do with a party or celebration

d. different, special

_b_   **3. contraptions**

In the same way, the seemingly innocent, aimless activities that your child engages in—making funny songs, inventing strange **contraptions** made of household odds and ends, drawing crazy cartoons—may be instrumental in helping to prepare the way for later accomplishments. (para. 2) (HINT: Think of the descriptors *strange* and *made of household odds and ends.*)

a. liquids or drinks

b. devices or gadgets, sometimes unusual

c. confusions, misunderstandings

d. lies, deceptive statements

_d_   **4. inevitably**

If a child feels that his creations will **inevitably** be subject to judgments . . . or comparisons . . . , he will either stop producing altogether or will simply make what other people want him to make. (para. 4) (HINT: Think of a word that would make the first part of the sentence lead to the last part.)

a. never

b. unlikely to occur

c. unpredictably

d. as expected, bound to happen

_a_   **5. uniqueness**

Uniqueness will be replaced by clichés. (para. 4) (HINT: What is the opposite of cliché?)

a. being one of a kind

b. boredom, disinterest

c. being uncontrollable, unruly

d. annoyance, of short temper

_c_   **6. clichés**

Uniqueness will be replaced by **clichés**. (para. 4) (HINT: What is the opposite of unique?)

a. excitement

b. insults, negative comments

c. overly familiar, commonplace

d. imaginary ideas, fantasy

_d_   **7. misconceptions**

Remember that the creative process is an uneven one, consisting of dead ends, **misconceptions**, errors and the occasional brilliant flash of insight. (para. 5) (HINT: Is this on the upside or downside of the creative process? What does the prefix *mis-* mean? What does the root word *concept* mean?)

a. bright ideas
b. lies and deception
c. complaints
d. mistaken thoughts

_b_   **8. unimpeded**

By allowing the entire process to occur **unimpeded** by your prejudices, you can honor your child's creativity and make it that much easier for him or her to find the right path to self-expression. (para. 5) (HINT: Consider the meaning of the entire sentence.)

a. limited, in small amounts
b. not hampered, able to move freely
c. following the rules and regulations
d. secretly, in private

_d_   **9. stagnation**

Your child may go through long periods of seeming **stagnation**, only to burst through with renewed vitality. Be patient! (para. 6) (HINT: Here the context clue is in the contrast. What is the opposite of *burst through with renewed vitality*?)

a. arrogance, stubbornness
b. extreme activity and movement
c. fright, fear of interacting with others
d. not moving, sluggish, dull

_a_   **10. dialogue**

This might turn into an ongoing visual **dialogue** or a pictorial story lasting several days. (para. 8) (HINT: What is the topic of this activity?)

a. conversation between two people
b. squabble or argument
c. contest or competition
d. problem or dilemma

_b_   **11. percussion**

Stock the area with art supplies, clay, science-kit materials, building blocks, **percussion** instruments, puppets, dress-up clothes. (para. 8) (HINT: What *kind* of instruments do children like?)

a. medical, pertaining to health care and medicine
b. items that make musical tones when struck
c. related to writing, such as pens and pencils
d. used for eating, such as forks and knives

_c_ **12. evoke**

Ask your child whimsical questions that **evoke** creative responses: What if everyone had an extra eye in the back of his head? What if dogs could talk? (para. 8)

a. criticize, find fault with
b. change or alter
c. bring out, draw forth
d. evaluate and assess

 **as you read**

Establish Your Purpose

Now, read and annotate the selection using the guidelines for active reading, and focus on the major points of information

Actively Process While You Read: Self-Monitored Reading

Monitor your comprehension as you read. (See Chapter 2, page 54.) Be sure to stop to reflect at the conclusion of each paragraph, and ask yourself the following questions:

- Did I understand what I have just read?
- What is the main idea of the paragraph?
- Am I ready to continue?

Exercise 3   **Processing While You Read**

Directions: Highlight the most important points in each paragraph. Then, write the key topics and main ideas in the spaces provided in the margins. Finally, underline or number the supporting details in the text.

Sparking Creativity in Your Child
By Thomas Armstrong, Ph.D.

1   When Julia was nine, she created an imaginary world of "weepals." There were one hundred sixty-four of these fantasy creatures, each related to the others in some way, and each with its own name, personality and physical characteristics. She even designed houses and furniture for them. Now, at the age of twenty-three, Julia manages a real-life social system. She coordinates the activities of several departments in a law firm. Childhood creativity was a key ingredient in Julia's grown-up success.

Notes
Topic _____
_____
_____
Main Idea _____
_____
_____
_____

Notes

Topic _____
_____
_____

Main Idea _____
_____
_____
_____

2   In the same way, the seemingly innocent, aimless activities that your child engages in—making up funny songs, inventing strange **contraptions** made of household odds and ends, drawing crazy cartoons—may be instrumental in helping to prepare the way for later accomplishments. Childhood is a time of natural creativity and curiosity. But while many people grow up and lose this precious gift in the "reasonable" world of adulthood, those who maintain a connection with their creative self find a world of satisfaction and richness that can't be measured. What can you do to foster this vital capacity in your own kids?

Topic _____
_____

Main Idea _____
_____
_____

3   **Nourish your own creativity.** If a child grows up in a household where the adults around him suffer from psychosclerosis (hardening of the mind), then he will likely come down with a bad case of it, too. Share with your child your own creations— poems, drawings, stories, even ones from your own childhood, if you still have them. Every day, vow to be a little bit whimsical and spontaneous: Create a funny voice, make up a silly dance, point out something around the house or in the neighborhood that you hadn't noticed before. Encourage new ways of seeing the world and **novel** ways of doing **conventional** things.

Topic _____
_____

Main Idea _____
_____
_____

4   **Avoid judgments, criticisms and comparisons. Evaluation** kills creativity. If a child feels that his creations will **inevitably** be subject to judgments ("You forgot to put a door on that house") or comparisons ("Put more color in your drawings, like your brother does"), he will either stop producing altogether or will simply make what other people want him to make. **Uniqueness** will be replaced by **clichés.**

Topic _____
_____

Main Idea _____
_____
_____

5   **Honor your child's individuality.** Accept her creations with an open mind, even if they seem flawed or incomplete. Remember that the creative process is an uneven one, consisting of dead ends, **misconceptions,** errors and the occasional brilliant flash of insight. By allowing the entire process to occur **unimpeded** by your prejudices, you can honor your child's creativity and make it that much easier for him or her to find the right path to self-expression.

Topic _____
_____

Main Idea _____
_____
_____

6   **Don't force your child to do something.** There are those who prefer to package creativity and market it like a new toy. But creativity can't be pushed and prodded. In fact, pressure can cause creativity to go into a permanent state of decline. Your child may go through long periods of seeming **stagnation** only to burst through with renewed vitality. Be patient!

Topic _____
_____

Main Idea _____
_____
_____

7   **Provide the resources they need.** You can't be creative in a vacuum: Children must be exposed to materials and experiences that trigger ideas and feelings. But remember, it doesn't take much to spark a child's creativity—building blocks, a cardboard box, a puppet, paper and crayons are often much better than the latest superhero action figure or electronic doll in encouraging creativity.

Topic _____
_____

Main Idea _____
_____
_____

8   Following are several simple-to-do activities you might want to try with your child at home. Being creative is fun. Sharing creative times with your child will not only help their capacity to use their imagination, but will give you opportunities to engage with your child, and enjoy time as a parent.

■ Invent-a-Machine. Give your child boxes of all different sizes, glue, scissors, a variety of buttons, knobs, pipe cleaners, string and other household items. Suggest he create his own machine or other construction (older kids may want to add battery operated bulbs and motors).

■ Pencil Talk. Take a large sheet of shelf paper, some pencils, markers or crayons, and have a "conversation" with your child. The catch: You can't talk; you have to draw what you want to say. This might even turn into an ongoing visual **dialogue** or a pictorial story lasting several days. Ask everyone in the family to join in.

■ Messing-Around Center. Set aside a special area of the house (a corner of your child's room is a good place) where he or she can engage in unstructured creative activities. Stock the area with art supplies, clay, science-kit materials, building blocks, **percussion** instruments, puppets, dress-up clothes.

■ Composer's Corner. Has your child shown an interest in music? You might buy or rent an inexpensive piano or even an electronic keyboard. Set up a corner where she can create her own melodies. How about recording her songs or giving a concert for the family?

■ Loonie Link-Ups. Invite your child to cut out pictures from magazines, and then take five or six unrelated pictures and make up a story that links the pictures together in a continuous narrative. Once you get things started, have your child tell his own stories.

■ Big Box Blow-Out. Get a large cardboard box from an appliance store and let your child decide what he'd like it to be. A spaceship? A house? A puppet theater? Let him paint or draw his own designs on it.

■ Record-O-Rama. Provide your child with a tape recorder, camera or camcorder, and let her create her own "stories" from the sounds and sights she puts together. Give her the opportunity (if she wishes) to present her production to the family.

■ World-Making. Using figurines, miniature buildings, plants, and other small shapes and materials, your child can create little towns or worlds; these can be set in a sandbox, on a sheet of plywood, or in a quiet corner of a room.

■ Silly Squiggles. Draw a simple abstract shape on a sheet of paper and ask your child to make up different things it could be (e.g., a straight line might be two ants carrying a piece of string, etc.); have your child create his own silly squiggles.

■ Kookie Questions. Ask your child whimsical questions that **evoke** creative responses: What if everyone had an extra eye in the back of his head? What if dogs could talk? Invite her to create her own questions.

■ TV Tales. Turn off a TV show (one that tells a story) ten minutes before it ends, and take turns making up your own endings to the plot (if you wish, you can record the remaining segment and compare your endings with those of the TV screenwriters).

■ Smudge Sightings. Go outside and look at the clouds, and together search for "pictures" in the billowy shapes. Other places to look for images of things: smudges on walls, scribbles on sheets of paper, the bark of trees.

Source: Adapted from Thomas Armstrong, Ph.D., "Sparking Creativity in Your Child," originally published in *Ladies Home Journal*, October 1993, © Meredith Corporation 1993. Used with permission from Meredith Corporation and Thomas Armstrong—http://www.thomasarmstrong.com. All Rights Reserved.

■ ◼ ■

 **after you read**

Review Important Points

Go over the major points immediately after you have read to help you to recall the content and record key ideas.

| Exercise 4 | Reviewing Important Points |

Directions: Choose the best answer for each of the following questions using information provided in the selection. Write your answers in the spaces provided.

b 1. The topic of the reading selection is:
   a. parenting effectively.
   b. enhancing creativity in one's children.
   c. how educators can promote creative thinking.
   d. the loss of creativity as we age.

c 2. What is the main idea, or thesis, of this selection?
   a. Childhood is a time of natural creativity and curiosity, but many people grow up and lose this precious gift as they become adults.
   b. Teaching creativity in the schools is important, and parents should demand that it occurs.
   c. Creativity creates a rich life, and there are many activities parents can initiate to foster creativity in their children.
   d. If parents don't help their child develop creative thinking, then they don't deserve to be parents.

d 3. In writing this article, the primary purpose of the author is to:
   a. entertain the reader.
   b. inform the reader.
   c. persuade the reader.
   d. instruct the reader.

b 4. In paragraph 1, the author tells about both the childhood and adulthood of Julia. In doing so, he uses the _____ writing pattern.
   a. definition
   b. comparison and contrast
   c. classification
   d. process

a 5. The main idea of paragraph 2 can be paraphrased as:
   a. People who stay connected with the creative selves of their childhood throughout their adult lives are likely to find a richness in living and attain many accomplishments.
   b. Childhood is a time of natural creativity and curiosity, and all children should be allowed to pursue their dreams.

    c. People who engage in seemingly aimless activities as a child are like to continue in the pursuit of aimless activities in adulthood.

    d. Many people grow up and lose their creativity.

_b_   **6. In paragraph 3, the author implies that:**

    a. We need to eat nutritious foods in order to raise healthy, creative children.

    b. Creative parents are likely to rear creative children.

    c. Even if your child is not creative, you can have fun being creative yourself.

    d. Your child will suffer a great loss if you haven't saved your own creations from your own childhood to share with him or her.

_b_   **7. What is the predominant writing pattern of paragraph 4?**

    a. definition

    b. cause and effect

    c. classification

    d. enumeration

_b_   **8. When the author recommends that parents honor their child's individuality in paragraph 4, he means that:**

    a. Parents should let children take care of themselves and not intrude.

    b. Parents should accept the creative effort of their children without judging or stopping it.

    c. Parents must listen to what their children say and obey their wishes.

    d. Parents must understand their own prejudices and try to get rid of them whenever possible.

_a_   **9. What kinds of resources does the author imply are best for sparking creativity in one's child?**

    a. simple, inexpensive items that can be used in many ways

    b. state of the art technology, so children will be prepared for the future

    c. action figures, so that children can make up their own stories about them

    d. no items at all, so that children can find their own materials

_c_ **10. Which of the following terms best describes the author's tone in the selection?**

    a. critical and concerned

    b. pessimistic and troubled

    c. straightforward and positive

    d. nostalgic and ironic

Organize the Information

Organizing the information from a reading selection shows you have understood it and can restate the material in your own way.

Some answers may vary.

Exercise 5   **Organizing the Information**

Directions: Refer back to the selection and Dr. Armstrong's "Simple To Do Activities" list. In collaboration with a classmate, complete the following chart, checking off the learning modalities that are used in each activity. Review the "Learning Styles" section in Chapter 1 to refresh your memory about learning modalities.

Activities to Enhance Creativity in Children

	Modalities		
Activity	**Tactile/ Kinesthetic**	**Verbal/Auditory**	**Visual/Spatial**
Invent-a-Machine	X		
Pencil Talk	X		X
Messing-Around Center	X		
Composer's Corner	X	X	
Loonie Line Up	X	X	X
Big Box Blow-Out	X		
Record-O-Rama		X	X
World-Making		X	
Silly Squiggles	X	X	X
Kookie Questions			X
TV Tales		X	X
Smudge Sightings			X

Integrate the Vocabulary

Make the new vocabulary *your* vocabulary.

Exercise 6A   **Using Context Clues**

Directions: Locate a word from the text box in Exercise 2 (page 400) that best completes the following sentences. Then write the word, or a form of the word, in the spaces provided.

1. I just love speaking with my best friend, Sarah. Our conversations are so interesting. She and I have the best _dialogues_ I have ever had with anyone.

2. My favorite section in the orchestra is the _percussion_ section. I like to listen to the beat of the drums, the crash of the cymbals, and the gentle twinkle of the triangle.

3. Uncle Jim was actually an eccentric inventor. He hoped to make millions of dollars marketing his inventions, from cat toys to tractor awnings. Unfortunately, his _contraptions_ never made it to the store shelves.

4. Martha Graham's _uniqueness_, both as a dancer and choreographer, made it _inevitable_ that she would become one of the most accomplished performers of our times.

5. The many _misconceptions_ Phillip had about the company hurt his chances of securing the position.

6. Fortunately, our plans for hiking in the Adirondack Mountains were _unimpeded_ by threats of stormy weather and falling temperatures, and we had a very pleasurable climb.

7. Although Maketa believed her essay was unique and well written, Professor Bice commented that it was unoriginal and filled with _clichés_.

8. Even though I had intended to take a _novel_ trip to the Alps over spring break, I changed my plans and took a more _conventional_ vacation, heading for Palm Beach, Florida, with several of my friends.

9. Dr. Farber's announcement that there would be no final exam in Philosophy 101 _evoked_ applause and cheers from all her students.

10. The _stagnation_ of the lake waters last summer led to a dangerous number of mosquitoes in our area during July and August.

Exercise 6B Learning Words' Multiple Meanings

Directions: Some of the vocabulary words listed in the selection have more than one meaning. Read each of the words that follow. Place a check next to the definition of the term *as it is used in the selection*. To make your decision, find and reread the word in the text. Use context clues to guide your thinking.

1. **convention**

   _X_ accepted usage, established practice or custom

   ____ a meeting, as of delegates, for matters of common concern

2. **novel**

   ____ a fictional, literary narrative of considerable length

   _X_ an unusually new or different kind

Make Personal Connections Through Writing and Discussion

Connect to the content on a personal level. How does it relate to you? How can you apply what you have read to other situations?

Exercise 7	**Making Personal Connections Through Writing and Discussion**

Responses will vary.

1. With a partner, take turns playing the role of parent and child. Complete either Pencil Talk, Silly Squiggles, or Kookie Questions. Then respond to the following questions in your journal. Share your written responses with your partner or others in your class.

   ■ Do you think you would have enjoyed these activities as a child?

   ■ Do you think the activities have value? In what ways?

   ■ Can you invent an activity of your own to enhance the creativity of a youngster?

   ■ How did it feel to participate in the activity? Was it fun? Difficult? In what way was it a challenge?

2. What has been your experience with creativity during your own education? In what ways has your creativity been encouraged or repressed in school? Discuss these questions with your classmates and/or enter responses in your journal.

Independent Reading
Selection 3

Charles
By Shirley Jackson

Shirley Jackson (1916–1965) was one of the most prolific, popular, and somewhat controversial writers of her time. Though best known for her provocative short story, "The Lottery," she wrote several novels (some of them considered horror stories) and numerous short stories, which focused on her reflections on marriage and raising children.

"Charles" was originally published in Mademoiselle, a women's magazine, in July 1948. It is the story of a young boy's early days in kindergarten and the experiences he reports to his parents. Read it to understand those experiences and the reactions of his teacher and parents. Aside from the intriguing plot events in "Charles," the reader gets a window into some of the customs and practices in public schools during the 1940s and 50s.

⏪ before **you read**

Answer the following questions before you read the selection.

1. What do you recall about your earliest days in kindergarten? Was going to school for the first time an adjustment? In what ways?

   _____

   _____

   _____

2. Do you think children always tell their parents the truth about their experiences at school? If not, why not?

   _____

   _____

   _____

Prepare to Read

Preview the short story "Charles" by Shirley Jackson. Remember, when you preview literature, you do so differently than when you preview a textbook. This short story has a brief editorial introduction and some biographical information about the author at the beginning. Read this information carefully to gain some insight into the story that follows. See Chapter 2 (page 50) for information about previewing literature.

| Exercise 1 | **Developing Preview Questions** |

Directions: Based on your previewing, write three questions you anticipate will be answered in the selection.   *Answers will vary.*

1. _____

2. _____

3. _____

| Exercise 2 | **Checking Out the Vocabulary** |

Directions: You will encounter the following words in bold type in this reading.

cynically	insolently	matronly	renounced
elaborately	institution*	raucous	simultaneously
incredulously	lapses	reformation	solemnly

*Denotes a word from the Academic Word List

Read each of the following sentences in which a vocabulary word from the selection appears in bold. Select the best definition of the word from the choices provided. Write the letter of your choice on the line provided.

_b_ **1. renounced**

The day my son Laurie started kindergarten he **renounced** corduroy overalls with bibs and began wearing blue jeans with a belt. (para. 1)

a. applauded, praised
b. gave up
c. followed, went along with
d. welcomed, embraced

_a_ **2. raucous**

He came home the same way, the front door slamming open, his cap on the floor, and the voice suddenly become **raucous** shouting, "Isn't anybody here?" (para. 2)

a. disagreeably harsh, loud and disorderly
b. confused, disoriented
c. varied, changing constantly
d. peaceful, calm

_c_ **3. insolently**

At lunch he spoke **insolently** to his father, spilled his baby sister's milk, and remarked that his teacher said we were not to take the name of the Lord in vain. (para. 3)

a. with reverence and respect
b. meekly, sheepishly
c. overbearing, insulting
d. foolishly, ridiculously

_d_ **4. simultaneously**

"Charles's mother?" my husband and I asked **simultaneously.** (para. 33)

a. in opposition or contradiction to one another
b. overly loud, boisterously
c. quietly, sullenly
d. existing or occurring at the same time

_b_ **5. solemnly**

He got **solemnly** back into his chair and said, picking up his fork, "Charles didn't even *do* exercises." (para. 33)

  a. inconsistent, very different
  b. seriously, gravely
  c. confusing, very difficult
  d. problematic, causing stress

_b_ **6. elaborately**

Laurie shrugged **elaborately.** (para. 39)

  a. minimally, with little attention to detail
  b. with complexity, ornately
  c. in a romantic way
  d. uncaringly

_d_ **7. institution**

With the third week of kindergarten Charles was an **institution** in our family; the baby was being a Charles when she cried all afternoon; Laurie did a Charles when he filled his wagon full of mud and pulled it through the kitchen; even my husband, when he caught his elbow in the telephone cord and pulled the telephone, an ashtray, and a bowl of flowers off the table, said, after the first minute, "Looks like Charles." (para. 41)

  a. an annoyance or intrusion.
  b. a shock, an unexpected result or event
  c. curtness, rudeness
  d. long established

_c_ **8. reformation**

During the third and fourth weeks it looked like a **reformation** in Charles; Laurie reported grimly at lunch on Thursday of the third week, "Charles was so good today the teacher gave him an apple." (para. 42)

  a. decline, downfall, demise
  b. confusion and misunderstanding
  c. complete change or overhaul
  d. questioning, interrogation

_a_ **9. incredulously**

"What happened?" I asked **incredulously.** (para. 45)

  a. in disbelief, not willing to accept what is true
  b. with great bitterness, hostility, and anger
  c. joyfully, with great glee and happiness
  d. regretful, with sorrow

_d_ **10. cynically**

"Wait and see," my husband said **cynically.** (para. 48)

  a. with joy and positive spirit
  b. without thought or consideration
  c. believing in the goodness of people
  d. in a doubting or distrustful way

_a_ **11. matronly**

At the meeting I sat restlessly, scanning each comfortable **matronly** face, trying to determine which one hid the secret of Charles. (para. 63)

a. that of a mature, dignified woman
b. old and withered
c. young, immature, and hopeful
d. that of an animal or creature of the wild

_d_ **12. lapses**

". . . With occasional **lapses,** of course." (para. 68)

a. distances around a track
b. total confusion or disorganization
c. worries or concerns
d. slight slips or errors

▶ as **you read**

Establish Your Purpose

Now, read and annotate the selection, using the guidelines for active reading. When reading a narrative, picture the setting and the plot events in your mind. Become familiar with the characters and the story line. Make note of the sequence of events and the culminating idea.

Actively Process as You Read: Independent Reading of a Narrative

Monitor your comprehension as you read. (See Chapter 2, page 54.) Stop to reflect at the conclusion of each paragraph.

Highlight the most important points. Write notes, responses, or questions that come to mind in the margin.

Charles
By Shirley Jackson

1   The day my son Laurie started kindergarten he **renounced** corduroy overalls with bibs and began wearing blue jeans with a belt; I watched him go off the first morning with the older girl next door, seeing clearly that an era of my life was ended, my sweet-voiced nursery-school tot replaced by a long-trousered, swaggering character who forgot to stop at the corner and wave good-bye to me.

2   He came home the same way, the front door slamming open, his cap on the floor, and the voice suddenly become **raucous** shouting, "Isn't anybody *here*?"

3   At lunch he spoke **insolently** to his father, spilled his baby sister's milk, and remarked that his teacher said we were not to take the name of the Lord in vain.

4   "How *was* school today?" I asked, elaborately casual.

5   "All right," he said.

6   "Did you learn anything?" his father asked.

7   Laurie regarded his father coldly. "I didn't learn nothing," he said.

8   "Anything," I said. "Didn't learn anything."

9   "The teacher spanked a boy, though," Laurie said, addressing his bread and butter. "For being fresh," he added, with his mouth full.

10   "What did he do?" I asked. "Who was it?"

11   Laurie thought. "It was Charles," he said. "He was fresh. The teacher spanked him and made him stand in a corner. He was awfully fresh."

12   "What did he do?" I asked again, but Laurie slid off his chair, took a cookie, and left, while his father was still saying, "See here, young man."

13   The next day Laurie remarked at lunch, as soon as he sat down, "Well, Charles was bad again today." He grinned enormously and said, "Today Charles hit the teacher."

14   "Good heavens," I said, mindful of the Lord's name, "I suppose he got spanked again?"

15   "He sure did," Laurie said. "Look up," he said to his father.

16   "What?" his father said, looking up.

17   "Look down," Laurie said. "Look at my thumb. Gee, you're dumb." He began to laugh insanely.

18   "Why did Charles hit the teacher?" I asked quickly.

19   "Because she tried to make him color with red crayons," Laurie said. "Charles wanted to color with green crayons so he hit the teacher and she spanked him and said nobody should play with Charles but everybody did."

20   The third day—it was a Wednesday of the first week—Charles bounced a see-saw on to the head of a little girl and made her bleed, and the teacher made him stay inside all during recess. Thursday Charles had to stand in a corner during story-time because he kept pounding his feet on the floor. Friday Charles was deprived of blackboard privileges because he threw chalk.

21   On Saturday I remarked to my husband, "Do you think kindergarten is too unsettling for Laurie? All this toughness, and bad grammar, and this Charles boy sounds like such a bad influence."

22   "It'll be alright," my husband said reassuringly. "Bound to be people like Charles in the world. Might as well meet them now as later."

23   On Monday Laurie came home late, full of news. "Charles," he shouted as he came up the hill; I was waiting anxiously on the front steps. "Charles," Laurie yelled all the way up the hill, "Charles was bad again."

24   "Come right in," I said, as soon as he came close enough. "Lunch is waiting."

25   "You know what Charles did?" he demanded following me through the door. "Charles yelled so in school they sent a boy in from first grade to tell the teacher she had to make Charles keep quiet, and so Charles had to stay after school. And so all the children stayed to watch him."

26   "What did he do?" I asked.

27   "He just sat there," Laurie said, climbing into his chair at the table. "Hi, Pop, y'old dust mop."

28   "Charles had to stay after school today," I told my husband. "Everyone stayed with him."

29   "What does this Charles look like?" my husband asked Laurie. "What's his other name?"

30   "He's bigger than me," Laurie said. "And he doesn't have any rubbers and he doesn't ever wear a jacket."

31   Monday night was the first Parent-Teachers meeting, and only the fact that the baby had a cold kept me from going; I wanted passionately to meet Charles's mother. On Tuesday Laurie remarked suddenly, "Our teacher had a friend come to see her in school today."

32   "Charles's mother?" my husband and I asked **simultaneously.**

33   "Naaah," Laurie said scornfully. "It was a man who came and made us do exercises, we had to touch our toes. Look." He climbed down from his chair and squatted down and touched his toes. "Like this," he said. He got **solemnly** back into his chair and said, picking up his fork, "Charles didn't even *do* exercises."

34   "That's fine," I said heartily. "Didn't Charles want to do exercises?"

35   "Naaah," Laurie said. "Charles was so fresh to the teacher's friend he wasn't *let* do exercises."

36   "Fresh again?" I said.

37   "He kicked the teacher's friend," Laurie said. "The teacher's friend just told Charles to touch his toes like I just did and Charles kicked him."

38   "What are they going to do about Charles, do you suppose?" Laurie's father asked him.

39   Laurie shrugged **elaborately.** "Throw him out of school, I guess," he said.

40   Wednesday and Thursday were routine; Charles yelled during story hour and hit a boy in the stomach and made him cry. On Friday Charles stayed after school again and so did all the other children.

41   With the third week of kindergarten Charles was an **institution** in our family; the baby was being a Charles when she cried all afternoon; Laurie did a Charles when he filled his wagon full of mud and pulled it through the kitchen; even my husband, when he caught his elbow in the telephone cord and pulled telephone, ashtray, and a bowl of flowers off the table, said, after the first minute, "Looks like Charles."

42   During the third and fourth weeks it looked like a **reformation** in Charles; Laurie reported grimly at lunch on Thursday of the third week, "Charles was so good today the teacher gave him an apple."

43   "What?" I said, and my husband added warily, "You mean Charles?"

44   "Charles," Laurie said. "He gave the crayons around and he picked up the books afterward and the teacher said he was her helper."

45   "What happened?" I asked **incredulously.**

46   "He was her helper, that's all," Laurie said, and shrugged.

47   "Can this be true, about Charles?" I asked my husband that night. "Can something like this happen?"

48 "Wait and see," my husband said **cynically.** "When you've got a Charles to deal with, this may mean he's only plotting."

49 He seemed to be wrong. For over a week Charles was the teacher's helper; each day he handed things out and he picked things up; no one had to stay after school.

50 "The P.T.A. meeting's next week again," I told my husband one evening. "I'm going to find Charles's mother there."

51 "Ask her what happened to Charles," my husband said. "I'd like to know."

52 "I'd like to know myself," I said.

53 On Friday of that week things were back to normal. "You know what Charles did today?" Laurie demanded at the lunch table, in a voice slightly awed. "He told a little girl to say a word and she said it and the teacher washed her mouth out with soap and Charles laughed."

54 "What word?" his father asked unwisely, and Laurie said, "I'll have to whisper it to you, it's so bad." He got down off his chair and went around to his father. His father bent his head down and Laurie whispered joyfully. His father's eyes widened.

55 "Did Charles tell the little girl to say *that*?" he asked respectfully.

56 "She said it *twice*," Laurie said. "Charles told her to say it *twice*."

57 "What happened to Charles?" my husband asked.

58 "Nothing," Laurie said. "He was passing out the crayons."

59 Monday morning Charles abandoned the little girl and said the evil word himself three or four times, getting his mouth washed out with soap each time. He also threw chalk.

60 My husband came to the door with me that evening as I set out for the P.T.A. meeting. "Invite her over for a cup of tea after the meeting," he said. "I want to get a look at her."

61 "If only she's there." I said prayerfully.

62 "She'll be there," my husband said. "I don't see how they could hold a P.T.A. meeting without Charles's mother."

63 At the meeting I sat restlessly, scanning each comfortable **matronly** face, trying to determine which one hid the secret of Charles. None of them looked to me haggard enough. No one stood up in the meeting and apologized for the way her son had been acting. No one mentioned Charles.

64 After the meeting I identified and sought out Laurie's kindergarten teacher. She had a plate with a cup of tea and a piece of chocolate cake; I had a plate with a cup of tea and a piece of marshmallow cake. We maneuvered up to one another cautiously, and smiled.

65 "I've been so anxious to meet you," I said. "I'm Laurie's mother."

66 "We're all so interested in Laurie," she said.

67 "Well, he certainly likes kindergarten," I said. "He talks about it all the time."

68 "We had a little trouble adjusting, the first week or so," she said primly, "but now he's a fine little helper. With occasional **lapses,** of course."

69 "Laurie usually adjusts very quickly," I said. "I suppose this time it's Charles's influence."

70 "Charles?"

71   "Yes," I said, laughing, "you must have your hands full in that kindergarten, with Charles."

72   "Charles?" she said. "We don't have any Charles in the kindergarten."

Source: "Charles," *The Lottery and Other Stories* by Shirley Jackson.

■ ■ ■

▶▶ after you read

Exercise 3   **Answering Your Preview Questions**

Directions: Look back at the questions you posed before your read the selection. If you have discovered the answers, write them on the lines provided.

Answers will vary.

1. _____

_____

2. _____

_____

3. _____

_____

Exercise 4   **Reviewing Important Points**

Directions: Choose the best answer for each of the following questions using the content provided in the story. You may need to go back and reread certain sections to be sure your responses are accurate.

_c_ 1. Who is the narrator of the story?

    a. Charles
    b. Laurie
    c. Laurie's mother
    d. Laurie's teacher

_b_ 2. What time period is covered in the story?

    a. Laurie's first year of kindergarten
    b. approximately the first six weeks of kindergarten.
    c. the 1940s
    d. the first few days of school

_d_ 3. Charles's inappropriate behaviors include all of the following *except:*

    a. hitting the teacher.
    b. throwing chalk.
    c. pounding his feet on the floor.
    d. writing curse words on his desk.

_c_ 4. The punishments Charles received at school included all of
the following *except:*

    a. standing in the corner.
    b. having his mouth washed out with soap.
    c. cleaning up the classroom.
    d. getting spanked.

_c_ 5. In hindsight, what could you conclude about Laurie's parents' understanding of their son?

    a. They knew he had emotional problems and gave him the
       appropriate support.
    b. They believed he had issues but that it was the school's
       responsibility to discipline their son.
    c. Because they loved their son, they ignored his inappropriate
       behaviors and did not recognize he had issues.
    d. They were uncaring parents and showed little concern for their
       son's needs.

_d_ 6. What written organizational pattern is used by Shirley Jackson to
present the events of the story as they occurred?

    a. chronology and sequence
    b. classification
    c. definition
    d. comparison and contrast

_c_ 7. By having Laurie identify Charles's behaviors and then reveal his
punishment, the author uses the _____ organizational writing
pattern.

    a. classification
    b. process
    c. cause and effect
    d. enumeration

_a_ 8. What is the overall tone used throughout the selection?

    a. surprised, but generally straightforward
    b. critical and persuasive
    c. somber and at times solemn
    d. impassioned and outraged

_a_ 9. Reading the very last line of the story, you can infer that:

    a. Laurie actually *is* Charles.
    b. The mother is in the wrong P.T.A. meeting.
    c. The school is confused about the names of their students.
    d. Laurie is an imaginary child.

_d_ **10. On several occasions, Laurie reports that all the rest of the children
in the class were told to stay with Charles when he stayed after
school. Why do you think Laurie said this?**

    a. to make his parents feel sorry for the other kids
    b. to show that the teacher was mean
    c. because he was confused
    d. to explain his own lateness and familiarity with the situation

_c_ 11. In hindsight, what tone is *really underlying* the conversation between Laurie's parents in paragraphs 21 and 22?

    a. critical

    b. nostalgic

    c. ironic

    d. farcical

_a_ 12. Based on what is shared in the story, why might Laurie have "made up" Charles?

    a. He knew he was misbehaving, but needed to share his experiences with his parents.

    b. He needed an imaginary friend to play with.

    c. Kids made fun of his name.

    d. He hated his teacher and wanted to take revenge on her.

Exercise 5   **Organizing the Information**

Directions: Read the story again. Then, working in small groups, complete the tables that follow. In the first table, record Charles's behaviors and his teacher's responses during the first month of school. In the second table, note Laurie's behaviors at home and his parents' reactions. Use the information you gathered in both tables to discuss the interventions of his teacher and his parents and their effectiveness.

Charles' Behavior at School and His Teacher's Responses

Day of Occurrence	Charles's Behavior	Teacher's Response
First day of school	• Very fresh to the teacher	*spanks Charles and makes him stand in the corner*
2ⁿᵈ day of school	• Charles hits the teacher because *she tried to make him color with red crayons but he wanted to color with green*	• Spanks Charles • Tells everyone not to play with Charles, but "everybody" did
3ʳᵈ day: Wednesday	• *Bounces a see-saw* on the head of a little girl	• *makes Charles stay in during recess*
4ᵗʰ day: Thursday	• Pounds feet on the floor	• *makes Charles stand in the corner during story-time*
5ᵗʰ day: Friday	• *Throws chalk*	• Deprives Charles of blackboard privileges
2ⁿᵈ week: Monday	• *Yells in school so loud that a first grade boy came in to complain*	• Makes Charles stay after school and all the other children to stay and watch him

Day of Occurrence	Charles's Behavior	Teacher's Response
2nd week: Tuesday	• Charles "refuses" _to do exercises to touch his toes_ • Is fresh to the teacher • Kicks the teacher's "friend"	
2nd week: Wednesday/ Thursday	• Yells _during story hour_ • Hits a boy in the stomach	
2nd week: Friday		• Keeps Charles after school (and all the other children stay as well)
3rd and 4th week	• Being good; helps _give out crayons_ and clean up _books_	• Gives Charles _an apple_ • Makes him the teacher's _helper_
Next Friday	• Tells a little girl to say a curse word—twice	• _Washes the girl's mouth out with soap_
Monday of PTA Meeting	• _Charles says the word himself_ • Throws _chalk_	• Washes Charles's mouth out with soap

Laurie's Behavior at Home and His Parents' Responses

Day of Occurrence	Laurie's Behavior	Parents' Response
First day of kindergarten	• Renounces _wearing overalls with a bib_ • Doesn't wave good-bye • Says he didn't learn "nothing" • _slides off_ chair, takes a cookie, and leaves	• Mom feels _an era of her life is ending_ • Dad corrects his language • Dad says, "See here young man."
Monday of following week	• Calls his father _"Y'old dust mop."_	• Doesn't respond, asks about Charles
3rd week	• Fills a wagon _with mud_ and pulls it _through the kitchen_	• Mom considers "a Charles" is an _institution_ in the household
Next Friday	• Joyfully whispers the curse words to his father	• Father "respectfully" asks, _"What happened to Charles?"_

| Exercise 6 | **Integrating the Vocabulary** |

Directions: Several of the vocabulary words used in the selection are adverbs. For example, "At lunch he spoke *insolently*" and "I asked *incredulously.*" You can easily change these words into adjectives by removing the suffix -*ly*. Thus, *insolently* becomes *insolent* and *incredulously* becomes *incredulous*.

Change the following words from adverbs to adjectives. Then fill in the blank in each of the following sentences with the adjective that best completes it.

cynically: *cynical*

elaborately: *elaborate*

enormously: *enormous*

incredulously: *incredulous*

insolently: *insolent*

simultaneously: *simultaneous*

solemnly: *solemn*

1. That burger was so *enormous* that I couldn't even finish half of it.

2. Everyone in my family was *solemn* at my grandfather's funeral.

3. Because she believed that her new car was overpriced, Tara's responses to the dealership's satisfaction survey were extremely *insolent* and critical.

4. We all sat there with our mouths open, feeling *incredulous* after watching a film on the potential effects of global warming on our planet.

5. Richard and his best friend, Sean, had a *simultaneous* reaction at the game; as soon as the touchdown was made, they each jumped up and cheered.

6. After years of being disappointed by the health care he received, Mr. Mather had become quite *cynical* about the benefits of regular trips to the doctor.

7. Monica overwhelmed me with the *elaborate* plans she had made for the weekend; I was hoping for some downtime.

| Exercise 7 | **Making Personal Connections Through Writing and Discussion** |

Directions: Think about yourself in relation to the short story you just read. Break into small groups. Each group can address one of the following questions. Have one person take notes on the ideas of the group, and then share these with the rest of the class.

Responses will vary.

1. Place yourself in the role of Laurie's mother at the conclusion of the story, when his teacher says, " We don't have any Charles in the kindergarten." Writing in the mother's voice, answer the following: What are you thinking at this moment? What questions do you have? How do you feel? What will you do now?

2. When people have difficulty dealing with change, we sometimes call this an adjustment reaction. Why do you think a child would behave as Laurie did during his first weeks of school?

3. Some of the interventions on the part of the school are old-fashioned, if not illegal, by today's standards. Nevertheless, Laurie was seemingly on his way to adjusting and improving his behavior. What do you think of the way the school handled "Charles"? What could they have done differently?

4. How do you think the parents handled their son? Citing specific reactions to his stories and his behavior at home, comment on their responses. What could they have done differently?

reflect AND respond

Now that you have read three selections related to *learning and school,* you have a broader and better understanding of the topic.

Directions: Complete a journal response for this module. Read the following questions. Select two to which you would like to respond. Write your responses on a separate piece of paper. Write at least one page.

1. What did you learn about issues related to learning, parenting, and/or schools?

2. How does this information apply to you? Make connections with your own experience. What do these readings make you think about?

3. Aside from handwriting, what other areas of instruction in schools are changing because of technology?

4. What else would you like to know about some of the topics discussed in this module?

Readings About the World of Work

Get Acquainted with the Issue

Selecting a major in college is the first step on your path to a career. Finding the right mentor to direct your passions and offer guidance will make this process easier. A mentor can also assist you with transitions to other colleges and career choices and can help you develop academic, interpersonal, and technical skills, too—all of which are essential in the workplace.

In this module, you will read three selections focusing on the workplace. The first is "Major-ly Unique: Lost in a Sea of English Major." The article discusses unique and unusual college majors offered by colleges nationwide. The second selection is titled "About That First Job." It gives some practical advice on preparing for your first occupation after college. The concluding selection is adapted from a business textbook. It describes the five qualities of an effective leader in the workplace.

Guided Reading

Major-ly Unique: Lost in a Sea of English Major

By Tracey Middlekauff

In this selection, Middlekauff discusses unusual and unique majors offered through-out the United States.

◀ before you read

Think about what you already know about a topic before you begin reading. Then you will be able to attach your new learning to this background knowledge and more easily understand the new information. (See Chapter 2, page 38.)

Discuss or write responses to the following questions about your *own* experience with selecting majors.

1. What major have you selected or are you thinking of choosing?
2. Skim your college catalogue. Define three major areas of study at your college about which you had no previous knowledge. Share and discuss your findings in class.

Prepare to Read

Preview the essay "Major-ly Unique" using the THIEVES strategy on page 40.

Exercise 1   **Previewing**

Directions: Complete the following items.

1. Take a look at the selection, and check off all the items that are available to you for preview.

     _X_ Title

     _X_ Headings

     _X_ Introduction

     _X_ Every first sentence in each paragraph

     ___ Visuals/vocabulary

     ___ End of chapter questions

     _X_ Summary/concluding paragraph

2. Actively preview the selection by reading and highlighting the items you have checked.

3. Based on your preview, place an "X" next to all those items you predict will be discussed in the selection.

Check Out the Vocabulary

You will find the following vocabulary words in bold type in the reading selection. Some are repeated more than once in the text. Do you know what these words mean? Knowing the meaning of all these words will increase your understanding of the material.

affiliated	boasts	equine	mainstream	sector*
aspiring	concentration*	hone	prestigious	thesis

*Denotes a word from the Academic Word List

Exercise 2   **Checking Out the Vocabulary**

Directions: Look at each word taken from the reading selection and read the sentences that follow. The first is from the selection, with a hint to its meaning, and the second one uses the word in an additional context. Choose the best definition for the word, and write the letter of the definition you select on the line provided.

_d_ 1. **sector**

   • Over the past 15 years, organic food has become the hottest **sector** in agriculture and it's only getting bigger. (para. 2) (HINT: The word *sector* refers to agriculture, marketing, and housing. What topic connects all these words?)

- The housing **sector** can be expected to bottom out if interest rates continue to increase.

    a. a geometric figure
    b. a portion of the military
    c. a body of people who form part of society
    d. a distinct area of business

_d_ 2. **concentration**

- Some schools, such as the University of Florida, offer organic agriculture **concentrations** within other majors, such as horticulture. (para. 2) (HINT: Look for a synonym clue.)
- I am currently taking allied health, psychology, and sociology courses, all of which are required in the nursing **concentration.**

    a. exclusive attention and focus
    b. memory and recall
    c. the amount of a specific substance in one area
    d. a major area of study

_a_ 3. **affiliated**

- They get hands-on experience working on a school-**affiliated,** community-supported organic farm. (para. 2) (HINT: There is a connection between the farm and the school. What is it?)
- Nassau Community College is one of the 64 two- and four-year campuses **affiliated** with SUNY, the State University of New York.

    a. organization associated with another
    b. independent member of a team
    c. intimately united in action
    d. solely supported by

_c_ 4. **mainstream**

- Organic agriculture is here, it's now, and it's **mainstream**. (para. 4) (HINT: Look at other parts of the sentence: It is *here* and *now*. Look at the parts of the compound word *mainstream*, especially *main*.)
- Cell phone use is so **mainstream** that many people have given up their land lines.

    a. providing water for crops
    b. belonging to current thought
    c. popular and current
    d. unusual and atypical

_d_ 5. **thesis**

- For his senior **thesis** project at Otis College of Art and Design in Southern California, Noordzy, class of 2007, developed a line of action figures. . . . (para. 5) (HINT: The word *thesis* describes a project completed in the last year of college. Look at what was involved in designing and completing the project.)

- For my master's **thesis,** I researched the impact of the media on second language acquisition.
    a. the central idea of a reading selection
    b. the subject of written discourse
    c. a factual and informative piece of writing
    d. original research presented by a candidate for a diploma or degree

_a_ 6. **equine**

- Thanks to the **equine** studies major at Lamar Community College in Lamar, Colo., that's exactly what he did. (para. 8) (HINT: Look at the heading, *Ride into the Sunset.* What does Dell ride? What is the overall topic of this paragraph? What other words refer to *equine* studies?)

- There are a variety of **equine** jobs available at the race track or working with trainers and horse owners.
    a. horse-related
    b. business
    c. healthcare
    d. water purification

_b_ 7. **boasts**

- Lamar **boasts** a 100 percent job placement rate. (para. 8) (HINT: How would you feel if you could place all those students who completed a particular major area of study? Would you feel good and satisfied?)

- Because of its high academic standards, John F. Kennedy High School **boasts** that 90 percent of its graduates continue on to two- or four-year colleges.
    a. speaks modestly
    b. speaks with pride
    c. speaks with excessive pride
    d. calls attention

_a_ 8. **prestigious**

- He's also won many **prestigious** and celebrated riding awards. Hendricks loved spending class time riding and training horses. (para. 9) (HINT: Look for a synonym clue.)

- The Nobel Prizes are widely regarded as the most **prestigious** awards given for intellectual achievement in the world.
    a. outstanding and prominent
    b. popular and widespread
    c. magical and dazzling
    d. valuable and expensive

_b_ 9. **aspiring**

- A handful of schools, including Green Mountain College in Vermont and the State University of New York, Plattsburgh, offer degrees in this field—a great major for **aspiring** adventure guides. (para. 12)

(HINT: These schools provide education and training for people who want to be adventure guides.)

- Many **aspiring** actors participate in high school and college plays, work at college radio or television stations, or perform with local community theater before they seek employment in the entertainment industry.
    - a. content
    - b. ambitious
    - c. hardly working
    - d. unemployed

_a_ **10. hone**

- If you want to get to Sesame Street, you will need to **hone** your puppet chop skills. (para. 13) (HINT: Look for a cause-and-effect clue. Read the rest of the paragraph to see what a BA in puppetry will provide.)
- You can **hone** your effective delivery of a speech with much practice.
    - a. perfect or work on
    - b. own or purchase
    - c. learn or acquire
    - d. polish or shine

 as **you read**

Establish Your Purpose

Now you are ready to read and annotate the selection "Major-ly Unique." Focus on major points of information. Read to learn about unique majors.

Actively Process While You Read: Guided Reading

Stop to think about the information as you read.

Exercise 3   **Processing While You Read**

Directions: Answer the questions that appear in bold print at the conclusion of each paragraph. This will help you monitor your reading process and understand the material.

Major-ly Unique: Lost in a Sea of English Major
By Tracey Middlekauff

---

1   Quick quiz: What are the two most popular college majors? Answer: Business and psychology. But what if those subjects don't thrill you? What if your interests are more specialized than that? Not to worry. Both two- and four-year colleges offer an

enormous variety of special majors. Students graduate with skills and knowledge that will truly set them apart in the job market.

Why do colleges offer a variety of majors?

Colleges offer a variety of majors because not all students are interested in the same majors. There are many unique concentrations.

2   Over the past 15 years, organic food has become the hottest **sector** in agriculture, and it's only getting bigger. Washington State University in Pullman is the first, and currently the only, U.S. school to offer a major in organic agricultural systems. (Some schools, such as the University of Florida, offer organic agriculture **concentrations** within other majors, such as horticulture.) At Washington State, organic agriculture students take classes in biology, chemistry, soil science, and economics. They get hands-on experience working on a school-**affiliated,** community-supported organic farm.

Nowadays, what is the most popular area in agriculture? How have colleges responded to this new sector?

Organic food is the most popular area in agriculture. Colleges have responded by offering majors or course work in organic agriculture and related areas of study.

3   Recent grad Jewlee Sullivan's goal is to grow her own food and run a small farm of her own. "I took a lot of science classes, like soil science and microbiology, and they were all fascinating," she says. "You get to be outside and work with your hands. . . . The farm changes every single day."

In preparation for her career in organic agriculture, which courses in science did Jewlee take?

Jewlee took soil science and microbiology.

Why does Jewlee want to grow her own food and run a small farm?

She likes being outdoors and doing manual work. She also likes the changing nature of the farm.

4   Getting a degree in organic agriculture doesn't mean you have to become a grower, although according to John Reganold, a professor of soil science at Washington State, "There are so many jobs in this field," he says. "You could work in the marketing and business **sector**, as a buyer or seller for an organic food company . . . [or] for the state Department of Agriculture." Major consumer-products companies, such as Kellogg's, are selling organic foods. Bottom line? "[Organic agriculture is] here, it's now, and it's **mainstream**," says Reganold, who predicts that other schools will add an organic agriculture major within the next couple of years. Check out the program online at afs.wsu.edu/organic.htm.

What are some career opportunities in organic agriculture?

Careers include marketing and business as a buyer and seller for an organic food company, the state Department of Agriculture, or major consumer-products companies.

Have Some Serious Fun

5   Does designing a plush toy, a doll, a toy car, or a game sound like a pretty good homework assignment? It's all in a day's work for a toy design major. Just ask Keith Noordzy. For his senior **thesis** project at Otis College of Art and Design in Southern California, Noordzy, class of 2007, developed a line of action figures that he describes as "kind of like 20,000 Leagues Under the Sea meets Mad Max."

What is Keith's final project as a toy major?

He designed a line of action figures.

6   Students in the toy-design program at Otis take intensive coursework in drawing, model making, brainstorming, concept development, digital rendering, and child psychology. Although toy designers rely on illustration skills, don't despair if that's not currently your strong suit. "By the time you get out of here, you will draw well!" says department chair Deborah Ryan. "We don't want to discourage creative people from applying, just because they don't think they have the drawing skills yet."

What happens if you have some great design ideas in toy-making but cannot draw that well?

The toy design program provides many courses to help students develop good drawing skills so they can successfully implement their ideas.

In addition to technical course work, what liberal arts course is required of toy design majors?

Toy design majors also take child psychology.

7   Graduates of the Otis program have gone on to work at big-name companies such as Crayola, Mattel, and Fisher-Price. Because only two schools offer this major—the other is the Fashion Institute of Technology in New York—admission to Otis is highly competitive. But there are other ways to get into the biz. Many art schools offer a major in industrial design with a **concentration** in toy design. For more info, check out artschools.org.

Why is it hard to get into Otis College of Art and Design?

Otis is the one of only two schools in the country to offer a major in toy design.

Ride into the Sunset

8   Dell Hendricks always loved horses. One day, a thought hit him: I like horses, so why not make a career out of it? Thanks to the **equine** studies major at Lamar Community College in Lamar, Colo., that's exactly what he did. At Lamar, students learn about everything from **equine** anatomy and riding to the business of managing a stable full of horses. According to lead instructor J. J. Rydberg, pros who know how to train and care for horses are in big demand. Case in point: Lamar **boasts** a 100 percent job placement rate.

How do students who major in equine studies fare in the job market?

They all find jobs.

9   Hendricks used his degree in horse training and management to build a successful breeding and training business in Texas. He's also won many **prestigious** and celebrated riding awards. Hendricks loved spending class time riding and training horses. "It was hard work attending classes and doing the program," he says. "But I enjoyed all of it." When considering schools, Hendricks says, look for instructors who have been successful in the industry, and make sure the program teaches horse health care.

What two pieces of advice does Hendricks give to anyone who is interested in an equine major?

Look for a college with a staff that is experienced in the horse business. Make sure the program offers courses in the health care of horses.

10   Dozens of two- and four-year schools offer **equine** or equestrian studies. For more information, check out www.horseschools.com.

11   And Now for Something Completely Different . . . Looking for a major as unique as you? Try on one of these for size!

Adventure Recreation or Expeditionary Studies

12   Imagine spending a good chunk of your college years backpacking, sea kayaking, and rock climbing—for credit! A handful of schools, including Green Mountain College in Vermont and the State University of New York, Plattsburgh, offer degrees in this field—a great major for **aspiring** adventure guides.

Which degree includes course work in kayaking and rock climbing?

A degree in adventure recreation or expeditionary studies requires such course work.

Puppetry

13   If you want to get to Sesame Street, you will need to **hone** your puppet chop skills. Though theater departments at some schools offer courses in puppetry, only two— the University of Connecticut and West Virginia University offer a bachelor of fine arts degree and training in such areas as puppet production techniques and marionette performance.

What are two examples of course work in puppetry?

Puppetry course work includes puppet production techniques and marionette performance.

Bagpiping

14   Not surprisingly, only one school in the United States—Carnegie Mellon University in Pittsburgh—offers a bachelor of fine arts degree in bagpiping. And it's not exactly the most popular major on campus. At one point, only one student was enrolled in the program.

Which college offers a degree in bagpiping?

Carnegie Mellon University offers a degree in bagpiping.

Popular Culture

15   You have a big exam tomorrow, so you're staying up all night to watch TV. Irresponsible? Not if your major is popular culture, which is offered at Bowling Green

State University in Ohio. A few schools, such as the University of Southern California, offer pop culture as a minor. But it's not just all about TV; along with going to class, reading, and writing papers, you'll have to watch movies and listen to music too!

What are some of the requirements of a popular culture major?

Requirements include watching TV, watching movies, listening to music, reading, and writing papers.

Traditional Eastern Arts

16   If nothing else, you'll graduate from this degree program feeling very mellow. Offered only at Naropa University in Boulder, Colo., the major offers three **concentrations**: T'ai-chi Ch'uan, yoga teacher training, or aikido. Class work includes meditation and traditional Eastern chanting.

What concentrations are offered in traditional Eastern arts at Naropa University?

Naropa offers T'ai-chi Ch'uan, yoga teacher training, and aikido.

A Singular Major

17   As an undergraduate at University in Bloomington, Will Shortz came up with a special for himself: enigmatology, the art and science of puzzle construction. His creativity paid off; Shortz went on to become the editor of the *New York Times* crossword puzzle. Many schools offer tailor-made majors, often called individualized-major programs, for those students whose academic interests are truly one-of-a-kind.

How do some colleges accommodate students whose majors are not available at their campuses?

They offer individualized programs, in which students can design their own majors.

Source: Adapted from Middlekauff, Tracey. "Major-ly Unique: Lost in a Sea of English Major? Not if You Graduate from One of These Unusual Programs." *Career World, a Weekly Reader publication* Sept. 2007: 23+. Web. 13 Jan. 2010. <http://find.galegroup.com/gtx/start.do?prodId=ITOF&userGroupName=sunynassau>.

■ ■ ■

 **after you read**

Review Important Points

Going over major points immediately after you read, while the information is fresh in your mind, will help you recall the content and record key ideas.

Exercise 4	**Reviewing Important Points**

Directions: Answer the following questions based on the information provided in the selection. You may need to go back to the article and reread certain portions to be sure your responses are correct and can be supported by information in the text. Write the letter of your choice in the space provided.

_b_ 1. **What is the overall message of this selection?**

    a. Most colleges only offer majors in liberal arts, such as business and psychology.

    b. Many colleges have majors in unique areas of concentration, such as toy design and equestrian studies, to suit the individual interests of their student population.

    c. Almost every college in the U.S. provides students with an opportunity to design a one-of-a-kind major.

    d. Organic agriculture has become the hottest major on college campuses today.

_a_ 2. **In this article, the author discusses all of the following unique majors** *except:*

    a. English, business, and psychology.

    b. equestrian studies.

    c. organic agricultural systems.

    d. enigmatology.

_c_ 3. **Students who major in organic agriculture at Washington State do their fieldwork:**

    a. outside the community.

    b. in the biology and chemistry labs.

    c. on an organic farm.

    d. on the college campus.

_b_ 4. **From paragraph 4, we can infer that opportunities for students who have degrees in organic agriculture are:**

    a. very limited.

    b. increasing.

    c. available only in business.

    d. bottoming out.

_d_ 5. **The purpose of paragraph 6 is to:**

    a. describe each of the required courses in toy design at Otis.

    b. discourage those with limited drawing skills from applying to their college.

    c. remind students that they need strong illustration skills in the workforce.

    d. encourage those who are creative but need work on drawing to apply to their program.

_d_ 6. Students who major in equine studies must take courses in:
  a. human anatomy.
  b. small business management.
  c. personal health.
  d. horseback riding.

_d_ 7. Degrees that allow you to be outdoors include all of the following *except:*
  a. organic agricultural systems.
  b. equine studies.
  c. expeditionary studies.
  d. bagpiping.

_b_ 8. According to the selection, which of the following two areas of concentration will provide you with a bachelor of fine arts?
  a. equestrian studies and organic agricultural systems
  b. bagpiping and puppetry
  c. adventure recreation and popular culture
  d. none of the above

_c_ 9. Which two programs of study have the least number of students enrolled?
  a. popular culture and puppetry
  b. yoga teacher training and aikido
  c. bagpiping and enigmatology
  d. expeditionary studies and bagpiping

_b_ 10. The overall pattern of organization of this selection is:
  a. cause and effect.
  b. enumeration.
  c. definition.
  d. comparison and contrast.

Organize the Information

Organizing the information you have learned from a reading selection shows you have understood it and can restate the material in a different way. You can use this reorganized material to help you study for exams and prepare for written assignments. (See Chapter 9.)

Exercise 5   **Organizing the Information**

Directions: Complete the last column of the following table (Possible Careers) with details from the reading about unique majors in college. (Note: If the article does not provide details, leave the section blank.)

Unique Majors in Colleges Throughout the U.S.

Major	Colleges	Required Course Work	Possible Careers
organic agricultural studies	Washington State	biology, chemistry, soil science, economics	*Run a farm, grower, marketing, major consumer-products companies, The state Department of Agriculture*
toy design	Otis College	drawing, model making, digital rendering, child psychology	*Major toy companies, such as Crayola, Mattel and Fischer-Price*
equine studies	Lamar C.C.	equine anatomy, riding, business management, horse health care	*Care and training horses, breeding*
expeditionary studies	Green Mountain College. State University of NY, Plattsburgh	backpacking, sea kayaking, rock climbing	*Adventure guide*
puppetry	University of Connecticut, West Virginia University	puppet production, marionette performance	*Sesame Street*
bagpiping	Carnegie Mellon University		
popular culture	Bowling Green State University	reading, writing papers, watching TV, and listening to music	
traditional Eastern arts	Naropa University	Meditation and Eastern chanting	*Yoga teacher*

Integrate the Vocabulary

Make the new vocabulary presented in the reading *your* vocabulary. In addition to learning the meaning of new words, you should also learn related word forms.

Exercise 6A   **Using Context Clues**

Directions: For each sentence, select the word from the text box on page 426 that is a synonym for the word or words in parentheses and best completes the sentence. Then write it in the space provided.

1. Technology is so (popular) _mainstream_____ in higher education that many colleges have developed extensive online programs.

2. The Nursing Program (speak with pride) _boasts_____ that more than 85 percent of its students complete their RN in two years.

3. The Fashion Buying Merchandising Department is (associated) _affiliated_____ with many local businesses that provide externships for their students.

4. It took Eric three months to complete his senior (original research for completion of a degree) _thesis_____ for his major in electrical engineering.

5. I declared my (major area of study) _concentration_____ in psychology after my sophomore year.

6. As an (ambitious) _aspiring_____ journalist, I took courses in literature, writing, communications, and the fine arts.

7. To get into the Respiratory Program, I need to (improve) _hone_____ my skills in science.

8. A good foundation in liberal arts is essential for a career in the business (area) _sector_____.

9. Harvard is the most (highly regarded) _prestigious_____ university in the United States.

10. Graduates of (horses) _equine_____ studies might find employment as veterinarian assistants, whose duties include moving and restraining animals and assisting with medications and treatments.

Exercise 6B   **Learning Words with Multiple Meanings**

Directions: Words with multiple meanings have different definitions. You need to use the context to discern the correct meaning. For example, in paragraph 6 the author writes, "Although toy designers rely on illustration skills, don't despair if that's not currently your strong **suit**. 'By the time you get out of here, you will draw well!' says department chair Deborah Ryan." The word *suit* has many different meanings. Here it is part of the idiomatic expression *strong suit*. A **strong suit** is an area in which a person excels. Following are four definitions of expressions with the word *suit*. In the sentences that follow, fill in the blanks with one of the expressions.

   strong suit: an area in which a person excels.

   (It) suits me (fine): It is fine with me.

   follow suit: to follow in the same pattern; to follow someone else's example.

the men in gray suits: men in business or politics who have a lot of power and influence although the public does not see them or know about them.

1. As usual, it is the *men in gray suits* who will decide the future of the industry.

2. Mary went to work for a bank, and Jane *followed suit*. Now, they are both head cashiers.

3. While his aptitude in math and science is weak, Anthony's *strong suit* is in the arts and humanities.

4. John: Is this seat okay?

    Mary: *This suits me just fine.* I always like to sit up front where I can hear better.

5. The Smiths went out to dinner, but the Browns *didn't follow suit.* They stayed home and watched T.V.

Make Personal Connections Through Writing and Discussion

When you make your new learning relevant to yourself in some way, it becomes more meaningful and easier to remember. Whenever you read, try to connect to the content on a personal level. How does it relate to you? How can you apply what you have read to other situations? What else would you like to know?

Exercise 7   **Making Personal Connections Through Writing and Discussion**

1. What major might you select if there were no restrictions or requirements to fulfill?

    An individualized major provides students with an opportunity to design and follow a personalized program of study. Write a proposal for your plan. Include information that explains what you want to do and why you want to do it. After you complete your proposal, share it with the members of your group, who will decide if yours is accepted.

2. Below you will find three additional unique majors adapted from http://mycollegeguide.org.

    Add these areas of concentration to the table you completed on page 436. Arrange the information as it appears on the table.

    Viticulture. You may be too young to drink wine, but you're not too young to make it! Cal Poly, in San Luis Obispo, California, offers a Wine and Viticulture major, where students will learn how to grow grapes and turn them into high-quality wine, using the school's 100-acre vineyard. Once you've finished the program, you'll finally be old enough to try your own wine—and you will be prepared to start your own winery.

    Professional Golf Management. If you love golf but aren't quite qualified to be a pro, consider running your own golf course. A degree in

Professional Golf Management from Penn State University will teach you how to do that. Courses include Turf Grass Management, Analysis of the Swing, and Golf Car Fleet Management. Students must pass a golfing proficiency test before being awarded with a diploma and a membership to the PGA. This is a good excuse to spend plenty of time out on the course (as scholarly research).

Food Science. Do you love chemistry and cooking? A degree in Food Science from Cornell University will allow you to combine these passions, teaching you about engineering, microbiology, chemistry and other scientific fields as applied to food. This is definitely not a lightweight major—you'll need to take calculus, organic chemistry, and microbiology to even begin the program—but it's a rewarding field. If you think coming up with Ben and Jerry's next flavor would be a dream job, this is the major for you.

Self-Monitored Reading
Reading Selection 2

About That First Job
By Rich Karlgaard

In this article, Karlgaard offers the reader advice about how to prepare for your first "real" job in the workforce.

before you read

Answers will vary. It's important to think about what you already know about a topic before you read. Answer the following questions before you read the selection.

1. Do you also work while you are attending classes? If so, what advice would you offer about the skills and attitudes necessary to enter the workforce?

   _____

   _____

2. From your own experiences and from the observation of others at work, what is an example of a good attitude that might lead to a promotion or a better-paying job?

   _____

   _____

Prepare to Read

Preview the reading selection by applying the THIEVES strategy (p. 40).

Exercise 1 **Previewing**

Directions: Based on your preview, respond to the following questions:

1. Why does the author think it was funny that he was being asked for advice about getting that first job?

   He did not know what he wanted to be in high school or college; he just had a passion for sports. He was an average student.

2. What advice does the author give about the world of work?

   Get an appreciation for reading. Follow your passions. Find a mentor. Act like an owner.

3. Who was one of his mentors?

   William F. Buckley, Jr.

Check Out the Vocabulary

You will encounter the following vocabulary words in this reading.

blotted out	marveled	pored	rival
bureaucracy	mechanism*	prose	shirked
careerist	mentor	realm	trivial

*Denotes a word from the Academic Word List

Exercise 2 **Checking Out the Vocabulary**

Directions: Look at each boldface word taken from the reading selection. Use the context of the sentence and the hint provided to select the best definition from the choices listed. Write the letter of your choice on the line provided.

_b_ **1. shirked**

At the library, I **shirked** my homework and pored over old bound volumes of these magazines. (para. 2) (HINT: Did the author complete his homework assignment?)

a. take charge of
b. get out of responsibility
c. shy away from
d. blame others for

_a_ **2. pored**

At the library I shirked my homework and **pored** over old bound volumes of these magazines. (para. 2) (HINT: Read the previous sentence.)

a. to read and study carefully
b. to look at steadily
c. to think about it intently
d. to fill one's mind completely

_d_ **3. prose**

It was there that I discovered the **prose** of H. L. Mencken and George Orwell. (para. 3) (HINT: Read the next sentence to find out who Mencken and Orwell are and what they do.)

a. poetry
b. speech
c. slang
d. writing

_c_ **4. mechanism**

And it needs a **mechanism** to express itself, just as a waterfall needs a turbine wheel to make electricity. (para. 5) (HINT: Look at the comparison. The turbine wheel is the mechanical device used to turn a waterfall into electricity. What means can be used to turn passion into action?)

a. a mechanical device
b. a gadget or instrument
c. an agency by which a purpose is accomplished
d. a psychological force that helps individuals with problems

_d_ **5. realm**

In the **realm** of school the best teachers and coaches know how to direct their students' passion and energy. (para. 5) (HINT: The author is making a general statement about school.)

a. a world of reality
b. a kingdom or country
c. a field of study
d. a sphere of activity

a   **6. mentor**

But careers don't work that way. In the world of jobs and careers, the student must find the **mentor.** (para. 5) (HINT: Read the previous sentence to find out what teachers and coaches can do for students. Read the next paragraph to learn more about what the author's mentors have done for him.)

a. an advisor
b. a psychologist
c. a wise man
d. a teacher

c   **7. trivial**

Sounds **trivial,** even silly, but it helped me and gave me confidence. (para. 6) (HINT: Look at the information between the commas; it provides a definition.)

a. of a small amount
b. of little substance or significance
c. of great importance
d. providing useful information

c   **8. marveled**

I **marveled** at how this guy could sell six-figure consulting packages while I was stuck in a four-figure piecemeal world. (para. 7) (HINT: How did the author feel when he saw how successful his friend was?)

a. to laugh at
b. to joke about
c. to be amazed at
d. to be angry about

d   **9. blotted out**

The company's big-picture goals may be **blotted out** by the narrower demands of the boss. (para. 9) (HINT: What happens to the broad goals of a company when a boss makes his own demands?)

a. destroyed
b. preserved
c. to make something stop upsetting you
d. to make something insignificant

c   **10. rival**

Maybe the boss just wants to upstage a **rival** or knock off early for golf. (para. 9) (HINT: The literal meaning of *upstage* means that when you move to the rear of the stage, you force the other actors to face away from the audience. Figuratively, you draw attention away from someone else.)

a. an equal
b. a friend
c. a competitor
d. an actor

_a_ **11. careerist**

This is a dangerous time for the young **careerist.** (para. 10) (HINT: The suffix *-ist* means "a person who.")

a. a professional person
b. a professional golfer
c. a supervisor
d. an employee

_c_ **12. bureaucracy**

This ownership view can get lost in the **bureaucracy.** (para. 10) (HINT: Read the next sentence. It mentions the all the tasks involved in getting work done at one's job.)

a. a government office
b. officials and governance
c. official procedures and red tape
d. authority

▶ as you read

Establish Your Purpose

Now, read and annotate the selection using the guidelines for active reading, and focus on the major points of information.

Actively Process While You Read: Self-Monitored Reading

Monitor your comprehension as you read. (See Chapter 2, page 54.) Be sure to stop to reflect at the conclusion of each paragraph, and ask yourself the following questions:

- Did I understand what I have just read?
- What is the main idea of the paragraph?
- Am I ready to continue?

Exercise 3   **Processing While You Read**

Directions: Highlight the most important points in each paragraph. Then write the key topics and main ideas in the spaces provided in the margins. Finally, underline or number the supporting details in the text.

About That First Job
By Rich Karlgaard

Notes
Topic _____
_____

1   This question always comes up at the end of a speech: "Given the dizzying pace of change in the economy, what careers should my kids pursue?"

Main Idea _____
_____

2   I always chuckle. The question is legitimate, of course, but the fact that I am being asked it is a bit funny, if you know me. In college, let alone high school, I had no clue as to what I wanted to do once I graduated. All I cared about was sports, track-and-field especially. That I wound up working for a magazine might have been predictable—might have been—from my twin passions at the time, *Sports Illustrated* and *Track & Field News.* I would read and reread each new issue to the point of memorization. At the library I **shirked** my homework and **pored** over old bound volumes of these magazines. Forget Mark Twain and Ernest Hemingway. The best American writer was sportswriter Dan Jenkins.

3   As a result of this goofballing, I graduated with low Bs and was clueless about careers. College friends headed off to law school, med school, divinity school . . . and I headed off to a security guard agency. My first job was to show up at 5:00 p.m., relieve the receptionist and sit in the lobby until midnight. It was there that I discovered the **prose** of H. L. Mencken and George Orwell. And lively contemporary writers, too, such as Tom Wolfe, George Gilder and P. J. O'Rourke. They were nothing like the sour postmodernists I had been force-fed in college.

4   The written word, I had come to appreciate (on my own and rather late), was everything. So here is my first piece of advice to parents: Get your kids to fall in love with reading. It doesn't matter what the writing is. What's key is that the kids claim it as their own. I know scholars who were intellectually awakened as teenagers by *Playboy* magazine interviews. Those are great interviews. A few years ago, a neighbor's kid was struggling in high school, despite an IQ score in the nosebleed zone. His passions were golf and basketball. "Fire the tutors," I told his mother. "Buy him subscriptions to *Sports Illustrated* and *Golf* magazines." She did. The boy was awakened. Now, he works for Lehman Brothers (nyse: LEH-new-people) in London.

Find the Right Mentors

5   Passion, like energy, is vital. Of course, passion must be captured and directed in order to accomplish actual work. And it needs a **mechanism** to express itself, just as a waterfall needs a turbine wheel to make electricity. In the **realm** of school the best teachers and coaches know how to direct their students' passion and energy. But careers don't work that way. In the world of jobs and careers, the student must find the **mentor.**

6   The **mentor** needn't be a boss. The **mentor** doesn't even have to know he's been selected as a **mentor.** Throughout my career, I've never told my **mentors** they were my **mentors.** I picked **mentors** because they had something I needed to learn. From one of my bosses, I learned how to match a jacket, shirt and tie. He always looked sharp; I wanted to look sharp, too, so I quietly observed the color of his clothing, the knot of his tie, the amount of shirt cuff showing. Sounds **trivial** and even silly, but it helped me and gave me confidence.

7   For several years during the mid-1980s, I worked for myself, making brochures for technology companies. I sublet space from a pal who ran a consulting firm. I **marveled** at how this guy could sell six-figure consulting packages while I was stuck in a four-figure piecemeal world. So I studied my friend. I would sneakily stand outside his office while he was on the phone schmoozing a client. I would read draft memos and proposals found by the copy machine. I was literally picking the guy's knowledge and methods off the floor.

8   Another **mentor**, unaware he was chosen, was William F. Buckley, Jr. One day in 1986 a friend got a call to pick up Buckley at the airport. He invited me along. Buckley, in town to debate George McGovern, was eager to learn about Silicon Valley. We brain-dumped all that we knew, and he nodded. And then he asked: "Is there a magazine that covers this?" Well, no, we said. "Maybe you should start one," he said. Two years later we did. My goal for *Upside* magazine was to marry a Dan Jenkins **prose** style with the subjects of technology startups and IPOs. And so to change the world, as Buckley had done with *National Review*.

Notes
Topic _____
_____
Main Idea _____
_____

Think Like an Owner

9   My last piece of advice is for your kid to learn to think like an owner. Your kid will get that first job and report to a foreman or a middle manager or someone lower on the totem pole. The company's big-picture goals may be **blotted out** by the narrower demands of the boss. Maybe the boss just wants to upstage a **rival** or knock off early for golf.

Topic _____
_____
Main Idea _____
_____

10   This is a dangerous time for the young **careerist.** It's when destructive habits can be learned. The worst of these mental habits is: restricting one's vision to the internal view of the company—that organizations and jobs exist for their own preservation. Actually, they exist to keep a customer and make a profit. This ownership view can get lost in the **bureaucracy.** I've seen too many talented people in their 40s and 50s who are stuck in their organizations, deeply frustrated. Ask them what they do, and you get a boring, task-oriented job description such as an h.r. department might write.

Topic _____
_____
Main Idea _____
_____

11   Even if your first job is sweeping floors, think like an owner.

Topic _____
_____
Main Idea _____
_____

Source: Adapted from Karlgaard, Rich. "About That First Job." *Forbes* 22 May 2006. Web. 13 Jan. 2010. <http://find.galegroup.com/gtx/start.do?prodId=ITOF&userGroupName=sunynassau>.

▶▶ after you read

Review Important Points

Going over the major points immediately after you have read, while the information is fresh in your mind, will help you to recall the content and record key ideas.

Exercise 4   **Reviewing Important Points**

Directions: Choose the best answer for each of the following questions using information provided in the selection. Write your answers in the spaces provided.

_a_ 1. The overall topic of this article is:
   a. providing advice for the first job.
   b. reading what interests you.
   c. finding the right mentor.
   d. thinking like an owner.

_c_ 2. From the details in paragraphs 2 and 3, we can infer that the author:
   a. decided to go to law school after college.
   b. graduated with a degree in physical education.
   c. was preoccupied with sports and not his studies.
   d. played on the track and field team in college.

<u>d</u> 3. **What was the author's first job after graduating from college?**

    a. coach in track and field
    b. physical education instructor
    c. sports editor
    d. security guard

<u>b</u> 4. **When did the author first become interested in contemporary literature?**

    a. in college
    b. after graduating from college
    c. in graduate school
    d. while working for *Sports Illustrated*

<u>b</u> 5. **In paragraph 4, what is the first piece of advice that the author offers to parents about their kids' reading habits?**

    a. Insist that your kids read assigned textbooks.
    b. Encourage them to read about subjects they enjoy.
    c. Buy a subscription to *Playboy* magazine.
    d. Foster a passion for reading literature.

<u>d</u> 6. **What is the main idea of paragraph 6?**

    a. A waterfall needs a turbine wheel to make electricity.
    b. Passion is critical for actual work.
    c. The best teachers direct a student's passion or energy.
    d. In school, the instructor or coach directs a student's passion, while at work it is the mentor.

<u>b</u> 7. **In paragraph 5, the *water* refers to the _____, and the *turbine wheel* is (are) the _____.**

    a. sports, career
    b. passion, teachers/coaches
    c. passion, mentor
    d. passion, energy

<u>d</u> 8. **Why did the author choose mentors throughout his career?**

    a. to develop effective communication skills
    b. to increase self-confidence
    c. to gain knowledge from successful individuals
    d. all of the above

<u>c</u> 9. **Why does the author recommend that kids should learn to think like an owner?**

    a. because the owner wants to keep a customer and make a profit
    b. because otherwise, people will stay at their jobs continuing to work for other people instead of aspiring to become the boss
    c. because people will waste their talents
    d. because if you don't, the boss may fire you.

<u>c</u> 10. **The overall pattern of organization is:**

    a. time or chronological order.
    b. definition and example.
    c. cause and effect.
    d. enumeration or listing.

Organize the Information

Organizing the information from a reading selection shows you have understood it and can restate the material in your own way.

Organizing the Information

Directions: In this selection, the author provides three pieces of advice that parents should offer to their kids in preparation for their first job. Complete the map that follows with details from the article.

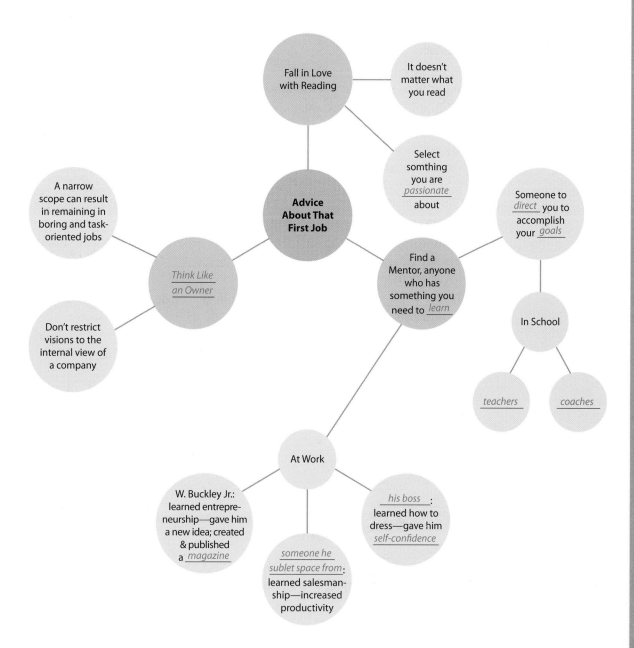

Fall in Love with Reading

It doesn't matter what you read

Select somthing you are *passionate* about

A narrow scope can result in remaining in boring and task-oriented jobs

Advice About That First Job

Someone to *direct* you to accomplish your *goals*

Think Like an Owner

Find a Mentor, anyone who has something you need to *learn*

Don't restrict visions to the internal view of a company

In School

teachers

coaches

At Work

W. Buckley Jr.: learned entrepreneurship—gave him a new idea; created & published a *magazine*

someone he sublet space from: learned salesmanship—increased productivity

his boss: learned how to dress—gave him *self-confidence*

Integrate the Vocabulary

Make the new vocabulary *your* vocabulary.

Exercise 6A   **Using Context Clues**

Directions: Using context clues, locate a word from the text box in Exercise 2 (page 440) that best completes the following sentences. Then write the word, or a form of the word, in the spaces provided.

1. I _pored_ through my textbook and all my class notes to prepare for my midterm in economics.

2. In my Early American Literature course, we are reading from the _prose_ of writers such as Poe, Emerson, and Thoreau.

3. The football game was almost forfeited until the _rival_ team showed up.

4. As a new _careerist_ in the field of marketing, I was required to attend a weeklong workshop.

5. I should have completed my business project; instead, I _shirked_ my responsibilities and went off to the movies.

6. My business professor has served as my _mentor_ throughout my college career, offering advice on career options and informing me of advanced educational opportunities.

7. I often _marveled_ at my classmate who was able to get 100 percent on every lab assignment.

8. It's unfortunate that a lot of great social programs to help the homeless are abandoned because of the _bureaucracy_ in the federal government.

9. In the _realm_ of the college, the dean usually makes the final decision about violations to the students' code of conduct.

10. Although some students see plagiarism as a _trivial_ matter, colleges may take disciplinary actions such as imposing probation, suspension, or expulsion.

11. I tried to _blot out_ how I was going to pass my psychology course and focused instead on writing a good paper for the next assignment.

12. A good _mechanism_ to generate ideas for an essay is brainstorming the topic.

Exercise 6B   **Learning Word Parts and Expanding Vocabulary**

Directions: Review the prefixes in the text box. Then match each word in column A with its meaning in column B. Write the letter of your answer in the spaces provided.

Review of Prefixes

inter-	between	*re-*	again, back
post-	after	*sub-*	below, under
pre-	before		

Column A	Column B
_d_ 1. postscript	a. an underlying or implicit meaning
_i_ 2. subconscious	b. an act that serves as a guide for future situations
_e_ 3. reimbursement	c. say or do again; repeat
_f_ 4. postbaccalaureate	d. a series of notes added to the end of a letter
_g_ 5. interdisciplinary	e. repayment for losses incurred
_b_ 6. precedence	f. an advanced degree after a B.A.
_h_ 7. recovery	g. combining two or more academic fields of study
_a_ 8. subtext	h. restore or return to a healthy state
_j_ 9. presuppose	i. operating in the mind beneath or beyond
_c_ 10. reiterate	j. to take for granted in advance

Make Personal Connections Through Writing and Discussion

Connect to the content on a personal level. How does it relate to you? How can you apply what you have read to other situations?

Exercise 7	**Making Personal Connections Through Writing and Discussion**

From the contacts you have already made in college, including professors, counselors, and coaches, who would you choose as a mentor? How could this individual help direct your passions and energy, guide you through college life, and assist you with your long-term goals? Write a paragraph in which you identify your mentor and describe the ways this person can help you stay on track in college and achieve your dreams.

_____

_____

_____

_____

_____

_____

_____

_____
_____
_____
_____
_____
_____
_____

Independent Reading
Selection 3

> ## Characteristics of Effective Leaders
> ### By Gareth R. Jones

This selection is adapted from an introductory business textbook. Within the chapter titled "Leadership, Influence, and Communication in Business," the author identifies five qualities of effective leaders. (Adapted from Introduction to Business: How Companies Create Value for People._)_

 before you read

Answer the following questions before you read the selection.

1. Have you ever served in a leadership position? Explain.

    _____
    _____

2. What do you believe are the qualities that make a good leader?

_____

_____

Prepare to Read

Preview "Characteristics of Effective Leaders" using the THIEVES technique.

| **Exercise 1** | **Developing Preview Questions** |

Directions: Based on your previewing, write *three* questions you anticipate will be answered in the selection.

Answers will vary.

1. _____

2. _____

3. _____

| **Exercise 2** | **Checking Out the Vocabulary** |

Directions: You will encounter the following vocabulary words in bold type in the reading selection.

| adept | enhance* | integrity* | proactive | renege |
| empathy | fostering | intuition | rapport | subordinates* |

*Denotes a word from Academic Word List

Read each of the following sentences in which a vocabulary word from the selection appears in bold. Select the best definition of the word from the choices provided. Write the letter of your choice on the line provided.

_c_ 1. Research has found that there are some personal characteristics or qualities that **enhance** the ability of *all* managers to function as effective leaders. (para. 1)

    a. make attractive
    b. raise the value
    c. improve the quality
    d. reduce the amount

_a_ 2. Indeed, managers who possess one or more of these qualities to a high degree might be particularly **adept** at one of the four leadership approaches. (para. 1)

    a. skillful
    b. awkward
    c. ineffective
    d. flexible

<u>d</u> 3. The first quality of an effective leader is ***intuition,*** *intelligence,* and the *cognitive ability* to process information and analyze a business problem, such as the need to identify what kind of leadership approach to use based on the characteristics of their employees and the work setting. (para. 2)

    a. prior knowledge
    b. sensitivity
    c. humor
    d. intelligence

<u>b</u> 4. Effective leaders demonstrate their confidence in their projects, however, and the ability of their **subordinates** to make them succeed. (para. 4)

    a. of inferior quality
    b. of lower rank
    c. of higher rank
    d. modifiers

<u>b</u> 5. A leader's ***ethics and moral integrity*** are also an important determinant of how effective he or she will be. (para. 5)

    a. perfectionism
    b. honesty
    c. trustworthiness
    d. bias

<u>a</u> 6. Leaders who play favorites, **renege** on their promises, or fail to reward good performance do not inspire confidence in their followers. (para. 5)

    a. fail to carry out a commitment
    b. keep and uphold
    c. surrender or give in
    d. break the rules

<u>c</u> 7. They seldom can persuade employees to act in a **proactive** way. (para. 5)

    a. showing energy and strength
    b. displaying aggressiveness
    c. acting in anticipation of future problems
    d. showing support for

<u>c</u> 8. A fifth characteristic of an effective leader is ***emotional intelligence and empathy,*** a person's ability to appreciate and understand the feelings and emotions of other people, as well as one's own, and to use this knowledge to guide one's behavior towards others. (para. 6)

    a. feelings of sorrow or sadness for another
    b. feelings of loyalty and devotion to another
    c. awareness and understanding the experiences of others
    d. showing no feelings at all

<u>d</u> 9. Some people seem to be "in control" of their own feelings and emotions and can use them in positive ways to build **rapport** with other people. (para. 6)

    a. a written record or account
    b. confidence or self-esteem

c. an agreement or accord

d. a connection or relationship

_b_ 10. Such leaders have a knack for smoothing over disputes, solving conflict, building cooperation, and **fostering** shared feelings that help build a strong corporate culture. (para. 6)

a. adopting

b. encouraging

c. increasing

d. diminishing

 # as **you read**

Establish Your Purpose

Read and annotate the selection below using the guidelines for active reading.

Actively Process as You Read: Independent Reading

Monitor your comprehension as you read. (See Chapter 2, page 54.)

Highlight the most important points. Write notes, responses, or questions that come to mind in the margin.

Characteristics of Effective Leaders
By Gareth R. Jones

---

1   Research has found that there are some personal characteristics or qualities that **enhance** the ability of *all* managers to function as effective leaders. Indeed, managers who possess one or more of these qualities to a high degree might be particularly **adept** at one of the four leadership approaches.

2   There are five important qualities or characteristics of effective leaders. The first quality of an effective leader is **intuition,** *intelligence,* and the *cognitive ability* to process information and analyze a business problem, such as the need to identify what kind of leadership approach to use based on the characteristics of their employees and the work setting. Employees are always "judging" their leaders. They respond favorably to leaders who demonstrate the ability to design good business plans and put them into action.

3   Effective leaders also display *energy, drive,* and a *need for achievement* to employees. These leaders show, through their own actions, their commitment to work hard and perform at a high level. They put in long hours and always seem to be in the right spot when problems arise, ready to put their cognitive and problem-solving abilities into action. Effective leaders never leave work before their employees on a regular basis.

4   Third, effective leaders tend to be *self-confident* and believe they are in control of their situation and that good things happen because of their *own* efforts. The future

success of a new company's business model, or of a new project in an established company, can never be predicted in advance. Effective leaders demonstrate their confidence in their projects, however, and the ability of their **subordinates** to make them succeed. Effective leaders don't give up, complain, or blame other people when problems arise—actions that show employees that they lack control of the situation. Instead, they build commitment by taking control of the situation and making quick decisions to correct problems. They encourage employees to believe in themselves and perform to the best of their abilities to help solve problems, something that often leads to success.

5   A leader's *ethics and moral **integrity*** are also an important determinant of how effective he or she will be. Leadership is about influence and persuasion. The willingness of followers to be persuaded is a function of their beliefs that the leader is a fair and honest person who can be trusted. Effective leaders want to protect the rights of their employees, and their personal reputation for making fair decisions is an important indicator of their moral integrity. Leaders who play favorites, **renege** on their promises, or fail to reward good performance do not inspire confidence in their followers. They seldom can persuade employees to act in a **proactive** way.

6   A fifth characteristic of an effective leader is *emotional intelligence and **empathy***, a person's ability to appreciate and understand the feelings and emotions of other people, as well as one's own, and to use this knowledge to guide one's behavior towards others. Some people seem to be "in control" of their own feelings and emotions and can use them in positive ways to build **rapport** with other people. Emotional intelligence helps a leader develop the social skills necessary to build good personal working relationships with individual employees and **cohesiveness** and cooperation among people who work in groups and teams. Such leaders have a knack for smoothing over disputes, solving conflict, building cooperation, and **fostering** shared feelings that help build a strong corporate culture.

7   In sum, the more of these characteristics that managers possess, the more likely they are to function effectively as leaders. Moreover, as we mentioned earlier, a person who has one or more of these qualities might be able to pursue a particular leadership approach particularly effectively.

8   To some degree the characteristics of an effective leader such as need for achievement, cognitive ability, self-confidence, or emotional intelligence are *personality characteristics* that people are born with. Nevertheless, most people can cultivate leadership qualities, and strengthen those they already possess if the put their minds to it and take advantage of opportunities that arise. We discussed in Chapter 3 how employees can seek mentors (commonly managers who are proven effective leaders) and by observing how they behave, learn effective leadership skills. Employees can also seek out leadership opportunities by taking on new job projects. In high school and college, students can practice their leadership skills by assuming positions in sports or social clubs or by volunteering to take on projects for local charities, hospitals, and so on. (Adapted from Jones 2007)

■ ■ ■

⏩ after you read

| Exercise 3 | **Answering Your Preview Questions** |

Directions: Look back at the questions you posed before you read the selection. If you have discovered the answers, write them on the lines provided. *Answers will vary.*

1. _____

_____

2. _____

_____

3. _____

_____

| Exercise 4 | **Reviewing Important Points** |

Directions: Choose the best answer for each of the following questions using the content provided in the reading. You may need to reread certain sections to be sure your responses are accurate.

_c_ 1. What is the overall main idea of this portion of the textbook?

   a. Effective leaders must possess the ability to process information.
   b. All managers have the qualities to become leaders.
   c. Possessing certain qualities will help improve the ability of all managers to serve as effective leaders.
   d. Students can cultivate leadership skills by volunteering to take on projects.

_b_ 2. What is the second characteristic of an effective leader?

   a. cognitive ability
   b. need for achievement
   c. internal locus of control
   d. moral integrity

_d_ 3. How do effective leaders demonstrate control of a situation in business?

   a. They don't attribute success to sheer luck.
   b. They don't blame others when a crisis arises.
   c. They make quick decisions to remediate a problem.
   d. All of the above.

_a_ 4. An effective leader possesses self-esteem and:

   a. promotes self-confidence in his employees.
   b. demands his employees follow his orders.
   c. takes complete authority in the success of a project.
   d. does not consider the suggestions of his employees to help solve problems.

_c_ 5. **In which paragraph does the author discuss the significance of honesty?**

   a. paragraph 1
   b. paragraph 2
   c. paragraph 5
   d. paragraph 8

_d_ 6. **What happens when a leader *lacks* integrity?**

   a. Others will not trust him.
   b. His reputation will be tarnished.
   c. Employees will not want to make decisions or take action.
   d. All of the above.

_d_ 7. **How does the quality of empathy impact the relationship between the leader and his employees?**

   a. The leader builds personal relationships with his subordinates outside of work.
   b. He supports the idea that workers solve their own conflicts.
   c. He participates in groups and teams.
   d. He encourages collaboration and teamwork.

_c_ 8. **The overall pattern of organization is:**

   a. order of importance.
   b. definition and example.
   c. listing and enumeration.
   d. cause and effect.

_a_ 9. **From paragraph 8, we can infer that _____ is *not* a characteristic with which you are born.**

   a. good ethics
   b. intelligence
   c. emotional intelligence
   d. drive

_c_ 10. **In what ways can students develop leadership qualities?**

   a. Find mentors and observe their behaviors.
   b. Devote free time to new projects.
   c. Assume leadership roles in athletics or clubs.
   d. Get a job in a hospital.

_a_ 11. **From this selection, we can infer that the information is based on:**

   a. studies and statistics.
   b. scientific research.
   c. the author of the textbook.
   d. the opinions of executives.

_d_ 12. **The tone of this selection is:**

   a. optimistic.
   b. serious.
   c. persuasive.
   d. informative.

| Exercise 5 | **Organizing the Information** |

Directions: Using the content of the reading selection, complete the outline that follows.

Five Qualities of Effective Leaders

I. Intuition, Intelligence, and Cognitive Ability

    A. Purpose

        1. to process information

        2. to analyze business problems

        3. to determine leadership approaches to use

            a. based on characteristics of employees

            b. depending on the work setting

    B. Effect on Employees

        1. Value leaders' ability to create good business

        2. *Respond positively to leaders who get things done*

II. Energy, Drive and Need for Achievement

    A. Show commitment to hard work

        1. *Work long hours*

        2. *Never leave before employees*

    B. Perform at a high level

        1. Always at the right place when a situation arises

        2. Ready to put cognitive and problem-solving skills into action

III. *Self-Confidence and Control*

    A. *Shows confidence in projects*

    B. *Believes employees will contribute to success*

    C. Crisis Control

        1. Attitude

            a. Doesn't give up

            b. Won't complain to others

            c. *Refrains from blaming others*

        2. Action

            a. Makes quick decisions to correct problems

            b. *Encourages employees to believe in themselves*

            c. *Supports subordinates in their abilities to help solve problems*

IV. Ethics and Moral Integrity

    A. *Leadership is about influence, persuasion and trust.*

    B. *Leaders want to maintain a good reputation with associates.*

C. They also want to engender trust with and confidence in their employees so they will perform well at their work.

    1. Make fair decisions

    2. Do not play favorites

    3. *Do not go back on promises*

    4. *Reward good performances*

V. *Emotional Intelligence and Empathy*

A. Definition

    1. *Appreciate and understand the emotions of other people and oneself*

    2. *Ability to use this knowledge to guide one's behavior toward others*

B. Impact

    1. Develop social skills necessary to build good working relationships with subordinates

       a. Engender cohesiveness among participants of groups

       b. *Possess the ability to negotiate disputes*

       c. *Build a strong corporate culture*

Exercise 6A   **Using the Context Clues**

Directions: Choose a word or a form of the word from the text box on page 451 to complete each of the following sentences. Write your choice in the spaces provided.

1. Nadine had said she would meet me after class, but she must have *reneged* on her promise because she was nowhere in sight.

2. To *enhance* my reading skills, I joined a weekly book club on campus.

3. Participating in a learning community helped me build a *rapport* with both my classmates and my professors.

4. Although I was fortunate to still have both parents, I *empathized* with my friend who had lost her mother in a car accident.

5. The college experience course served to *foster* self-confidence in my ability to succeed in college.

6. If I want to get an A in sociology, I had better be *proactive* and bring my paper over to the writing center before I submit it to my instructor.

7. I am pretty *adept* at computer skills, so my professor asked me to help him design his online course.

8. Being a psychology major, I am quite *intuitive* about issues and information that relate to learning disorders.

9. I doubted my friend's _integrity_____ when he said he was sick and then was spotted at the beach.

10. Although   my   boss   leaves   work   early   on   Fridays,   the _subordinates_____ must stay until 5 p.m.

| **Exercise 6B** | **Learning Word Parts and Expanding Your Vocabulary** |

Directions: Being familiar with the meaning of word parts will often provide you with a clue to the meaning of a new and unfamiliar word. In this selection, the ending -*ship* (as in the word *leadership*) means the act or instance. Other meanings of -*ship* are a quality or condition, status or office, or skill or capacity. After reading the following sentences and definitions, write the word that best fits each definition in the space provided.

apprenticeship — Before Thomas started his own plumbing business, he completed an **apprenticeship** with his uncle.

authorship — Her **authorship** of the news article was in question.

censorship — The producer of a local news network opposed any **censorship** of her show because she believes in freedom of speech.

entrepreneurship — If you are planning a new business, remember that innovation and newness is an integral part of any **entrepreneurship.**

internship — During the summer of my junior year, I received an **internship** at a law firm in New York City.

mentorship — A lot of major companies offer **mentorship** programs for their new employees.

ownership — The new **ownership** of the restaurant made a lot of major changes to the menu.

partnership — In a law firm **partnership**, several lawyers engage in a practice together; the primary purpose is to advise their clients on legal matters and represent them in civil or criminal cases.

1. _apprenticeship_____ work for another to learn a trade

2. _censorship_____ the act or process of banning something considered objectionable

3. _mentorship_____ a formal relationship between an individual and a professional in which the professional furthers his/her goals or career with knowledge and skills

4. _entrepreneurship_____ the act of starting a new business

5. _authorship_____ with reference to an author, creator, or producer of a work

6. _internship_____ a formal program to provide practical experience for a beginner in a profession or career.

7. _ownership_____ the fact of being an owner of an object or business

8. _partnership_ a contract between two individuals or more who agree to furnish money and labor and share in profits and losses of a business venture

| **Exercise 7** | **Making Personal Connections Through Writing and Discussion** |

Directions: Think about yourself in relation to the essay you just read. Read the description of three candidates for the position of vice president at Gold Instruments Company. Based on "Characteristics of Effective Leaders," which applicant would you hire for the job? Support your opinion for or against each candidate with specific statements from the selection. Then record your selection and reasons on the spaces provided.

Candidate A

- Has been described as a hardworking employee, working overtime when necessary
- Has a regular golf game every Tuesday at 5 p.m.
- Was mentored by the CEO
- Coached Little League
- Volunteered at Mercy Hospital

Candidate B

- Negotiated with employees for a raise, rather than risk losing them to a picket line
- Provides incentives to employees who bring in the most sales
- Has fired employees for missing project deadlines
- Was active in community service—headed up a fund-raising project for senior citizens
- Was suspended from school for plagiarism but was reinstated later without penalties

Candidate C

- Graduated with honors from a top-tier university
- Often works weekends
- Provides 10 sick days for personal illness
- Gives bonuses to all his employees
- Was president of the Student Council

The best candidate is _____ .

Reasons:

_____

_____

⌐reflect AND respond ⌐

Now that you have read three selections related to the world of work, you have a broader and better understanding of the topic.

Directions: Complete a journal response for this module. Read the following questions. Select two to which you would like to respond. Write your responses on a separate piece of paper. Write at least one page.

1. What did you learn about the selection of majors, jobs and careers, and leadership qualities?

2. How does this information apply to you? Make connections to your own experience(s). What do these readings make you think about?

3. What else would you like to know about some of the topics discussed in this module?

Readings About Physical Health and Well-Being

Get Acquainted with the Issue

Going to college is stimulating and invigorating, yet also demanding. It is important that you stay as healthy as possible during this time so that you can take on these challenges. Exercising regularly, eating a nutritious diet, and avoiding the intake of harmful substances, such as cigarettes, drugs, and alcohol, will go a long way to support your overall health. Health is a combination of your physical, mental, and emotional well-being. You can read more about issues impacting your emotional well-being in Module 7.

In this module, you will read selections that deal with topics related to your physical health. In "Brain Stays Young into Old Age if You Stay Physically Fit," you will learn about the benefits of exercise on your mental abilities. In the paired readings for "Should the Legal Drinking Age Be Lowered to 18?" you will read opposing views on the controversial issue of the appropriate drinking age in the United States.

Guided Reading
Reading Selection 1

Brain Stays Young into Old Age
if You Stay Physically Fit

Medical News Today

This article, from an online health news website, discusses the importance of exercise to maintaining good mental functioning as you age.

⏪ before you read

Think about what you already know about a topic before you begin reading. Then you will be able to attach your new learning to this background knowledge and more easily understand the new information. (See Chapter 2, page 38.)

Discuss or write your responses to the following questions about your *own* experiences on the topic of exercise and aging.

1. Do you exercise regularly? If so, how? Why?

2. Consider those older than you. In what ways are they physically active? Do you think it is possible to stay physically fit well into your seventies, eighties, or even nineties?

3. If you knew that a grandparent or elderly person in your life could benefit mentally by staying physically fit, what would you recommend?

Prepare to Read

Preview the selection "Brain Stays Young into Old Age if You Stay Physically Fit," using the THIEVES strategy on page 40.

Exercise 1   **Previewing**

Directions: Complete the following items.

1. Take a look at the selection, and check off all the items that are available to you for preview.

   X   Title

   ___ Headings

   X   Introduction

   X   Every first sentence in each paragraph

   X   Visuals/vocabulary

   ___ End of chapter questions

   X   Summary/concluding paragraph

2. Actively preview the selection by reading and highlighting the items you have checked.

3. Based on your preview, place an "X" next to all those items you predict will be discussed in the selection.

   X   a. Staying physically fit has intellectual as well as physical benefits.

   ___ b. Older Americans need to take vitamins to support their health.

   X   c. Dr. Arthur Kramer did some research in the field of fitness and mental functioning.

   X   d. In addition to supporting brain functioning, aerobic exercise improves the health of your heart.

   X   e. At least two kinds of experiments were conducted to study this.

   ___ f. Experiments on the brain are carried out on children as well.

Check Out the Vocabulary

You will find the following vocabulary words in bold type in the reading selection. Some are repeated more than once in the text. Do you know what some of these words mean? Knowing the meaning of all these words will increase your understanding of the material.

| aerobic | cardiovascular | dementia | institute* | | neurons |
| assessed* | cognitive* | enhance* | mental function* | synapses |

*Denotes a word from the Academic Word List

Exercise 2   **Checking Out the Vocabulary**

Directions: Look at each word taken from the reading selection. Read each sentence that follows. Choose the best definition for the word, and write the letter of the definition you select on the line provided

_b_ **1. aerobic**

This is known as **aerobic** fitness. (para. 1) (HINT: Read the paragraph. What does it have to do with?)

a. having to do with the air and flight
b. involving increasing oxygen use for body functioning, often through movement and exercise
c. concerned with older groups of people
d. related to thinking, studying, and reasoning

_c_ **2. institute**

Dr. Arthur Kramer, from the Beckman **Institute** at the University of Illinois, said . . . (para. 2) (HINT: Think about what might exist at a university. In what context might a researcher work?)

a. prison for the criminally insane
b. asylum for the mentally ill
c. organization for study or a particular purpose
d. gym and physical fitness center

_d_ **3. enhance**

. . . fitness can **enhance** brain and mental function . . . (para. 2) (HINT: Would this be something positive or negative?)

a. welcome
b. decrease, make less important
c. minimize, make smaller
d. heighten, increase in value or desirability

_a_ **4. mental function**

. . . fitness can enhance brain and **mental function**. (para. 2) (HINT: mental has to do with the mind; function refers to activity)

a. the activities of the brain
b. school work
c. relating to insanity
d. physical activities, as in a fitness center

_a_ **5. cognitive**

If you do this or the equivalent amount of movement, your **cognitive** function will be enhanced. (para. 2) (HINT: Read sentence 2 in paragraph 1. Also, consider the meaning of mental function.)

a. intellectual activity such as thinking, reasoning, or remembering
b. emotional issues, such as anxiety, depression, or love
c. physical activities, such as running and jogging
d. recreational endeavors, such as vacationing and dining out

_b_ **6. neurons**

Apart from improving blood flow to the brain, it also helps the formation of new **neurons**, or brain cells. (para. 3) (HINT: Notice the use of the definition context clue signal word *or.*)

a. bombs
b. brain cells
c. friendships
d. blood cells

_d_ **7. synapses**

Exercising also increases the number of connections, called **synapses**, between the neurons. (para. 7) (HINT: The word is defined in the phrase preceding it. The term *between* also is a clue.)

a. the central part of a neuron
b. the outer layer of a nerve cell
c. blood in the brain cell
d. the connections between nerve cells

_c_ **8. dementia**

Researchers observed forty-one older adults who had no **dementia**. (para. 5) (HINT: Use context clues. Pay attention to the word *no.*)

a. a condition related to devil worship
b. a progressive condition of making preparations for something
c. a progressive condition of failing mental functioning
d. referring to physical strength

_b_ **9. assessed**

They completed a variety of exercise tests and their fitness was **assessed**. (para. 5) (HINT: Think of what the purpose of exercise tests would be.)

a. monitored
b. measured or evaluated
c. weakened
d. strengthened

_a_ **10. cardiovascular**

At the end of the six months the aerobic group had better **cardiovascular** health. (para. 7) (HINT: Are you familiar with a cardio workout? What does it relate to? What kind of doctor is a cardiologist?)

a. the heart and flow of blood through the body
b. the lungs
c. mental well-being
d. cognitive ability

 **as you read**

Establish Your Purpose

Now you are ready to read and annotate the selection, "Brain Stays Young into Old Age if You Stay Physically Fit." Focus on major points of information. Read to learn how and why researchers came to the conclusion revealed in the title.

Actively Process While You Read: Guided Reading

Stop and think about the information as you read.

Exercise 3   **Processing While You Read**

Directions: Answer the questions that appear in bold print at the conclusion of each paragraph. This will help you monitor your reading process and understand the material.

> # Brain Stays Young into Old Age if You Stay Physically Fit
> Medical News Today

1 Researchers have discovered that the aging brain benefits from physical fitness. According to a new study, the fitter older people are the better their mental abilities are. This is known as **aerobic** fitness.

What is the main idea of the paragraph?

The main idea is that physical fitness helps the brain as people get older.

2 Dr. Arthur Kramer, from the Beckman **Institute** at the University of Illinois, said that fitness can **enhance** brain and **mental function**. You do not need to run marathons or do giant workouts. Even moderate physical activity keeps the brain young. Walking two or three miles a week would be enough to keep your brain in tip-top condition. If you do this or the equivalent amount of movement, your **cognitive** function will be **enhanced**.

What kind of activity can enhance cognitive function?

Moderate physical activity, such as walking a few miles a week, is all that is needed.

3   Scientists have known for a while that **aerobic** training has a positive effect on the brains of older animals. This occurs for several reasons. Apart from improving blood flow to the brain, it also helps the formation of new **neurons**, or brain cells. Exercising also increases the number of connections, called **synapses**, between the **neurons**.

Why has aerobic training positively effected the brains of older animals?

It improves the blood flow to the brain, helps form new neurons, and increases the number of synapses between the neurons.

4   What scientists did not know until now was whether this applied to humans as well. Kramer's study was conducted to address this issue. The findings can be found in the journal *Proceedings of the National Academy of Sciences.*

What did Kramer hope to find out in his study?

He wanted to know if the effects of exercise that were seen in animals would be the same for humans.

The Study

5   The researchers carried out two sets of experiments with older groups of adults. In the first experiment on which data was collected, researchers observed forty-one older adults who had no **dementia**. They completed a variety of exercise tests and their fitness was **assessed**. Next, their brain activity was measured while they performed mental tasks that challenged their **cognitive**, or mental and thinking skills. Those who were fitter physically were able to carry out the **cognitive** tasks better. The part of the brain that is involved in focusing and paying attention worked significantly better in these people.

Who was studied in the first experiment?

forty-one older adults without dementia

What was discovered?

The adults who were in better physical shape did better on the cognitive tasks, especially in focusing and paying attention.

6   In the next experiment, another group of older adults was divided into two parts. One part had to do stretching and toning activities for several days during a week. The other part of the group was instructed in doing mild **aerobic** activities. These included movements like walking, but not major workouts. The groups maintained these activities over a period of six months.

What was the difference in the kind of exercising done by each of the two groups in this part of the study?

One group did stretching and toning activities, whereas the other group did mild aerobic activities like walking.

How long did the study last?

for six months

7   At the end of the six months the **aerobic** group had better **cardiovascular** health. Their attention activity was also much better than the stretching and toning group. The aerobic group had better blood supply and activity in part of the brain that deals with attention. The stretching and toning group, on the other hand, saw no improvement in their brain or attention activities.

Which group saw the most benefits at the end of the study?

the aerobic group

How did they benefit?

They had better cardiovascular health and attention activity.

■ ■ ■

 **after you read**

Review Important Points

Going over major points immediately after you read, while the information is fresh in your mind, will help you recall the content and record key ideas.

Exercise 4 **Reviewing Important Points**

Directions: Answer the following questions based on the information provided in the selection. You may need to go back to the text and reread certain portions to be sure your responses are correct and can be supported by information in the text. Write the letter of your choice in the space provided.

_b_ 1. **What is the author's overall message in this selection?**

   a. Adults should take up exercise so that they are in better physical condition during their older years.

   b. Being physically fit has long-term benefits for the brain and cognitive abilities.

   c. Some researchers believe that the benefits of exercise in animals are similar to the benefits in human beings.

   d. Everyone needs to exercise.

_d_ 2. **The positive effects of aerobic training on the brains of animals are caused by:**

   a. improved blood flow to the brain.

   b. the formation of new brain cells.

   c. the increased number of synapses.

   d. all of the above.

_a_ 3. **We can infer that all of the following would be examples of moderate physical activity except:**

   a. running a marathon.

   b. walking your dog around the block.

   c. going up and down the steps in your home several times a day.

   d. taking a leisurely bike ride after dinner.

_c_ 4. **According to paragraph 5, the cognitive ability that was most impacted by physical fitness focused on:**

   a. short-term ability.

   b. reasoning and critical thinking.

   c. focusing and paying attention.

   d. long-term memory.

_a_   5. The purpose of paragraphs 5–7 is to:

   a. explain how the study was conducted and give the results.
   b. criticize the study.
   c. tell ways in which people can exercise to improve their cognition.
   d. none of the above.

_d_   6. In paragraph 6, by discussing the different types of exercise activities used by each part of the group, the author uses the writing pattern of:

   a. definition.
   b. cause and effect.
   c. listing.
   d. comparison and contrast.

_c_   7. The implied main idea of paragraph 6 is that:

   a. The groups in the study did different types of exercise.
   b. The study lasted six months.
   c. Mild aerobic exercise is the most important.
   d. Stretching and toning was completed several days a week.

_b_   8. The topic of paragraph 7 is:

   a. cardiovascular health.
   b. the results of the six month study.
   c. aerobic exercise and blood flow.
   d. the aerobic group.

_b_   9. The overall organizational pattern of this article is:

   a. time order.
   b. cause and effect.
   c. listing.
   d. definition.

_c_ 10. From this article, we can infer that:

   a. Senior citizens should be careful not to overexert themselves when exercising.
   b. The more strenuous an activity, the more impact it will have on your mental functioning.
   c. It is a good idea to stay physically active and fit throughout your entire life.
   d. Stretching and toning are valuable aerobic activities.

Organize the Information

Organizing the information you have learned from a reading selection shows you have understood it and can restate the material in a different way. You can use this reorganized material to help you study for exams and prepare for written assignments. (See Chapter 9.)

| **Exercise 5** | **Organizing the Information** |

Directions: Using the reading selection, including the results of the study results, make a list of at least *five* positive effects of aerobic exercise on the brain, health, and/or cognitive skills.

Answers may vary.

1. improves blood flow to the brain, 2. helps the formation of new neurons, 3. increases the number of synapses, 4. improves ability to focus and pay attention, 5. better cardiovascular health

Integrate the Vocabulary

Make the new vocabulary presented in the reading YOUR vocabulary. In addition to learning the meaning of new words, you should also learn related word forms.

| **Exercise 6A** | **Using Context Clues** |

Directions: For each sentence, select the word from the text box on p. 465 that is a synonym for the word or words in parentheses and best completes the sentence. Then write it in the space provided.

1. I was saddened to learn that my grandmother had been diagnosed with (a progressive condition that affects cognitive functioning) *dementia* and would now live in a facility to care for her special needs.

2. To (improve the quality of) *enhance* her schoolwork, the college freshman decided to attend several sessions at the tutorial help center on campus.

3. Wanting to continue his studies in behavioral psychology, Bob enrolled in the new (formal organization for professional study) *institute* that recently opened in the next town.

4. Professor Brown informed the class that the biology exam would include the identification of the parts of (brain cells) *neurons*, including the (connections to one another) *synapses*.

5. Exercise that is (involving the increased use of oxygen through repeated movements) *aerobic* is great for improving (heart and circulatory system) *cardiovascular* health.

6. Before enrolling in college, all potential students are required to take a placement exam to (measure) *assess* their achievement in reading, math, and writing.

7. Although Brian recovered physically from the car accident, his head injury left a long-term impairment to his (intellectual capacity, including thinking, reasoning, and memory) *cognitive* ability. His (capacity to use his mind productively) *mental function* would never be the same.

| **Exercise 6B** | **Learning Synonyms or Similar Expressions** |

Directions: Writers often use synonyms or other expressions to restate important terms in selections. Scan the article and list the synonyms for "cognition." Then check the dictionary or a thesaurus for additional synonyms.

Located in the Text: Words that mean **cognition**— *mental abilities, thinking skills, mental function*

Found in the Dictionary or Thesaurus: Synonyms for **cognition**— *mental processes, knowing, the process of thinking*

Make Personal Connections Through Writing and Discussion

When you make your new learning relevant to yourself in some way, it becomes more meaningful and easier to remember. Whenever you read, try to connect to the content on a personal level. How does it relate to you? How can you apply what you have read to other situations? What else would you like to know?

| Exercise 7 | **Making Personal Connections** |

Responses will vary.

Create a list of *five* moderate aerobic activities you could integrate into your life.

1. _____

2. _____

3. _____

4. _____

5. _____

Self-Monitored Reading
Reading Selection 2

> # Should the Legal Drinking Age Be Lowered to 18?
> ## Yes! Drinking "Licenses" Promote Responsible Behavior
> ### By David J. Hanson

This is the first of two essays, presented as paired readings, in a professional pub-lication for college faculty called AFT On Campus. *It presents one point of view on whether or not the legal drinking age should be lowered. What do you think? David J. Hanson is professor emeritus of sociology at the State University of New York at Potsdam.*

◀◀ before you read

Answer the following questions before you read the selection.   *Answers will vary.*

1. What do you think the legal age to drink alcohol should be? Why?
   _____
   _____

2. Do you think young adults should be required to obtain a license in order to drink alcoholic beverages? Why or why not?
   _____
   _____

3. Do you think that drinking alcohol early in life can have long-lasting, negative effects? If so, in what ways?
   _____
   _____

Prepare to Read

Preview the reading selection by applying the THIEVES strategy (p. 40).

Exercise 1   Previewing

Directions: Based on your preview, respond to the following questions:

1. What is the author's point of view concerning lowering the drinking age?
   He's in favor of it.

2. What method of monitoring young adult drinkers is suggested by Profes-sor John McCardell?
   He suggests issuing drinking licenses to 18- to 20-year-old adults who have completed an alcohol education course.

3. What two arguments against his opinion will the author address in his article?
   He will discuss whether or not alcohol is harmful to young brains and the idea that those who begin drinking young are likely to experience problems later in life.

Check Out the Vocabulary

You will encounter the following words in this reading. They are in bold type in the selection. Are you already familiar with some of them? Knowing the meaning of this vocabulary will increase your comprehension of the material.

> compliance   correlation   formerly   incrementally   preexisting
>
> consume*   emeritus   graduated   moderation   underlying*
>
> *Denotes a word from the Academic Word List

Exercise 2   **Checking Out the Vocabulary**

Directions: Look at each boldface word taken from the reading selection. Use the context of the sentence and the hint provided to select the best definition from the choices listed. Write the letter of your choice on the line provided.

_b_ 1. **emeritus**

Professor **Emeritus** John McCardell, formerly of Middlebury College, is now the director of ChooseResponsibility.org. (para. 2) (HINT: He used to be at Middlebury, now he is elsewhere.)

a. currently holding an important position
b. no longer in a position, but still holding rank or title
c. in competition for a teaching position
d. fired from one's position of rank

_a_ 2. **formerly**

. . . John McCardell, **formerly** of Middlebury College, is now the director . . . (para. 2) (HINT: Think of the opposite of now.)

a. previously, in the past
b. having graduated from
c. president
d. thrown out of

_a_ 3. **graduated**

Such licenses might be **graduated**, like a learner's permit is a step with privileges en route to obtaining a driver's license. (para. 2) (HINT: Look at the comparison, "like a learner's permit is a step . . . ," and think of the meaning of *gradually.*)

a. progressive, in steps
b. finished with school
c. available in grade school
d. all at once

_c_ 4. **incrementally**

Restrictions could be lifted **incrementally**, little by little. (para. 2) (HINT: Look at the preceding sentence in the text. Also, think about the meaning of *little by little.*)

a. occurring in giant leaps
b. rarely ever changing
c. occurring in small changes or amounts
d. in an unfair manner

_d_ **5. compliance**

More and more freedoms to consume alcohol would be allowed, after successful **compliance** with all the many conditions. (para. 2) (HINT: Think logically about under what circumstances increased freedoms would be allowed.)

a. going against, in opposition to
b. making fun of
c. complaining about
d. going along with, conformity in fulfilling requirements

_a_ **6. moderation**

Actually, there's no evidence that drinking in **moderation** damages developing brains. (para. 3) (HINT: Think logically about what would make sense here.)

a. limited amount, without intensity or severity
b. modern times, present day
c. a great deal, in large quantities
d. in secret

_c_ **7. consume**

And the frequently cited research on the subject uses rats and people who are alcohol abusers—not young people who **consume** in moderation. (para. 3) (HINT: What are the young people doing with the alcohol?)

a. fight
b. abuse
c. to eat or drink in quantity
d. distribute

_c_ **8. correlation**

What about the fact that those who begin drinking at an early age are more likely to experience drinking problems later in life? This **correlation** appears to result from preexisting personality factors that have been identified. (para. 4) (HINT: Look at the sentence that precedes the word. What is being established?)

a. shocking event or outcome
b. correction or editorial review
c. relationship or association, occurring together beyond chance
d. negative result

_d_ **9. preexisting**

This correlation appears to result from **preexisting** personality factors . . . (para. 4) (HINT: Look at the word parts. The prefix *pre-* means *before* and the root, *exist*, means to be or to live.)

a. complicated
b. harmful personality factors
c. prehistoric
d. in place from earlier or before

_a_ 10. **underlying**

The idea that a person would consider, or want, to begin to drink early in life speaks to the **underlying** problems that they already have. (para. 4) (HINT: The prefix *under-* means beneath or below.)

a. beneath, below the surface, the basic foundation
b. untruthful
c. extreme, monumental
d. many and various

▶ as you read

Establish Your Purpose

Now, read and annotate the selection using the guidelines for active reading, and focusing on the major points of information.

Actively Process While You Read: Self-Monitored Reading

Monitor your comprehension as you read. (See Chapter 2, page 54.) Be sure to stop to reflect at the conclusion of each paragraph, and ask yourself the following questions:

■ Did I understand what I have just read?
■ What is the main idea of the paragraph?
■ Am I ready to continue?

Exercise 3   **Processing While You Read**

Directions: Highlight the most important points in each paragraph. Then, write the key topics and main ideas in the spaces provided in the margins. Finally, underline or number the supporting details in the text.

Should the Legal Drinking Age Be Lowered?
Yes! Drinking "Licenses" Promote Responsible Behavior
By David J. Hanson

Notes
Topic _____
_____ 1
Main Idea _____
_____
_____

Imagine that we prepared young people for driving the way we "prepare" them for drinking—if they choose to do so when they come of age. We would tell them that safe driving requires physical maturity and coordination, knowledge of rules of the road, driving experience that we won't give them because they're not ready, and emotional maturity that they don't have. Then, when they reached a certain age, we would issue them licenses and tell them that it's much safer to take public transportation. We hope they don't drive, but that if they do they should be careful and try to stay out of accidents.

Create Responsibility

2   Professor **Emeritus** John McCardell, **formerly** of Middlebury College, is the director of ChooseResponsibility.org. He proposes that we consider issuing drinking licenses to 18- to 20-year-old adults who have completed a specified alcohol-education course. They also must never have been found guilty of violating, or breaking, a state's alcohol laws. Such licenses might be **graduated**, in the way a learner's permit is a step with privileges en route to obtaining a driver's license. Restrictions could be lifted **incrementally**, little by little. More and more freedoms to consume alcohol would be allowed, after successful **compliance** with all the many conditions.

Some Myths About Alcohol Consumption

3   What about the argument that alcohol damages young brains? Actually, there's no evidence that drinking in **moderation** damages developing brains. If it did, most Italians, French, Greeks, Spaniards, Portuguese and many others would be suffering mental defects. And the frequently cited research on the subject uses rats and people who are alcohol abusers—not young people who **consume** in moderation.

4   What about the fact that those who begin drinking at an early age are more likely to experience drinking problems later in life? This **correlation** appears to result from **preexisting** personality factors that have been identified. The idea that a person would consider, or want, to begin to drink early in life speaks to the **underlying** problems that they already have. In fact, psychologists have been able to observe preschoolers and predict accurately which ones will begin drinking earlier and will later have problems.

5   It's time to rethink our approach to alcohol education and public policy.

Source: Adapted from David J. Hanson, "Should the Legal Drinking Age Be Lowered? Yes! Drinking 'Licenses' Promote Responsible Behavior," *AFT On Campus*, Vol. 28, No. 2, November/December 2008, p. 3.

■ ■ ■

 **after you read**

Review Important Points

Going over the major points immediately after you have read, while the information is fresh in your mind, will help you recall the content and record key ideas.

| Exercise 4 | **Reviewing Important Points** |

Directions: Choose the best answer for each of the following questions using information provided in the selection. Write your answers in the spaces provided.

_b_ 1. The topic of the reading selection is:

    a. raising the legal drinking age.
    b. lowering the legal drinking age.
    c. prohibiting teenage drinking.
    d. encouraging teen use of alcohol.

_d_ 2. What is the main idea, or thesis, of this selection?

    a. The legal drinking age should be raised, as young people are not mature enough to handle alcohol.
    b. No one under 20 years of age should be permitted to drink alcohol.
    c. Drinking among young people is on the rise and is causing many problems on the road.
    d. The legal drinking age should be lowered, provided responsible behavior is taught and monitored through the issue of drinking licenses.

_c_ 3. The primary purpose of the author is to:

    a. entertain the reader.
    b. inform the reader.
    c. persuade the reader.
    d. instruct the reader.

_b_ 4. In paragraph 1, the author relates hypothetically preparing young people to drive with the way we prepare them to drink to make his point. The writing pattern he uses is:

    a. definition.
    b. comparison and contrast.
    c. classification.
    c. cause and effect.

_a_ 5. The main idea of paragraph 2 is that:

    a. We should issue licenses to drink to those who have taken the appropriate course, much like we issue driver's licenses.
    b. People getting a drinking license must never have committed a crime.
    c. Drinking licenses should be issued to those over 21.
    d. Compliance with conditions should lead to more freedoms.

_a_ 6. In paragraph 3, the main idea is that:

    a. Alcohol in moderation does not cause brain damage.
    b. Moderate drinking does, indeed, cause brain damage in young adults.
    c. Young people always abuse alcohol.
    d. Rats should not be used in research on alcoholism.

_b_ 7. The topic sentence of paragraph 3 is the:

    a. first sentence.
    b. second sentence.
    c. third sentence.
    d. fourth sentence.

_b_ 8. We can infer from the argument in paragraph 3 that the author believes:
   a. All research with rats is invalid.
   b. Many Europeans drink at an early age.
   c. Moderate drinking can sometimes cause brain damage.
   d. Studies on alcohol abusers should be used to gather data on this topic.

_c_ 9. How does the author respond to the concern that those who begin drinking at an early age are more likely to experience drinking problems later on in life?
   a. He thinks that people are overestimating the problem.
   b. He believes that psychologists should observe preschoolers to get a better handle on the situation.
   c. He believes that alcohol abuse is caused by personality factors that appear early on, rather than because of the freedom to drink at an earlier age.
   d. He thinks that preschoolers who try alcohol will have drinking problems later in life.

_a_ 10. We can say that the author of this selection appears to be:
   a. biased.
   b. stubborn.
   c. objective.
   d. foolish.

Organize the Information

Organizing the information from a reading selection shows you have understood it and can restate the material in your own way.

| Exercise 5 | **Organizing the Information** |

Directions: Complete the following outline. Write your answers in the spaces provided.

> ### Should the Drinking Age Be Lowered?
> **Yes! Drinking "Licenses" Promote Responsible Behavior**

I. Create Responsibility

  A. Proposal of _John McCardell_

    1. Professor Emeritus of _Middlebury College_

    2. Director of _ChooseResponsibility.org_

  B. Issue _drinking licenses_

    1. To those adults aged _18_ to _20_

      a. Have completed _an alcohol education course_

      b. Never found guilty of _violating a state's alcohol laws_

2. Graduated
   a. Like a _learner's permit_
   b. Incrementally, _restrictions_ would be lifted.
   c. More and more freedom to consume alcohol after _compliance_ with the many conditions

II. Myths About Consumption
   A. Alcohol damages _young brains_ .
      1. _Europeans_ who tend to drink early are not brain damaged.
      2. Research that supports this was done on _rats_ and _alcohol abusers_ , not young people who use alcohol in _moderation_ .
   B. Those who drink early are more likely to experience drinking problems later.
      1. The correlation is based on preexisting _personality factors_ .
      2. The factors begin as early as _preschool_ , rather than starting because of an earlier drinking age.

Integrate the Vocabulary

Make the new vocabulary *your* vocabulary.

Exercise 6A   Using Context Clues

Directions: Locate a word from the text box in Exercise 2 (page 474) that best completes the following sentences. Then write the word, or a form of the word, in the spaces provided.

1. Not managing one's time effectively is an _underlying_ cause for difficulties in college.

2. The college insists that all students who wish to register for and remain in class are in _compliance_ with the regulations about immunizations and the submission of required documents.

3. Rather than go on a diet, Dr. Fender recommends that young adults watch the amounts of any food they _consume_ and eat all foods with carbohydrates and sugars in _moderation_ .

4. There is a high _correlation_ between lack of physical exercise and depression, so to feel better, get up and be active!

5. Rabbi Jacobs was awarded the title Rabbi _Emeritus_ upon her retirement from the congregation after serving for 20 years.

6. Health insurance companies are criticized for denying insurance coverage to people who have a _preexisting_ condition before they want to enroll in plan.

7. Janice decided to organize her room in small _increments_ . She would begin with her closet, move onto her desk, and finally tackle the piles of laundry.

8. Income tax rates in the United States are _graduated_ _____. The more one earns, the higher percentage of income one pays to the government.

9. Brian certainly has come a long way. _Formerly_ _____ a cashier at the supermarket, he now owns a chain of convenience stores all over the country.

| Exercise 6B | **Learning Words' Multiple Meanings** |

Directions: Several of the vocabulary words listed in the selection have more than one meaning. Read these words below. Place a check next to the definition of the term *as it is used in the selection*. To make your decision, find and reread the word as it is used in the text. Use context clues to guide your thinking.

1. **graduated**

    ____ to earn a degree from an educational institution

    _X_ progressive, to occur in increments

2. **moderation**

    ____ the presiding over a public forum, debate, or program

    _X_ not in an extreme, excessive, or intense way

3. **consume**

    _X_ eat or drink

    ____ use up, do away with completely

Make Personal Connections Through Writing and Discussion

Connect to the content on a personal level. How does it relate to you? How can you apply what your have read to other situations?

| Exercise 7 | **Making Personal Connections Through Writing and Discussion** |

Responses will vary.

1. What do you think about the idea of issuing licenses for young adults to consume alcohol? Would you want such an opportunity if you are under-age right now? Do you think it is a wise solution to an ongoing issue?

    _____
    _____
    _____
    _____
    _____

2. In small groups, discuss your answers to the following questions with other students, and then share your responses with the whole class.

    ■ What is the legal age to consume alcohol in your state? Do you think it is appropriate?

    ■ What do most people feel about the idea of drinking licenses?

    ■ What are some other alternatives for creating responsible drinking?

    ■ Do you think drinking at an earlier age will cause problems later on?

Independent Reading
Selection 3

> ## Should the Drinking Age Be Lowered to 18?
> **No! It's Not Safe for Youth, nor on the Roads**
>
> By William De Jong

This essay counters, or opposes, the preceding selection. It is written by a professor of social and behavioral sciences at Boston University School of Public Health. Read it to discover Professor De Jong's arguments in favor of maintaining the legal drinking age at 21.

◀ before you read

Answer the following questions before you read the selection.

1. Do you believe that 18 year olds are responsible enough to monitor their use of alcoholic beverages? Why or why not?

   _____

   _____

2. What would you say to those who believe that if teens are permitted to drink alcohol, there will be an even greater number of alcohol-related car accidents, injuries, and death?

   _____

   _____

Prepare to Read

Preview the reading selection using the THIEVES strategy (p. 40).

| Exercise 1 | **Developing Preview Questions** |

Directions: Based on your previewing, write *three* questions you anticipate   *Answers may vary.*
will be answered in the selection.

1. _____

2. _____

3. _____

| Exercise 2 | **Checking Out the Vocabulary** |

Directions: You will encounter the following words in bold type in this reading.

> colleague*   epidemiologist   initiative*   overseas*   proponents
>
> emulate*   fluctuated*   mounted   predictably*   uniform*
>
> *Denotes a word from the Academic Word List

Read each of the following sentences in which a vocabulary word from the selection appears in bold. Select the best definition of the word from the choices provided, and write the letter of your choice on the line provided.

_b_ **1. colleague**

Talk to my public health **colleagues** about the proposal to lower the minimum legal drinking age to 18 . . . (para. 1)

a. employer, boss
b. co-worker, associate in a profession
c. instructor
d. friend or companion

_d_ **2. mounted**

When the death toll **mounted**, Congress passed legislation in 1984 to pressure the states to adopt an age-21 law . . . (para. 2)

a. decreased, lessened
b. stayed the same
c. varied, went up and down
d. increased in amount or extent

_c_ **3. initiative**

Members of the Amethyst **Initiative**—college presidents who have called for a renewed debate about lowering the legal drinking age—are sincere in believing that the age-21 law doesn't work. (para. 3)

    a. resource center entry into a group

    b. protest group

    c. an introductory step in review, organization, or study

    d. government agency

_a_ **4. epidemiologist**

University of Minnesota **epidemiologists** . . . reviewed 132 research studies . . . (para. 3)

    a. a medical professional who deals with the spread and control of disease

    b. a psychologist who studies animals and animal behavior

    c. a researcher who studies agriculture

    d. a physician who deals with alcohol and substance abuse

_b_ **5. uniform**

Their conclusion is that a **uniform** national age-21 law has reduced both youth alcohol use and alcohol-related traffic crashes. (para. 3)

    a. inconsistent, very different

    b. consistent, not varying

    c. confusing, very difficult

    d. problematic, causing stress

_b_ **6. fluctuated**

Rates of heavy drinking among college students have **fluctuated** very little since the federal legislation was passed. (para. 4)

    a. stay the same

    b. shift back and forth

    c. consistently improve

    d. consistently decrease

_d_ **7. predictably**

Predictably, an evaluation study showed that this policy change caused a big increase in traffic crashes and injuries among 15- to 19-year olds. (para. 5)

    a. in a manner that is annoying

    b. in a manner that is shocking

    c. in a manner that is rude

    d. in a manner that could be expected

_c_ **8. overseas**

Don't Look **Overseas** (section heading)

    a. within the United States

    b. on the North American continent

    c. beyond or across the sea or ocean

    d. in the sky above the water

_a_ **9. proponent**

Proponents of a lower drinking age want us to emulate France, Italy, and other European nations where there is a lower drinking age, or none at all. (para. 6)

    a. one who argues in favor of something

    b. one who argues against something

c. one who is extremely angry about something

d. one who is very joyful about something

<u>d</u> **10. emulate**

Proponents of a lower drinking age want us to **emulate** France, Italy, and other European nations . . . (para. 6)

a. strive to destroy

b. strive to erase

c. strive to move away from

d. strive to equal

 as **you read**

Establish Your Purpose

Read and annotate the selection using the guidelines for active reading. Identify the reasons why the author is against lowering the legal drinking age.

Actively Process as You Read: Independent Reading

Monitor your comprehension as you read. (See Chapter 2, page 54.) Be sure to stop to reflect at the conclusion of each paragraph.

Highlight the most important points. Write notes, responses, or questions that come to mind in the margins.

Should the Drinking Age Be Lowered to 18?
No! It's Not Safe for Youth, nor on the Roads
By William De Jong

---

1   Talk to my public health **colleagues** about the proposal to lower the minimum legal drinking age to 18, and this is what you'll hear: "I can't believe we're even talking about this."

2   Why the strong reaction? We tried this experiment in the 1970s. When the death toll **mounted**, Congress passed legislation in 1984 to pressure the states to adopt an age-21 law, which has saved thousands of lives.

Look at the Research

3   Members of the Amethyst **Initiative**—college presidents who have called for a renewed debate about lowering the legal drinking age—are sincere in believing that the age-21 law doesn't work. They are badly mistaken. University of Minnesota **epidemiologists** Alexander Wagenaar and Traci Toomey reviewed 132 research studies published between 1960 and 1999. Their conclusion is that a **uniform** national age-21 law has reduced both youth alcohol use and alcohol-related traffic crashes.

4   Point by point, the Amethyst Initiative's supporters have it wrong. Has the age-21 law led to an increase in college student drinking? According to the University of Michigan's *Monitoring the Future Study,* the answer is no. Rates of heavy drinking among college students have **fluctuated** very little since the federal legislation was passed.

5   Will lowering the legal drinking age to 18 result in fewer alcohol-related problems? Again, the answer is no. We learned this from our experience in the United States, but we also have more recent history to draw upon. In 1999, New Zealand reduced its legal drinking age from 20 to 18. **Predictably**, an evaluation study showed that this policy change caused a big increase in traffic crashes and injuries among 15- to 19-year-olds.

Don't Look Overseas

6   **Proponents** of a lower drinking age want us to **emulate** France, Italy, and other European nations where there is a lower drinking age, or none at all. Parents introduce alcohol to their children at a younger age. Does this reduce binge drinking?

7   The answer is no. According to the European School Survey Project on Alcohol and Other Drugs, a majority of these countries have higher percentages of youth who report heavy alcohol use and drinking to intoxication than the United States.

8   The age-21 law is working for us. Let's leave it alone.

Source: Adapted from William De Jong, "Should the Legal Drinking Age Be Lowered to 18? No! It's Not Safe for Youth, nor on the Roads," *AFT On Campus,* Vol. 28, No. 2, November/December 2008, p. 3.

■ ■ ■

▶▶ after **you read**

| **Exercise 3** | **Answering Your Preview Questions** |

Directions: Look back at the questions you posed after previewing the selection. If you have discovered the answers, write them on the lines provided.

1. _____
   _____

2. _____
   _____

3. _____
   _____

| **Exercise 4** | **Reviewing Important Points** |

Directions: Choose the best answer for each of the following questions using information provided in the selection. You may need to reread certain sections to be sure your responses are accurate.

_c_ 1. The title of this selection indicates that the author:
  a. is in favor of lowering the drinking age.
  b. believes we should research the benefits of lowering the drinking age.
  c. has at least two important reasons for not lowering the drinking age.
  d. sees both sides of the issue and has not made up his mind.

_a_ 2. From paragraph 2, we can infer that:
  a. Lowering the legal drinking age has already been tried and more driving accidents occurred.
  b. Congress has been exploring the idea of lowering the drinking age since the 1970s.

   c. The legal drinking age was already lowered in 1984.

   d. Fewer deaths because of drinking while driving occurred during the 1970s.

_c_ 3. **The Amethyst Initiative is:**

   a. a group of college presidents who believe the drinking age should be raised.

   b. a group of college presidents who believe the age-21 law should be maintained.

   c. a group of college presidents who believe the current laws should be reviewed with the intent of lowering the drinking age.

   d. a group of college presidents who believe underage drinking causes increased alcohol-related traffic crashes.

_b_ 4. **The research of Wagenaar and Toomey finds that a uniform national age-21 law:**

   a. increased the amount of alcohol abuse among young adults.

   b. reduced alcohol intake and related car accidents among young adults.

   c. has no direct effect on alcohol-related car crashes.

   d. supports the views of the Amethyst Initiative.

_a_ 5. **The main idea of paragraph 4 is that:**

   a. Setting the legal drinking age at 21 does not increase the amount of college drinking.

   b. Setting the drinking age at 21 promotes drinking among college students.

   c. The age-21 law for the legal consumption of alcohol has had some impact on the amount of drinking among college students.

   d. Heavy drinking on colleges campuses has fluctuated greatly over the years.

_d_ 6. **The first sentence in paragraph 4 is an example of:**

   a. a fact.

   b. an inference.

   c. an objective statement.

   d. an opinion.

_a_ 7. **In paragraph 5, the author uses the example of New Zealand to show that reducing the legal drinking age:**

   a. increases the number of automobile accidents among young drivers.

   b. decreases the number of automobile accidents among young drivers.

   c. has had no impact on the number of traffic crashes and injuries.

   d. leads to increased amounts of drinking among even younger citizens.

_b_ 8. **The overall writing pattern of paragraph 5 is:**

   a. definition.

   b. cause and effect.

   c. classification.

   d. sequence.

_a_ 9. By reading paragraphs 6–7, we conclude that the heading, "Don't Look Overseas" implies that:

    a. In Europe, where there is a lower drinking age, there is a higher percentage of alcohol abuse among youth than in the United States, so we shouldn't pattern our laws after those countries.

    b. We should make our own decisions, and never look to others to tell us what to do.

    c. In Europe, where children begin consuming alcohol at an earlier age, they learn how to manage their drinking.

    d. Because individual freedoms are important, we should look the other way when some people abuse alcohol, and not create laws based on the lack of control by just a few.

_c_ 10. The author supports his point of view primarily by presenting:

    a. the opinions of others.

    b. facts.

    c. research findings.

    d. personal anecdotes.

_d_ 11. The overall tone of the selection can be described as:

    a. hostile and outraged.

    b. humorous with some sarcasm.

    c. sad and solemn.

    d. persuasive yet informative.

Exercise 5   **Organizing the Information**

Directions: Using your notes and annotations, complete the following chart, which identifies the research and findings noted in the article that support the author's view that the drinking age should not be lowered.

Should the Drinking Age Be Lowered to 18? No!

Research	Findings
1. Wagenaar and Toomey Research Studies, 1960–1999	*A uniform national age-21 law has reduced youth alcohol use and alcohol-related accidents.*
2. *University of Michigan, "Monitoring the Future" Study*	Raising the drinking age does not lead to heavier binge drinking on college campuses.
3. *New Zealand Evaluation Study, 1999*	When the drinking age was lowered to 18 there was a large increase in traffic crashes and injuries among 15- to 19–year-olds.
4. European School Survey Project on Alcohol and Other Drugs	*In a majority of European nations, where the drinking age is lower or none at all, there is a higher percentage of youth who report heavy alcohol use than in the United States.*

| Exercise 6 | **Using Context Clues** |

Directions: Select a pair of words from the text box on page 483 that best completes each of the following sentences.

1. Always wanting to _emulate_____ her older brother who had grad-uated from Harvard, Karen was, _predictably_____, overcome with happiness when she received her letter of acceptance in the mail yesterday.

2. _Epidemiologists_____ from around the world gathered at the Global Conference on Infectious Diseases to discuss their concern about the _mounting_____ number of AIDS cases in developing nations.

3. For the first time since the company was established, my _colleagues_____ and I decided to develop an _initiative_____ that would address the unsanitary conditions that have existed in the cafeteria for the last 10 years.

4. My dreams of traveling _overseas_____ have not _fluctuated_____ since I first studied European history.

5. Some _proponents_____ of changes in the tax laws are in favor of a single, _uniform_____ rate for income taxes for all, no matter what one earns for a living.

| Exercise 7 | **Making Personal Connections Through Writing and Discussion** |

Directions: Think about yourself in relation to the article you just read.   *Responses will vary.*

1. You have read two articles on the drinking age, with opposing points of view. Which author, Professor Hanson or Professor De Jong, do you think presented the stronger argument? Why so?

2. Is there a middle ground on the issue of lowering the drinking age? What ideas can you offer that were not covered in either article?

3. What is your college's policy on the use of alcohol on campus? You might want to look into your college's Code of Conduct.

⌐reflect AND respond⌐

Having read three selections about *physical health and well-being,* you now have a broader and better understanding of the topic.

Directions: Complete a journal response for this module. Read the following ques-tions. Select two to which you would like to respond. Then write your responses on a separate piece of paper. Write at least one page.

1. What did you learn about issues related to your physical health and well-being?

2. How does this information apply to you? Make connections with your own expe-rience. What do these readings make you think about?

3. How can you relate what you have read to other situations? Are there other activities you can do or precautions you can take to care for your physical health? Make connections to other readings, course work, or current events.

4. What else would you like to know about this topic?

Readings About Emotional Well-Being

Get Acquainted with the Issue

The question "How do you feel?" often expresses interest in a person's emotional state as much as his or her physical condition. When things are going well, we experience feelings of love, excitement, joy, and contentment. Unfortunately, life is not always rosy, and we feel anger, anxiety, fear, and depression at times. Recognizing and managing such emotions can be quite a challenge. The capacity to do so is important because a connection exists between our emotional well-being and our body's physical health.

In this module you will read three selections that address different ways of managing or treating emotions. The first selection, "Eco-Therapy for Environmental Depression," describes a simple solution to modern-day stressors. In the second selection, "Overcoming Phobias," the author explains how the application of a new therapeutic method has helped him address his worst fear. The module concludes with a portion from an introductory psychology textbook, titled "Client-Centered Therapy." It describes a type of "humanistic" therapy that focuses on the connection between a patient and his or her therapist. While you read, consider your own feelings about each of the approaches. Do you think you would benefit from any of the interventions?

Guided Reading

'Eco-Therapy' for Environmental Depression: Go Jump Off a Pier
By Bryan Walsh

This article is from Time Magazine. *It reports on current events and trends in society. Read it to find out about some eco-friendly ideas to combat depression, stress, and anxiety.*

◀◀ before you read

Think about what you already know about a topic before you begin reading. Then you will be able to attach your new learning to this background knowledge and more easily understand the new information. (See Chapter 2, page 38.)

Discuss or write responses to the following questions about your ways of dealing with stress.

1. What do you typically do to combat feelings of stress or anxiety?

2. In what ways do you experience or interact with nature? How do you usually feel afterward?

3. What would you say to those who believe that spending more time in the great outdoors can improve your mood?

Prepare to Read

Preview the selection "'Eco-Therapy' for Environmental Depression: Go Jump Off a Pier" using the THIEVES strategy on page 40.

Exercise 1   **Previewing**

Directions: Complete the following items.

1. Look through the selection, and check off all the items that are available for preview.

    _X_ Title

    ___ Headings

    _X_ Introduction

    _X_ Every first sentence in each paragraph

    _X_ Visuals/vocabulary

    ___ End of chapter questions

    _X_ Summary/concluding paragraph

2. Actively preview the selection by reading and highlighting the items you have checked.

3. Based on your preview, place an "X" next to those items you predict will be discussed in the selection.

    _X_ a. that going outside can help mental problems

    _X_ b. how we have been involved with nature in the past

    ___ c. the causes of mental problems

    _X_ d. some ways to reconnect with nature

    _X_ e. the findings of a study at the University of Essex

    ___ f. a list of parks and preserves across the globe

Check Out the Vocabulary

You will find the following vocabulary words in bold type in the reading selection. Some are repeated more than once in the text. Do you know what these words mean? Knowing the meaning of all these words will increase your understanding of the material.

alienation	embedded	enhancer	glimpse	practical
dominate*	endangered	evolved*	interact*	relentless

*Denotes a word from the Academic Word List

| Exercise 2 | **Checking Out the Vocabulary** |

Directions: Look at each word taken from the reading selection. Read the sentences that follow. The first is from the selection, with a hint to its meaning, and the second uses the word in an additional context. Choose the best definition for the word, and write the letter of the definition you select on the line provided.

___c___ 1. alienation

- A new and growing group of psychologists believes that many of our modern-day mental problems, including depression, stress, and anxiety, can be traced in part to society's increasing **alienation** from nature. (para. 1) (HINT: Consider the root word, *alien*. Does it imply being close and familiar, or distant and unfamiliar?)

- Even though Rhonda ended her relationship with Carl, she had hoped to remain friends, rather than experience his **alienation** caused by his feelings of anger and rejection.

    a. hostility and anger
    b. worship and devotion
    c. estrangement, withdrawal after a former attachment
    d. traveling far to a foreign land

___b___ 2. evolved

- Eco-therapists point out that human beings have **evolved** in synchrony with nature for millions of years . . . (para. 3) (HINT: Think of a word you know that includes this root. What does *evolution* refer to?)

- Jenna's diligence and commitment to her studies throughout her four years at college enabled her to **evolve** into quite a scholar, planning her application for graduate school and a career in law.

    a. danced and sang
    b. develop, produce by natural progression
    c. been in conflict with or opposition to
    d. seen in the future, predicted

___d___ 3. interact

- [W]e are hard-wired to **interact** with our environment—with the air, water, plants, and other animals. (para. 3) (HINT: Read the sentence in the text that follows. It implies the opposite meaning, providing a contrast clue.)

- Professor Connors enjoys nothing more than seeing his students **interact** with one another in class; of course, when they are discussing physics and not the latest movie.

    a. to destroy, tear down
    b. to use up, take from
    c. to mock or make fun of
    d. to engage, to act upon one another

_c_ 4. dominate

- [The rise] of the Internet and other technologies, like iPhones and BlackBerrys, that **dominate** our lives . . . (para. 3) (HINT: Use the sentences before and after this sentence to help. What do the words "regulate" and "push us" imply?)
- Caroline's tendency to **dominate** every conversation gradually caused her friends to stop phoning, and even begin to stay away entirely.
  a. end quickly
  b. cause harm to, hurt
  c. rule, control
  d. delay, slow down

_d_ 5. glimpse

- Today, more than half of the world's population lives in cities, and many people barely ever get a **glimpse** of green. (para. 5) (HINT: Think of the context. What word could substitute for glimpse?)
- Jerome was so curious about Shana's new boyfriend that although he got only a **glimpse** of him in the car, he was thrilled to finally picture his face.
  a. touch or feel
  b. photograph or drawing
  c. hope or wish
  d. a fleeting view or look

_d_ 6. embedded

- "People were **embedded** in nature once," says Buzzell-Saltzman. (para. 5) (HINT: The author uses this word to reiterate how we used to be involved with or connected to nature.)
- The nail was so deeply **embedded** in the wood that no amount of pulling was able to remove it.
  a. in conflict with
  b. next to, near by
  c. fatigued by, worn out by
  d. enclosed in or surrounded closely by

_a_ 7. enhancer

- Of course, it's no secret that regular exercise is a powerful mood **enhancer** . . . (para. 7) (HINT: In the preceding sentence, the author uses the term "antidepressant." How would this impact one's mood?)
- Reviewing class notes every evening is certainly an **enhancer** for learning and remembering the new material.
  a. something that heightens or increases the value, quality, or intensity
  b. something that inhibits or slows down an action
  c. something that creates problems or complications
  d. something that erases or gets rid of information

_c_ 8. practical

- [E]co-therapy [may be more than] a **practical** psychological treatment . . . (para. 8) (HINT: Think of your prior knowledge. What does a "practical solution" to a problem mean?)

- Rather than going for looks and style, Jenna decided to purchase shoes for her camping trip that would be more **practical** and comfortable.

    a. intricate and complex
    b. costly, expensive
    c. useful, purposeful
    d. cheap, inexpensive

_a_ **9. relentless**

- And with worsening climate change and a **relentless** drumbeat of bad news about our endangered environment, it seems our eco-anxiety may be far from being cured. (para. 8) (HINT: If something is not going to be cured, does it mean it will stop or continue to go on?)
- The falling snow seemed **relentless**, leaving us wondering if classes would be canceled over the next two days.

    a. not ending in severity, intensity, strength, or pace
    b. annoying, causing problems and difficulties
    c. stopping and going, intermittent
    d. mild, gentle

_c_ **10. endangered**

- And with worsening climate change and a relentless drumbeat of bad news about our **endangered** environment, it seems our eco-anxiety may be far from being cured. (para. 8) (HINT: Consider the root "danger." What would the entire word mean when describing the environment?)
- Overfishing freshwater salmon has caused such a significant decrease in their population that certain species are now considered **endangered.**

    a. dangerous, harmful for one's heath
    b. plentiful, abundant
    c. in trouble, on the risk of falling apart
    d. poisoned, tainted

 as you read

Establish Your Purpose

Now, you are ready to read and annotate the selection, "'Eco-Therapy' for Environmental Depression: Go Jump Off a Pier." Focus on major points of information. Read to learn the meaning of eco-therapy and how it can help us all feel better emotionally.

Actively Process While You Read: Guided Reading ⏸

Stop and think about the information as you read.

| Exercise 3 | **Processing While You Read** |

Directions: Answer the questions that appear in bold print at the conclusion of each paragraph. This will help you monitor your reading process and understand the material.

from the pages of

TIME

'Eco-Therapy' for Environmental Depression: Go Jump Off a Pier

By Bryan Walsh

1   Depressed people often need someone to hug. On occasion, that someone may just be a tree. A new and growing group of psychologists believes that many of our modern-day mental problems, including depression, stress and anxiety, can be traced in part to society's increasing **alienation** from nature. The solution? Get outside and enjoy it.

What do some psychologists consider to be the cause for many of our current emotional problems?

Some psychologists believe that our disconnect with nature is the cause of many emotional problems.

2   Therapists have long focused their treatments on the patient's insides—whether through medications like Prozac, practices like meditation to calm the mind, or old-fashioned couch-bound therapy by the hour. Practitioners of the growing field of eco-therapy, on the contrary, believe that patient care must include time spent in the great outdoors. "It's psychotherapy—as if nature really mattered," says Linda Buzzell-Saltzman, a psychologist and the founder of the International Association for Eco-therapy, which currently lists slightly more than 100 official members.

What do practitioners in the field of eco-therapy believe we should do to feel less stressed?

They believe we should spend more time outdoors, connecting with nature.

What organization supports this point of view, and who is its founder?

The International Association for Ecotherapy supports this view. Linda Buzzell-Saltzman, a psychologist, is its founder.

3   Eco-therapists point out that human beings have **evolved** in synchrony with nature for millions of years and that we are hard-wired to **interact** with our environment—with the air, water, plants, and other animals. But in the past two centuries, beginning with the Industrial Revolution, people have been steadily removed from the natural world. Our lives are regulated not by the sun or moon but instead by the factory clock. Recently it's gotten worse with the rise of the Internet and other technologies, like iPhones and BlackBerrys, that **dominate** our lives, pushing us even further from any appreciation of our natural surroundings.

What do eco-therapists identify as having caused our alienation from nature?

They believe that people have steadily been removed from the natural world. This began with the Industrial Revolution. The rise of the Internet and other technologies has made it worse. These push us away from our natural surroundings.

4   "We began to get the impression that we were somehow above and separate from nature," says Craig Chalquist. He is an instructor at John F. Kennedy University in San Francisco and co-editor with Buzzell-Saltzman of the new book *Ecotherapy: Healing with Nature in Mind.*

What concern has instructor Craig Chalquist raised?

He says that we are under the impression that somehow we are above and separate from nature.

5   Today, more than half of the world's population lives in cities, and many people barely ever get a **glimpse** of green. At the same time, human beings appear to be doing their best to destroy what remains of the earth by contributing to climate change—a problem that itself causes some people deep anxiety. But what the average person feels as stress or depression, eco-therapists suggest, is a longing for our natural home. "People were **embedded** in nature once," says Buzzell-Saltzman. "We've lost that, and we're paying the price."

What two concerns does the author raise regarding our involvement with nature?

He says that many people barely have any connection with nature at all and that, at the same time, humans are contributing to climate change and the destruction of the earth.

6   Getting it back doesn't have to be difficult, according to eco-therapists, most of whom, unsurprisingly, practice in California. Patients' treatment typically begins with starting a nature journal in which they record how much time they spend outside. The results can often be shocking, says Buzzell-Saltzman. "Some patients find they spend less than 15 to 30 minutes a day outside, other than walking to and from their cars," she says. Eco-therapists counsel patients to slow down and reconnect with nature. They suggest hiking, gardening or simply taking walks outdoors. Therapy sessions may also take place outdoors—in a park, for example—rather than inside yet another office. "We can use the natural world to be part of the healing process," says Chalquist. "We have to acknowledge that we're part of this, not the master of it."

What are some strategies identified in the paragraph that are used by eco-therapists to help people get involved with nature?

They can keep a nature journal, recording the time they spend outside. They also suggest hiking, gardening, or taking walks. Sessions can take place outside, too.

7   If such prescriptions sound a little simplistic, consider this: A 2007 study by researchers at the University of Essex in England found that a daily dose of walking outside could be as effective as taking antidepressant drugs for treating mild to moderate depression. Of course, it's no secret that regular exercise is a powerful mood **enhancer** although researchers noted that a similar routine of walking in a crowded shopping mall did not have the same impact and the boost in vitamin D production in people who spent more time outside in the sun surely helped as well.

What does the author suggest is as effective as a dose of antidepressant?

He suggests taking a walk.

8   It may be that eco-therapy is less a **practical** psychological treatment than a timely idea that connects common feelings of loneliness and stress with the fact that the world in which we live is slowly becoming something it shouldn't be. And with worsening climate change and a **relentless** drumbeat of bad news about our **endangered** environment, it seems our eco-anxiety may be far from being cured. "Ultimately, what we need to do is change human behavior," says Buzzell-Saltzman—a commonsense recommendation for humans as well as the environment.

What is the author's final conclusion?

He believes that we need to change human behavior in order to help ourselves as well as the environment.

■ ■ ■

 **after you read**

Review Important Points

Going over major points immediately after you read, while the information is fresh in your mind, will help you recall the content and record key ideas.

Exercise 4   **Reviewing Important Points**

Directions: Answer the following questions based on the content of the selection. You may need to go back and reread certain portions to be sure your responses are correct and can be supported by information in the text. Write the letter of your choice in the space provided.

_c_ 1. **What is the overall thesis of this selection?**
   a. Eco-therapists oppose the use of medications to improve mental health.
   b. Technology is the cause of a lot of stress and depression in our lives.
   c. Interacting with the natural environment is important for our emotional health and well-being.
   d. Human beings have evolved in harmony with nature for millions of years.

_c_ 2. **Examples of therapeutic intervention that have focused on the patient's "interior" cited in the selection include all of the following *except*:**
   a. medications, like Prozac.
   b. meditation.
   c. electroshock therapy.
   d. talk-therapy.

_b_ 3. **The statement in paragraph 2, "Practitioners of the growing field of eco-therapy, on the contrary, believe that patient care must include time spent in the great outdoors" integrates the written organizational pattern of:**
   a. cause and effect.
   b. comparison and contrast.
   c. sequence/chronology.
   d. classification.

_c_ 4. The predominant writing pattern used to convey the main idea of paragraph 3 is:

    a. cause and effect.
    b. classification.
    c. comparison and contrast.
    d. definition.

_c_ 5. The implied main idea of paragraph 3 can be paraphrased as:

    a. Eco-therapists say that human beings have grown in harmony with nature since the beginning of mankind.
    b. Our lives have begun to be controlled by industry, factory life, and the Internet.
    c. The rise of industry and technologies have gradually taken us further and further away from appreciating and interacting with our natural world.
    d. The use of technologies, such as the Internet and smart phones, has lead to an increase in mental illness and emotional distress.

_b_ 6. In paragraph 5, the statement "At the same time, human beings appear to be doing their best to destroy what remains of the earth . . ." is an example of:

    a. a fact.
    b. an opinion.
    c. a statistic.
    d. none of the above.

_a_ 7. The topic of paragraph 6 is:

    a. getting back to nature.
    b. a nature journal.
    c. the healing process.
    d. mastering nature.

_a_ 8. The main idea of paragraph 7 is stated in the:

    a. first sentence.
    b. second sentence.
    c. third sentence.
    d. last sentence.

_b_ 9. The overall tone of the selection can be described as:

    a. critical and negative.
    b. informative and hopeful.
    c. humorous and ironic.
    d. entertaining and sarcastic.

_c_ 10. We can infer from the last paragraph that the author:

    a. believes we are on a path to destruction and the environment and emotional health are severely endangered.
    b. will be leaving this country to find a better place to live.
    c. hopes people begin to make adjustments in the way they treat themselves and the environment.
    d. human behavior will never change.

Organize the Information

Organizing the information you have learned from a reading selection shows you have understood it and can restate the material in a different way. You can use this reorganized material to help you study for exams and prepare for written assignments. (See Chapter 9.)

> **Exercise 5**   **Organizing the Information**

Directions: Review the reading selection. Generate a list of five recommendations for incorporating nature into one's life suggested within the text.

1. _Keep a nature journal, increasing the amount of time spent outside._ .
2. _Go on a hike._ .
3. _Do gardening._ .
4. _Take walks outdoors._ .
5. _Spend time in the sun._ .

Integrate the Vocabulary

Make the new vocabulary presented in the reading *your* vocabulary. In addition to learning the meaning of new words, you should also learn related word forms.

> **Exercise 6**   **Using Context Clues**

Directions: Fill in the two blanks in each sentence below with words, or forms of the words, from the text box on page 492.

1. Unable to resolve his long-standing resentments, Robert's continued _alienation_ from his brothers and sisters is now _endangering_ his relationship with the entire family.
2. The _relentless_ rain and high humidity of the islands _dominated_ the memories of our summer vacation in the tropics.
3. Professor Wilson had the ability to _enhance_ the quality of her lectures by _embedding_ several jokes within each of the topics she discussed.
4. Although I was hoping to _interact_ with Jared, my best friend throughout high school, he was so in demand at our reunion that I caught just a brief _glimpse_ of him as he walked past my table.
5. Over time, taking the bus has _evolved_ as a _practical_ solution to the problem of finding a parking space for my car on campus.

Make Personal Connections Through Writing and Discussion

When you make your new learning relevant to yourself in some way, it becomes more meaningful and easier to remember. Whenever you read, try to connect to the content on a personal level. How does it relate to you? How can you apply what you have read to other situations? What else would you like to know?

| **Exercise 7** | **Making Personal Connections** |

Directions: Write your personal response to each of the following questions. Then share your responses in a small group or with the rest of the class. Do others feel similarly?

1. What is your opinion of eco-therapy? Do you believe it to be a practical psychological treatment? Why or why not?

   _____
   _____
   _____
   _____
   _____

Answers will vary.

2. What other "practical" suggestions might you offer someone who is feeling lonely, anxious, or depressed?

   _____
   _____
   _____
   _____
   _____

Self-Monitored Reading
Reading Selection 2

> ## Why Overcoming Phobias Can Be So Daunting
> By Lev Grossman

This article is from Time Magazine. *Think about the method described by the author to rid himself of his phobia. Consider your own fears and whether the interventions described might help you.*

◀ before you read

Answer the following questions before you read the selection.

Answers will vary.

1. What are some common fears or phobias that impact people today?

   _____

   _____

2. What do you suspect are the causes of those phobias?

   _____

   _____

3. From your own life experience or study, what are some methods that can help people combat their phobias?

   _____

   _____

Prepare to Read

Preview the reading selection by applying the THIEVES strategy (p. 40).

Exercise 1   Previewing

Directions: Based on your preview, respond to the following questions:

1. What is the author's purpose in writing this article?
   The author is going to describe different strategies currently being used to help people overcome phobias.

2. Identify three methods you anticipate will be described.
   1. CBT. 2. Memory-reconsolidation. 3. Traditional talk therapy.

3. From your preview, what do you learn about the author's success in curing his phobia?
   The author has not been able to get rid of his phobia. He is still living with it.

Check Out the Vocabulary

You will encounter the following words in this reading. They are in bold type in the selection. Are you already familiar with some of them? Knowing the meaning of these vocabulary terms will increase your comprehension of the material.

ambient	departed	induced*	profound
arbitrary*	documented*	irrational*	reliable*
daunting	dread	neuroses	traumatic

* Denotes a word from the Academic Word List

Exercise 2   Checking Out the Vocabulary

Directions: Look at each boldface word taken from the reading selection. Read each pair of sentences that follows in which the word appears. The first sentence is from the reading. The second gives you additional context to help you figure out the meaning of the word. Select the best definition of the word from the choices. Write the letter of your choice on the line provided.

_a_ 1. **daunting**
   • Why Overcoming Phobias Can Be So **Daunting** (title)
   • That first semester in a large urban university was **daunting** for Carmine, who had graduated from a small town high school nestled in the countryside.
      a. overwhelming, intimidating
      b. pleasant, enjoyable
      c. expensive, costly
      d. damaging, destructive

_b_ 2. **irrational**
   • I'm filled with overpowering, **irrational** dread by the sight or sound of another human being eating or drinking. (para. 1)
   • Justin made so many **irrational** decisions about dating during his college years, leading to extremely difficult situations, that he chose to remain single all throughout his twenties.
      a. powerful, with great force
      b. lacking reason or clarity, not rational
      c. thoughtful, carefully considered
      d. fanciful, fun-loving

_b_ 3. **dread**
   • I'm filled with overpowering, irrational **dread** by the sight or sound of another human being eating or drinking. (para. 1)
   • Tonia filled with **dread** upon realizing she had forgotten all about the exam on Chapter Two that Professor Connor began distributing at the start of biology class.
      a. feeling of joy and happiness
      b. feeling of great fear, extreme reluctance to meet or face something
      c. feeling of anger and resentment
      d. feeling of exhaustion or fatigue

_c_ 4. **ambient**
   • I do well in restaurants where there's a lot of **ambient** noise and distraction, but one-on-one meals are a minefield. (para. 2)
   • Because the **ambient** chatter and music emanating from his sister's room was so distracting to Carlos, he chose to study in the library where he was always assured of complete quiet.
      a. restful, quiet
      b. helpful, supportive
      c. surrounding, encompassing
      d. confusing, problematic

_d_ 5. **profound**
- I like to think of my brain as **profound** and mysterious, full of demons and neuroses and fascinating dreams that I can bore my co-workers with. (para. 4)
- After dating for six months, Gerald realized that his initial connection and attraction for Kara had evolved into **profound** feelings of love and respect.
  - a. superficial, existing on the surface
  - b. frightening, causing worry and concern
  - c. overloaded, overwhelming
  - d. with depth, extending deeply and with great meaning

_c_ 6. **neuroses**
- I like to think of my brain as profound and mysterious, full of demons and **neuroses** and fascinating dreams that I can bore my co-workers with. (para. 4)
- Ironically, it probably has become normal to have one or two **neuroses,** given the complicated and demanding world in which many of us live.
  - a. severe mental illnesses
  - b. brain cells attached with dendrites
  - c. mild personality disorders or mental disturbances
  - d. bad habits and behaviors

_d_ 7. **reliable**
- It's **reliable** and well documented. (para. 4)
- Though there were problems in the early stages of its development, today digital thermometers have become quite **reliable** in their capacity to measure temperature.
  - a. questionable, unclear
  - b. complicated and confusing
  - c. not truthful, full of deceit
  - d. dependable, giving the same result on successive trials

_b_ 8. **documented**
- It's reliable and well **documented.** (para. 4)
- Freshman college students learn the importance of using **documented** sources in their research papers.
  - a. creative and original
  - b. having substantial support with reliable references
  - c. handy, easily accessible
  - d. written in hard copy, rather than electronically

_b_ 9. **traumatic**
- According to a study published in December in *Nature,* when a person's phobia gets activated, there's a period immediately afterward when the **traumatic** memory that the phobia is based on becomes vulnerable. (para. 5)

- Soldiers who witness the death of comrades, or who suffer severe injury on the battlefield, often need time to heal emotionally from those **traumatic** events.
    - a. light-hearted
    - b. psychologically damaging, experiencing a high degree of stress
    - c. unusual or odd, unexpected
    - d. unique, one of a kind

<u>*a*</u> 10. **arbitrary**

- The participants in the *Nature* study were first trained to fear a certain **arbitrary** stimulus—they were shown colored cards while receiving mild electric shocks . . . (para. 6)
- With no formal seating plan at the dinner to follow, we found seats wherever there was room, filling the tables in an **arbitrary** way.
    - a. depending on individual choice, not according to rule, plan, or law
    - b. structure, orderly, preplanned manner
    - c. combative, argumentative, rather hostile way
    - d. foolish, silly, childlike manner

<u>*c*</u> 11. **induced**

- I would calmly try to separate the sight and sound of a person eating from the fear it **induced** in me. (para. 7)
- Odd as it may seem, the doctors **induced** a coma-like existence during the early stages of Bob's recuperation, so that he would not be in pain from his injuries and could heal quietly before beginning other treatment.
    - a. to lure, lead someone into a new experience
    - b. to halt, or put an end to
    - c. to bring about through stimulation or influence
    - d. to challenge

<u>*a*</u> 12. **departed**

- In one session, Dr. N **departed** from the CBT script and suggested I try to visualize the fear as a creature. (para. 9)
- Though the stormy weather had been a concern, fortunately our plane **departed** on time and the flight was smooth and comfortable.
    - a. to leave, to move in another or alternative direction
    - b. to settle in or land
    - c. to criticize and find fault with
    - d. to become uncontrollable

▶ as **you read**

Establish Your Purpose

Now, read and annotate the selection on page 506, using the guidelines for active reading, and focus on the major points of information.

Actively Process While You Read: Self-Monitored Reading

Monitor your comprehension as you read. (See Chapter 2, page 54.) Be sure to stop to reflect at the conclusion of each paragraph, and ask yourself the following questions:

- Did I understand what I have just read?
- What is the main idea of the paragraph?
- Am I ready to continue?

Exercise 3   **Processing While You Read**

Directions: Highlight the most important points in each paragraph. Then write the key topics and main ideas in the spaces provided in the margins. Finally, underline or number the supporting details in the text.

from the pages of

TIME

Why Overcoming Phobias Can Be So Daunting
By Lev Grossman

Notes

Topic _____

_____

Main Idea _____

_____

1   Let's get this out of the way right up front: I'm afraid of people eating. Some people are scared of snakes or flying or heights or other things that can actually be dangerous. I'm filled with overpowering, **irrational dread** by the sight or sound of another human being eating or drinking. It doesn't make any more sense to me than it does to you. But that's what a phobia is: a fear that has nothing to do with logic or common sense.

Topic _____

_____

Main Idea _____

_____

2   Weird as it sounds, phobias are not that unusual. According to a study published in 2008 by the National Institute of Mental Health, 8.7% of people in the United States over the age of 18 have a specific phobia of some kind or other. It doesn't take much to set mine off. A swig from a water bottle can do it, or someone chewing gum. Every morning when I get on the subway, I scan the passengers like an air marshal looking for terrorists. At any moment, somebody could whip out a bagel or a danish. I do well in restaurants, where there's a lot of **ambient** noise and distraction, but one-on-one meals are a minefield. And don't get me started on popcorn. When I go to a movie theater, every movie is a horror movie.

Topic _____

_____

Main Idea _____

_____

3   The treatment for a phobia like mine is simple and routine, and I avoided it for as long as humanly possible. That's because it involves deliberately, systematically exposing yourself to the thing you fear. It's part of cognitive behavioral therapy, or CBT. It's a very practical kind of therapy—it has no truck with mystical Freudian mumbo-jumbo. CBT views your symptoms not as clues to the secrets locked in your tormented unconscious but as a set of learned behaviors and bad habits that you can be trained to give up. As far as CBT is concerned, my phobia was just a piece of bad neural wiring that needed troubleshooting.

Topic _____

_____

Main Idea _____

_____

4   That isn't a model of my brain that I feel especially comfortable with. I like to think of my brain as **profound** and mysterious, full of demons and **neuroses** and fascinating dreams that I can bore my co-workers with. But when you're fighting a phobia, CBT is your weapon of choice. It's **reliable** and well **documented**. Insurance companies love it. Often you can cure a phobia like mine in about 12 sessions.

5   Researchers at New York University have even gone beyond CBT. According to a study published in December in *Nature,* when a person's phobia gets activated, there's a period immediately afterward when the **traumatic** memory that the phobia is based on becomes vulnerable. During that time—which lasts about six hours—you can reshape the memory, rewrite it in a way that removes the fear.

6   The results of memory-reconsolidation experiments are impressive. The participants in the *Nature* study were first trained to fear a certain **arbitrary** stimulus—they were shown colored cards while receiving mild electric shocks—then reconditioned during the reconsolidation period. The fear went away. It was still gone when the participants were retested a year later.

7   For now, this is all still in the realm of research. In my case, my psychiatrist—let's call him Dr. N—practices something called psychodynamic psychotherapy, which is more like psychoanalysis. But for the purposes of treating my phobia, he turned himself into a cognitive-behavioral therapist. For each session, I would arrive with groceries and watch while he ate them. I would calmly try to separate the sight and sound of a person eating from the fear it **induced** in me. I would try to retrain my brain to be unafraid of something that there was no reason to be afraid of in the first place.

8   And it worked—up to a point. As the treatment went on, I began to catch my first glimpses of what it might be like to live without wanting to cross the street every time I saw a stranger holding an ice cream cone. But they were just that: glimpses. The spell always faded, and I didn't know how to make it last.

9   In one session, Dr. N **departed** from the CBT script and suggested I try to visualize the fear as a creature. As soon as he said that, I saw it: a primitive, eyeless monster visible only to me, like the gremlin on the wing of the airplane in *The Twilight Zone.* When Dr. N took a sip of milk, the creature would reach out and touch the carton. When it touched the carton, I felt the fear.

10   Try making it let go, Dr. N said. Don't let it touch the carton. It took a lot of effort, but I did it. The creature wanted to touch the milk, but if I tried, I could stop it. When I did, the fear went away. I practiced that—letting the creature reach for something, making it stop, making it back away. The better I got at controlling the creature, the easier my phobia was to control. I even talked to it. I asked it what it wanted and why it wouldn't leave me alone. It wasn't CBT, but it was working.

11   The day may come when psychiatrists can wipe out phobias at will, like erasing a whiteboard. Who knows? But I suspect that my phobia is a more complicated animal than the ones they worked with at NYU. It goes back a lot further and down a lot deeper than colored cards and electric shocks.

12   For now, I'm still living with it. For whatever reason, my treatment has not been successful. I can't always make the fear go away. Maybe that means there's more to the problem than bad wiring. There are feelings down there too—old, dark, unmapped feelings—and I'm going to have to deal with them before the fear leaves me alone.

Notes

Topic _____

_____

Main Idea _____

_____

Topic _____

_____

Main Idea _____

_____

Topic _____

_____

Main Idea _____

_____

Topic _____

_____

Main Idea _____

_____

Topic _____

_____

Main Idea _____

_____

Topic _____

_____

Main Idea _____

_____

Topic _____

_____

Main Idea _____

_____

Topic _____

_____

Main Idea _____

_____

My phobia is a part of me—an ugly part, by the looks of it. I'm going to have to get to know that demon better. Because it's not going to leave till it's good and ready.

■ ■ ■

 **after you read**

Review Important Points

Go over the major points immediately after you have read to help you recall the content and record key ideas.

Exercise 4   **Reviewing Important Points**

Directions: Choose the best answer for each of the following questions using information provided in the selection. Write your answers in the spaces provided.

_c_ 1. In paragraph 1, by giving examples and telling the meaning of phobia, the author uses the overall writing pattern of:

    a. comparison and contrast.

    b. cause and effect.

    c. definition.

    d. sequence.

_a_ 2. The first sentence of paragraph 2, is supported by a fact in:

    a. the second sentence.

    b. the third sentence.

    c. the forth sentence.

    d. the last sentence.

_c_ 3. The author has a phobia of:

    a. restaurants.

    b. relationships.

    c. people eating or drinking.

    d. planes and subways.

_d_ 4. To paraphrase the approach of CBT as a treatment for phobias, we can say it asks patients to:

    a. totally eliminate the object of their fear from their lives.

    b. imagine the fear as a bird, flying away from their lives.

    c. speak with a therapist regularly about the unconscious cause of the fear.

    d. repeatedly expose themselves to their fear and develop new responses and behaviors.

_a_ 5. The main idea of paragraph 4 is:

    a. CBT has been found to be an effective cure for phobias.

    b. Insurance companies love CBT.

c. The author thinks his brain is full of demons and neuroses.

d. CBT has not really been that successful in dealing with phobias.

c 6. The topic of paragraphs 5 and 6 is _____, a method of intervening as soon as a traumatic event occurs to prevent the development of a phobia.

    a. arbitrary stimulation

    b. electroshock therapy

    c. memory-reconsolidation

    d. the nature study

b 7. Why might you infer that Dr. N "departed from the CBT script" and suggested the author try to visualize his fear as a creature?

    a. He was doing research on phobias and wanted to try out another possible cure.

    b. The CBT was not entirely effective in helping his patient so he attempted another approach.

    c. He was becoming bored with the CBT method and wanted something new.

    d. Visualizations are more effective than cognitive behavioral therapy.

c 8. What does the author conclude as the reason CBT did not cure his phobia?

    a. CBT is really a form of quackery.

    b. Dr. N is probably not qualified to treat people with his disorder.

    c. His fear is complicated and very deep-seated.

    d. In general, psychotherapy doesn't work.

a 9. The thesis of the selection is:

    a. Although not always effective, cognitive behavioral therapy is a valuable tool used by therapists to help people cure their phobias.

    b. People should not trust therapists suggesting CBT to cure phobias, but rather should look for alternative interventions.

    c. Visualization is an important alternative to CBT.

    d. Phobias are common throughout the United States, and we must do something to cure them.

a 10. The author's primary purpose is to inform us of CBT and other interventions to cure phobias. He does so primarily with:

    a. some facts and personal anecdote.

    b. statistics and case studies.

    c. testimonials from various patients.

    d. documents from psychological research.

Organize the Information

Organizing the information from a reading selection shows you have understood it and can restate the material in your own way.

Organizing the Information

Directions: Refer back to the selection, reviewing each paragraph. Complete the following chart, describing four types of therapies mentioned in the selection that are used to treat phobias. Fill in the blanks to identify the therapy and/or its general method of intervention. Then, with a partner, discuss the therapies and your feelings about each one. What might work best for you, if you had a phobia?

Some answers may vary.

Treating Phobias

Therapy	Description
Cognitive Behavioral Therapy (CBT)	■ Deliberately, systematically expose the patient to <u>their fear</u>. ■ View symptoms as <u>learned behaviors</u> and <u>bad habits</u> that can be trained to give up.
Talk Therapy	Therapist and patient review a person's early life to understand and confront the <u>roots of a traumatic event and fear</u>.
<u>Memory-Reconsolidation</u>	"Reshape" a traumatic memory within six hours after a phobia has been activated. This <u>removes</u> the fear.
Visualization	The patient is instructed to <u>visualize</u> the fear or phobia as an object or "creature" that can then be <u>controlled</u> by the patient.

Integrate the Vocabulary

Make the new vocabulary *your* vocabulary.

Using Context Clues

Directions: Using context clues, fill in the blanks to complete the following passage using words, or forms of the words, from the text box in Exercise 2 (page 502).

When he was seven, Brian had a _____<u>traumatic</u>_____ encounter with a cat. Happily attempting to hug his neighbor's pet, the cat hissed harshly and then scratched Brian's hand, drawing blood. The memory of that day has had a deep and _____<u>profound</u>_____ effect on Brian. Now 25, though mentally healthy in every other way, he _____<u>dreads</u>_____ the idea of being around felines. His _____ _neuroses_ _____ about cats of all kinds even _____ _induced_ _____ him to give up free tickets to the Broadway show *The Lion King*. _____ _Irrational_ _____ as it seems, Brian just couldn't bear sitting in a theater that had so many "cats" in the cast. It was _____ _daunting_ _____ for him. In fact, when at the zoo last summer, the _____ _ambient_ _____ sound of the lion's roar in the Wild Cat exhibit fostered Brian's early _____ _departure_ _____ from the African Exhibit entirely. Though there has never been a _____ _documented_ _____ case of a cat escaping, Brian fled that area and waited for his friends in the Snake Hall, fearing the wrath of a wild cat. _____ _Arbitrary_ _____ as it seems, all his friends know that if a cat, or even a person dressed in a cat costume, is anywhere nearby, Brian will _____ _reliably_ _____ leave the scene.

Exercise 6B **Recognizing Figurative Language**

Directions: Throughout the selection, the author uses similes and metaphors to help you understand his experiences with his phobia. Following are sentences from the text that include similes and metaphors. Beneath each, write the literal meaning of the italicized figure of speech. You might want to collaborate with a partner.

1. I scan the passengers *like an air marshal looking for terrorists.* (para. 2)
   He intently and nervously looks for anyone eating or drinking, as though they had a "bomb."

2. . . . I saw a primitive, eyeless monster, visible only to me, *like the gremlin on the wing of the airplane in* The Twilight Zone. (para. 9)
   The phobia was like a frightening monster that no one could see except him.

3. The day may come when psychiatrists can wipe out phobias at will, *like erasing a whiteboard.* (para. 10)
   Phobias may be removed quickly and easily.

4. I do well in restaurants, where there's a lot of ambient noise and distraction, but **one-on-one meals** *are a minefield.* (para. 2)
   Eating with just one other person has a lot of potential but unforeseen danger.

5. When I go to a movie theater, *every movie is a horror movie.* (para. 2)
   Because there is so much eating in a movie theater, seeing any movie can be just awful and scary for the author.

6. *CBT is your weapon of choice.* (para. 4)
   Cognitive Behavioral Therapy is a preferred method for dealing with phobias.

Make Personal Connections Through Writing and Discussion

Connect to the content on a personal level. How does it relate to you? How can you apply what you have read to other situations?

| Exercise 7 | **Making Personal Connections Through Writing and Discussion** |

Responses will vary.

1. Phobias, or irrational fears, seem to plague many people. The article focuses on one method to treat phobias, and mentions several others. With a partner in discussion, or in a written response in a journal, answer the following questions. Share your written response with your partner or others in your class.

   ■ What is your opinion of CBT? Do you think it makes sense as a treatment for phobias?

   ■ Do you have a phobia, or know anyone who does? If you were going to apply a CBT technique, what would you do or recommend? Could you "treat" the phobia with a visualization as Dr. N suggested for the author? What would you suggest?

2. Can you think of any other "therapies" not mentioned in the article that could address a person's phobia? Consider a student who had a phobia of elevators. What could you suggest? Discuss these with your classmates and/or enter responses in your journal.

Independent Reading
Selection 3

> ## Humanistic Psychotherapies: Client-Centered Therapy
> ### By Michael Passer and Ronald Smith
> Adapted from *Psychology, The Science of Mind and Behavior*

 before you read ⏸

Answer the following questions before you read the selection.

1. What do you know about the field of psychotherapy?

   _____

   _____

   _____

2. What qualities in a psychologist or therapist do you believe would be most helpful to a client seeking emotional support? Explain.

   _____

   _____

   _____

Prepare to Read

Preview the adapted chapter excerpt using the THIEVES strategy (p. 40).

| Exercise 1 | **Developing Preview Questions** |

Directions: Based on your previewing, write *three* questions you anticipate *Answers will vary.* will be answered in the selection.

1. _____
2. _____
3. _____

| Exercise 2 | **Checking Out the Vocabulary** |

You will encounter the following words in bold type in this reading.

attributes*	consistency*	empathy	insights*	resources*
climate	distorted*	fostering	perceptions*	theorists

*Denotes a word from the Academic Word List

Read each sentence from the selection in which a vocabulary word appears in bold. Select the best definition of the word from the choices provided. Write the letter of your choice on the line provided.

_b_ **1. theorists**

Humanistic **theorists** view humans as capable of consciously controlling their actions and taking responsibility for their choices and behaviors. (para. 1)

a. people who perform miracles
b. people who propose plausible or scientifically acceptable principles to explain behavior and occurrences
c. people who ask questions about the nature of the universe
d. people who often contradict accepted principles and scientific explanations

_b_ **2. resources**

These theorists also believe that everyone possesses inner **resources** for self-healing and personal growth and that disordered behavior reflects a blocking of the natural growth process. (para. 1)

a. bodily organs
b. natural sources of capability or expertise
c. medications and remedies
d. beliefs and ideas

_d_ **3. distorted**

This blocking is brought about by **distorted** perceptions, lack of aware-ness about feeling, or a negative self-image. (para. 1)

a. grandiose, self-absorbed
b. fearful, timid, very afraid
c. clear, concise, accurate
d. inaccurate, twisted out of true meaning

_a_ **4. perceptions**

This blocking is brought about by distorted **perceptions**, lack of aware-ness about feeling, or a negative self-image. (para. 1)

a. mental image or awareness based on interpretation
b. evidence based on fact
c. self-loathing and hatred
d. belief based on experience

_c_ **5. insights**

It is directed at helping clients to become aware of feelings as they occur rather than to achieve **insights** into the childhood origins of those feelings. (para. 2)

a. memories and recollections
b. joy and elation
c. power to see or understand situations intuitively
d. weakness in the capacity to remember

_d_ **6. fostering**

He began to focus his attention on the kind of therapeutic environment that seemed most effective in **fostering** self-exploration and personal growth (Bozarth et al., 2002). (para. 3)

a. stopping, preventing
b. limiting, causing delay or problems
c. placing in another location, away from the original source
d. nurturing, promoting growth and development

_b_ **7. attributes**

Roger's research and experiences as a therapist identified three impor-tant and interrelated therapist **attributes**. (para. 3)

a. physical features
b. qualities, characteristics
c. strategies, methods
d. office locations

_c_ **8. empathy**

Empathy, the willingness and ability to view the world through the client's eyes, is a second vital factor. (para. 3)

a. capacity to think outside the box
b. capacity to have unusual insight and vision
c. capacity for sensitivity and experiencing the feeling of others
d. capacity to put others before oneself, unselfish

<u>*a*</u> 9. consistency

Genuineness refers to **consistency** *between the way the therapist feels and the way her or she behaves.* (para. 3)

a. agreement or harmony
b. contradiction
c. annoyance
d. inaccuracy

<u>*d*</u> 10. climate

They create a **climate** in which the client feels accepted, understood, and free to explore attitudes and feelings without fear of being judged or rejected. (para. 4)

a. weather conditions
b. happy and comfortable place
c. air quality
d. prevailing condition or atmosphere

▶ as you read

Establish Your Purpose

Read and annotate the selection using the guidelines for active reading.

Actively Process as You Read: Independent Reading of a Textbook Selection

Monitor your comprehension as you read. (See Chapter 2, page 54.) Think about the attributes of a therapist involved in client-centered therapy. Imagine the conversation between therapist and client. Highlight the most important points. In the margin, write notes, responses, or questions that come to mind.

⏸

> ## Humanistic Psychotherapies: Client-Centered Treatment
> ### By Michael Passer and Ronald Smith

1   Humanistic **theorists** believe humans are capable of consciously controlling their actions and taking responsibility for their choices and behaviors. These theorists also believe that everyone possesses inner **resources** for self-healing and personal growth and that disordered behavior reflects a blocking of the natural growth process. This blocking is brought about by **distorted perceptions**, lack of awareness about feelings, or a negative self-image.

2   Unlike psychoanalytic theorists who see behavior as a result of unconscious processes, humanistic therapists focus primarily on the present and the future, instead of

the past. The therapy is directed at helping clients to become aware of feelings as they occur rather than to achieve **insights** into the childhood origins of those feelings.

Client-Centered Therapy

3   The best-known and most widely used humanistic therapy is the *client-centered* (now sometimes called *person-centered*) approach developed by Carl Rogers (1959, 1980). In the 1940s, Rogers began to depart from psychoanalytic methods, which focused on people's pasts. He became convinced that the important active ingredient in therapy is the relationship that develops between client and therapist. He began to focus his attention on the kind of therapeutic environment that seemed most effective in **fostering** self-exploration and personal growth (Bozarth et al., 2002). Rogers' research and experiences as a therapist identified three important and interrelated therapist **attributes.**

■ *Unconditional positive regard is communicated when the therapist shows that he or she genuinely cares about and accepts the client, without judgment or evaluations.* The therapist communicates a trust in the client's ability to work through her or his problems. In part, this is communicated in the therapist's refusal to offer advice or guidance.

■ *Empathy, the willingness and ability to view the world through the client's eyes,* is a second vital factor. The therapist comes to sense the feelings and meanings experienced by the client and communicates this understanding. The therapist reflects back to the client what she or he is communicating—perhaps by rephrasing something the client has just said in a way that captures the meaning and emotion involved.

■ *Genuineness refers to* **consistency** *between the way the therapist feels and the way he or she behaves.* The therapist must be open enough to express his or her own feelings honestly, whether positive or negative. A therapist can express displeasure with a client's behavior, however, and at the same time communicate acceptance of the client as a person. For example, a therapist might say, "I feel frustrated with the way you handled that situation because I want things to work out better than that for you."

4   Rogers believed that when therapists can express these three key attributes, they create a **climate** in which the client feels accepted, understood, and free to explore attitudes and feelings without fear of being judged or rejected. The client experiences the courage and freedom to grow. These therapeutic attributes are exhibited in the following excerpt from one of Rogers' therapy sessions.

> *Client*: I cannot be the kind of person I want to be. I guess maybe I haven't the guts or the strength to kill myself, and if someone else would relieve me of the responsibility or I would be in an accident—I just don't want to live.
>
> *Rogers*: At the present time things look so black that you can't see much point in living. (Note the use of empathic reflection and the absence of any criticism.)
>
> *Client*: Yes, I wish I'd never started this therapy. I was happy when I was living in my dream world. There I could be the kind of person I wanted to be. But now there is such a wide, wide gap between my ideal and what I am. . . . (Notice how the client responds to reflection with more information.)
>
> *Rogers*: It's really tough digging into this like you are, and at times the shelter of your dream world looks more attractive and comfortable. (Reflection.)
>
> *Client*: My dream world or suicide. . . . So I don't see why I should waste your time coming in twice a week—I'm not worth it—what do you think?

Rogers: It's up to you . . . It isn't wasting my time. I'd be glad to see you whenever you come, but it's how you feel about it . . . (Note the genuineness in stating an honest desire to see the client and the unconditional positive regard in trusting her capacity and responsibility for choice.)

Client: You're not going to suggest that I come in more often? You're not alarmed and think I ought to come in every day until I get out of this?

Rogers: I believe you're able to make your own decision. I'll see you whenever you want to come. (Trust and positive regard.)

Client: (Note of awe in her voice.) I don't believe you are alarmed about—I see—I may be afraid of myself but you aren't afraid for me. (She experiences the therapist's confidence in her.)

Rogers: You say you are afraid of yourself and are wondering why I don't seem to be afraid for you. (Reflection.)

Client: You have more confidence in me that I have. I'll see you next week, maybe.

(Based on Rogers 1951) (The client did not attempt suicide.)

5   Rogers believed that as clients experience a constructive, therapeutic relationship, they exhibit increased self-acceptance, greater self-awareness, enhanced self-reliance, increased comfort with other relationships, and improved life functioning. (Rogers, 1959). Research supports the idea that the therapist's characteristics do, indeed, have a strong effect on the outcome of psychotherapy. It is most likely to be successful when the therapist is perceived as genuine, warm, and empathic. (Sachese & Ellito 2002)

■ ■ ■

 **after you read**

| **Exercise 3** | **Answering Your Preview Questions** |

Directions: Look back at the questions you posed before you read the selection. If you have discovered the answers, write them on the lines provided.

1. _____   *Answers will vary.*

   _____

2. _____

   _____

3. _____

   _____

| **Exercise 4** | **Reviewing Important Points** |

Directions: Choose the best answer for each of the following questions using the information provided in the selection. Write your answers in the spaces provided.

_c_ 1. By first introducing the beliefs of humanistic theorists, and then discussing client-centered therapy, the authors incorporate the organizational writing pattern of:

  a. sequence.
  b. comparison and contrast.
  c. classification.
  d. cause and effect.

_d_ 2. The difference between humanistic therapy and psychodynamic therapy is that humanistic therapy:

  a. focuses on the present and future, rather than the past.
  b. is directed at helping clients become aware of feelings as they occur, rather than focus on past feelings of childhood.
  c. believes that all people possess the power to control their actions, choices, and behaviors.
  d. all of the above.

_a_ 3. The topic of paragraph 3 is:

  a. Carl Rogers and client-centered therapy.
  b. the right kind of therapeutic environment.
  c. humanistic therapy.
  d. the relationship between patient and therapist.

_c_ 4. The bulleted list within paragraph 3 identifies and defines:

  a. traits all clients must have to achieve mental health.
  b. qualities every good doctor should possess.
  c. three important therapist attributes, according to Carl Rogers.
  d. none of the above.

_b_ 5. The attribute in which the therapist communicates a trust in the client's ability to work through his or her own issues is called:

  a. empathy.
  b. unconditional positive regard.
  c. client-centered environment.
  d. genuineness.

_a_ 6. The main idea of paragraph 4 is expressed:

  a. in the first sentence.
  b. in the second sentence.
  c. in the third sentence.
  d. nowhere; it is unstated.

_a_ 7. From the excerpt of one of Rogers' therapy sessions, we can infer that:

  a. Carl Rogers himself expressed the three attributes he valued in his work.
  b. Carl Rogers was unable to apply the attributes he identified as important.
  c. Rogers was generally insensitive to the needs of his client.
  d. The patient may have actually committed suicide after the session.

_b_ 8. We can infer from the last paragraph that the work of Carl Rogers:
   a. is considered outdated and unacceptable.
   b. is still respected and used in treatment today.
   c. is unlikely to be successful because most therapists are not genuine, warm, and empathic.
   d. is criticized by most therapists.

_c_ 9. The overall purpose of this excerpt is to:
   a. amuse and entertain the reader with the excerpt from Carl Rogers' therapy session.
   b. persuade the reader that the client-centered therapy of Carl Rogers is the most important of the humanistic therapies.
   c. inform the reader of the client-centered therapeutic approach developed by Carl Rogers.
   d. instruct the reader on how to conduct a client-centered therapy session.

_d_ 10. What is the overall tone of the selection?
   a. nostalgic and thoughtful
   b. disappointed and critical
   c. biased and upset
   d. straightforward and neutral

Exercise 5   ## Organizing the Information

Directions: Complete the semantic map that follows to graphically reorganize the key points of the selection.

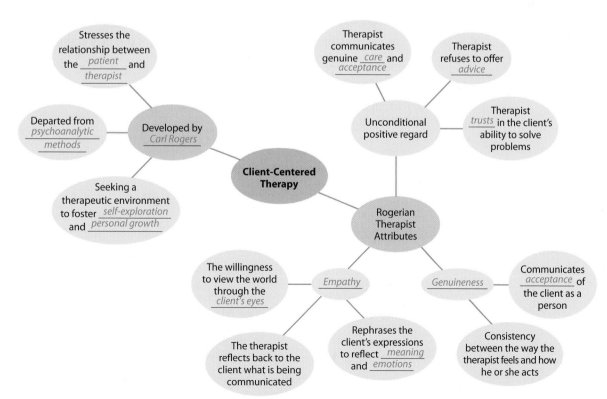

Exercise 6	**Integrating the Vocabulary**

Directions: Answer the following questions, each of which includes a vocabulary word, or form of the word, from the selection. Write a complete sentence for your response, *restating* the word in the context of your answer.

Answers will vary.

1. Based on your own knowledge, what do **theorists** believe are possible causes of global warming?

   Some theorists believe that global warming . . .

   _____

2. What personal **resources** have you developed to help yourself succeed in college?

   _____

   _____

3. How might abusive parents **distort** the self image of their child?

   _____

   _____

4. What are your general **perceptions** of your professors this semester?

   _____

   _____

5. Have you gained any **insights** into your capabilities as a student since beginning college? What are they?

   _____

   _____

6. What kind of environment do you think **fosters** good study habits ?

   _____

   _____

7. Identify the **attributes** you look for in a close friend.

   _____

   _____

8. Do you consider yourself to be an **empathic** person? How so?

   _____

   _____

9. What is an example in your life in which your beliefs are **consistent** with your behavior?

   _____

   _____

10. What kind of classroom **climate** do you find most conducive to learning?

    _____

    _____

Exercise 7   **Making Personal Connections Through Writing and Discussion**

Directions: Think about yourself in relation to the selection. Share your responses in pairs or within a small group.

1. Consider the three attributes Rogers identified as important for a therapist to possess. Which of these would you say you exhibit the most in dealing with others? Explain with an example.

2. With a partner, take the role of therapist and client. Read aloud the dialogue of Rogers' therapy session excerpted in the selection. When you finish, discuss it with your partner. What is your reaction to the exchange? How did you feel in your role? What do you think of the "Rogerian" approach?

Responses will vary.

⌐°reflect AND respond⌐

Now that you have read three selections about interventions for *emotional well-being*, you have a broader and better understanding of the topic.

Directions: Complete a journal response for this module. Read the following questions. Select two to which you would like to respond. Write your responses on a separate piece of paper. Write at least one page.

1. What interesting information did you learn about eco-therapy to deal with stress and depression, cognitive-behavioral therapy to combat phobias, and/or client-centered therapy to help people with their emotional problems?

2. How does this information apply to you? Make connections with your own experience(s). What approach do you value the most? What do these readings make you think about?

3. What else would you like to know about some of the topics discussed in this module?

Readings About Relationships

Get Acquainted with the Issue

Relationships come in many forms. As we go out into the world, the number and range of our relationships expand. As a college student, perhaps you have forged relationships with fellow students, professors, or support staff. And if you are not or have never been involved in a romantic relationship, the odds are that you will be in the future.

Many areas of study in college focus on aspects of relationships. Psychology looks at how people grow in their capacity to interact with one another. Sociology views patterns of relationships among different cultures and societies. Anthropology explores how people from various cultures and civilizations relate with one another. Your college studies will often tap into relationships, whether they are characters in literature, leaders in history, inventors in science, or explorers of the universe. When you learn about people, you learn about relationships.

In this module you will read three selections focusing on relationships. The first is an adapted section of a sociology textbook. Called "Courtship and Mate Selection," the selection discusses various ways people from different cultures find life companions. The second selection, "Friendship: Awkward Encounters of the Friendly Kind," is an article excerpted from a popular magazine. It gives practical advice on maintaining a good relationship with close friends. The concluding selection is about an unusual father and son relationship. Adapted from a memoir by Osama bin Laden's fourth son, Omar, it describes a remote father who puts his politics above his family. Think about your own relationships as you read about others.

Guided Reading
Reading Selection 1

Courtship and Mate Selection
By Richard T. Schaefer

This article is adapted from an introductory sociology textbook. Within a chapter titled "The Family and Intimate Relationships," it describes different cultural views about selecting a life partner for marriage.

⏪ **before you read**

⏸

Think about what you already know about a topic before you begin reading. Then you will be able to attach your new learning to this background knowledge and more easily understand the new information. (See Chapter 2, p. 38.)

Discuss or write responses to the following questions about your *own* views on choosing a mate.

1. What qualities in a potential life partner do you consider to be most important?
2. Would you ever entrust the decision of finding your future partner to another person?
3. What would you say to those whose tradition says that they must marry the person that is selected for them by their parents?

Prepare to Read

Now preview the selection, "Courtship and Mate Selection," using the THIEVES strategy on page 40.

Exercise 1   Previewing

Directions: Complete the following items.

1. Take a look at the selection and check off all the items that are available to you for preview.

    _X_ Title

    _X_ Headings

    _X_ Introduction

    _X_ Every first sentence in each paragraph

    ___ Visuals/vocabulary

    ___ End of chapter questions

    _X_ Summary/concluding paragraph

2. Actively preview the selection by reading and highlighting the items you have checked.

3. Based on your preview, place an "X" next to those items you predict will be discussed in the selection.

    _X_ a. Courtship and mate selection.

    _X_ b. Homogamy and how it relates to mate selection.

    _X_ c. The love relationship as part of mate selection.

    ___ d. The percentages of divorce in marriage around the world.

    _X_ e. Arranged marriage in other cultures and the United States.

    ___ f. Cultures in which marriage is forbidden.

Check Out the Vocabulary

You will find the following vocabulary words in bold font in the reading selection. Some are repeated more than once in the text. Do you know what these words mean? Knowing the meaning of all of these words will increase your understanding of the material.

benign	homogenous	priority	relent
designated	intimate	rationale	trend
engage	precede*	reinforce*	universal

*Denotes a word from the Academic Word List

Exercise 2   **Checking Out the Vocabulary**

Directions: Look at each word taken from the reading selection. Read the sentences that follow. The first is from the selection, with a hint to its meaning, and the second one uses the word in an additional context. Choose the best definition for the word, and write the letter of the definition you select on the line provided.

_a_ **1. trend**

- An unmistakable **trend** in mate selection is that the process appears to be taking longer today than in the past. (para. 1) (HINT: It is going on today, rather than in the past.)
- Wearing sports caps with the brim in the back began as a **trend,** but is now typical today among high school and college students.

    a. a tendency to go in a certain way or direction
    b. a rebellion
    c. a problem or conflict
    d. a mistake or error

_b_ **2. engage**

- Today's generation of college students seems more likely to "hook up" or cruise in large packs than to **engage** in the romantic dating relationships of their parents and grandparents. (para. 2) (HINT: The phrase "than to" implies a contrast.)
- Professor McNair loves to **engage** her students in heated debates in class, discussing controversial issues, so that everyone gets involved and participates.

    a. put down, demean
    b. take part in, carry on an activity
    c. confuse or complicate the situation
    d. poke fun at, ridicule

__d__ **3. homogenous**

- Though some people may follow the **homogenous** pattern, others observe the rule that opposites attract. (para. 3) (HINT: Use the contrast clue, signaled by the words *though* and *others*. Also, what does the word part "homo" mean?)
- Though there are exceptions, populations in developing countries are generally **homogenous** regarding levels of education and gross family income.

  a. hof a different and opposite kind or nature
  b. of a romantic nature
  c. unpredictable, without reason or explanation
  d. of the same or similar kind or nature

__c__ **4. rationale**

- Parents in the United States tend to value love highly as a **rationale** for marriage, and they encourage their children to develop intimate relationships based on love and affection. (para. 4) (HINT: Use your own background knowledge. What is love considered to be when it comes to marrying in this country?)
- Malcolm's **rationale** for partying the night before the exam was that he had studied extensively over the last four days and felt completely prepared.

  a. recognition
  b. wish or hope
  c. underlying reason or basis
  d. underlying remedy for something

__b__ **5. intimate**

- Parents in the United States tend to value love highly as a rationale for marriage, and they encourage their children to develop **intimate** relationships based on love and affection. (para. 4) (HINT: What kind of relationships would these be?)
- According to psychologist and researcher R. J. Sternberg, complete love involves an **intimate** relationship, with passion and commitment.

  a. marked by power and importance
  b. marked by closeness, familiarity and warmth
  c. marked by anger and confrontation
  d. marked by mistrust and doubt

__d__ **6. reinforce**

- Songs, films, books, magazines, television shows and even cartoons and comic books **reinforce** the theme of love. (para. 4) (HINT: What does the prefix *re-* mean?)
- In order to **reinforce** his recall of the mathematical formulas, Pete recited them aloud as he wrote them three times.

  a. to diminish
  b. to remember

c. to change
d. to strengthen

_c_ 7. **universal**

- Though most people in the United States take the importance of falling in love for granted, the coupling of love and marriage is by no means a cultural **universal**. (para. 5) (HINT: Think of your sense of the term, *universe*. What is it generally known to include?)
- A **universal** facial expression for happiness is the smile.

  a. uncommon, unique to a few
  b. relating to the planets and galaxies
  c. including all without limit, everywhere and everyone
  d. related to the movies and motion pictures

_d_ 8. **priority**

- Many of the world's cultures give **priority** to mate selection factors other than romantic feelings. (para. 5) (HINT: Read the previous sentence. What can you conclude? Are romantic feelings at the top of the list? If not, then are others considered more important?)
- During the registration period, the advisement office gives **priority** to students who are in their last semester before graduation and allows them to register before all other students.

  a. a negative judgment or rating
  b. authority and power
  c. less time than required to achieve a task
  d. a preferential rating, something above all other alternatives

_a_ 9. **designated**

- Among the Sikhs and Hindus who have immigrated from India, and among Muslims and Hasidic Jews, young people allow their parents or **designated** matchmakers to find spouses within their ethnic community. (para. 7) (HINT: How would you describe someone who you gave permission to make a decision on your behalf?)
- Because Raphael injured his wrist, the coach **designated** Jason to bat for him during the season's playoff games.

  a. indicated for a specific purpose
  b. withdrew support for
  c. demanded participation
  d. to ask or request

_c_ 10. **benign**

- In its most **benign** form, this custom is a kind of elopement in which the man whisks off his girlfriend. (para. 9) (HINT: Compared to being abducted against your will, another form of *ala kachuu*, how would you describe the form being discussed?)
- Though Janice thought it was **benign** to use phrases from her friend's paper in her own, her professor considered it plagiarism.

a. problematic, serious, causing harm
b. joyous, playful, fun filled
c. harmless, mild, unthreatening
d. worrisome and annoying

_b_ 11. relent

- Many of them—perhaps 80 percent—eventually **relent** to their kidnapping. (para. 9) (HINT: Read the next two sentences. What can you infer for the meaning of relent?)

- Students begged Professor Miller to **relent** on the number of papers and exams he demanded in History 203. Five papers and six exams felt like just too much!

    a. became stronger, increase in intensity, make demands
    b. become less severe, let up, slacken, give in
    c. become aimless and lost, without direction
    d. become noncaring, uninvolved, without purpose

_c_ 12. precede

- For these women, though love may well develop over time, romantic love does not **precede** marriage. (para. 9) (HINT: Based on what occurs in this situation what can you infer *precede* means? Also, consider the meaning of the prefix *pre-*.)

- The completion of all noncredited classes must **precede** registration for advanced courses in English and Math.

    a. to belong, to become part of
    b. to follow, to come after
    c. to come before, to come ahead of
    d. to cancel, to make unauthorized

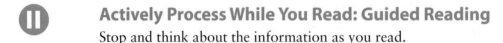

▶ as you read

Establish Your Purpose

Now you are ready to read and annotate the excerpt "Courtship and Mate Selection." Focus on major points of information. Read to learn the various factors that impact the selection of lifelong partners in America and in other cultures.

⏸ Actively Process While You Read: Guided Reading

Stop and think about the information as you read.

Exercise 3   **Processing While You Read**

Directions: Answer the questions that appear in bold print at the conclusion of each paragraph. This will help you monitor your reading process and understand the material.

Courtship and Mate Selection
By Richard Schaefer

1   An unmistakable **trend** in mate selection is that the process appears to be taking longer today than in the past. Many factors, including concerns about financial security and personal independence, have contributed to this delay in marriage. Most people are now well into their twenties before they marry, both in the United States and in other countries.

What trend has impacted our culture regarding the age at which people marry?
People are marrying at a comparatively older age than in the past, well into their twenties.

The Love Relationship

2   Today's generation of college students seems more likely to "hook up" or cruise in large packs than to **engage** in the romantic dating relationships of their parents and grandparents. Still, at some point in their adult lives, the great majority of today's students will meet someone they love. They are then likely to enter into a long-term relationship that focuses on creating a family.

Before entering into a romantic relationship, what is typical of today's generation of college students.
College students tend to casually hook up, or go out in large groups of people rather than on romantic dates.

3   Homogamy is the conscious or unconscious tendency to select a mate with personal characteristics similar to one's own. It is a factor that plays a large part in mate selection. The "like marries like" rule can be seen in couples with similar personalities and cultural interests. However, mate selection is unpredictable. Though some people may follow the **homogenous** pattern, others observe the rule that opposites attract.

What is homogamy? Is it always a factor in selection of a mate?
Homogamy is the conscious or unconscious tendency to choose a mate with personal characteristics similar to one's own. Sometimes it is a factor in picking a partner, but not always. People sometimes are attracted to their opposite.

4   Parents in the United States tend to value love highly as a **rationale** for marriage, and they encourage their children to develop **intimate** relationships based on love and affection. Songs, films, books, magazines, television shows and even cartoons and comic books **reinforce** the theme of love. At the same time, our society expects parents and peers to help a person confine his or her search for a mate to "socially acceptable" members of the opposite sex.

What is identified as the primary rationale for marriage in the United States?
The primary rationale for marriage in the United States is love.

Alternatives to Love in Other Cultures

5   Though most people in the United States take the importance of falling in love for granted, the coupling of love and marriage is by no means a cultural **universal.** Many of the world's cultures give **priority** to mate selection factors other than romantic feelings.

What is the main idea of this paragraph?

Not all cultures think romantic feelings are the most important reason for marriage.

_____

Arranged Marriages

6   In many societies, *arranged marriages* are engineered by parents or religious authorities. Economic considerations play a significant role. The newly married couple is expected to develop a feeling of love *after* the legal union is formalized, if at all.

Who orchestrates the arranged marriages in many societies? What is a primary consideration?

Parents or religious authorities often are involved in arranged marriages. An important consideration is economics or finances.

_____

7   Even within the United States, some subcultures carry on the arranged marriage practice of their native cultures. Among the Sikhs and Hindus who have immigrated from India, and among Muslims and Hasidic Jews, young people allow their parents or **designated** matchmakers to find spouses within their ethnic community. As one young Sikh declared, "I will definitely marry who my parents wish. They know me better than I know myself."

Are marriages ever arranged in the United States? How so?

There are arranged marriages in the United States. Young people coming from cultures that have a tradition of arranged marriages allow their parents or designated matchmakers to find mates for them within their ethnic community.

_____

High-Tech Connections

8   Young people who have come to the United States without their families often turn to the Internet to find partners who share their background and goals. Matrimonial ads for the Indian community run on such Web sites as SuitableMatch.com and Indolink.com. As one Hasidic Jewish woman noted, the system of arranged marriages "isn't perfect, and it doesn't work for everyone, but this is the system we know and trust, the way we couple, and the way we learn to love. So it works for most of us." (R. Segall 1998).

How is the Internet used in finding partners of suitable ethnic backgrounds?

There are several sites where young people who have immigrated to the United States without family can post matrimonial ads specifically within a particular ethnic background.

_____

A Kidnapped Bride?

9   In some societies, neither the parents nor the bride has a say in whom she marries. Since at least the 12th century, men in the central Asian nation of Kyrgyzstan have literally kidnapped their future wives from the street. This is a custom known as *ala kachuu*. It translates roughly as "grab and run." In its most **benign** form, this custom is a kind of elopement in which the man whisks off his girlfriend. Men do it to avoid the "bride price" that parents often demand in return for their consent. But as of 2005, one-third of the brides in Kyrgyzstan had been abducted against their will. Many of them—perhaps 80 percent—eventually **relent** to their kidnapping. This is often at their parents' urging. For these women, though love may well develop over time, romantic love does not **precede** marriage. (Craig Smith 2005)

What is the custom of ala kachuu?

It is a custom in central Asia in which a man "whisks" off his girlfriend to avoid a bride price that is often demanded by the woman's parents. Unfortunately, it has turned into a practice of abducting brides against their will in many cases.

_____

■ ■ ■

 after you read

Review Important Points

Going over major points immediately after you read, while the information is fresh in your mind, will help you recall the content and record key ideas.

| Exercise 4 | **Reviewing Important Points** |

Directions: Answer the following questions based on the content of the selection. You may need to go back and reread certain portions to be sure your responses are correct and can be supported by information in the text. Write the letter of your choice in the space provided.

_c_ **1. What is the thesis of this selection?**
   a. Homogamy plays a major role in mate selection in the United States
   b. Love is the critical reason for marriage.
   c. Mate selection can take on many forms and varies in different cultures.
   d. Mate selection is often carried out by parents in many societies.

_d_ **2. The main idea of the first paragraph is that:**
   a. not as many people are marrying as in the past.
   b. people are not interested in marriage.
   c. in most countries, people are marrying at a younger age than in the past.
   d. in most countries, people are delaying marriage until they are older.

_b_ 3. The topic of paragraph 3 is homogamy. What is the primary organizational pattern used by the author to discuss it?

    a. cause and effect
    b. definition
    c. sequence/chronology
    d. classification

_c_ 4. Which of the following details *does not* support the main idea of paragraph 4?

    a. Parents encourage children to develop intimate relationships based on love and affection.
    b. Songs and films reinforce the theme of love.
    c. Parents and peers help confine a search for a mate to those who are "socially acceptable."
    d. Even cartoons and comic books focus on love.

_a_ 5. All of the following are mentioned as factors in arranged marriages *except*:

    a. being close to home.
    b. economic reasons.
    c. having a spouse from within the same ethnic community.
    d. believing parents can make a wise choice for a partner.

_b_ 6. In arranged marriages, the expectation is that if love occurs, it will do so:

    a. before marriage.
    b. after marriage.
    c. during the marriage ceremony.
    d. none of the above.

_a_ 7. The main idea of paragraph 8 is stated in the:

    a. first sentence.
    b. second sentence.
    c. third sentence.
    d. last sentence.

_a_ 8. That as of 2005, one-third of the brides in Kyrgyzstan had been abducted against their will, is an example of a:

    a. fact.
    b. opinion.
    c. informed opinion.
    d. biased statement.

_b_ 9. The topic of the last paragraph is:

    a. elopement.
    b. a custom called *ala kachuu*.
    c. runaway brides.
    d. kidnapping.

<u> c </u> 10. We can infer that *ala kachuu:*

    a. would be enjoyed by women in the United States.

    b. will soon be legalized in America.

    c. would not be tolerated in this country.

    d. is a custom we might incorporate in the near future.

Organize the Information

Organizing the information you have learned from a reading selection shows you have understood it and have the ability to restate the material in a different way. You can use this reorganized material to help you study for exams and prepare for written assignments. (See Chapter 9.)

Exercise 5 **Organizing the Information**

Directions: Using the content of the reading selection, complete the following outline.

> # Courtship and Mate Selection

I. Trends in Mate Selection

    A. Taking _longer_ than in the past

        1. concerns about _financial security_

        2. desire for personal independence

    B. Delay marriage until _well into twenties_

II. The Love Relationship

    A. Majority of students today will meet someone they _love_

        1. Will enter _into a long-term relationship_

        2. Focus _on creating a family_

    B. _Homogamy_

        1. The conscious or unconscious tendency to select a mate with personal _characteristics_ similar to one's own

            a. personalities

            b. _cultural interests_

        2. Some may follow the homogenous pattern

        3. Others observe the rule that _opposites attract_

    C. U.S. parents value love as a _rationale_ for marriage

        1. Encourage _intimate_ relationships based on love and affection

        2. Many cultural reinforcements

            a. _songs_

            b. _books_

    c. _magazines_

    d. _TV shows_

    e. cartoons and _comic books_

III. Alternatives to Love in Other Cultures

    A. Arranged marriage

        1. Engineered by _parents or religious authorities_

        2. _Economic_ considerations

        3. Hopefully will develop feelings of love _after_ the legal union

        4. Occurs in the United States within subcultures

            a. _Sikhs_ and _Hindus_ from India

            b. _Muslims_

            c. _Hasidic Jews_

    B. Internet search

        1. Used by young people in the United States without _families_

        2. Use the Internet to find partners with similar _backgrounds_ and _goals_.

    C. _Ala kachuu_

        1. Practice of literally _kidnapping future wives from the street_

        2. Began during _the 12th century_ in _central Asian nation of Kyrgyzstan_

        3. Translates as _"grab and run"_

        4. Benign form

            a. similar to _elopement_; man whisks off his girlfriend

            b. avoids the _"bride price"_ demanded for parental consent

        5. Severe form

            a. 1/3 of the brides had been _abducted against their will_

            b. Often with parental urging, most brides _relent to their kidnapping_

            c. Romantic love surely does not _precede_ marriage

Integrate the Vocabulary

Make the new vocabulary presented in the reading _your_ vocabulary. In addition to learning the meaning of new words, you should also learn related word forms.

Exercise 6   **Using Context Clues**

Directions: Complete the following paragraph by filling in the blanks with a word or form of the word from the text box on page 525.

An educational _____trend_____ during the 1950s and 60s was to group students of similar abilities into the same classroom. Making classes _____homogenous_____ was an important _____priority_____ for many school districts during that time. It was a widespread practice that became almost _____universal_____.

One _____rationale_____ behind the grouping was that students with common needs and intellectual ability would likely interact and _____engage_____ with one another and form close and _____intimate_____ relationships easily. Also, the teacher could use similar strategies for everyone to strengthen and _____reinforce_____ the learning. Students would be _____designated_____ for certain classes based on their level of achievement, often measured on exams that were taken _____preceding_____ a student's entry into a school.

More recently, rather than seen as beneficial, if not _____benign_____, the practice lost favor. For many, it was discriminatory and unsound. Supporters had to _____relent_____ to change. Educators have since adopted thinking that calls for diversity in classes. Students of varying abilities and backgrounds are learning to work together, and teachers are incorporating better strategies to teach them.

Make Personal Connections Through Writing and Discussion

When you make your new learning relevant to yourself in some way, it becomes more meaningful and easier to remember. Whenever you read, try to connect to the content on a personal level. How does it relate to you? How can you apply what you have read to other situations? What else would you like to know?

Exercise 7   Making Personal Connections

Directions: Write your personal response to each of the following questions. Then share your responses in a small group or with the rest of the class. Do others feel similarly?

1. How important is homogamy to you? List four characteristics that you would like to have in common with a life mate or partner.   *Answers will vary.*

_____
_____
_____
_____

2. The author includes a quote from a young Sikh who says, "I will definitely marry who my parents wish. They know me better than I know myself." Is there any part of this statement that could apply to you? Why or why not?

_____
_____
_____
_____

Self-Monitored Reading
Reading Selection 2

Friendship: Awkward Encounters
of the Friendly Kind

By Carlin Flora

This excerpt is taken from an article published in a popular magazine called Psychology Today. As you read it, consider the nature of some of your own friendships. Are any of the situations familiar?

◀◀ before you read

Answers will vary.   Answer the following questions before you read the selection.

1. What do you consider to be the benefits of a good friendship?

   _____

   _____

2. What are some of the pitfalls or problems adult friends may typically encounter?

   _____

   _____

3. From your own life experience, what are three suggestions you would offer to help people maintain good friendships?

   _____

   _____

Prepare to Read

Preview the reading selection by applying the THIEVES strategy (p. 40).

Exercise 1   **Previewing**

Directions: Based on your preview, respond to the following questions:

1. What is the author's purpose in writing this article?

   The author is going to provide pointers about maintaining good friendships.
   _____

2. Identify three main issues in friendships that the author is likely to discuss.

   1. How friendships change or grow apart

   2. What are some problems we encounter when trying to be helpful to friends?

   3. How to be friends with the opposite sex

3. From your preview, identify some of the benefits of friendship.

   Answers will vary. Some examples: They make us happier and healthier. Friends help us when

   we are down or depressed. We feel good about ourselves when we can help a friend. We can

   benefit from the different relationship styles in men and women when we have friends of the

   opposite sex.

Check Out the Vocabulary

You will encounter the following words in this reading. They are in bold font in the selection. Are you already familiar with some of them? Knowing the meaning of these vocabulary terms will increase your comprehension of the material.

embroiled	individuate	mosaic	rift
gender*	inherently*	myriad	schism
heterogeneous	intervention*	presume*	taint

*Denotes a word from the Academic Word List

Exercise 2   **Checking Out the Vocabulary**

Directions: Look at each word taken from the reading selection. Read each pair of sentences that follows in which the word appears. The first sentence is from the reading. The second gives you additional context to help you figure out the meaning of the word. Select the best definition of the word from the choices. Write the letter of your choice on the line provided.

_b_ **1. rift**

- The unspoken **rift** kept them out of touch for almost two years. (para. 2)
- During their childhood, ongoing jealousy and anger caused such a **rift** between the brothers that, even in adulthood, they never could resolve their differences.

a. a secret or lie
b. a space in between, a break in association
c. a lawsuit against another person
d. a dangerous situation, a problem

_d_ 2. myriad

- And there are a **myriad** situations in between. (para. 3)
- Despite trying a **myriad** of solutions, Jack could not stop the water from leaking into the living room.

a. one hundred
b. unexpected
c. unconventional
d. a great number

_b_ 3. mosaic

- Longtime friends can be invaluable, as they often understand your **mosaic** of experiences and emotional makeup. (para. 4)
- Janice loves the **mosaic** of cultures, ethnicities, and lifestyles on her community college campus—so different from the sameness of students she experienced in her high school.

a. memories, thoughts of times gone by
b. variety, diversity of different ideas or aspects coming together to form a whole
c. similarities, things that people have in common with one another
d. tiles set in grout to form a picture or design

_c_ 4. individuate

- The question . . . is whether you can accept the trade-offs that occur when friends **individuate**. (para. 5)
- After being unemployed and living at home since graduating from college, Aaron's finally getting his own apartment and signing a contract for a well-paying job at the publishing company were big steps enabling him to **individuate** from his parents.

a. to rebel, create conflict
b. to make fun of, mock
c. to form into a distinct entity, become independent
d. to seek support and understanding

_a_ 5. heterogeneous

- The more **heterogeneous** our circle, . . . the more reward, the more access, and the more opportunities we reap. . . . (para. 5)
- Karina loves the **heterogeneous** nature of big cities, rather than the similarities among the people she experienced while living in the suburbs.

a. consisting of mixed or dissimilar parts or ingredients
b. consisting of similar or like parts or ingredients
c. chaotic, frantic, disorganized
d. calm, peaceful, regimented and in order

_c_ 6. schism
   • That's why Terri Apter, a psychologist at the University of Cambridge, recommends confronting small conflicts head-on, to avoid a **schism**. (para. 6)
   • One of the worst **schisms** ever experienced by the United States was the Civil War, during which our country was divided into two, and so many died in battle.
      a. war, combat situations
      b. breakdown, demise, crumbling
      c. division, separation
      d. illness, widespread disease

_d_ 7. taint
   • If you're hurt that your friend didn't invite you to her barbecue or tell you about her promotion, say so, in a nondefensive tone before built-up resentments **taint** all of your interactions. (para. 6)
   • The pharmaceutical company issued an international recall for the batches of aspirin that had been accidentally **tainted** with a harmful chemical.
      a. get into, infuse, infiltrate
      b. complicate, make confusing
      c. complain, express negativity or doubt
      d. contaminate, touch or affect with something bad or harmful

_b_ 8. embroiled
   • It feels good to comfort a friend who is stressed out, lovesick, or **embroiled** in family conflict. (para. 9)
   • Though she tried to avoid it, her emotions flared and Sharon could not help but get **embroiled** in the argument with her co-workers over schedules and time off.
      a. avoidant, staying away from
      b. involved in conflict, disorder, or confusion
      c. mocking or making fun of
      d. hateful over, angered

_d_ 9. presume
   • Don't **presume** that what you do will be a cure. You wouldn't **presume** that if it were pneumonia. (para. 11)
   • Because he had completed all his assignments, George mistakenly **presumed** he would receive an A in the course; he neglected to consider his grade on the final exam.
      a. demand or insist upon
      b. explain in detail
      c. celebrate ahead of time
      d. expect or assume, suppose to be true without proof

_a_ 10. intervention
   • Think before pulling an **intervention**. (para. 12)
   • It was felt that some kind of **intervention** was in order to help Justin stop the binge drinking and partying he was involved in on a regular basis.

　　　　a. the act of coming in-between to prevent harm or improve conditions
　　　　b. the act of withdrawing or falling back
　　　　c. the imposition of a penalty or consequence
　　　　d. changing or altering a situation or dilemma

　c　**11. inherently**
- Opposite sex friends can benefit from the **inherently** different relationship styles that men and women tend to display." (para 17)
- Marissa didn't need to be taught good manners; she **inherently** was polite, kind, and respectful of others.
　　　　a. always, consistently
　　　　b. oddly, unusually
　　　　c. intrinsically, belonging by nature, inborn
　　　　d. rarely, intermittently at best

　c　**12. gender**
- A lot of research shows that regardless of **gender,** the more we pursue closeness, the happier we are in that friendship. (para 17)
- Not knowing the **gender** of her friend's new baby, Leslie avoided a gift with pink or blue, and bought a teddy bear all dressed in yellow.
　　　　a. likes and dislikes
　　　　b. ability, intellect
　　　　c. sex type, male or female
　　　　d. height and weight

▶ as you read

Establish Your Purpose

Now, read and annotate the selection using the guidelines for active reading, and focus on the major points of information.

❙❙ Actively Process While You Read

Monitor your comprehension as you read. (See Chapter 2, page 54.) Be sure to stop to reflect at the conclusion of each paragraph, and ask yourself the following questions:

- Did I understand what I have just read?
- What is the main idea of the paragraph?
- Am I ready to continue?

Exercise 3　**Processing While You Read**

Directions: Highlight the most important points in each paragraph. Then write the key topics and main ideas in the spaces provided in the margins. Finally, underline or number the supporting details in the text.

Friendship: Awkward Encounters of the Friendly Kind
By Carlin Flora

1   Caleb, a photographer, and Mike, a musician, met at an arts festival and became fast friends, eventually laying down roots just blocks from each other in New York City. When Caleb slipped into a scary bout of depression, he leaned on Mike. "We saw each other almost every day," recalls Caleb. "I was having a hard time being alone, so I followed him around. He tried to entertain me, and we discussed my fears about what was happening. I felt like he compromised his own life because he was spending so much time on me."

2   After Caleb came out of his depression, the two drifted apart. Caleb thought Mike would appreciate the break; he also started dating a woman Mike disapproved of. Mike felt badly, believing Caleb left him when he was no longer needed. The unspoken **rift** kept them out of touch for almost two years. Finally they patched things up, but only after Caleb received "a pretty big lecture about what I'd done by 'disappearing.'"

3   Solid friendships make us happier and healthier. In our late-marrying, highly mobile society they're more important than ever as pillars of support. But like any human entanglement, they can cause pain and confusion. For every tale of loyalty and sacrifice, there's a story of betrayal and heartbreak. And there are **myriad** situations in between. Here are some pointers about maintaining good friendships.

Growing Apart

"I feel awkward and self-conscious sharing my life with her, and I'm not that interested in hers. When we were teenagers, we'd stay up all night talking."

4   Longtime friends can be invaluable, as they often understand your **mosaic** of experiences and emotional makeup. But how do you sustain a relationship if your primary-school bosom buddy is off reforesting the developing world while you are prancing around parties in stiletto heels?

5   We tend to choose friends based on who's close by and similar to us. The question, according to Judith Sills, a Philadelphia-based clinical psychologist, is whether you can accept the trade-offs that occur when friends **individuate**. "The more **heterogeneous** our circle," says Sills, "the more rewards, the more access, and the more opportunities we reap. We also reap more discomfort, though. So expect to feel annoyed or threatened on occasion when you have a diverse group of friends."

6   Friendship is accordion-like: Sometimes you'll be close, sometimes you'll be distant, and sometimes you'll revert back to being close. Or not. It can be heartrending to realize that a friendship has petered out. That's why Terri Apter, a psychologist at the University of Cambridge, recommends confronting small conflicts head-on, to avoid a **schism**. If you're hurt that your friend didn't invite you to her barbecue or tell you about her promotion, say so, in a nondefensive tone, before built-up resentments **taint** all of your interactions.

Notes

Topic _____

_____

Main Idea _____

_____

_____

Topic _____

_____

Main Idea _____

_____

_____

Topic _____

_____

Main Idea _____

_____

_____

Topic _____

_____

Main Idea _____

_____

_____

Topic _____

_____

Main Idea _____

_____

_____

Topic _____

_____

Main Idea _____

_____

_____

Notes

Topic _____
Main Idea _____
_____

7   Also, examine your own changed feelings. Let's say a single woman's best friend gets married and has a son. The new mom ignores all her friend's e-mails, cuts short her phone calls, and shows up late to coffee dates. The single woman gets critical: "She's so boring now." But really, she's feeling neglected. It would be better, Sills says, if she were to think, "My friend is not as available to me as she used to be, but life is long. Someday I may have kids, and I'll want her understanding then." When you do reconnect, you'll both bring new experiences to the interaction.

Topic _____
Main Idea _____
_____

8   Accept that friendships erode but then sometimes rebuild. Communicate hurt feelings. Appreciate chums who aren't like you. Wouldn't a life filled with clones bore you?

Lending a Hand to a Friend in Need

I'm sorry to show up at this hour, but I don't know what I'd do without you. I'm so upset."

Topic _____
Main Idea _____
_____

9   It feels good to comfort a friend who is stressed out, lovesick, or **embroiled** in family conflict. But if a pal's bad day stretches into weeks or months, how can you help? "Clearly communicate that you are there for him or her," says Beverley Fehr, author of *Friendship Processes*. Listening is usually more appreciated than giving advice. While men tend to appreciate practical support in hard times (rake his lawn, pick up some groceries), women value emotional support (give a hug and point out how well she's taking it all).

Topic _____
Main Idea _____
_____

10   Friends often fall into respective roles of "saint" and "sinner," Sills observes. The sinner reels from crisis to crisis, reporting all the drama. The saint dependably, patiently, takes it all. Sometimes the saint will need to set limits. If the sinner is constantly whining about a job but refuses to look for another one, the saint could say, "You know I'm happy to hear from you, but it's clear that you're not ready to leave this job. I keep getting caught lecturing you and I don't like that, so let's not talk about that topic anymore."

Topic _____
Main Idea _____
_____

11   If your pal is not merely down about a specific event, but clinically depressed, your friend will likely need professional guidance to feel better. However, just being there is important and soothing—even if it doesn't cause a noticeable positive change in your friend, says Martha Manning, a clinical psychologist and author of *Undercurrents: A Life Beneath the Surface*, a memoir of her own severe depression. "Friends think: 'I know this person really well. If I try hard and I try a lot of things, I can bring them back,'" says Manning. But people set on "fixing" a depressed friend risk making her feel even more helpless. "Don't **presume** that what you do will be a cure. You wouldn't presume that if it were pneumonia."

Topic _____
Main Idea _____
_____

12   Think before pulling an **intervention**. Listening is usually the friendliest thing you can do. But don't let yourself become a limitless dumping ground for complainers, either. If a friend is depressed, show up and pitch in, but don't expect to make it all better.

Getting Chummy with the Opposite Sex

"Well, yeah, I mean, of course I think she's pretty. And we always laugh so much. But wouldn't getting together ruin our friendship?"

Topic _____
Main Idea _____
_____
Topic _____
Main Idea _____
_____

13   All friendships start with a spark of mutual attraction. But does that mean that opposite-sex friends have to be lusting after each other? "Not necessarily," says Sills. However, we get the reassurance that we can still be attractive without the extreme complication of having an affair.

14   Things get sticky, of course, when your friend wants to turn the fellowship into a romance, and you absolutely do not. Or when your partner suspects your opposite-sex pal's intentions are less than honorable. Or when the world at large refuses to accept that you are "just friends." These challenges are pesky, but they are not huge obstacles.

15   When you're facing a buddy who wants more, respond to any early signs of romantic interest, and ward them off without humiliating the person. For example, you might say, "You're watching another game? Good thing we're not a couple—I wouldn't be able to stand your sports obsession."

16   When one friend is waiting for another to suddenly fall in love with him or her, a nasty power imbalance develops that can threaten the relationship, Pelusi warns. If you're the one waiting, Pelusi suggests working through your own sensitivity to rejection so you can deal with it. Both people should "shift their expectations of what a friend should be. That way, they'll open up possibilities of deepening the friendship."

17   Opposite-sex friends can benefit from the **inherently** different relationship styles that men and women tend to display. "Women's friendships evolve around self-disclosure and personal feelings and emotions," says Fehr. "When men are friends with women, they tend to be more open and self-disclosing than they would be with a man. A lot of research shows that regardless of **gender**, the more we pursue closeness, the happier we are in that friendship." For their part, women can learn how to relax and be more spontaneous from their male pals.

18   Don't shy away from opposite-sex friendships. A tame flirtation is a psychic boost; you can handle its challenges, and you'll each learn from keeping mixed-sex company.

Notes

Topic _____

Main Idea _____

_____

Topic _____

Main Idea _____

_____

Topic _____

Main Idea _____

_____

Topic _____

Main Idea _____

_____

■ ■ ■

▶ after you read

Review Important Points

Going over the major points immediately after you have read, while the information is fresh in your mind, will help you recall the content and record key ideas.

Exercise 4   **Reviewing Important Points**

Directions: Choose the best answer for each of the following questions using information provided in the selection. Write your answers in the spaces provided.

_c_ 1. The anecdote in first two introductory paragraphs illustrates the following point:
   a. People are prone to depression.
   b. Most people are critical of one another.
   c. Friendships have their ups and downs.
   d. It's difficult keeping friends.

_a_ 2. From paragraph 3, we can infer that the author believes the following is true:
   a. Though sometimes difficult, friendships are valuable and worth working at.
   b. Friendships are valuable but are not worth the effort it may take to maintain them.

c. Most friendships include betrayal and heartbreak, and there's not much one can do to maintain a good friendship in the long run.

d. Good friends are hard to find, so you should try to maintain a friendship at any cost.

_a_ 3. **The overall purpose of the selection is to:**

a. inform the reader about ways to maintain friendships.

b. persuade the reader to make good friends.

c. criticize people who don't pursue friendships.

d. entertain the reader with anecdotes about friends.

_d_ 4. **In paragraph 5, the author uses the _____ writing pattern.**

a. definition

b. comparison and contrast

c. classification

d. cause and effect

_a_ 5. **The advice that psychologist Terri Apter gives to avoid rifts in relationships can be paraphrased in the following way:**

a. Express your feelings or concerns in a clear, upfront way, as they occur, rather than letting them build up inside you and hurt all your interactions.

b. Tackle any problems directly and strongly so that your friend doesn't take advantage of you.

c. Tell your friend everything on your mind so that you can get invited to his or her barbecues more often.

d. Always be sure to congratulate your friend on accomplishments, such as promotions.

_d_ 6. **Which paragraph provides a brief summary of the section, "Growing Apart?"**

a. paragraph 5

b. paragraph 6

c. paragraph 7

d. paragraph 8

_a_ 7. **What does the author consider to be the most important way to "be there" for a friend?**

a. listening

b. providing therapy

c. lending money

d. all of the above

_c_ 8. **By identifying and discussing the roles of friends as either "saints" or "sinners," in paragraph 10, the author is using the writing pattern of:**

a. cause and effect.

b. sequence.

c. classification.

d. definition.

_a_ 9. **The topic sentence of paragraph 17 is the:**

a. first sentence.

b. second sentence.

c. third sentence.

d. last sentence.

_d_ **10. The overall tone of the selection is best described as:**

a. critical and persuasive.

b. pessimistic and troubled.

c. straightforward and negative.

d. informative and positive.

Organize the Information

Organizing the information from a reading selection shows you have understood it and can restate the material in your own way.

| Exercise 5 | **Organizing the Information** |

Directions: Refer back to the selection, reviewing each paragraph. From these, make a list of recommendations for maintaining good friendships indicated by the author. Note the paragraph from which you find the recommendation. Share your list with a partner or a group. Discuss whether you feel each recommendation is a good one, and why or why not.

Some answers may vary.

Maintaining Good Friendships

Paragraph	Recommendation
6	Confront small conflicts head-on in a nondefensive tone.
7	Examine your own changed feeling and make adjustments.
8	Accept that friendships erode but then rebuild sometimes. Communicate hurt feelings. Appreciate friends who aren't like you.
9	Communicate that you are there for your friend. Listen. Provide practical support to men and emotional support to women.
10	Don't try to "fix" your friend. Recommend professional support when someone is clinically depressed.
14	If you are friends with someone of the opposite sex, and see signs of a romantic interest, ward them off without humiliating the person.
16	Work though your own fears of rejection if you are the one interested in your opposite-sex friend.
17, 18	Pursue closeness with friends of the opposite sex; you can learn a lot.

Integrate the Vocabulary

Make the new vocabulary *your* vocabulary.

Exercise 6   **Using Context Clues**

Directions: Fill in the two blanks in each of the following sentences with words, or forms of the words, from the text box on page 537.

1. You shouldn't _____*presume*_____ that one is of the female _____*gender*_____ just because the person paints his or her bedroom pink.

2. Maxine must _____*inherently*_____ be a lawyer or a prizefighter; she's always _____*embroiled*_____ in some kind of battle, argument or dispute.

3. Jonathan and Mark have had a _____*rift*_____ about who deserves the largest bedroom in their apartment for so long that I am afraid it will cause a permanent _____*schism*_____ in their relationship.

4. Superintendent Foster strongly opposed measures to create a class for students with disabilities in her district, fearing it would _____*taint*_____ the nature of the _____*heterogeneous*_____ classrooms she worked so hard to establish.

5. The _____*myriad*_____ of tourists who flock to Manhattan during the holiday season adds to the _____*mosaic*_____ of ethnicities and cultures that make up New York City.

6. Though Mrs. Conklin hoped for some sort of _____*intervention*_____ to stop her daughter from taking a cross-country road trip when she was eighteen, the concerned mom acknowledged that it was the next step on her child's path to _____*individuate*_____ and grow.

Make Personal Connections Through Writing and Discussion

Connect to the content on a personal level. How does it relate to you? How can you apply what you have read to other situations?

Exercise 7   **Making Personal Connections Through Writing and Discussion**

1. The article discusses three general issues involved in maintaining friendships: dealing with changes in the relationship, tending to the needs of a friend, and special problems that arise within an opposite-sex friendship. With a partner in discussion, or in a written response in a journal, answer the following questions. Share your written response with your partner or others in your class. *Responses will vary.*

    ■ Have you ever had to deal with either of these situations? Tell about it. What happened? How did it resolve?

    ■ What suggestions could you offer for any of the issues that the author did not mention?

2. Can you think of any other issues that are inherent in most friend-ships and that were not discussed in the article? What are they? What recommendations would you offer to help it? Discuss these with your classmates and/or enter responses in your journal.

Independent Reading
Selection 3

The Last Word: Growing up bin Laden
by Naiwa bin Laden, Omar bin Laden, and Jean Sasson

This book excerpt discusses a son's recollections of childhood experiences with his dad. As you read, consider what you know about the father, Osama bin Laden. What do Omar's stories reveal about their relationship?

◀ before you read

Answer the following questions before you read the selection.

1. Identify a significant memory you have about one of your parents. Do you think it has an effect on you today? In what way?

_____

_____

2. How do you think the children of criminals, or of people who notorious for a harmful act, are impacted?

_____

_____

Prepare to Read

Preview the adapted excerpt from *Growing Up bin Laden*, a book by Osama bin Laden's fourth son, Omar. Remember, when you preview literature, you do so differently than when you preview a textbook. This memoir is without headings. However, note the title and "lead" atop the article. Consider the first paragraph as an introduction, and look at the first sentences of subsequent paragraphs to preview the content. See Chapter 2, page 50, for information about previewing literature.

Exercise 1   **Developing Preview Questions**

Answers will vary.   **Directions:** Based on your previewing, write *three* questions you anticipate will be answered in the selection.

1. _____

2. _____

3. _____

Check Out the Vocabulary

Exercise 2   **Checking Out the Vocabulary**

Directions: You will encounter the following words in bold type in this reading.

compound	incessantly	martyrdom	proclamation
feat	indulge	piety	relish
goading	infraction	primitive	reverently

Read each of the following sentences in which a vocabulary word from the selection appears in bold. Select the best definition of the word from the choices provided, and write the letter of your choice on the line.

__b__ **1. feat**

He once confessed that he had mastered the **feat** during a time of great mental turmoil when he was 10 years old, after his biological father had been killed in an airplane accident. (para. 3)

   a. impossible, like a miracle
   b. accomplishment, remarkable achievement
   c. unexpected, unprecedented
   d. speech, announcement

__a__ **2. piety**

My father's **piety** made him strict about the way we lived. (para. 4)

   a. devoutness, dutifulness in religion
   b. cleanliness
   c. compulsiveness
   d. pity, sadness

_c_ 3. relish

He appeared to **relish** seeing his young sons suffer, reminding us that it was good for us to know what it felt like to be hungry or thirsty, to do without while others had plenty. (para. 4)

a. be upset and troubled
b. to desire or wish for
c. to enjoy or delight in something
d. to be confused about

_d_ 4. infraction

As time passed, he began caning me and my brothers for the slightest **infraction**. (para. 5)

a. mistake or error
b. question or request
c. hug or kiss
d. violation, breaking of a rule

_c_ 5. primitive

On Tora Bora mountain, at the **primitive** compound he chose as our new home, I served as his personal tea boy for three or four months. (para. 10)

a. urban, citylike
b. elaborate, lavish
c. basic, rudimentary
d. annoying, bothersome

_d_ 6. compound

On Tora Bora mountain, at the primitive **compound** he chose as our new home, I served as his personal tea boy for three or four months. (para. 10)

a. apartment building
b. a substance make of two or more chemical elements
c. alleyway or long hall
d. living quarters with several segments

_a_ 7. incessantly

I talked **incessantly** about automobiles, goading my dear mother and stepfather, Muhammad Atta, to desperation. (para. 14)

a. continually, without stopping or interruption
b. with anger and annoyance
c. incomprehensibly, nonsensically
d. respectfully and quietly

_c_ 8. goading

I talked incessantly about automobiles, **goading** my dear mother and stepfather, Muhammad Atta, to desperation. (para. 14)

a. tickling, poking
b. wishing, hoping for
c. inciting or rousing, driving one toward
d. questioning, asking

_b_   9. **indulge**

"As you know," he said, "Muhammad was never a man of wealth, and he could not afford to **indulge** me." (para. 15)

a. beat or batter
b. to humor, gratify, give in to desires
c. punish or chastise
d. transport or carry

_d_   10. **martyrdom**

My father's talk that day was about the joy of **martyrdom,** how it was the greatest honor for a Muslim to give his life to the cause of Islam. (para. 18)

a. a positive spirit
b. thoughtlessness
c. the goodness of society
d. extreme suffering

_a_   11. **reverently**

That's when one of my youngest brothers, one too young to comprehend the concept of life and death, got to his feet, nodded **reverently** in my father's direction, and took off running for the mosque. (para. 21)

a. worshipful, with great respect
b. with negativity and bitterness
c. joyful, happily
d. frightened, fearful

_d_   12. **proclamation**

My father's **proclamation** had been given: His love for his sons did not sink further than the outer layer of his flesh. (para. 23)

a. directions or orders
b. apology
c. request or invitation
d. official or formal announcement

▶ as **you read**

Establish Your Purpose

Read and annotate the selection using the guidelines for active reading. When reading a narrative, picture the setting and the plot events in your mind. Become familiar with the characters and the story line. Make note of the sequence of events and the culminating idea.

Actively Process as You Read

Monitor your comprehension as you read (see Chapter 2, page 54). As you read the memoir, imagine the events in your mind. Stop and reflect at the conclusion of each paragraph. Highlight the most important points. In the margin, write notes, responses, or questions that come to mind.

The Last Word: Growing Up bin Laden
The Last Word
Thursday, November 12, 2009

In a new book, Osama bin Laden's fourth son, Omar, describes a father who always put jihad above family.

1   MY FATHER WAS not always a man who hated. My father was not always a man hated by others. History shows that he was once loved by many people. Despite our differences today, I am not ashamed to admit that, as a young boy growing up in Saudi Arabia and Sudan, I worshipped my father, whom I believed to be not only the most brilliant but also the tallest man in the world. I would have to go to Afghanistan as a teenager to meet a man taller than my father. In truth, I would have to go to Afghanistan to truly come to know my father.

2   My father was accustomed to being No. 1 in everything he did. He was the most skilled horseman, the fastest runner, the best driver, the top marksman. Many people found my father to be a genius, particularly when it came to mathematical skills. He was so well known for the skill that men would come to our home and ask him to match wits against a calculator. He never failed.

3   His phenomenal memory fascinated many who knew him. On occasion, he would entertain those who would ask by reciting the Koran word for word. He once confessed that he had mastered the **feat** during a time of great mental turmoil when he was 10 years old, after his biological father had been killed in an airplane accident.

4   My father's **piety** made him strict about the way we lived. In the early 1980s, when we lived in Jeddah, Saudi Arabia, one of the hottest cities in a country known for its hot climate, he would not allow my mother to turn on the air conditioning. Nor would he allow her to use the refrigerator. He announced: "Islamic beliefs are corrupted by modernization." He appeared to **relish** seeing his young sons suffer, reminding us that it was good for us to know what it felt like to be hungry or thirsty, to do without while others had plenty. Why? Those with plenty would grow up weak men, he said, unable to defend themselves.

5   You might have guessed that my father was not an affectionate man. Nothing sparked his fatherly warmth. He never cuddled with me or my brothers. I tried to force him to show affection and was told that I made a pest of myself. In fact, my annoying behavior encouraged him to start carrying his signature cane. As time passed, he began caning me and my brothers for the slightest **infraction**.

6   Thankfully, my father had a different attitude when it came to the females in our family. I never heard him raise his voice in anger to my mother or shout at my sisters. He reserved all the harsh treatment for his sons.

7   I remember one particular time, during the period he became a leader in resisting the Soviet occupation of Afghanistan, when he had been away for longer than usual. I was desperate for his attention. He was sitting on the floor quietly studying intricate military maps when I suddenly ran past him, laughing loudly, skipping. He waved me away, saying in a stern voice, "Omar, go out of the room." I darted out the door and stared at him for a few moments; then, unable to hold back my excitement, I burst back into the room, laughing, skipping, performing a few more tricks. Finally, after the fourth or fifth repetition

of my bouncing appearance, my exasperated father looked at me and ordered me in his quiet voice, "Omar, go and gather all your brothers. Bring them to me." I leapt with glee, believing that I had tempted my father away from his military work. I gathered up each of my brothers, speaking rapidly: "Come! Father wants to see us all! Come!"

8   My father ordered us to stand in a line. He stood calmly, watching as we gathered, one hand clutching his wooden cane. I was grinning happily, certain that something very special was about to happen. He sometimes played a game with us in which each son's goal was to pick up a hat from the ground and return to the starting line before my father could catch him. On this day, I stood in restless anticipation, wondering what sort of new game he was about to teach us.

9   There would be no game. Shame, anguish, and terror surged throughout my body as he raised his cane and began to walk the human line, beating each of his sons in turn. My father never raised his soft voice as he reprimanded my brothers, striking them with the cane as his words kept cadence, "You are older than your brother Omar. You are responsible for his

bad behavior. I am unable to complete my work because of his badness." I was in the greatest anguish when he paused before me. I was very small at the time. He appeared taller than the trees. Despite the fact that I had witnessed him beating my brothers, I could not believe that my father was going to strike me with that heavy cane. But he did.

10   YEARS LATER, WHEN the government of Sudan in 1996 forced my father to leave the home we had made in Khartoum, he selected me, his fourth son, as the only member of the family to accompany him as he traveled to Afghanistan seeking a place to relocate. On Tora Bora mountain, at the **primitive compound** he chose as our new home, I served as his personal tea boy for three or four months. Believe me, I was happy to have responsibilities, for the boredom of life on Tora Bora eludes description. Being by his side for nearly every moment of the day and night gave me a good insight into my father's true character. For all of my childhood, he had remained a distant figure, but in Afghanistan I was often one of only three or four people he felt he could trust completely. His trust was not misplaced, for though I hated what he did, hated the militant operations that he and his Egyptian allies endorsed, he was still my father, and I would never betray him. I learned more about my father's life during those few months than during all the years of my early life combined.

11   Although my father was so serious that he rarely spoke of personal events, there were times in Afghanistan when he relaxed, pulling me with him into his early life. "Omar, come, I want to tell you a story," he would say, patting the cotton mat beside him. The stories I liked best of all had to do with his father, Mohammed bin Laden. My father kept the long-dead Grandfather bin Laden on a pedestal. "Omar," he'd say, "your grandfather was a genius, who helped build the Kingdom of Saudi Arabia, bringing the country out of the sand."

12   My father did not know my grandfather well. In our culture, it is not uncommon for men, particularly the wealthy, to have four wives simultaneously. Since my father was not one of my grandfather's eldest sons, he was not in a position to see his father regularly but instead saw him only when all of the sons were summoned at once.

13   Once, my father told me a story about his strict father striking him, almost knocking him down, because he had failed to line up in correct height order alongside his many brothers. "I never forgot the pain of that blow, both physically and mentally," he said.

14   He told me that he spoke privately with his father only once. My father was 9 at the time and had decided that he wanted his own automobile. "I had an early love for cars," he said to me. "I talked **incessantly** about automobiles, **goading** my dear mother and stepfather, Muhammad Attas, to desperation."

15   "As you know," he said, "Muhammad was never a man of wealth, and he could not afford to **indulge** me. But after months of my pestering my dear mother, Muhammad announced that he was going to ask for an audience with my biological father, so that I could express my wish to the only man who had the power to make it happen."

16   My father said he was "devastated" when his father announced that he would buy him a bicycle instead. He said he rode the red bicycle only a few times before giving it to a younger brother.

17   Several weeks later, though, my father received what he called the biggest shock of his life. "A shiny new car was delivered to our home in Jeddah! For me!" he said. "That was the happiest day of my young life."

18   THREE YEARS AFTER those unusual days we had together on Tora Bora mountain, my father called a meeting of all his fighters. My father's talk that day was about the joy of **martyrdom,** how it was the greatest honor for a Muslim to give his life to the cause of Islam. As he spoke, I looked around the room, studying the faces of the fighters. The older fighters looked a bit bored, but the men newest to al Qaida had a kind of glow on their faces.

19   When the meeting ended, my father called for all his sons to gather, even the youngest. He was in a rare good mood. In an excited voice, he told us, "My sons. Sit, sit, gather in a circle. I have something to tell you." Once we were at his feet, my father said, "There is a paper on the wall of the mosque. This paper is for men who are good Muslims, men who volunteer to be suicide bombers."

20   He looked at us with anticipation shining in his eyes. No one spoke or moved a muscle. So my father repeated what he had said. "My sons, there is a paper on the wall of the mosque. This paper is for men who volunteer to be suicide bombers. Those who want to give their lives for Islam must add their names to the list."

21   That's when one of my youngest brothers, one too young to comprehend the concept of life and death, got to his feet, nodded **reverently** in my father's direction, and took off running for the mosque. That small boy was going to volunteer to be a suicide bomber.

22   I was furious, finally finding my voice. "My father, how can you ask this of your sons?" Over the past few months, my father had become increasingly unhappy with me. I was turning out to be a disappointment, a son who did not want power, who wanted peace, not war. He stared at me with evident hostility. "Omar, this is what you need to know, my son. You hold no more a place in my heart than any other man or boy in the entire country." He glanced at my brothers. "This is true for all of my sons."

23   My father's **proclamation** had been given: His love for his sons did not sink further than the outer layer of his flesh. At last I knew exactly where I stood. My father hated his enemies more than he loved his sons.

From the book *Growing Up bin Laden* by Naiwa bin Laden, Omar bin Laden, and Jean Sasson. ©2009 by The Sasson Corporation.

■ ■ ■

 **after you read**

Exercise 3   **Answering Your Preview Questions**

Directions: Look back at the questions you posed before you read the selection. If you have discovered the answers, write them on the lines provided.

Answers will vary.

1. _____

_____

2. _____

_____

3. _____

_____

Exercise 4   **Reviewing Important Points**

Directions: Choose the best answer for each of the following questions using the information provided in the selection. Write your answers in the spaces provided.

_a_ 1. Paragraphs 1–3 help us understand that the author:

a. had respect and admiration for his father as a young child.
b. always regarded his father in a negative light.
c. thought his father was conceited and self-absorbed.
d. never understood his father.

_b_ 2. The main idea of paragraphs 2 and 3 is that Osama bin Laden:

a. was a fast runner.
b. had many recognized talents and a phenomenal memory.
c. never failed at mathematical calculations.
d. knew the Koran by heart.

_d_ 3. The topic of paragraph 4 is:

a. the heat of Saudi Arabia.
b. Islamic beliefs.
c. the negative impact of modernization.
d. the strict nature of bin Laden.

_c_ 4. What does the author say caused the strictness imposed by his father?

a. his father's overall depression
b. the fact that his father was beaten as a young child
c. his father's piety and religious beliefs
d. his father's value of hunger and thirst

_b_ 5. In paragraphs 5 and 6, the author uses the comparison and contrast writing pattern:

   a. to show his father's attitude and treatment of older and younger members of the family.
   b. to show his father's different attitude and treatment of males and females in the family.
   c. to show his father's affectionate nature to his younger brothers.
   d. to show the different reasons that brought about the punishment of caning.

_c_ 6. From the anecdote recounted in paragraphs 7 thorough 9, what can you infer the author felt at the conclusion of the "game" he anticipated?

   a. extreme joy and jubilation
   b. worry and anxiety
   c. deep disappointment and sadness
   d. annoyance and impatience

_d_ 7. During the time he spent at Tora Bora with his father, Omar learns the following:

   a. Like Omar, Osama bin Laden thought of his own father as a genius and leader.
   b. His father was impacted, physically and mentally, by a beating he received from Omar's grandfather for a minor infraction.
   c. Osama bin Laden rarely spoke personally with his own father.
   d. All of the above.

_b_ 8. From the stories recounted, we might infer that the way Osama bin Laden treated his son was:

   a. contrary to the way bin Laden himself was raised.
   b. learned from Osama bin Laden's own upbringing.
   c. a break in the family's tradition.
   d. actually against bin Laden's true belief system.

_a_ 9. In paragraph 18, why does the author refer to the time with his father on Tora Bora Mountain as "unusual"?

   a. His father shared personal stories with him and he learned more about his father's life during those months than during all the other years of his life combined.
   b. It was odd to be living in a primitive compound in the mountains.
   c. Though his father was usually serious, on the mountain he behaved in a lighthearted and silly manner.
   d. Osama bin Laden revealed that he resented his father just as Omar resented his.

_c_ 10. In what country is Tora Bora mountain?

   a. Egypt
   b. Pakistan
   c. Afghanistan
   d. Saudi Arabia

___c___ 11. The topic of the last segment of the selection (paragraphs 18–23), is Osama bin Laden's belief in:

    a. terrorism.
    b. child abuse.
    c. martyrdom.
    d. suicide.

___c___ 12. What does the author conclude as the reason his father would recruit his own sons as suicide bombers?

    a. There weren't enough soldiers in his military to do the job.
    b. His father was a cold and heartless man.
    c. His father hated his enemies more than he loved his sons.
    d. His father has become increasingly unhappy with his children.

___c___ 13. By retelling the events in the order in which they occurred, what is the primary writing pattern of the selection?

    a. definition
    b. cause and effect
    c. sequence
    d. classification

___b___ 14. What is the overall mood and tone of the memoir?

    a. content, calm and neutral
    b. hurtful, somber and ironic
    c. uplifting, positive and hopeful
    d. confused, nostalgic and surprised

Exercise 5   **Organizing the Information**

Directions: In several places in the memoir, forms of irony are revealed—directly in a statement or in the unfolding of the events. The opposite of what one might think or expect occurs. Notice signal words such as *although, though, however, despite*. Read through the selection again. Complete the following chart. Quote directly, or paraphrase, the ironic events or comments and indicate their location in the text. Share and discuss your entries with a partner or in a small group.

Responses will vary.

Paragraph	Example of Irony
1	*Despite our differences today, I am not ashamed to admit that as a young boy, I worshipped my father.*
4	*Though they lived in one of the hottest places, Omar's father would not allow his mother to use air conditioning or a refrigerator.* *Bin Laden "appeared to relish seeing his young sons suffer, reminding us that it was good for us to know what it felt like to be hungry or thirsty, to do without while others had plenty. . . ."*

9	*"Despite the fact that I had witnessed him beating my brothers, I could not believe that my father was going to strike me with that heavy cane, but he did."*
10	*". . . for though I hated what he did, hated the militant operations that he and his Egyptian allies endorsed, he was still my father, and I would never betray him."*
11	*"Although my father was so serious that he rarely spoke of personal events, there were times in Afghanistan when he relaxed, pulling me with him into his early life."*
19	Omar's father was in a "rare good mood" and spoke in an excited voice as he told his sons about becoming suicide bombers.
22	*"Omar, this is what you need to know, my son. You hold no more a place in my heart than any other man or boy in the entire country."*
23	*"My father hated his enemies more than he loved his sons."*

Integrate the Vocabulary

Exercise 6A | **Using Context Clues**

Directions: Answer the following questions, each of which includes a vocabulary word or form of the word, from the selection. Write a complete sentence for your response, *restating* the word in the context of your answer.

1. What is the most unusual **feat** you have ever accomplished?
   The most unusual feat I have ever accomplished is . . . _____ *Responses will vary.*

2. Did Omar believe his father was a **pious** person?

   _____

3. What is something you **relish** doing when you have free time?

   _____

4. What **infraction** of your school's code of conduct have you observed?

   _____

5. What are some types of **primitive** living spaces that exist today?

   _____

6. Is your family wealthy enough to own a **compound**, like the Kennedys in Hyannis, Massachusetts?

   _____

7. What type of **incessant** behavior do you find particularly annoying?

   _____

8. Has anyone attempted to **goad** you into doing something you really didn't want to do?

   _____

9. If you had the money and the time, in what would you **indulge**?

   _____

10. What is your reaction to the idea of **martyrdom**?

   _____

11. Who in your life is treated **reverently**?

   _____

12. If you could, what **proclamation** would you make about one of the policies in your college?

   _____

| **Exercise 6B** | **Words with Multiple Meanings** |

Directions: The words listed below from the selection have more than one meaning. Read these words and place a check next to the definition of the term *as it is used in the selection.* To make your decision, find and reread the word as it is used in the text. Use context clues to guide your thinking.

1. relish

   ____ a condiment added to food to add zest and flavor

   _X_ taking enjoyment or delight in something

2. compound

   ____ a substance composed of two or more chemical elements

   _X_ living quarters with several portions for different inhabitants

   ____ to put together by combining parts

| **Exercise 7** | **Making Personal Connections Through Writing and Discussion** |

Responses will vary.

Directions: Think about yourself in relation to the memoir you just read. Break into small groups. Each group can address one of the following questions. Have one person take notes on the ideas of the group, and share these with the rest of the class.

1. Place yourself in the role of Omar. What would you want to say to your father after learning you and your brothers had no more a place in his heart than any other man or boy in the country?

2. The author occasionally uses figurative language in the text. Paraphrase the literal meaning of the following expressions.

   ■ I would have to go to Afghanistan as a teenager to meet a man taller than my father.

   ■ He was so well known for the skill that men would come to our home and ask him to match wits against a calculator. He never failed.

- I was very small at the time. He appeared taller than the trees.
- His love for his sons did not sink further than the outer layer of his flesh.

3. Osama bin Laden told Omar he was struck by his own father because he failed to line up in correct height order beside his brothers. He never forgot both the physical and mental pain he felt. He also revealed that, except for one time, he never spoke privately with his father. Like Omar, he also thought of his father as a genius.

    How do you think bin Laden's upbringing influenced his own parenting? Do you think people parent their children in the way they were treated by their own parents, intentionally or not? How so?

4. Why do you think Omar wrote this memoir? What do you think he feels for his father today? If they were together, what kind of relationship would they have?

⌐reflect AND respond ⌐

Now that you have read three selections about *relationships*, you have a broader and better understanding of the topic.

Directions: Complete a journal response for this module. Read the following questions. Select two to which you would like to respond. Write your responses on a separate piece of paper. Write at least one page.

1. What interesting information did you learn about issues related to mate selection, maintaining friendships, or the father/son relationship of Osama and Omar bin Laden?

2. How does this information apply to you? Make connections with your own experience(s). What do these readings make you think about?

3. What else would you like to know about some of the topics discussed in this module?

Working with Word Parts and Compound Words

Using context clues is one way to discover the meaning of an unfamiliar word. Another method for unlocking its meaning is to analyze word parts. **Word parts**—roots, prefixes, and suffixes—are used to make up most of the words we use every day. In English, many words are formed by adding to the **root** word, which is the part that contains the basic meaning or definition of the word. Parts that are attached to the beginning of a word are called **prefixes**. They add meaning to the root word. Parts that come after the root are called **suffixes**; they can indicate the part of speech or change the meaning of the word. A **compound word** is made when two words are joined to form a new word. Academic disciplines commonly use compound words, often hyphenating them.

Word Parts

The word *prejudicial* is composed of three word parts: a prefix, a root, and a suffix.

Prefix	Root	Suffix
pre-	judis	(i)al

The meaning of the prefix *pre-* is *before*.
The meaning of the root *judis* is *judge*.
The suffix *-ial* means *like or having the quality of*.

From studying these word parts, we can work out that **prejudicial** means *having the quality of making judgments before*. An actual dictionary definition for the word **prejudicial** is *causing an unfavorable opinion or feeling formed beforehand or without knowledge, thought, or reason*. As you can see, a simple analysis of the word parts may lead you to a pretty good understanding of an unfamiliar word.

Prefixes

Are you familiar with any of these word parts? If so, write an example with each of the ones you know.

***com-, con-, co-, col-* (with, together)** *community, convict, cooperate, collect*

***dis-* (negative)** *disagree, disallow, dishonest, dislike*

***ex-* (out, away from)**	*exit, extra, extraordinary, excommunicate*
***re-* (back, again)**	*repeat, remind, review, rewrite*
***sub-* (under, below)**	*subway, submarine, subtract, substitute*

Prefixes are located at the beginning of words and change the meaning of root words. For example, when the prefix *pre-* (before) is added to the root word *sumere* (take up), the word **presume** is formed, meaning *accepting without proof*. And if you add the prefix *re-* (again) to the root word *sumere*, the word becomes **resume** and the meaning changes *to take up again*.

Can you think of any other words that contain the prefix *pre-*?

1. *prefix*
2. *prejudge*
3. *preceding*
4. *preview*
5. *preconceived*

Common Prefixes

Prefix	Meaning	Example	Definition
ante-	before	antebellum	before the war
anti-	against	antifreeze	liquid used to guard against freezing
auto-	self	automatic	self-acting or self-regulating
bene-	good	benefit	an act of kindness; a gift
circum-	around	circumscribe	to draw a line around; to encircle
contra-	against	contradict	to speak against
de-	reverse, remove	defoliate	remove the leaves from a tree
dis-	apart, not	dislocate, distaste	to unlodge, to dislike
dys-	bad	dysfunctional	not functioning
ecto-	outside	ectoparasite	parasite living on the exterior of animals
endo-	within	endogamy	marriage within the tribe
ex-	out	excavate	to dig out
extra-	beyond	extraterrestrial	beyond the earth
hyper-	over	hypertension	high blood pressure
hypo-	under	hypotension	low blood pressure
in-	in	interim	in between
inter-	between	intervene	come between
intra-	within	intramural	within bounds of a school
intro-	in, into	introspect	to look within, as one's own mind

macro-	large	macroscopic	large enough to be observed by the naked eye
mal-	bad	maladjusted	badly adjusted
micro-	small	microscopic	so small that one needs a microscope to observe
neo-	new	neolithic	new stone age
non-	not	nonconformist	one who does not conform
pan-	all	pantheon	a temple dedicated to all gods
poly-	many	polygonal	having many sides
post-	after	postgraduate	after graduating
pre-	before	precede	to go before
pro-	for	proponent	a supporter
proto-	first	prototype	first or original model
pseudo-	false	pseudonym	false name; esp., an author's pen-name
re-, red-	back again	rejuvenate	to make young
re-, red-	together	reconnect	to put together again
retro-	backward	retrospect	a looking back on things
sub-	under	submerge	to put under water
super-	above	superfine	extra fine
tele-	far	telescope	seeing or viewing afar
trans-	across	transalpine	across the Alps

(Common prefixes table adapted from Walter Pauk. *How to Study in College*, 4E. © 1989 Wadsworth, a part of Cengage Learning, Inc. Reproduced by permission. www.cengage.com/permissions.)

USING PREFIXES

Directions: Several prefixes mean **not**. They appear in words like, *il*legal, *im*proper, *in*opportune, and *ir*relevant. Match the words in the column on the left with their definitions in the column on the right, and write your answers in the spaces provided.

Column 1	Column 2
<u>g</u> 1. illiterate	a. not by one's own choice
<u>e</u> 2. illogical	b. deprived of reason and sound judgment
<u>h</u> 3. immature	c. not cautious, unsound
<u>d</u> 4. immoral	d. not conforming to the patterns of socially acceptable behavior
<u>c</u> 5. imprudent	e. contrary to the rules of logic
<u>f</u> 6. injustice	f. unfairness
<u>j</u> 7. inconclusive	g. unable to read or write
<u>a</u> 8. involuntary	h. emotionally underdeveloped
<u>b</u> 9. irrational	i. not reliable or trustworthy
<u>i</u> 10. irresponsible	j. without final results or outcome

Number or Amount Prefixes

uni-	one	*semi-*	half, part
mono-	one	*equi-*	equal
bi-, di-, duo-	two	*multi-, poly-*	many
tri-	three		
dec-	ten		
centi-	hundred		
milli-	thousand		

The best way to learn prefixes is to study them in groups based on their meaning. In the following exercise, you will practice using prefixes that mean number or amount.

USING NUMBER PREFIXES

Directions: Underline the number or amount prefix of the boldface word. Then write a number or amount that best completes each of the following sentences.

Example: A **mono**theistic person believes in <u>one</u> God.

1. An individual who is **bilingual** speaks _____*two*_____ languages.
2. The **Pentagon** is a _____*five*_____-sided building.
3. People who practice **polygamy** have _____*many*_____ spouses.
4. America's **bicentennial** took place in 1976; it celebrated our _____*200th*_____ birthday.
5. A **decade** is a period of _____*ten*_____ years.
6. The U.S. is a **multicultural** society. In other words, people from _____*many*_____ ethnic groups reside in this country.
7. The debate went on for hours, but the decision was **unanimous**. We finally arrived at _____*one*_____ opinion.
8. An **equalitarian** is a person who supports _____*equal*_____ rights and responsibilities.
9. A **semiskilled** worker is one who is _____*partially*_____ trained or experienced, not yet meeting the expected level of skill.
10. In today's busy world, it is sometimes necessary to **multitask** or handle _____*many*_____ tasks at one time.

Roots

Are you familiar with any of these roots? If so, write a word that contains each of these roots.

audi (to hear) *audition, auditory*

bene (good) *benefit, benevolent*

bio (life) *biography, biology*

dic, dict (say, tell) *dictation, dictionary*

graph (write) *autograph, paragraph*

path (feeling) *sympathy, empathy*

ped (child) *pediatrician, pediatrics*

phil (love) *philosophy, philology*

tel (far away) *telephone, telegraph*

A **root** or stem is the basic part of a word to which other parts are added. The meaning of a word changes by the addition of prefixes and/or suffixes. For example, the root word *dict* means *to say or tell*. Attach the prefix *pre-*, meaning *before*, and you have the word **predict**—*to tell in advance*. Attach the prefix *contra-*, meaning *against*, and you have **contradict**—*to say the opposite of*. Attach the prefix *in-*, meaning *toward*, and you have **indict**—*to charge with a crime*. Now let's attach the suffix *-ment*, meaning *the act of*, *state of*, and *result of* an action, and you have **indictment**—*a charge or accusation*—or finally the suffix *-ee*, meaning *one who receives*, and you have **indictee**—*one who has received an indictment*.

Becoming familiar with common roots will help you to figure out the meanings of many new and unfamiliar words and terms.

Common Word Roots

Root	Meaning	Example	Definition
agri	field	agronomy	field-crop production and soil management
anthropo	man	anthropology	the study of man
astro	star	astronaut	one who travels in interplanetary space
bio	life	biology	the study of life
cardio	heart	cardiac	pertaining to the heart
cede	go	precede	to go before
chromo	color	chromatology	the science of colors
demos	people	democracy	government by the people
derma	skin	epidermis	the outer layer of skin

(continued)

Common Word Roots (*continued*)

dyna	power	dynamic	characterized by power and energy
geo	earth	geology	the study of the earth
helio	sun	heliotrope	any plant that turns toward the sun
hydro	water	hydroponics	growing of plants in water reinforced with nutrients
hypno	sleep	hypnosis	a state of sleep induced by suggestion
ject	throw	eject	to throw out
magni	great, big	magnify	to enlarge, to make bigger
man(u)	hand	manuscript	written by hand
mono	one	monoplane	airplane with one wing
ortho	straight	orthodox	right, true, straight opinion
pod	foot	pseudopod	false foot
psycho	mind	psychology	study of the mind in any of its aspects
pyro	fire	pyrometer	an instrument for measuring temperatures
script	write	manuscript	hand written
terra	earth	terrace	a raised platform of earth
thermo	heat	thermometer	instrument for measuring heat
zoo	animal	zoology	the study of animals

(Common word roots table adapted from Walter Pauk. *How to Study in College,* 4E. © 1989 Wadsworth, a part of Cengage Learning, Inc. Reproduced by permission. www.cengage.com/permissions.)

USING ROOTS

Directions: Look at the following meanings of the common roots that relate to people and life. Then write the words in the box next to their correct definitions.

bio life	*frat* brother	*mater* mother	*nas, nat* born
demo people	*gen* birth, race	*pater* father	*anthropo* man
ethno center			

anthropology	demographics	genocide	patriotic
biodiversity	ethnography	matriarch	
democratize	fratricide	naturalize	

1. <u>fratricide</u>   act of killing one's brother
2. <u>naturalize</u>   adapt or accustom to a place or new surroundings

3. _patriotic_____ loyal and devoted

4. _ethnography_____ branch of anthropology that deals with the scientific description of specific human cultures

5. _anthropology_____ science that deals with the origins, physical and cultural development, biological characteristics, and social customs and beliefs of humankind

6. _matriarch_____ female head of a family

7. _democratize_____ make a society characterized by formal equality of rights and privileges

8. _genocide_____ the deliberate destruction of an entire race or nation

9. _demographics_____ study of the characteristics of human populations, such as size, growth, density, distribution, and vital statistics

10. _biodiversity_____ term that describes the number of different species that live within a particular ecosystem

Suffixes

Are you familiar with any of these word endings? If so, write an example using each one.

-ion, -sion, -tion (state, condition, act, quality) _nation, tension, information_____
-er, -or, -ist (a person or thing that does something) _teacher, instructor, chemist_____
–ed, -ing _interested, interesting_____

Suffixes are groups of letters attached to the root or end of a word. A suffix can indicate what part of speech (noun, verb, adjective, and adverb) a word is. When different suffixes are added to certain words, the part of speech will change (e.g., verb → noun). Often, spelling changes are involved. At times, a suffix can also change the meaning of a word. Look at the following examples.

react (verb, to do something back) + _-ion_ →	reaction (noun, something done back)
+ _-ary_ →	reactionary (adjective, opposing political or social change)
lie (verb, to say something false) + _-ar_ →	liar (noun, a person who does not tell the truth)
honest (adjective, truthful) + _-y_ →	honesty (noun, having the quality of being honest)
prejudice (noun, unreasonable feeling) + _-ial_ →	prejudicial (adjective, causing injurious feelings)

Look at the verbs in the following list, and add the suffixes _-ion, -sion, -ation_ or _-tion_ (action) to change them into nouns. You may want to check the dictionary for correct spellings.

Verbs	Nouns
1. add	*addition*
2. culminate	*culmination*
3. decide	*decision*
4. educate	*education*
5. explain	*explanation*
6. inform	*information*
7. initiate	*initiation*
8. organize	*organization*
9. revise	*revision*
10. saturate	*saturation*

The suffixes *-an, -ar, -er,* and *-ist* also mean a person who does something. Look at the following examples and write in additional words that contain the same suffix.

-or tutor _____, _____, _____

-an librarian _____, _____, _____

-ar scholar _____, _____, _____

-er philosopher _____, _____, _____

-ist psychologist _____, _____, _____

Common Suffixes

Suffix	Meaning	Example
Used to Form Nouns		
-age, -ance, -cy, -ence, -ion, -ism, -ity, -ment, -ness, -tion, -tude, -ure	state, condition, act, quality	action, adjustment, assistance, attitude, bankruptcy, communism, conversation, intelligence, kindness, mixture, percentage, sanity
-an, -ar, -er, -ist, -or	a person or thing that does something	librarian, liar, scholar, dispatcher, dispenser, cartoonist, administrator
-cle, -cule	small	corpuscle, molecule
-ology	study of	sociology
Used to Form Adverbs		
-ly	in the manner of	slowly, unlikely

Suffix	Meaning	Example
Used to Form Nouns or Adjectives		
-ful	full of	teaspoonful, helpful
-ant, -ary, -ent, -ery, -ory	one who, quality of, place for	assistant, adversary, recipient, robbery, advisory
Used to Form Adjectives		
-able, -ible	able to be	memorable, flexible
-ac, -al, -an, -en, -em, -ic, -eous, -ious, -ous	like, having the quality related to	democratic, minimal, American, brazen, western, Islamic, courteous, anxious, boistrous
-ive	one who is, that which is	additive, aggressive
-less	full of	useless, worthless
Used to Form Verbs		
-ate, -en, -ify, -ize	to make	liberate, weaken, magnify, criticize

(Adapted from www1.fccj.edu/lchandouts/communicationshandouts/vocabularyhandouts/V-3.doc)

USING SUFFIXES

Directions: Below you will find vocabulary words used in Chapter 3. For each of them, underline the suffix, write the part of speech (noun, adjective, adverb, or verb) and write the meaning of the suffix as it appears in the charts. Finally, write a definition of the word.

1. advocacy *noun, state or condition*

    Definition: *act of recommending something*

2. affirmative *adjective, that which*

    Definition: *that which is favorable*

3. anthropology *noun, study of*

    Definition: *the study of humankind in terms or origin, physical and cultural development, biological characteristics, social customs and beliefs*

4. collaborate *verb, to make*

    Definition: *to work with one another*

5. competence *noun, state or condition*

    Definition: *the state of possessing knowledge or a required skill*

6. discrimination *noun, state or quality*

    Definition: *a denial of equal rights because of prejudice*

7. disproportion<u>ately</u> *adverb, in the manner of* _____

   Definition: *in an unequal manner, out of proportion* _____

8. divers<u>ity</u> *noun, state, condition or quality* _____

   Definition: *the state of being different in terms of ethnic, racial, cultural, gender or ability* _____

9. plural<u>istic</u> *adjective, having the quality related to, like* _____

   Definition: *the quality of a social organization in which diversity of racial or religious or ethnic or cultural groups is tolerated* _____

10. stigmat<u>ize</u> *verb, make* _____

    Definition: *to characterize in a negative way, brand or label* _____

Compound Words

A compound word is made when two words are joined together to form a new word. You are already familiar with many compound words used in spoken and written language—for example, *freshman, course work,* and *textbook.* Academic disciplines commonly use compound words, often hyphenating them. Understanding the separate words can assist you in your quest for the right meaning of an unfamiliar word or term.

Example

freethinker   free + thinker = one who forms opinions on the basis of reason independently of authority

viewpoint   view + point = point of view, attitude

peacemaker   peace + maker = a person, group, or nation that tries to make peace, especially by reconciling parties who disagree, quarrel, or fight.

DECODING COMPOUND WORDS

Directions: Match the following compound words with their definitions. Remember to consider the meaning of each portion of the compound word to find the correct definition.

<u>d</u>   1. a **foreshadowing** incident in the novel   a. protect

<u>e</u>   2. an **outgrowth** of stereotyping   b. native soil

<u>f</u>   3. an **uprising** in Afghanistan   c. gang leader

<u>g</u>   4. an **upsurge** in crime statistics   d. prediction

<u>b</u>   5. **homeland** security   e. consequence, result

<u>c</u>   6. the **ringleader** of revolutionary activities   f. unrest, revolt

<u>a</u>   7. to **safeguard** his property from vandals   g. increase, rise

Working with Resources and Strategies to Improve Vocabulary

To help you read effectively and build your college vocabulary, you can use many resources and strategies. Consult a **dictionary** to find the exact meaning of new words, search for related word forms, and find synonyms for new vocabulary. Use a **glossary,** an alphabetical list of words that relate to specialized topics or specific disciplines, to locate the meaning of new and unfamiliar terminology. Go to a thesaurus to discover **synonyms** or **antonyms.**

Using Dictionaries

In Chapter 3, you learned the importance of using context clues to figure out the meaning of unfamiliar words while you are reading. After you read, it is a good idea to consult a dictionary. Good collegiate dictionaries, such as *Merriam-Webster's Collegiate Dictionary,* or an electronic one, such as *Franklin's Dictionary & Thesaurus,* are helpful tools. The Web has a wide range of online dictionaries, too. At www.Merriam-Webster.com, and www.dictionary.com, you can find definitions, synonyms, word origins, and even pronunciation sound cues. Many online dictionaries also provide the etymology of words so that you can learn a word's origin and understand the word parts it contains.

Consider the following entry from *The New American Webster Handy Dictionary.*

word (werd) *n.*

1. a sound or combination of sounds, or its graphic representation, expressing an idea; a term. **2.** (*pl*) speech; written words; a song lyric; a quarrel **3.** information; a report; a command; a signal or password; a motto. **4.** promise. **5.** (cap. Holy Scripture. **6.** (*Computers*) the string of bytes which is treated by a computer.

(From Albert H. Morehead, Loy Morehead, and Philip D. Morehead, eds., *The New American Webster Handy Dictionary*, 3rd ed. [New York: Signet, 1995], 747.)

Guide Words
woodcut workday
Entry Word [this refers to *word*]
Parts of Speech [this refers to the *n*]
Pronunciation [this refers to *werd*]

Word Meaning

Etymology   Etymology: Middle English, from Old English; akin to Old High German *wort* word, Latin *verbum*, Greek *eirein* to say, speak, Hittite *weriya-* to call, name. Date: before 12th century

(By permission. From Merriam-Webster's Collegiate® Dictionary, Eleventh Edition ©2010 by Merriam-Webster, Incorporated [www.Merriam-Webster.com].)

Guide Words

Guide words are the two words that appear at the top of each dictionary page. They help you determine if the word you are looking for is located on the page. In this dictionary, the entry for *word* is found on the page with the guide words *woodcut* and *workday*.

Parts of Speech

For each entry, a dictionary gives you the **part of speech** of the word, usually in an abbreviated form, as shown in the table below.

Parts of Speech

Noun *(n.)* a word indicating a person, place, or thing
　　We should all embrace all *diversity*.

Verb *(v.)* a word that expresses action or existence
　　The notion of diversity *includes* acceptance and respect for each individual's unique differences.

Adjective *(adj.)* a word that is used to qualify (describe) or limit the meaning of a noun
　　Few societies have a more *diverse* population than the United States.

Adverb *(adv.)* a word that is used to qualify or limit a verb or adjective or another adverb
　　The *widely* diverse student body differs in terms of age, ethnicity, culture, language, and ability.

Pronoun *(pron.)* a word that replaces a noun that was previously stated (like *he* or *she*)
　　As a college student, *you* can learn about diverse cultures through courses in anthropology, sociology, history and communications.

Preposition *(prep.)* a word that shows the relationship between a noun and a verb, an adjective, or another noun that typically describes a relationship as *in, on, by, to, since*.
　　Celebrate diversity, the differences *in* gender, race, ethnicity, sexual orientation, physical disabilities, learning styles and all disabilities.

Pronunciation

How to **pronounce** a word is shown after it, in parentheses. If more than one pronunciation is included, the first one is usually the most common or preferred. Use the guide to the pronunciation section (located at the beginning of your dictionary or at the bottom on the page) to understand the symbols used for the vowel sounds. For example, in "wərd" the *e* is pronounced like the *e* in the word *her*. From the pronunciation entry, you will also learn how many syllables a word contains.

Word Meaning

It is not uncommon to find words in English with multiple meanings. For instance, the entry for *word* on page A-11 has six meanings. Look at the following sentences. The numbers in parentheses refer to the definition in the dictionary entry that corresponds to the correct meaning of *word* as it is used in each sentence.

I would like to have a **word** with you after class. (4)
Actions speak louder than **words.** (2)

Remember that you still need to consider the context of the word you are looking up because many words have more than one meaning. When you search for definitions, find the one that fits best and substitute it for the word in the sentence. If it makes sense, you have probably selected the appropriate definition. Also consider the part of speech of the word you are looking up, because many words can be used in different forms (see page A-12).

Etymology

The etymology feature of a dictionary refers to the word origin or history of the word. For example, *word* comes from Old or Middle English and dates back to the twelfth century.

UNDERSTANDING AND USING DICTIONARY ENTRIES

Directions: Use the dictionary entry that follows for the noun form of the word *subject* to complete items 1–5. Then, for items 6–10, write the definition of the word *subject* as it is used in the sentence, using context clues.

Entry Word: **sub·ject**
Pronunciation: \səb-jikt, -(,)jekt\
Part of Speech: *noun*

Etymology: Middle English *suget, subget,* from Anglo-French, from Latin *subjectus* one under authority & *subjectum* subject of a proposition, from masculine & neuter respectively of *subjectus,* past participle of *subicere* to subject, literally, to throw under, from *sub-* + *jacere* to throw

Date: 14th century

1 : one that is placed under authority or control: as

   a : VASSAL

   b (1) : one subject to a monarch and governed by the monarch's law
   (2) : one who lives in the territory of, enjoys the protection of, and owes
   allegiance to a sovereign power or state

2 **a** : that of which a quality, attribute, or relation may be affirmed or in
   which it may inhere

   b : SUBSTRATUM; *especially* : material or essential substance

   c : the mind, ego, or agent of whatever sort that sustains or assumes the
   form of thought or consciousness

3 **a** : a department of knowledge or learning

   b : MOTIVE, CAUSE

   c (1) : one that is acted on <the helpless *subject* of their cruelty> (2) : an
   individual whose reactions or responses are studied (3) : a dead **body** for
   anatomical study and dissection

   d (1) : something concerning which something is said or done <the
   subject of the essay> (2) : something represented or indicated in a
   work of art

   e (1) : the term of a logical proposition that denotes the entity of which
   something is affirmed or denied; *also* : the entity denoted (2) : a word or
   word group denoting that of which something is predicated

   f : the principal melodic phrase on which a musical composition or
   movement is based

(By permission. From *Merriam-Webster's Collegiate® Dictionary*, Eleventh Edition ©2010 by Merriam-Webster,
Incorporated [www.Merriam-Webster.com].)

1. There are _____*two*_____ ways to pronounce the word *subject.*
2. The word *subject* contains _____*two*_____ syllables.
3. The entry *subject* originates from _____*three*_____ languages.
4. The word *subject* dates back to the __*14th century*__ .
5. There are _____*three*_____ main definitions listed for the noun form of
   the word *subject.*

   What is the meaning of the word *subject* as it is used in the following
   sentences?
6. I studied the **subject** of economics in high school.
   an area of knowledge and learning

7. The **subject** of my research paper is diversity in the college classroom.
   something concerning which something is said or done

8. The King's **subjects** were required to bow as they entered his presence.
   those who live in the territory of, enjoy the protection of, and owe allegiance to a sovereign
   power

9. During Hitler's reign of terror, many ethnic groups were helpless **subjects** of his cruelty.

   people placed under authority or control

10. In the Milgram Experiment, all the **subjects** in the study thought they were really administering shocks to the other participants.

    individuals whose reactions or responses are studied

Using Textbook Glossaries

Glossaries contain alphabetical lists of words that relate to specialized topics or specific disciplines. In the majority of college textbooks, they are located in the back of the book. Most often, they contain the same words that are in bold print and/or are defined in marginal notes in the body of the text. When reading textbooks, a glossary can be more useful than a dictionary because the definitions relate directly to your course work, and you don't have to search for a meaning that seems to fit the context of a word with which you are unfamiliar.

Following are two examples taken from the glossary of a sociology textbook. These terms may not be found in a traditional dictionary. The numbers in parentheses refer students to a more in-depth discussion of each of these terms in the body of the textbook.

Cultural relativism   The viewing of people's behavior from the perspective of their own culture. (67)

Labeling theory   An approach to deviance that attempts to explain why certain people are seen as deviants while others engaged in the same behavior are not. (169)

(Schaefer 2007)

Using a Thesaurus

A dictionary will assist you in reading and understanding academic language and college-level vocabulary, and a glossary will define the terminology used in a specific discipline. A thesaurus, however, will be more useful when you are looking for a synonym. **Synonyms** are words that have similar meanings to each other. A **thesaurus** is a book of synonyms (usually organized alphabetically), which often also contain **antonyms,** or words that have opposite meanings. A thesaurus can be very helpful when you are looking for the precise word to clearly express an idea, when you are paraphrasing a section of your textbook, or when you are writing a summary of an article or assignment you have read. Knowing more about the words you are studying can also help you in recalling the meanings of new words.

Roget's Twenty-First Century Thesaurus, Franklin's Electronic Dictionary, word-processing programs, or online dictionaries can be consulted for synonyms and antonyms. These words add interest and variety to your writing assignments. Instead of repeating the same word throughout a piece of writing, a thesaurus will provide you with a choice of many words that have the same or similar meanings. Just remember that you will still have to use context clues before you select a synonym or antonym for an unfamiliar word when writing a paraphrase or summary!

The following sentence comes from Philip Chiu's essay, "The Myth of the Model Minority."

> We read in newspapers how **diligent** they (Chinese Americans) are in terms of working and saving.

Look at the following entry for the word ***diligent.*** See how many words have similar meanings.

Entry Word:	diligent
Part of Speech:	*adjective*
Definition:	persevering, hard-working
Synonyms:	active, assiduous, attentive, busy, careful, conscientious, constant, eager, eager beaver, earnest, grind*, indefatigable, industrious, laborious, occupied, operose, painstaking, persistent, persisting, pertinacious, plugging, sedulous, steadfast, studious, tireless, unflagging, unrelenting, untiring
Antonyms:	inactive, indifferent, languid, lazy, lethargic, negligent

(From *Roget's 21st Century Thesaurus.* Dell Publishing, 2010.)

Now you can effectively paraphrase the previous sentence as:

> Newspaper articles have reported that Chinese Americans are *conscientious* workers and *earnest* in saving money.

USING A THESAURUS

Directions: Using the previous entry, select a synonym or antonym for the word ***diligent*** as it is used in each of the following sentences, and write it in the space provided.

1. To succeed in college studies, students must be _____*studious*_____ in completing their reading assignments and preparing for exams.

2. College students who are _____*negligent*_____ will fall behind in their course work, end up performing poorly on tests, and may even be dropped from classes.

3. The newly arriving immigrants found employment because of their
   _____*persistent*_____ efforts to learn the English language as quickly
   as possible.
4. During the Holocaust, the German SS were _____*indefatigable*_____ in
   maintaining records of their mass murders.
5. Meanwhile, the Jewish victims who were persecuted were
   _____*occupied*_____ in trying to maintain faith and a sense of com-
   munity in the remaining ghettos throughout Eastern Europe.

Strategies for Building a College-Level Vocabulary

You can use a number of strategies to build your college vocabulary.

- **Use your college textbooks.** While you are reading, underline new and unfamiliar words, and use context clues or your knowledge of word parts to discern their meaning. After you finish reading, check a dictionary for the appropriate meaning and pronunciation. Looking over the word origin or etymology can also help you remember the new word.
- **Read a daily newspaper.** Journalists often use a bank of vocabulary words to write about broad topics such as elections, terrorism, natural disasters, business, etc. The language used in newspapers is usually repeated and recycled, and readers will find that running or continuing stories often use a lot of the same vocabulary. It's a good idea to learn these new words.

Following is a list of some vocabulary words that relate to **terrorism.** Some of these words have different meanings in other contexts. For example, you may have encountered the word *cell* in your biology class, where it refers to a basic unit of living matter, but when a journalist talks about terrorism, a *cell* means a group of three to five terrorists.

- cell
- civil war
- coalition
- fundamentalist
- counter-terrorism
- domestic terrorism
- hijacking
- kidnapping
- opposition forces
- refugee
- skyjacking
- state terrorism
- suicide bombings
- theocracy

How many of these words do you already know? Start a newspaper vocabulary log, and organize the vocabulary in terms of content. When you encounter a new word, write it in the appropriate section.

Here is an example of an entry in a newspaper log. The following word was found in an article about terrorism. Review your own list of new words weekly.

Terrorism

Date	Word	Definition	Sentence
8/7/09	**cell**	a group of 3–5 terrorists, usually used in the plural form	To ensure security, the members of adjacent terrorist **cells** usually don't know each other or the identity of their leadership.

■ **Use online resources.** Many online sources present opportunities for learning new vocabulary. One is *The New York Times* Word of the Day (http://learning.blogs.nytimes.com/category/word-of-the-day). Another site that presents an especially fun and challenging way to learn new vocabulary is *FreeRice* (a nonprofit website run by the United Nations Food Program) located at www.freerice.com. For each answer you get right, the site donates 10 grains of rice to help end hunger.

■ **Read a wide variety of material.** Although you will be quite busy reading for your college course work, take some time to read your favorite magazines and authors. Add new words to your *Personal Vocabulary Journal* (see page A-20).

■ **Use vocabulary workbooks.**

  ■ *Vocabulary Connections: High Frequency Words*, 1st Edition, by Marianne C. Reynolds

  ■ *Vocabulary Connections: Word Parts,* 1st Edition, by Marianne C. Reynolds

  ■ *Vocabulary Connections: Academic Words*, 1st Edition, by Marianne C. Reynolds

Techniques for Learning Vocabulary

After building your vocabulary with new words, there are many ways to recall and learn these new words. From the following list, select the technique that best suits your needs and learning styles.

1. **Use index cards or flash cards.**

   ■ List new vocabulary or terminology on an index card for easy review and study.

   ■ Write the new word on the blank side of the card and the definition on the lined side.

   ■ For vocabulary words, write synonyms and original sentences using the word. For terminology, provide examples, their context or source, and a picture or diagram that helps you remember the meaning of the word.

   ■ Review these words right after you write them down. Then, review them regularly until you have mastered them.

   Here are two examples for learning a new word through the use of index cards.

Side 1

---

xenophobia

ze-no-fo-be-ah

Side 2

Part of Speech: noun

Definition: fear of strangers

Root: *xeno-* stranger, *phob-* fear

Related forms: xenophobe (noun), xenophobic (adjective)

Related Words: xenophile (kind to people from other culture or with other customs)

Sentence: After arriving in the United States as an immigrant, I was surprised by the level of *xenophobia*.

Side 1

diversity (di-vur-si-tee)

Side 2

---

meaning: the political and social policy of encouraging tolerance for people of different backgrounds

example: Because the United States has become a country of many cultures and ethnic groups, we should embrace *diversity*.

---

2. **Create a split page for new vocabulary words or terms.**

   ■ Write the new word or term in the left-hand column and the definition of the word on the right.

   ■ Add any extra information that will help you remember this word, such as examples, your own sentences, or pictures.

   Here is an example of a split page entry:

Ethnocentrism (noun) (eth-nō-ˈsen-trism) **ethnocentric** (adjective)	is the belief that one's own race or ethnic group is the most important and that some or all aspects of its culture are superior to those of other groups. It is coupled with a generalized contempt for members of other groups. Ethnocentrism may manifest itself in attitudes of superiority or sometimes hostility. Violence, discrimination, proselytizing, and verbal aggressiveness are other means whereby ethnocentrism may be expressed. (*The Columbia Encyclopedia*, Sixth Edition, 2008.) *The Columbia Encyclopedia*, Sixth Edition. Copyright 2008 Columbia University Press. ex. You can overcome ethnocentrism in college by enrolling in courses in pluralism and diversity, by cultivating friendships with people from other cultures, and by joining multicultural clubs.

3. **Create a *Personal Vocabulary Journal* of new words or terminology.**

   ■ Use a spiral notebook.

   ■ Label it *Personal Vocabulary Journal.*

   ■ Date each page.

   ■ From your lecture notes, textbook reading, or other reading sources, compile a list of words you need to learn.

   ■ Include definitions, examples, sentences, etc.

   ■ Review these words and terms regularly.

4. **Store new words in an electronic folder.**

   ■ In your word-processing program, create a file for new vocabulary and/or terminology. Include definitions, sentences, sources, examples, and so on to help you remember these words.

Active Textbook Reading

Learn about your emotional health as you complete activities in Chapter 2, "Get Ready to Read: Active Reading Strategies for Managing College Texts." The chapter in this Appendix is from the freshman experience textbook entitled *Peak Performance: Success in College and Beyond* by Sharon Ferrett.

2

Expand Your Emotional Intelligence

LEARNING OBJECTIVES

In this chapter, you will learn to

2.1 Describe emotional intelligence and the key personal qualities

2.2 Explain the importance of good character, including integrity, civility, and ethics

2.3 Display responsibility, self-management, and self-control

2.4 Develop self-esteem and confidence

2.5 Incorporate a positive attitude and motivation

2.6 Use goal setting as a motivational tool

2.7 List the benefits of a higher education

2.8 Overcome the obstacles to staying positive and motivated

Focus on **CHARACTER**, not just *skills*.

T HERE IS A TENDENCY TO DEFINE INTELLIGENCE AS A SCORE ON AN IQ TEST OR THE SAT OR AS SCHOOL GRADES. Educators have tried to predict who will succeed in college and have found that high school grades, achievement test scores, and ability are only part of the picture. Emotional intelligence and maturity have more effect on school and job success than traditional scholastic measures. In fact, research has indicated that persistence and perseverance are major predictors of college success. A landmark study by the American College Test (ACT) indicated that the primary reasons for first-year students' dropping out of college were not academic but, rather, were emotional difficulties, such as feelings of inadequacy, depression, loneliness, and a lack of motivation or purpose.

Employers also list a positive attitude, motivation, honesty, the ability to get along with others, and the willingness to learn as more important to job success than a college degree or specific skills. In Chapter 1, you learned that SCANS identifies many personal qualities as important competencies for success in the workplace. These qualities and competencies are also essential for building and maintaining strong, healthy relationships throughout life. Essential personal qualities should be viewed as a foundation on which to build skills, experience, and knowledge.

In this chapter, you will learn the importance of emotional intelligence and why character is so important for school and job success. You will also develop personal strategies for maintaining a positive attitude and becoming self-motivated. You may realize that you are smarter than you think. You are smarter than your test scores or grades. Success in your personal life, school, and career is more dependent on a positive attitude, motivation, responsibility, self-control, and effort than on inborn abilities or a high IQ. Peak performers use the whole of their intelligence—and so can you.

Emotional Intelligence and Maturity

Emotional intelligence is the ability to understand and manage yourself and relate effectively to others. **Maturity** is the ability to control your impulses, to think beyond the moment, and to consider how your words and actions affect yourself and others before you act. Emotional intelligence has become a popular topic as we learn more about the importance of personal qualities, communication, the management of feelings, and social competence. Researchers have demonstrated that people who have developed a set of traits that adds to their maturity level increase their sense of well-being, help them get along with others, and enhance their school, job, and life success.

The ability to regulate emotions is vital for school and job success. Emotional maturity contributes to competent behavior, problem-solving ability, socially appropriate behavior, and good communication. Being unaware of or unable to control emotions often accompanies restlessness, a short attention span, negativism, impulsiveness, and distractibility. Clearly, having emotional intelligence distinguishes peak performers from mediocre ones. Becoming more emotionally mature involves three stages:

1. Self-awareness—tuning in to yourself
2. Empathy—tuning in to others
3. Change—tuning in to results

Character First: Integrity, Civility, and Ethics

Good **character** is an essential personal quality for true success in school, work, and life. A person of good character has a core set of principles that most of us accept as constant and relatively noncontroversial. These principles include fairness, honesty, respect, responsibility, caring, trustworthiness, and citizenship. Recent surveys of business leaders indicate that dishonesty, lying, and lack of respect are top reasons for on-the-job difficulties. If an employer believes that an employee lacks integrity, all of that person's positive qualities—from skill and experience to productivity and intelligence—are meaningless. Employers usually list honesty or good character as an essential personal quality, followed by the ability to relate to and get along with others. A number of books have been written by successful top executives who claim that good character, honesty, and a strong value system are what make you an effective leader. All the corporate scandals seen in the news lately are testimonials that business leaders with poor values will eventually meet their demise.

Following The Golden Rule (treating others as we want to be treated) is a simple way to weave integrity and civility into our everyday lives. The word *integrity* comes from the Latin word *integre,* meaning "wholeness." Integrity is the integration of your principles and actions. In a sense, people who have integrity "walk the talk." They consistently live up to their highest principles. Integrity is not adherence to a rigid code but, rather, an ongoing commitment to being consistent, caring, and true to doing what is right. Not only is integrity understanding what is right, but it is also the courage to do it even when it is difficult.

Civility is a set of tools for interacting with others with respect, kindness, and good manners, or etiquette. However, civility is more than good manners and politeness. It includes the many sacrifices we make each day in order to live together peacefully. **Empathy**—understanding and compassion for others—is essential for integrity and civility. You can practice civility in your classes by being on time, turning off your cell phone, staying for the entire class, and listening to the instructor and other students when they speak.

> " Character is like a tree and reputation like its shadow. The shadow is what we think of it; the tree is the real thing. "
>
> ABRAHAM LINCOLN
> *U.S. president*

WORDS TO SUCCEED

> 66 The measure of a man's character is what he would do if he knew he never would be found out. 99
>
> THOMAS MACAULAY
> *British writer and politician*

Ethics are the principles of conduct that govern a group or society. Since a company's reputation is its most important asset, most organizations have a written code of ethics that deals with how people are expected to behave and treat others. It is your responsibility to know and understand the code of ethics at your place of employment and at school. Look in your school's catalog for statements regarding academic integrity, honesty, cheating, and plagiarism. **Cheating** is using or providing unauthorized help in test taking or on projects. **Plagiarism** is considered a form of cheating, since it is presenting someone else's ideas as if they were your own. Know the consequences of your behavior, which could result in an *F* grade, suspension, expulsion, or firing from a job. You always have the choice of telling the truth, being prepared, talking with the instructor, and being responsible for your own work.

Personal qualities, especially honesty, are very important to consider when you think of hiring someone to work for a business you own. Let's say that a candidate sends in an outstanding resume. She has a college degree, experience, and a great personality, and she is positive and motivated, but you find out that she stole from her last employer. No matter how bright or talented someone is, you may realize you cannot have a dishonest person working for you.

There is no universal code of ethics, and many questions about ethical issues do not have clear-cut answers. For example, taking money out of a cash drawer is clearly dishonest, but what about coming in late to work, padding your expense account, or using someone else's words without giving credit?

You will be faced with situations in your personal, school, and business lives that will force you to make decisions that will be viewed as either ethical or unethical. Sometimes it is not easy. At one time or another, everyone is faced with situations that demand tough decisions. Consider the following situations.

Scenarios on Character

Peggy Lyons has a midterm test to take. This test will determine 50 percent of her final grade. She has been very busy at home and has not attended class or her study group for the past week. She knows she probably won't do well on the test, but she needs a good grade. She knows the instructor is fair and has been asking about her. Someone Peggy met in the cafeteria tells her she can buy a copy of the test. She's tempted. What do you think she will do? What would you do?

While in college, Rey Armas has been working part-time at an electronics store. Rey's supervisor, Joe, has worked in the store for 10 years. Joe is 50 and has a family. This is his only means of support. Rey has discovered that Joe is stealing some of the electronics components to sell on the side. Rey likes Joe. What should Rey do? What would you do?

Tora Veda is up late, working on a term paper. She debates whether she should take the time to cite references. Her instructor warns the class about plagiarism, but,

Personal Evaluation Notebook 2.1

Character and Ethics

Integrity and honesty are essential qualities. It is important for you to assess and develop them as you would any skill. Use critical thinking to answer these questions.

1. What is the most difficult ethical dilemma you have faced in your life?

   _____

2. Do you have a code of ethics that helps guide you when making decisions? Explain.

   _____

3. When did you learn about honesty?

   _____

4. Who have you known that is a role model for displaying integrity and honesty?

   _____

5. Do you have a code of ethics at your college? Where did you find it? (Hint: Check your school's catalog or ask the dean of students for a copy.)

   _____

6. Does your company have a code of ethics? How do employees access it?

   _____

7. If you were the chief executive officer (CEO) or owner of a small company, what would you want to include in your code of ethics?

   _____

8. How would you make certain that employees understood and honored your company's code of ethics?

   _____

because some of her information came off the Internet, she doesn't think it should be a big deal. What should she do? What would you do?

Peggy, Rey, and Tora are all faced with tough decisions. Their final decisions will be viewed by others as either ethical or unethical and carry consequences, such as being fired, getting an *F* in the course, or even being suspended or expelled from school. They will have to call on their own personal code of ethics. When defining their code and their subsequent actions, they may find the following questions helpful. You, too, may find them helpful when developing a code of ethics.

- Is this action against the law?
- Is this action against company policy or code of behavior?

Personal Evaluation Notebook ✐ 2.2

Skills and Personal Qualities

1. Jot down the skills, personal qualities, and habits you are learning and demonstrating in each of your classes.

Skills	Personal Qualities	Habits
_____	_____	_____
_____	_____	_____
_____	_____	_____

2. Pretend that you own your own business. List the skills and personal qualities you would want in the employees you hire.

Type of business: _____

Employees' Skills	Employees' Personal Qualities
_____	_____
_____	_____
_____	_____

- How would this situation read if reported on the front page of the newspaper?
- How would you explain this to your mother? To your child?
- What might be the negative consequences?
- Are you causing unnecessary harm to someone?
- If unsure, have you asked a trusted associate outside of the situation?
- Are you treating others as you would want to be treated?

Remember, unethical behavior rarely goes unnoticed!

Responsibility

Peak performers take responsibility for their thoughts, state of mind, and behavior. They don't blame others for their problems but, rather, use their energy to solve them. They are persistent and patient. They know they must exert a consistent amount of high effort to achieve their goals. They keep their word and agreements. When they say they are going to do something, they keep their commitment. People can depend on them.

Examples of being responsible include showing up prepared and on time for work, meetings, study teams, and so on; paying bills and repaying loans on time; and cleaning up personal messes at home and elsewhere. Responsible people own up to

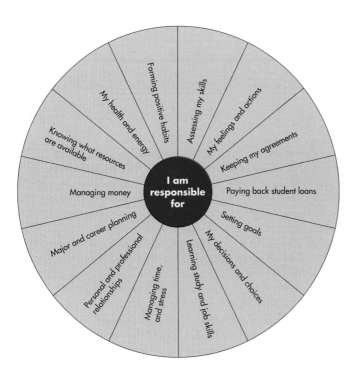

Figure **2.1**
Personal Responsibilities

What you do or don't do in one area of life can affect other areas of your life and other people. *What one area of personal responsibility would you improve?*

their mistakes and do what they can to correct them. The model in **Figure 2.1** illustrates many important interrelated personal responsibilities.

Other personal qualities related to responsibility include perseverance, punctuality, concentration, attention to details, follow-through, and high standards. What you do or don't do in one area of your life affects other areas of your life and other people.

Peak performers realize they are responsible for their attitudes and actions, and they know they have the power to change them. A negative attitude is sometimes the result of not coping effectively with change, conflict, and frustration. Emotional, physical, and social changes are part of the growing process at any age. Learning to adjust to frustration and discouragement can take many forms. Some people withdraw or become critical, cynical, shy, sarcastic, or unmotivated. Blame, excuses, justification, and criticism of others are devices for those who cannot accept personal responsibility for their behavior and state of mind. Acknowledge your feelings and attitudes. Decide if they support your goals; if they do not, choose a state of mind and actions that support you.

Being responsible creates a sense of integrity and a feeling of self-worth. For example, if you owe money to a friend, family member, or bank, take responsibility for repaying the loan. If you have a student loan, repay it on schedule or make new arrangements with the lender. Not repaying can result in years of guilt and embarrassment, as well as a poor credit rating. It is important to your self-worth to know you are a person who keeps commitments and assumes responsibility.

Self-Control

> 66 Holding on to anger is like grasping a hot coal with the intent of throwing it at someone else; you are the one who gets burned. 99
>
> BUDDHA

If anger were a disease, there would be an epidemic in this country. Road rage, spousal and child abuse, and a lack of civility are just a few examples of anger. Emotionally mature people know how to control their thoughts and behaviors and how to resolve conflict. Conflict is an inevitable part of school and work, but it can be resolved in a positive way. Following are tips for trying to redirect and transform your anger:

1. **Calm down.** Step back from the situation and take a deep breath. Take the drama out of the situation and observe what is happening, what behavior is triggering angry emotions, and what options you have in responding in appropriate and positive ways. If you lash out without thinking and attack verbally, you may cause serious harm to your relationship. You cannot take back words once they are spoken. Resist the urge to overreact.

2. **Clarify and define.** Determine exactly with whom or what you are angry and why. What specific behavior in the other person is causing you to feel angry or frustrated? Determine whose problem it is. For example, your instructor may have an annoying tone and style of lecturing. If a behavior annoys only you, perhaps it is something you alone need to address.

3. **Listen with empathy and respect.** Empathy includes the ability to listen, understand, and respond to the feelings and needs of others. Take the tension out of the conflict by really listening and understanding the other person's point of view. Communicate that you have heard and understood by restating the other person's position. Respect yourself as well. Ask yourself how you feel. Are you tired, hot, hungry, frustrated, rushed, or ill? If so, you may not want to deal with your anger until you feel better. Sometimes getting a good night's sleep or having a good meal will put the situation into perspective, and your anger will dissolve.

4. **Use "I" statements.** Take ownership of your feelings. Using "I" statements—direct messages you deliver in a calm tone with supportive body language—can diffuse anger. You are not blaming another person but, rather, expressing how a situation affects you. For example, you can say, "Carlos, when I hear you clicking your pen and tapping it on the desk, I'm distracted from studying." This is usually received better than saying, "Carlos, you're so rude and inconsiderate. You must know that you're annoying me when you tap your pen."

5. **Focus on one problem.** Don't pounce on every annoying behavior you can think of to dump on the person. Let's continue with the example in Tip 4: "In addition to clicking your pen, Carlos, I don't like how you leave your dishes in the sink, drop your towels in the bathroom, and make that annoying little sound when you eat." Work to resolve only one behavior or conflict at a time.

6. **Focus on win-win solutions.** How can you both win? Restate the problem and jot down as many different creative solutions as possible that you can both agree on.

7. **Reward positive behavior.** As you use praise and reinforce positive behaviors, you will find that the person will exert less resistance. You can now be more direct about the specific behaviors and ask for a commitment: "Julie, if you could be here right at 8:00, we could get through this study session in 2 hours.

Can we agree on this?" Focus on behavior, not personality or name calling, which just angers you and antagonizes the other person. Don't let anger and conflict create more stress in your life and take a physical and emotional toll. You can learn to step back automatically from explosive situations and control them, rather than let your emotions control you. **Peak Progress 2.1** explores how you can use the Adult Learning Cycle to manage your emotions.

Self-Esteem and Confidence

Self-esteem is how you feel about yourself. Peak performers have developed self-respect and confidence and believe in themselves. They assess themselves honestly and focus on their strengths. They constantly learn new skills and competencies that build their confidence. They accept responsibility for their attitudes and behavior. They know that blame and anger do not solve problems.

Peak Progress

2.1

Applying the Adult Learning Cycle to Self-Control

The Adult Learning Cycle can help you increase your emotional intelligence. For example, you may have felt the same angry and frustrated feelings mentioned in the Self-Management exercise on the first page of this chapter. It could be because someone cut you off or you've lost your keys, you may have three papers due, or you are so overwhelmed with school, work, and family that your motivation dropped and you developed a negative attitude.

1. **RELATE. Why do I want to learn this?** What personal meaning and interest does controlling my anger have for me? Has it been a challenge for me? Has it hurt important relationships in my personal life or at school or work? How will controlling my anger help me in those situations?

2. **OBSERVE. How does this work?** I can learn a lot about anger management by watching, listening, and engaging in trial and error. Whom do I consider to be an emotionally mature person? Whom do I respect because of his or her patience, understanding, and ability to deal with stressful events? When I observe the problems that people around me have in their lives, how do they exhibit their emotional maturity in general and anger specifically?

3. **REFLECT. What does this mean?** Test new ways of behaving and break old patterns. Explore creative ways to solve problems rather than getting angry. Gather and assess information about anger management and reflect on what works and doesn't work.

4. **DO. What can I do with this?** Learn by doing and finding practical applications for anger management. Practice the seven steps outlined on pages 52–53. Apply the ABC Method of Self-Management to specific situations to determine positive outcomes.

5. **TEACH. Whom can I share this with?** Talk with others and share experiences. Demonstrate to and teach others the methods you've learned. Model by example.

Now return to Stage 1 and realize your accomplishment in taking steps to control your anger better.

People with a positive self-esteem have the confidence that allows them to be more open to new experiences and accepting of different people. They tend to be more optimistic. They are more willing to share their feelings and ideas with others and are willing to tolerate differences in others. Because they have a sense of self-worth, they do not find it necessary to put down or discriminate against others.

Confidence can develop from

- Focusing on your strengths and positive qualities and finding ways to bolster them. Be yourself and don't compare yourself with others.
- Learning to be resilient and bouncing back after disappointments and setbacks. Don't dwell on mistakes or limitations. Accept them, learn from them, and move on with your life.
- Using affirmations and visualizations to replace negative thoughts and images.
- Taking responsibility for your life instead of blaming others. You cannot control other people's behavior, but you have complete control over your own thoughts, emotions, words, and behavior.
- Learning skills and competencies that give you opportunities and confidence in your abilities. It is not enough to feel good about yourself; you must also be able to do what is required to demonstrate that you are a competent, honest, and responsible person. The more skills and personal qualities you acquire, the more competent and confident you will feel.
- Focusing on giving, not receiving, and make others feel valued and appreciated. You will increase your self-esteem when you make a contribution.
- Creating a support system by surrounding yourself with confident and kind people who feel good about themselves and who make you feel good about yourself.

A Positive Attitude and Personal Motivation

There is an old story about three men working on a project in a large city in France. A curious tourist asks them, "What are you three working on?" The first man says, "I'm hauling rocks." The second man says, "I'm laying a wall." The third man says with pride, "I'm building a cathedral." The third man has a sense of vision of the whole system. When college and work seem as tedious as hauling rocks, focus on the big picture.

A positive attitude is essential for achieving success in school, in your career, and in life. Your attitude, more than any other factor, influences the outcome of a task. **Motivation** is the inner drive that moves you to action. Even when you are discouraged or face setbacks, motivation can help you bounce back and keep on track. You may have skills, experience, intelligence, and talent, but you will accomplish little if you are not motivated to direct your energies toward specific goals.

A positive attitude results in enthusiasm, vitality, optimism, and a zest for living. When you have a positive attitude, you are more likely to be on time, alert in meetings and class, and able to work well even when you have an unpleasant assignment. A positive attitude encourages

- Higher productivity
- An openness to learning at school and on the job
- School and job satisfaction
- Creativity in solving problems and finding solutions
- The ability to work with diverse groups of people
- Enthusiasm and a "can do" outlook
- Confidence and higher self-esteem
- The ability to channel stress and increase energy
- A sense of purpose and direction

A negative attitude can drain you of enthusiasm and energy, and it can result in absenteeism, tardiness, and impaired mental and physical health. In addition, people who have a negative attitude may

- Feel that they are victims and are helpless to make a change
- Focus on the worst that can happen in a situation
- Blame external circumstances for their attitudes
- Focus on the negative in people and situations
- Look at adversity as something that will last forever
- Be angry and blame other people

> " It is better to light a candle than curse the darkness. "
>
> ELEANOR ROOSEVELT
> *U.S. first lady and political leader*

WORDS TO SUCCEED

How Needs and Desires Influence Attitudes and Motivation

One of the deepest needs in life is to become all that you can be by using all of your intelligence and potential. Abraham Maslow, a well-known psychologist, developed the theory of a hierarchy of needs. According to his theory, there are five levels of universal needs. **Figure 2.2** on the next page illustrates these levels, moving from the lower-order needs—physiological and safety and security needs—to the higher-order needs—the needs for self-esteem and self-actualization. The lower-order needs must be met first before satisfying the higher-order needs. For example, it may be difficult for you to participate in hobbies that foster your self-respect if you don't have enough money for food and rent. For some people, the lower-order needs include a sense of order, power, or independence. The higher levels, which address social and self-esteem factors, include the need for companionship, respect, and a sense of belonging.

As your lower-order needs are satisfied and cease to motivate you, you begin to direct your attention to the higher-order needs for motivation. As you go up the

Figure 2.2

Maslow's Hierarchy of Needs

Maslow's theory states that most people need to satisfy the universal basic needs before considering the higher-order needs. *Which level of needs is motivating you right now?*

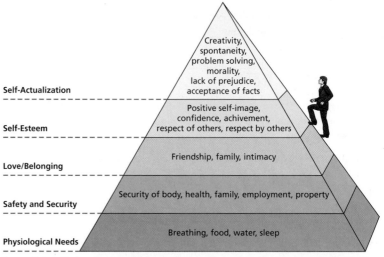

Self-Actualization — Creativity, spontaneity, problem solving, morality, lack of prejudice, acceptance of facts

Self-Esteem — Positive self-image, confidence, achivement, respect of others, respect by others

Love/Belonging — Friendship, family, intimacy

Safety and Security — Security of body, health, family, employment, property

Physiological Needs — Breathing, food, water, sleep

Source: Maslow, Abraham H., Frager, Robert D. (Editor), Fadiman, James (Editor), "Hierarchy of Needs," from *Motivation and Personality,* 3rd ed., ©1987. Pearson Education, Inc.

Personal Evaluation Notebook  2.3

Needs, Motivation, and Commitment

1. What needs motivate you at this time?

   _____

   _____

2. What do you think will motivate you in 20 years?

   _____

   _____

3. Complete this sentence in your own words: "For me to be more motivated, I need . . ."

   _____

   _____

4. Describe a time in your life when you were committed to something—such as a goal, a
   project, an event, or a relationship—that was important to you.

   _____

   _____

5. Regarding your answer to Question 4, what were the main factors that kept you
   motivated?

   _____

   _____

ladder of higher-order needs, you'll find that you're learning for the joy of new ideas and the confidence that comes from learning new skills and competencies. You have more energy and focus for defining and pursuing your dreams and goals. You want to discover and develop your full potential. You not only love learning new ideas but also value emotional maturity, character, and integrity. You are well on the path to self-actualization. According to Maslow, self-actualizing people embrace the realities of the world rather than deny or avoid them. They are creative problem solvers who make the most of their unique abilities to strive to be the best they can be. Complete **Personal Evaluation Notebook 2.3** to assess what motivates you.

Motivational Strategies

Keeping yourself motivated isn't always easy with all the pressures you may be feeling from school, work, family, and so on. However, there are some key motivational strategies you can put into action:

1. **Act as if you were motivated.** Attitude can influence behavior, and behavior can influence attitude. The way you act every day can affect your self-esteem, and your self-esteem can affect the things you do. You can attempt to change your behavior anytime. You don't need to wait until your attitude changes or until you feel motivated to begin the positive behaviors. Act as if you were already motivated.

   For example, pretend you are performing in a movie. Your character is a positive, motivated student. How do you enter the room? Are you smiling? What are your breathing, posture, and muscle tension like? What kinds of gestures and facial expressions do you use to create this character? What kinds of friends does this person enjoy being with? Try acting out the part when you wake up in the morning and throughout the day. If you develop positive study and work habits and do them consistently, even when you don't feel like it, you'll be successful, and this will create a positive state of mind. You are what you do consistently. Positive habits create success.

2. **Use affirmations.** Any discussion of motivation must include your self-talk, what you say to yourself throughout the day. Once you start paying attention to your self-talk, you may be amazed at how much of it is negative. Throughout the day, countless thoughts, images, and phrases go through your brain almost unnoticed, but they have a tremendous influence on your mood and attitude. The first step, then, is to replace negative self-talk with affirmations or positive self-talk. For example, don't say, "I won't waste my time today." That just reminds you that you have a habit of wasting time. Instead, affirm, "I am setting goals and priorities and achieving the results I want. I have plenty of

energy to accomplish all that I choose to do, and I feel good when I'm organized and centered." Complete **Personal Evaluation Notebook 2.4** to determine if your self-talk needs to become more positive.

3. **Use visualization.** As we explored in Chapter 1, visualization is seeing things
in your mind's eye by organizing and processing information through pictures
and symbols. You imagine yourself behaving in certain ways, so that behavior
will become real. For example, businessman Calvin Payne knows the power of
visualization. Before he graduated from college, he bought his graduation cap
and gown and kept them in his room. He visualized himself crossing the stage
in his gown to accept his diploma. This visual goal helped him when he suffered setbacks, frustration, and disappointments. He graduated with honors
and now incorporates visualization techniques in his career.

   Most right-brain dominant people are visual and use imagery a great deal.
They can see scenes in detail when they read or daydream. In fact, their imagery is like a movie of themselves, with scenes of how they will react in certain
situations, or a replay of what has occurred in the past. These images are rich
in detail, expansive, and ongoing. Left-brain dominant people tend to use
imagery less, but using imagery is a technique that can be learned, developed,
and practiced.

   Visualization will help you see problems through formulas; read a recipe
and see and taste the finished food; read blueprints and visualize the building;
and see scenes and characters through narratives. You can also use mental
imagery to create a positive, calm, and motivated state of mind.

4. **Use goals as motivational tools.** Just as an athlete visualizes crossing the finish
line, you, too, can visualize your final goal. Working toward your goal can be a
great motivator; however, you first must know what your goal is. **Peak Progress
2.3** will help you distinguish the difference between a desire and a goal and
between long-term and short-term goals.

Peak Progress

2.3

Setting Goals

There is an old saying: "If you don't know where you are going, any road will take you there." The key, then, is to figure out where you are going, and then you can determine the best way to get there. Goal setting will help you do that. But goals provide more than direction and a clear vision for the future. When appropriately understood and applied, they are very effective motivators.

It is helpful first to distinguish between goals and desires. Identifying what you want out of life (that is, creating your mission statement, as discussed in Chapter 1) is certainly an important step in developing effective goals, but the goals themselves are not mere desires; rather, they are specific, measurable prescriptions for action. For example, if you want to be financially secure, you should start by identifying the actions that will help you fulfill that desire. Knowing that financial security is tied to education, you might make college graduation your first long-term goal. However, be careful how you construct this goal. "My goal is to have a college degree" is passive and vague. On the other hand, "I will earn my Bachelor of Science degree in computer technology from State University by June 2011" prescribes a clear course of action that can be broken down easily into sequences of short-term goals, which then can be broken down into manageable daily tasks.

Note that your long-term goal always comes first. Discomfort with long-term commitment sometimes leads people to try to address short-term goals first. Do not fall into this trap. Remember that short-term goals are merely steps toward achieving the long-term goal. As such, they cannot even exist by themselves. To understand this better, try to imagine driving to an unfamiliar city and then using a road map without having first determined where you are going. It cannot be done. You must know where you are going before you can plan your route (as illustrated on the next page).

Peak performers have an internal **locus of control**—they believe that they have control over their lives and that their rewards or failures are a result of their behavior, choices, character, or efforts. They are able to delay gratification and cope effectively with stress. Many people who have less school and job success have an **external locus of control**—they credit outside influences, such as fate, luck, or other people, with their success or failure. They are impulsive about immediate pleasures and are easily swayed by the influences of others. If you practice responsibility and discipline every day in small ways, your internal locus of control will grow and you will be achieving your goals and writing your own life script, rather than living the script written by your parents, circumstances, or society. In Chapter 3, we will explore using your goals to plan how to use your time effectively.

The following are some points to remember:

- Desires are not goals.
- Goals prescribe action.
- Effective goals are specific.
- Goal setting always begins with a long-term goal.
- Short-term goals are the steps in achieving the long-term goal.
- Daily tasks are the many specific actions that fulfill short-term goals.

(continued)

Setting Goals *(concluded)*

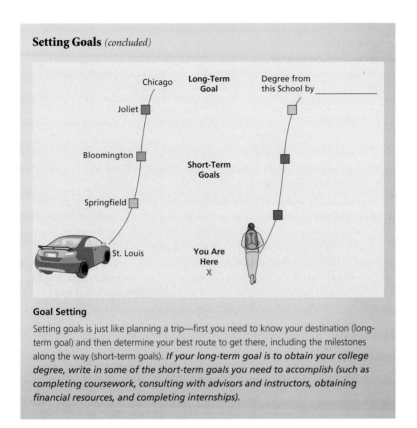

Goal Setting

Setting goals is just like planning a trip—first you need to know your destination (long-term goal) and then determine your best route to get there, including the milestones along the way (short-term goals). *If your long-term goal is to obtain your college degree, write in some of the short-term goals you need to accomplish (such as completing coursework, consulting with advisors and instructors, obtaining financial resources, and completing internships).*

Often, peak performers not only visualize goals but also write them down. Try keeping yours in your wallet, taping them on your bathroom mirror, or putting them on yellow sticky notes around your computer screen. Without a specific goal, it's not easy to find the motivation, effort, and focus required to go to classes and complete assignments. Make certain your goals are realistic. Achieving excellence doesn't mean attaining perfection or working compulsively toward impossible goals. If you try to be a perfectionist, you set yourself up for frustration, which can lead to decreased motivation, lowered productivity, increased stress, and failure.

5. **Understand expectations.** You will be more motivated to succeed if you understand what is expected of you in each class. Most instructors hand out a syllabus on the first day. Review it carefully and keep a copy in your class notebook. Review the syllabus with a study partner and clarify expectations with your instructor. Meet with your academic advisor to review general college and graduation requirements. College is different from high school and, the more you understand expectations, the more focused you'll be on reaching your goals.

6. **Study in teams.** Success in the business world depends on team skills—the sharing of skills, knowledge, confidence, and decision-making abilities. The term *synergy* means that the whole is greater than the sum of the parts. It means seeing and using the whole system, not just isolated parts. You can increase your school and job success by learning, studying, and working in teams. You can also

   - Teach each other material and outline main points
   - Read and edit each other's reports
   - Develop sample quizzes and test each other
   - Learn to get along with and value different people (we will explore healthy relationships in more detail in Chapter 12)

7. **Stay physically and mentally healthy.** It is difficult to motivate yourself if you don't feel well physically or emotionally. If you are ill, you will miss classes, fall behind in studying, or both. Falling behind can cause you to worry and feel stressed. Talk out your problems, eat well, get plenty of exercise and rest, and create a balance of work and play.

8. **Learn to reframe.** You don't have control over many situations or the actions of others, but you do have total control over your responses. **Reframing** is choosing to see a situation in a new way. For example, to pay for school, Joan

Bosch works at a fast-food hamburger place. She could have chosen to see this in a negative way; instead, she sees it in a positive way. She has reframed this work situation to focus on essential job skills. She is learning to be positive, dependable, hardworking, service-oriented, flexible, and tolerant.

9. **Reward yourself.** The simplest tasks can become discouraging without rewards for progress and for completion. Set up a system of appropriate rewards and consequences. Decide what your reward will be when you finish a project. For an easier task, the reward might be small, such as a snack, a hot shower, or a phone call to a friend. For a larger project, the reward might be going out to dinner, a movie, or a museum or throwing a small party. What are some rewards that would motivate you?

10. **Make learning relevant.** You will be more motivated if you understand the benefits of gaining knowledge and learning new skills in your coursework and the ways they will relate to your performance on the job. You may be attending college just because you love to learn and meet new people. However, it's more likely that you are enrolled to acquire or enhance your knowledge and skills, which will increase your marketability in the workforce.

The Benefits of Higher Education

As just mentioned, you will be more motivated in your schoolwork—and more likely to graduate and excel—if you understand how attending college benefits you both today and in the future.

HIGHER EDUCATION ENCOURAGES CRITICAL THINKING

Higher education has its roots in the liberal arts. Many years ago, being an educated person meant having a liberal arts education. *Liberal* comes from the Latin root word *liber,* which means "to free." A broad education is designed to free people to think and understand themselves and the world around them. The liberal arts include such areas as the arts, the humanities, the social sciences, mathematics, and the natural sciences. Classes in philosophy, history, language, art, and geography focus on how people think, behave, and express themselves in our culture and in the world. The liberal arts integrate many disciplines and provide a foundation for professional programs, such as criminal justice, electronics, computer systems, business, medicine, and law.

Technology is no longer a separate field of study from liberal arts but is an important tool for educated people. Employers want professionals who are creative problem solvers, have good critical thinking skills, can communicate and work well with others, can adapt to change, and understand our complex technical and social world. Liberal arts classes can help make a skilled professional a truly educated professional by providing an integration and understanding of history, culture, ourselves, and our world.

HIGHER EDUCATION IS A SMART FINANCIAL INVESTMENT

As mentioned earlier, you will be more motivated to put in long hours of studying when you feel the goal is worth it. Higher education is an excellent investment.

> **"**Education's purpose is to replace an empty mind with an open one.**"**
>
> MALCOLM FORBES
> *Publisher*

WORDS TO SUCCEED

Figure 2.4

Annual Earnings and Education

Statistically, the level of your education is directly related to your income. These figures are average earnings for the U.S. population. Incomes vary within each category. *What other advantages, besides a good job and income, do you think education offers?*

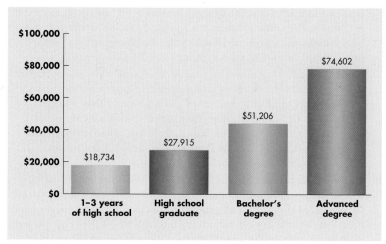

SOURCE: U.S. Census Bureau, U.S. Department of Commerce, 2005.

No one can take your education away from you, and it can pay large dividends. College graduates earn an average of well over $800,000 more in a lifetime than do high school graduates. (See **Figure 2.4**.) Although graduating from college or a career school won't guarantee you a great job, it pays off with more career opportunities, better salaries, more benefits, more job promotions, increased workplace flexibility, better workplace conditions, and greater job satisfaction. Many career centers at colleges make a commitment to help their students find employment.

Society and the workplace benefit when people improve their literacy. Various reports from the U.S. Department of Labor indicate that people who attend at least 2 years of college tend to

- Make better decisions
- Be willing to learn new skills
- Have more hobbies and leisure activities
- Have a longer life expectancy
- Be healthier
- Be more involved in the community
- Have more discipline and perseverance
- Have more self-confidence
- Learn to adapt to change

HIGHER EDUCATION PREPARES YOU FOR LIFE ON THE JOB

As you've no doubt noticed, the connection between school and job success is a major theme in this book. What you learn in school correlates directly with

Peak Progress

2.5

Skills for School and Career

Keep the following skills in mind as you see the connection between school and job success.

Skills	School Application	Career Application
Basic skills	Foundation for schoolwork	Foundation for work tasks
Motivation	Motivated to attend classes	Motivated to excel at work
Thinking skills	Solve case studies, equations	Solve work problems
Creativity	Creative experiments	Creative work solutions
Control of time	Homework first	Work priorities in order
Control of money	Personal budget	Departmental budgets
Writing	Writing papers	Writing reports, memos
Speeches	Classroom speeches	Presentations
Test taking	Tests in classes	Performance reviews
Information	Selecting class information	Selecting work information
Learning	Learning for classes	Learning job skills
Systems	Learning college system	Learning organization
Resources	Using college resources	Using work resources
Technology	Using computers for papers	Using computers for work

finding and keeping a job, as well as succeeding in a chosen career. As you go through school, think about how the skills, personal qualities, and habits you are learning and demonstrating in class are related to job and life success. **Peak Progress 2.5** includes a number of skills and qualities you are learning, practicing, and enhancing in your coursework and indicates how you will use them on the job.

As you develop your time- and stress-management skills, which we will explore in more detail later in this text, you will see improvement in your habits in school and on the job. Time management may help you show up for class on time and be prepared every day, thus leading to better grades. Punctuality in school will carry over to punctuality for work. Stress management may help you get along better with your roommates, instructors, or co-workers. Learning how to succeed in the school or college system can serve as a model for working effectively in organizational systems. Do you think you are maximizing your strengths, skills, and personal qualities? See **Peak Progress 2.6** on page 66 to determine what kind of student/worker you are and to determine what you need to do to improve your performance.

Peak Progress

2.6

What Kind of Student/Worker Are You?

A peak performer or an *A* student

- Is alert, actively involved, and eager to learn
- Consistently does more than required
- Consistently shows initiative and enthusiasm
- Is positive and engaged
- Can solve problems and make sound decisions
- Is dependable, prompt, neat, accurate, and thorough
- Attends work/class every day and is on time and prepared

A good worker or a *B* student

- Frequently does more than is required
- Is usually attentive, positive, and enthusiastic
- Completes most work accurately, neatly, and thoroughly
- Often uses critical thinking to solve problems and make decisions
- Attends work/class almost every day and is usually on time and prepared

An average worker or a *C* student

- Completes the tasks that are required
- Shows a willingness to follow instructions and learn
- Is generally involved, dependable, enthusiastic, and positive
- Provides work that is mostly thorough, accurate, and prompt
- Misses some work/classes

A problem worker or a *D* student

- Usually does the minimum of what is required
- Has irregular attendance, is often late, or is distracted
- Lacks a positive attitude or the ability to work well with others
- Often misunderstands assignments and deadlines
- Lacks thoroughness
- Misses many days of work/classes

An unacceptable worker or an *F* student

- Does not do the work that is required
- Is inattentive, bored, negative, and uninvolved
- Is undependable and turns in work that is incorrect and incomplete
- Misses a significant amount of work/classes

Overcome Obstacles

Don't Get Discouraged

Even peak performers sometimes feel discouraged and need help climbing out of life's valleys. Creating and maintaining a positive state of mind and learning self-management do not happen by reading a book, attending a lecture, or using a few strategies for a day or two. It takes time and effort. Everyone gets off course now and then, but the key is to realize that setbacks are part of life. Don't allow setbacks to make you feel as if you have failed and can no longer reach your goal. Find a formula that works for you to create a positive and resourceful mind.

Peak Progress 2.7 shows that a lack of personal qualities has a direct effect on the main reasons students don't graduate. If you think, "I'll be more motivated as soon as I graduate and get a real job," you may never develop the necessary qualities and skills to achieve that. Starting today, you should

- Focus on being motivated and positive
- Focus on your successes and accomplishments
- Surround yourself with positive, supportive, and encouraging friends
- Tell yourself, "This is a setback, not a failure"
- Learn self-control and self-management strategies
- Make certain you are physically renewed; get more rest, exercise more, and every day do something that you love

> 66 I've missed more than 9,000 shots in my career. I've lost almost 300 games. 26 times, I've been trusted to take the game winning shot and missed. I've failed over and over and over again in my life. And that is why I succeed. 99
>
> MICHAEL JORDAN
> *Professional basketball player*

WORDS TO SUCCEED

2.7

The Most Common Reasons Students Do Not Graduate

Between 30 and 50 percent of all college freshmen never graduate. The top reasons are

1. Poor study skills and habits
2. Lack of time-management skills
3. Lack of preparation for the demands and requirements of college
4. Inability to handle the freedom at college
5. Too much partying
6. Lack of motivation or purpose
7. Failure to attend class regularly
8. Failure to ask for help early
9. Lack of effort and time spent in studying
10. Failure to take responsibility for education (such as getting to know instructors, knowing expectations, setting goals, understanding deadlines, making up tests, redoing papers)

- Replace negative and limiting thoughts and self-talk with affirmations and positive visualization
- Collect short stories about people who were discouraged, received negative messages, and bounced back

Create Positive Mind Shifts

Your beliefs and expectations about yourself can either limit or expand your success. Other people's expectations of you may cause you to redefine who you think you are and what you think you are capable of achieving. You may start to believe what you tell yourself or hear from others again and again, which may be limiting your thinking.

For example, Steve Delmay comes from a long line of lumber mill workers. Although they have lived for generations in a college town, his family has never had anything to do with the college. Steve was expected to go to work at the mill right after high school. He never thought about other options. However, during his senior year in high school, he attended Career Day. He met instructors and students from the local college who were friendly, supportive, and encouraging. His world opened up, and he saw opportunities he had never considered before. Steve experienced a major mind shift. Although he had to overcome a lack of support at home, he is now a successful college student with a bright future.

Creative problem solving can expand your mind and shift your thinking, so that you can see new possibilities and broader and more exciting horizons. College is an ideal time to develop your natural creativity and explore new ways of thinking. Try the following:

1. **Create a support system.** Without support and role models, you may question whether you can be successful. First-generation college students, women in technical programs, and men in nursing programs may feel uncomfortable and question whether they belong. Cultural minorities, veterans, and physically challenged or returning students may feel that they don't belong. Some students may be told that they are not college material. You can find encouragement with a support system of positive and accepting people. Join a variety of clubs. Make friends with diverse groups of students, instructors, and community leaders.

2. **Reprogram your mind.** Affirmations and visualization can create a self-fulfilling prophecy. If you think of yourself as a success and are willing to put in the effort, you will be successful. Focus on your successes and accomplishments and overcome limitations. For example, if you need to take a remedial math class, take it and don't label yourself as "dumb" or "math-impaired." Instead, focus on how improved your math skills will be.

3. **Use critical thinking.** Question limiting labels and beliefs. Where did they come from and are they accurate? Be mentally active and positive.

4. **Use creative thinking.** Ask yourself, "What if?" Explore creative ways of achieving your goals. Find out how you learn best and adopt positive habits.

5. **Take responsibility.** You are responsible for your thoughts, beliefs, and actions. You can question, think, and explore. You can achieve almost anything you dream.

6. **Learn new skills.** Focus on your strengths, but be willing to learn new skills and competencies continually. Feeling competent is empowering.

7. **Use the whole of your intelligence.** You definitely are smarter than you think you are. Use all your experiences and personal qualities to achieve your goals. Develop responsibility, self-control, dependability, sociability, character, manners, and all the other qualities necessary for school, job, and life success.

TAKING CHARGE

Summary

In this chapter I learned to:

- **Use the whole of my intelligence.** Developing emotional maturity and strong personal qualities is just as, if not more, important to my future success as learning new skills and information. Essential personal qualities include character, responsibility, self-management and self-control, self-esteem, confidence, attitude, and motivation.

- **Focus on character first.** Strong leaders are those who have an equally strong set of values. Having personal integrity gives me the courage to do the right thing, even when it is difficult. I display civility and empathy by interacting with family, friends, and colleagues with respect, kindness, good manners, empathy, and compassion. It's important for me to have a personal code of ethics that I follow in all facets of my life.

- **Take responsibility for my thoughts, actions, and behaviors.** I don't blame others for my setbacks, and I focus my energy on positive solutions. Others can depend on me to keep my commitments.

- **Manage and control my emotions, anger, and negative thoughts.** Conflict is an inevitable part of life, but it can be resolved in a positive way. Steps I can follow to redirect my negative thoughts and anger are (1) calm down; (2) clarify and define; (3) listen with empathy and respect; (4) use "I" statements; (5) focus on one problem; (6) focus on win-win solutions; and (7) reward positive behavior.

- **Develop self-esteem and confidence.** Through self-assessment, I understand my strengths and will continue to learn new skills and competencies that will build my confidence.

- **Maintain a positive attitude and keep myself motivated.** A positive attitude is essential for achieving success, and it influences the outcome of a task more than any other factor. Motivation is the inner drive that moves me to action. Working toward goals increases my motivation. Maslow's hierarchy of needs shows that I can fulfill my higher needs for self-esteem and self-actualization only when I have fulfilled my more basic needs first. The motivation cycle further demonstrates how affirmations, visualization, and self-talk affect my physical responses and behavior.

- **Realize the benefits of higher education.** Higher education has its roots in the liberal arts. Liberal arts classes can help make me a truly educated professional by providing an integration and understanding of history, culture, ourselves, and our world. My pursuit of a higher education should pay off with more career opportunities, a higher salary, more benefits, more job promotions, increased workplace flexibility, better workplace conditions, and greater job satisfaction. I will become more prepared for life on the job.

- **Overcome the barriers to staying positive and motivated.** Discouragement is the number one barrier to motivation. Setbacks will occur, but I will focus on my successes and accomplishments, surround myself with supportive and encouraging people, keep physically renewed, and replace negative self-talk with positive affirmations and visualization.

- **Create positive mind shifts and expand my comfort zone.** My beliefs and perceptions must be realistic. If they aren't, I must refocus my expectations in order to achieve my goals. I should not allow my beliefs to limit my potential, and I will use critical thinking techniques to expand my mind and comfort zone.

Performance Strategies

Following are the top 10 strategies for expanding your emotional intelligence and personal qualities:

- Cultivate character and integrity.
- Create a personal code of ethics.
- Take responsibility for your thoughts, actions, and behaviors.
- Practice self-control.

- Develop positive self-esteem and confidence.
- Determine personal motivators.
- Use goals as motivational tools.
- Reward yourself for making progress and strive for excellence, not perfection.
- Create positive mind shifts.
- Expand your comfort zone.

Tech for Success

Take advantage of the text's Web site at **www.mhhe.com/ ferrett7e** for additional study aids, useful forms, and convenient and applicable resources.

- **Ethics information on the Web.** Search for articles on ethics, business etiquette, and codes of ethics.

  Check out different businesses, the military, government agencies, and colleges to find out if each has a code of ethics. Print some samples and bring them to class. What do all the codes of ethics have in common?

- **Online discussion groups.** When you are interested in a topic or goal, it's very motivating to interact with others who have the same interests. Join a discussion group or

listserv and share your knowledge, wisdom, and setbacks with others. You will learn their stories and strategies in return.

- **Goal-setting examples.** Although your goals should be personal, sometimes it helps to see how others have crafted theirs. This may inspire you to realize that setting goals isn't a difficult task—it just takes thinking critically about what you want out of life. A number of resources on the Web provide goal-setting ideas on everything from becoming more financially responsible to learning a second language.

Study Team Notes

Career*in*focus

Jacqui Williams
SALES REPRESENTATIVE

Related Majors: Business, Marketing, Public Relations

Positive Attitudes at Work

As a sales representative for a large medical company, Jacqui Williams sells equipment, such as X-ray and electrocardiograph (EKG) machines, to hospitals nationwide. Her job requires travel to prospective clients, where she meets with buyers to show her products and demonstrate their installation and use. Because Jacqui cannot take the large machines with her, she relies on printed materials and a laptop computer, from which she can point out the new aspects of the machines she sells. The sales process usually takes several months and requires more than one trip to the prospective client.

Jacqui works on commission, being paid only when she makes a sale. Because she travels frequently, Jacqui must be able to work independently without a lot of supervision. For this reason, being personally motivated is a strong requirement for her position. Jacqui has found that the best way to remain motivated is to believe in the products she sells. Jacqui keeps up on the latest in her field by reading technical information and keeping track of the competition. She sets sales goals and then rewards herself with a short vacation.

Because personal relations with buyers are so important, Jacqui is careful about her appearance. While traveling, she keeps a positive mind-set through affirmations, and she gets up early to eat a healthy breakfast and exercise in the hotel gym. She uses integrity by presenting accurate information and giving her best advice, even if it means not making a sale. Her clients would describe Jacqui as positive and helpful, someone whom they look forward to seeing and whose advice they trust.

CRITICAL THINKING In what way does having integrity, good character, and a code of ethics enhance a sales representative's business?

(From Sharon Ferrett, *Peak Performance: Success in College and Beyond,* 7th ed., pp. 45–72. McGraw-Hill, 2007.)

Appendix 4

Applications of Skills

On the pages that follow, four-part worksheets guide you through the process of applying many of the skills you have learned in this textbook. Use the cover sheet to monitor your progress. You may photocopy these pages and use them in your subject areas courses or as part of an assignment in your reading class.

Target a course in which you are currently enrolled that has an assigned textbook to which you can apply the exercises. If you are not taking such a class, you may practice your skills on the complete textbook chapter from *The Art of Public Speaking*, "Speaking in Public" that follows the worksheets here. You may also apply the strategy to the chapter from *Peak Performance: Success in College and Beyond*, found in Appendix 3.

Application of Skills: Active Textbook Reading

Cover Sheet

Name: _____   Semester: _____

Targeted Course: _____   Instructor: _____

Author: _____   Textbook Title: _____

Enter the due dates for each part and check each as you complete it.

Part I: Survey the Text to familiarize yourself with its organization and features.

- **Worksheet I**   Date Due _____   Completed _____
- **Evaluation**   Date Due _____   Completed _____

Part II: Preview a Chapter of your choice from the text.

- **Worksheet II**   Date Due _____   Completed _____
- **Evaluation**   Date Due _____   Completed _____

Part III: Read Actively, Highlight, and Annotate your text.

- **Worksheet III**   Date Due _____   Completed _____
- **Evaluation**   Date Due _____   Completed _____

Part IV: Recite, Review, Rehearse to enhance your knowledge and recall.

- **Worksheet IV**   Date Due _____   Completed _____
- **Evaluation**   Date Due _____   Completed _____

Application of Skills: Active Textbook Reading

Name: _____   Targeted Course: _____

Author: _____   Textbook Title: _____

Part I Worksheet: Survey the Text (See Chapter 2.)

The worksheet will guide you in evaluating the organization of one of your textbooks. Being familiar with the features of your texts will help you use them efficiently to access information and to understand the content.

I.   IDENTIFY TOPICS FOR READING AND STUDY

A. Look over the **Table of Contents**. Copy the first five chapter titles.
     Then, write what you expect to learn from each chapter.

Chapter 1: _____

I expect to learn: _____

_____

Chapter 2: _____

I expect to learn: _____

_____

Chapter 3: _____

I expect to learn: _____

_____

Chapter 4: _____

I expect to learn: _____

_____

Chapter 5: _____

I expect to learn: _____

_____

B. Which topics, if any, have you already studied? _____

_____

C. Did you find any topics that you knew nothing about? What are they?

_____

_____

D. How are the chapters arranged: **sequentially, chronologically** or **topically?**

_____

_____

II. TEXTBOOK FEATURES:

A. **Look through your textbook.** Check off any of the features that are included in your textbook.

_____ **Title Page**

_____ **Table of Contents**

_____ **Preface**

_____ **Index**

_____ **Glossary**

_____ **Appendix**

_____ **Bibliography, Resources, or Works Cited**

_____ **Webliography**

_____ **Acknowledgments**

_____ Other: _____

B. Which textbook feature(s) will be most useful to your reading and study? Explain.

_____

_____

_____

C. **Look through a chapter.** Place a check next to each feature of your textbook that will support your reading and study.

_____ **Introduction**

_____ **Chapter Objective**

_____ **Chapter Outline**

_____ **Vocabulary Word Lists** (terminology)

_____ **Headings and Subheadings**

_____ **Marginal Notes**

_____ **Text Boxes**

_____ **Graphic Organizers** (outlines, maps, charts)

_____ **Visual Aids** (diagrams, photos, drawings, maps)

_____ **End of Chapter Questions**

_____ **Chapter Summary or Key Points**

_____ **Resources or Suggested Readings**

_____ Other:_____

III. ADDITIONAL FEATURES:

A. Which supplementary material is available for your text? Check below.

_____ study guides   _____ companion website

_____ supplemental readings   _____ CD-ROM

_____ workbooks   _____ other _____

B. Which of the indicated supplemental materials might you use in your course work? Explain.

_____

_____

NOW, EVALUATE the process for <u>Surveying the Text.</u>

Do you think this strategy is worthwhile? How do you think this technique will help you to improve your performance in your targeted course? Write at least one paragraph in which you answer these questions and explain your responses.

_____

_____

_____

_____

_____

Application of Skills: Active Textbook Reading

Name: _____   Targeted Course: _____

Author: _____   Textbook Title: _____

Part II Worksheet: <u>Preview a Chapter</u> (See Chapter 2.)

Prepare for your reading. The worksheet will guide you through the previewing process. You will determine the topic and general organization of a textbook chapter, access your prior knowledge, and plan your reading and study time.

PHOTOCOPY THE FIRST THREE PAGES OF YOUR SELECTED CHAPTER AND ATTACH THEM TO THIS SHEET. COMPLETE THE FOLLOWING QUESTIONS BASED ON <u>PREVIEW-ING THE ENTIRE CHAPTER.</u>

1. Why are you reading this chapter at this time? (assignment, test preparation, research, report writing)

    _____

2. What is the **title** of the chapter? _____

3. What do you already know about the topic? _____

    _____

    _____

4. Is there an **introduction**? _____ On what page(s)? _____ How many paragraphs? _____

    What did you learn about the chapter from reading the introduction?

    _____

    _____

5. Read and highlight the major **headings and subheadings** of the chapter.

6. Read and underline the **first sentence in each paragraph.**

7. List and briefly describe any **illustrations, charts, diagrams, tables** or other visual aids presented.

    _____

    _____

    _____

    _____

    _____

8. Are **vocabulary** words presented? _____How? _____

9. Is there a **chapter summary**? _____ On what page?_____ How many paragraphs? _____

10. How much time will you allot to the actual reading of this chapter based on your preview? _____

11. Based on your complete preview, briefly describe what this chapter *will be about*, what it *will discuss*, and what you *predict* you will learn. Use the back of this page if needed.

_____

_____

_____

_____

_____

_____

_____

_____

_____

NOW, EVALUATE the process for <u>Previewing a Chapter.</u>

Do you think this strategy is worthwhile? How do you think this technique will help you to improve your performance in your targeted course? Write at least one paragraph in which you answer these questions and explain your responses.

_____

_____

_____

_____

_____

_____

_____

_____

_____

_____

Application of Skills: Active Textbook Reading

Name: _____   Targeted Course: _____

Author: _____   Textbook Title: _____

Part III Worksheet: <u>Read Actively, Highlight, and Annotate</u> (See Chapter 2.)

Using the chapter you previewed in Part II, photocopy pages that include at least five headings or subheadings. Then, read with a purpose. First, list each heading and then phrase each one as a question. Next, read, highlight, and annotate to find your answers, determine main ideas, and locate important details. Finally, return to this page and paraphrase your responses to your own question. Attach your annotated pages to this sheet.

Heading 1 _____

Question _____

_____

Response _____

_____

_____

_____

Heading 2 _____

Question _____

_____

Response _____

_____

_____

_____

Heading 3 _____

Question _____

_____

Response _____

_____

_____

_____

Heading 4 _____

Question _____

_____

Response _____

_____

_____

_____

Heading 5 _____

Question _____

_____

Response _____

_____

_____

_____

NOW, EVALUATE the process for <u>Reading Actively, Highlighting, and Annotating.</u>

Do you think this strategy is worthwhile? How do you think this technique will help you to improve your performance in your targeted course? Write at least one paragraph in which you answer these questions and explain your responses.

_____

_____

_____

_____

_____

_____

_____

_____

_____

_____

_____

_____

Application of Skills: Active Textbook Reading

Name: _____   Targeted Course: _____

Author: _____   Textbook Title: _____

Part IV Worksheet: <u>**Recite, Review, Rehearse**</u>

To successfully prepare for exams, you need to review all of the material, rehearse it, write it, recite it, and test yourself. In preparation for writing, you need to understand the content and be able to present it in an organized way.

A. Use the same chapter you used for Parts II and III or a chapter you have just been assigned to read in your targeted course. Photocopy the entire chapter, and read and annotate it completely. Then, develop an outline, create a map, or write a comprehensive summary using the guidelines found in Chapter 9. Attach your annotated photocopies and outline, map, or summary to this worksheet.

B. Using your outline, map, or summary of the material, create five "study questions" that might appear on an exam. These should be questions that focus on the most important concepts and information. Do *not* write short-answer questions or multiple-choice questions. Write essay-type questions that cover broad areas of content. (See Chapter 10.) Then, write the answers to your questions on a separate piece of paper. Attach them to this assignment.

<u>**Study Questions and Answers**</u>

Textbook: _____

Chapter: _____

1. _____

   _____

   _____

   _____

2. _____

   _____

   _____

   _____

3. _____

   _____

   _____

   _____

4. _____

_____

_____

_____

5. _____

_____

_____

_____

NOW, EVALUATE the process of <u>Recite, Review, Rehearse.</u>

Do you think this strategy is worthwhile? How do you think this technique will help you to improve your performance in your targeted course? Write at least one paragraph in which you answer these questions and explain your responses.

_____

_____

_____

_____

_____

_____

_____

_____

_____

_____

_____

_____

_____

_____

_____

_____

_____

Speaking in Public

The Power of Public Speaking

The Tradition of Public Speaking

Similarities Between Public Speaking and
  Conversation

Differences Between Public Speaking and
  Conversation

Developing Confidence: Your Speech Class
  Nervousness Is Normal
  Dealing with Nervousness

Public Speaking and Critical Thinking

The Speech Communication Process
  Speaker
  Message
  Channel
  Listener
  Feedback
  Interference
  Situation
  The Speech Communication Process:
    Example with Commentary

Public Speaking in a Multicultural World
  Cultural Diversity in the Modern World
  Cultural Diversity and Public Speaking
  Avoiding Ethnocentrism

2

Growing up in rural Tennessee, Van Jones had no intention of becoming a public speaker. Studying journalism at the University of Tennessee at Martin, he hoped one day to report the news, not to make it. Nevertheless, he soon found himself drawn to campus politics, and he became a vocal member of the student body.

After attending law school, Jones joined the San Francisco–based Lawyers Committee for Human Rights to work on problems confronting inner-city communities. A few years later he established the Ella Baker Center for Human Rights, a nonprofit organization dedicated to promoting opportunity in urban America.

But Jones didn't stop there. Over the years, he combined human rights initiatives with his interest in environmental justice. Today, he is president of Green for All, which focuses on creating green-collar jobs throughout America. In 2007 he worked with members of the U.S. House of Representatives to pass the Green Jobs Act, which approved $125 million to train environmentally conscious workers.

How has Jones achieved all this? Partly through his legal training and dauntless spirit. But just as important is his ability to communicate with people through public speaking, which has been the primary vehicle for spreading his message. He has been described as "one of the most powerful and inspiring prophetic voices of our time." Audiences are moved "by his heart, inspired by his commitment, and rocked by his eloquence."

If you had asked Van Jones early in his life, "Do you see yourself as a major public speaker?" he probably would have laughed at the idea. Yet today he gives more than 100 presentations a year. Along the way, he has lectured at Harvard and Columbia and has addressed the U.S. Conference of Mayors, the National Symposium on Climate Change, and the World Economic Forum. More than a few pundits have suggested that elective office might be in his future.

The Power of Public Speaking

connectlucas.com
View John F. Kennedy, Martin Luther King, Ronald Reagan, Barbara Jordan, and other speakers in the online Media Library for this chapter (Video Clip 1.1)

Throughout history people have used public speaking as a vital means of communication. What the Greek leader Pericles said more than 2,500 years ago is still true today: "One who forms a judgment on any point but cannot explain" it clearly "might as well never have thought at all on the subject."[1] Public speaking, as its name implies, is a way of making your ideas public—of sharing them with other people and of influencing other people.

During modern times many women and men around the globe have spread their ideas and influence through public speaking. In the United States, the list includes Franklin Roosevelt, Billy Graham, Cesar Chavez, Barbara Jordan, Ronald Reagan, Martin Luther King, Hillary Clinton, and Barack Obama. In other countries, we see the power of public speaking employed by such people as former British Prime Minister Margaret Thatcher, South African leader Nelson Mandela, Burmese democracy champion Aung San Suu Kyi, and Kenyan environmentalist and Nobel Prize winner Wangari Maathai.

As you read these names, you may think to yourself, "That's fine. Good for them. But what does that have to do with me? I don't plan to be a president or a preacher or a crusader for any cause." Nevertheless, the need for public speaking will almost certainly touch you sometime in your life—maybe tomorrow, maybe not for five years. Can you imagine yourself in any of these situations?

You are one of seven management trainees in a large corporation. One of you will get the lower-management job that has just opened. There is to be a large staff meeting at which each of the trainees will discuss the project he or she has been developing. One by one your colleagues make their presentations. They have no experience in public speaking and are intimidated by the higher-ranking managers present. Their speeches are stumbling and awkward. You, however, call upon all the skills you learned in your public speaking course. You deliver an informative talk that is clear, well reasoned, and articulate. You get the job.

One of your children has a learning disability. You hear that your local school board has decided, for budget reasons, to eliminate the special teacher who has been helping your child. At an open meeting of the school board, you stand up and deliver a thoughtful, compelling speech on the necessity for keeping the special teacher. The school board changes its mind.

You are the assistant manager in a branch office of a national company. Your immediate superior, the branch manager, is about to retire, and there will be a retirement dinner. All the executives from the home office will attend. As his close working associate, you are asked to give a farewell toast at the party. You prepare and deliver a speech that is both witty and touching—a perfect tribute to your boss. After the speech, everyone applauds enthusiastically, and a few people have tears in their eyes. The following week you are named branch manager.

connectlucas.com
To read the words of famous speakers, log on to the Top 100 American Speeches of the 20th Century in the online Research Library.

Fantasies? Not really. Any of these situations could occur. In a survey of 480 companies and public organizations, communication skills—including public speaking—were ranked first among the personal qualities of college graduates sought by employers. In another survey, college graduates in the work force were asked to rank the skills most essential to their career development. What was at the top of their list? Oral communication.[2]

The importance of such skill is true across the board—for accountants and architects, teachers and technicians, scientists and stockbrokers. Even in highly specialized fields such as civil and mechanical engineering, employers consistently rank the ability to communicate above technical knowledge when deciding whom to hire and whom to promote. The ability to speak effectively is so prized that college graduates are increasingly being asked to give a presentation as part of their job interview.

Nor has the growth of the Internet and other new technologies reduced the need for public speaking. As one communication consultant states, "There are more avenues to reach people than ever before, but there's no substitute for face-to-face communication." To be successful, says business leader Midge Costanza, you must have "the ability to stand on your feet, either on a one-to-one basis or before a group, and make a presentation that is convincing and believable."[3]

The same is true in community life. Public speaking is a vital means of civic engagement. It is a way to express your ideas and to have an impact on issues that matter in society. As a form of empowerment, it can—and often does—make a difference in things people care about very much. The key phrase here is "make a difference." This is what most of us want to do in life—to make a difference, to change the world in some small way. Public speaking offers you an opportunity to make a difference in something you care about very much.

The Tradition of Public Speaking

Given the importance of public speaking, it's not surprising that it has been taught and studied around the globe for thousands of years. Almost all cultures have an equivalent of the English word "orator" to designate someone with special skills in public speaking. The oldest known handbook on effective speech was written on papyrus in Egypt some 4,500 years ago. Eloquence was highly prized in ancient India, Africa, and China, as well as among the Aztecs and other pre-European cultures of North and South America.[4]

In classical Greece and Rome, public speaking played a central role in education and civic life. It was also studied extensively. Aristotle's *Rhetoric,* composed during the third century B.C.E., is still considered the most important work on its subject, and many of its principles are followed by speakers (and writers) today. The great Roman leader Cicero used his speeches to defend liberty and wrote several works about oratory in general.

Over the centuries, many other notable thinkers have dealt with issues of rhetoric, speech, and language—including the Roman educator Quintilian, the Christian preacher St. Augustine, the medieval writer Christine de Pizan, the British philosopher Francis Bacon, and the American critic Kenneth Burke.[5] In recent years, communication researchers have provided an increasingly scientific basis for understanding the methods and strategies of effective speech.

Your immediate objective is to apply those methods and strategies in your classroom speeches. What you learn, however, will be applicable long after you leave college. The principles of public speaking are derived from a long tradition and have been confirmed by a substantial body of research. The more you know about those principles, the more effective you will be in your own speeches—and the more effective you will be in listening to the speeches of other people.

Similarities Between Public Speaking and Conversation

How much time do you spend each day talking to other people? The average adult spends about 30 percent of her or his waking hours in conversation. By the time you read this book, you will have spent much of your life perfecting the art of conversation. You may not realize it, but you already employ a wide range of skills when talking to people. These skills include the following:

1. *Organizing your thoughts logically.* Suppose you were giving someone directions to get to your house. You wouldn't do it this way:

When you turn off the highway, you'll see a big diner on the left. But before that, stay on the highway to Exit 67. Usually a couple of the neighbors' dogs are in the street, so go slow after you turn at the blinking light. Coming from your house you get on the highway through Maple Street. If you pass the taco stand, you've gone too far. The house is blue.

Instead, you would take your listener systematically, step by step, from his or her house to your house. You would organize your message.

2. *Tailoring your message to your audience.* You are a geology major. Two people ask you how pearls are formed. One is your roommate; the other is your nine-year-old niece. You answer as follows:

To your roommate: "When any irritant, say a grain of sand, gets inside the oyster's shell, the oyster automatically secretes a substance called nacre, which is principally calcium

Many skills used in conversation also apply in public speaking. As you learn to speak more effectively, you may also learn to communicate more effectively in other situations.

carbonate and is the same material that lines the oyster's shell. The nacre accumulates in layers around the irritant core to form the pearl."

To your niece: "Imagine you're an oyster on the ocean floor. A grain of sand gets inside your shell and makes you uncomfortable. So you decide to cover it up. You cover it with a material called mother-of-pearl. The covering builds up around the grain of sand to make a pearl."

3. *Telling a story for maximum impact.* Suppose you are telling a friend about a funny incident at last week's football game. You don't begin with the punch line ("Keisha fell out of the stands right onto the field. Here's how it started. . . ."). Instead, you carefully build up your story, adjusting your words and tone of voice to get the best effect.

4. *Adapting to listener feedback.* Whenever you talk with someone, you are aware of that person's verbal, facial, and physical reactions. For example:

You are explaining an interesting point that came up in biology class. Your listener begins to look confused, puts up a hand as though to stop you, and says "Huh?" You go back and explain more clearly.

A friend has asked you to listen while she practices a speech. At the end you tell her, "There's just one part I really don't like—that quotation from the attorney general." Your friend looks very hurt and says, "That was my favorite part!" So you say, "But if you just worked the quotation in a little differently, it would be wonderful."

Each day, in casual conversation, you do all these things many times without thinking about them. You already possess these communication skills. And these are among the most important skills you will need for public speaking.

Similarities Between Public Speaking and Conversation   **7**

To illustrate, let's return briefly to one of the hypothetical situations at the beginning of this chapter. When addressing the school board about the need for a special teacher:

- You *organize* your ideas to present them in the most persuasive manner. You steadily build up a compelling case about how the teacher benefits the school.

- You *tailor your message* to your audience. This is no time to launch an impassioned defense of special education in the United States. You must show how the issue is important to the people in that very room—to their children and to the school.

- You tell your story for *maximum impact*. Perhaps you relate an anecdote to demonstrate how much your child has improved. You also have statistics to show how many other children have been helped.

- You *adapt to listener feedback*. When you mention the cost of the special teacher, you notice sour looks on the faces of the school board members. So you patiently explain how small that cost is in relation to the overall school budget.

In many ways, then, public speaking requires the same skills used in ordinary conversation. Most people who communicate well in daily talk can learn to communicate just as well in public speaking. By the same token, training in public speaking can make you a more adept communicator in a variety of situations, such as conversations, classroom discussions, business meetings, and interviews.

Differences Between Public Speaking and Conversation

Despite their similarities, public speaking and everyday conversation are not identical. Imagine that you are telling a story to a friend. Then imagine yourself telling the story to a group of seven or eight friends. Now imagine telling the same story to 20 or 30 people. As the size of your audience grows, you will find yourself adapting to three major differences between conversation and public speaking:

1. *Public speaking is more highly structured.* It usually imposes strict time limitations on the speaker. In most cases, the situation does not allow listeners to interrupt with questions or commentary. The speaker must accomplish her or his purpose in the speech itself. In preparing the speech, the speaker must anticipate questions that might arise in the minds of listeners and answer them. Consequently, public speaking demands much more detailed planning and preparation than ordinary conversation.

2. *Public speaking requires more formal language.* Slang, jargon, and bad grammar have little place in public speeches. As angry as he is about industrial pollution, when Van Jones speaks to a congressional committee, he doesn't say, "We've damn well got to stop the greedy creeps who pollute low-income communities just to make a few more bucks." Listeners usually react negatively to speakers who do not elevate and polish their language when addressing an audience. A speech should be "special."

3. *Public speaking requires a different method of delivery.* When conversing informally, most people talk quietly, interject stock phrases such as "like" and "you know," adopt a casual posture, and use what are called vocalized pauses ("uh," "er," "um"). Effective public speakers, however, adjust their voices to be heard clearly throughout the audience. They assume a more erect posture. They avoid distracting mannerisms and verbal habits.

With study and practice, you will be able to master these differences and expand your conversational skills into speechmaking. Your speech class will provide the opportunity for this study and practice.

Developing Confidence: Your Speech Class

One of the major concerns of students in any speech class is stage fright. We may as well face the issue squarely. Many people who converse easily in all kinds of everyday situations become frightened at the idea of standing up before a group to make a speech.

If you are worried about stage fright, you may feel better knowing that you are not alone. A 2001 Gallup Poll asked Americans to list their greatest fears. Forty percent identified speaking before a group as their top fear, exceeded only by the 51 percent who said they were afraid of snakes. A 2005 survey produced similar results, with 42 percent of respondents being terrified by the prospect of speaking in public. In comparison, only 28 percent said they were afraid of dying.[6]

stage fright
Anxiety over the prospect of giving a speech in front of an audience.

In a different study, researchers concentrated on social situations and, again, asked their subjects to list their greatest fears. Here is how they answered:[7]

Greatest Fear	Percent Naming
A party with strangers	74
Giving a speech	70
Asked personal questions in public	65
Meeting a date's parents	59
First day on a new job	59
Victim of a practical joke	56
Talking with someone in authority	53
Job interview	46

Again, speechmaking ranks near the top in provoking anxiety.

NERVOUSNESS IS NORMAL

If you feel nervous about giving a speech, you are in very good company. Some of the greatest public speakers in history have suffered from stage fright, including Abraham Lincoln, Margaret Sanger, and Winston Churchill. The famous Roman orator Cicero said: "I turn pale at the outset of a speech and quake in every limb and in my soul."[8] Oprah Winfrey, Conan O'Brien, and Jay Leno all report being anxious about speaking in public. Early in his career, Leonardo DiCaprio was so nervous about giving an acceptance speech that he hoped he would not win the Academy Award for which he had been nominated. Eighty-one percent of business executives say public speaking is the most nerve-wracking experience they face.[9] What comedian Jerry Seinfeld said in jest sometimes seems literally true: "Given a choice, at a funeral most of us would rather be the one in the coffin than the one giving the eulogy."

Actually, most people tend to be anxious before doing something important in public. Actors are nervous before a play, politicians are nervous before a campaign speech, athletes are nervous before a big game. The ones who succeed have learned to use their nervousness to their advantage. Listen to American gymnast Shawn Johnson speaking after her balance beam routine in the women's apparatus finals at the 2008 Olympic Games in Beijing: "I was so nervous I couldn't get anything right in warm ups. But I wanted to do my best and end on a good note." Putting her butterflies to good use, Johnson ended on a good note, indeed, by scoring 16.225 points to win the gold medal.

Much the same thing happens in speechmaking. Most experienced speakers have stage fright before taking the floor, but their nervousness is a healthy sign that they are getting "psyched up" for a good effort. Novelist and lecturer I. A. R. Wylie explains, "Now after many years of practice I am, I suppose, really a 'practiced speaker.' But I rarely rise to my feet without a throat constricted with terror and a furiously thumping heart. When, for some reason, I *am* cool and self-assured, the speech is always a failure."[10]

In other words, it is perfectly normal—even desirable—to be nervous at the start of a speech. Your body is responding as it would to any stressful situation—by producing extra *adrenaline*. This sudden shot of adrenaline is what makes your heart race, your hands shake, your knees knock, and your skin perspire. Every public speaker experiences all these reactions to some extent. The question is: How can you control your nervousness and make it work for you rather than against you?

adrenaline
A hormone released into the bloodstream in response to physical or mental stress.

DEALING WITH NERVOUSNESS

Rather than trying to eliminate every trace of stage fright, you should aim at transforming it from a negative force into what one expert calls *positive nervousness*—"a zesty, enthusiastic, lively feeling with a slight edge to it. . . . It's still nervousness, but it feels different. You're no longer victimized by it; instead, you're vitalized by it. You're in control of it."[11]

Don't think of yourself as having stage fright. Instead, think of it as "stage excitement" or "stage enthusiasm."[12] It can help you get focused and energized in the same way that it helps athletes, musicians, and others get primed for a game or a concert. Think of it as a normal part of giving a successful speech.

Here are six time-tested ways you can turn your nervousness from a negative force into a positive one.

positive nervousness
Controlled nervousness that helps energize a speaker for her or his presentation.

Acquire Speaking Experience

You have already taken the first step. You are enrolled in a public speaking course, where you will learn about speechmaking and gain speaking experience. Think back to your first day at kindergarten, your first date, your first day

The need for public speaking arises in many situations. Here Dr. Jim Thomas explains the surgical procedures used in a pioneering operation at Children's Medical Center in Dallas, Texas.

at a new job. You were probably nervous in each situation because you were facing something new and unknown. Once you became accustomed to the situation, it was no longer threatening. So it is with public speaking. For most students, the biggest part of stage fright is fear of the unknown. The more you learn about public speaking and the more speeches you give, the less threatening speechmaking will become.

Of course, the road to confidence will sometimes be bumpy. Learning to give a speech is not much different from learning any other skill—it proceeds by trial and error. The purpose of your speech class is to shorten the process, to minimize the errors, to give you a nonthreatening arena—a sort of laboratory—in which to undertake the "trial."

Your teacher recognizes that you are a novice and is trained to give the kind of guidance you need to get started. In your fellow students you have a highly sympathetic audience who will provide valuable feedback to help you improve your speaking skills. As the class goes on, your fears about public speaking will gradually recede until they are replaced by only a healthy nervousness before you rise to speak.[13]

Prepare, Prepare, Prepare

Another key to gaining confidence is to pick speech topics you truly care about—and then to prepare your speeches so thoroughly that you cannot help but be successful. Here's how one student combined enthusiasm for his topic with thorough preparation to score a triumph in speech class:

Jesse Young was concerned about taking a speech class. Not having any experience as a public speaker, he got butterflies in his stomach just thinking about talking in front of an audience. But when the time came for Jesse's first speech, he was determined to make it a success.

Jesse chose Habitat for Humanity as the topic for his speech. He had been a volunteer for the past three years, and he believed deeply in the organization and its mission. The purpose of his speech was to explain the origins, philosophy, and activities of Habitat for Humanity.

As Jesse spoke, it became clear that he was enthusiastic about his subject and genuinely wanted his classmates to share his enthusiasm. Because he was intent on communicating with his audience, he forgot to be nervous. He spoke clearly, fluently, and dynamically. Soon the entire class was engrossed in his speech.

Afterward Jesse admitted that he had surprised even himself. "It was amazing," he said. "Once I passed the first minute or so, all I thought about were those people out there listening. I could tell that I was really getting through to them."

How much time should you devote to preparing your speeches? A standard rule of thumb is that each minute of speaking time requires one to two hours of preparation time—perhaps more, depending on the amount of research needed for the speech. This may seem like a lot of time, but the rewards are well worth it. One professional speech consultant estimates that proper preparation can reduce stage fright by up to 75 percent.[14]

If you follow the techniques suggested by your teacher and in the rest of this book, you will stand up for every speech fully prepared. Imagine that the day for your first speech has arrived. You have studied your audience and selected a topic you know will interest them. You have researched the speech thoroughly and practiced it several times until it feels absolutely comfortable. You have even tried it out before two or three trusted friends. How can you help but be confident of success?

Think Positively

Confidence is mostly the well-known power of positive thinking. If you think you can do it, you usually can. On the other hand, if you predict disaster and doom, that is almost always what you will get. This is especially true when it comes to public speaking. Speakers who think negatively about themselves and the speech experience are much more likely to be overcome by stage fright than are speakers who think positively. Here are some ways you can transform negative thoughts into positive ones as you work on your speeches:

Negative Thought	Positive Thought
I wish I didn't have to give this speech.	This speech is a chance for me to share my ideas and gain experience as a speaker.
I'm not a great public speaker.	No one's perfect, but I'm getting better with each speech I give.
I'm always nervous when I give a speech.	Everyone's nervous. If other people can handle it, I can too.
No one will be interested in what I have to say.	I have a good topic and I'm fully prepared. Of course they'll be interested.

Many psychologists believe that the ratio of positive to negative thoughts in regard to stressful activities such as speechmaking should be at least five to one. That is, for each negative thought, you should counter with a minimum of five positive ones. Doing so will not make your nerves go away completely, but it will help keep them under control so you can concentrate on communicating your ideas rather than on brooding about your fears and anxieties.

Use the Power of Visualization

Visualization is closely related to positive thinking. It is used by athletes, musicians, actors, speakers, and others to enhance their performance in stressful situations. How does it work? Listen to long-distance runner Vicki Huber:

visualization
Mental imaging in which a speaker vividly pictures himself or herself giving a successful presentation.

> Right before a big race, I'll picture myself running, and I will try and put all of the other competitors in the race into my mind. Then I will try and imagine every possible situation I might find myself in . . . behind someone, being boxed in, pushed, shoved or cajoled, different positions on the track, laps to go, and, of course, the final stretch. And I always picture myself winning the race, no matter what happens during the event.

Of course, Huber doesn't win every race she runs, but research has shown that the kind of mental imaging she describes can significantly increase athletic performance.[15] It has also shown that visualization can help speakers control their stage fright.[16]

The key to visualization is creating a vivid mental blueprint in which you see yourself succeeding in your speech. Picture yourself in your classroom rising to speak. See yourself at the lectern, poised and self-assured, making eye contact with your audience and delivering your introduction in a firm, clear voice. Feel your confidence growing as your listeners get more and more caught up in what you are saying. Imagine your sense of achievement as you conclude the speech knowing you have done your very best.

As you create these images in your mind's eye, be realistic but stay focused on the positive aspects of your speech. Don't allow negative images to eclipse the positive ones. Acknowledge your nervousness, but picture yourself overcoming it to give a vibrant, articulate presentation. If one part of the speech always seems to give you trouble, visualize yourself getting through it without any hitches. And be specific. The more lucid your mental pictures, the more successful you are likely to be.

As with your physical rehearsal of the speech, this kind of mental rehearsal of the speech should be repeated several times in the days before you speak. It doesn't guarantee that every speech will turn out exactly the way you envision it—and it certainly is no substitute for thorough preparation. But used in conjunction with the other methods of combating stage fright, it is a proven way to help control your nerves and to craft a successful presentation.

Know That Most Nervousness Is Not Visible

Many novice speakers are worried about appearing nervous to the audience. It's hard to speak with poise and assurance if you think you look tense and insecure. One of the most valuable lessons you will learn as your speech class proceeds is that only a fraction of the turmoil you feel inside is visible on the outside. "Your nervous system may be giving you a thousand shocks," says one experienced speaker, "but the viewer can see only a few of them."[17]

Even though your palms are sweating and your heart is pounding, your listeners probably won't realize how tense you are—especially if you do your best to act cool and confident on the outside. Most of the time when students confess after a speech, "I was so nervous I thought I was going to die," their classmates are surprised. To them the speaker looked calm and assured.

Knowing this should make it easier for you to face your listeners with confidence. As one student stated after watching a videotape of her first classroom speech, "I was amazed at how calm I looked. I assumed everyone would be able to see how scared I was, but now that I know they can't, I won't be nearly so nervous in the future. It really helps to know that you look in control even though you may not feel that way."

Don't Expect Perfection

It may also help to know that there is no such thing as a perfect speech. At some point in every presentation, every speaker says or does something that does not come across exactly as he or she had planned. Fortunately, such moments are usually not evident to the audience. Why? Because the audience does not know what the speaker *plans* to say. It hears only what the speaker *does* say. If you momentarily lose your place, reverse the order of a couple statements, or forget to pause at a certain spot, no one need be the wiser. When such moments occur, just proceed as if nothing happened.

One of the biggest reasons people are concerned about making a mistake in a speech is that they view speechmaking as a performance rather than an act of communication. They feel the audience is judging them against a scale of absolute perfection in which every misstated word or awkward gesture will count against them. But speech audiences are not like judges in a violin recital or an ice-skating contest. They are not looking for a virtuoso performance, but for a well-thought-out address that communicates the speaker's ideas clearly and directly. Sometimes an error or two can actually enhance a speaker's appeal by making her or him seem more human.[18]

As you work on your speeches, make sure you prepare thoroughly and do all you can to get your message across to your listeners. But don't panic about being perfect or about what will happen if you make a mistake. Once you free your mind of these burdens, you will find it much easier to approach your speeches with confidence and even with enthusiasm.

Besides stressing the six points just discussed, your teacher will probably give you several tips for dealing with nervousness in your first speeches. They may include:

- Be at your best physically and mentally. It's not a good idea to stay up until 2:00 A.M. partying with friends or cramming for an exam the night before your speech. A good night's sleep will serve you better.

- As you are waiting to speak, quietly tighten and relax your leg muscles, or squeeze your hands together and then release them. Such actions help reduce tension by providing an outlet for your extra adrenaline.

- Take a couple slow, deep breaths before you start to speak. Most people, when they are tense, take short, shallow breaths, which only reinforces their anxiety. Deep breathing breaks this cycle of tension and helps calm your nerves.

- Work especially hard on your introduction. Research has shown that a speaker's anxiety level begins to drop significantly after the first 30 to 60

Terrified early in his career by the prospect of giving a public speech, today Leonardo DiCaprio is an accomplished speaker who confidently addresses audiences around the globe.

seconds of a presentation.[19] Once you get through the introduction, you should find smoother sailing the rest of the way.

- Make eye contact with members of your audience. Remember that they are individual people, not a blur of faces. And they are your friends.

- Concentrate on communicating with your audience rather than on worrying about your stage fright. If you get caught up in your speech, your audience will too.

- Use visual aids. They create interest, draw attention away from you, and make you feel less self-conscious.

If you are like most students, you will find your speech class to be a very positive experience. As one student wrote on her course evaluation at the end of the class:

I was really dreading this class. The idea of giving all those speeches scared me half to death. But I'm glad now that I stuck with it. It's a small class, and I got to know a lot of the students. Besides, this is one class in which I got to express *my* ideas, instead of spending the whole time listening to the teacher talk. I even came to enjoy giving the speeches. I could tell at times that the audience was really with me, and that's a great feeling.

Over the years thousands of students have developed confidence in their speechmaking abilities. As your confidence grows, you will be better able to stand before other people and tell them what you think and feel and know—and to make them think and feel and know those same things. The best part about confidence is that it nurtures itself. After you score your first triumph, you will be that much more confident the next time. And as you become a more confident public speaker, you will likely become more confident in other areas of your life as well.

Checklist   Speaking with Confidence

YES	✓	NO	
☐		☐	1. Am I enthusiastic about my speech topic?
☐		☐	2. Have I thoroughly developed the content of my speech?
☐		☐	3. Have I worked on the introduction so my speech will get off to a good start?
☐		☐	4. Have I worked on the conclusion so my speech will end on a strong note?
☐		☐	5. Have I rehearsed my speech orally until I am confident about its delivery?
☐		☐	6. Have I worked on turning negative thoughts about my speech into positive ones?
☐		☐	7. Do I realize that nervousness is normal, even among experienced speakers?
☐		☐	8. Do I understand that most nervousness is not visible to the audience?
☐		☐	9. Am I focused on communicating with my audience, rather than on worrying about my nerves?
☐		☐	10. Have I visualized myself speaking confidently and getting a positive response from the audience?

connectlucas.com
This checklist is also available in the online Speech Tools for this chapter.

Public Speaking and Critical Thinking

That guy at the party last night really owned me when we were talking about the economy. I know my information is right, and I'm sure his argument didn't make sense, but I can't put my finger on the problem.

I worked really hard on my term paper, but it's just not right. It doesn't seem to hang together, and I can't figure out what's wrong.

Political speeches are so one-sided. The candidates sound good, but they all talk in slogans and generalities. It's really hard to decide who has the best stands on the issues.

critical thinking
Focused, organized thinking about such things as the logical relationships among ideas, the soundness of evidence, and the differences between fact and opinion.

Have you ever found yourself in similar situations? If so, you may find help in your speech class. Besides building confidence, a course in public speaking can develop your skills as a critical thinker. Those skills can make the difference between the articulate debater and the pushover, the A student and the C student, the thoughtful voter and the coin tosser.

What is critical thinking? To some extent, it's a matter of logic—of being able to spot weaknesses in other people's arguments and to avoid them in your own. It also involves related skills such as distinguishing fact from opinion, judging the credibility of statements, and assessing the soundness of evidence. In the broadest sense, critical thinking is focused, organized thinking—the ability to see clearly the relationships among ideas.[20]

If you are wondering what this has to do with your public speaking class, the answer is quite a lot. As the class proceeds, you will probably spend a good deal of time organizing your speeches. While this may seem like a purely mechanical exercise, it is closely interwoven with critical thinking. If the structure of your speech is disjointed and confused, odds are that your thinking is also disjointed and confused. If, on the other hand, the structure is clear and cohesive, there is a good chance your thinking is too. Organizing a speech is not just a matter of arranging the ideas you already have. Rather, it is an important part of shaping the ideas themselves.

What is true of organization is true of many aspects of public speaking. The skills you learn in your speech class can help you become a more effective thinker in a number of ways. As you work on expressing your ideas in clear, accurate language, you will enhance your ability to think clearly and accurately. As you study the role of evidence and reasoning in speechmaking, you will see how they can be used in other forms of communication as well. As you learn to listen critically to speeches in class, you will be better able to assess the ideas of speakers (and writers) in a variety of situations.[21]

To return to the examples at the beginning of this section:

The guy at the party last night—would well-honed critical thinking skills help you find the holes in his argument?

The term paper—would better organization and a clear outline help pull it together?

Political speeches—once you get past the slogans, are the candidates drawing valid conclusions from sound evidence?

If you take full advantage of your speech class, you will be able to enhance your skills as a critical thinker in many circumstances. This is one reason public speaking has been regarded as a vital part of education since the days of ancient Greece.

The Speech Communication Process

As you begin your first speeches, you may find it helpful to understand what goes on when one person talks to another. Regardless of the kind of speech communication involved, there are seven elements—speaker, message, channel, listener, feedback, interference, and situation. Here we shall focus on how these elements interact when a public speaker addresses an audience.

SPEAKER

Speech communication begins with a speaker. If you pick up the telephone and call a friend, you are acting as a speaker. (Of course, you will also act as a listener when your friend is talking.) In public speaking, you will usually present your entire speech without interruption.

speaker
The person who is presenting an oral message to a listener.

Your success as a speaker depends on *you*—on your personal credibility, your knowledge of the subject, your preparation of the speech, your manner of speaking, your sensitivity to the audience and the occasion. But successful speaking also requires enthusiasm. You can't expect people to be interested in what you say unless you are interested yourself. If you are truly excited about your subject, your audience is almost sure to get excited along with you. You can learn all the techniques of effective speechmaking, but before they can be of much use, you must first have something to say—something that sparks your own enthusiasm.

MESSAGE

message
Whatever a speaker communicates to someone else.

The message is whatever a speaker communicates to someone else. If you are calling a friend, you might say, "I'll be a little late picking you up tonight." That is the message. But it may not be the only message. Perhaps there is a certain tone in your voice that suggests reluctance, hesitation. The underlying message might be "I really don't want to go to that party. You talked me into it, but I'm going to put it off as long as I can."

Your goal in public speaking is to have your *intended* message be the message that is *actually* communicated. Achieving this depends both on what you say (the verbal message) and on how you say it (the nonverbal message).

Getting the verbal message just right requires work. You must narrow your topic down to something you can discuss adequately in the time allowed for the speech. You must do research and choose supporting details to make your ideas clear and convincing. You must organize your ideas so listeners can follow them without getting lost. And you must express your message in words that are accurate, clear, vivid, and appropriate.

Besides the message you send with words, you send a message with your tone of voice, appearance, gestures, facial expression, and eye contact. Imagine that one of your classmates gets up to speak about student loans. Throughout her speech she slumps behind the lectern, takes long pauses to remember what she wants to say, stares at the ceiling, and fumbles with her visual aids. Her intended message is "We must make more money available for student loans." But the message she actually communicates is "I haven't prepared very well for this speech." One of your jobs as a speaker is to make sure your nonverbal message does not distract from your verbal message.

CHANNEL

channel
The means by which a message is communicated.

The channel is the means by which a message is communicated. When you pick up the phone to call a friend, the telephone is the channel. Public speakers may use one or more of several channels, each of which will affect the message received by the audience.

Consider a speech to Congress by the President of the United States. The speech is carried to the nation by the channels of radio and television. For the radio audience the message is conveyed entirely by the President's voice. For the television audience the message is conveyed by both the President's voice and the televised image. The people in Congress have a more direct channel. They not only hear the President's voice as amplified through a microphone, but they also see him and the setting firsthand.

In a public speaking class your channel is the most direct of all. Your classmates will see you and hear you without any electronic intervention.

LISTENER

listener
The person who receives the speaker's message.

The listener is the person who receives the communicated message. Without a listener, there is no communication. When you talk to a friend on the phone, you have one listener. In public speaking you will have many listeners.

The critical thinking skills you develop in researching and organizing your speeches can be applied in many forms of communication, including meetings and group projects.

Everything a speaker says is filtered through a listener's *frame of reference*—the total of his or her knowledge, experience, goals, values, and attitudes. Because a speaker and a listener are different people, they can never have exactly the same frame of reference. And because a listener's frame of reference can never be exactly the same as a speaker's, the meaning of a message will never be exactly the same to a listener as to a speaker.

You can easily test the impact of different frames of reference. Ask each of your classmates to describe a chair. If you have 20 classmates, you'll probably get 20 different descriptions. One student might picture a large, overstuffed easy chair, another an elegant straight-backed chair, yet another an office chair, a fourth a rocking chair, and so on. Even if two or more envision the same general type—say, a rocking chair—their mental images of the chair could still be different. One might be thinking of an early American rocker, another of a modern Scandinavian rocker—the possibilities are unlimited. And "chair" is a fairly simple concept. What about "patriotism" or "freedom"?

Because people have different frames of reference, a public speaker must take great care to adapt the message to the particular audience being addressed. To be an effective speaker, you must be *audience-centered*. You will quickly lose your listeners' attention if your presentation is either too basic or too sophisticated. You will also lose your audience if you do not relate to their experience, interests, knowledge, and values. When you make a speech that causes listeners to say "That is important to *me*," you will almost always be successful.

frame of reference
The sum of a person's knowledge, experience, goals, values, and attitudes. No two people can have exactly the same frame of reference.

FEEDBACK

When the President addresses the nation on television, he is engaged in one-way communication. You can talk back to the television set, but the President won't hear you. Most situations, however, involve *two-way* communication. Your listeners don't simply absorb your message like human sponges. They send back messages of their own. These messages are called feedback.

feedback
The messages, usually nonverbal, sent from a listener to a speaker.

In public speaking there is plenty of feedback to let you know how your message is being received. Do your listeners lean forward in their seats, as if paying close attention? Do they applaud in approval? Do they laugh at your jokes? Do they have quizzical looks on their faces? Do they shuffle their feet and gaze at the clock? The message sent by these reactions could be "I am fascinated," "I am bored," "I agree with you," "I don't agree with you," or any number of others. As a speaker, you need to be alert to these reactions and adjust your message accordingly.

Like any kind of communication, feedback is affected by one's frame of reference. How would you feel if, immediately after your speech, all your classmates started to rap their knuckles on the desks? Would you run out of the room in despair? Not if you were in a European university. In many parts of Europe, students rap their knuckles on their desks to show admiration for a classroom lecture. You must understand the feedback to be able to deal with it.

INTERFERENCE

interference
Anything that impedes the communication of a message. Interference can be external or internal to listeners.

Interference is anything that impedes the communication of a message. When you talk on the telephone, sometimes there is static, or wires get crossed so that two different conversations are going on at once. That is a kind of interference.

In public speaking there are two kinds of interference. One, like the static or crossed wires in a phone conversation, is *external* to the audience. Many classrooms are subject to this kind of interference—from traffic outside the building, the clatter of a radiator, students conversing in the hall, a room that is stifling hot or freezing cold. Any of these can distract listeners from what you are saying.

A second kind of interference is *internal* and comes from within your audience. Perhaps one of your listeners has a toothache. She may be so distracted by the pain that she doesn't pay attention to your speech. Another listener could be worrying about a test in the next class period. Yet another could be brooding about an argument with his girlfriend.

As a speaker, you must try to hold your listeners' attention despite these various kinds of interference. In the chapters that follow you will find many ways to do this.

SITUATION

situation
The time and place in which speech communication occurs.

The situation is the time and place in which speech communication occurs. Conversation always takes place in a certain situation. Sometimes the situation helps—as when you propose marriage over an intimate candlelight dinner. Other times it may hurt—as when you try to speak words of love in competition with a blaring stereo. When you have to talk with someone about a touchy issue, you usually wait until the situation is just right.

Public speakers must also be alert to the situation. Certain occasions—funerals, church services, graduation ceremonies—require certain kinds of speeches. Physical setting is also important. It makes a great deal of difference whether a speech is presented indoors or out, in a small classroom or in a gymnasium, to a densely packed crowd or to a handful of scattered souls. When you adjust to the situation of a public speech, you are only doing on a larger scale what you do every day in conversation.

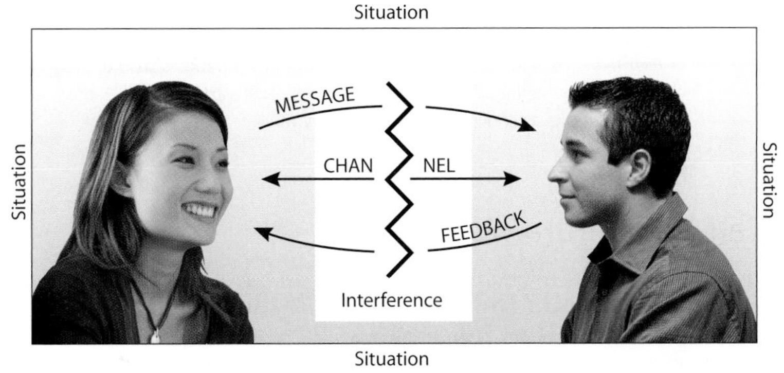

Situation

• **FIGURE 1.1**

    Now let us look at a complete model of the speech communication process, as shown in Figure 1.1 above.[22]

THE SPEECH COMMUNICATION PROCESS: EXAMPLE WITH COMMENTARY

The following example shows how the various components of the speech communication process interact:

Situation	It was 5:15 P.M., and the fall sales conference of OmniBrands, Inc., had been going on all day. A series of new-product presentations to buyers from the company's largest customers had taken much longer than expected.
Speaker	Alyson Kaufman was worried. As a marketing manager for fragrances, she was the last speaker of the day. When Alyson rose to address the audience, she knew she faced a difficult situation. She had been allotted 45 minutes to introduce her products, and the meeting was scheduled to end in 15 minutes. What's more, holiday sales of her entire product line depended in large part on this presentation.
Channel Interference	Alyson stepped to the microphone and began to speak. She could see members of the audience looking at their watches, and she knew they were eager to get to dinner after a long day of presentations.
Adapting to Interference	"Good afternoon," Alyson said, "and thanks for your attention. I know everyone is ready for dinner—I certainly am. I was given 45 minutes for my presentation—okay, everybody groan—but with your kind cooperation, I'll do my best to finish in under half an hour. I think you'll find the time well worth your while, because the products I am going to tell you about will seriously boost your holiday sales." Alyson was relieved to see several people smiling as they settled back in their seats.
Message	Now that she had the audience's attention, Alyson presented each new product as briefly as she could. She streamlined her planned presentation to emphasize the features that would be most appealing to the buyers and the ones they would be most likely to remember. She ended by handing out samples of the products and promising to contact anyone who needed more information. She quickly added her e-mail address to her PowerPoint slides and was encouraged to see people writing it down.

Feedback   As promised, Alyson finished in under half an hour. "And that wraps it up!" she concluded. "Let's eat!" Later, the marketing director complimented Alyson on dealing so well with a tough situation. "You did a great job," the marketing director said. "Next year, we'll try to make all the presentations as concise and efficient as yours."

Public Speaking in a Multicultural World

CULTURAL DIVERSITY IN THE MODERN WORLD

The United States has always been a diverse society. In 1673 a visitor to what is now New York City was astonished to find that 18 languages were spoken among the city's 8,000 inhabitants. By the middle of the 19th century, so many people from so many lands had come to the United States that novelist Herman Melville exclaimed, "You cannot spill a drop of American blood without spilling the blood of the whole world."[23]

One can only imagine what Melville would say today! The United States has become the most diverse society on earth. For more than a century, most immigrants to the U.S. were Europeans—Irish, Germans, English, Scandinavians, Greeks, Poles, Italians, and others. Together with African Americans, they made America the "melting pot" of the world.[24] Today another great wave of immigration—mostly from Asia and Latin America—has transformed the United States into what one writer calls "the first universal nation," a multicultural society of unmatched diversity.[25]

The diversity of life in the United States can be seen in cities and towns, schools and businesses, community groups, and houses of worship all across the land. Consider the following:

- There are 195 nations in the world, and every one of them has someone living in the United States.

- Houston has two radio stations that broadcast solely in Vietnamese and a daily newspaper that prints in Chinese.

- Nearly 60 percent of the people in Miami were born outside the United States.

- More than 47 million people in the U.S. speak a language other than English at home.

These kinds of developments are not limited to the United States. We live in an age of international multiculturalism. The Internet allows for instant communication everywhere around the world. CNN is broadcast to more than 1 billion people globally. International air travel has made national boundaries almost meaningless. All nations are becoming part of a vast global village. For example:

- There are 77,000 transnational corporations around the world, and they account for more than 30 percent of the world's economic output.

- McDonald's sells twice as many hamburgers and French fries abroad than it does in the United States; Nike makes 63 percent of its sales through exports.

- France has as many Muslims as practicing Catholics; radio CHIN in Toronto, Canada, broadcasts in 31 languages.

- In Geneva, Switzerland, there are so many people from around the world that nearly 60 percent of the school population is non-Swiss.

CULTURAL DIVERSITY AND PUBLIC SPEAKING

Diversity and multiculturalism are such basic facts of life that they can play a role in almost any speech you give. Consider the following situations: A business manager briefing employees of a multinational corporation. A minister sermonizing to a culturally diverse congregation. An international student explaining the customs of his land to students at a U.S. university. A teacher addressing parents at a multiethnic urban school. These are only a few of the countless speaking situations affected by the cultural diversity of modern life.

Speechmaking becomes more complex as cultural diversity increases. Part of the complexity stems from the differences in language from culture to culture. Nothing separates one culture from another more than language. Language and culture are so closely bound that "we communicate the way we do because we are raised in a particular culture and learn its language, rules, and norms."[26]

The meanings attached to gestures, facial expressions, and other nonverbal signals also vary from culture to culture. Even the gestures for such basic messages as "hello" and "goodbye" are culturally based. The North American "goodbye" wave is interpreted in many parts of Europe and South America as the motion for "no," while the Italian and Greek gesture for "goodbye" is the same as the U.S. signal for "come here."[27]

Many stories have been told about the fate of public speakers who fail to take into account cultural differences between themselves and their audiences. Consider the following scenario:[28]

The sales manager of a U.S. electronics firm is in Brazil to negotiate a large purchase of computers by a South American corporation. After three days of negotiations, the sales manager holds a gala reception for all the major executives to build goodwill between the companies.

As is the custom on such occasions, time is set aside during the reception for an exchange of toasts. When it is the sales manager's turn to speak, he praises the Brazilian firm for its many achievements and talks eloquently of his respect for its president and other executives. The words are perfect, and the sales manager can see his audience smiling in approval.

And then—disaster. As the sales manager closes his speech, he raises his hand and flashes the classic U.S. "OK" sign to signal his pleasure at the progress of the negotiations. Instantly the festive mood is replaced with stony silence; smiles turn to icy stares. The sales manager has given his Brazilian audience a gesture with roughly the same meaning as an extended middle finger in the United States.

The next day the Brazilian firm announces it will buy its computers from another company.

As this story illustrates, public speakers can ill afford to overlook their listeners' cultural values and customs. The methods of effective speech explained throughout this book will be helpful to you in speaking to culturally diverse audiences. Here we need to stress the importance of avoiding the ethnocentrism

Public speaking is a vital mode of communication in most cultures around the world. Here French finance minister Christine Lagarde addresses the World Economic Forum in Davos, Switzerland.

that often blocks communication between speakers and listeners of different cultural backgrounds.

AVOIDING ETHNOCENTRISM

ethnocentrism
The belief that one's own group or culture is superior to all other groups or cultures.

Ethnocentrism is the belief that our own group or culture—whatever it may be—is superior to all other groups or cultures. Because of ethnocentrism, we identify with our group or culture and see its values, beliefs, and customs as "right" or "natural"—in comparison to the values, beliefs, and customs of other groups or cultures, which we tend to think of as "wrong" or "unnatural."[29]

Ethnocentrism is part of every culture, and it can play a positive role in creating group pride and loyalty. But it can also lead to prejudice and hostility toward different racial, ethnic, or cultural groups. To be an effective public speaker in a multicultural world, you need to keep in mind that all people have their special beliefs and customs.

Avoiding ethnocentrism does not mean you must agree with the values and practices of all groups and cultures. At times you might try to convince people of different cultures to change their traditional ways of doing things—as speakers from the United Nations seek to persuade farmers in Africa to adopt more productive methods of agriculture, or as delegates from the U.S. and China attempt to influence the other country's trade policies.

If such speakers are to be successful, however, they must show respect for the cultures of the people they address. They need to adapt their message to the cultural values and expectations of their listeners.

When you work on your speeches, be alert to how cultural factors might affect the way listeners respond. As we shall see in Chapter 5, for classroom speeches you can use audience-analysis questionnaires to learn about the backgrounds and opinions of your classmates. For speeches outside the classroom, the person who invites you to speak can usually provide information about the audience.

As we shall see throughout this book, there are many Internet resources for public speakers. One of those resources is an extensive collection of speeches from world history, which you can access at the History Place: Great Speeches Collection (www.historyplace.com/speeches/previous.htm).

Thousands of people in the United States earn their living as professional public speakers. You can learn about their activities at the National Speakers Association Web site (www.nsaspeaker.org/).

Internet Connection
www.connectlucas.com

Once you know about any cultural factors that might affect your listeners' response, try to put yourself in their place and to hear your message through their ears. If there is a language difference, avoid words or phrases that might cause misunderstanding. When researching the speech, keep an eye out for supporting materials that will relate to a wide range of listeners. Also, consider using visual aids. As we shall see in Chapter 13, they can be especially helpful in bridging a gap in language or cultural background.

When delivering your speech, be alert to feedback that might indicate the audience is having trouble grasping your ideas. If you see puzzled expressions, restate your point to make sure it is understood. With some audiences, you can encourage feedback by asking, "Am I making myself clear?" or "Did I explain this point fully enough?"

If you pose such questions, however, be aware that listeners from different cultures may respond quite differently. Most Arabs, North Americans, and Europeans will give you fairly direct feedback if you ask for it. Listeners from Asian and Caribbean countries, on the other hand, may not respond, out of concern that doing so will show disrespect for the speaker. (See Chapter 5 for a full discussion of audience analysis and adaptation.)

Finally, we should note the importance of avoiding ethnocentrism when listening to speeches. As we shall see in Chapters 2 and 3, speech audiences have a responsibility to listen courteously and attentively. When you listen to a speaker from a different cultural background, be on guard against the temptation to judge the speaker on the basis of his or her appearance or manner of delivery. Too often we form opinions about people by the way they look or speak rather than by what they *say*. No matter what the cultural background of the speaker, you should listen to her or him as attentively as you would want your audience to listen to you.[30]

SUMMARY

Public speaking has been a vital means of personal empowerment and civic engagement throughout history. The need for effective public speaking will almost certainly touch you sometime in your life. Your speech class will give you training in researching topics, organizing your ideas, and presenting yourself skillfully. This training is invaluable for every type of communication.

There are many similarities between public speaking and daily conversation, but public speaking is also different from conversation. First, it usually imposes strict time limitations and requires more detailed preparation than does ordinary conversation.

Second, it requires more formal language. Listeners react negatively to speeches loaded with slang, jargon, and bad grammar. Third, public speaking demands a different method of delivery. Effective speakers adjust their voices to the larger audience and work at avoiding distracting physical mannerisms and verbal habits.

One of the major concerns of students in any speech class is stage fright. Your class will give you an opportunity to gain confidence and make your nervousness work for you rather than against you. You will take a big step toward overcoming stage fright if you think positively, prepare thoroughly, visualize yourself giving a successful speech, keep in mind that most nervousness is not visible to the audience, and think of your speech as communication rather than as a performance in which you must do everything perfectly.

A course in public speaking can also help develop your skills as a critical thinker. Critical thinking helps you organize your ideas, spot weaknesses in other people's reasoning, and avoid them in your own.

The speech communication process includes seven elements—speaker, message, channel, listener, feedback, interference, and situation. The speaker is the person who initiates a speech transaction. Whatever the speaker communicates is the message, which is sent by means of a particular channel. The listener receives the communicated message and provides feedback to the speaker. Interference is anything that impedes the communication of a message, and the situation is the time and place in which speech communication occurs. The interaction of these seven elements determines the outcome in any instance of speech communication.

Because of the diversity of modern life, many—perhaps most—of the audiences you address will include people of different cultural backgrounds. When you work on your speeches, be alert to how such factors might affect the responses of your listeners and adapt your message accordingly. Above all, avoid the ethnocentric belief that your own culture or group is superior to all others. Also keep in mind the importance of avoiding ethnocentrism when listening to speeches. Accord every speaker the same courtesy and attentiveness you would want from your listeners.

KEY TERMS

stage fright *(9)*	channel *(18)*
adrenaline *(10)*	listener *(18)*
positive nervousness *(10)*	frame of reference *(19)*
visualization *(13)*	feedback *(19)*
critical thinking *(16)*	interference *(20)*
speaker *(17)*	situation *(20)*
message *(18)*	ethnocentrism *(24)*

REVIEW QUESTIONS

connectlucas.com
For further review, go to the Study Questions in the online Study Aids for this chapter.

After reading this chapter, you should be able to answer the following questions:

1. In what ways is public speaking likely to make a difference in your life?

2. How is public speaking similar to everyday conversation?

3. How is public speaking different from everyday conversation?

4. Why is it normal—even desirable—to be nervous at the start of a speech?

5. How can you control your nervousness and make it work for you in your speeches?

6. What are the seven elements of the speech communication process? How do they interact to determine the success or failure of a speech?

7. What is ethnocentrism? Why do public speakers need to avoid ethnocentrism when addressing audiences with diverse cultural, racial, or ethnic backgrounds?

EXERCISES FOR CRITICAL THINKING

1. Think back on an important conversation you had recently in which you wanted to achieve a particular result. (*Examples:* Asking your employer to change your work schedule; explaining to a friend how to change the oil and filter in a car; attempting to talk your spouse or partner into buying the computer you like rather than the one he or she prefers.) Work up a brief analysis of the conversation.

    In your analysis, explain the following: (1) your purpose in the conversation and the message strategy you chose to achieve your purpose; (2) the communication channels used during the conversation and how they affected the outcome; (3) the interference—internal or external—you encountered during the conversation; (4) the steps you took to adjust to feedback; (5) the strategic changes you would make in preparing for and carrying out the conversation if you had it to do over again.

2. Divide a sheet of paper into two columns. Label one column "Characteristics of an Effective Public Speaker." Label the other column "Characteristics of an Ineffective Public Speaker." In the columns, list and briefly explain what you believe to be the five most important characteristics of effective and ineffective speakers. Be prepared to discuss your ideas in class.

3. On the basis of the lists you developed for Exercise 2, candidly evaluate your own strengths and weaknesses as a speaker. Identify the three primary aspects of speechmaking you most want to improve.

Applying *the* **Power** *of* **Public Speaking**

It's been three years since you graduated from college. After gaining experience as an administrative assistant at a major office equipment manufacturer, you've just been promoted to marketing manager for office copiers. Though you have occasionally given brief reports to other members of your work team, you're now facing your first speech to a large audience. At your company's annual sales meeting, you will address the sales force about the company's new multifunction printer/copiers, and how to sell them to dealers such as Office Depot and OfficeMax.

You're pleased to have this opportunity and you know it shows the company's faith in your abilities. Yet the closer you get to the day of the speech, the harder it is to control the butterflies in your stomach. There will be 200 people in your audience, including all the sales managers and regional managers, in addition to the sales force. All eyes will be on you. It's important that you come across as confident and well informed, but you're afraid your stage fright will send the opposite message. What strategies will you use to control your nerves and make them work for you?

Credits

Text and Line Art Credits

CHAPTER 1 **Pages 4–7:** Adapted from Josh Johnson, "Study Secrets for College Success," from *Campus Life*, 2002. Copyright 2002 Josh Johnson. Used by permission. **Pg. 23:** Adapted from Colin Rose (1987), Accelerated Learning, acceleratedlearning.com. Used with permission. **Pgs. 28–29:** Robert Feldman, *P.O.W.E.R. Learning*, 4th ed., Pg. 416. Copyright © 2009 The McGraw-Hill Companies. Used with permission.

CHAPTER 2 **Pages 46–47:** Jan Hunt, "'Learning Disorder'? Just Say No!," http://www.naturalchild.org/jan_hunt/learning_disorder.html#1276491242. Used with permission of the author. **Pg. 52:** Mitch Albom, *Tuesdays with Morrie*, Pg. 1–2. Copyright © 1997 by Mitch Albom. New York: Doubleday, 1997. **Pgs. 59–61:** Adapted from Howard Gardner, "Workshop: Tapping into Multiple Intelligence." Courtesy WNET.ORG, http://www.teachersfirst.com/getsource.cfm?id=6775, © 2004 Educational Broadcasting Corpg.

CHAPTER 3 **Pages 71–72, 75–81, 85, 88:** Adapted from Richard T. Schaefer, *Sociology*, 10th ed. Copyright © 2007 The McGraw-Hill Companies. Used with permission. **Pgs. 72, 82:** Adapted from Saundra Hybels & Richard L. Weaver, *Communicating Effectively*, 9th ed. Copyright © 2009 The McGraw-Hill Companies. Used with permission. **Pgs. 73–74:** Robert Feldman, *PG.O.W.E.R. Learning*, 4th ed. Copyright © 2009 The McGraw-Hill Companies. Used with permission. **Pg. 74:** Adapted from Sharon Ferret, *Peak Performance: Success in College & Beyond*, 7th ed. Copyright © 2010 The McGraw-Hill Companies. Used with permission. **Pgs. 75, 80:** Adapted from Dale B. Hahn, Wayne A. Payne, and Ellen B. Lucas, *Focus on Health*, 8th ed. Copyright © 2007 The McGraw-Hill Companies. Used with permission. **Pg. 76:** Adapted from J. Sterling Warner and Judith Hilliard, *Visions across the Americas: Short Essays for Composition*, 7th Edition. Heinle, 2010. **Pg. 78:** Terry F. Pettijouhn II and Amy S. Walter, College Student Journal, June, 2008. **Pg. 79:** Adapted from Alan Brinkley, *American History: A Survey*, 12th ed. Copyright © 2007 The McGraw-Hill Companies. **Pg. 81:** Adapted from Stan F. Shaw, Sally S. Scott, and Joan M. McGuire, "Teaching College Students with Learning Disabilities," *ERIC EC Digest* #E618, November 2001. **Pgs. 82–83:** Adapted from Associated Press, "Overweight kids face widespread stigma," 7/12/2007. **Pg. 83:** Burns, Lisbeth Fisher, "A Trait, Not an Illness," *Newsday CITY Edition*, 8 January 1995, Z.38. **Pg. 83:** Jennifer Maloney, "Little people ask FCC to ban the word 'midget' on TV," *Newsday*, July 5, 2009.

CHAPTER 4 **Pages 98–99, 102–103, 107, 111–112, 114:** Adapted from Sharon Ferret, *Peak Performance: Success in College & Beyond*, 7th ed. Copyright © 2010 The McGraw-Hill Companies. Used with permission. **Pgs. 100–101, 121–123:** Robert Feldman, *PG.O.W.E.R. Learning*, 4th ed. Copyright © 2009 The McGraw-Hill Companies. Used with permission. **Pgs. 104–106, 108–110, 115–119:** Adapted from Dale B. Hahn, Wayne A. Payne, and Ellen B. Lucas, *Focus on Health*, 8th ed. Copyright © 2007 The McGraw-Hill Companies. Used with permission. **Pg. 113, 118:** William PG. Cunningham and Mary Ann Cunningham, *Environmental Science: A Global Concern*. Copyright © 2008 The McGraw-Hill Companies.

CHAPTER 5 **Pg. 127:** Robert Feldman, *PG.O.W.E.R. Learning*, 4th ed. Copyright © 2009 The McGraw-Hill Companies. Used with permission. **Pgs. 127, 131–132, 143–148:** Adapted from Michael W. Passer and Ronald E. Smith, *Psychology: The Science of Mind and Behavior*, 3rd ed. Copyright © 2007 The McGraw-Hill Companies. Used with permission. **Pgs. 128–129, 133, 136–137, 139–143, 148:** Adapted from Dale B. Hahn, Wayne A. Payne, and Ellen B. Lucas, *Focus on Health*, 8th ed. Copyright © 2007 The McGraw-Hill Companies. Used with permission. **Pgs. 134–135, 144:** Adapted from Sharon Ferret, *Peak Performance: Success in College & Beyond*, 7th ed. Copyright © 2010 The McGraw-Hill Companies. Used with permission.

CHAPTER 6 **Pages 166–167, 172–173, 176–177:** Robert Feldman, *PG.O.W.E.R. Learning*, 4th ed., Pg. 198, 419. Copyright © 2009 The McGraw-Hill Companies. Used with permission. **Pg. 170:** Robert Feldman, *PG.O.W.E.R. Learning*, 4th ed., Pg. 407. Copyright © 2009 The McGraw-Hill Companies. Used with permission. **Pg. 174:** Richard T. Schaefer, *Sociology*, 10th ed., Fig. 16.1, Pg. 407. Copyright © 2007 The McGraw-Hill Companies. Used with permission. **Pg. 174:** Richard T. Schaefer, *Sociology*, 10th ed., Pg. 161. Copyright © 2007 The McGraw-Hill Companies. Used with permission.

CHAPTER 7 **Pages 186, 188–189, 199:** Robert Feldman, *P.O.W.E.R. Learning*, 4th ed. Copyright © 2009 The McGraw-Hill Companies. Used with permission. **Pgs. 186–187, 189:** Adapted from Sharon Ferret, *Peak Performance: Success in College & Beyond*, 7th ed. Copyright © 2010 The McGraw-Hill Companies. Used with permission. **Pgs. 190, 200:**

November/December 2008, American Federation of Teachers. Reprinted with permission. **Pgs. 483–484:** Adapted from William De Jong, "Should the Legal Drinking Age Be Lowered to 18? No! It's Not Safe For Youth, Nor on the Roads," © *AFT On Campus*, November/December 2008, American Federation of Teachers. Reprinted with permission.

MODULE 7   Pages 513–515: Adapted from Michael W. Passer and Ronald E. Smith, "Humanistic Psychotherapies: Client Centered Treatment," *Psychology: The Science of Mind and Behavior*, 3rd ed., Pgs. 578–79. Copyright © 2007 The McGraw-Hill Companies. Used with permission.

MODULE 8   Pages 527–529: Adated from Richard T. Schaefer, *Sociology*, 10th ed., Pgs. 302–303. Copyright © 2007 The McGraw-Hill Companies. Used with permission. **Pgs. 539–541:** Adapted from Carlin Flora, "Friendship: Awkward Encounters of the Friendly Kind," *Psychology Today*, May 1, 2009. Reprinted with permission from Psychology Today Magazine (Copyright © 2009 Sussex Publishers, LLC). **Pgs. 549–551:** Naiwa bin Laden, Omar bin Laden, and Jean Sasson, from GROWING UP BIN LADEN, copyright © 2009 by The Sasson Corporation and reprinted by permission of St. Martin's Press, LLC and the authors.

APPENDIX 1   Page A-8–A-9: Suffixes, adapted from Communications Lab, Florida State College at Jacksonville, http://www1.fccj.org/lchandouts/communicationshandouts/vocabularyhandouts/V-3.doc. Used with permission.

APPENDIX 2   Page A-11: From NEW AMERICAN WEBSTER'S HANDY COLLEGE DICTIONARY by Philip D. Morehead and Andrew T. Morehead, copyright 1951 (renewed), © 1955, 1956, 1957, 1961 by Albert H. Morehead, 1972, 1981, 1985, 1995 by Philip D. Morehead and Andrew T. Morehead. Used by permission of Dutton Signet, a division of Penguin Group

(USA) Inc. **Pg. A-15:** Richard T. Schaefer, *Sociology,* 10th ed. Copyright © 2007 The McGraw-Hill Companies. Used with permission. **Pg. A-16:** Thesaurus entry for "diligent," from *Roget's 21st Century Thesaurus* © 2010 The Philip Lief Group, Dell Publishing. Used with permission. **Pg. A-20:** Definitions of "Ethnocentrism" and "ethnocentric," adapted from *Columbia Encyclopedia* 6th ed., by Paul Lagasse, Lora Goldman, and Archie Hobson (eds.). Copyright © 2008 Columbia University Press. Reprinted with permission of the publisher.

APPENDIX 3   Pages A-21–A-48: Sharon Ferret, *Peak Performance: Success in College & Beyond*, 7th ed., Pgs. 45–72. Copyright © 2010 The McGraw-Hill Companies. Used with permission. **Pg. A-32:** Maslow, Abraham H.; Frager, Robert D. (Editor); Fadiman, James (Editor), *Motivation and Personality*, 3rd, ©1987. Printed and Electronically reproduced by permission of Pearson Education, Inc., Upper Saddle River, New Jersey.

APPENDIX 4   Pg. A-56–A-81: Stephen Lucas, *The Art of Public Speaking*, 10th ed., Pgs. 2–27. Copyright © The McGraw-Hill Companies. Used with permission.

PHOTO CREDITS

CHAPTER 1   Pages 2–3: © Tom Stewart/Corbis; **Pg. 5:** © Ingram Publishing / Alamy; **Pg. 10:** © Stockbyte/Gety Images; **Pg. 13:** © Getty Images / Digital Vision; **Pg. 16:** © Comstock Images/ JupiterImages; **Pg. 19:** © Digital Vision/Getty Images; **Pg. 25:** © Loungepark/The Image Bank/Getty Images; **Pg. 26:** © Getty Images / Digital Vision; **Pg. 28:** © Rubberball/Getty Images

CHAPTER 2   Pages 32–33: © John Cumming/Iconica /Getty Images; **Pg. 35:** © Aurora Photos / Alamy; **Pg. 40:** © Image Source/Getty Images; **Pg. 41:** © Photodisc / Getty Images; **Pg. 43:** © Jose Luis Pelaez Inc /Getty images; **Pg. 44:** © Tetra Images / Alamy; **Pg. 46:**

© Rubberball Productions/Getty Images; **Pg. 51:** (top and bottom) Jacket Cover and Table of Contents from Tuesdays with Morrie by Mitch Albom, copyright © 1997 by Mitch Albom. Used by permission of Doubleday, a division of Random House, Inc.; **Pg. 54:** © John Cumming/Getty Images; **Pg. 58:** © PhotoAlto/Alix Minde/Getty Images; Pg. 60: © CMCD/Getty Images; **Pg. 62:** © Fuse/Getty Images; **Pg. 65:** © Clarissa Leahy/Getty Images

CHAPTER 3   Pages 68–69: © Beaux Arts / Alamy; **Pg. 70:** © C. Devan/Corbis; **Pg. 72:** Moodboard/Alamy; **Pg. 78:** © George Doyle & Claran Griffin/Getty Images; **Pg. 80:** © Image Source/Corbis; **Pg. 83:** © Amy Sussman/Getty Images for Discovery; **Pg. 85:** © Image Source/Getty Images; **Pg. 88:** Library of Congress, Prints and Photographs Division (LC-USZ62-95442); **Pg. 90:** © Photo by Chip Somodevilla/Getty Images

CHAPTER 4   Pages 92–93: © Dirk Anschutz/Stone /Getty Images; **Pg. 97:** © Science Photo Library/Getty Images; **Pg. 98:** © Javier Pierini/Getty Images; **Pg. 100:** © C Squared Studios/Getty Images; **Pg. 102:** © Janis Christie/Getty Images; **Pg. 106:** © David Harry Stewart/Getty Images; **Pg. 108:** © Ken Karp for MMH; **Pg. 110:** © Jack Mann/Getty Images; **Pg. 117:** © RubberBall / SuperStock; **Pg. 120:** © Rubberball/Getty Images; **Pg. 122:** © ScienceVU, Inc/Visuals Unlimited/Corbis

CHAPTER 5   Pages 124–125: © Danita Delimont / Alamy; **Pg. 126:** © Allison Michael Orenstein/Getty Images; **Pg. 128:** © Yellow Dog Productions Inc. /Getty Images; **Pg. 132:** © Stockbyte/PunchStock; **Pg. 134:** © Mark Harmel/Getty Images; **Pg. 138:** © BananaStock/PunchStock; **Pg. 140:** © BananaStock/PunchStock; **Pg. 142:** © Liquidlibrary/PictureQuest; **Pg. 144:** © Jessica Peterson/Getty Images; **Pg. 147:** © Chris Hondros/Getty Images

CHAPTER 6   Pages 150–151: © WorldFoto/Alamy; **Pg. 155:** © 2007 Getty Images, Inc.; **Pg. 161:** © Jeff

Index